Financial Markets and Institutions

13th Edition

Jeff Madura

Florida Atlantic University

⁂ CENGAGE

Australia • Brazil • Mexico • Singapore • United Kingdom • United States

Financial Markets and Institutions,
Thirteenth Edition

Jeff Madura

Sr. VP, Higher Ed Product, Content, and Market Development: Erin Joyner

VP, Product Management: Mike Schenk

Sr. Product Manager: Aaron Arnsparger

Content Manager: Christopher Valentine

Digital Delivery Lead: Mark Hopkinson

Learning Designer: Brittany Waitt

Marketing Manager: Christopher Walz

Marketing Coordinator: Sean Messer

Production Service/Composition: SPi Global

Art Director: Chris Doughman

Cover Designer: Chris Doughman

Cover and Internal Image: © Eloi Omella/iStock

Intellectual Property Analyst: Ashley Maynard

Intellectual Property Project Manager: Carly Belcher

Library of Congress Control Number: 2019948095

ISBN: 978-0-357-13079-7

Cengage
200 Pier 4 Boulevard
Boston, MA 02210
USA

Cengage is a leading provider of customized learning solutions with employees residing in nearly 40 different countries and sales in more than 125 countries around the world. Find your local representative at **www.cengage.com.**

Cengage products are represented in Canada by Nelson Education, Ltd.

To learn more about Cengage platforms and services, register or access your online learning solution, or purchase materials for your course, visit **www.cengage.com.**

Printed in United State of America
1 2 3 4 5 6 7 24 23 22 21 20

This text is dedicated to Best Friends Animal Society in Kanab, Utah, for its commitment to, compassion for, and care of more than 1,500 animals, many of which were previously homeless. Best Friends has established an ambitious campaign to save all healthy dogs and cats in the United States by 2025 (prevent healthy cats and dogs from being euthanized due to excessive population).

Most of the royalties the author receives from this edition of the text will be invested in a fund that will ultimately be donated to Best Friends Animal Society and other humane societies. In the last several years, this fund has donated more than $500,000 to Best Friends to support a new healthcare facility for Best Friends, sponsor a Public Broadcasting Service (PBS) documentary on the efforts of Best Friends to help animal societies, save dogs that were abandoned during Hurricane Harvey in Houston during 2017, and create an online information network in 2019 for people who want to help dogs. This fund has also donated more than $100,000 to other animal care societies, including Friends of Greyhounds (Fort Lauderdale, FL), Florida Humane Society (Pompano Beach, FL), Greyhound Pets of America in Central Florida (Melbourne, FL), Tri-County Humane Society (Boca Raton, FL), and Doris Day Animal League (Washington, DC).

Brief Contents

Contents

PART 5: Derivative Security Markets — 317

Preface

Financial markets finance much of the expenditures by corporations, governments, and individuals. Financial institutions are the key intermediaries in financial markets because they transfer funds from savers to the individuals, firms, or government agencies that need funds. *Financial Markets and Institutions,* 13th Edition, describes financial markets and the financial institutions that serve those markets. It provides a conceptual framework that can be used to understand why markets exist. Each type of financial market is described with a focus on the securities that are traded and the participation by financial institutions.

Today, many financial institutions offer all types of financial services, such as banking, securities services, mutual fund services, and insurance services. Each type of financial service is unique, however. Therefore, the discussion of financial services in this book is organized by type of financial service that can be offered by financial institutions.

Intended Market

This text is suitable for undergraduate and master's-level courses in financial markets, or financial institutions. To maximize students' comprehension, some of the more difficult questions and problems should be assigned in addition to the special applications at the end of each chapter.

Organization of the Text

Part 1 (Chapters 1 through 3) introduces the key financial markets and financial institutions, explains why interest rates change over time, and explains why yields vary among securities. Part 2 (Chapters 4 and 5) describes the functions of the Federal Reserve System (the Fed) and explains how its monetary policy influences interest rates and other economic conditions. Part 3 (Chapters 6 through 9) covers the major debt security markets, Part 4 (Chapters 10 through 12) describes equity securities markets, and Part 5 (Chapters 13 through 16) covers the derivative security markets. Each chapter in Parts 3 through 5 focuses on a particular market. The integration of each market with other markets is stressed throughout these chapters. Part 6 (Chapters 17 through 20) concentrates on commercial banking, and Part 7 (Chapters 21 through 26) covers all other types of financial services provided by financial institutions.

Courses that emphasize financial markets should focus on the first five parts (Chapters 1 through 16); however, some chapters in the section on commercial banking are also relevant. Courses that emphasize financial institutions and financial services should focus on Parts 1, 2, 6, and 7, although some background on securities markets (Parts 3, 4, and 5) may be helpful.

Professors may wish to focus on certain chapters of this book and skip others, depending on the intended coverage of the course they are teaching. Chapters can be rearranged without a loss in continuity. Regardless of the order in which chapters are studied, it is highly recommended that some questions and exercises from each chapter be assigned. These exercises may serve as a focal point for class discussion.

Coverage of Major Concepts and Events

Numerous concepts relating to recent events and current trends in financial markets are discussed throughout the chapters. These include the following:

- Concerns about systemic risk
- Behavioral finance in financial markets
- Expert networks used to access information
- Use of high frequency trading and robots ("bots") to trade securities
- "Crowdfunding" as a popular financing method for businesses
- Changes in Federal Reserve operations and communication to financial markets
- The increasing popularity of virtual currencies
- Challenges in valuing companies that attempt to go public
- Performance of venture capital and private equity funding
- Emergence of private stock exchanges
- Dark pools used to trade stocks
- Governance in financial markets
- Value-at-risk applications
- Emergence of hedge funds
- Stress tests imposed on commercial banks
- Pension underfunding

Each chapter is self-contained, so professors can use classroom time to focus on the more complex concepts and rely on the text to cover the other concepts.

Features of the Text

The features of the text are as follows:

FINANCIAL REFORM

ETHICS

GLOBAL ASPECTS

- **Part-Opening Diagram.** A diagram is provided at the beginning of each part to illustrate generally how the key concepts in that part are related.
- **Objectives.** A bulleted list at the beginning of each chapter identifies the key concepts in that chapter.
- **Examples.** Examples are provided to reinforce key concepts.
- **Financial Reform.** A Financial Reform icon in the margin indicates a discussion of financial reform as it applies to the topics covered in the chapter.
- **Ethics.** An Ethics icon in the margin indicates financial ethics topics covered in the chapter.
- **Global Aspects.** A Global Aspects icon in the margin indicates international coverage of the topic being discussed.
- **Summary.** A bulleted list at the end of each chapter summarizes the key concepts. This list corresponds to the list of objectives at the beginning of the chapter.
- **Point/Counterpoint.** A controversial issue is introduced, along with opposing arguments on that issue, and students are asked to offer their opinion.
- **Questions and Applications.** The Questions and Applications section at the end of each chapter tests students' understanding of the key concepts. These exercises may serve as homework assignments or study aids in preparation for exams.
- **Critical Thinking Question.** At the end of each chapter, students are challenged to use their critical thinking skills by writing a short essay on a specific topic that was discussed in the chapter.
- **Interpreting Financial News.** At the end of each chapter, students are challenged to interpret comments made in the media about the chapter's key concepts. This gives students practice in analyzing announcements by the financial media.

- *Managing in Financial Markets.* At the end of each chapter, students are placed in the position of financial managers and must make decisions about specific situations related to the key concepts in that chapter.
- *Flow of Funds Exercise.* A running exercise is provided at the end of each chapter to illustrate how a manufacturing company relies on all types of financial markets and financial services provided by financial institutions.
- *Internet/Excel Exercises.* At the end of each chapter, exercises introduce students to applicable information available on various websites, encourage them to apply Excel as a tool for examining related topics, or a combination of these. For example, the exercises allow students to assess yield curves, risk premiums, and stock volatility.
- *Problems.* Selected chapters include problems to test students' computational skills.
- *WSJ Exercise.* This exercise appears at the end of selected chapters and gives students an opportunity to apply information provided in *The Wall Street Journal* to specific concepts explained in that chapter.
- *Integrative Problems.* An integrative problem at the end of each part integrates the key concepts of chapters within that part.
- *Comprehensive Project.* This project, found in Appendix A, requires students to apply real data to several key concepts described throughout the book.
- *Midterm and Final Self-Examinations.* At the end of Chapter 16, a midterm self-exam is offered to test students' knowledge of financial markets. At the end of Chapter 26, a final self-exam is offered to test students' knowledge of financial institutions. An answer key is provided so that students can evaluate their answers after they take the exam.

The concepts in each chapter can be reinforced by using one or more of the features just listed. Professors' use of these features will vary depending on the level of their students and the course goals. A course that focuses mostly on financial markets may emphasize tools such as the WSJ Exercises and Part 1 of the Comprehensive Project (on taking positions in securities and derivative instruments). In contrast, a course that focuses on financial institutions may assign an exercise in which students must review recent annual reports (see Part 2 of the Comprehensive Project) to determine how a particular financial institution's performance is affected by its policies, industry regulations, and economic conditions. In addition, the Internet/Excel Exercises on financial institutions give students practice in assessing the operations and performance of financial institutions.

New to this Edition: MindTap

MindTap™, Cengage's fully online, highly personalized learning experience combines readings, multimedia activities, and assessments into a singular Learning Path. MindTap™ guides students through their course with ease and engagement with a learning path that includes an Interactive Chapter Reading, Algorithmic Practice Problems, and Homework Assignments powered by Aplia. These homework problems include rich explanations and instant grading, with opportunities to try another algorithmic version of the problem to bolster confidence with problem solving. Instructors can personalize the Learning Path for their students by customizing the robust suite of resources and adding their own content via apps that integrate into the MindTap™ framework seamlessly with Learning Management Systems.

Supplements to the Text

To access the instructor resources, go to **www.cengage.com/login**, log in with your faculty account username and password, and use **ISBN 9780357130797** to search for and add instructor resources to your account Bookshelf.

- *Instructor's Manual.* Revised by the author, the instructor's manual contains the chapter outline for each chapter and a summary of key concepts for discussion as well as answers to the end-of-chapter Questions and Problems.
- *Test Bank.* The expanded test bank, which has also been revised by the author, contains a large set of questions in multiple-choice or true/false format, including content questions as well as problems.
- *Cognero™ Test Bank.* Cengage Learning Testing Powered by Cognero™ is a flexible, online system that allows you to author, edit, and manage test bank content from multiple Cengage Learning solutions; create multiple test versions in an instant; and deliver tests from your LMS, your classroom, or wherever you want. The Cognero™ Test Bank contains the same questions that are in the Microsoft® Word Test Bank. All question content is now tagged according to Tier I (Business Program Interdisciplinary Learning Outcomes) and Tier II (Finance-Specific) standards topic, Bloom's Taxonomy, and difficulty level.
- *PowerPoint Slides.* The PowerPoint slides clarify content and provide a solid guide for student note-taking. In addition to the regular notes slides, a separate set of exhibit-only PowerPoint slides is available.

Additional Course Tools

Cengage Learning Custom Solutions

Whether you need print, digital, or hybrid course materials, Cengage Learning Custom Solutions can help you create your perfect learning solution. Draw from Cengage Learning's extensive library of texts and collections, add or create your own original work, and create customized media and technology to match your learning and course objectives. Our editorial team will work with you through each step, allowing you to concentrate on the most important thing—your students. Learn more about all our services at **www.cengage.com/custom.**

Acknowledgments

Several professors reviewed previous versions of this text and influenced its content and organization. They are acknowledged in alphabetical order:

Ibrihim Affaneh, Indiana University of Pennsylvania

Michael H. Anderson, University of Massachusetts–Dartmouth

Henry C. F. Arnold, Seton Hall University

James C. Baker, Kent State University

Gerald Bierwag, Florida International University

Carol Billingham, Central Michigan University

Randy Billingsley, Virginia Tech University

Rita M. Biswas, SUNY–Albany

Howard W. Bohnen, St. Cloud State University

Paul J. Bolster, Northeastern University

M. E. Bond, University of Memphis

Carol Marie Boyer, Long Island University–C. W. Post Campus

Alka Bramhandkar, Ithaca College

Emile J. Brinkman, University of Houston–University Park

Christopher L. Brown, Western Kentucky University

Bill Brunsen, Eastern New Mexico University

Sarah Bryant, George Washington University

James B. Burnham, Duquesne University

Paul Bursik, St. Norbert College

Deanne Butchey, Florida International University

William Carner, University of Missouri–Columbia

Joseph Cheng, Ithaca College

William T. Chittenden, Northern Illinois University

C. Steven Cole, University of North Texas

M. Cary Collins, University of Tennessee

Mark Correll, University of Colorado

Wayne C. Curtis, Troy State University

Julie Dahlquist, University of Texas–San Antonio

Steven Dobson, California Polytechnic State University

Robert M. Donchez, University of Colorado–Boulder

Lynne Pierson Doti, Chapman University

Richard J. Dowen, Northern Illinois University

Imad Elhaj, University of Louisville

James Felton, Central Michigan University

Donald Flagg, University of Tampa

Stuart Fletcher, Appalachian State University

George C. Fowler, York County Community College

Norman Frost, Loyola University of Maryland

Clifford L. Fry, University of Houston

Ramesh Garg, Eastern Michigan University

Edward K. Gill, California State University–Chico

Claire G. Gilmore, St. Joseph's University

Owen Gregory, University of Illinois–Chicago

Paul Grier, SUNY–Binghamton

Ann Hackert, Idaho State University

John Halloran, University of Notre Dame

Gerald A. Hanweck, George Mason University

Rodney Hardcastle, Pacific Union College

Wei He, Mississippi State University

Hildegard R. Hendrickson, Seattle University

Bradley K. Hobbs, Florida Gulf Coast University

Jerry M. Hood, Loyola University–New Orleans

Ronald M. Horowitz, Oakland University

Paul Hsueh, University of Central Florida

Carl D. Hudson, Auburn University

John S. Jahera, Jr., Auburn University

Rob James, Boston University

Mel Jameson, University of Nevada

Shane Johnson, Louisiana State University

Jody Jones, Oklahoma Christian University

Jan Jusko, College of Staten Island

Richard H. Keehn, University of Wisconsin–Parkside

James B. Kehr, Miami University of Ohio

David F. Kern, Arkansas State University

Elinda F. Kiss, University of Maryland Robert H. Smith School of Business

James W. Kolari, Texas A&M University

Vladimir Kotomin, University of Wisconsin–Eau Claire

Robert A. Kunkel, University of Wisconsin–Oshkosh

George Kutner, Marquette University

Robert Lamy, Wake Forest University

David J. Leahigh, King's College

David N. Leggett, Bentley College

William Lepley, University of Wisconsin–Green Bay

Andrew Light, Liberty University

Morgan Lynge, Jr., University of Illinois

Pawan Madhogarhia, Pennsylvania State University

Judy E. Maese, New Mexico State University

Timothy A. Manuel, University of Montana

L. R. Martindale, Texas A&M University

Joseph S. Mascia, Adelphi University

Robert W. McLeod, University of Alabama

Kathleen S. McNichol, LaSalle University

James McNulty, Florida Atlantic University

Charles Meiburg, University of Virginia

Jose Mercado-Mendez, Central Missouri State University

Edward Miseta, Penn State–Erie

Clay M. Moffett, University of North Carolina–Wilmington

Kenneth Moran, Harding University

J. K. Mullen, Clarkson University

Neil Murphy, Virginia Commonwealth University

Srinivas Nippani, Texas A&M University–Commerce

Hossein Noorain, Boston University & Wentworth Institute of Technology
Dale Osborne, University of Texas–Dallas
Coleen Pantalone, Northeastern University
Thomas H. Payne, University of Tennessee–Chattanooga
Sarah Peck, University of Iowa
Chien-Chih Peng, Morehead State University
Micki Pitcher, Olivet College
D. Anthony Plath, University of North Carolina–Charlotte
Barbara Poole, Roger Williams University
Rose Prasad, Central Michigan University
Xiaoling Pu, Kent State University
Mitchell Ratner, Rider University
David Rayome, Northern Michigan University
Alan Reichert, Cleveland State University
Kenneth L. Rhoda, LaSalle University
Nivine Richie, University of North Carolina–Wilmington
Antonio J. Rodriguez, Texas A&M International University
Lawrence C. Rose, Massey University
Jack Rubens, Bryant College
Atul K. Saxena, Georgia Gwinnett College
Jeff Schultz, Christian Brothers University
Robert Schweitzer, University of Delaware
Mehmet Sencicek, University of New Haven
Kilman Shin, Ferris State University

Ahmad Sorhabian, California State Polytechnic University–Pomona
Andrew Spieler, Hofstra University
K. P. Sridharan, Delta State University
S. R. Stansell, East Carolina University
Richard W. Stolz, University of South Carolina Upstate
Richard S. Swasey, Northeastern University
John Thornton, Kent State University
Olaf J. Thorp, Babson College
James D. Tripp, University of Tennessee–Martin
K. C. Tseng, California State University–Fresno
Harry J. Turtle, University of Manitoba
Emre Unlu, University of Nebraska
Cevdet Uruk, University of Memphis
Geraldo M. Vasconcellos, Lehigh University
John Walker, Kutztown University
Michael C. Walker, University of Cincinnati
Charles Walwyn, SUNY–Maritime
Fang Wang, West Virginia University
Bruce Watson, Wellesley College
Jennifer Westbrook, University of Alabama–Huntsville
David A. Whidbee, Washington State University
Alex H. Wilson, University of Arizona
Colin Young, Bentley College
Stephen Zera, California State University–San Marcos
Mei "Miranda" Zhang, Mercer University

In addition, many friends and colleagues offered useful suggestions for this edition, including Kevin Brady (St. Thomas University), Inga Chira (California State University, Northridge), Sean Davis (University of North Florida), David Dubofsky (University of Louisville), Bob Duever, Luis Garcia-Feijoo (Florida Atlantic University), Victor Kalafa, Pat Lewis, Marek Marciniak (West Chester University), Robert McLeod (University of Alabama), Thanh Ngo (East Carolina University), Fred Olmsted, Arjan Premti (University of Wisconsin–Whitewater), Steve Spratt, Jurica Susnjara (Texas State University), Mike Suerth (Monitor Liability Managers), and Nik Volkov (Mercer University).

I appreciate the help and support from the people at Cengage, including Aaron Arnsparger (Sr. Product Manager), Christopher Walz (Marketing Manager), Christopher Valentine (Content Manager), and Brittany Waitt (Learning Designer).

Jeff Madura
Florida Atlantic University

About the Author

Dr. Jeff Madura is presently Emeritus Professor of Finance at Florida Atlantic University. He has written several successful finance texts, including *International Financial Management* (now in its 13th edition). His research on financial markets and institutions has been published in numerous journals, including *Journal of Financial and Quantitative Analysis*; *Journal of Banking and Finance*; *Journal of Money, Credit and Banking*; *Financial Management*; *Journal of Financial Research*; *Journal of Financial Services Research*; and *Financial Review*. Dr. Madura has received multiple awards for excellence in teaching and research, and he has served as a consultant for international banks, securities firms, and other multinational corporations. He has served as a director for the Southern Finance Association and Eastern Finance Association, and he is also former president of the Southern Finance Association.

PART 1
Overview of the Financial Environment

Part 1 of this book focuses on the flow of funds across financial markets, interest rates, and security prices. Chapter 1 introduces the key financial markets and the financial institutions that participate in those markets. Chapter 2 explains how various factors influence interest rates and how interest rate movements in turn affect the values of securities purchased by financial institutions. Chapter 3 identifies factors other than interest rates that influence security prices. Participants in financial markets use this information to value securities and make investment decisions within financial markets.

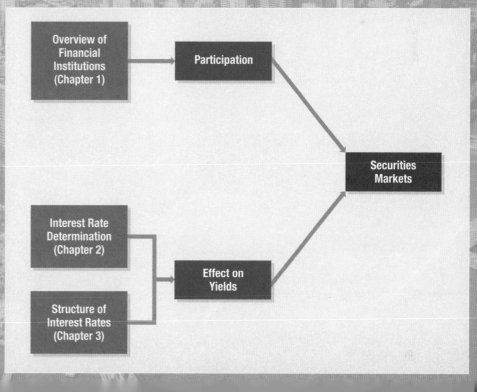

1

Role of Financial Markets and Institutions

CHAPTER OBJECTIVES

The specific objectives of this chapter are to:

- Describe the types of financial markets that facilitate the flow of funds.

- Describe the types of securities traded within financial markets.

- Describe the role of financial institutions within financial markets.

- Explain how financial institutions are exposed to systemic risk.

A **financial market** is a market in which financial assets (securities) such as stocks and bonds can be purchased or sold. Funds are transferred in financial markets when one party purchases financial assets previously held by another party. Financial markets facilitate the flow of funds, thereby allowing for financing and investing by households, firms, and government agencies. This chapter provides some background on financial markets and on the financial institutions that participate in them.

1-1 Role of Financial Markets

Financial markets transfer funds from those parties who have excess funds to those parties who need funds. They enable college students to obtain student loans, families to obtain mortgages, businesses to finance their growth, and governments to finance many of their expenditures. Many households and businesses with excess funds are willing to supply funds to financial markets because they earn a return on their investment. If funds were not supplied, the financial markets would not be able to transfer funds to those who need them.

Those participants who receive more money than they spend are referred to as **surplus units** (or investors). They provide their net savings to the financial markets. Those participants who spend more money than they receive are referred to as **deficit units**. They access funds from financial markets so that they can spend more money than they receive. Many individuals provide funds to financial markets in some periods and access funds in other periods.

EXAMPLE

College students are typically deficit units, as they often borrow from financial markets to support their education. After they obtain their degree, graduates may earn more income than they spend and become surplus units by investing their excess funds. A few years later, they may become deficit units again when they purchase a home. At this stage, they may provide funds to and access funds from financial markets simultaneously. That is, they may periodically deposit savings in a financial institution while also borrowing a large amount of money from a financial institution to buy a home. ●

Many deficit units such as firms and government agencies access funds from financial markets by issuing **securities**, which represent a claim on the issuer. **Debt securities** represent debt (also called *credit*, or *borrowed funds*) incurred by the issuer. Deficit units that issue the debt securities are borrowers. The surplus units that purchase debt securities are creditors, and they receive interest on a periodic basis (such as every six months). Debt securities have a maturity date, at which time the surplus units can redeem the securities and receive the principal (face value) from the deficit units that issued them.

Equity securities (also called *stocks*) represent equity or ownership in the firm. Some businesses prefer to issue equity securities rather than debt securities when they need funds but might not be financially capable of making the periodic interest payments required for debt securities. For example, a new social media company might want to reinvest all of its profits in the business to support its growth, so it would prefer to sell shares of stock in the company (issue equity securities) rather than make interest payments on debt securities.

1-1a Accommodating Corporate Finance Needs

A key role of financial markets is to accommodate corporate finance activity. Corporate finance (also called financial management) involves corporate decisions such as how much funding to obtain and which types of securities to issue when financing operations. The financial markets serve as the mechanism whereby corporations (acting as deficit units) can obtain funds from investors (acting as surplus units).

1-1b Accommodating Investment Needs

Another key role of financial markets is accommodating surplus units who want to invest in either debt or equity securities. Investment management involves decisions by investors regarding how to invest their funds. The financial markets offer investors access to a wide variety of investment opportunities, including securities issued by the U.S. Treasury and government agencies as well as securities issued by corporations.

Financial institutions (discussed later in this chapter) serve as intermediaries within the financial markets. They channel funds from surplus units to deficit units. For example, they channel funds received from individuals to corporations. In this way, they connect the investment management activity with the corporate finance activity, as shown in Exhibit 1.1. They also commonly serve as investors and channel their own funds to corporations.

Primary versus Secondary Markets　**Primary markets** facilitate the issuance of new securities. Thus, they allow corporations to obtain new funds, and offer a means by which investors can invest funds. **Secondary markets** facilitate the trading of existing securities, which allows investors to change their investments by selling securities that they own and buying other securities. Many types of debt securities have a secondary market, so that investors who initially purchased them in the primary market do not have to hold them until maturity. Primary market transactions provide funds to the initial issuer of securities; secondary market transactions do not.

Exhibit 1.1　How Financial Markets Facilitate Corporate Finance and Investment Management

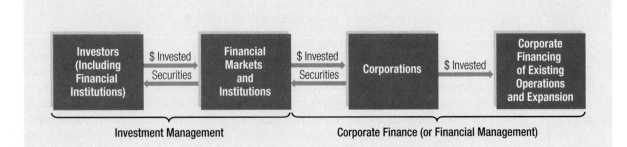

EXAMPLE

Last year, Riverto Co. had excess funds and invested in newly issued Treasury debt securities with a 10-year maturity. This year, it will need $15 million to expand its operations. The company decides to sell its holdings of Treasury debt securities in the secondary market, even though those securities will not mature for nine more years. It receives $5 million from the sale. It also issues its own debt securities in the primary market today so that the company can obtain an additional $10 million. Riverto's debt securities have a 10-year maturity, so investors that purchase them can redeem them at maturity (in 10 years) or sell them before that time to other investors in the secondary market. ●

An important characteristic of securities that are traded in secondary markets is **liquidity**, which is the degree to which securities can easily be liquidated (sold) without a loss of value. Some securities have an active secondary market, meaning that there are many willing buyers and sellers of the security at a given moment in time. Investors often prefer highly liquid securities so that they can easily sell the securities whenever they want (without a loss in value). An active secondary market is especially desirable for debt securities that have a long-term maturity, because it allows investors flexibility to sell them at any time prior to maturity. Many investors would not even consider investing in long-term debt securities if they were forced to hold these securities until maturity.

Treasury securities are liquid because they are frequently issued by the U.S. Treasury, and many investors want to invest in them. Therefore, investors who previously purchased Treasury securities can sell them at any time.

1-2 Securities Traded in Financial Markets

Securities can be classified as money market securities, capital market securities, or derivative securities.

1-2a Money Market Securities

Money markets facilitate the sale of short-term debt securities by deficit units to surplus units. The securities traded in this market are referred to as **money market securities**, meaning that they are debt securities that have a maturity of one year or less. These securities generally have a relatively high degree of liquidity, not only because of their short-term maturity but also because they are desirable to many investors and commonly have an active secondary market. Money market securities tend to have a low expected return but also a low degree of credit (default) risk. Common types of money market securities include Treasury bills (issued by the U.S. Treasury), commercial paper (issued by corporations), and negotiable certificates of deposit (issued by depository institutions).

1-2b Capital Market Securities

Capital markets facilitate the sale of long-term securities by deficit units to surplus units. The securities traded in this market are referred to as **capital market securities**. Capital market securities are commonly issued to finance the purchase of capital assets, such as buildings, equipment, or machinery. Three frequently encountered types of capital market securities are bonds, mortgages, and stocks.

WEB

www.investinginbonds
.com
Data and other
information about
bonds.

Bonds   Bonds are long-term debt securities issued by the Treasury, government agencies, and corporations to finance their operations. They provide a return to investors in the form of interest income (coupon payments) every six months. Because bonds represent debt, they specify the amount and timing of interest and principal payments to investors who purchase them. At maturity, investors holding the debt securities are paid the principal. Bonds commonly have maturities of between 10 and 20 years.

Treasury bonds are perceived to be free from default risk because they are issued by the U.S. Treasury. In contrast, bonds issued by corporations are subject to default (credit) risk because the issuer could default on its obligation to repay the debt. These bonds must offer a higher expected return than Treasury bonds to compensate investors for that default risk.

Bonds can be sold in the secondary market if investors do not want to hold them until maturity. Because the prices of debt securities change over time, they may be worth less when sold in the secondary market than when they were purchased.

Mortgages Mortgages are long-term debt obligations created to finance the purchase of real estate. Residential mortgages are obtained by individuals and families to purchase homes. Financial institutions serve as lenders by providing residential mortgages in their role as a financial intermediary. They can pool deposits received from surplus units and lend those funds to an individual who wants to purchase a home. Before granting a mortgage, these lenders assess the likelihood that the borrower will repay the loan based on certain criteria such as the borrower's income level relative to the value of the home. They offer prime mortgages to borrowers who qualify based on these criteria. The home serves as collateral in the event that the borrower is not able to make the mortgage payments.

Subprime mortgages are offered to some borrowers who do not have sufficient income to qualify for prime mortgages or who are unable to make a down payment. Subprime mortgages carry a higher risk of default, so the lenders providing these mortgages charge a higher interest rate (and additional up-front fees) to compensate for that factor. Subprime mortgages received much attention in 2008 because of their high default rates, which led to the credit crisis. Many lenders are no longer willing to provide subprime mortgages, and recent regulations (described later in this chapter) have raised the minimum qualifications necessary to obtain a mortgage.

Commercial mortgages are long-term debt obligations created to finance the purchase of commercial property. Real estate developers rely on commercial mortgages so that they can build shopping centers, office buildings, or other facilities. Financial institutions serve as lenders by providing commercial mortgages. By channeling funds from surplus units (depositors) to real estate developers, they serve as financial intermediaries and facilitate the development of commercial real estate.

Mortgage-Backed Securities Mortgage-backed securities are debt obligations representing claims on a package of mortgages. Many types of mortgage-backed securities exist. In their simplest form, the investors who purchase these securities receive monthly payments that are made by the homeowners on the mortgages backing the securities.

EXAMPLE

Mountain Savings Bank originates 100 residential mortgages for home buyers and will service the mortgages by processing the monthly payments. However, the bank does not want to use its own funds to finance the mortgages, so it issues mortgage-backed securities representing this package of mortgages to eight financial institutions that are willing to purchase all of these securities. Each month, when Mountain Savings Bank receives interest and principal payments on the mortgages, it passes those payments on to the eight financial institutions that purchased the mortgage-backed securities and thereby provided the financing to the homeowners. If some of the homeowners default on their mortgages, the payments will be reduced, as will the return on investment earned by the financial institutions that purchased the mortgage-backed securities. The securities they purchased are backed (collateralized) by the mortgages.

If Mountain Savings Bank is not experienced at issuing mortgage-backed securities, another financial institution may participate by bundling Mountain's 100 mortgages with mortgages originated by other institutions. Then the financial institution issues mortgage-backed securities that represent all the mortgages in the bundle. Any investor that purchases these mortgage-backed securities is partially financing the 100 mortgages at Mountain Savings Bank and all the other mortgages in the bundle that are backing these securities. ●

During the 2004–2006 period, housing prices increased rapidly, and many financial institutions used their funds to purchase mortgage-backed securities, some of which represented bundles of subprime mortgages. These financial institutions incorrectly presumed that the homes would serve as sufficient collateral if the mortgages defaulted. In 2008, many borrowers with subprime mortgages defaulted and home prices plummeted, which meant that the collateral was not adequate to cover the credit provided. Consequently, the values of mortgage-backed securities also plummeted, and the financial institutions holding these securities experienced major losses.

Stocks   Stocks (or equity securities) represent partial ownership in the corporations that issue them. They are classified as capital market securities because they have no maturity; therefore they serve as a long-term source of funds. Investors who purchase stocks (referred to as stockholders or shareholders) issued by a corporation in the primary market can sell the stocks to other investors at any time in the secondary market. However, some corporate stocks are more liquid than others. Millions of shares of stocks of large corporations are traded in the secondary market on any given day, as there are many investors who are willing to buy them. Stocks of small corporations are less liquid, because the secondary market for these stocks is not as active.

Some corporations provide income to their stockholders by distributing a portion of their quarterly earnings in the form of dividends. Other corporations retain and reinvest all of their earnings in their operations, which increases the company's growth potential.

As corporations grow and increase in value, the value of their stock increases; investors can then earn a capital gain from selling the stock for a higher price than they paid for it. Thus, investors can earn a return from stocks in the form of both periodic dividends (if there are any) and a capital gain when they sell the stock. However, stocks are subject to risk because their future prices are uncertain. When a firm performs poorly, its stock price commonly declines, resulting in negative returns to investors.

1-2c **Derivative Securities**

WEB

www.cboe.com
Information about
derivative securities.

Like money market and capital market securities, derivative securities are traded in financial markets. **Derivative securities** are financial contracts whose values are derived from the values of underlying assets (such as debt securities or equity securities). Many derivative securities enable investors to engage in speculation and risk management.

Speculation   Derivative securities allow an investor to speculate on movements in the value of the underlying assets without having to purchase those assets. Some derivative securities allow investors to benefit from an increase in the value of the underlying assets, whereas others allow investors to benefit from a decrease in the assets' value. Investors who speculate in derivative contracts can achieve higher returns than if they had speculated in the underlying assets, but they are also exposed to higher risk.

Risk Management   By investing in derivative securities that will generate gains if the value of the underlying assets declines, financial institutions and other firms can use derivative securities to reduce their exposure to the risk that the value of their existing investments in those assets may decline. Thus, if a firm maintains investments in bonds, it can take specific positions in derivative securities that will generate gains if those bonds' value declines. In this way, derivative securities can be used to reduce a firm's risk. Put simply, the loss on the bonds is offset by the gains on the derivative securities.

1-2d **Valuation of Securities**

Each type of security generates a unique stream of expected cash flows to investors. The valuation of a security is measured as the present value of its expected cash flows, discounted at a rate that reflects the uncertainty surrounding the cash flows.

Debt securities are easier to value than equity securities because they promise to provide investors with specific payments (interest and principal) until they mature. The stream of cash flows generated by stocks is more difficult to estimate because some stocks do not pay dividends; instead, investors receive cash flows only when they sell the stocks, which occurs at different times for different investors. Since the valuation of a stock at a future point in time is uncertain, so is the selling price of a stock at a future point in time. Investors often rely on financial statements issued by firms when assessing how stock prices might change in the future. In particular, investors rely on accounting reports of a firm's revenues, expenses, and earnings as a basis for estimating that company's future cash flows. Firms with publicly traded stock are required to disclose financial information and financial statements to the public.

Impact of Information on Valuation Investors can attempt to estimate the future cash flows that they will receive by obtaining information that may influence a security's future cash flows. The valuation process is illustrated in Exhibit 1.2.

Some investors rely mostly on economic or industry information to value a security, whereas others rely more on financial statements provided by the firm, or published opinions about the firm's management. When investors receive new information about a security that clearly indicates the likelihood of higher cash flows or less uncertainty surrounding the cash flows, they revise their valuations of that security upward, consequently increasing the demand for the security. In addition, investors that previously purchased that security and were planning to sell it in the secondary market may decide not to sell.

Exhibit 1.2   Use of Information to Make Investment Decisions

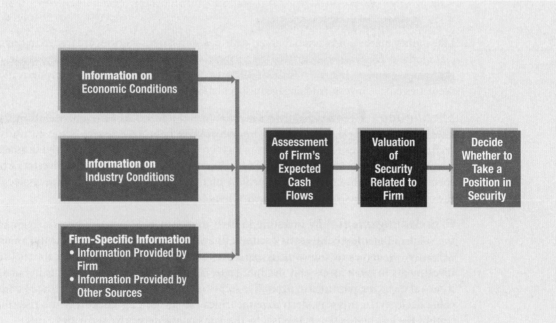

This results in a smaller supply of that security for sale (by investors who had previously purchased it) in the secondary market. In turn, the market price of the security rises to a new equilibrium level.

Conversely, when investors receive unfavorable information, they reduce the expected cash flows or increase the discount rate used in valuation. Their valuations of the security are revised downward, which results in a lower demand and an increased supply of that security for sale in the secondary market. Consequently, the equilibrium price declines.

In an **efficient market**, securities are rationally priced. If a security is clearly under-valued based on public information, some investors will capitalize on the discrepancy by purchasing that security. This strong demand for the security will push the security's price higher until the discrepancy disappears. The investors who recognized the discrepancy will be rewarded with higher returns on their investment. Their actions to capitalize on valuation discrepancies typically push security prices toward their proper price levels, based on the information that is available.

Efficiency in the stock market is enhanced by the amount of information that is easily accessible. Prices of securities are quoted online and can be obtained at any given moment by investors. For some securities, investors can track the actual sequence of transactions. Furthermore, orders to buy or sell many types of securities can be submitted online, which expedites the adjustment in security prices to new information.

WEB

finance.yahoo.com
Market quotations and overview of financial market activity.

Impact of Behavioral Finance on Valuation　In some cases, a security may be mispriced because of the psychology involved in the decision making. **Behavioral finance is the application of psychology to financial decision making.** It can offer a reason why markets are not always efficient. Behavioral finance can sometimes explain why a security's price moved abruptly, even though public information about the company's expected future cash flows did not change.

EXAMPLE

In recent years, after several states legalized the recreational use of marijuana, some companies with very little experience in any business related to marijuana announced that they were positioned to capitalize on the expected growth in this market. Many investors wanted to benefit from this potential growth and quickly purchased the stocks of companies in the newly emerging industry. However, some investors did not carefully check the business plan, operations, or financial condition of these companies. Consequently, the strong demand by investors for stocks of marijuana companies without much experience caused their stock prices to increase dramatically, only for those prices to crash after investors subjected their prospects to a closer review. ●

Behavioral finance can even be used to explain abrupt stock price movements in the entire stock market. In some periods, investors seem to be excessively optimistic about stock market conditions, and their stock-buying frenzy can push the prices of the entire stock market higher. This leads to a stock price bubble, which subsequently bursts once investors consider fundamental characteristics that affect a firm's expected future cash flows rather than hype when valuing stocks.

Uncertainty Surrounding Valuation of Securities　Even if markets are efficient, the valuation of a firm's security is subject to much uncertainty because investors have limited information available to value that security. However, a firm's managers may possess information about its financial condition that is not available to investors, a situation known as **asymmetric information**. Furthermore, although all investors can access the same public information about a firm, they may interpret it in different ways, which leads to different valuations of the firm and uncertainty surrounding the firm's stock price.

The higher the degree of uncertainty about a security's proper valuation, the higher the risk is from investing in that security. From the perspective of an investor who purchases a security, risk represents the potential deviation of the security's actual return from what was expected. For any given type of security, risk levels among the issuers of that security can vary.

Nike stock provides cash flows to investors in the form of quarterly dividends and capital gains when an investor sells the stock. Both the future dividends and the future stock price are uncertain. Thus, the cash flows the Nike stock will provide to investors over a future period are uncertain, which means the return from investing in Nike stock over that period is uncertain.

Yet the cash flow provided by Nike's stock is less uncertain than that provided by a small, young, publicly traded technology company. Because the return on the technology stock over a particular period is more uncertain than the return on Nike stock, the technology stock has more risk. ●

1-2e **Securities Regulations on Financial Disclosure**

Many regulations exist that attempt to ensure that businesses disclose accurate financial information, so that investors participating in financial markets can more properly value stocks and debt securities issued by firms. In addition, securities regulations attempt to ensure that the information disclosed by firms is made available to all prospective investors, so that no investors have an unfair information advantage over other investors.

Securities Act of 1933 The Securities Act of 1933 was intended to ensure complete disclosure of relevant financial information on publicly offered securities and to prevent fraudulent practices in selling these securities.

Securities Exchange Act of 1934 The Securities Exchange Act of 1934 extended the disclosure requirements to secondary market issues. It also declared illegal a variety of deceptive practices, such as issuing misleading financial statements and engaging in trading strategies designed to manipulate the market price. In addition, it established the Securities and Exchange Commission (SEC) to oversee the securities markets, and the SEC has implemented additional regulations over time. Securities laws seek only to ensure full disclosure of information and thereby protect against fraud; they do not prevent investors from making poor investment decisions.

Sarbanes-Oxley Act of 2002 Firms that have issued stock and debt securities are required have their financial statements audited by independent auditors (not their own employees) to verify that their financial information is accurate. However, some auditors might be motivated to ignore any misleading information disclosed by a firm so that they can receive more business from that firm in the future. Furthermore, the executives of the company can benefit from misleading information because their compensation may be tied to the company's reported profits or its stock price. In response to several well-documented cases of fraudulent financial reporting by companies that were not detected by auditors, the U.S. Congress enacted the Sarbanes-Oxley Act of 2002. It imposed restrictions to ensure proper auditing by auditors and proper oversight of the audit by the firm's board of directors. It also required key executives of the company to sign off on the financial statements, and imposed penalties on them if financial fraud was later detected. By establishing these rules, regulators tried to eliminate or at least reduce the amount of asymmetric information surrounding each publicly traded firm.

ETHICS

Nevertheless, some companies continue to engage in fraudulent financial reporting. Such behavior is unfair to investors who trust the financial reports and may overpay when purchasing the securities issued by such companies. If investors do not trust financial disclosures by companies, they may be unwilling to participate in financial markets. The lack of trust can cause markets to be less liquid due to very limited investor participation.

GLOBAL
ASPECTS

1-2f International Financial Markets

Financial markets are continuously being developed throughout the world to improve the transfer of securities between surplus and deficit units. The financial markets are much more developed in some countries than in others, and they also vary in terms of their liquidity.

The level of liquidity in each country's financial markets is influenced by local securities laws regarding financial disclosure. In general, countries that require more financial disclosure tend to have more liquid financial markets, as investors are more willing to participate when they can obtain more information about the firms whose securities they trade.

Each country has its own laws regarding shareholder rights. Investors may be more willing to participate in their country's financial markets if they have the right to bring a lawsuit against a local firm that engaged in fraudulent financial disclosure.

The enforcement of securities laws also varies from country to country. Investors may be more willing to participate in financial markets if they believe that the securities laws are being strictly enforced. Conversely, investors may avoid their country's markets if the local government fails to enforce the laws that protect investors.

International Integration of Financial Markets

Under favorable economic conditions, the international integration of financial markets allows governments and corporations easier access to funding from creditors or investors in other countries to support their growth. In addition, investors and creditors in any country can benefit from the investment opportunities available in other countries.

Conversely, under unfavorable economic conditions, the international integration of financial markets allows one country's financial problems to adversely affect other countries. When the U.S. stock market experiences an abrupt decline, financial institutions outside the United States that invest in U.S. stocks are adversely affected.

Role of Foreign Exchange Market

International financial transactions typically require the exchange of currencies. When U.S. investors purchase German stock, their U.S. dollars are converted to euros. When they sell the stock, the euros they receive will be converted back to dollars. The **foreign exchange market** facilitates these kinds of exchanges involving different currencies. Many financial institutions serve as intermediaries in the foreign exchange market by matching up participants who want to exchange one currency for another. Some of these financial institutions also serve as dealers by taking positions in currencies to accommodate foreign exchange requests.

Like securities, most currencies have a market-determined price (exchange rate) that changes in response to supply and demand. If the aggregate demand by corporations, government agencies, and individuals for a given currency shifts suddenly, or if the aggregate supply of that currency for sale (to be exchanged for another currency) changes abruptly, the price of the currency (exchange rate) will change. The exchange rate of a currency can fluctuate substantially over time, which in turn affects the return earned by investors who invest in securities in international financial markets. U.S. investors benefit when the currency denominating a foreign security that they purchased appreciates against the dollar over their investment horizon.

1-3 Role of Financial Institutions

Because financial markets are **imperfect**, securities buyers and sellers do not have full access to all possible information. Individuals with available funds usually are not capable of identifying creditworthy borrowers to whom they could lend those funds. In addition, they do not have the expertise to assess the creditworthiness of potential borrowers. Financial institutions are needed to resolve these kinds of limitations caused by market imperfections. They accept funds from surplus units and channel the funds to deficit units. Without financial institutions, the information and transaction costs of financial market transactions would be excessive. Financial institutions can be classified as depository and nondepository institutions.

1-3a Role of Depository Institutions

Depository institutions accept deposits from surplus units and provide credit to deficit units through loans and purchases of securities. They are popular financial institutions for the following reasons:

- They offer deposit accounts that can accommodate the amount and liquidity characteristics desired by most surplus units.
- They repackage funds received from deposits to provide loans of the size and maturity desired by deficit units.
- They are willing to accept the risk of default on loans that they provide.
- They have more expertise than individual surplus units in evaluating the creditworthiness of prospective deficit units.
- They diversify their loans among numerous deficit units, which means they can absorb defaulted loans better than individual surplus units could.

To appreciate these advantages, consider what the flow of funds from surplus units to deficit units would be like if depository institutions did not exist. Each surplus unit would have to identify a deficit unit desiring to borrow the precise amount of funds available for the precise time period in which funds would be available. Furthermore, each surplus unit would have to perform the credit evaluation of the potential borrower and incur the risk of default. Under these conditions, many surplus units would likely hold their funds closely rather than channel them to deficit units. Hence, the flow of funds from surplus units to deficit units would be disrupted.

When a depository institution offers a loan, it is acting as a creditor, just as if it had purchased a debt security. The loan agreement is less marketable in the secondary market than a debt security, however, because the loan agreement is personalized for the particular borrower and contains detailed provisions that can differ significantly among loans. Potential investors would need to review all provisions before purchasing loans in the secondary market.

A more specific description of each depository institution's role in the financial markets follows.

Commercial Banks   In aggregate, commercial banks are the most dominant type of depository institution. They serve surplus units by offering a wide variety of deposit accounts, and they transfer deposited funds to deficit units by providing direct loans or purchasing debt securities. Commercial bank operations are exposed to risk because their loans and many of their investments in debt securities are subject to the risk of default by the borrowers.

Commercial banks serve both the private and public sectors; their deposit and lending services are utilized by households, businesses, and government agencies. Some commercial banks (including Bank of America, JPMorgan Chase, Citigroup, and Wells Fargo) have more than $1 trillion in assets.

Some commercial banks receive more funds from deposits than they need to make loans or invest in securities. Other commercial banks need more funds to accommodate customer requests than the amount of funds that they receive from deposits. The **federal funds market** facilitates the flow of funds between depository institutions (including banks). A bank that has excess funds can lend to a bank with deficient funds for a short-term period, such as one to five days. In this way, the federal funds market facilitates the flow of funds from banks that have excess funds to banks that need funds.

Commercial banks are subject to regulations that are intended to limit their exposure to the risk of failure. In particular, banks are required to maintain a minimum level of capital, relative to their size, so that they have a cushion to absorb possible losses from defaults on some loans provided to households or businesses. The Federal Reserve ("the Fed") serves as a regulator of banks.

WEB

www.fdic.gov
Information and news about banks and savings institutions.

Savings Institutions   Savings institutions, which are sometimes referred to as thrift institutions, are another type of depository institution. Savings institutions include savings and loan associations (S&Ls) and savings banks. Like commercial banks, savings institutions take deposits from surplus units and then channel these deposits to deficit units. Savings banks are similar to S&Ls except that they have more diversified uses of funds. Over time, this difference, which was once quite pronounced, has narrowed.

Savings institutions can be owned by shareholders, but most are mutual (depositor owned). Like commercial banks, savings institutions rely on the federal funds market to lend their excess funds or to borrow funds on a short-term basis.

Whereas commercial banks concentrate on commercial (business) loans, savings institutions concentrate on residential mortgage loans. In most cases, mortgage loans are perceived to exhibit a relatively low level of risk.

Credit Unions   Credit unions differ from commercial banks and savings institutions in that they (1) are nonprofit enterprises and (2) restrict their business to credit union members, who share a common bond (such as a common employer or union). Like savings institutions, they are sometimes classified as thrift institutions in an effort to distinguish them from commercial banks. Because of the "common bond" characteristic, credit unions tend to be much smaller than other depository institutions. They use most of their funds to provide loans to their members. Some of the largest credit unions (e.g., the Navy Federal Credit Union, the State Employees Credit Union of North Carolina, the Pentagon Federal Credit Union) have assets of more than $20 billion.

1-3b **Role of Nondepository Financial Institutions**

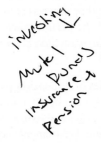

Nondepository institutions generate funds from sources other than deposits but also play a major role in financial intermediation. These institutions are briefly described here and are covered in more detail in Part 7.

Finance Companies   Most finance companies obtain funds by issuing securities and then lend those funds to individuals and small businesses. The functions of finance companies and depository institutions overlap, although each type of institution concentrates on a particular segment of the financial markets (as explained in the chapters devoted to these institutions).

Mutual Funds   Mutual funds sell shares to surplus units and use the funds received to purchase a portfolio of securities. They are the dominant nondepository financial institution when measured in total assets. Some mutual funds concentrate their investments in capital market securities, such as stocks or bonds. Others, known as **money market mutual funds**, concentrate in money market securities. By investing in mutual funds and money market funds, small savers are able to invest in a diversified portfolio of securities while committing only a relatively small amount of money to each security.

Securities Firms   Securities firms provide a wide variety of functions in financial markets. Some securities firms act as a **broker**, executing securities transactions between two parties for a commission (or markup). The commission as a percentage of the transaction amount will likely be higher for less common transactions, because more time is needed to match up buyers and sellers. The commission will also likely be higher for transactions involving relatively small amounts, so that the broker will be adequately compensated for the time required to execute the transaction.

Securities firms also often act as **dealers**, making a market in specific securities by maintaining an inventory of securities. Whereas a broker's income is mostly based on commissions, a dealer's income is influenced by the performance of the security portfolio maintained. Some dealers also provide brokerage services and therefore earn income from both types of activities.

In addition to brokerage and dealer services, securities firms may provide underwriting and advising services. The underwriting and advising services are commonly referred to as *investment banking*, and the securities firms that specialize in these services are sometimes referred to as *investment banks*. Some securities firms place newly issued securities for corporations and government agencies; this task differs from traditional brokerage activities because it involves the primary market. When securities firms **underwrite** newly issued securities, they may either sell the securities for a client at a guaranteed price or simply sell the securities at the best price they can get for their client.

Some securities firms offer advisory services on mergers and other forms of corporate restructuring. In addition to helping a company plan its restructuring, the securities firm executes the change in the client's capital structure by placing the securities issued by the company.

Insurance Companies   Insurance companies provide individuals and firms with insurance policies that reduce the financial burden associated with death, illness, and damage to property. These companies charge fees (called premiums) in exchange for the insurance that they provide. They invest the funds received in the form of premiums until the funds are needed to cover insurance claims. Insurance companies commonly invest these funds in stocks or bonds issued by corporations or in bonds issued by the government. By financing the needs of deficit units in this way, they serve as important financial intermediaries. Their overall performance is linked to the performance of the stocks and bonds in which they invest. Large insurance companies include State Farm, Allstate, Travelers, CNA Financial, and Liberty Mutual.

Pension Funds   Many corporations and government agencies offer pension plans to their employees. The employees and sometimes their employers periodically contribute funds to the plan, and pension funds manage the money until the individuals withdraw the funds for their retirement. The money that is contributed to individual retirement accounts is commonly invested by the pension funds in stocks or bonds issued by corporations or in bonds issued by the government. Thus, pension funds are important financial intermediaries that finance the needs of deficit units.

1-3c Comparison of Roles among Financial Institutions

The role of financial institutions in facilitating the flow of funds from individual surplus units (investors) to deficit units is illustrated in Exhibit 1.3. Surplus units are shown on the left side of the exhibit, and deficit units are shown on the right. Three different flows of funds from surplus units to deficit units are depicted in the exhibit. One set of flows represents deposits from surplus units that are transformed by depository institutions into loans for deficit units. A second set of flows represents purchases of securities (commercial paper) issued by finance companies that are transformed into finance company loans for deficit units. A third set of flows reflects the purchases of shares issued by mutual funds, which are used by the mutual funds to purchase debt and equity securities of deficit units.

The deficit units also receive funding from insurance companies and pension funds. Because insurance companies and pension funds purchase massive amounts of stocks and bonds, they finance much of the expenditures made by large deficit units, such as corporations and government agencies. Financial institutions such as commercial banks, insurance companies, mutual funds, and pension funds take charge of investing funds that they have received from surplus units, so they are often referred to as *institutional investors*.

Securities firms are not shown in Exhibit 1.3, but they play an important role in facilitating the flow of funds. Many of the transactions between the financial institutions and deficit units are executed by securities firms. Furthermore, some funds flow directly from surplus units to deficit units as a result of security transactions, with securities firms serving as brokers.

Exhibit 1.3 Comparison of Roles among Financial Institutions

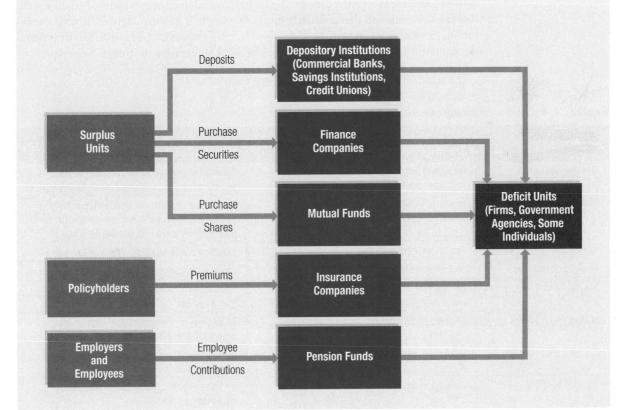

In recent years, the flow of funds has been facilitated by peer-to-peer lending websites that enable persons with excess money to make loans to persons needing funds. The website verifies information about a potential borrower such as employment, income, and credit rating and assigns the borrower a risk score. Lenders can then offer loans with the interest rate based on the borrower's risk.

Institutional Role as a Monitor of Publicly Traded Firms   In addition to filling the roles described in Exhibit 1.3, financial institutions serve as monitors of publicly traded firms. Because insurance companies, pension funds, and some mutual funds are major investors in stocks, they can influence the management of publicly traded firms. In recent years, many large institutional investors have publicly criticized specific firms for poor management, which has resulted in corporate restructuring or even the firing of executives in some cases. Thus, institutional investors not only provide financial support to companies, but also exercise some degree of corporate control over them. By serving as activist shareholders, they can help ensure that managers of publicly held corporations make appropriate decisions that are in the best interests of the shareholders.

1-3d Relative Importance of Financial Institutions

Financial institutions hold assets equal to approximately $70 trillion. Among depository institutions, commercial banks hold the most assets, with nearly $17 trillion in aggregate. Among nondepository institutions, mutual funds hold the largest amount of assets, with approximately $18 trillion in aggregate.

Exhibit 1.4 summarizes the main sources and uses of funds for each type of financial institution. Households with savings are served by depository institutions. Households with deficient funds are served by depository institutions and finance companies. Large corporations and governments that issue securities obtain financing from all types of financial institutions. Several agencies regulate the various types of financial institutions, and the various regulations may give some financial institutions a comparative advantage over others.

Exhibit 1.4   Summary of Institutional Sources and Uses of Funds

FINANCIAL INSTITUTIONS	MAIN SOURCES OF FUNDS	MAIN USES OF FUNDS
Commercial banks	Deposits from households, businesses, and government agencies	Purchases of government and corporate securities; loans to businesses and households
Savings institutions	Deposits from households, businesses, and government agencies	Purchases of government and corporate securities; mortgages and other loans to households; some loans to businesses
Credit unions	Deposits from credit union members	Loans to credit union members
Finance companies	Securities sold to households and businesses	Loans to households and businesses
Mutual funds	Shares sold to households, businesses, and government agencies	Purchases of long-term government and corporate securities
Money market funds	Shares sold to households, businesses, and government agencies	Purchases of short-term government and corporate securities
Insurance companies	Insurance premiums and earnings from investments	Purchases of long-term government and corporate securities
Pension funds	Employer/employee contributions	Purchases of long-term government and corporate securities

1-3e Consolidation of Financial Institutions

In recent years, some financial institutions have merged in an effort to achieve economies of scale. By increasing the volume of services produced with a given infrastructure, the average cost of providing the services (such as loans) can be reduced.

Historically, each kind of financial service (such as banking, mortgages, brokerage, and insurance) was provided by a different type of financial institution due to regulations that prevented firms from offering a range of services. As these regulations were loosened over the last 20 years, firms that had specialized in one service expanded into other financial services. By becoming a financial conglomerate, they could capitalize on economies of scope. As financial institutions spread into other financial services, the competition for customers desiring the various types of financial services increased. In turn, prices of financial services declined in response to the competition.

Exhibit 1.5 depicts the typical organizational structure of a financial conglomerate. Although the operations of each type of financial service are commonly managed separately, a financial conglomerate offers advantages to customers who prefer to obtain all of their financial services from a single financial institution. Because a financial conglomerate is more diversified, it may be less exposed to a possible decline in customer demand for any single financial service. Many commercial banks now offer an expansive set of financial services.

Global Consolidation of Financial Institutions   Many financial institutions have expanded internationally to capitalize on their expertise. Notably, commercial banks, insurance companies, and securities firms have all expanded through international mergers. An international merger between financial institutions enables the merged company to offer the services of both entities to its entire customer base. For example, a U.S. commercial bank may specialize in lending while a European securities firm specializes

Exhibit 1.5   Organizational Structure of a Financial Conglomerate

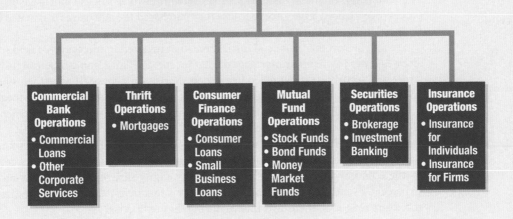

in services such as underwriting securities. A merger between the two entities allows the U.S. bank to provide its services to the European customer base (clients of the European securities firm) and allows the European securities firm to offer its services to the U.S. customer base. By combining specialized skills and customer bases, the merged financial institutions can offer more services to clients and gain an international customer base.

The adoption of the euro by 19 European countries has increased business between those countries and created a more competitive environment in Europe. European financial institutions, which had primarily competed with other financial institutions based in their own country, recognized that they would now face more competition from financial institutions in other countries with the development of the eurozone.

Many other financial institutions have attempted to benefit from opportunities in emerging markets. For example, some large securities firms have expanded into many countries to offer underwriting services for firms and government agencies. The need for this service has increased most dramatically in countries where businesses have been privatized. In addition, commercial banks have expanded into emerging markets to provide loans. Although this move allows them to capitalize on opportunities in these countries, it also exposes them to financial problems in these countries.

1-4 Systemic Risk among Financial Institutions

Given the frequent business transactions between the various types of financial institutions, financial problems that occur at one or a few financial institutions can quickly spread to others. **Systemic risk** is defined as the spread of financial problems among financial institutions and across financial markets that could cause a collapse in the financial system. It exists because financial institutions invest their funds in similar types of securities and therefore have similar exposure to large declines in the prices of these securities. Furthermore, they commonly engage in various loan and guarantee arrangements that cause one financial institution to rely on others for payment. The subsequent bankruptcy of one large financial institution can cause defaults on payments to several other financial institutions, which might reduce their ability to cover their respective obligations to other financial institutions. This can result in bankruptcy for many financial institutions.

During the credit crisis of 2008 and 2009, mortgage defaults affected financial institutions in several ways. First, many financial institutions that originated mortgages shortly before the crisis sold them to other financial institutions (i.e., commercial banks, savings institutions, mutual funds, insurance companies, securities firms, and pension funds). Therefore, even financial institutions that were not involved in the mortgage origination process experienced large losses because they purchased the mortgages originated by other financial institutions.

Second, many other financial institutions that invested in mortgage-backed securities received lower payments as mortgage defaults occurred. Third, some financial institutions (especially securities firms) relied heavily on short-term debt to finance their operations and used their holdings of mortgage-backed securities as collateral. But when the prices of mortgage-backed securities plummeted, they could not issue new short-term debt to pay off the principal on maturing debt.

Fourth, as mortgage defaults increased, there was an excess of unoccupied housing. There was no need to construct new homes, so construction companies laid off many employees. As the economy weakened, the prices of many equity securities declined by more than 40 percent. Eventually, most financial institutions that invested heavily in equities experienced large losses on their investments during the credit crisis.

The U.S. government intervened in an attempt to improve the economy and rescued some financial institutions. It also imposed new regulations on the mortgage markets (as explained in Chapter 9) in an effort to prevent a similar type of credit crisis from occurring in the future.

Summary

- Financial markets facilitate the transfer of funds from surplus units to deficit units. Because funding needs vary among deficit units, different types of financial markets have been established. The primary market allows for the issuance of new securities, and the secondary market allows for the sale of existing securities.

- Securities can be classified as money market (short-term) securities or capital market (long-term) securities. Common capital market securities include bonds, mortgages, mortgage-backed securities, and stocks. The valuation of a security represents the present value of future cash flows that it is expected to generate. New information that indicates a change in expected cash flows or degree of uncertainty affects the prices of securities in the financial markets.

- Depository and nondepository institutions help to finance the needs of deficit units. The main depository institutions are commercial banks, savings institutions, and credit unions. The main nondepository institutions are finance companies, mutual funds, pension funds, and insurance companies.

- Many financial institutions have been consolidated (due to mergers) into financial conglomerates, in which they serve as subsidiaries of the conglomerate while conducting their specialized services. In this way, some financial conglomerates are able to provide all types of financial services. Consolidation allows for economies of scale and scope, which can enhance cash flows and increase the financial institution's value. In addition, consolidation can diversify the institution's services and increase its value by reducing risk.

- Financial institutions are subject to systemic risk, because they commonly invest in the same types of securities and are similarly exposed to conditions that could cause the prices of those securities to decline substantially. The credit crisis of 2008 and 2009 illustrates how massive mortgage defaults can cause a major decline in the prices of mortgage-backed securities and equity securities, which are investments commonly held by many types of financial institutions.

Point/Counterpoint

Will Computer Technology Cause Financial Intermediaries to Become Extinct?

Point Yes. Financial intermediaries benefit from access to information. As information becomes more accessible, individuals will have the information they need before investing or borrowing funds. They will not need financial intermediaries to make their decisions.

Counterpoint No. Individuals rely not only on information but also on expertise. Some financial intermediaries specialize in credit analysis so that they can make wise choices when offering loans. Surplus units will continue to provide funds to financial intermediaries, rather than make direct loans, because they are not capable of credit analysis even if more information about prospective borrowers is available. Some financial intermediaries no longer have physical buildings for customer service, but they still require agents who have the expertise to assess the creditworthiness of prospective borrowers.

Who Is Correct? Use the Internet to learn more about this issue and then formulate your own opinion.

Questions and Applications

1. **Surplus and Deficit Units** Explain the meaning of surplus units and deficit units. Provide an example of each. Which types of financial institutions do you deal with? Explain whether you are acting as a surplus unit or a deficit unit in your relationship with each financial institution.

2. **Types of Markets** Distinguish between primary and secondary markets. Distinguish between money and capital markets.

3. **Imperfect Markets** Distinguish between perfect and imperfect security markets. Explain why the existence of imperfect markets creates a need for financial intermediaries.

4. **Efficient Markets** Explain the meaning of efficient markets. Why might we expect markets to be efficient most of the time? In recent years, several securities firms have been guilty of using inside information when purchasing securities, thereby achieving returns well above the norm (even when accounting for risk). Does this suggest that the security markets are not efficient? Explain.

5. **Securities Laws** What was the purpose of the Securities Act of 1933? What was the purpose of the Securities Exchange Act of 1934? Do these laws prevent investors from making poor investment decisions? Explain.

6. **International Barriers** Discuss why many financial institutions have expanded internationally in recent years. What advantages can be obtained through an international merger of financial institutions?

7. **Stock Valuation** What type of information do investors rely on when determining the proper value of stocks?

8. **Securities Firms** What are the functions of securities firms? Many securities firms employ brokers and dealers. Distinguish between the functions of a broker and those of a dealer, and explain how each type of professional is compensated.

9. **Mis-valued Marijuana Stocks** Explain why some stocks in the marijuana industry were mis-valued when several states legalized the recreational use of marijuana.

10. **Marketability** Commercial banks use some funds to purchase securities and other funds to make loans. Why are the securities more marketable than the loans in the secondary market?

11. **Depository Institutions** Explain the primary use of funds by commercial banks versus savings institutions.

12. **Credit Unions** With regard to the profit motive, how are credit unions different from other financial institutions?

13. **Nondepository Institutions** Compare the main sources and uses of funds for finance companies, insurance companies, and pension funds.

14. **Mutual Funds** What is the function of a mutual fund? Why are mutual funds popular among investors? How does a money market mutual fund differ from a stock or bond mutual fund?

15. **Secondary Market for Debt Securities.** Why is it important for long-term debt securities to have an active secondary market?

Advanced Questions

16. **Comparing Financial Institutions** Classify the types of financial institutions mentioned in this chapter as either depository or nondepository. Explain the general difference between depository and nondepository institutions as sources of funds. It is often said that all types of financial institutions have begun to offer services that were previously offered only by certain types. Consequently, the operations of many financial institutions are becoming more similar. Nevertheless, performance levels still differ significantly among types of financial institutions. Why?

17. **Financial Intermediation** Look in a business periodical for news about a recent financial transaction involving two financial institutions. For this transaction, determine the following:

a. How will each institution's balance sheet be affected?

b. Will either institution receive immediate income from the transaction?

c. Who is the ultimate user of funds?

d. Who is the ultimate source of funds?

18. **Role of Accounting in Financial Markets** Integrate the roles of accounting, regulation, and financial market participation. That is, explain how financial market participants rely on accounting and why regulatory oversight of the accounting process is necessary.

19. Factors That Influence Liquidity Which factors influence a security's liquidity?

20. Impact of Credit Crisis on Institutions Explain why mortgage defaults during the credit crisis in 2008 and 2009 adversely affected financial institutions that did not originate the mortgages. What role did these institutions play in financing the mortgages?

21. Impact of Fraudulent Financial Reporting on Market Liquidity Explain why financial markets may be less liquid if companies are not forced to provide accurate financial reports.

22. Impact of a Country's Laws on Its Market Liquidity Describe how a country's laws can influence the degree of its financial market liquidity.

23. Global Financial Market Regulations Assume that countries A and B are of similar size, that they have similar economies, and that the government debt levels of both countries are within reasonable limits. Assume that the regulations in country A require complete disclosure of financial reporting by issuers of debt in that country, whereas regulations in country B do not require much disclosure of financial reporting. Explain why the government of country A is able to issue debt at a lower cost than the government of country B.

24. Influence of Financial Markets Some countries do not have well-established markets for debt securities or equity securities. Why do you think this can limit the development of the country, business expansion, and growth in national income in these countries?

25. Impact of Systemic Risk Different types of financial institutions commonly interact. Specifically, they may provide loans to each other and take opposite positions on many different types of financial agreements, whereby one will owe the other based on a specific financial outcome. Explain why these kinds of relationships create concerns about systemic risk.

26. Uncertainty Surrounding Stock Price Assume that your publicly traded company attempts to be completely transparent about its financial condition, and provides thorough information about its debt, sales, and earnings every quarter. Explain why there still may be much uncertainty surrounding your company's stock price.

27. Financial Institutions' Roles as Intermediaries Explain how each type of financial institution serves as a financial intermediary.

28. Systemic Risk During a Financial Crisis Explain why financial institutions are highly exposed to systemic risk during a financial crisis.

Critical Thinking Question

Impact of Financial Crisis on Market Liquidity During a financial crisis, liquidity in financial markets declines dramatically, and many surplus units no longer participate in financial markets. Yet, if the markets are efficient, securities prices should decline due to existing economic conditions, which should make these securities appealing to potential investors. Nevertheless, many investors typically are no longer willing to participate in the financial markets under these conditions. Write a short essay that explains the logic behind why participants may temporarily disappear during a financial crisis even though security prices are low, causing illiquidity in financial markets.

Interpreting Financial News

"Interpreting Financial News" tests your ability to comprehend common statements made by Wall Street analysts and portfolio managers who participate in the financial markets. Interpret the following statements.

a. "The price of Apple stock will not be affected by the announcement that its earnings have increased as expected."
b. "The lending operations at Bank of America should benefit from strong economic growth."
c. "The brokerage and underwriting performance at Goldman Sachs should benefit from strong economic growth."

Managing in Financial Markets

Utilizing Financial Markets As a financial manager of a large firm, you plan to borrow $70 million over the next year.

a. What are the most likely ways in which you can borrow $70 million?
b. Assuming that you decide to issue debt securities, describe the types of financial institutions that may purchase these securities.
c. How do individuals indirectly provide the financing for your firm when they maintain deposits at depository institutions, invest in mutual funds, purchase insurance policies, or invest in pensions?

Flow of Funds Exercise

Roles of Financial Markets and Institutions

This continuing exercise focuses on the interactions of a single manufacturing firm (Carson Company) in the financial markets. It illustrates how financial markets and institutions are integrated and facilitate the flow of funds in the business and financial environment. At the end of every chapter, this exercise provides a list of questions about Carson Company that requires the application of concepts presented in the chapter as they relate to the flow of funds.

Carson Company is a large manufacturing firm in California that was created 20 years ago by the Carson family. It was initially financed with an equity investment by the Carson family and 10 other individuals. Over time, Carson Company obtained substantial loans from finance companies and commercial banks. The interest rates on those loans are tied to market interest rates and are adjusted every six months. Thus, Carson's cost of obtaining funds is sensitive to interest rate movements.

The company has a credit line with a bank in case it suddenly needs additional funds for a temporary period. It has purchased Treasury securities that it could sell if it experiences any liquidity problems.

Carson Company has assets valued at approximately $50 million and generates sales of nearly $100 million per year. Some of its growth is attributed to its acquisitions of other firms. Because it expects the U.S. economy to be strong in the future, Carson plans to grow by expanding its business and by making more acquisitions. It expects that it will need substantial long-term financing and plans to borrow additional funds either through obtaining loans or by issuing bonds. It is also considering issuing stock to raise funds in the next year. Carson closely monitors conditions in financial markets that could affect its cash inflows and cash outflows and thereby affect its value.

a. In what way is Carson a surplus unit?

b. In what way is Carson a deficit unit?

c. How might finance companies facilitate Carson's expansion?

d. How might commercial banks facilitate Carson's expansion?

e. Why might Carson have limited access to additional debt financing during its growth phase?

f. How might securities firms facilitate Carson's expansion?

g. How might Carson use the primary market to facilitate its expansion?

h. How might it use the secondary market?

i. If financial markets were perfect, how might this factor have allowed Carson to avoid financial institutions?

j. The loans that Carson has obtained from commercial banks stipulate that Carson must receive the bank's approval before pursuing any large projects. What is the purpose of this condition? Does this condition benefit the owners of the company?

Internet/Excel Exercises

1. Review the information for the common stock of IBM, using the website finance.yahoo.com. Search for the ticker symbol "IBM." The main goal at this point is to become familiar with the information that you can obtain at this website. Review the data shown for IBM stock. Compare the price of IBM stock based on its last trade with the price range for the year. Is the price near its high or low price? What is the total value of IBM stock (Market Cap)? What is the average daily trading volume (Avg Volume) of IBM stock? Click on "5Y" just above the stock price chart to see IBM's stock price movements over the last five years. Describe the trend in IBM's stock over this period. At what points were the stock price the highest and lowest?

2. Repeat the questions in exercise 1 for the Children's Place, Inc. (ticker symbol "PLCE"). Explain how the market capitalization and trading volume for PLCE differ from those for IBM.

WSJ Exercise

Differentiating between Primary and Secondary Markets

Review the different tables relating to stock markets and bond markets that appear in the *Wall Street Journal*. Explain whether each of these tables is focused on the primary or secondary markets.

Online Articles with Real-World Examples

Find a recent practical article online that describes a real-world example regarding a specific financial institution or financial market that reinforces one or more concepts covered in this chapter.

If your class has an online component, your professor may ask you to post your summary of the article there and provide a link to the article so that other students can access it. If your class is live, your professor may ask you to summarize your application of the article in class. Your professor may assign specific students to complete this assignment or may allow any students to do the assignment on a volunteer basis.

For recent online articles and real-world examples related to this chapter, consider using the following search terms (be sure to include the prevailing year as a search term to ensure that the online articles are recent):

1. secondary market AND liquidity
2. secondary market AND offering
3. money market
4. bond offering
5. stock offering
6. valuation AND stock
7. market efficiency
8. financial AND regulation
9. financial institution AND operations
10. financial institution AND governance

2

Determination of Interest Rates

CHAPTER OBJECTIVES

The specific objectives of this chapter are to:

- Apply the loanable funds theory to explain why interest rates change.

- Identify the most relevant factors that affect interest rate movements.

- Explain how to forecast interest rates.

WEB

www.bloomberg.com
Information on interest rates in recent months.

An interest rate reflects the rate of return that a creditor receives when lending money, or the rate that a borrower pays when borrowing money. Because interest rates change over time, so does the rate earned by the creditors who provide loans and the rate paid by the borrowers who obtain loans. Interest rate movements have a direct influence on the market values of debt securities, such as money market securities, bonds, and mortgages. They also have an indirect influence on equity security values because they can affect economic conditions, and therefore influence the cash inflows to corporations. Since interest rates represent the cost of borrowing, they directly affect corporate cash outflow payments on debt.

Interest rate movements also affect the value of most financial institutions. They influence the cost of funds to depository institutions and the interest received on some loans by financial institutions. Since financial institutions commonly invest in securities, the market value of their investment portfolios is affected by interest rate movements. Managers of financial institutions attempt to anticipate interest rate movements and commonly restructure their assets and liabilities to capitalize on their expectations. Individuals also attempt to anticipate interest rate movements so that they can estimate the potential cost of borrowing or the potential return from investing in various debt securities.

2-1 Loanable Funds Theory

The **loanable funds theory**, commonly used to explain interest rate movements, suggests that the market interest rate is determined by factors controlling the supply of and demand for loanable funds. This theory is especially useful for explaining movements in the general level of interest rates for a particular country. Furthermore, it can be used (along with other concepts) to explain why interest rates for some debt securities of a given country vary, which is the focus of the next chapter. The phrase "demand for loanable funds" is widely used in financial markets to refer to the collective borrowing activities of households, businesses, and governments. This chapter describes the sectors that commonly affect the demand for loanable funds and then describes the sectors that supply loanable funds to the markets. Finally, the demand and supply concepts are integrated to explain interest rate movements.

Exhibit 2.1   Relationship between Interest Rates and Household Demand (D_h) for Loanable Funds at a Given Point in Time

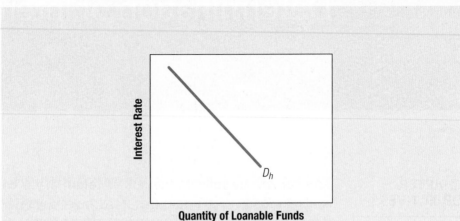

2-1a Household Demand for Loanable Funds

Households commonly demand loanable funds to finance their housing expenditures. In addition, they finance the purchases of automobiles and household items, which results in installment debt. As the aggregate level of household income rises, so does installment debt, because households are more comfortable financing expenses when their income is relatively high. The level of installment debt as a percentage of disposable income has been increasing over time, although it is generally lower in recessionary periods.

An inverse relationship exists between the interest rate and the quantity of loanable funds demanded by households. At any moment in time, households (in aggregate) demand a greater quantity of loanable funds at lower rates of interest; in other words, they are willing to borrow more money at lower interest rates.

EXAMPLE

Consider the household demand-for-loanable-funds schedule (also called the *demand curve*) in Exhibit 2.1, which shows how the amount of funds that would be demanded depends on the interest rate at a given point in time. Various events can cause household borrowing preferences to change over time, thereby shifting the demand curve. For example, if tax rates on household income are expected to decrease significantly in the future, households might believe that they can more easily afford future loan repayments and thus be willing to borrow more funds. Under this scenario, the quantity of loanable funds demanded by households at any particular interest rate would be greater as a result of the tax rate change. This represents an outward shift (to the right) in the demand curve. ●

WEB

www.treasurydirect.gov
Information on the U.S.
government's debt.

2-1b Business Demand for Loanable Funds

Businesses need funds to invest in long-term assets. Business investment in new projects should be greater when interest rates are low, as the cost of financing potential projects should be low. Consequently, businesses will demand a greater quantity of loanable funds at a given point in time if interest rates are lower, as illustrated in Exhibit 2.2.

2-1c Government Demand for Loanable Funds

Whenever a government's planned expenditures cannot be completely covered by its incoming revenues from taxes and other sources, it demands loanable funds. Municipal (state and local) governments issue municipal bonds to obtain these kinds of funds; the

Exhibit 2.2   Relationship between Interest Rates and Business Demand (D_b) for Loanable Funds at a Given Point in Time

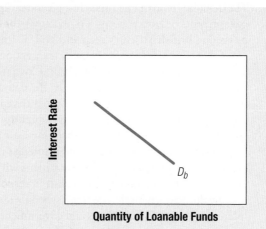

Quantity of Loanable Funds

federal government and its agencies issue Treasury securities and federal agency securities. These securities constitute government debt.

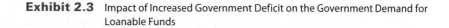
The federal government's expenditure and tax policies are generally thought to be independent of interest rates. Thus, the federal government's demand for funds is **interest-inelastic**, or insensitive to interest rates. In contrast, municipal governments sometimes postpone proposed expenditures if the cost of financing is too high, implying that their demand for loanable funds is somewhat sensitive to interest rates.

Like household and business demand, government demand for loanable funds can shift in response to various events.

EXAMPLE

The federal government's demand-for-loanable-funds schedule is represented by D_{g1} in Exhibit 2.3. If new laws are passed that cause a net increase of $200 billion in the deficit, the federal government's demand for loanable funds will increase by that amount. In the graph, this new demand schedule is represented by D_{g2}. ●

Exhibit 2.3   Impact of Increased Government Deficit on the Government Demand for Loanable Funds

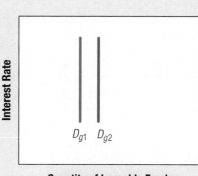

Quantity of Loanable Funds

2-1d Foreign Demand for Loanable Funds

The demand for loanable funds in a given market also includes foreign demand by foreign governments or corporations. For example, the British government may obtain financing by issuing British Treasury securities to U.S. investors; this represents British demand for U.S. funds. Because foreign financial transactions are becoming so common, they can have a significant impact on the demand for loanable funds in any given country. A foreign country's demand for U.S. funds (i.e., the country's preference to borrow U.S. dollars) is influenced by, among other factors, the difference between its own interest rates and U.S. rates. Other things being equal, a larger quantity of U.S. funds will be demanded by foreign governments and corporations if their domestic interest rates are high relative to U.S. rates. As a result, for a given set of foreign interest rates, the quantity of U.S. loanable funds demanded by foreign governments or firms will be inversely related to U.S. interest rates.

The foreign demand curve can shift in response to economic conditions. For example, assume the original foreign demand schedule is represented by D_{f1} in Exhibit 2.4. If foreign interest rates rise, foreign firms and governments will likely increase their demand for U.S. funds, as represented by the shift from D_{f1} to D_{f2}.

2-1e Aggregate Demand for Loanable Funds

The aggregate demand for loanable funds is the sum of the quantities demanded by the separate sectors at any given interest rate, as shown in Exhibit 2.5. Because most of these sectors are likely to demand a larger quantity of funds at lower interest rates (other things being equal), it follows that the aggregate demand for loanable funds is inversely related to the prevailing interest rate. If the demand schedule of any sector changes, the aggregate demand schedule will also be affected.

2-1f Supply of Loanable Funds

The term "supply of loanable funds" is commonly used to refer to funds provided to financial markets by savers. The household sector is the largest supplier of such funds, but loanable funds are also supplied by some government units that temporarily generate more tax revenues than they spend or by some businesses whose cash inflows exceed outflows during a particular period. Although households as a group are a net supplier of loanable funds, governments and businesses are net demanders of loanable funds.

Exhibit 2.4   Impact of Increased Foreign Interest Rates on the Foreign Demand for U.S. Loanable Funds

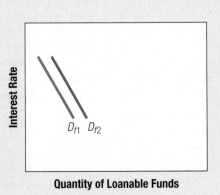

Exhibit 2.5   Determination of the Aggregate Demand Curve for Loanable Funds

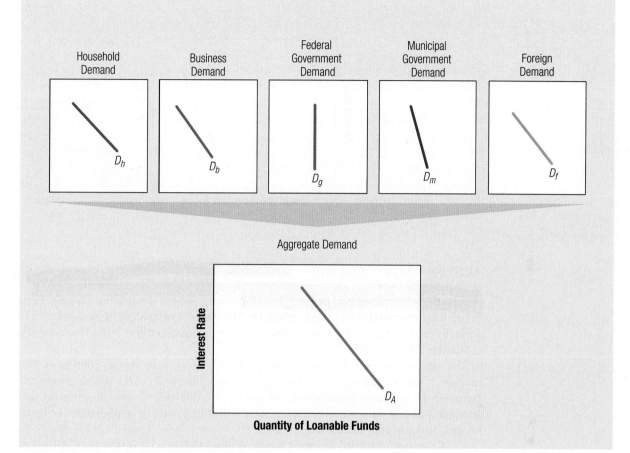

Suppliers of loanable funds are willing to supply more funds at a given point in time if the interest rate (the reward for supplying funds) is higher, other things being equal. This means that the supply-of-loanable-funds schedule (also called the supply curve) is upward sloping, as shown in Exhibit 2.6. A supply of loanable funds exists at even a very low interest rate because some households choose to postpone consumption until later years, even when the reward (interest rate) for saving is low. Foreign households, governments, and businesses commonly supply funds to their domestic markets by purchasing domestic securities. In addition, they have been major suppliers of funds to the U.S. government by purchasing large amounts of Treasury securities. The large foreign supply of funds to the U.S. market is due in part to the high saving rates of foreign households.

Effects of the Fed
The supply of loanable funds in the United States is also influenced by the monetary policy implemented by the Federal Reserve System. The Fed conducts monetary policy in an effort to control U.S. economic conditions. By affecting the supply of loanable funds, the Fed's monetary policy affects interest rates (as will be described shortly). In turn, by influencing interest rates, the Fed is able to influence the amount of money that corporations and households are willing to borrow and spend.

Exhibit 2.6   Aggregate Supply Curve for Loanable Funds

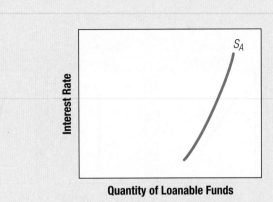

Aggregate Supply of Funds   The aggregate supply schedule of loanable funds represents the combination of all sector supply schedules along with the supply of funds provided by the Fed's monetary policy. The steep slope of the aggregate supply curve in Exhibit 2.6 means that it is interest-inelastic. The quantity of loanable funds demanded is normally expected to be more elastic (more sensitive to interest rates) —than the quantity of loanable funds supplied.

The supply curve can shift inward or outward in response to various conditions. For example, if the tax rate on interest income decreases, the supply curve will shift outward as households save more funds at each possible interest rate level. Conversely, if the tax rate on interest income increases, the supply curve will shift inward as households save fewer funds at each possible interest rate level.

In this section, minimal attention has been given to financial institutions. Although financial institutions play a critical intermediary role in channeling funds, they are not the ultimate suppliers of funds. Any change in a financial institution's supply of funds results only from a change in habits of the households, businesses, or governments that supply those funds.

2-1g Equilibrium Interest Rate

An understanding of equilibrium interest rates is necessary to assess how various events can affect interest rates. In reality, several different interest rates are present at a given point in time because some borrowers pay a higher rate than others. At this point, however, our focus is on the forces that cause the general level of interest rates to change, because interest rates across borrowers tend to change in the same direction. The determination of an equilibrium interest rate is presented first from an algebraic perspective and then from a graphical perspective. Following this presentation, several examples are offered to reinforce the concept.

Algebraic Presentation   The equilibrium interest rate is the rate that equates the aggregate demand for funds (aggregate quantity of funds demanded) with the aggregate supply of loanable funds. The aggregate demand for funds (D_A) can be written as

$$D_A = D_h + D_b + D_g + D_m + D_f$$

where

D_h = household demand for loanable funds

D_b = business demand for loanable funds

D_g = federal government demand for loanable funds

D_m = municipal government demand for loanable funds

D_f = foreign demand for loanable funds

The aggregate supply of funds (S_A) can likewise be written as

$$S_A = S_h + S_b + S_g + S_m + S_f$$

where

S_h = household supply of loanable funds

S_b = business supply of loanable funds

S_g = federal government supply of loanable funds

S_m = municipal government supply of loanable funds

S_f = foreign supply of loanable funds

If interest rates were extremely low at a given point in time, D_A would likely exceed S_A because the low interest rate would be appealing to borrowers, but not to savers. Conversely, if interest rates were very high at a given point in time, D_A would likely be less than S_A because the high interest rate would be appealing to savers, but not to borrowers.

At any given point in time, there should be an interest rate level that is equally appealing to borrowers and savers in aggregate. At that interest rate, an equilibrium occurs because $D_A = S_A$. As time passes, conditions can change that will affect either D_A or S_A, thereby disrupting the equilibrium.

EXAMPLE   Assume that recent conditions have increased the desire by various sectors to borrow, resulting in a larger D_A. When the aggregate demand for loanable funds increases without a corresponding increase in aggregate supply, the equilibrium situation has been disrupted because D_A now exceeds S_A. At the previous equilibrium interest rate, there will be a shortage of loanable funds. Consequently, interest rates will rise, causing savers to provide an additional supply of loanable funds. Interest rates will continue to rise until savers have supplied sufficient funds to accommodate the excess demand, creating a new equilibrium. ●

An equilibrium situation could also be disrupted by a change in condition that alters the quantity of funds supplied.

EXAMPLE   Assume an initial equilibrium situation is disrupted because recent conditions have increased the desire by various sectors to supply loanable funds. At the previous equilibrium interest rate, there will be an excess supply of loanable funds. Consequently, interest rates will decline until the quantity of loanable funds demanded has risen to a level that offsets the increased supply of loanable funds. A new equilibrium situation will be established at this point. ●

In many cases, both supply and demand for loanable funds are changing. Given an initial equilibrium situation, the equilibrium interest rate should rise when $D_A > S_A$ and fall when $D_A < S_A$.

Exhibit 2.7   Interest Rate Equilibrium

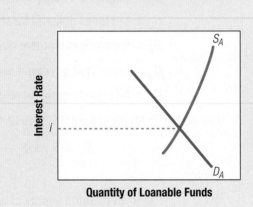

Quantity of Loanable Funds

Graphical Presentation   By combining the aggregate demand and aggregate supply curves of loanable funds (refer to Exhibits 2.5 and 2.6), it is possible to compare the total amount of funds that would be demanded to the total amount of funds that would be supplied at any particular interest rate. Exhibit 2.7 illustrates the combined demand and supply schedules. At the equilibrium interest rate of i, the supply of loanable funds is equal to the demand for loanable funds.

At any interest rate greater than i, there is a surplus of loanable funds. Some potential suppliers of funds will be unable to successfully supply their funds at the prevailing interest rate. Once the market interest rate decreases to i, however, the quantity of funds supplied is sufficiently reduced and the quantity of funds demanded is sufficiently increased so that there is no longer a surplus of funds. When a disequilibrium situation exists, market forces should cause an adjustment in interest rates until equilibrium is achieved.

If the prevailing interest rate is less than i, there will be a shortage of loanable funds; borrowers will not be able to obtain all the funds that they desire at that rate. The shortage of funds will cause the interest rate to increase, resulting in two reactions. First, more savers will enter the market to supply loanable funds because the reward (interest rate) is now higher. Second, some potential borrowers will decide not to demand loanable funds at the higher interest rate. Once the interest rate rises to i, the quantity of loanable funds supplied has increased and the quantity of loanable funds demanded has decreased to the extent that a shortage no longer exists. Thus, an equilibrium position is achieved once again.

2-2 Factors That Affect Interest Rates

A number of underlying economic forces can cause a change in either the supply of or the demand for loanable funds. The following economic factors influence this supply and demand, thereby influencing interest rates.

2-2a Impact of Economic Growth on Interest Rates

Changes in economic conditions cause a shift in the demand curve for loanable funds, which affects the equilibrium interest rate.

When economic conditions become more favorable, businesses' expected cash flows for their proposed projects will increase. More of these projects will then have expected returns that exceed a business's particular required rate of return (the *hurdle rate*). As additional projects become acceptable as a result of the more favorable economic forecasts, demand for loanable funds will increase, causing an outward shift (to the right) in the demand curve.

The improvement in economic conditions may also affect the supply-of-loanable-funds schedule, but it is difficult to know in which direction it will shift. If the increased expansion by businesses leads to more income for construction crews and other workers, the quantity of savings (loanable funds supplied) could increase regardless of the interest rate, causing an outward shift in the supply schedule. Conversely, the increased income may be used for consumption rather than savings. Thus, there is no assurance that the volume of savings will actually increase. Even if such a shift in the supply-of-loanable-funds schedule does occur, it will likely be of smaller magnitude than the shift in the demand schedule.

Overall, the expected impact of the increased expansion by businesses is an outward shift in the demand curve but no obvious change in the supply schedule. In Exhibit 2.8, notice that the shift in the aggregate demand curve to D_{A2} causes an increase in the equilibrium interest rate to i_2. ●

Just as economic growth puts upward pressure on interest rates, an economic slowdown puts downward pressure on the equilibrium interest rate.

A slowdown in the economy will cause the demand curve to shift inward (to the left), reflecting less demand for loanable funds at any given interest rate. The supply curve may shift a little, but the direction of that shift is uncertain. Although some households may try to increase their savings to prepare for possible layoffs, the economic slowdown could reduce other households' ability to save. In either case, any shift that does occur is likely to be minor relative to the shift in demand. The equilibrium interest rate is therefore expected to decrease, as illustrated in Exhibit 2.9. ●

2-2b Impact of Inflation on Interest Rates

Changes in inflationary expectations can affect interest rates by altering the amount of spending by households or businesses. Decisions to spend affect both the amount saved (supply of funds) and the amount borrowed (demand for funds).

Assume the U.S. inflation rate is expected to increase. In this scenario, households that supply funds may reduce their savings at any interest rate level so that they can make more purchases now before prices rise. This shift in behavior is reflected by an inward shift (to the left) in the supply curve of loanable funds. In addition, households and businesses may be willing to borrow more funds at any interest rate level so that they can purchase products now before prices increase. This is reflected by an outward shift (to the right) in the demand curve for loanable funds. These shifts are illustrated in Exhibit 2.10. The new equilibrium interest rate is higher because of these shifts in saving and borrowing behavior. ●

Exhibit 2.8   Impact of Increased Expansion by Firms

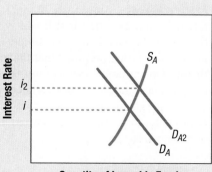

Exhibit 2.9   Impact of an Economic Slowdown

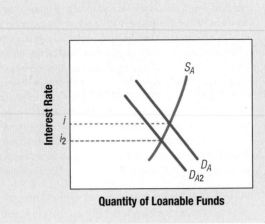

Exhibit 2.10   Impact of an Increase in Inflationary Expectations on Interest Rates

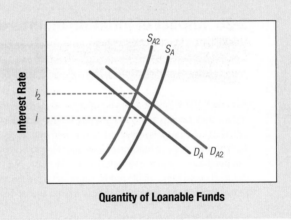

Fisher Effect   More than 70 years ago, Irving Fisher proposed a theory of interest
rate determination that is still widely used today. Fisher's theory does not contradict
the loanable funds theory, but simply offers an additional explanation for interest rate
movements. Fisher proposed that the nominal interest rate (the interest rate quoted by a
financial institution) on savings must be sufficient to compensate savers in two ways. First,
it must compensate for a saver's reduced purchasing power because of anticipated inflation
over the period in which funds are saved. Second, it must provide an additional premium
to savers for forgoing present consumption. Thus, the nominal interest rate is composed
of these two factors:

$$i = E(\text{INF}) + i_R$$

where

$$i = \text{nominal rate of interest}$$
$$E(\text{INF}) = \text{expected inflation rate}$$
$$i_R = \text{real interest rate}$$

This relationship between interest rates and expected inflation is often referred to as the Fisher effect. The difference between the nominal interest rate and the expected inflation rate is referred to as the **real interest rate** because it measures the rate of interest earned by a saver after adjusting for the expected loss in purchasing power (due to expected inflation) over the time period of concern.

The preceding equation can be rearranged to express the real interest rate as

$$i_R = i - E(\text{INF})$$

WEB

www.federalreserve
.gov/monetarypolicy
/fomc.htm
Information on how the
Fed controls the money
supply.

To the extent that the real rate of interest is very stable over time, the Fisher effect suggests that the nominal interest rate should rise in response to an increase in expected inflation.

Throughout this text, the term "interest rate" will be used to represent the *nominal*, or *quoted*, rate of interest. Keep in mind, however, that because of the Fisher effect, high interest rates will not necessarily result in a higher real rate of interest.

2-2c Impact of Monetary Policy on Interest Rates

The Federal Reserve can affect the supply of loanable funds by increasing or reducing the total amount of deposits held at commercial banks or other depository institutions. The process by which the Fed adjusts the money supply is described in Chapter 4. When the Fed revises the money supply, it revises the supply of loanable funds, which affects interest rates.

EXAMPLE
When economic conditions are weak, the Fed may believe that it can stimulate the economy by reducing interest rates, which may encourage businesses and households to borrow more funds (at the appealing lower interest rate). To do so, the Fed increases the money supply in the banking system. The increase in the supply of loanable funds (represented as an outward shift in the supply curve) places downward pressure on interest rates. ●

To reduce the money supply, the Fed reduces the supply of loanable funds in the banking system. Assuming no change in demand, this action places upward pressure on interest rates.

EXAMPLE
Exhibit 2.11 plots U.S. interest rates over recent decades and illustrates how they have been affected by the forces of monetary policy. During the period 2005–2007, U.S. economic growth increased and interest rates rose.

However, when the credit crisis that began in 2008 caused the economy to weaken substantially, the Fed responded by substantially increasing the supply of loanable funds in the banking system over the next several years. Consequently, U.S. interest rates declined to extremely low levels, which the Fed hoped would encourage businesses and households to borrow and spend more money. Ultimately, the Fed's strategy helped to stimulate the U.S. economy. ●

2-2d Impact of the Budget Deficit on Interest Rates

When the federal government enacts fiscal policies that result in more expenditures made than tax revenues collected, the budget deficit is increased. Because of large budget deficits in recent years, the U.S. government has been a major participant in the demand for loanable funds. A higher federal government deficit increases the quantity of loanable funds

Exhibit 2.11 U.S. Interest Rates Over Time

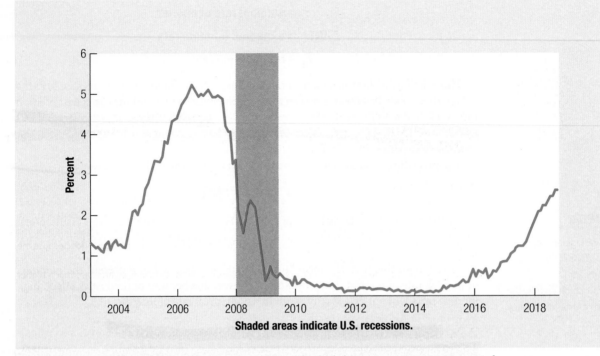

Shaded areas indicate U.S. recessions.

Note: *Rate shown is for Treasury bills with a one-year maturity. The shaded area represents a recession period.*
Source: *Board of Governors of the Federal Reserve.*

demanded at any prevailing interest rate, which represents an outward shift in the demand curve. Assuming that all other factors are held constant, interest rates will rise in such a scenario. Given a finite amount of loanable funds supplied to the market (through savings), excessive government demand for these funds tends to "crowd out" the private demand (by consumers and corporations) for funds. The federal government may be willing to pay whatever is necessary to borrow these funds, but the private sector may not. This impact is known as the **crowding-out effect**. Exhibit 2.12 illustrates the flow of funds between the federal government and the private sector.

Exhibit 2.12 Flow of Funds between the Federal Government and the Private Sector

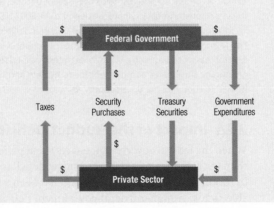

An increase in the budget deficit might also cause the supply curve to shift a little, but the direction of that shift is uncertain. Much research has been conducted on this issue and has generally shown that, when holding other factors constant, higher budget deficits place upward pressure on interest rates.

2-2e Impact of Foreign Flows of Funds on Interest Rates

Since a currency's interest rate depends on the demand for and the supply of loanable funds in that currency, the interest rate of one currency typically differs from the interest rates of other currencies.

EXAMPLE

WEB

http://fred.stlouisfed.org
Time series of various interest rates provided by the Federal Reserve Economic Databank.

WEB

http://fred.stlouisfed.org
Current interest rates and trends of historical interest rates for various debt securities.

The supply and demand curves for the U.S. dollar and for Brazil's currency (which is called the Brazilian *real*) are compared for a given point in time in Exhibit 2.13. Although the demand curve for loanable funds should be downward sloping for every currency and the supply schedule should be upward sloping, the actual positions of these curves vary among currencies. Notice that the demand and supply curves are farther to the right for the dollar than for the Brazilian real. The amount of U.S. dollar–denominated loanable funds supplied and demanded is much greater than the amount of Brazilian real–denominated loanable funds because the U.S. economy is much larger than Brazil's economy.

Observe also that the positions of the demand and supply curves for loanable funds are much higher for the Brazilian real than for the dollar. The supply schedule for loanable funds denominated in Brazilian real shows that hardly any amount of savings would be supplied when interest rate levels are low, because the relatively high inflation rate in Brazil encourages households to spend more of their disposable income before prices increase. In essence, this factor discourages households from saving unless the interest rate is sufficiently high. In addition, the demand for loanable funds denominated in Brazilian real shows that borrowers are willing to borrow even at relatively high rates of interest because they want to make purchases now before prices increase. Brazilian businesses may be willing to pay 15 percent interest on a loan to purchase machines whose prices may increase 20 percent by the following year.

Because of the different positions of the demand and supply curves for the two currencies shown in Exhibit 2.13, the equilibrium interest rate is much higher for the Brazilian real than for the dollar. As the demand and supply schedules change over time for a specific currency, so will the equilibrium interest rate of that currency. ●

Exhibit 2.13 Demand and Supply Curves for Loanable Funds Denominated in U.S. Dollars and Brazilian Real

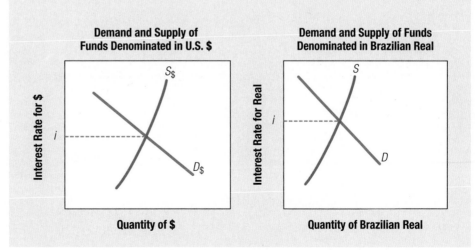

2-3 Forecasting Interest Rates

Exhibit 2.14 summarizes the key factors that are evaluated when forecasting interest rates. With an understanding of how each factor affects interest rates, it becomes possible to forecast how interest rates may change in the future. When forecasting household demand for loanable funds, it may be necessary to assess consumer credit data to determine the borrowing capacity of households. The potential supply of loanable funds provided by households may be determined in a similar manner by assessing factors that affect the earning power of households.

Business demand for loanable funds can be forecasted by assessing future plans for corporate expansion and the future state of the economy. Federal government demand for loanable funds could be influenced by the economy's future state because it affects both the tax revenues to be received and the amount of unemployment compensation to be paid out—factors that affect the size of the government deficit. The Federal Reserve System's money supply targets may be assessed by reviewing public statements about the Fed's future objectives, although those statements tend to be rather vague.

To forecast future interest rates, the net demand for funds (ND) should be forecast:

$$ND = D_A - S_A = (D_h + D_b + D_g + D_m + D_f) - (S_h + S_b + S_g + S_m + S_f)$$

If the forecasted level of ND is positive or negative, then a disequilibrium will exist temporarily. If ND is positive, the disequilibrium will be corrected by an upward adjustment in interest rates; if ND is negative, the disequilibrium will be corrected by a downward adjustment. The larger the forecasted magnitude of ND, the larger the adjustment in interest rates will be.

Some analysts focus more on changes in D_A and S_A than on estimating their aggregate levels. For example, assume that today the equilibrium interest rate is 7 percent. This interest rate will change only if D_A and S_A change to create a temporary disequilibrium. If the government demand for funds (D_g) is expected to increase substantially and if no other components are expected to change, D_A will exceed S_A, placing upward pressure on interest rates. In such a case, the forecast of future interest rates can be derived without estimating every component of D_A and S_A.

Exhibit 2.14   Framework for Forecasting Interest Rates

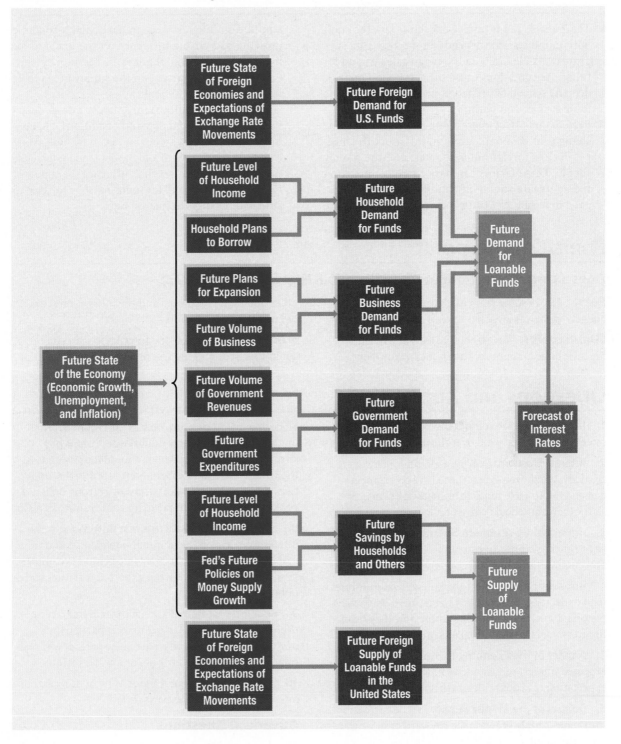

Summary

- The loanable funds framework shows how the equilibrium interest rate depends on the aggregate supply of available funds and the aggregate demand for funds. As conditions cause the aggregate supply or demand schedules to change, interest rates gravitate toward a new equilibrium.

- Factors that affect interest rate movements include changes in economic growth, inflation, the budget deficit, foreign interest rates, and the money supply. These factors can have a strong impact on the aggregate supply of funds and/or the aggregate demand for funds, thereby affecting the

equilibrium interest rate. In particular, economic growth has a strong influence on the demand for loanable funds, and changes in the money supply have a strong impact on the supply of loanable funds.

- Given that the equilibrium interest rate is determined by supply and demand conditions, changes in the interest rate can be forecasted by forecasting changes in the supply of and the demand for loanable funds. Thus, the factors that influence the supply of funds and the demand for funds must be forecast to anticipate changes in interest rates.

Point/Counterpoint

Does a Large Fiscal Budget Deficit Result in Higher Interest Rates?

Point   No. In some years (such as 2014), the fiscal budget deficit was large but interest rates were very low.

Counterpoint   Yes. When the federal government borrows large amounts of funds, it can crowd out

other potential borrowers, and the interest rates are bid up by the deficit units.

Who Is Correct?   Use the Internet to learn more about this issue and then formulate your own opinion.

Questions and Applications

1. **Interest Rate Movements** Explain why interest rates changed as they did over the past year.

2. **Interest Elasticity** Explain what is meant by interest elasticity. Would you expect the federal government's demand for loanable funds to be more or less interest-elastic than household demand for loanable funds? Why?

3. **Impact of Government Spending** If the federal government planned to expand the space program, how might this change affect interest rates?

4. **Impact of a Recession** Explain why interest rates tend to decrease during recessionary periods. Review historical interest rates to determine how they reacted to recessionary periods. Explain this reaction.

5. **Impact of the Economy** Explain how the expected interest rate in one year depends on your expectation of economic growth and inflation.

6. **Impact of the Money Supply** Would increasing the money supply growth place upward or downward pressure on interest rates?

7. **Impact of Exchange Rates on Interest Rates** Assume that if the U.S. dollar strengthens, it can

place downward pressure on U.S. inflation. Based on this information, how might expectations of a strong dollar affect the demand for loanable funds in the United States and U.S. interest rates? Is there any reason to think that expectations of a strong dollar could also affect the supply of loanable funds? Explain.

8. **Nominal versus Real Interest Rate** What is the difference between the nominal interest rate and the real interest rate? What is the logic behind the implied positive relationship between expected inflation and nominal interest rates?

9. **Real Interest Rate** Estimate the real interest rate over the last year. If financial market participants overestimate inflation in a particular period, will real interest rates be relatively high or low? Explain.

10. **Forecasting Interest Rates** Why do forecasts of interest rates made by experts differ?

Advanced Questions

11. **Impact of Stock Market Crises** During periods when investors suddenly become fearful that stocks are overvalued, they dump their stocks and the stock market

experiences a major decline. During these periods, interest rates also tend to decline. Use the loanable funds framework discussed in this chapter to explain how a massive sell-off of stocks leads to lower interest rates.

12. Impact of Expected Inflation How might expectations of higher prices in the United States affect the demand for loanable funds, the supply of loanable funds, and interest rates in the United States? Offer a logical explanation of why such an impact on interest rates in the United States might spread to other countries.

13. Global Interaction of Interest Rates Why might you expect the interest rate movements of various industrialized countries to be more highly correlated in recent years than they were in earlier years?

14. Impact of War War tends to cause significant reactions in financial markets. Why might a war in the Middle East place upward pressure on U.S. interest rates? Why might some investors expect a war like this to place downward pressure on U.S. interest rates?

15. Impact of September 11 Offer an argument for why the terrorist attacks on the United States on September 11, 2001, could have placed downward pressure on U.S. interest rates. Offer an argument for why those attacks could have placed upward pressure on U.S. interest rates.

16. Impact of Government Spending Jayhawk Forecasting Services analyzed several factors that could affect interest rates in the future. Most factors were expected to place downward pressure on interest rates. Jayhawk also expected that, although the annual budget deficit was to be cut by 40 percent from the previous year, the deficit would still be very large. Because Jayhawk believed that the deficit's impact would more than offset the effects of other factors, it forecast interest rates to increase by 2 percentage points. Comment on Jayhawk's logic.

17. Decomposing Interest Rate Movements The interest rate on a one-year loan can be decomposed into a one-year, risk-free (free from default risk) component and a risk premium that reflects the potential for default on the loan in that year. A change in economic conditions can affect the risk-free rate and the risk premium. The risk-free rate is usually affected by changing economic conditions to a greater degree than is the risk premium. Explain how a weaker economy will likely affect the risk-free component, the risk premium, and the overall cost of a one-year loan obtained by (a) the Treasury and (b) a corporation. Will the

change in the cost of borrowing be more pronounced for the Treasury or for the corporation? Why?

18. Forecasting Interest Rates Based on Prevailing Conditions Consider the prevailing conditions for inflation (including oil prices), the economy, the budget deficit, and the Fed's monetary policy that could affect interest rates. Based on these conditions, do you think interest rates will likely increase or decrease during this semester? Offer some logic to support your answer. Which factor do you think will have the greatest impact on interest rates?

19. Impact of Economic Crises on Interest Rates When economic crises in countries are due to a weak economy, local interest rates tend to be very low. However, if the crisis is caused by an unusually high rate of inflation, the interest rate tends to be very high. Explain why.

20. U.S. Interest Rates during the Credit Crisis During the credit crisis of 2008 and 2009, U.S. interest rates were extremely low, which enabled businesses to borrow at a low cost. Holding other factors constant, this should have resulted in a higher number of feasible projects, which should have encouraged businesses to borrow more money and expand. Yet many businesses that had access to loanable funds were unwilling to borrow during the credit crisis. What other factor changed during this period that more than offset the potentially favorable effect of the low interest rates on project feasibility, thereby discouraging businesses from expanding?

21. Political Influence on Interest Rates Offer an argument for why a political regime that favors having a large government bureaucracy will cause interest rates to be higher. Offer at least one example of why a political regime that favors having a large government bureaucracy will cause interest rates to be lower. [*Hint:* Recognize that the government intervention in the economy can influence other factors that affect interest rates.]

22. Impact of Stock Market Uncertainty Consider a period in which stock prices are very high, such that investors begin to think that stocks are overvalued and their valuations are very uncertain. If investors decide to move their money into much safer investments, how would this affect general interest rate levels? In your answer, use the loanable funds framework to explain how the supply of or demand for loanable funds would be affected by the investor actions, and how this force would affect interest rates.

23. **Impact of the European Economy** Use the loanable funds framework to explain how European economic conditions might affect U.S. interest rates.

Critical Thinking Question

Forecasting Interest Rates Given your knowledge of how interest rates are influenced by various factors reflecting the demand for funds and the supply of funds available in the credit markets, write a short essay to explain how and why interest rates will change over the next three months.

Interpreting Financial News

Interpret the following comments made by Wall Street analysts and portfolio managers.

a. "The flight of funds from bank deposits to U.S. stocks will pressure interest rates."
b. "Since Japanese interest rates have recently declined to very low levels, expect a reduction in U.S. interest rates."
c. "The cost of borrowing by U.S. firms is dictated by the degree to which the federal government spends more than it taxes."

Managing in Financial Markets

Forecasting Interest Rates As the treasurer of a manufacturing company, your job is to forecast the direction of interest rates. Your company plans to borrow funds, and it may use the forecast of interest rates to determine whether it should obtain a loan with a fixed interest rate or a floating interest rate. The following information can be considered when assessing the future direction of interest rates.

- Economic growth has been high over the last two years, but you expect that it will be stagnant over the next year.
- Inflation has been 3 percent over each of the last few years, and you expect that it will be about the same over the next year.
- The federal government has announced major cuts in its spending, which should have a major impact on the budget deficit.
- The Federal Reserve is not expected to affect the existing supply of loanable funds over the next year.
- The overall level of savings by households is not expected to change.

a. Given the preceding information, assess how the demand for and the supply of loanable funds would be affected, if at all, and predict the future direction of interest rates.
b. Your company can obtain a one-year loan at a fixed rate of 8 percent or a floating-rate loan that is currently at 8 percent but for which the interest rate would be revised every month in accordance with general interest rate movements. Which type of loan is more appropriate based on the information provided?
c. Assume that Canadian interest rates have abruptly risen just as you have completed your forecast of future U.S. interest rates. Consequently, Canadian interest rates are now 2 percentage points above U.S. interest rates. How might this specific situation place pressure on U.S. interest rates? Considering this situation along with the other information provided, would you change your forecast of the future direction of U.S. interest rates?

Problems

1. **Nominal Rate of Interest** Suppose the real interest rate is 6 percent and the expected inflation rate is 2 percent. What would you expect the nominal rate of interest to be?

2. **Real Interest Rate** Suppose that Treasury bills are currently paying 9 percent and the expected inflation rate is 3 percent. What is the real interest rate?

Flow of Funds Exercise

How the Flow of Funds Affects Interest Rates

Recall that Carson Company has obtained substantial loans from finance companies and commercial banks. The interest rate on the loans is tied to market interest rates and is adjusted every six months. Thus, Carson's cost of obtaining funds is sensitive to interest rate movements. Given its expectations that the U.S. economy will strengthen, Carson plans to grow in the future by expanding and by making acquisitions. Carson expects that it will need substantial long-term financing to pay for this growth, and it plans to borrow additional funds either through existing loans or by issuing bonds. The company is also considering the possibility of issuing stock to raise funds in the next year.

a. Explain why Carson should be very interested in future interest rate movements.

b. Given Carson's expectations, do you think the company anticipates that interest rates will increase or decrease in the future? Explain.

c. If Carson's expectations of future interest rates are correct, how would this affect its cost of borrowing on its existing loans and on its future loans?

d. Explain why Carson's expectations about future interest rates may affect its decision about when to borrow funds and whether to obtain floating-rate or fixed-rate loans.

Internet/Excel Exercises

1. Go to http://fred.stlouisfed.org/categories. Under "Money, Banking, & Finance," select "Interest Rates" and then select the three-month Treasury-bill series (secondary market). Describe how this rate has changed in recent months. Using the information in this chapter, explain why the interest rate changed as it did.

2. Using the same website, retrieve data at the beginning of the last 20 quarters for interest rates (based on the three-month Treasury-bill rate) and the producer price index for all commodities (under "Prices") and place the data in two columns of an Excel spreadsheet. Derive the change in interest rates on a quarterly basis. Then derive the percentage change in the producer price index on a quarterly basis, which serves as a measure of inflation. Apply regression analysis in which the change in interest rates is the dependent variable and inflation is the independent variable (see Appendix B for information about applying regression analysis). Explain the relationship that you find. Does it appear that inflation and interest rate movements are positively related?

WSJ Exercise

Forecasting Interest Rates

Review information about the credit markets in a recent issue of *The Wall Street Journal*. Identify the factors that are given attention because they may affect future interest rate movements. Then create your own forecasts as to whether interest rates will increase or decrease from now until the end of the school term, based on your assessment of any factors that affect interest rates. Explain your forecast.

Online Articles with Real-World Examples

Find a recent practical article available online that describes a real-world example regarding a specific financial institution or financial market that reinforces one or more concepts covered in this chapter.

If your class has an online component, your professor may ask you to post your summary of the article there and provide a link to the article so that other students can access it. If your class is live, your professor may ask you to summarize your application of the article in class. Your professor may assign specific students to complete this assignment or may allow any students to do the assignment on a volunteer basis.

For recent online articles and real-world examples related to this chapter, consider using the following search terms (be sure to include the prevailing year as a search term to ensure that the online articles are recent):

1. budget deficit AND interest rate

2. flow of funds AND interest rate

3. Federal Reserve AND interest rate

4. economic growth AND interest rate

5. inflation AND interest rate

6. monetary policy AND interest rate

7. supply of savings AND interest rate

8. business expansion AND interest rate

9. demand for credit AND interest rate

10. interest rate AND forecast

3
Structure of Interest Rates

CHAPTER OBJECTIVES

The specific objectives of this chapter are to:

- Describe how characteristics of debt securities cause their yields to vary.

- Demonstrate how to model the appropriate yield for any particular debt security.

- Explain the theories behind the term structure of interest rates (relationship between the term to maturity and the yield of securities).

The annual interest rate offered at any given time varies among debt securities. Individual and institutional investors must understand why quoted yields vary so that they can determine whether the extra yield on a given security outweighs any unfavorable characteristics. Likewise, financial managers of corporations or government agencies in need of funds must understand why quoted yields of debt securities vary at a given point in time so that they can estimate the yield they would have to offer so as to sell new debt securities.

3-1 Why Debt Security Yields Vary

Debt securities offer different yields because they exhibit different characteristics that influence the yield to be offered. The yields on debt securities are affected by the following characteristics:

- Credit (default) risk
- Liquidity
- Tax status
- Term to maturity

The yields on bonds may also be affected by special provisions of those bonds, as described in Chapter 7.

In general, securities with unfavorable characteristics must offer higher yields to entice investors to buy them. Although the difference in yields may seem small, the impact on the issuer can be significant. If a company has to pay an extra 1 percent (100 basis points) on $30 million worth of bonds that it wants to issue, that extra percentage point reflects $300,000 in additional interest expenses per year.

3-1a Credit (Default) Risk

Because most securities are subject to the risk of default, investors must consider the credit-worthiness of the security issuer. Although investors always have the option of purchasing risk-free Treasury securities, they may prefer other securities if the yield compensates them for the credit risk. Thus, if all other characteristics besides credit risk are equal, securities with a higher degree of credit risk must offer a credit risk premium (higher yield above the Treasury bond yield) if they are to attract investors.

EXAMPLE

Investors can purchase a Treasury bond with a 10-year maturity that presently offers an annualized yield of 7 percent if they hold the bond until maturity. Alternatively, investors can purchase bonds that are being issued by Zanstell Co. Although Zanstell is in good financial condition, there is a small possibility that the company could file for bankruptcy during the next 10 years, in which case it would stop making payments to investors who purchased the bonds. Thus, there is a small possibility that investors could lose most of their investment in these bonds. The only way that investors would even consider purchasing bonds issued by Zanstell is if the annualized yield offered on these bonds is higher than the Treasury bond yield. Zanstell's bonds presently offer a yield of 8 percent, which reflects a 1 percentage point credit risk premium. At this yield, some investors may be willing to purchase Zanstell's bonds because they think the company should have sufficient cash flows to repay its debt over the next 10 years. ●

Use of Ratings Agencies to Assess Credit Risk

Investors can personally assess the creditworthiness of corporations that issue bonds, but they may prefer to rely on bond ratings provided by rating agencies. These ratings are based on a financial assessment of the issuing corporation, with a focus on whether the corporation will receive sufficient cash flows over time to cover its payments to bondholders. The higher the rating on the bond, the lower the perceived credit risk is.

WEB

www.moodys.com
Credit rating
information.

The rating agencies charge the issuers of debt securities a fee for assessing the credit risk of those securities. The ratings are then provided through various financial media outlets at no cost to investors. The most popular rating agencies are Moody's Investors Service and Standard & Poor's Corporation; Exhibit 3.1 summarizes their rating classification schedules. The ratings issued by Moody's range from Aaa for the highest quality to C for the lowest quality, and those issued by Standard & Poor's range from AAA to D. Because these rating agencies use different methods to assess the creditworthiness of firms and state governments, a particular bond could be rated at a different quality level by each agency. However, the differences are usually small.

Commercial banks typically invest only in **investment-grade bonds**, which are bonds rated as Baa or better by Moody's and as BBB or better by Standard & Poor's. Other financial institutions, such as pension funds and insurance companies, might invest in bonds that are rated lower and offer the potential for higher returns.

At a given point in time, the credit risk premium offered on a corporate bond is higher for bonds that are rated lower and, therefore, are more likely to default. The credit risk premium might be 1 percent on highly rated corporate bonds, 2.5 percent on medium-quality corporate bonds, and 5 percent on low-quality bonds.

Exhibit 3.1   Rating Classification by Rating Agencies

DESCRIPTION OF SECURITY	RATINGS ASSIGNED BY:	
	MOODY'S	STANDARD & POOR'S
Highest quality	Aaa	AAA
High quality	Aa	AA
High–medium quality	A	A
Medium quality	Baa	BBB
Medium–low quality	Ba	BB
Low quality (speculative)	B	B
Poor quality	Caa	CCC
Very poor quality	Ca	CC
Lowest quality (in default)	C	D

Credit Ratings and Risk Premiums over Time   Rating agencies can change bond ratings over time in response to changes in the issuing firm's financial condition. In addition, economic conditions can change, which can influence the ability of a corporation to repay its debt. During weak economic conditions, corporations generate reduced cash flows and may struggle to cover their debt obligations. The credit risk premium required by investors to invest in corporate bonds then rises because of concerns that the firms' credit risk is rising.

For example, medium-quality bond yields might contain a credit risk premium of 2.5 percent during normal economic conditions, but contain a credit risk premium of 5 percent or higher during a recession. Many corporations whose bonds are rated Baa or lower are unwilling to issue bonds during a recession because of the high credit risk premium they would have to pay to bondholders.

Accuracy of Credit Ratings   The ratings issued by the agencies are opinions, not guarantees. Bonds that are assigned a low credit rating experience default more frequently than bonds assigned a high credit rating, which suggests that the rating can be a useful indicator of credit risk. However, credit rating agencies do not always detect firms' financial problems.

Credit rating agencies were criticized for being too liberal in their assignment of ratings on debt issued shortly before the credit crisis of 2008 and 2009, as many highly rated debt issues defaulted over the next few years. The credit rating agencies might counter that they could not have anticipated the credit crisis and that they used all the information available to them when assigning ratings to new securities. Yet because credit rating agencies are paid by the issuers of debt securities, and not by the investors who purchase those securities, agencies may have a natural incentive to assign high ratings. Doing so facilitates a firm's issuing of debt securities, which in turn may enable the rating agency to attract more business from other issuers of debt securities.

In response to these criticisms, credit rating agencies made some changes to improve their rating processes and their transparency. They now disclose more information about how they derived their credit ratings. They also give more attention to sensitivity analysis in which they assess how a bond issuer's creditworthiness might change in response to abrupt changes in the economy. In addition, employees of each rating agency who work in sales and marketing are not allowed to influence the ratings assigned by the agency.

FINANCIAL REFORM

Oversight of Credit Rating Agencies   The Financial Reform Act of 2010 established the Office of Credit Ratings within the Securities and Exchange Commission to regulate credit rating agencies. The act mandated that the credit rating agencies disclose their rating performance over time and that they establish internal controls to ensure that their process of assigning ratings is more transparent. The act also allows investors to sue an agency for issuing credit ratings that the agency should have known were inaccurate.

3-1b Liquidity

Investors prefer securities that are *liquid*, meaning that they can be easily converted to cash without a loss in value. Thus, if all other characteristics are equal, securities with less liquidity must offer a higher yield to attract investors. Debt securities with a short-term maturity or an active secondary market have greater liquidity. Investors who need a high degree of liquidity (because they may need to sell their securities for cash at any moment) prefer liquid securities, even if it means accepting a lower return on their investment. Investors who will not need their funds until the securities mature are more willing to invest in securities with less liquidity so that they can earn a slightly higher return.

3-1c Tax Status

Investors are more concerned with after-tax income than with before-tax income earned on securities. Debt securities differ considerably in their tax status. The interest paid on Treasury securities is subject to federal income tax but is exempt from state income tax, whereas the interest on most municipal securities issued by state and local governments is exempt from federal tax and from state tax in the state that issued them. Interest on corporate debt securities is subject to both federal and state income tax. Because states impose different income tax rates, a particular security's after-tax yield may vary with the investor's location.

If all other characteristics are similar, taxable securities must offer a higher before-tax yield than do tax-exempt securities. The extra compensation required for taxable securities depends on the tax rates of individual and institutional investors. Investors in high tax brackets benefit most from tax-exempt securities.

When assessing the expected yields of various securities with similar risk and maturity, it is common to convert them into an after-tax form, as follows:

$$Y_{at} = Y_{bt}(1 - T)$$

where

$$Y_{at} = \text{after-tax yield}$$
$$Y_{bt} = \text{before-tax yield}$$
$$T = \text{investor's marginal tax rate}$$

Investors retain only a percentage $(1 - T)$ of the before-tax yield once taxes are paid.

EXAMPLE Consider a taxable security that offers a before-tax yield of 8 percent. When converted to after-tax terms, the yield will be reduced by the tax percentage. The precise after-tax yield depends on the tax rate T. If the investor's tax rate is 20 percent, then the after-tax yield will be

$$Y_{at} = Y_{bt}(1 - T)$$
$$= 8\%(1 - 0.2)$$
$$= 6.4\%$$

Exhibit 3.2 presents after-tax yields based on a variety of tax rates and before-tax yields. For example, a taxable security with a before-tax yield of 4 percent will generate an after-tax yield of 3.60 percent to an investor in the 10 percent tax bracket, 3.12 percent to an investor in the 22 percent tax bracket, and so on. This exhibit shows why investors in high tax brackets are attracted to tax-exempt securities. ●

Exhibit 3.2   After-Tax Yields Based on Various Tax Rates and Before-Tax Yields

	BEFORE-TAX YIELD			
TAX RATE	2%	4%	6%	8%
10%	1.80%	3.60%	5.40%	7.20%
22	1.56	3.12	4.68	6.24
32	1.36	2.72	4.08	5.44
37	1.26	2.52	3.78	5.04

Computing the Equivalent Before-Tax Yield   In some cases, investors wish to determine the before-tax yield necessary to match the after-tax yield of a tax-exempt security with a similar risk and maturity. This can be done by rearranging the terms of the previous equation:

$$Y_{bt} = \frac{Y_{at}}{1 - T}$$

WEB

www.treasury.gov
Treasury yields among different maturities.

For instance, suppose that a firm in the 20 percent tax bracket is aware of a tax-exempt security that is paying a yield of 8 percent. To match this after-tax yield, taxable securities must offer a before-tax yield of

$$Y_{bt} = \frac{Y_{at}}{1 - T} = \frac{8\%}{1 - 0.2} = 10\%$$

3-1d Term to Maturity

WEB

www.gurufocus.com
Search for "yield curve" to find the most recent yield curve.

The **term structure of interest rates** defines the relationship between possible terms to maturity and the annualized yield for a debt security at a specific moment in time while holding other factors constant. The Treasury yield curve graphically illustrates the term structure of interest rates at a given point in time for Treasury securities. Since Treasury securities are perceived to have no credit risk, the difference in their annualized yields is mostly attributed to their term to maturity. Similarly, the annualized yield that a corporation has to offer when issuing its debt securities is influenced by the maturity of the debt securities that it issues. Explanations for the shape of the term structure of interest rates are provided later in this chapter.

3-2 Modeling the Yield to be Offered on a Debt Security

When a company wants to issue debt, it needs to consider all the characteristics just described so that it can determine the appropriate yield to offer that will entice investors to buy its debt securities. The following model incorporates the key characteristics for determining the appropriate yield to be offered on a debt security:

$$Y_n = R_{f,n} + CP + LP + TA$$

where

Y_n = **annualized yield of an *n*-year debt security**

$R_{f,n}$ = **annualized yield (return) of an *n*-year Treasury (risk-free) security with the same term to maturity as the debt security of concern**

CP = **credit risk premium to compensate for credit risk**

LP = **liquidity premium to compensate for less liquidity**

TA = **adjustment due to the difference in tax status**

Special provisions applicable to bonds also may be included, as described in Chapter 7. The model presented here controls for the term to maturity by matching the maturity of the debt security with that of a risk-free Treasury security.

EXAMPLE   Assume that Elizabeth Co. plans to issue 10-year bonds. It wants to determine the yield that it must offer to successfully sell its debt securities. First, it checks the annualized yield on a risk-free (Treasury) bond with the same 10-year term to maturity, which is presently 6 percent. Next, Elizabeth Co. must consider how its characteristics affect the premiums that it needs to offer (above the prevailing risk-free Treasury security with the same maturity) to sell its debt securities. Assume Elizabeth Co. believes that a 2.1 percent credit risk premium, a 0.4 percent liquidity premium, and a 0.2 percent tax adjustment are necessary to persuade investors to purchase its bonds. The appropriate yield to be offered on the bonds is

$$Y_n = R_{f,n} + DP + LP + TA$$
$$= 6\% + 2.1\% + 0.4\% + 0.2\%$$
$$= 8.7\%$$

●

Corporations can apply a similar model to estimate the yield that they would have to offer on short-term debt securities, such as commercial paper. The main difference is that they should include the prevailing risk-free yield of a short-term rather than a long-term Treasury security in the model.

The appropriate yield to offer on any particular debt security will change over time, because of changes in the risk-free rate, credit premium, liquidity premium, and tax adjustment factors. Some corporations may postpone their plans to issue debt securities until the economy improves and the required premium for credit risk decreases. However, the yield that they need to offer could increase if the yield on Treasury securities with a similar maturity has risen by that point in time. In other words, any savings from a slightly smaller credit risk premium could be offset by a higher risk-free rate.

3-3 A Closer Look at the Term Structure

Of all the factors that affect the yields offered on debt securities, the one that is most difficult to understand is *term to maturity*. For this reason, a more comprehensive explanation of the relationship between term to maturity and annualized yield (referred to as the term structure of interest rates) is necessary.

Various theories have been proposed to explain the relationship between the maturity and the annualized yield of securities. Three of these theories are explained in this section.

3-3a Pure Expectations Theory

According to pure expectations theory, the term structure of interest rates is determined solely by expectations of interest rates.

Impact of an Expected Increase in Interest Rates   To understand how interest rate expectations may influence the yield curve, assume that the annualized yields of short-term and long-term risk-free securities are similar and that investors are willing to invest in either short-term or long-term risk-free securities. If these investors believe that interest rates will rise in the near future, they will invest their funds mostly in the short-term risk-free securities so that they can soon reinvest their funds in securities that offer higher yields after interest rates increase. Their actions cause funds to flow into the short-term market and away from the long-term market. The large supply of funds in the short-term market will force annualized yields down, while the reduced supply of long-term funds forces long-term yields up. Hence, the yield curve will shift as shown in Panel A of Exhibit 3.3.

Even though the annualized short-term yields become lower than the annualized long-term yields, investors in short-term funds are satisfied because they expect interest rates to rise. They will make up for the lower short-term yield when the short-term securities mature, and they reinvest at a higher rate (if interest rates rise) at maturity.

Exhibit 3.3   How Interest Rate Expectations Affect the Yield Curve

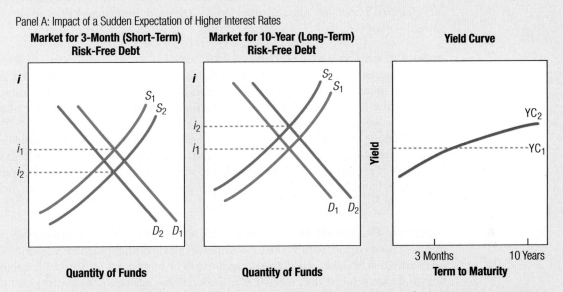

Panel A: Impact of a Sudden Expectation of Higher Interest Rates

$E(\uparrow i) \rightarrow$ Supply of funds provided by investors ↑ in short-term (such as 3 months) markets, and ↓ in long-term (such as 10 years) markets. Demand for funds by borrowers ↑ in long-term markets and ↓ in short-term markets. Therefore, the yield curve becomes upward sloping as shown here.

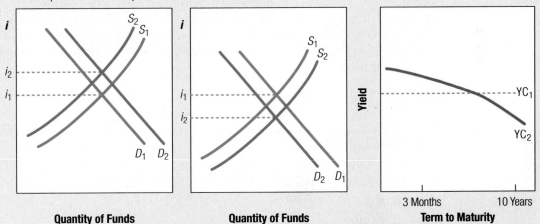

Panel B: Impact of a Sudden Expectation of Lower Interest Rates

$E(\downarrow i) \rightarrow$ Supply of funds provided by investors ↑ in long-term (such as 10 years) markets, and ↓ in short-term (such as 3 months) markets. Demand for funds by borrowers ↑ in short-term markets and ↓ in long-term markets. Therefore, the yield curve becomes downward sloping as shown here.

Assuming that the borrowers who plan to issue securities also expect interest rates to increase, they will prefer to lock in the present interest rate over a long period of time. Thus, borrowers will generally prefer to issue long-term securities rather than short-term securities. This results in a relatively small demand for short-term funds. Consequently, there is downward pressure on the yield of short-term funds. The corresponding increase in the demand for long-term funds by borrowers places upward pressure on long-term funds. Overall, the expectation of higher interest rates changes the demand for funds and the supply of funds in different maturity markets, which forces the original flat yield curve (labeled YC_1 in the rightmost graph) to pivot upward (counterclockwise) and become upward sloping (YC_2).

Impact of an Expected Decline in Interest Rates If investors expect interest rates to decrease in the future, they will prefer to invest in long-term funds rather than short-term funds because they can lock in today's higher interest rate before interest rates fall. Borrowers will prefer to borrow short-term funds so that they can refinance at a lower interest rate once interest rates decline.

Based on the expectation of lower interest rates in the future, the supply of funds provided by investors will be low for short-term funds and high for long-term funds. This will place upward pressure on short-term yields and downward pressure on long-term yields, as shown in Panel B of Exhibit 3.3. Overall, the expectation of lower interest rates causes the yield curve to pivot downward (clockwise).

Algebraic Presentation Investors monitor the yield curve to determine the rates that exist for securities with various maturities. They can either purchase a security with a maturity that matches their investment horizon or purchase a security with a shorter term and then reinvest the proceeds at maturity. They may select the strategy that they believe will generate a higher return over the entire investment horizon. This could affect the prices and yields of securities with different maturities, so that the expected return over the investment horizon is similar regardless of the strategy used. If investors were indifferent to maturities, the return of any security should equal the compounded yield of consecutive investments in shorter-term securities. That is, a two-year security should offer a return that is similar to the anticipated return from investing in two consecutive one-year securities. A four-year security should offer a return that is competitive with the expected return from investing in two consecutive two-year securities or four consecutive one-year securities, and so on.

EXAMPLE

To illustrate these equalities, consider the relationship between interest rates on a two-year security and a one-year security as follows:

$$(1 + {}_t i_2)^2 = (1 + {}_t i_1)(1 + {}_{t+1} r_1)$$

where

$${}_t i_2 = \text{known annualized interest rate of a two-year security as of time } t$$

$${}_t i_1 = \text{known annualized interest rate of a one-year security as of time } t$$

$${}_{t+1} r_1 = \text{one-year interest rate that is anticipated as of time } t + 1 \text{ (one year ahead)}$$

In this expression, the term *i* represents a quoted (known) rate, whereas *r* represents a rate that will be quoted at some point in the future, so its value is uncertain. The left side of the equation represents the compounded yield to investors who purchase a two-year security, and the right side represents the anticipated compounded yield from purchasing a one-year security and reinvesting the proceeds in a new one-year security at the end of one year. If time t is today, then $_{t+1}r_1$ can be estimated by rearranging terms:

$$1 + _{t+1}r_1 = \frac{(1 + _t i_2)^2}{1 + _t i_1}$$

$$_{t+1}r_1 = \frac{(1 + _t i_2)^2}{1 + _t i_1} - 1$$

The term $_{t+1}r_1$, referred to as the **forward rate**, is commonly estimated and assumed to represent the market's forecast of the future interest rate.

Here is a numerical example. Assume that, as of today (time t), the annualized two-year interest rate is 10 percent and the one-year interest rate is 8 percent. The forward rate is then estimated as follows:

$$_{t+1}r_1 = \frac{(1 + 0.10)^2}{1 + 0.08} - 1$$
$$= 0.1203704$$

This result implies that, one year from now, a one-year interest rate must equal about 12.037 percent for consecutive investments in two one-year securities to generate a return similar to that of a two-year investment. If the actual one-year rate beginning one year from now (that is, at time $t + 1$) is greater than 12.037 percent, the return from two consecutive one-year investments will exceed the return on a two-year investment. ●

The forward rate is sometimes used as an approximation of the market's consensus interest rate forecast. The reason is that, if the market had a different perception, the demand and supply of today's existing two-year and one-year securities would adjust to capitalize on this information. Of course, there is no guarantee that the forward rate will forecast the future interest rate with perfect accuracy.

The greater the difference between the implied one-year forward rate and today's one-year interest rate, the greater the change in the one-year interest rate that is expected to occur. If the term structure of interest rates is solely influenced by expectations of future interest rates, the following relationships hold:

SCENARIO	STRUCTURE OF YIELD CURVE	EXPECTATIONS ABOUT THE FUTURE INTEREST RATE
1. $_{t+1}r_1 > _t i_1$	Upward slope	Higher than today's rate
2. $_{t+1}r_1 = _t i_1$	Flat	Same as today's rate
3. $_{t+1}r_1 < _t i_1$	Downward slope	Lower than today's rate

Forward rates can be determined for securities with various maturities. The relationships described here can be applied when assessing the change in the interest rate of a security with any particular maturity.

The previous example can be expanded to solve for other forward rates. The equality specified by the pure expectations theory for a three-year horizon is

$$(1 + _t i_3)^3 = (1 + _t i_1)(1 + _{t+1}r_1)(1 + _{t+2}r_1)$$

where

$$_t i_3 = \text{annualized interest rate of a three-year security as of time } t$$

$$_{t+2} r_1 = \text{one-year interest rate that is anticipated as of time } t + 2 \text{ (two years ahead)}$$

All other terms were defined previously. By rearranging terms, we can isolate the forward rate of a one-year security beginning two years from now:

$$1 + {}_{t+2}r_1 = \frac{\left(1 + {}_t i_3\right)^3}{\left(1 + {}_t i_1\right)\left(1 + {}_{t+1}r_1\right)}$$

$$_{t+2}r_1 = \frac{\left(1 + {}_t i_3\right)^3}{\left(1 + {}_t i_1\right)\left(1 + {}_{t+1}r_1\right)} - 1$$

If the one-year forward rate beginning one year from now ($_{t+1}r_1$) has already been estimated, then this estimate can be combined with actual one-year and three-year interest rates to estimate the one-year forward rate two years from now. Recall that our previous example assumed $_t i_1 = 8$ percent and estimated $_{t+1}r_1$ to be approximately 12.037 percent.

EXAMPLE

Assume that a three-year security has an annualized interest rate of 11 percent (that is, $_t i_3 = 11$ percent). Given this information, the one-year forward rate two years from now can be calculated as follows:

$$_{t+2}r_1 = \frac{\left(1 + {}_t i_3\right)^3}{\left(1 + {}_t i_1\right)\left(1 + {}_{t+1}r_1\right)} - 1$$

$$= \frac{\left(1 + 0.11\right)^3}{\left(1 + 0.08\right)\left(1 + 0.12037\right)} - 1$$

$$= \frac{1.367631}{1.21} - 1$$

$$= 13.02736\%$$

Thus, the market anticipates that, two years from now, the one-year interest rate will be 13.02736 percent. ●

The yield curve can also be used to forecast annualized interest rates for periods other than one year. For example, the information provided in the last example could be used to determine the two-year forward rate beginning one year from now.

According to pure expectations theory, a one-year investment followed by a two-year investment should offer the same annualized yield over the three-year horizon as a three-year security that could be purchased today. This relation is expressed as follows:

$$\left(1 + {}_t i_3\right)^3 = \left(1 + {}_t i_1\right)\left(1 + {}_{t+1}r_2\right)^2$$

where $_{t+1}r_2$ is the annual interest rate of a two-year security anticipated as of time $t + 1$. By rearranging terms:

$$\left(1 + {}_{t+1}r_2\right)^2 = \frac{\left(1 + {}_t i_3\right)^3}{1 + {}_t i_1}$$

EXAMPLE

Recall that today's annualized yields for one-year and three-year securities are 8 percent and 11 percent, respectively. With this information, $_{t+1}r_2$ is estimated as follows:

$$\left(1 + {}_{t+1}r_2\right)^2 = \frac{\left(1 + {}_ti_3\right)^3}{1 + {}_ti_1}$$

$$= \frac{\left(1 + 0.11\right)^3}{1 + 0.08}$$

$$= 1.266325$$

$$1 + {}_{t+1}r_2 = \sqrt{1.266325}$$

$$= 1.1253$$

$${}_{t+1}r_2 = 0.1253$$

Thus, the market anticipates an annualized interest rate of about 12.53 percent for two-year securities beginning one year from now. ●

Pure expectations theory is based on the premise that forward rates are unbiased estimators of future interest rates. If forward rates are biased, investors can attempt to capitalize on the bias.

EXAMPLE

In the previous numerical example, the one-year forward rate beginning one year ahead was estimated to be approximately 12.037 percent. If the forward rate was thought to contain an upward bias, the expected one-year interest rate beginning one year ahead would actually be less than 12.037 percent. Therefore, investors with funds available for two years would earn a higher yield by purchasing two-year securities rather than purchasing one-year securities for two consecutive years. However, their actions would trigger an increase in the price of two-year securities and a decrease in the price of one-year securities; the yields of these securities would then move inversely with the price movements. Ultimately, any attempt by investors to capitalize on the forward rate bias would essentially eliminate the bias. ●

If forward rates are unbiased estimators of future interest rates, financial market efficiency is supported and the information implied by market rates about the forward rate cannot be used to generate abnormal returns. In response to new information, investor preferences would change, yields would adjust, and the implied forward rate would adjust as well.

If a long-term rate is expected to equal a geometric average of consecutive short-term rates covering the same time horizon (as is suggested by pure expectations theory), long-term rates would likely be more stable than short-term rates. As expectations about consecutive short-term rates change over time, the average of these rates would be less volatile than the individual short-term rates. Thus, long-term rates would be much more stable than short-term rates.

3-3b Liquidity Premium Theory

Some investors may prefer to own short-term rather than long-term securities because a shorter maturity represents greater liquidity. Therefore, they may be willing to hold long-term securities only if compensated by a premium for the lower degree of liquidity. Although long-term securities can be liquidated prior to maturity, their prices are more sensitive to interest rate movements. Short-term securities are normally considered to be more liquid because they are more likely to be converted to cash without a loss in value.

The preference for the more liquid short-term securities places upward pressure on the slope of a yield curve. Liquidity may be a more critical factor to investors at some times than at others, and the liquidity premium will accordingly change over time. As it does, the yield curve will change in tandem. The model that explains these movements is called liquidity premium theory (or liquidity preference theory).

Exhibit 3.4 contains three graphs that reflect the existence of both expectations theory and a liquidity premium. Each graph shows different interest rate expectations held by the market. Regardless of the interest rate forecast, the yield curve is affected in a similar manner by the liquidity premium.

Estimation of the Forward Rate Based on a Liquidity Premium   When expectations theory is combined with liquidity theory, the yield on a security will not necessarily be equal to the yield from consecutive investments in shorter-term securities over the same investment horizon. For example, the yield on a two-year security is now determined as

$$\left(1 + {}_t i_2\right)^2 = \left(1 + {}_t i_1\right)\left(1 + {}_{t+1} r_1\right) + LP_2$$

where LP_2 denotes the liquidity premium on a two-year security. The yield generated from the two-year security should exceed the yield from consecutive investments in one-year securities by a premium that compensates the investor for less liquidity. The relationship between the liquidity premium and term to maturity can be expressed as follows:

$$0 < LP_1 < LP_2 < LP_3 < \ldots < LP_{20}$$

where the subscripts represent years to maturity. This implies that the liquidity premium would more strongly affect the difference between annualized interest rates on one-year and 20-year securities than the difference between one-year and two-year securities.

If liquidity influences the yield curve, the forward rate overestimates the market's expectation of the future interest rate. A more appropriate formula for the forward rate would

Exhibit 3.4   Impact of Liquidity Premium on the Yield Curve under Three Different Scenarios

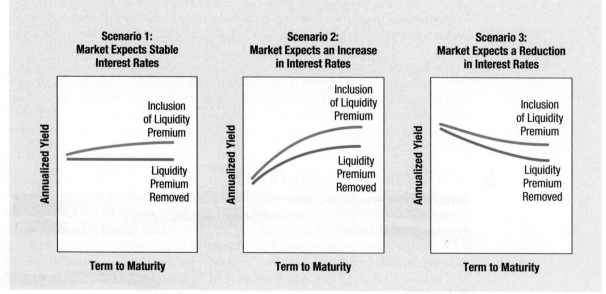

account for the liquidity premium. By rearranging terms in the previous equation for forward rates, the one-year forward rate can be derived as follows:

$$_{t+1}r_1 = \frac{\left(1 + {}_ti_2\right)^2}{1 + {}_ti_1} - 1 - \frac{LP_2}{1 + {}_ti_1}$$

EXAMPLE

Reconsider the example where $i_1 = 8$ percent and $i_2 = 10$ percent, and assume that the liquidity premium on a two-year security is 0.5 percent. The one-year forward rate can then be derived from this information as follows:

$$_{t+1}r_1 = \frac{\left(1 + {}_ti_2\right)^2}{1 + {}_ti_1} - 1 - \frac{LP_2}{1 + {}_ti_1}$$

$$= \frac{(1.10)^2}{1.08} - 1 - \frac{0.005}{1 + 0.08}$$

$$= 0.11574$$

This estimate of the one-year forward rate is lower than the estimate derived in the previous related example in which the liquidity premium was not considered. The previous estimate (12.037 percent) of the forward rate probably overstates the market's expected interest rate because it did not account for a liquidity premium. Thus, forecasts of future interest rates implied by a yield curve are reduced slightly when accounting for the liquidity premium. ●

Even with the existence of a liquidity premium, yield curves could still be used to interpret interest rate expectations. A flat yield curve would indicate that the market is expecting a slight decrease in interest rates (without the effect of the liquidity premium, the yield curve would have had a slight downward slope). A slight upward slope would indicate no expected change in interest rates. If the liquidity premium were removed, this yield curve would be flat.

3-3c Segmented Markets Theory

According to the segmented markets theory, investors and borrowers choose securities with maturities that satisfy their forecasted cash needs. Pension funds and life insurance companies may generally prefer long-term investments that coincide with their long-term liabilities. Commercial banks may prefer more short-term investments to coincide with their short-term liabilities. If investors and borrowers participate only in the maturity market that satisfies their particular needs, then markets are segmented. That is, investors (or borrowers) will shift from the long-term market to the short-term market, or vice versa, only if the timing of their cash needs changes. According to segmented markets theory, the choice of long-term versus short-term maturities is determined more by investors' needs than by their expectations of future interest rates.

EXAMPLE

Assume that most investors have funds available to invest for only a short period of time, so that they desire to invest primarily in short-term securities. Also assume that most borrowers need funds for a long period of time, so that they desire to issue mostly long-term securities. The result will be downward pressure on the yield of short-term securities and upward pressure on the yield of long-term securities. Overall, the scenario described would create an upward-sloping yield curve.

Now consider the opposite scenario, in which most investors wish to invest their funds for a long period of time while most borrowers need funds for only a short period of time. According to segmented markets theory, this situation will cause upward pressure on the yield of short-term securities and downward pressure on the yield of long-term securities. If the supply of funds provided by investors and the demand for funds by borrowers were better balanced between the short-term and long-term markets, the yields of short- and long-term securities would be more similar. ●

Yields of securities with various maturities should be influenced in part by the desires of investors and borrowers to participate in the maturity market that best satisfies their needs. A corporation that needs additional funds for 30 days would not consider issuing long-term bonds for such a purpose. Likewise, savers with short-term funds would avoid some long-term investments (for example, 10-year certificates of deposit) that cannot be easily liquidated.

Limitation of the Theory   A limitation of segmented markets theory is that some borrowers and savers have the flexibility to choose among various maturity markets. Corporations that need long-term funds may initially obtain short-term financing if they expect interest rates to decline, and investors with long-term funds may make short-term investments if they expect interest rates to rise. Moreover, some investors with short-term funds may be willing to purchase long-term securities that have an active secondary market.

Implications   Although markets are not completely segmented, the preference for particular maturities can affect the prices and yields of securities with different maturities, thereby affecting the yield curve's shape. For this reason, the theory of segmented markets seems to explain the yield curve's shape, but is not the sole explanation.

A more flexible variant of segmented markets theory, known as preferred habitat theory, offers a compromise explanation for the term structure of interest rates. It proposes that, although investors and borrowers may normally concentrate on a particular maturity market, certain events may cause them to wander from their "natural" market. Preferred habitat theory acknowledges that natural maturity markets may influence the yield curve, but it also recognizes that interest rate expectations could entice market participants to stray from their natural, preferred markets.

3-3d Integrating the Term Structure Theories

Much research has been conducted on the term structure of interest rates and has offered considerable insight into the various theories. Although the results of research differ, at least some evidence suggests that expectations theory, liquidity premium theory, and segmented markets theory all have some validity.

To understand how all three theories can simultaneously affect the yield curve, first assume the following conditions:

1. Investors and borrowers who select security maturities based on anticipated interest rate movements currently expect interest rates to rise.
2. Most borrowers are in need of long-term funds, whereas most investors have only short-term funds to invest.
3. Investors prefer more liquidity to less.

The first condition, which is related to expectations theory, suggests the existence of an upward-sloping yield curve (other things being equal); see curve E in Exhibit 3.5. The segmented markets information (condition 2) also favors the upward-sloping yield curve. When conditions 1 and 2 are considered simultaneously, the appropriate yield curve may look like curve E + S in the exhibit. The third condition (regarding liquidity) would then place a higher premium on the longer-term securities because of their lower degree of liquidity. When this condition is included with the first two, the yield may be represented by curve E + S + L.

In this example, all conditions place upward pressure on long-term yields relative to short-term yields. In reality, offsetting conditions may be present: One condition may put downward pressure on the slope of the yield curve, while other conditions cause upward pressure. If condition 1 in the example here were revised so that future interest rates were expected to decline, then this condition (by itself) would result in a downward-sloping yield curve. When

Exhibit 3.5   Effect of Conditions in an Example Yield Curve

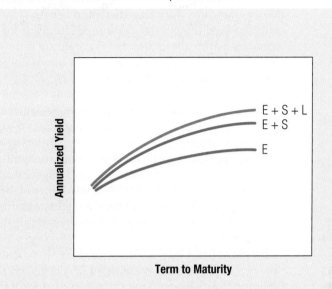

combined with the other conditions, which imply an upward-sloping curve, the result would be a partial offsetting effect. The actual yield curve would exhibit a downward slope if the effect of the interest rate expectations dominated the combined effects of segmented markets and a liquidity premium. In contrast, an upward slope would occur if the liquidity premium and segmented markets effects dominated the effects of interest rate expectations.

3-3e Use of the Term Structure

The term structure of interest rates is used to forecast interest rates, to forecast recessions, and to make investment and financing decisions.

Forecasting Interest Rates   At any point in time, the shape of the yield curve can be used to assess the general expectations of investors and borrowers about future interest rates. Recall from expectations theory that an upward-sloping yield curve generally results from expectation of higher interest rates, whereas a downward-sloping yield curve generally results from expectation of lower interest rates. Expectations about future interest rates must be interpreted cautiously, however, because liquidity and specific maturity preferences could influence the yield curve's shape. Despite these caveats, it is generally believed that interest rate expectations are a major factor contributing to the yield curve's shape. Thus the curve's shape should provide a reasonable indication (especially once the liquidity premium effect is taken into account) of the market's expectations about future interest rates.

Forecasting Recessions   Some analysts believe that flat or inverted yield curves indicate a recession will occur in the near future. The rationale for this belief is that, given a positive liquidity premium, such yield curves reflect the expectation of lower interest rates. This condition, in turn, is commonly associated with expectations of a reduced demand for loanable funds, which could be attributed to expectations of a weak economy. In March 2007, the yield curve exhibited a slight negative slope that caused some market participants to forecast a recession; a recession did begin in December 2007 and was followed by the credit crisis in 2008 and 2009.

Making Investment and Financing Decisions   If the yield curve is upward sloping, some investors may attempt to benefit from the higher yields on longer-term securities even though they have funds to invest for only a short period of time. The secondary market allows investors to implement this strategy, which is known as *riding the yield curve*. The risk of this strategy is the uncertainty in the price at which the securities can be sold in the near future.

The yield curve is commonly monitored by financial institutions whose liability maturities are distinctly different from their asset maturities. Consider a bank that obtains much of its funds through short-term deposits and uses those funds to provide long-term loans or purchase long-term securities. An upward-sloping yield curve is favorable to the bank because annualized short-term deposit rates are significantly lower than annualized long-term investment rates. The bank's spread is higher than it would be if the yield curve were flat. However, if it believes that the upward slope of the yield curve indicates higher interest rates in the future (as predicted by expectations theory), then the bank will expect its cost of liabilities to increase over time because future deposits would be obtained at higher interest rates.

Similarly, firms may use the yield curve in making financing decisions. An upward-sloping yield curve might encourage a firm to borrow short-term securities even though it needs funds for a longer term, in the hope that when the debt matures in the near future, it can be refinanced at a relatively low yield.

3-3f How the Yield Curve Has Changed over Time

Yield curves at various dates are illustrated in Exhibit 3.6. The yield curve is usually upward sloping, but a slight downward slope has sometimes been evident (as is the case with the curve for March 21, 2007). The yield curves for the last few years have been very low, reflecting a low annualized interest rate at any possible time to maturity.

Exhibit 3.6   Yield Curves at Various Points in Time

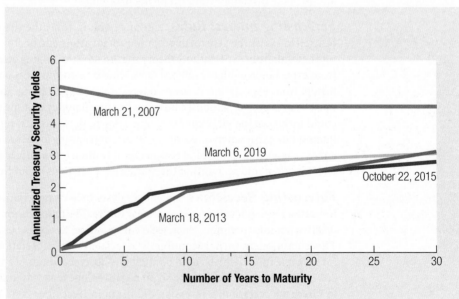

Source: Federal Reserve.

3-3g International Structure of Interest Rates

Because the factors that affect the shape of the yield curve can vary among countries, the yield curve's shape at any given time also varies among countries. Each country has a different currency with its own interest rate levels for various maturities, and each country's interest rates are based on conditions of supply of and demand for loanable funds in its own currency. Nevertheless, interest rate movements across countries tend to be positively correlated as a result of internationally integrated financial markets. Consequently, interest rate changes in one country may affect interest rates in another country. Because a foreign interest rate may affect domestic interest rates, some investors estimate the forward interest rate in a foreign country in an attempt to predict the future interest rate in that country.

Summary

- Quoted yields of debt securities at any given time may vary for the following reasons. First, securities with higher credit (default) risk must offer a higher yield. Second, securities that are less liquid must offer a higher yield. Third, taxable securities must offer a higher before-tax yield than do tax-exempt securities. Fourth, securities with longer maturities will offer a different yield (not consistently higher or lower) than securities with shorter maturities.

- Any particular debt security can be estimated by first determining the risk-free yield that is currently offered by a Treasury security with a similar maturity. Then adjustments are made that account for credit risk, liquidity, tax status, and other provisions.

- The term structure of interest rates can be explained by three theories. The pure expectations theory suggests that the shape of the yield curve is dictated by interest rate expectations. The liquidity premium theory suggests that securities with shorter maturities have greater liquidity and, therefore, should not have to offer as high a yield as do securities with longer terms to maturity. The segmented markets theory suggests that investors and borrowers have different needs that cause the demand and supply conditions to vary across different maturities. Consolidating the theories suggests that the term structure of interest rates depends on interest rate expectations, investor preferences for liquidity, and the unique needs of investors and borrowers in each maturity market.

Point/Counterpoint

Should a Yield Curve Influence a Borrower's Preferred Maturity of a Loan?

Point   Yes. If there is an upward-sloping yield curve, then a borrower should pursue a short-term loan to capitalize on the lower annualized rate charged for a short-term period. The borrower can obtain a series of short-term loans rather than a single loan to match the desired maturity.

Counterpoint   No. The borrower will face uncertainty regarding the interest rate charged on subsequent loans that are needed. An upward-sloping yield curve suggests that interest rates may rise in the future, which will cause the cost of borrowing to increase. Overall, the cost of borrowing may be higher when using a series of loans than when matching the debt maturity to the time period in which funds are needed.

Who Is Correct?   Use the Internet to learn more about this issue and then formulate your own opinion.

Questions and Applications

1. Characteristics That Affect Security Yields Identify the relevant characteristics of any security that can affect its yield.

2. Impact of Credit Risk on Yield How does high credit risk affect the yield offered securities?

3. Impact of Liquidity on Yield Discuss the relationship between the yield and the liquidity of securities.

4. Tax Effects on Yields Do investors in high tax brackets or those in low tax brackets benefit more from tax-exempt securities? Why? At a given point in time, which offers a higher before-tax yield: municipal bonds or corporate bonds? Why? Which has the higher after-tax yield? If taxes did not exist, would Treasury bonds offer a higher or lower yield than municipal bonds with the same maturity? Why?

5. Pure Expectations Theory Explain how a yield curve would shift in response to a sudden expectation of rising interest rates, according to the pure expectations theory.

6. Forward Rate What is the meaning of the forward rate in the context of the term structure of interest rates? Why might forward rates consistently overestimate future interest rates? How could such a bias be avoided?

7. Pure Expectations Theory Assume an expectation of lower interest rates in the future arises quite suddenly. What would be the effect on the shape of the yield curve? Explain.

8. Liquidity Premium Theory Explain the liquidity premium theory.

9. Impact of Liquidity Premium on Forward Rate Explain how consideration of a liquidity premium affects the estimate of a forward interest rate.

10. Segmented Markets Theory If a downward-sloping yield curve is mainly attributed to segmented markets theory, what does that suggest about the demand for and supply of funds in the short-term and long-term maturity markets?

11. Segmented Markets Theory If the segmented markets theory causes an upward-sloping yield curve, what does this imply? If markets are not completely segmented, should we dismiss the segmented markets theory as even a partial explanation for the term structure of interest rates? Explain.

12. Preferred Habitat Theory Explain the preferred habitat theory.

13. Yield Curve Which factors influence the shape of the yield curve? Describe how financial market participants use the yield curve.

Advanced Questions

14. Segmented Markets Theory Suppose that the U.S. Treasury decides to finance its deficit with mostly long-term funds. How could this decision affect the term structure of interest rates? If short-term and long-term markets were segmented, would the Treasury's decision have a more or less pronounced impact on the term structure? Explain.

15. Yield Curve Assuming that liquidity and interest rate expectations are both important for explaining the shape of a yield curve, what does a flat yield curve indicate about the market's perception of future interest rates?

16. Global Interaction among Yield Curves Assume that the yield curves in the United States, France, and Japan are flat. If the U.S. yield curve suddenly becomes positively sloped, do you think the yield curves in France and Japan would be affected? If so, how?

17. Multiple Effects on the Yield Curve Assume that (1) investors and borrowers expect that the economy will weaken and that inflation will decline, (2) investors require a small liquidity premium, and (3) markets are partially segmented and the Treasury currently has a preference for borrowing in short-term markets. Explain how each of these forces would affect the term structure, holding other factors constant. Then explain the effect on the term structure overall.

18. Effect of Crises on the Yield Curve During some crises, investors shift their funds out of the stock market and into money market securities for safety, even if they do not fear that interest rates will rise. Explain how and why these actions by investors affect the yield curve. Is the shift best explained by expectations theory, liquidity premium theory, or segmented markets theory?

19. How the Yield Curve May Respond to Prevailing Conditions Consider how economic conditions affect the credit risk premium. Do you think the credit risk premium will likely increase or decrease during this semester? How do you think the yield curve will change during this semester? Offer some logic to support your answers.

20. Assessing Interest Rate Differentials among Countries In countries experiencing high inflation, the annual interest rate may exceed 50 percent; in other countries, such as the United States and many European countries, annual interest rates are typically less than 10 percent. Do you think such a large difference in interest rates is due primarily to country-specific differences in the risk-free rates or in the credit risk premiums? Explain.

21. Applying the Yield Curve to Risky Debt Securities Assume that the yield curve for Treasury bonds has a slight upward slope, starting at 6 percent for a 10-year maturity and slowly rising to 8 percent for a 30-year maturity. Create a yield curve that you believe would exist for A-rated bonds and a corresponding yield curve for B-rated bonds.

22. Changes to Credit Rating Process Explain how credit rating agencies have changed their rating processes following criticism of their ratings during the credit crisis.

Critical Thinking Question

How a Credit Crisis Can Paralyze Credit Markets The key components of a market interest rate are the risk-free rate and the credit risk premium. During a credit crisis, these two components may change substantially, but in different ways. Write a short essay that describes how the risk-free rate and the risk premium may change during a credit crisis. Explain why the financial markets can become paralyzed during a crisis. Is it because of changes in the risk-free rate or changes in the risk premium?

Interpreting Financial News

Interpret the following comments made by Wall Street analysts and portfolio managers.

a. "An upward-sloping yield curve persists because many investors stand ready to jump into the stock market."

b. "Low-rated bond yields rose as recession fears caused a flight to quality."

c. "The shift from an upward-sloping yield curve to a downward-sloping yield curve is sending a warning about a possible recession."

Managing in Financial Markets

Monitoring Yield Curve Adjustments As an analyst at a bond rating agency, you have been asked to interpret the implications of the recent shift in the yield curve. Six months ago, the yield curve exhibited a slight downward slope. Over the last six months, long-term yields declined while short-term yields remained the same. Analysts said that the shift was due to revised expectations of interest rates.

a. Given the shift in the yield curve, does it appear that firms increased or decreased their demand for long-term funds over the last six months?

b. Interpret what the shift in the yield curve suggests about the market's changing expectations of future interest rates.

c. Recently, an analyst argued that the underlying reason for the yield curve shift is that many large U.S. firms anticipate a recession. Explain why an anticipated recession could force the yield curve to shift as it has.

d. What could the specific shift in the yield curve signal about the ratings of existing corporate bonds? Which types of corporations would be most likely to experience a change in their bond ratings as a result of this shift in the yield curve?

Problems

1. Forward Rate

a. Assume that, as of today, the annualized two-year interest rate is 13 percent and the one-year interest rate is 12 percent. Use this information to estimate the one-year forward rate.

b. Assume that the liquidity premium on a two-year security is 0.3 percent. Use this information to estimate the one-year forward rate.

2. Forward Rate Assume that, as of today, the annualized interest rate on a three-year security is 10 percent and the annualized interest rate on a two-year security is 7 percent. Use this information to estimate the one-year forward rate two years from now.

3. Forward Rate If $_ti_1 > {_ti_2}$, what is the market consensus forecast about the one-year forward rate one year from now? Is this rate above or below today's one-year interest rate? Explain.

4. After-Tax Yield You need to choose between investing in a one-year municipal bond with a 7 percent yield and a one-year corporate bond with an 11 percent yield. If your marginal federal income tax rate is 30 percent and no other differences exist between these two securities, which would you invest in?

5. Deriving Current Interest Rates Assume that interest rates for one-year securities are expected to be 2 percent today, 4 percent one year from now, and 6 percent two years from now. Using only pure expectations theory, what are the current interest rates on two-year and three-year securities?

6. Commercial Paper Yield

a. A corporation is planning to sell its 90-day commercial paper to investors by offering an 8.4 percent yield. If the three-month Treasury bill's annualized rate is 7 percent, the credit risk premium is estimated to be 0.6 percent, and there is a 0.4 percent tax adjustment, then what is the liquidity premium on the commercial paper?

b. Suppose that, because of unexpected changes in the economy, the credit risk premium increases to 0.8 percent. Assuming that no other changes occur, what is the appropriate yield to be offered on the commercial paper?

7. Forward Rate

a. Determine the forward rate for various one-year interest rate scenarios if the two-year interest rate is 8 percent, assuming no liquidity premium. Explain the relationship between the one-year interest rate and the one-year forward rate while holding the two-year interest rate constant.

b. Determine the one-year forward rate for the same one-year interest rate scenarios described in question (a) while assuming a liquidity premium of 0.4 percent. Does the relationship between the one-year interest rate and the forward rate change when the liquidity premium is considered?

c. Determine how the one-year forward rate would be affected if the quoted two-year interest rate rises, while both the quoted one-year interest rate and the liquidity premium are held constant. Explain the logic of this relationship.

d. Determine how the one-year forward rate would be affected if the liquidity premium rises and if the quoted one-year interest rate is held constant. What if the quoted two-year interest rate is held constant? Explain the logic of this relationship.

8. After-Tax Yield Determine how the after-tax yield from investing in a corporate bond is affected by higher tax rates, holding the before-tax yield constant. Explain the logic of this relationship.

9. Debt Security Yield

a. Determine how the appropriate yield to be offered on a security is affected by a higher risk-free rate. Explain the logic of this relationship.

b. Determine how the appropriate yield to be offered on a security is affected by a higher default risk premium. Explain the logic of this relationship.

Flow of Funds Exercise

Influence of the Structure of Interest Rates

Recall that Carson Company has obtained substantial loans from finance companies and commercial banks. The interest rates on these loans are tied to the six-month Treasury bill rate (and includes a risk premium) and are adjusted every six months. Therefore, Carson's cost of obtaining funds is sensitive to interest rate movements. The company expects that the U.S. economy will strengthen, so it plans to grow in the future by expanding its business and by making acquisitions. Carson anticipates needing substantial long-term financing to pay for its growth and plans to borrow additional funds, either through loans or by issuing bonds; it is also considering issuing stock to raise funds in the next year.

a. Assume that the market's expectations for the economy are similar to Carson's expectations. Also assume that the yield curve is primarily influenced by interest rate expectations. Would the yield curve be upward sloping or downward sloping? Why?

b. If Carson could obtain more debt financing for its 10-year projects, would it prefer to obtain credit at a long-term fixed interest rate or at a floating rate? Why?

c. If Carson attempts to obtain funds by issuing 10-year bonds, explain what information would help the company estimate the yield it would have to pay on 10-year bonds. That is, which key factors would influence the rate that Carson has to pay on its 10-year bonds?

d. If Carson attempts to obtain funds by issuing loans with floating interest rates every six months, explain what information would help the company estimate the yield it would have to pay over the next 10 years. That is, which key factors that would

influence the rate that Carson has to pay over the 10-year period?

e. An upward-sloping yield curve suggests that the initial rate that financial institutions could charge on a long-term loan to Carson would be higher than the initial rate that they could charge on a loan that floats in accordance with short-term interest rates. Does this imply that creditors should prefer offering Carson a fixed-rate loan to offering it a floating-rate loan? Explain why Carson's expectations of future interest rates are not necessarily the same as those of some financial institutions.

Internet/Excel Exercises

1. Assess the shape of the yield curve by going to the website www.gurufocus.com and searching for "yield curve." Is the Treasury yield curve upward or downward sloping? What is the yield of a 90-day Treasury bill? What is the yield of a 30-year Treasury bond?

2. Based on the various theories attempting to explain the yield curve's shape, what could explain the difference between the yields of the 90-day Treasury bill and the 30-year Treasury bond? Which theory, in your opinion, is the most reasonable? Why?

WSJ Exercise

Interpreting the Structure of Interest Rates

a. Explaining Yield Differentials Using the most recent issue of *The Wall Street Journal*, review the yields for the following securities:

TYPE	MATURITY	YIELD
Treasury	10-year	—
Corporate: high-quality	10-year	—
Corporate: medium-quality	10-year	—
Municipal (tax-exempt)	10-year	—

If credit (default) risk is the only reason for the yield differentials, then what is the credit risk premium on the corporate high-quality bonds? On the medium-quality bonds?

During a recent recession, high-quality corporate bonds offered a yield of 0.8 percent above Treasury bonds, while medium-quality bonds offered a yield of about 3.1 percent above Treasury bonds. How do these yield differentials compare to the differentials today? Explain the reason for any change.

b. Examining Recent Adjustments in Credit Risk Using the most recent issue of *The Wall Street Journal*, review the corporate debt section showing the high-yield issue with the biggest price decrease.

- Why do you think there was such a large decrease in price?
- How does this decrease in price affect the expected yield for any investors who buy bonds now?

c. Determining and Interpreting Today's Term Structure Using the most recent issue of *The Wall Street Journal*, review the yield curve to determine the approximate yields for the following maturities:

TERM TO MATURITY	ANNUALIZED YIELD
1 year	—
2 years	—
3 years	—

Assuming that the differences in these yields are due solely to interest rate expectations, determine the one-year forward rate as of one year from now and the one-year forward rate as of two years from now.

d. Assessing the Treasury Yield Curve *The Wall Street Journal* provides a "Treasury Yield Curve." Use this curve to describe the market's expectations about future interest rates. If a liquidity premium exists, how would this affect your perception of the market's expectations?

Online Articles with Real-World Examples

Find a recent practical article available online that describes a real-world example regarding a specific financial institution or financial market that reinforces one or more concepts covered in this chapter.

If your class has an online component, your professor may ask you to post your summary of the article there and provide a link to the article so that other students can access it. If your class is live, your professor may ask you to summarize your application of the article in class. Your professor may assign specific students to complete this assignment or may allow any students to do the assignment on a volunteer basis.

For recent online articles and real-world examples related to this chapter, consider using the following search terms (be sure to include the prevailing year as a search term to ensure that the online articles are recent):

1. credit risk
2. credit ratings AND risk
3. risk premium
4. yield curve
5. yield curve AND interest rate
6. interest rate AND liquidity premium
7. interest rate AND credit risk
8. rating agency AND risk
9. term structure AND maturity
10. yield curve AND financing

PART 1 INTEGRATIVE PROBLEM

Interest Rate Forecasts and Investment Decisions

This problem requires an understanding of how economic conditions affect interest rates and bond yields (Chapters 1, 2, and 3). Your task is to use information about existing economic conditions to forecast U.S. and Canadian interest rates. The following information is available to you.

1. Over the past six months, U.S. interest rates have declined and Canadian interest rates have increased.

2. The U.S. economy has weakened over the past year, while the Canadian economy has improved.

3. The U.S. saving rate (proportion of income saved) is expected to decrease slightly over the next year; the Canadian saving rate will remain stable.

4. The U.S. and Canadian central banks are not expected to implement any policy changes that would have a significant impact on interest rates.

5. You expect the U.S. economy to strengthen considerably over the next year but still be weaker than it was two years ago. You expect the Canadian economy to remain stable.

6. You expect the U.S. annual budget deficit to increase slightly from last year but be significantly less than the average annual budget deficit over the past five years. You expect the Canadian budget deficit to be about the same as last year.

7. You expect the U.S. inflation rate to rise slightly but still remain below the relatively high levels of two years ago; you expect the Canadian inflation rate to decline.

8. Based on some events last week, most economists and investors around the world (including you) expect the U.S. dollar to weaken against the Canadian dollar and against other foreign currencies over the next year. This expectation was already accounted for in your forecasts of inflation and economic growth.

9. The yield curve in the United States currently exhibits a consistent downward slope. The yield curve in Canada currently exhibits an upward slope. You believe that the liquidity premium on securities is quite small.

Questions

1. Using the information available to you, forecast the direction of U.S. interest rates.
2. Using the information available to you, forecast the direction of Canadian interest rates.
3. Assume that the perceived risk of corporations in the United States is expected to increase. Explain how the yield of newly issued U.S. corporate bonds will change to a different degree than will the yield of newly issued U.S. Treasury bonds.

PART 2
The Fed and Monetary Policy

The chapters in Part 2 explain how the Federal Reserve System (the Fed) affects economic conditions. Because the policies implemented by the Fed can influence securities prices, they are closely monitored by financial market participants. By assessing the Fed's policies, market participants can more accurately value securities and make more effective investment and financing decisions.

Financial Market Assessment of Possible Monetary Policy Actions by the Fed (Chapter 4) → Impact of Monetary Policy (Chapter 5) → Expectations of Economic Conditions → Expectations of Securities Prices → Decisions to Buy or Sell Securities

Decisions by Firms about When to Issue Securities

4

Functions of the Fed

The specific objectives of this chapter are to:

- Describe the organizational structure of the Fed.

- Describe how the Fed controls the money supply.

- Explain how the Fed revised its lending role in response to the credit crisis of 2008.

- Explain how monetary policy is used in other countries.

During the late 1800s and early 1900s, the United States experienced several banking panics. In 1913, in an effort to enhance the safety of the U.S. banking system, the government enacted the Federal Reserve Act, which created the **Federal Reserve System**. Today, the Fed is involved (along with other agencies) in regulating large commercial banks and savings institutions, as is discussed in Chapter 18.

As the central bank of the United States, the Fed is responsible for conducting national monetary policy in an attempt to achieve full employment and price stability (low or zero inflation) in the United States. Because the Fed's monetary policy has a major influence on interest rates, it has a major influence on financial markets and institutions.

4-1 Organizational Structure of the Fed

The Fed as it exists today has five major components:

- Federal Reserve district banks
- Member banks
- Board of Governors
- Federal Open Market Committee (FOMC)
- Advisory committees

4-1a Federal Reserve District Banks

The 12 Federal Reserve districts are identified in Exhibit 4.1, along with the city where each district bank is located. The New York district bank is considered the most important because many large banks are located in this district. Commercial banks that become members of the Fed are required to purchase stock in their **Federal Reserve district bank**. This stock, which is not traded in a secondary market, pays a maximum dividend of 6 percent annually.

Each Fed district bank has nine directors. The three Class A directors are employees or officers of a bank in that district and are elected by member banks to represent member banks. The three Class B directors are not affiliated with any bank and are elected by member banks to represent the public. Finally, the three Class C directors are not affiliated with any bank and are appointed by the Board of Governors (to be discussed shortly). The president of each Fed district bank is appointed by the three Class B and three Class C directors representing that district.

Exhibit 4.1 Locations of Federal Reserve District Banks

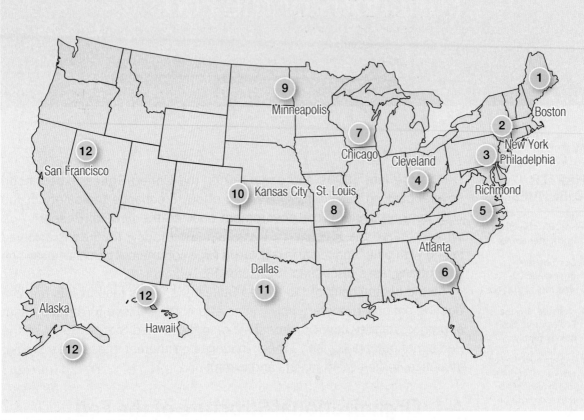

Source: Federal Reserve Bulletin.

Fed district banks facilitate operations within the banking system by clearing checks, replacing old currency, and providing loans (through the so-called discount window) to depository institutions in need of funds. They also collect economic data and conduct research on commercial banking and economic trends.

WEB

www.federalreserve.gov
Background on the
Board of Governors,
board meetings, board
members, and the
structure of the Fed.

4-1b Member Banks

Commercial banks can elect to become member banks if they meet specific requirements. All national banks (chartered by the Comptroller of the Currency) are required to be members of the Fed, but other banks (chartered by their respective states) are not. Currently, about 38 percent of all banks are members; these banks account for approximately 70 percent of all bank deposits.

4-1c **Board of Governors**

The **Board of Governors** (sometimes called the Federal Reserve Board) is made up of seven individual members with offices in Washington, D.C. Each member is appointed by the president of the United States and serves a nonrenewable 14-year term. This long term is thought to reduce political pressure on the governors, thereby encouraging the development of policies that will benefit the U.S. economy over the long run. The board members' terms are staggered so that one member's term expires in every even-numbered year.

WEB

www.federalreserve
.gov/monetarypolicy
/fomc.htm
Find information about
the Federal Open Market
Committee (FOMC).

One of the seven board members is selected by the president to be the Federal Reserve chair for a four-year term, which may be renewed. The chair has no more voting power than any other member but may have more influence. Jerome Powell is currently the chair of the Fed.

As a result of the Financial Reform Act of 2010, one of the seven board members is designated by the president to be the vice chair for supervision; this member is responsible for overseeing the financial institutions that the Fed regulates and for developing policy recommendations concerning that regulation for the Board of Governors. The vice chair reports to Congress semiannually.

The Board of Governors participates in setting margin requirements, which indicate the minimum percentage of an investment in securities that must be with investor's cash. The board also has the power to revise reserve requirements imposed on depository institutions. Most importantly, the board has a major influence on monetary policy, as discussed later in this chapter.

4-1d **Federal Open Market Committee**

The **Federal Open Market Committee (FOMC)** is made up of the seven members of the Board of Governors plus the presidents of five Fed district banks (the New York district bank plus four of the other 11 Fed district banks as determined on a rotating basis). Presidents of the seven remaining Fed district banks typically participate in the FOMC meetings but are not allowed to vote on policy decisions. The chair of the Board of Governors serves as chair of the FOMC.

The main goals of the FOMC are to achieve stable economic growth and price stability (low inflation). Realizing these goals would stabilize financial markets and interest rates. The FOMC attempts to achieve its goals by controlling the money supply, as described shortly.

4-1e **Advisory Committees**

The Federal Advisory Council consists of one member from each Federal Reserve district who represents the banking industry. Each district's member is elected each year by the board of directors of the respective district bank. The council meets with the Board of Governors in Washington, D.C., at least four times a year and makes recommendations about economic and banking issues.

The Community Depository Institutions Advisory Council (CDIAC; formerly called the Thrift Institutions Advisory Council) is made up of 12 members who represent savings banks, savings and loan associations, and credit unions. Its purpose is to offer views on issues specifically related to these institutions. It meets with the Board of Governors twice a year.

The Community Advisory Council was formed in 2015 to complement the two councils on the financial services industry. Its 15 members offer diverse views on economic circumstances and the financial services needs of consumers and communities, with particular emphasis on low- and moderate-income populations. The Community Advisory Council meets with the Board of Governors twice a year.

Exhibit 4.2 Integration of Federal Reserve Components

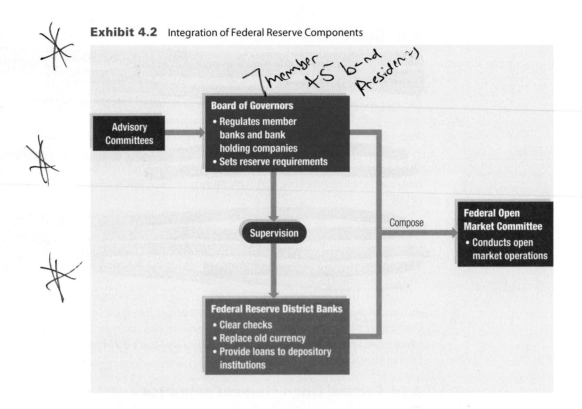

4-1f **Integration of Federal Reserve Components**

Exhibit 4.2 shows the relationships among the various components of the Federal Reserve System. The advisory committees advise the board, while the board oversees the operations of the district banks. The board and representatives of the district banks make up the FOMC.

4-1g **Consumer Financial Protection Bureau**

The Financial Reform Act of 2010 established the Consumer Financial Protection Bureau as an independent agency that is housed within the Federal Reserve but is independent of the other Fed committees. The bureau's director is appointed by the president, with the consent of the Senate. The bureau is responsible for regulating financial products and services, including online banking, certificates of deposit, and mortgages. In theory, it can act quickly to protect consumers from deceptive practices rather than waiting for Congress to pass new laws. Financial services administered by auto dealers are exempt from the Consumer Financial Protection Bureau's oversight. The bureau's Consumer Education and Engagement Division works to improve consumers' financial literacy.

FINANCIAL REFORM

WEB

www.federalreserve
.gov/monetarypolicy
/fomccalendars.htm
Provides minutes of
FOMC meetings. Notice
from the minutes how
much attention is
given to any economic
indicators that can be
used to anticipate future
economic growth or
inflation.

4-2 **Fed Control of the Money Supply**

As noted earlier, the Fed implements monetary policy with the goals of achieving full employment, low or zero inflation, and moderate long-term interest rates. Through its monetary policy, the Fed can influence the U.S. economy in multiple ways.

First, because the Fed's monetary policy affects interest rates, it has a strong influence on the cost of borrowing by households and thus affects the amount of monthly payments on mortgages, car loans, and other loans. In this way, monetary policy influences the amount of funds borrowed and spent by households.

WEB

www.clevelandfed.org
Features economic and
banking topics.

Second, monetary policy affects the cost of borrowing by businesses, thereby influencing how much money businesses are willing to borrow to support or expand their operations. Through its effect on the amount of spending by households and businesses, monetary policy influences the aggregate demand for products and services in the United States, which in turn influences the national income level and employment level. Because aggregate demand can affect the price level of products and services, the Fed indirectly influences the price level and hence the rate of inflation in the United States.

Third, because the Fed's monetary policy affects interest rates and therefore the return that is required by investors on investments, it can influence the prices of debt and equity securities. It can also indirectly affect the prices of equity securities by shaping economic conditions, which influence the future cash flows generated by publicly traded businesses.

In these ways, the Fed's monetary policy can have a major impact on households, businesses, and investors. Financial market participants closely monitor the Fed's actions so that they can anticipate how interest rates will be affected. They then use this information to forecast economic conditions and securities' prices. The relationship between the money supply and economic conditions is discussed in detail in the following chapter. First, it is important to understand *how* the Fed controls the money supply.

4-2a Decision Process

The FOMC meets eight times a year. At each meeting, targets for the money supply growth level and the interest rate level are determined, and actions are taken to implement the monetary policy dictated by the FOMC. If the Fed wants to consider changing its targets for money supply growth or interest rates before its next scheduled meeting, it may hold a conference-call meeting.

Pre-Meeting Economic Reports   Approximately two weeks before the FOMC meeting, FOMC members receive the **Beige Book**, which is a consolidated report of regional economic conditions in each of the 12 districts. Each Federal Reserve district bank is responsible for reporting its regional conditions, and all of these reports are included in the Beige Book.

Approximately one week before the FOMC meeting, participants receive analyses of the economy and economic forecasts. Thus, participants have a great deal of information to study before the meeting takes place.

Economic Presentations   The seven members of the Board of Governors, the 12 presidents of the Fed district banks, and staff members (typically economists) of the Board of Governors attend each FOMC meeting. The meeting begins with presentations by the staff members about current economic conditions and recent economic trends. These presentations include data and trends related to wages, consumer prices, unemployment, gross domestic product, business inventories, foreign exchange rates, interest rates, and financial market conditions.

The staff members also assess production levels, business investment, residential construction, international trade, and international economic growth. This assessment is conducted to predict economic growth and inflation in the United States, assuming that the Fed does not adjust its monetary policy. For example, a decline in business inventories may lead to an expectation of stronger economic growth, because firms will need to boost their production to replenish inventories. Conversely, an increase in inventories may indicate that firms will reduce their production, and possibly their workforces as well. An increase in business investment indicates that businesses are expanding their production capacity and are likely to increase production in the future. An increase in economic growth in foreign countries is important because a portion of the rising incomes in those countries will be spent on U.S. products or services.

Much attention is also given to any factors that can affect inflation. For example, oil prices are closely monitored because they affect the cost of producing and transporting many products. A decline in business inventories when production is near full capacity may indicate an excessive demand for products that will pull prices up. This condition indicates the potential for higher inflation because firms may raise the prices of their products when they are producing near full capacity and experience shortages. Firms that attempt to expand their capacity under these conditions will have to raise wages to attract additional qualified employees. Because these firms will incur higher costs from raising wages, they will, in turn, raise the prices of their products. The Fed becomes concerned when several indicators suggest that higher inflation is likely.

The staff members typically base their forecasts for economic conditions on the assumption that the prevailing monetary growth level will continue in the future. When it is highly likely that the monetary growth level will be changed, they provide forecasts for economic conditions under different monetary growth scenarios. Their goal is to provide facts and economic forecasts, not to make judgments about the appropriate monetary policy.

Once the presentations are completed, the FOMC members, including both voting and nonvoting members, discuss what the Fed's monetary policy should be. The chair of the Fed may offer a recommendation and usually has some influence over the other members. The participants are commonly given three options for monetary policy, which are intended to cover a range of the most reasonable policies and should include at least one policy that is satisfactory to each member.

FOMC Decisions   After the discussion, the voting members of the FOMC vote on whether the federal funds rate target should be changed. Most decisions are unanimous, but it is not unusual to have one or two dissenting votes.

The federal funds rate is the rate charged by banks on short-term loans to each other. Even though this rate is determined by the banks that participate in the federal funds market, it is subject to the supply of and demand for funds in the banking system. Thus, the Fed influences the federal funds rate by revising the supply of funds in the banking system. The target may be specified as a specific point estimate, such as 2.5 percent, or as a range, such as from 2.5 to 2.75 percent.

Because all short-term interest rates are affected by the supply of and demand for funds in the banking system, the Fed's actions will affect not just the federal funds rate, but other interest rates as well. If the FOMC is concerned that the economy is weak and if it is not concerned about inflation, it would recommend that the Fed implement a monetary policy to reduce the federal funds rate.

Exhibit 4.3 shows how the federal funds rate was reduced near the end of 2007 when signs of the credit crisis and recession in 2008 became noticeable. In December 2008, the Fed set the target for the federal funds rate at a range between 0 and 0.25 percent. The goal was to stimulate the economy by reducing interest rates to their minimum level in an effort to encourage more borrowing and spending by households and businesses. The Fed maintained the federal funds rate within this range over the 2009–2015 period; other interest rates were also low during this period.

When there is evidence of a very strong economy and the potential for inflation, the Fed tends to implement a monetary policy that will increase the federal funds rate (and therefore other interest rates as well). Such a policy aims to reduce any inflationary pressure that is attributed to excess demand for products and services. Ideally, this

Exhibit 4.3   Federal Funds Rate over Time

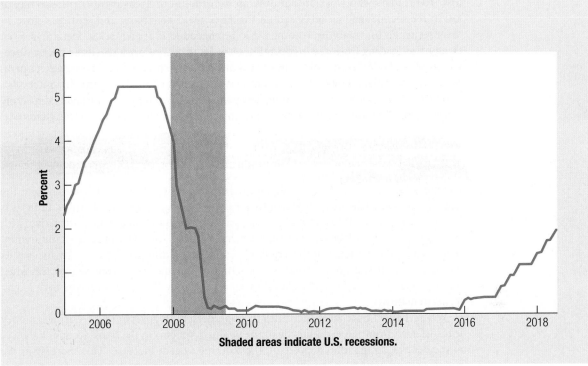

Shaded areas indicate U.S. recessions.

Source: Board of Governors, Federal Reserve.

policy will reduce inflationary pressure without having an adverse effect on the economy. Exhibit 4.3 shows that the Fed has raised the federal funds rate by a small amount several times since 2016.

FOMC Statement   Following the FOMC meeting, the committee issues a clear detailed statement that summarizes its conclusion. In recent years, the FOMC has acknowledged the importance of this statement, which is used (along with other information) by many participants in the financial markets to generate forecasts of the economy. Voting members vote not only on the proper monetary policy but also on the corresponding communication (statement) of that policy to the public. The statement provided by the committee following each meeting is widely publicized in the news media and can be accessed on Federal Reserve websites.

Minutes of FOMC Meeting   Within three weeks of an FOMC meeting, the minutes for that meeting are provided to the public and made accessible on Federal Reserve websites. These minutes commonly illustrate the different points of view held by various participants at the FOMC meeting.

www.treasurydirect.gov
Treasury note and bond
auction results.

4-2b Role of the Fed's Trading Desk

If the FOMC determines that a change in its monetary policy is appropriate, its decision is forwarded to the **Trading Desk** (or the **Open Market Desk**) at the New York Federal Reserve District Bank through a statement called the **policy directive**.

After receiving a policy directive from the FOMC, the manager of the Trading Desk instructs traders who work at that desk on the amount of Treasury securities to buy or sell in the secondary market based on the directive. The buying and selling of government securities (through the Trading Desk) is referred to as open market operations. Even though the Trading Desk at the Federal Reserve Bank of New York receives a policy directive from the FOMC only eight times a year, it continuously conducts open market operations to control the money supply in response to ongoing changes in bank deposit levels.

The FOMC is not limited to issuing new policy directives only on its scheduled meeting dates. It can hold additional meetings at any time to consider changing the federal funds rate.

Fed Purchase of Treasury Securities

When traders at the Trading Desk at the New York Fed are instructed to *lower* the federal funds rate, they purchase Treasury securities in the secondary market. First, they contact securities dealers to obtain their list of Treasury securities for sale, including the denomination and maturity of each security, and the dealer's ask quote (the price at which the dealer is willing to sell the security). From this list, the traders attempt to purchase those Treasury securities that are most attractive (with the lowest prices for whatever maturities are desired) until they have purchased the amount requested by the manager of the Trading Desk. The Trading Desk frequently focuses its purchases on Treasury bills (Treasury securities with a maturity of one year or less when initially issued by the Treasury), but it may also consider Treasury securities with longer terms to maturity.

When the Fed purchases securities through dealers in government securities, money is transferred from the Fed (outside of the banking system) to the bank account balances of the dealers, so the total deposits in the banking system increase. This increase in the supply of funds within the banking system places downward pressure on the federal funds rate. The Fed continues this process of increasing the money supply in the banking system until the federal funds rate declines to the new targeted level. Such activity, which is initiated by the FOMC's policy directive, is referred to as a *loosening* of money supply growth.

The Fed's purchase of government securities has a different impact than a purchase by another investor would have because the Fed's purchase results in additional bank deposits (increased money supply) and, therefore, allows banks to offer more loans to businesses and individuals. Conversely, the purchase of government securities by someone other than the Fed (such as an investor) merely results in offsetting account balance positions at commercial banks. For example, as investors purchase Treasury securities in the secondary market, their bank balances decline, while the bank balances of the sellers of the Treasury securities increase.

Fed Sale of Treasury Securities

If the FOMC's policy directive instructs the Trading Desk at the New York Fed to *increase* the federal funds rate, its traders sell government securities (obtained from previous purchases) to dealers in government securities. The securities are sold to the dealers that submit the highest bids. As the dealers pay for the securities, money is transferred from the dealers to the Fed, and the dealers' bank account balances are reduced. Thus, the total amount of funds in the banking system is reduced by the market value of the securities sold by the Fed. This reduction in the supply of funds in the banking system places upward pressure on the federal funds rate (and other interest rates as well). Such activity is referred to as a *tightening* of money supply growth.

Dynamic versus Defensive Open Market Operations

The Trading Desk's open market operations to either reduce or increase the federal funds rate are classified as **dynamic**, because they are intended to have a lasting impact on economic conditions.

Exhibit 4.4   Comparison of Money Supply Measures

MONEY SUPPLY MEASURES
M1 = currency + checking deposits
M2 = M1 + savings deposits, MMDAs, overnight repurchase agreements, Eurodollars, and small time deposits
M3 = M2 + institutional money market mutual funds, large time deposits, and repurchase agreements and Eurodollars lasting more than one day

WEB

www.federalreserve.gov
Click on " Data" to
obtain Federal Reserve
statistical releases.

The Trading Desk also implements **defensive** open market operations, which are simply intended to offset the impact of temporary conditions on the amount of funds in the banking system. For example, if the Fed anticipates an unusually large amount of deposit withdrawals during specific holidays, it may wish to temporarily inject funds into the banking system. Under these conditions, the Trading Desk may engage in **repurchase agreements**, in which it purchases Treasury securities from securities dealers (to temporarily inject funds into the banking system) with an agreement to sell back the securities at a specified date in the near future.

4-2c Control of M1 versus M2

When the Fed conducts open market operations to adjust the money supply, it must also consider the measure of money on which it will focus. For the Fed's purposes, the optimal form of money should (1) be controllable by the Fed and (2) have a predictable impact on economic variables when adjusted by the Fed. The most narrow form of money, known as **M1**, includes currency held by the public and checking deposits (such as demand deposits, negotiable order of withdrawal [NOW] accounts, and automatic transfer balances) at depository institutions. The M1 measure does not include all funds that can be used for transactions purposes. For example, checks can be written against a **money market deposit account (MMDA)** offered by depository institutions or against a money market mutual fund. In addition, funds can easily be withdrawn from savings accounts to make transactions. For this reason, a broader measure of money, called **M2**, also deserves consideration. It includes everything in M1 as well as savings accounts and small time deposits, MMDAs, and some other items. Another measure of money, called **M3**, includes everything in M2 plus large time deposits and other items. Although even broader measures of money exist, M1, M2, and M3 receive the most attention. Exhibit 4.4 compares these measures of money.

The M1 money measure is more volatile than M2 or M3. Because M1 can change simply owing to changes in the types of deposits maintained by households, M2 and M3 are more reliable measures for monitoring and controlling the money supply.

4-2d How Open Market Operations Affect All Interest Rates

Even though the Fed focuses solely on controlling a targeted federal funds rate, it has a major influence on all types of interest rates, which means it also has a major influence on economic conditions. When the Fed increases the supply of funds in the banking system by purchasing Treasury bills, banks have more funds available, and this should naturally place downward pressure on the federal funds rate. However, the Fed's actions have additional effects. Since banks now have more funds available, they may want to put their excess funds to work by offering new loans to businesses and households. They may lower their loan rates in an effort to appeal to potential borrowers. They may also lower the interest rates offered on deposits.

When the Fed buys Treasury bills as a means of increasing the money supply, it places upward pressure on those securities' market prices. Because Treasury bills offer a fixed value to investors at maturity, a higher price translates into a lower yield for investors who buy them and hold them until maturity. As the yields on Treasury bills and bank deposits decline, investors will move some of their funds into other short-term debt securities (such as commercial paper), but then the yields of those securities will also decline.

Thus, the Fed's open market operations reduce not only the federal funds rate, but also the rates (or yields) on bank deposits, bank loans, T-bills, and other short-term debt securities. Consequently, the cost of financing to businesses, households, and government agencies is reduced, which may encourage them to borrow and spend more money, which can stimulate the economy.

If open market operations are used to reduce bank funds, the opposite effects occur. There is upward pressure on the federal funds rate, on the loan rates charged to households and firms, on the interest rates offered to bank depositors, and on the yields of debt securities.

4-2e **Alternative Monetary Policy Tools**

Along with open market operations, the Fed could consider adjusting its reserve requirement ratio or changing the primary credit rate available through its lending facility as a means of controlling the money supply.

Adjusting the Reserve Requirement Ratio   Depository institutions are subject to a **reserve requirement ratio**, which is the proportion of their deposit accounts that must be held as required reserves (funds held in reserve). This ratio is set by the Fed's Board of Governors. Most depository institutions are required to maintain 10 percent of their transaction accounts (such as checking accounts) and a smaller proportion of their other savings accounts as required reserves.

Because the reserve requirement ratio affects the degree to which the money supply in the banking system can change in response to an injection of new deposits, it is considered a monetary policy tool. If the Board of Governors reduces the reserve requirement ratio, a bank will have to hold a smaller proportion of its new deposits as reserves and, therefore, can make more loans. As the borrowers spend these loans, some of the funds will return to depository institutions in the form of new deposits, which can be used to make more loans. As this cycle plays out, it stimulates the economy. Conversely, a higher reserve requirement ratio means that depository institutions must hold a larger proportion of their new deposits as reserves, so an initial injection of funds will multiply by a smaller amount.

However, an adjustment in the reserve requirement ratio could cause erratic shifts in the money supply. Consequently, the Fed normally relies on open market operations rather than adjustments in the reserve requirement ratio when controlling the money supply.

The Fed's Lending Facility   The Fed maintains a lending facility (sometimes called the discount window) through which it provides short-term loans (usually overnight) to depository institutions. It charges a lower interest rate (called the *primary credit rate*) to the most creditworthy depository institutions and a higher interest rate (called the *secondary credit rate*) to depository institutions that not as creditworthy. This facility was historically viewed as a potential monetary policy tool because it could affect the money supply. Specifically, if the Fed adjusted its lending rates downward, it might encourage depository institutions to borrow more money from the Fed, which would lead to a greater amount of funds injected into the banking system. Conversely, if the

Fed adjusted its lending rates downward, it might discourage depository institutions from borrowing from the Fed, which would reduce the amount of funds injected into the banking system.

The Fed no longer considers its lending facility as a potential monetary policy tool, since its open market operations are more effective at controlling money supply. Nevertheless, the lending facility can still be an important source of liquidity for some depository institutions.

4-3 The Fed's Intervention during the Credit Crisis

During and after the credit crisis of 2008, the Fed not only engaged in traditional open market operations to reduce interest rates, but also implemented various nontraditional strategies in an effort to improve economic conditions.

4-3a Fed Loans to Facilitate the Rescue of Bear Stearns

In March 2008, the Fed provided funding to Bear Stearns that enabled it to avoid filing for bankruptcy. Bear Stearns was a securities firm, not a depository institution, so ordinarily it would not have been allowed to borrow funds from the Fed. However, it was a major provider of clearing operations for many types of financial transactions conducted by firms and individuals. If it had gone bankrupt, those financial transactions might have been delayed, potentially creating liquidity problems for many individuals and firms that were to receive cash as a result of the transactions. On March 16, 2008, the Fed provided a loan to JPMorgan Chase that was passed through to Bear Stearns. This ensured that the clearing operations would continue and avoided liquidity problems.

4-3b The Fed's Strategy of Quantitative Easing

In theory, the Fed's monetary policy of purchasing short-term Treasury securities can lower interest rates, encourage more borrowing and spending, and therefore stimulate the economy. However, during the credit crisis in 2008, short-term interest rates were already close to zero, so the Fed's ability to resolve the crisis by lowering short-term interest rates was limited.

In addition, institutional investors were concerned about possible defaults on various types of risky debt securities, so they reduced their participation in these debt markets. It was difficult for potential borrowers to borrow funds even though interest rates were very low, because institutional investors were unwilling to provide funding through the purchase of debt securities. If credit is not available for the potential borrowers, then those potential borrowers cannot spend money, so the economy cannot be stimulated. Furthermore, some potential corporate borrowers needed funds simply to survive.

Starting in 2008, the Fed implemented a variety of innovative strategies that were intended to have favorable effects on the economy, beyond what would be achieved by the Fed's traditional monetary policy of purchasing short-term Treasury securities. These strategies are broadly referred to as **quantitative easing**. The term "quantitative" reflects that the Fed allocated a specific quantity of money to purchase specific types of debt securities each month, while the term "easing" indicates that this "easy money" or "loose money" policy was designed to flood specific debt markets with funds.

The quantitative easing strategies were unique because they were not focused solely on purchases of short-term Treasury securities, as in the Fed's traditional monetary policy. The Fed also purchased long-term Treasury securities as well as debt securities that exhibited credit (default) risk. By purchasing these securities, the Fed was attempting to increase liquidity in specific markets for risky debt securities and reduce long-term interest rates.

Some of the more well-known examples of quantitative easing used to improve economic conditions during the credit crisis and beyond are described next.

Fed Purchases of Mortgage-Backed Securities   One of the Fed's main concerns during the credit crisis in 2008 was that the market values of mortgage-backed securities had weakened substantially due to the high default rate on mortgages. Therefore, at that time, the Fed's quantitative easing strategy was heavily focused on purchasing mortgage-backed securities. It expended more than $30 billion to purchase mortgage-backed securities every month, and by 2010, it was holding more than $2 trillion of mortgage-backed securities. Many financial institutions were heavily exposed to mortgages during the credit crisis, but were able to reduce their exposure by selling some of their mortgage-backed securities to the Fed.

As the Fed increased its purchases of mortgage-backed securities, the prices of these securities rose. In addition, investors slowly began to invest again in the risky debt securities markets, which resulted in higher liquidity in the market for these securities. In this way, the Fed's actions helped to stabilize the housing market. The Fed continued to periodically purchase mortgage-backed securities through 2014.

Fed's Purchase of Bonds Backed by Loans   In 2008, the Fed created a term asset-backed security loan facility (TALF) that purchased high-quality bonds backed by consumer loans, credit card loans, or automobile loans. The secondary market for these types of loans had dried up during the credit crisis, because investors were concerned that borrowers would default on such loans. Consequently, financial institutions stopped making consumer loans because they could not easily sell the loans in the secondary market. The TALF provided loans to institutional investors that purchased these types of loans. In this way, the Fed encouraged financial institutions to offer new consumer loans.

Fed's Purchase of Commercial Paper   During 2008 and 2009, the Fed used another form of quantitative easing in which it purchased a large amount of commercial paper. Under normal circumstances, it did not purchase commercial paper, but it implemented this strategy during the credit crisis to offset the reduction in the market demand for commercial paper due to investors' fears of defaults. Those fears were triggered in part by the failure of Lehman Brothers (a very large securities firm) in 2008, which caused Lehman to default on the commercial paper that it had previously issued. The Fed recognized that some of these debt securities had low risk, yet the financial markets were paralyzed by fear of potential default. The Fed's willingness to purchase commercial paper restored trading and liquidity in the commercial paper market.

Fed's Purchase of Long-Term Treasury Securities   The Fed's normal open market operations focus on purchasing short-term Treasury securities, but from 2010 through 2014, it also purchased a large amount of long-term Treasury notes and bonds. The Fed took this action because although short-term interest rates were close to zero in 2010, many large expenditures by corporations and individuals are subject to long-term interest rates. The Fed attempted to reduce long-term interest rates to encourage more long-term borrowing by corporations for capital expenditures and by individuals to purchase homes. The Fed's purchases of long-term securities were intended to reduce long-term Treasury bond yields, which would indirectly result in lower long-term borrowing rates. This strategy is discussed in more detail in Chapter 5.

4-3c Perceptions of the Fed's Intervention during the Crisis

While the Fed took much initiative to improve economic conditions during the credit crisis, opinions vary on exactly what the Fed should have done to improve the economy. Many of the Fed's actions during the credit crisis involved the purchasing of securities either to lower interest rates (traditional monetary policy) or to restore liquidity in the markets for various types of risky debt securities. The Fed's focus was on improving conditions in financial markets, which was expected to increase the flow of funds from financial markets to corporations or individuals.

However, some critics argue that the Fed's actions addressed only the financial institutions, but ignored other sectors of the economy. Some of this criticism points to the very high compensation that some financial institutions (such as some securities firms) paid to their employees. Critics contend that if these securities firms could afford to pay such high salaries, they should not have needed to be bailed out by the government.

The Fed might respond that it did not bail out Lehman Brothers when it failed in September 2008. In addition, the Fed's actions to restore liquidity in the debt markets did not just help financial institutions, but were necessary to ensure that all types of corporations could obtain funding to support or expand operations, and that individuals could obtain funding to purchase homes or automobiles. Such funding is needed for corporations and individuals to increase their spending, which can stimulate the economy and create jobs.

4-4 Global Monetary Policy

Each country has its own central bank that conducts monetary policy. The central banks of industrialized countries tend to have somewhat similar goals, which essentially reflect price stability (low inflation) and economic growth (low unemployment). Resources and conditions vary among countries, however, so a given central bank may focus more on a particular economic goal. Like the Fed, the central banks of other industrialized countries commonly use open market operations to control their money supply and influence economic conditions.

Because country economies are largely integrated on a global scale, the Fed must consider economic conditions in other major countries when assessing the U.S. economy. The Fed may be most effective when it coordinates its activities with those of the central banks of other countries. Central banks commonly work together when they intervene in the foreign exchange market, but conflicts of interest can make it difficult for them to coordinate monetary policies.

4-4a A Single Eurozone Monetary Policy

One of the goals of the European Union (EU) has been to establish a single currency (the euro) for its members. In 2002, 12 European countries replaced their national currencies with the euro, and seven more countries have adopted the euro since then.

The European Central Bank (ECB), based in Frankfurt, Germany, is responsible for setting monetary policy for all European countries that use the euro as their currency. This bank's objective is to control inflation in the participating countries and to stabilize (within reasonable boundaries) the value of the euro with respect to other major currencies. Thus, the ECB's monetary goals of price and currency stability are similar to those of individual countries around the world; they differ in that they are focused on a group of countries rather than a single country.

WEB

www.ecb.europa.eu
Provides links to the European Central Bank and other foreign central banks.

Limitations of Monetary Policy in the Eurozone   Because all countries participating in the eurozone are subject to the monetary policy imposed by the ECB, each participating country no longer has full control over the monetary policy implemented within its borders at any given time. Thus, any participating country cannot solve local economic problems with its own monetary policy.

Furthermore, the monetary policy implemented by the ECB in a particular period may enhance economic conditions in some countries and adversely affect others. For example, consider an ECB policy that is intended to slow economic growth in an effort to reduce inflationary pressure. This policy might be perfect for the eurozone countries that presently have high inflation and strong economic growth, but it would not be suitable for a country that has negligible inflation, a weak economy, and high unemployment. Each participating country is still able to apply its own fiscal policy (tax and government expenditure decisions) in an effort to solve its economic problems.

Summary

- The key components of the Federal Reserve System are the Board of Governors and the Federal Open Market Committee. The Board of Governors determines the reserve requirements on account balances at depository institutions. It is also an important subset of the Federal Open Market Committee (FOMC), which determines U.S. monetary policy. The FOMC's monetary policy has a major influence on interest rates and other economic conditions.

- The Fed uses open market operations (the buying and selling of securities) as a means of adjusting the money supply. The Fed purchases securities to increase the money supply and sells them to reduce the money supply.

- In response to the credit crisis, the Fed provided indirect funding to Bear Stearns (a large securities firm)

so that it did not have to file for bankruptcy. In an effort to stimulate the economy and lower long-term interest rates, the Fed engaged in quantitative easing, which involved purchasing long-term Treasury securities and risky debt securities such as mortgage-backed securities. It also purchased commercial paper issued by corporations. In addition, the Fed created various facilities for providing funds to financial institutions and other corporations.

- Each country has its own central bank, which is responsible for conducting monetary policy to achieve economic goals such as low inflation and low unemployment. Nineteen countries in Europe have adopted a single currency, which means that all of these countries are subject to the same monetary policy.

Point/Counterpoint

Should There Be a Global Central Bank?

Point   Yes. A global central bank could serve all countries in the manner that the European Central Bank now serves several European countries. With a single central bank, there could be a single monetary policy across all countries.

Counterpoint   No. A global central bank could create a global monetary policy only if a single currency

were used throughout the world. Moreover, all countries would not agree on the monetary policy that would be appropriate.

Who Is Correct?   Use the Internet to learn more about this issue and then formulate your own opinion.

Questions and Applications

1. **The Fed** Briefly describe the origin of the Federal Reserve System. Describe the functions of the Fed district banks.

2. **FOMC** What are the main goals of the Federal Open Market Committee? How does it attempt to achieve these goals?

3. **Open Market Operations** Explain how the Fed increases the money supply through open market operations.

4. **Policy Directive** What is the policy directive, and who carries it out?

5. **Beige Book** What is the Beige Book, and why is it important to the FOMC?

6. **Reserve Requirements** How is money supply growth affected by an increase in the reserve requirement ratio?

7. **Control of Money Supply** Describe the characteristics that a measure of money should have if it is to be manipulated by the Fed.

8. **FOMC Economic Presentations** What is the purpose of the economic presentations made during an FOMC meeting?

9. **Open Market Operations** Explain how the Fed can use open market operations to reduce the money supply.

10. **Effect on Money Supply** Why do the Fed's open market operations have a different effect on the money supply than do transactions between two depository institutions?

11. **Fed's Indirect Influence on Many Types of Interest Rates** The Fed focuses its control on the federal funds rate, yet indirectly influences many other types of interest rates. Explain.

12. **The Fed versus Congress** Should the Fed or Congress decide the fate of large financial institutions that are near bankruptcy?

13. **Bailouts by the Fed** Do you think that the Fed should have bailed out large financial institutions during the credit crisis?

14. **The Fed's Impact on Unemployment** Explain how the Fed's monetary policy affects the unemployment level.

15. **The Fed's Impact on Home Purchases** Explain how the Fed influences the monthly mortgage payments on homes. How might the Fed indirectly influence the total demand for homes by consumers?

16. **The Fed's Impact on Security Prices** Explain how the Fed's monetary policy may indirectly affect the prices of equity securities.

17. **Impact of FOMC Statement** How might the FOMC statement (issued following the committee's meeting) stabilize financial markets more than if no statement were provided?

18. **Fed Facility Programs during the Credit Crisis** Explain how the Fed's facility programs improved liquidity in some debt markets.

19. **Consumer Financial Protection Bureau** As a result of the Financial Reform Act of 2010, the Consumer Financial Protection Bureau was established and housed within the Federal Reserve. Explain the role of this bureau.

20. **Eurozone Monetary Policy** Explain why participating in the eurozone causes a country to give up its independent monetary policy and control over its domestic interest rates.

21. **The Fed's Power** What should be the Fed's role? Should it focus only on monetary policy? Or should it engage in the trading of various types of securities in an attempt to stabilize the financial system when securities markets are suffering from investor fears and the potential for high credit (default) risk?

22. **Fed Purchases of Mortgage-Backed Securities** Explain the motivation behind the Fed's policy of purchasing massive amounts of mortgage-backed securities during the 2008 credit crisis. What could this policy accomplish that the Fed's traditional monetary policy might not accomplish?

23. **The Fed's Purchases of Commercial Paper** Why and how did the Fed intervene in the commercial paper market during the 2008 credit crisis?

24. **The Fed's Trading of Long-Term Treasury Securities** Why did the Fed purchase long-term Treasury securities in 2010, and how did this strategy differ from the Fed's usual operations?

25. The Fed and TALF What was TALF, and why did the Fed create it?

26. The Fed's Quantitative Easing Strategies Explain how the Fed's "quantitative easing" strategies differed from its traditional strategy of buying short-term Treasury securities.

Critical Thinking Question

The Fed's Intervention during the Crisis The Fed intervened heavily during the 2008 credit crisis. Write a short essay explaining whether you believe the Fed's intervention improved conditions in financial markets or made conditions worse.

Interpreting Financial News

Interpret the following statements made by Wall Street analysts and portfolio managers.

a. "The Fed's future monetary policy will be dependent on the economic indicators to be reported this week."
b. "The Fed's role is to take the punch bowl away just as the party is coming alive."
c. "Inflation will likely increase because real short-term interest rates currently are negative."

Managing in Financial Markets

Anticipating the Fed's Actions As a manager of a large U.S. firm, one of your assignments is to monitor U.S. economic conditions so that you can forecast the demand for products sold by your firm. You realize that the Federal Reserve implements monetary policy whereas the federal government implements spending and tax policies (fiscal policy) in order to influence economic growth and inflation. However, it is difficult to achieve high economic growth without igniting inflation. Although the Fed is often said to be independent of the administration in office, there is much interaction between monetary and fiscal policies.

Assume that the economy is currently stagnant and that some economists are concerned about the possibility of a recession. Yet some industries are experiencing high growth, and inflation is higher this year than in the previous five years. Assume that the Fed chair's term will expire in four months and that the president will have to appoint a new chair (or reappoint the existing chair). It is widely known that the existing chair would like to be reappointed. Also assume that next year is an election year for the administration.

a. Given the circumstances, do you expect that the administration will be more concerned about increasing economic growth or reducing inflation?
b. Given the circumstances, do you expect that the Fed will be more concerned about increasing economic growth or reducing inflation?
c. Your firm is relying on you for some insight into how the government will influence economic conditions and hence the demand for your firm's products. Given the circumstances, what is your forecast of how the government will affect economic conditions?

Flow of Funds Exercise

Monitoring the Fed

Recall that Carson Company has obtained substantial loans from finance companies and commercial banks. The interest rate on the loans is tied to market interest rates and is adjusted every six months. Expecting a strong U.S. economy, Carson plans to grow by expanding its business and by making acquisitions. The company expects that it will need substantial long-term financing, and it plans to borrow additional funds either through loans or by issuing bonds. Carson Company is also considering issuing stock to raise funds in the next year.

Given its large exposure to interest rates charged on its debt, Carson closely monitors Fed actions. It subscribes to a special service that attempts to monitor the Fed's actions in the Treasury security markets. Carson recently received an alert from the service indicating that the Fed has been selling large holdings of its Treasury securities in the secondary Treasury securities market.

a. How should Carson interpret the actions by the Fed? That is, will these actions place upward or downward pressure on the price of Treasury securities? Explain.
b. Will these actions place upward or downward pressure on Treasury yields? Explain.
c. Will these actions place upward or downward pressure on interest rates? Explain.

Internet/Excel Exercise

Assess the current structure of the Federal Reserve System by using the website www.federalreserve.gov/monetarypolicy/fomc.htm.

Go to the minutes of the most recent meeting. Who is the current chair? Who is the current vice chair? How many people attended the meeting? Describe the main issues discussed at the meeting.

WSJ Exercise

Reviewing Fed Policies

Review recent issues of *The Wall Street Journal* and search for any comments that relate to the Fed. Does it appear that the Fed may attempt to revise the federal funds rate? If so, how and why?

Online Articles with Real-World Examples

Find a recent practical article available online that describes a real-world example regarding a specific financial institution or financial market that reinforces one or more concepts covered in this chapter.

If your class has an online component, your professor may ask you to post your summary of the article there and provide a link to the article so that other students can access it. If your class is live, your professor may ask you to summarize your application of the article in class. Your professor may assign specific students to complete this assignment or may allow any students to do the assignment on a volunteer basis.

For recent online articles and real-world examples related to this chapter, consider using the following search terms (be sure to include the prevailing year as a search term to ensure that the online articles are recent):

1. Federal Reserve AND interest rate
2. Federal Reserve AND monetary policy
3. Board of Governors
4. FOMC meeting
5. FOMC AND interest rate
6. Federal Reserve AND policy
7. Federal Reserve AND open market operations
8. money supply AND interest rate
9. open market operations AND interest rate
10. Federal Reserve AND economy

5

Monetary Policy

CHAPTER OBJECTIVES

The specific objectives of this chapter are to:

- Describe the input used to determine monetary policy.

- Explain the effects due to the Fed's implementation of a stimulative monetary policy.

- Explain the effects due to the Fed's implementation of a restrictive monetary policy.

- Explain the trade-off involved in monetary policy.

- Describe how financial market participants respond to the Fed's policies.

- Explain how monetary policy is affected by the global environment.

Chapter 4 discussed the Federal Reserve System and the ways that it controls the money supply, information essential to financial market participants. It is just as important for participants to know how changes in the money supply affect the economy, which is the subject of this chapter.

5-1 Input Used to Determine Monetary Policy

Recall from Chapter 4 that the Federal Open Market Committee (FOMC) is responsible for determining monetary policy. Also recall that the Fed's goals are to achieve a low level of inflation and a low level of unemployment. These goals are consistent with the goals of most central banks, although the stated goals of some central banks are more broadly defined (for example, "achieving economic stability"). After assessing economic conditions and identifying the main concerns about the economy, the FOMC determines the monetary policy that would alleviate its concerns. It changes the money supply growth to influence interest rates, which then affect the level of aggregate borrowing and spending by households and firms. The level of aggregate spending, in turn, affects demand for products and services, which then affects both price levels (inflation) and the unemployment level.

At one extreme, if the unemployment rate is very high while inflation is low, the Fed will enact a stimulative (expansionary) monetary policy to increase economic growth (in an effort to reduce the unemployment rate). At the other extreme, if inflation is very high while the unemployment rate is very low, the Fed will enact a restrictive monetary policy so as to reduce inflation. However, economic conditions are rarely at either of these two extremes, so the Fed is challenged to fine-tune the economy in a manner that achieves low unemployment (high economic growth) and low inflation simultaneously.

Given the Fed's goals of controlling economic growth and inflation, it considers the indicators of these economic variables before deciding on the proper monetary policy to implement.

5-1a Indicators of Economic Growth

The Fed monitors indicators of economic growth because high economic growth creates a more prosperous economy and can result in lower unemployment. Gross domestic product (GDP), which measures the total value of goods and services produced during a specific period, is measured each month. It serves as the most direct indicator of economic growth in the United States. The level of production adjusts in response to changes in consumers' demand for goods and services. A high production level indicates strong economic growth and can result in an increased demand for labor (lower unemployment).

The Fed also monitors national income, which is the total income earned by firms and individual employees during a specific period. A strong demand for U.S. goods and services results in a large amount of revenue for firms. To accommodate the demand for their products and services, firms hire more employees or increase the work hours of their existing employees. In consequence, the total income earned by employees rises.

The unemployment rate is monitored as well, because one of the Fed's primary goals is to maintain a low rate of unemployment in the United States. However, the unemployment rate does not necessarily indicate the degree of economic growth: It measures only the number (not the types) of jobs that are being filled. It is possible to have a substantial reduction in unemployment during a period of weak economic growth if new, low-paying jobs are created during that period. In addition, the unemployment rate does not include discouraged workers who have given up looking for jobs, so the unemployment rate may decline during a period of weak economic growth because many people have left the labor force.

Several other indexes serve as indicators of growth in specific sectors of the U.S. economy; these include an industrial production index, a retail sales index, and a home sales index. A composite index combines various indexes to indicate economic growth across sectors. In addition to the many indicators reflecting recent conditions, the Fed may use forward-looking indicators (such as consumer confidence surveys) to forecast future economic growth.

Index of Leading Economic Indicators   Among the economic indicators widely followed by market participants are the indexes of leading, coincident, and lagging economic indicators, which are published by the Conference Board. **Leading economic indicators** are used to predict future economic activity. Usually, three consecutive monthly changes in the same direction in these indicators suggest a turning point in the economy. **Coincident economic indicators** tend to reach their peaks and troughs at the same time as business cycles. **Lagging economic indicators** tend to rise or fall a few months after business-cycle expansions and contractions.

The Conference Board is an independent, not-for-profit, membership organization whose stated goal is to create and disseminate knowledge about management and the marketplace to help businesses strengthen their performance and better serve society. It conducts research, convenes conferences, makes forecasts, assesses trends, and publishes information and analyses. Exhibit 5.1 summarizes the Conference Board's leading, coincident, and lagging indexes.

5-1b Indicators of Inflation

The Fed closely monitors price indexes and other indicators to assess the U.S. inflation rate.

Producer and Consumer Price Indexes   The producer price index reflects prices at the wholesale level, whereas the consumer price index reflects prices paid by consumers (retail level). There is a lag time of about one month after the period being measured due to the time required to compile price information for the indexes. Nevertheless, financial markets closely monitor the price indexes because they may be used to forecast inflation, which affects nominal interest rates and the prices of some securities. Agricultural price indexes reflect recent price movements in grains, fruits, and vegetables. Housing price indexes reflect recent price movements in homes and rental properties.

Another index closely watched by the Fed is the personal consumption expenditures index, which measures a wide range of household spending. In monitoring inflation indexes, the Fed generally pays particular attention to "core" inflation, which excludes food and energy prices. These prices tend to be very volatile, as a flood or a drought could

Exhibit 5.1   The Conference Board's Indexes of Leading, Coincident, and Lagging Indicators

Leading Index
1. Average weekly hours, manufacturing
2. Average weekly initial claims for unemployment insurance
3. Manufacturers' new orders, consumer goods and materials
4. Index of new orders from consumers
5. Manufacturers' new orders, nondefense capital goods
6. Building permits, new private housing units
7. Stock prices, 500 common stocks
8. Credit index of various financial market measures
9. Interest rate spread, 10-year Treasury bonds less federal funds
10. Index of consumer expectations
Coincident Index
1. Employees on nonagricultural payrolls
2. Personal income less transfer payments
3. Industrial production
4. Manufacturing and trade sales
Lagging Index
1. Average duration of unemployment
2. Inventories to sales ratio, manufacturing and trade
3. Labor cost per unit of output, manufacturing
4. Average prime rate
5. Commercial and industrial loans
6. Consumer installment credit to personal income ratio
7. Consumer price index for services

temporarily affect food prices or political unrest could cause oil production to fall for a short time. After these kinds of short-term events end, food and energy prices tend to move back to more stable levels.

Other Inflation Indicators   In addition to price indexes, several other indicators of inflation are available. Wage rates are periodically reported in various regions of the United States. Because wages and prices are highly correlated over the long run, wages can indicate price movements. Rising oil prices can signal future inflation because they affect the costs of some forms of production as well as transportation costs and the prices paid by consumers for gasoline.

The price of gold is closely monitored because gold prices tend to move in tandem with inflation. Some investors buy gold as a hedge against future inflation. In consequence, a rise in gold prices may signal the market's expectation that inflation will increase.

Indicators of economic growth might also be used to indicate inflation. For example, the release of favorable information about economic growth at a time of full employment may arouse concerns about inflation, because any excess demand for products cannot be accommodated with extra supply when businesses are already at full capacity. Thus, businesses might respond to the excess demand by raising prices. This type of inflation is referred to as **demand-pull inflation**, because it occurs as a result of excessive demand (spending) that pulls up prices of products and services. Any economic reports that hint of possible demand-pull inflation are closely assessed by the Fed. The financial markets can be adversely affected by such reports, because investors anticipate that the Fed will have to increase interest rates to reduce the inflationary momentum.

5-2 Implementing a Stimulative Monetary Policy

When the Fed decides to implement a stimulative monetary policy, it uses open market operations to inject funds into the banking system, in an effort to reduce interest rates. The Fed hopes that these lower interest rates will encourage more businesses and households to borrow and spend money, which can stimulate the economy.

To increase the supply of funds in the banking system, the Fed purchases Treasury securities in the secondary market. As the investors who sell their Treasury securities receive payment from the Fed, their account balances at financial institutions increase without any offsetting decrease in the account balances of any other financial institutions. The result is a net increase in the total supply of loanable funds in the banking system.

5-2a How a Stimulative Monetary Policy Reduces Interest Rates

To illustrate how the injection of funds into the banking system affects interest rates, the left graph of Exhibit 5.2 shows the demand for loanable funds (D_1) and the supply of loanable funds (S_1) before the Fed implements its monetary policy, which results in an equilibrium interest rate (i_1). If the Fed's stimulative monetary policy leads to a \$5 billion increase in loanable funds, then the quantity of loanable funds supplied will now be \$5 billion higher at any possible interest rate level. In response, the supply curve for loanable funds shifts outward to S_2 in the left graph of Exhibit 5.2.

Exhibit 5.2   Effects of an Increased Money Supply

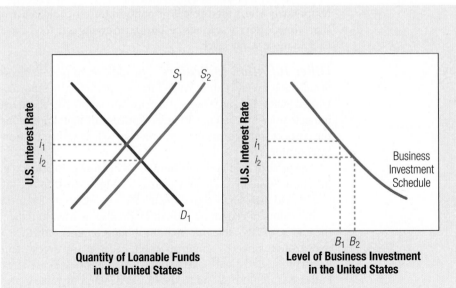

Given the shift in the supply curve for loanable funds, the quantity of loanable funds supplied exceeds the quantity of loanable funds demanded at the interest rate level i_1. The equilibrium interest rate in the left graph of Exhibit 5.2 will therefore decline to i_2, the level at which the quantities of loanable funds supplied and demanded are equal. As shown in the right graph of Exhibit 5.2, once the equilibrium interest rate declines to i_2, the level of business investment in new projects increases to B_2. The reason for the impact in the right graph of Exhibit 5.2 is that the lower interest rate results in a lower cost of financing for businesses, so that more of their potential projects become feasible.

When depository institutions experience an increase in their supply of funds due to the Fed's stimulative monetary policy, they have more funds than they need at prevailing interest rates. In this situation, depository institutions that commonly obtain very short-term loans (such as one day) in the federal funds market may not need to borrow as many funds. Thus, the extra supply of funds provided by the Fed places downward pressure on the federal funds rate, such as reducing that rate from 3 percent to 2.75 percent. Depository institutions may also lower the rate that they offer on deposits. Because their cost of funds (based on the rate they pay on deposits) is now lower, depository institutions are willing to charge lower loan rates to businesses. They also reduce their rates on loans in an attempt to attract more potential borrowers to make use of the newly available funds.

The Fed's stimulative monetary policy actions also reduce the Treasury yield (or rate). When the Fed purchases a large amount of Treasury securities, the strong demand results in a higher price for Treasury securities and, therefore, a lower the yield (or rate) to be earned by any investors who invest in Treasury securities at the higher prevailing price.

5-2b How Lower Interest Rates Increase Business Investment

The right graph of Exhibit 5.2 depicts the typical relationship between the interest rate on loanable funds and the current level of business investment. This inverse relation arises because firms are more willing to expand when interest rates are relatively low. Given an initial equilibrium interest rate i_1, the level of business investment before the Fed implements its monetary policy is B_1.

A lower interest rate on business loans triggered by the Fed's stimulative monetary policy causes an increase in the level of business investment from B_1 to B_2 in the right graph of Exhibit 5.2. That is, businesses are willing to pursue additional projects now that their cost of financing is lower. The increase in business investment represents new business spending that can stimulate the economy.

Another way to understand the effects of a stimulative monetary policy on the business cost of debt is to consider the influence of the risk-free rate on all interest rates. Recall from Chapter 3 that the yield for a security with a particular maturity is primarily based on the risk-free rate (the Treasury rate) for that same maturity plus a credit risk premium. Thus, the financing rate on a business loan is based on the risk-free rate plus a premium that reflects the credit risk of the business that is borrowing the money. Assume that a business with a low level of risk pays a credit risk premium of 3 percentage points when borrowing money. If the prevailing Treasury (risk-free) security rate is 5 percent on an annualized basis, that business would be able to obtain funds at 8 percent (5 percent risk-free rate plus 3 percent credit risk premium). However, if the Fed implements a stimulative monetary policy that reduces the Treasury security rate to 4 percent, the business would be able to borrow funds at 7 percent (4 percent risk-free rate plus 3 percent credit risk premium).

Businesses with other degrees of credit risk will also be affected by the Fed's monetary policy. Consider a business with moderate risk that pays a credit premium of 4 percentage points above the risk-free rate to obtain funds. When the Treasury (risk-free) rate is

5 percent, this business is able to borrow funds at 9 percent (5 percent risk-free rate plus 4 percent credit risk premium). However, if the Fed implements a stimulative monetary policy that reduces the Treasury security rate to 4 percent, the business will be able to borrow funds at 8 percent (4 percent risk-free rate plus 4 percent credit risk premium).

Thus, as a result of the Fed's stimulative monetary policy, all businesses (regardless of their risk level) will be able to borrow funds at lower rates. When they consider possible investments such as expanding their product line or building a new facility, they may be more willing to implement some projects as a result of the lower cost of funds.

5-2c How Lower Interest Rates Lower the Business Cost of Equity

Many businesses rely on equity as another key source of capital. Monetary policy can also influence the cost of equity. The cost of a firm's equity is based on the risk-free rate plus a risk premium that reflects the sensitivity of the firm's stock price movements to general stock market movements. This concept is discussed in more detail in Chapter 11, but the main point for now is that the firm's cost of equity is positively related to the risk-free rate. Therefore, if the Fed can reduce the risk-free rate by 1 percentage point, it can reduce a firm's cost of equity by 1 percentage point.

5-2d Summary of Stimulative Monetary Policy Effects

In summary, the Fed's ability to stimulate the economy is due to its effects on the Treasury (risk-free) rate, which influences the cost of debt and the cost of equity as shown in Exhibit 5.3. As the Fed reduces the risk-free rate, it reduces a firm's cost of borrowing (debt) and a firm's cost of equity, and therefore reduces its cost of capital. If a firm's cost of capital is reduced, its required return on its business investment is reduced. In turn, more of the possible projects that a firm considers will become feasible and will be implemented.

As firms implement more projects, they spend more money, and that extra spending results in higher income to individuals or other firms that receive the proceeds.

Exhibit 5.3 How the Fed Can Stimulate the Economy

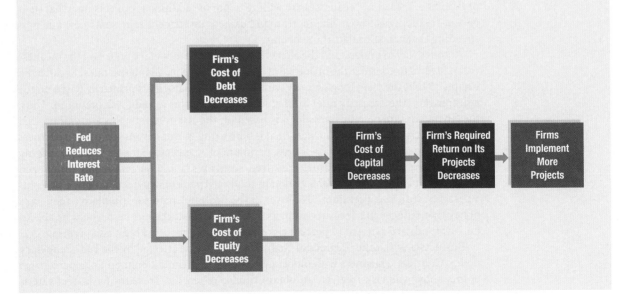

Firms may also hire more employees to expand their businesses, which generates more income for those new employees. Those employees will spend some of their new income, and that spending then provides income to the individuals or firms that receive the proceeds.

When interest rates decline, households are also able to borrow at lower loan rates. This may encourage households to borrow more funds, and therefore spend more funds, which can help stimulate the economy. It also may make a mortgage loan easier to afford for homeowners who have adjustable-rate mortgages.

Note that when the Fed implements a stimulative monetary policy to create more jobs, it is not using its money to purchase products or services. It is not telling firms that they must hire more employees. Instead, its stimulative monetary policy reduces the cost of funds, which encourages businesses and households to spend more money. As firms and households increase their spending, they stimulate the economy and create jobs.

EXAMPLE

In the 2005–2007 period, some depository institutions used very liberal standards when providing home buyers with mortgage loans. While this allowed many people to buy homes, it also led to many personal bankruptcies of homeowners who were not able to meet their mortgage payments. In the ensuing credit crisis in 2008, many homeowners had to sell their homes, as they could not afford them. The excessive supply of homes for sale halted the construction of new homes and led to massive layoffs in the construction industry and related industries. In addition, interest rates had been rising, which made it even more difficult for homeowners with adjustable-rate mortgages to make their mortgage payments.

The Fed implemented a stimulative monetary policy in the 2008–2009 period by reducing the federal funds rate several times, bringing the rate down from 5.25 percent to close to zero. However, even with such a major decline in interest rates, the recovery occurred only slowly. Although lower interest rates can reduce the payments on adjustable-rate mortgages, it did not lead to a major increase in the demand for new homes, because many homeowners could not afford the homes that they were in. Given the excess supply of homes, there was no need to build new homes, which meant that construction companies did not need to hire additional employees.

Although the economy improved in 2010, it remained weak for the next several years, prompting the Fed to continue its stimulative monetary policy (with the federal funds rate close to zero) until 2016. In 2014–2015, businesses and households began to borrow and spend more funds, and the unemployment rate declined. During the 2016–2018 period, the economy improved substantially. ●

5-2e Why a Stimulative Monetary Policy Might Fail

Although a stimulative monetary policy is normally desirable when the economy is weak, it is not always effective, for the reasons described next.

Fed's Limited Ability to Control Long-Term Interest Rates   The annualized yields on Treasury securities can vary among maturities (as discussed in Chapter 3). While the Fed was able to reduce short-term Treasury rates to near zero with its stimulative monetary policy over the 2010–2015 period, this did not have much impact on those businesses that prefer to borrow at long-term fixed interest rates. These borrowers incur a cost of debt that is highly influenced by the long-term Treasury rates, rather than the short-term Treasury rates. Thus, if the Fed wants to reduce the rate that these potential borrowers would pay for fixed-rate loans with 10-year maturities, it might need a monetary policy that reduces the yield on Treasury securities with 10-year maturities (which reflects the 10-year risk-free rate). However, since the Fed commonly buys and sells Treasury bills (with maturities of one year or less) when engaging in monetary policy, it might not be able to completely control long-term Treasury yields (and therefore other long-term interest rates).

Limited Credit Provided by Banks   The ability of the Fed to stimulate the economy is influenced to some extent by the willingness of depository institutions to lend funds. Even if the Fed increases the level of bank funds during a weak economy, banks may be unwilling to extend credit to some potential borrowers, leading to a *credit crunch.*

Banks provide loans only after confirming that the borrower's future cash flows will be adequate to make loan repayments. In a weak economy, the future cash flows of many potential borrowers are more uncertain, causing a reduction in loan applications (demand for loans) and in the number of loan applicants that meet a bank's qualification standards.

Banks and other lending institutions have a responsibility to their depositors, shareholders, and regulators to avoid loans that are likely to default. Because default risk rises during a weak economy, some potential borrowers will be unable to obtain loans. Some firms may have already reached their debt capacity, so they are restricted from borrowing more money, even if loan rates are reduced. These firms may believe that any additional debt could increase their likelihood of bankruptcy. In consequence, they may delay their spending until the economy has improved.

Other firms may qualify for loans only if they pay high-risk premiums to cover their default risk. If potential borrowers do not qualify or are unwilling to incur the high-risk premiums, the Fed's monetary policy may have only limited effects.

Similarly, households that commonly borrow to purchase vehicles, homes, and other products may prefer to avoid borrowing more money during weak economies, even if interest rates are low. Individuals who are unemployed are not in a position to borrow more money. And even if those who are employed can obtain loans from financial institutions, they may believe that they are already at their debt capacity. They may worry that their jobs are not secure due to the weak economy, and they may prefer not to increase their debt until economic conditions improve and they feel more confident about their employment.

So, while the Fed hopes that the lower interest rates will encourage more borrowing and spending to stimulate the economy, the potential spenders (firms and households) may delay their borrowing until the economy improves. But the economy may not improve unless firms and households increase their spending. Although the Fed can lower interest rates, it cannot necessarily force firms or households to borrow more money. If the firms and households do not borrow more money, they will not be able to spend more money. Thus, if banks do not lend out the additional funds that have been pumped into the banking system by the Fed, the economy will not be stimulated.

EXAMPLE   As described previously, during the credit crisis that began in 2008, the Fed attempted to stimulate the economy by using monetary policy to reduce interest rates. Initially, that monetary policy had only a negligible effect. Firms were unwilling to borrow even at low interest rates because they did not want to expand while economic conditions were so weak. In addition, commercial banks raised the standards necessary to qualify for loans so that they would not repeat the mistakes (such as liberal lending standards) that had led to the credit crisis. Consequently, the amount of new loans resulting from the Fed's stimulative monetary policy was limited, and therefore the amount of new spending was limited as well. ●

Low Return on Savings   Some savers, such as retirees, rely heavily on their interest income to cover their periodic expenses. When interest rates are close to zero, interest income is close to zero, and retirees who rely on interest income have to restrict their spending. This effect can partially offset the expected stimulative effect of lower interest rates. Some retirees may decide to invest their money in alternative instruments (such as in stocks) instead of as bank deposits when interest rates are low. However, many alternative investments are risky, and retirees could experience losses on their retirement funds.

Adverse Effects on Inflation

When a stimulative monetary policy is implemented, the increase in money supply growth may cause an increase in inflationary expectations, which may limit the impact on interest rates.

Assume that the U.S. economy is very weak, and suppose the Fed responds by using open market operations (purchasing Treasury securities) to increase the supply of loanable funds. This action is supposed to reduce interest rates and increase the level of borrowing and spending. However, some evidence indicates that high money supply growth may lead to higher inflation over time. To the extent that businesses and households recognize that an increase in money supply growth will cause higher inflation, they will revise their inflationary expectations upward as a result. This effect is often referred to as the **theory of rational expectations**. Higher inflationary expectations encourage businesses and households to increase their demand for loanable funds (as explained in Chapter 2) so that they can borrow and make planned expenditures before price levels increase. This increase in demand reflects a rush to make planned purchases now.

These effects of the Fed's monetary policy are shown in Exhibit 5.4. The result is an increase in both the supply of loanable funds and the demand for those funds. The effects are offsetting, so the Fed may not be able to reduce interest rates for a sustained period of time. If the Fed cannot force interest rates lower with an active monetary policy, it will be unable to stimulate an increase in the level of business investment. Business investment will increase only if the cost of financing is reduced, making some proposed business projects feasible. If the increase in business investment does not occur, economic conditions will not improve. ●

Because the effects of a stimulative policy could be disrupted by expected inflation, an alternative approach is a passive monetary policy that allows the economy to correct itself rather than relying on the Fed's intervention. Interest rates should ultimately decline in a weak economy even without a stimulative monetary policy because the demand for loanable funds should decline as economic growth weakens. In this case, interest rates would

Exhibit 5.4   Effects of an Increased Money Supply According to Rational Expectations Theory

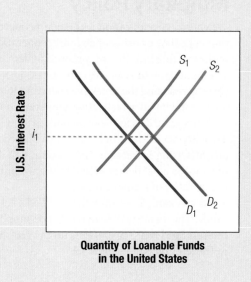

decline without a corresponding increase in inflationary expectations, so the interest rates may stay lower for a sustained period of time. Consequently, the level of business investment should ultimately increase, which should lead to a stronger economy and more jobs.

The major criticism of a passive monetary policy is that the weak economy could take years to correct itself. During a slow economy, interest rates might not decrease until a year later if the Fed played a passive role and did not intervene to stimulate the economy. Most people would probably prefer that the Fed take an active role in improving economic conditions, rather than assume a passive role and simply hope that the economy will correct itself.

Lagged Effects of Monetary Policy   Three lags involved in monetary policy can make the Fed's job more challenging. First, the **recognition lag** is the delay between the time a problem arises and the time it is recognized. Most economic problems are initially revealed by statistics, not actual observation. Because economic statistics are reported only periodically, they will not immediately signal a problem. For example, the unemployment rate is reported monthly. A sudden increase in unemployment may not be detected until the end of the month, when statistics finally reveal the problem.

The difference between the time a serious problem is recognized and the time the Fed implements a policy to resolve that problem is known as the **implementation lag**. Then, even after the Fed implements a policy, there will be an **impact lag** until the policy has its full impact on the economy. For example, an adjustment in money supply growth may have an immediate impact on the economy to some degree, but its full impact may not occur until a year or so after the adjustment.

These lags hinder the Fed's control of the economy. To see how, suppose the Fed uses a stimulative policy to stimulate the economy and reduce unemployment. By the time the implemented monetary policy begins to take effect, the unemployment rate may have already reversed and may now be trending downward. In this situation, the stimulative policy may no longer be needed and may even cause the economy to overheat, leading to inflation.

5-3 Implementing a Restrictive Monetary Policy

When excessive inflation is the main concern, the Fed can implement a restrictive (tight-money) policy by using open market operations to reduce money supply growth. A portion of the existing inflation may represent demand-pull inflation, which is caused by excessive economic growth that pulls up prices. The Fed can attempt to reduce economic growth, thereby reducing the excessive spending that can lead to this type of inflation.

To implement a restrictive monetary policy, the Fed can sell some of its holdings of Treasury securities in the secondary market. As investors make payments to purchase these Treasury securities, their account balances at depository institutions decrease without any offsetting increase in the account balances of any other depository institutions. The outcome is a net decrease in deposit accounts (money), which results in a net decrease in the quantity of loanable funds.

As an example, assume that the Fed's action causes a decrease of $5 billion in loanable funds. The quantity of loanable funds supplied will now be $5 billion lower at any possible interest rate level. This reflects an inward shift in the supply curve from S_1 to S_2, as shown in the left graph of Exhibit 5.5.

Exhibit 5.5 Effects of a Reduced Money Supply

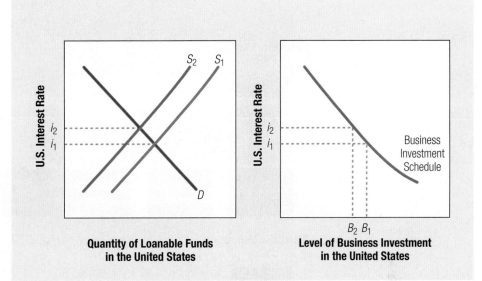

Given the inward shift in the supply curve for loanable funds, the quantity of loanable funds demanded exceeds the quantity of loanable funds supplied at the original interest rate level (i_1). In turn, the interest rate will increase to i_2, the level at which the quantities of loanable funds supplied and demanded are equal.

Depository institutions raise not only the rate charged on loans in the federal funds market but also the interest rates on deposits and on household and business loans. If the Fed's restrictive monetary policy increases the Treasury rate from 5 to 6 percent, a firm that must pay a risk premium of 4 percentage points must now pay 10 percent (6 percent risk-free rate plus 4 percent credit risk premium) to borrow funds. All firms and households that consider borrowing money incur a higher cost of debt as a result of the Fed's restrictive monetary policy. The effect of the Fed's monetary policy on loans to households and businesses is important, because the Fed's ability to affect the amount of spending in the economy stems from its influence on the rates charged on household and business loans.

The higher interest rate level increases the corporate cost of financing new projects and, therefore, causes a decrease in the level of business investment from B_1 to B_2 in the right graph of Exhibit 5.5. As economic growth is slowed by this reduction in business investment, inflationary pressure may be reduced.

5-3a **Comparing a Restrictive versus Stimulative Monetary Policy**

Exhibit 5.6 summarizes how the Fed can affect economic conditions through its influence on the supply of loanable funds. The top part of the exhibit illustrates a stimulative (loose-money) monetary policy intended to boost economic growth, and the bottom part illustrates a restrictive (tight-money) monetary policy intended to reduce inflation.

Exhibit 5.6 How Monetary Policy Can Affect Economic Conditions

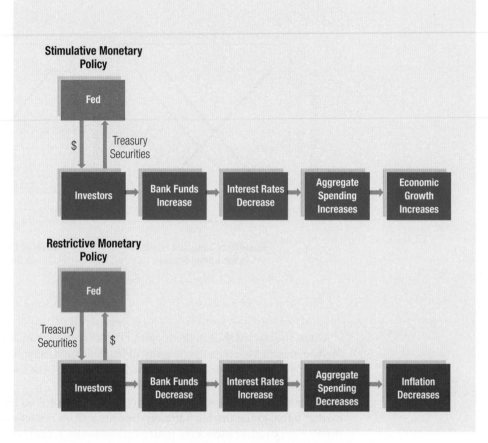

5-4 Trade-off in Monetary Policy

Ideally, the Fed would like to achieve both a very low level of unemployment and a very low level of inflation in the United States. The U.S. unemployment rate should be low in a period when U.S. economic conditions are strong. Inflation will likely be relatively high at this time, however, because wages and price levels tend to increase when economic conditions are strong. Conversely, inflation may be lower when economic conditions are weak, but unemployment will be relatively high. It is difficult, if not impossible, for the Fed to cure both problems simultaneously.

5-4a Impact of Other Forces on the Trade-off

Other forces may also affect the trade-off faced by the Fed. Consider a situation in which, because of specific cost factors (for example, an increase in energy costs), inflation will be at least 3 percent, no matter which type of monetary policy the Fed implements. Assume that, because of the number of unskilled workers and people "between jobs," the unemployment rate will be at least 4 percent. A stimulative policy will stimulate the economy sufficiently to maintain unemployment at that minimum level of 4 percent. However, such a stimulative policy may also cause additional inflation beyond the 3 percent level. Conversely, a restrictive policy could prevent inflation from rising above 3 percent, but unemployment would likely rise above the 4 percent minimum.

Exhibit 5.7   Trade-off between Reducing Inflation and Unemployment

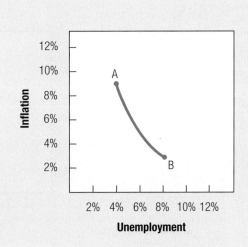

This trade-off is illustrated in Exhibit 5.7. In the scenario depicted in the figure, the Fed can use a very stimulative (loose-money) policy that is expected to result in point A (9 percent inflation and 4 percent unemployment), or it can use a highly restrictive (tight-money) policy that is expected to result in point B (3 percent inflation and 8 percent unemployment). Alternatively, it can implement a compromise policy that will result in some point along the curve between A and B.

Historical data on annual inflation and unemployment rates show that when one of these problems worsens, the other does not automatically improve. Both variables can rise or fall simultaneously over time. Nevertheless, this does not negate the trade-off faced by the Fed. It simply means that some outside factors have affected inflation or unemployment or both.

EXAMPLE

Recall that the Fed could have achieved point A, point B, or some other point along the curve connecting these two points in Exhibit 5.7 during a particular time period. Now assume that oil prices have increased substantially such that the minimum inflation rate will be, say, 6 percent. In addition, assume that various training centers for unskilled workers have been closed, leaving a higher number of unskilled workers. This forces the minimum unemployment rate to 6 percent. Now the Fed's trade-off position has changed. The Fed's new set of possibilities is shown as curve CD in Exhibit 5.8. Note that the points reflected on curve CD are not as desirable as the points along curve AB that were previously attainable. No matter which type of monetary policy the Fed uses, both the inflation rate and the unemployment rate will be higher than in the previous time period. This is not the Fed's fault. In fact, the Fed still faces a trade-off: between point C (11 percent inflation, 6 percent unemployment) and point D (6 percent inflation, 10 percent unemployment), or some other point along curve CD. ●

WEB

www.federalreserve.
gov/monetarypolicy/
openmarket.htm
Shows recent changes in
the federal funds target
rate.

When inflation is high and unemployment is low, or when unemployment is high and inflation is low, FOMC members tend to agree on the type of monetary policy that should be implemented. However, when both inflation and unemployment are relatively high, more disagreement arises among the members about the proper monetary policy to implement. Some members would likely argue for a restrictive policy to prevent inflation from rising, whereas other members would suggest that a stimulative policy should be implemented to reduce unemployment even if it results in higher inflation.

Exhibit 5.8   Adjustment in the Trade-off between Unemployment and Inflation over Time

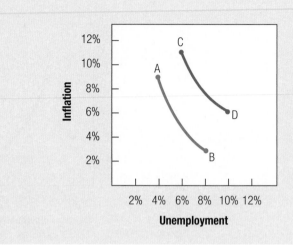

5-4b How Monetary Policy Responds to Fiscal Policy

The Fed's assessment of the trade-off between reducing unemployment versus inflation becomes more complicated when fiscal policy is considered. Although the Fed has the power to make decisions without the approval of the presidential administration, its monetary policy is commonly influenced by the administration's fiscal policies. If fiscal policies create large budget deficits, this may place upward pressure on interest rates. Under these conditions, the Fed may be concerned that the higher interest rates caused by fiscal policy could dampen the economy, and it may therefore feel pressured to use a stimulative monetary policy to reduce interest rates.

Exhibit 5.9 presents a framework for explaining how monetary policy and fiscal policies affect interest rates. Although fiscal policy typically shifts the demand for loanable funds, monetary policy normally has a larger impact on the supply of loanable funds. In some situations, a presidential administration has enacted a fiscal policy that caused the Fed to reassess its trade-off between focusing on inflation versus unemployment, as explained next.

5-4c Proposals to Focus on Inflation

Some well-respected economists have proposed that when weighing the trade-off between inflation and unemployment, the Fed should focus more on controlling inflation than on unemployment. Ben Bernanke, the chair of the Fed from 2006 to 2014, has made some arguments in favor of inflation targeting. The Fed might be better able to control inflation if it could concentrate on inflation without having to worry as much about the unemployment rate. In addition, the Fed's role would be more transparent, and there would be less uncertainty in the financial markets about how the Fed would respond to specific economic conditions.

However, inflation targeting also has some disadvantages. First, the Fed could lose credibility if the U.S. inflation rate deviated substantially from the Fed's target inflation rate. Factors such as oil prices could cause high inflation regardless of the Fed's targeted

Exhibit 5.9   Framework for Explaining How Monetary Policy and Fiscal Policy Affect Interest Rates over Time

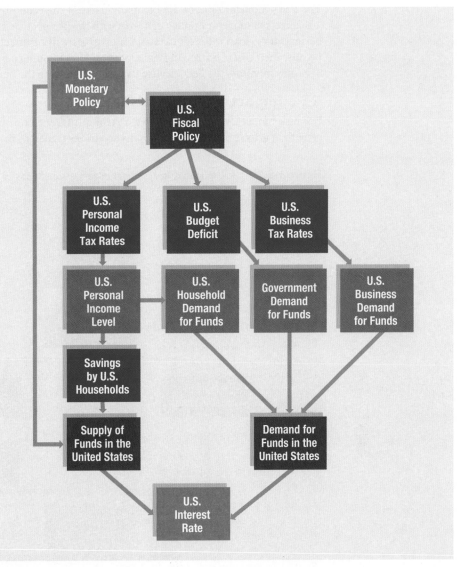

inflation rate. Second, focusing mostly on inflation could result in a much higher unemployment level. Bernanke has argued, however, that inflation targeting could be flexible enough that the employment level would still be given consideration.

Some Fed members might argue that the inflation targeting proposal is not much different from the Fed's existing monetary policy. During the 2008–2015 period when unemployment was clearly the Fed's biggest concern, inflation did not receive much attention in monetary policy meetings because the focus was on stimulating the economy in an effort to reduce unemployment. While some Fed members might argue for an inflation targeting policy in the long run, they tend to change their focus toward reducing unemployment when the United States is experiencing very weak economic conditions.

5-5 Monitoring the Impact of Monetary Policy

The Fed's monetary policy affects many parts of the economy, as shown in Exhibit 5.10. The effects of monetary policy can vary with the perspective. Households monitor the Fed because their loan rates on cars and mortgages will be affected. Firms monitor the Fed because their cost of borrowing from loans and from issuing new bonds will be affected. The Treasury monitors the Fed because its cost of financing the budget deficit will be affected.

5-5a Impact on Financial Markets

Because monetary policy can have a strong influence on interest rates and economic growth, it affects the valuation of most securities traded in financial markets. Changes in

Exhibit 5.10   How Monetary Policy Affects Financial Conditions

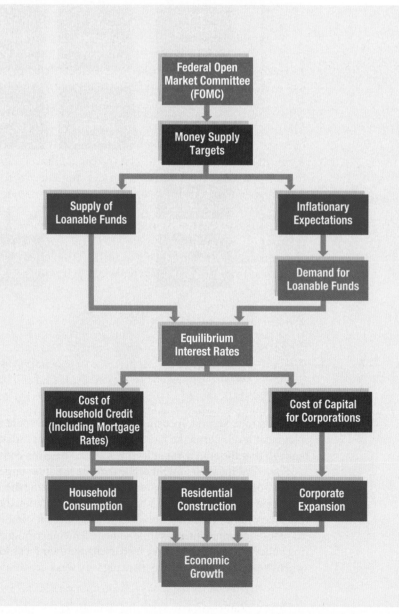

the values of existing bonds are inversely related to interest rate movements. Consequently, investors who own bonds (Treasury, corporate, or municipal) or fixed-rate mortgages are adversely affected when the Fed raises interest rates, but enjoy better prospects when the Fed reduces interest rates (as explained in Chapter 8).

The values of stocks (discussed in Chapter 11) also are commonly affected by interest rate movements, but these effects are not as consistent as they are for bonds.

EXAMPLE

Suppose the Fed lowers interest rates because the economy is weak. If investors anticipate that this action will enhance economic growth, they may expect that firms will generate higher sales and earnings in the future. In turn, the values of stocks would increase in response to this favorable information. However, the Fed's decision to reduce interest rates could make investors realize that economic conditions are worse than they thought. In this case, the Fed's actions could signal that corporate sales and earnings may weaken, and the values of stocks would decline because of the negative information. ●

WEB

www.federalreserve.
gov/monetarypolicy/
fomccalendars.htm
Schedule of FOMC
meetings and minutes
of previous FOMC
meetings.

To appreciate the potential impact of the Fed's actions on financial markets, go to any financial news website during the week in which the FOMC holds its meeting. You will see predictions of whether the Fed will attempt to change interest rates, by how much, and how that change will affect the financial markets.

The Fed's Focus on Improving Liquidity in Debt Markets in 2008–2014

During the credit crisis of 2008, many institutional investors were unwilling to purchase risky debt securities such as mortgage-backed securities, corporate bonds, or commercial paper; the result was a pronounced decline in market liquidity for these types of securities. Although the Fed's purchases of Treasury securities can reduce the risk-free (Treasury) rate, those actions do not necessarily ensure liquidity in risky debt markets at a time when there is general fear about defaults on risky debt.

To counteract this fear, from 2008 through 2014, the Fed implemented a strategy referred to as **quantitative easing** (described in Chapter 4), in which it purchased a specific dollar amount of a specific type of debt securities each month. This strategy was unique because it deviated from the traditional monetary policy of purchasing only Treasury securities. By purchasing risky debt securities such as mortgage-backed securities and commercial paper, the Fed was attempting to boost investor confidence and increase liquidity in the markets for these securities.

The Fed's Communication to Financial Markets

After the Federal Open Market Committee holds a meeting to determine its monetary policy, it announces its conclusion through an *FOMC statement.* The statement is available at www.federalreserve.gov, and it may have relevant implications for security prices. The following excerpt illustrates the type of communication provided by the FOMC when explaining its decision to implement a stimulative monetary policy:

> *The Federal Open Market Committee decided to reduce its target for the federal funds rate by 0.25%. Economic growth has weakened this year, and indicators suggest more pronounced weakness in the last four months. The Committee expects that the weakness will continue. Inflation is presently low and is expected to remain at very low levels. Thus, there is presently a bias toward correcting the economic growth, without as much concern about inflation. Voting for the FOMC monetary policy action were [list of voting members provided here].*

This statement could possibly cause the prices of debt securities such as bonds to rise because it suggests that interest rates will decline.

Exhibit 5.11 Impact of Monetary Policy across Financial Markets

TYPE OF FINANCIAL MARKET	RELEVANT FACTORS INFLUENCED BY MONETARY POLICY	KEY INSTITUTIONAL PARTICIPANTS
Money market	• Secondary market values of existing money market securities • Yields on newly issued money market securities	Commercial banks, savings institutions, credit unions, money market funds, insurance companies, finance companies, pension funds
Bond market	• Secondary market values of existing bonds • Yields offered on newly issued bonds	Commercial banks, savings institutions, bond mutual funds, insurance companies, finance companies, pension funds
Mortgage market	• Demand for housing and therefore the demand for mortgages • Secondary market values of existing mortgages • Interest rates on new mortgages • Risk premium on mortgages	Commercial banks, savings institutions, credit unions, insurance companies, pension funds
Stock market	• Required return on stocks and therefore the market values of stocks • Projections for corporate earnings and therefore stock values	Stock mutual funds, insurance companies, pension funds
Foreign exchange	• Demand for currencies and therefore the values of currencies, which in turn affect currency option prices	Institutions that are exposed to exchange rate risk

The following excerpt illustrates the type of communication provided by the FOMC about its decision to implement a restrictive monetary policy:

> *The Federal Open Market Committee decided to raise its target for the federal funds rate by 0.25%. Economic growth has been strong so far this year, but inflation has been rising. The Committee expects that a more restrictive monetary policy is needed to address inflation risks. The Committee will respond to changes in economic prospects as needed to support the attainment of its objectives. Voting for the FOMC monetary policy action were [list of voting members provided here].*

The type of influence that monetary policy can have on each financial market is summarized in Exhibit 5.11. Financial market participants closely review the FOMC statements to interpret the Fed's future plans and to assess how the monetary policy will affect security prices. Sometimes the markets fully anticipate the Fed's actions. In this case, prices of securities should adjust to the anticipated news before the meeting, and they will not adjust further when the Fed's decision is announced.

5-6 Global Monetary Policy

Financial market participants must recognize that the type of monetary policy implemented by the Fed is somewhat dependent on various international factors, as explained next.

5-6a **Impact of the Dollar**

A weak dollar can stimulate U.S. exports because it reduces the amount of foreign currency needed by foreign companies to obtain dollars to purchase U.S. exports. A weak dollar also discourages U.S. imports because it increases the dollars needed to obtain foreign currency to purchase imports. As a consequence, a weak dollar can stimulate the U.S. economy. In addition, it tends to exert inflationary pressure in the United States because it reduces foreign competition. The Fed can afford to be less aggressive with a stimulative monetary policy if the dollar is weak, because a weak dollar can itself provide some stimulus to the U.S. economy. Conversely, a strong dollar tends to reduce inflationary pressure but also dampens the U.S. economy. Therefore, if U.S. economic conditions are weak, a strong dollar will not provide the stimulus needed to improve conditions, so the Fed may need to implement a stimulative monetary policy.

5-6b Impact of Global Economic Conditions

The Fed recognizes that economic conditions are integrated across countries, so it considers prevailing global economic conditions when conducting monetary policy. When global economic conditions are strong, foreign countries purchase more U.S. products and can stimulate the U.S. economy. When global economic conditions are weak, the foreign demand for U.S. products weakens.

During the credit crisis that began in 2008, the United States and many other countries experienced very weak economic conditions. The Fed's decision to lower U.S. interest rates and stimulate the U.S. economy was partially driven by these weak global economic conditions. The Fed recognized that the United States would not receive any stimulus (such as a strong demand for U.S. products) from other countries where income and aggregate spending levels were also relatively low.

5-6c Transmission of Interest Rates

Each country has its own currency (except for countries in the eurozone) and its own interest rate, which is based on the supply of and demand for loanable funds in that currency. Investors residing in one country may attempt to capitalize on high interest rates in another country. If an upward pressure on U.S. interest rates can be offset by foreign inflows of funds, then the Fed may not feel compelled to use a stimulative policy. However, if foreign investors reduce their investment in U.S. securities, the Fed may be forced to intervene so as to prevent interest rates from rising.

Just as U.S. monetary policy indirectly affects other countries' economies through its effects on the U.S. economy, monetary policies in other countries can indirectly affect the U.S. economy. For example, when the European Central Bank (ECB) uses a stimulative monetary policy to boost the economies of countries in the eurozone, this decision can increase the European demand for U.S. products and can boost the U.S. economy.

Given the international integration of money and capital markets, a government's budget deficit can affect interest rates in various countries. This concept, referred to as **global crowding out**, is illustrated in Exhibit 5.12. An increase in the U.S. budget deficit causes an outward shift in the federal government's demand for U.S. funds and, therefore, in the aggregate demand for U.S. funds (from D_1 to D_2 in the left graph). This crowding-out effect forces the U.S. interest rate to increase from i_1 to i_2 if the supply curve (S) is unchanged. As U.S. rates rise, they attract funds from investors in other countries, such as Germany and Japan. As foreign investors use more of their funds to invest in U.S. securities, the supply of available funds in their respective countries declines. Consequently, there is upward pressure on non-U.S. interest rates as well, as shown in the second and third graphs in Exhibit 5.12. The impact will be most pronounced in countries whose investors are most likely to find the higher U.S. interest rates attractive. The possibility of global crowding out has caused national governments to criticize one another for large budget deficits.

Exhibit 5.12   Global Crowding Out

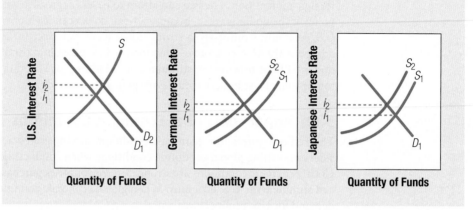

Summary

- The Fed uses monetary policy to achieve its goals of low inflation and low unemployment (strong economic growth). By using monetary policy, the Fed can affect the interaction between the demand for money and the supply of money, which affects interest rates, aggregate spending, economic growth, and inflation.

- A stimulative monetary policy involves increasing money supply growth, which reduces the federal funds rate and other interest rates. This policy is intended to encourage more borrowing and spending by businesses and households, which can increase economic growth.

- A restrictive monetary policy involves reducing money supply growth, which increases the federal funds rate and other interest rates. This policy is intended to discourage more borrowing and spending by businesses and households, which can reduce economic growth. Such a strategy is intended to reduce excessive demand for products and services that could cause demand-pull inflation.

- The Fed faces a trade-off when implementing monetary policy. Given a possible trade-off, the Fed tends to pinpoint its biggest concern (unemployment versus inflation) and assess whether the potential benefits of any proposed monetary policy outweigh the potential adverse effects.

- Because monetary policy can have a strong influence on interest rates and economic growth, it affects the valuation of most securities traded in financial markets. Financial market participants attempt to forecast the Fed's future monetary policies and the effects of these policies on economic conditions. When the Fed implements monetary policy, financial market participants attempt to assess how their security holdings will be affected and adjust their security portfolios accordingly.

- The Fed's monetary policy must take into account the global economic environment. A weak dollar may increase U.S. exports, thereby stimulating the U.S. economy. If economies of other countries are strong, this can also increase U.S. exports and boost the U.S. economy. Thus, if international conditions can provide some stimulus to the U.S. economy, the Fed may not have to implement a stimulative monetary policy. Conversely, the Fed may consider a more aggressive monetary policy to fix a weak U.S. economy if international conditions are weak, because in that case the Fed cannot rely on other economies to boost the U.S. economy.

Point/Counterpoint

Can the Fed Prevent U.S. Recessions?

Point   Yes. The Fed has the power to reduce market interest rates and can use such adjustments to encourage more borrowing and spending. In this way, it stimulates the economy.

Counterpoint   No. When the economy is weak, individuals and firms are unwilling to borrow regardless of the interest rate. As a consequence, borrowing (by those who are qualified) and spending will not be influenced by the Fed's actions. The Fed should not intervene but rather allow the economy to work itself out of a recession.

Who Is Correct?   Use the Internet to learn more about this issue and then formulate your own opinion.

Questions and Applications

1. **Impact of Monetary Policy** How does the Fed's monetary policy affect economic conditions?

2. **Trade-off of Monetary Policy** Describe the economic trade-off faced by the Fed in achieving its economic goals.

3. **Choice of Monetary Policy** When does the Fed use a stimulative monetary policy, and when does it use a restrictive monetary policy? What is a criticism of a stimulative monetary policy? What is the risk of using a monetary policy that is too restrictive?

4. **Active Monetary Policy** Describe an active monetary policy.

5. **Passive Monetary Policy** Describe a passive monetary policy.

6. **Fed Control** Why might the Fed have difficulty controlling the economy in the manner desired? Be specific.

7. **Lagged Effects of Monetary Policy** Compare the recognition lag and the implementation lag.

8. **Fed's Control of Inflation** Assume that the Fed's primary goal is to reduce inflation. How can it use open market operations to achieve this goal? What is a possible adverse effect of such action by the Fed (even if it achieves the goal)?

9. **Monitoring Money Supply** Why do financial market participants closely monitor money supply movements?

10. **Monetary Policy during the Credit Crisis** Describe the Fed's monetary policy response to the credit crisis that began in 2008.

11. **Impact of Money Supply Growth** Explain why an increase in the money supply can affect interest rates in different ways. Include the potential impact of the money supply on the supply of and the demand for loanable funds when answering this question.

12. **Confounding Effects** Which factors might be considered by financial market participants who are assessing whether an increase in money supply growth will affect inflation?

13. **Fed Response to Fiscal Policy** Explain how the Fed's monetary policy could depend on the fiscal policy that is implemented.

Advanced Questions

14. **Interpreting the Fed's Monetary Policy** When the Fed increases the money supply to lower the federal funds rate, will the cost of capital to U.S. companies be reduced? Explain how the segmented markets theory regarding the term structure of interest rates (as explained in Chapter 3) could influence the degree to which the Fed's monetary policy affects long-term interest rates.

15. **Monetary Policy Today** Assess the economic situation today. Is the current presidential administration more concerned with reducing unemployment or inflation? Does the Fed have a similar opinion? If not, is the administration publicly criticizing the Fed? Is the Fed publicly criticizing the administration? Explain.

16. **Impact of Foreign Policies** Why might a foreign government's policies be closely monitored by investors in other countries, even if the investors plan no investments in that country? Explain how monetary policy in one country can affect interest rates in other countries.

17.   Monetary Policy during a War Consider a discussion during FOMC meetings in which there is a weak economy and a war, with potential major damage to oil wells. Explain why this possible effect would have received much attention at the FOMC meetings. If this possibility was perceived to be highly likely at the time of the meetings, explain how it may have complicated the decision about monetary policy at that time. Given the conditions stated in this question, would you suggest that the Fed use a restrictive monetary policy or a stimulative monetary policy? Support your decision logically and acknowledge any adverse effects of your decision.

18.   Economic Indicators Stock market conditions serve as a leading economic indicator. If the U.S. economy is in a recession, what are the implications of this indicator? Why might this indicator be inaccurate?

19.   How the Fed Should Respond to Prevailing Conditions Consider the current economic conditions, including inflation and economic growth. Do you think the Fed should increase interest rates, reduce interest rates, or leave interest rates at their present levels? Offer some logic to support your answer.

20.   Impact of Inflation Targeting by the Fed Assume that the Fed adopts an inflation targeting strategy. Describe how the Fed's monetary policy would be affected by an abrupt 15 percent rise in oil prices in response to an oil shortage. Do you think an inflation targeting strategy would be more or less effective in this situation than a strategy of balancing inflation concerns with unemployment concerns? Explain.

21.   Predicting the Fed's Actions Assume the following conditions. The last time the FOMC met, it decided to raise interest rates. At that time, economic growth was very strong, so inflation was relatively high. Since the last meeting, economic growth has weakened, and the unemployment rate will likely rise by 1 percentage point over the quarter. The FOMC's next meeting is tomorrow. Do you think the FOMC will revise its targeted federal funds rate? If so, how?

22.   The Fed's Impact on the Housing Market In periods when home prices declined substantially, some homeowners blamed the Fed. In other periods, when home prices increased, homeowners gave credit to the Fed. How can the Fed have such a large impact on home prices? How could news of a substantial increase in the general inflation level affect the Fed's monetary policy and thereby affect home prices?

23.   Targeted Federal Funds Rate The Fed uses a targeted federal funds rate when implementing monetary policy. However, the Fed's main purpose in its monetary policy is typically to have an impact on the aggregate demand for products and services. Reconcile the Fed's targeted federal funds rate with its goal of having an impact on the overall economy.

24.   Monetary Policy during the Credit Crisis During the credit crisis of 2008, the Fed used a stimulative monetary policy. Why do you think the total amount of loans to households and businesses did not increase as much as the Fed had hoped? Are the lending institutions to blame for the relatively small increase in the total amount of loans extended to households and businesses?

25.   Stimulative Monetary Policy during a Credit Crunch Explain why a stimulative monetary policy might not be effective during a weak economy in which there is a credit crunch.

26.   Response of Firms to a Stimulative Monetary Policy In a weak economy, the Fed commonly implements a stimulative monetary policy to lower interest rates, and presumes that firms will be more willing to borrow money. Even if banks are willing to lend such funds, why might such a presumption about the willingness of firms to borrow be wrong? What are the consequences if the presumption is wrong?

27.   Fed Policy Focused on Long-Term Interest Rates Why might the Fed want to focus its efforts on reducing long-term interest rates rather than short-term interest rates during a weak economy? Explain how it might use a monetary policy focused on influencing long-term interest rates. Why might such a policy also affect short-term interest rates in the same direction?

28.   Impact of Monetary Policy on Cost of Capital Explain the effects of a stimulative monetary policy on a firm's cost of capital.

29.   Effectiveness of Monetary Policy Which circumstances might cause a stimulative monetary policy to be ineffective?

Critical Thinking Question

The Fed and the Government's Fiscal Policy   The Fed attempts to use monetary policy to control the level of inflation and economic growth in the United States. Write a short essay on how the government's fiscal policy can make the Fed's role more difficult. Specifically, assume that the administration plans to implement a new program that will expand the government benefits provided to most people in the country. The new program will likely increase the budget deficit. Discuss the impact of this policy on interest rates, and explain how this makes the Fed's role more challenging.

Interpreting Financial News

Interpret the following statements made by Wall Street analysts and portfolio managers.

a. "Lately, the Fed's policies are driven by gold prices and other indicators of the future rather than by recent economic data."
b. "The Fed cannot boost money growth at this time because of the weak dollar."
c. "The Fed will be forced to accommodate the excessive borrowing triggered by fiscal policy."

Managing in Financial Markets

Forecasting Monetary Policy   As a manager of a firm, you are concerned about a potential increase

in interest rates, which would reduce the demand for your firm's products. The Fed is scheduled to meet in one week to assess economic conditions and set monetary policy. Economic growth has been high, but inflation has also increased from 3 percent to 5 percent (annualized) over the last four months. The level of unemployment is so low that it cannot go much lower.

a. Given the situation, is the Fed likely to adjust monetary policy? If so, how?
b. Recently, the Fed has allowed the money supply to expand beyond its long-term target range. Does this affect your expectation of what the Fed will decide at its upcoming meeting?
c. Suppose the Fed has just learned that the Treasury will need to borrow a larger amount of funds than originally expected. Explain how this information may affect the degree to which the Fed changes its monetary policy.

Flow of Funds Exercise

Anticipating Fed Actions

Recall that Carson Company has obtained substantial loans from finance companies and commercial banks. The interest rate on the loans is tied to market interest rates and is adjusted every six months. Because of its expectations of a strong U.S. economy, Carson plans to grow in the future by expanding the business and by making acquisitions. It expects that it will need substantial long-term financing and plans to borrow additional funds either through loans or by issuing bonds. The company may also issue stock to raise funds in the next year.

An economic report recently highlighted the strong growth in the economy, which has led to nearly full employment. In addition, the report estimated that the annualized inflation rate increased to 5 percent, up from 2 percent last month. The factors that caused the higher

inflation (shortages of products and shortages of labor) are expected to continue.

a. How will the Fed's monetary policy change based on the report?
b. How will the likely change in the Fed's monetary policy affect Carson's future performance? Could it affect Carson's plans for future expansion?
c. Explain how a tight monetary policy could affect the amount of funds borrowed at financial institutions by deficit units such as Carson Company. How might it affect the credit risk of these deficit units? How might it affect the performance of financial institutions that provide credit to such deficit units as Carson Company?

Internet/Excel Exercises

1. Go to the website www.federalreserve.gov/monetarypolicy/fomc.htm to review the activities of the FOMC. Succinctly summarize the minutes of the last FOMC meeting. What did the FOMC discuss at that meeting? Did the FOMC make any changes in the current monetary policy? What is the FOMC's current monetary policy?

2. Is the Fed's present policy focused more on stimulating the economy or on reducing inflation? Or is the present policy evenly balanced? Explain.

3. Using the website http://fred.stlouisfed.org, retrieve interest rate data at the beginning of the last 20 quarters for the federal funds rate and the three-month Treasury bill rate, and place the data in two columns of an Excel spreadsheet. Derive the change in interest rates on a quarterly basis. Apply regression analysis in which the quarterly change in the T-bill rate is the dependent variable (see Appendix B for more information about using regression analysis). If the Fed's effect on the federal funds rate influences other interest rates (such as the T-bill rate), there should be a positive and significant relationship between the interest rates. Is there such a relationship? Explain.

WSJ Exercise

Market Assessment of Fed Policy

Review a recent issue of *The Wall Street Journal* and then summarize the market's expectations about future interest rates. Are these expectations based primarily on the Fed's monetary policy or on other factors?

Online Articles with Real-World Examples

Find a recent practical article available online that describes a real-world example regarding a specific financial institution or financial market that reinforces one or more concepts covered in this chapter.

If your class has an online component, your professor may ask you to post your summary of the article there and provide a link to the article so that other students can access it. If your class is live, your professor may ask you to summarize your application of the article in class. Your professor may assign specific students to complete this assignment or may allow any students to do the assignment on a volunteer basis.

For recent online articles and real-world examples related to this chapter, consider using the following search terms (be sure to include the prevailing year as a search term to ensure that the online articles are recent):

1. index of leading economic indicators
2. consumer price index AND Federal Reserve
3. inflation AND Federal Reserve
4. inflation AND monetary policy
5. Fed policy AND economy
6. federal funds rate AND economy
7. federal funds rate AND inflation
8. monetary policy AND budget deficit
9. monetary policy AND press release
10. monetary policy AND value of the dollar

PART 2 INTEGRATIVE PROBLEM

Fed Watching

This problem requires an understanding of the Fed (Chapter 4) and monetary policy (Chapter 5). It also requires an understanding of how economic conditions affect interest rates and securities' prices (Chapters 2 and 3).

Like many other investors, you are a "Fed watcher" who constantly monitors any actions taken by the Fed to revise monetary policy. You believe that three key factors affect interest rates. Assume that the most important factor is the Fed's monetary policy. The second most important factor is the state of the economy, which influences the demand for loanable funds. The third factor is the level of inflation, which also influences the demand for loanable funds. Because monetary policy can affect interest rates, it affects economic growth as well. By controlling monetary policy, the Fed influences the prices of all types of securities.

The following information is available to you:

- Economic growth has been consistently strong over the past few years, but is beginning to slow down.
- Unemployment is as low as it has been in the past decade, but has risen slightly over the past two quarters.
- Inflation has been about 5 percent annually for the past few years.
- The dollar has been strong.
- Oil prices have been very low.

Yesterday, an event occurred that you believe will cause much higher oil prices in the United States and a weaker U.S. economy in the near future. You plan to determine whether the Fed will respond to the economic problems that are likely to develop.

You have reviewed previous economic slowdowns caused by a decline in the aggregate demand for goods and services and found that each slowdown precipitated a stimulative policy by the Fed. Inflation was 3 percent or less in each of the previous economic slowdowns. Interest rates generally declined in response to these policies, and the U.S. economy improved.

Assume that the Fed's philosophy regarding monetary policy is to maintain economic growth and low inflation. There does not appear to be any major fiscal policy forthcoming that will have a major effect on the economy. In consequence, the future economy is up to the Fed. The Fed's present policy is to maintain a 2 percent annual growth rate in the money supply. You believe that the economy is headed toward a recession unless the Fed adopts a very stimulative monetary policy, such as a 10 percent annual growth rate in the money supply.

The general consensus of economists is that the Fed will revise its monetary policy to stimulate the economy for three reasons: (1) It recognizes the potential costs of higher unemployment if a recession occurs, (2) it has consistently used a stimulative policy in the past to prevent recessions, and (3) the administration has been pressuring the Fed to use a stimulative monetary policy. Although you will consider the economists' opinions, you plan to make your own assessment of the Fed's future policy. Two quarters ago, GDP declined by 1 percentage point. Last quarter, GDP declined again by 1 percentage point. Thus, there is clear evidence that the economy has recently slowed down.

Questions

1. Do you think that the Fed will use a stimulative monetary policy at this point? Explain.
2. You maintain a large portfolio of U.S. bonds. You believe that if the Fed does not revise its monetary policy, the U.S. economy will continue to decline. If the Fed stimulates the economy at this point, you believe that you would be better off with stocks than with bonds. Based on this information, do you think you should switch to stocks? Explain.

PART 3
Debt Security Markets

Part 3 focuses on how debt security markets facilitate the flow of funds from surplus units to deficit units. Chapter 6 examines money markets for investors and borrowers trading short-term securities. Chapters 7 and 8 deal with the bond markets, and Chapter 9 covers the mortgage markets. Because some financial market participants trade securities in all of these markets, there is much interaction among them, as emphasized throughout the chapters.

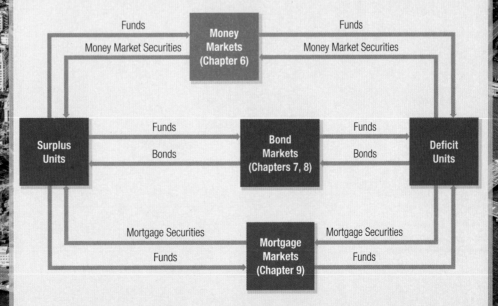

6

Money Markets

The specific objectives
of this chapter are to:

- Describe the
  features of the most
  popular money
  market securities.

- Explain how money
  markets are used
  by institutional
  investors.

- Explain how money
  markets have
  become globally
  integrated.

Money markets are used to facilitate the transfer of short-term funds from individuals, corporations, or governments with excess funds to those with deficient funds. Even investors who focus on long-term securities tend to hold some money market securities. Money markets enable financial market participants to maintain liquidity.

6-1 Money Market Securities

Money market securities are debt securities with a maturity of one year or less. They are issued in the primary market, using a telecommunications network, by the Treasury, corporations, and financial intermediaries that wish to obtain short-term financing. The means by which money markets facilitate the flow of funds are illustrated in Exhibit 6.1. The U.S. Treasury issues money market securities (Treasury bills) and uses the proceeds to finance the budget deficit. Corporations issue money market securities and use the proceeds to support their existing operations or to expand their operations. Financial institutions issue money market securities and bundle the proceeds to make loans to households or corporations. Thus, the funds obtained through money market securities are channeled to support household purchases, such as cars and homes, and to support corporate investment in buildings and machinery. The Treasury and some corporations commonly pay off their debt from maturing money market securities with the proceeds from issuing new money market securities. In this way, they are able to finance expenditures for long periods of time even though money market securities have short-term maturities. Overall, money markets allow households, corporations, and the U.S. government to increase their expenditures; in essence, the markets finance economic growth.

Money market securities are commonly purchased by corporations (including financial institutions), other institutional investors, and government agencies that have funds available for a short-term period. Most money market securities are issued in very large denominations, so they generally are purchased by firms and other institutional investors. Because money market securities have a short-term maturity and can typically be sold in the secondary market, they provide liquidity to investors. Most firms and financial institutions maintain some holdings of money market securities for this reason. Popular money market securities include the following options:

- Treasury bills (T-bills)
- Commercial paper
- Negotiable certificates of deposit
- Repurchase agreements

Exhibit 6.1   How Money Markets Facilitate the Flow of Funds

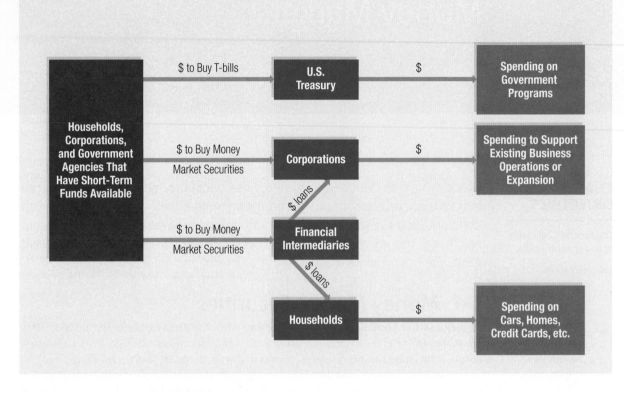

- Federal funds
- Banker's acceptances

Each of these instruments is described in this section.

6-1a Treasury Bills

When the U.S. government needs to borrow funds, the U.S. Treasury frequently issues short-term securities known as Treasury bills. The Treasury issues T-bills with 4-week, 13-week, and 26-week maturities on a weekly basis. It periodically issues T-bills with terms shorter than 4 weeks, which are called *cash management bills.* It also issues T-bills with a 1-year maturity on a monthly basis. Treasury bills were formerly issued in paper form but are now maintained electronically.

Investors in Treasury Bills   Depository institutions commonly invest in T-bills so that they can retain a portion of their funds in assets that can easily be liquidated if they suddenly need to accommodate deposit withdrawals. Other financial institutions invest in T-bills in case they need cash because their cash outflows exceed their cash inflows. Individuals with substantial savings invest in T-bills for liquidity purposes. Many individuals invest in T-bills indirectly by investing in money market funds, which in turn purchase large amounts of T-bills. Corporations invest in T-bills so that they have easy access to funding if they suddenly incur unanticipated expenses.

Credit Risk of Treasury Bills   Treasury bills are attractive to investors because they are backed by the federal government and, therefore, are virtually free of credit (default) risk. This is a very desirable feature, because investors do not have to spend time assessing the risk of the issuer, as they do with other issuers of debt securities.

Liquidity of Treasury Bills   Another attractive feature of T-bills is their liquidity, which is due to their short maturity and strong secondary market. At any given time, many institutional investors are participating in the secondary market by purchasing or selling existing T-bills. Thus, investors can easily obtain cash by selling their T-bills in the secondary market. Government securities dealers serve as intermediaries in the secondary market by buying existing T-bills from investors who want to sell them, or selling them to investors who want to buy them. These dealers profit by purchasing the bills at a slightly lower price than the price at which they sell them.

Pricing Treasury Bills   The par value (the amount received by investors at maturity) of T-bills is $1,000 and multiples of $1,000. Because T-bills do not pay interest, they are sold at a discount from par value, and the gain to the investor holding a T-bill until maturity is the difference between par value and the price paid.

   The price that an investor will pay for a T-bill with a particular maturity depends on the investor's required rate of return on that T-bill. That price is determined as the present value of the future cash flows to be received. The value of a T-bill is the present value of the par value. Thus, investors are willing to pay a price for a one-year T-bill that ensures the amount they receive a year later will generate their desired return.

EXAMPLE

If investors require a 4 percent annualized return on a one-year T-bill with a $10,000 par value, the price that they are willing to pay is

$$P = \$10{,}000/1.04$$
$$= \$9{,}615.38$$

   If the investors require a higher return, they will discount the $10,000 at that higher rate of return, which will result in a lower price that they are willing to pay today. You can verify this by estimating the price based on a required return of 5 percent and then on a required return of 6 percent. ●

   To price a T-bill with a maturity shorter than one year, the annualized return can be reduced by the fraction of the year in which funds will be invested.

EXAMPLE

If investors require a 4 percent annualized return on a six-month T-bill, this reflects a 2 percent unannualized return over six months. The price that they will be willing to pay for a T-bill with a par value of $10,000 is therefore

$$P = \$10{,}000/1.02$$
$$= \$9{,}803.92$$ ●

Yield from Investing in Treasury Bills   Because T-bills do not offer coupon payments and are sold at a discount from par value, their yield is influenced by the difference between the selling price and the purchase price. If an investor purchases a newly issued T-bill and holds it until maturity, the return is based on the difference between the par value and the purchase price. If the T-bill is sold prior to maturity, the return is based on the difference between the price for which the bill was sold in the secondary market and the purchase price. The annualized yield from investing in a T-bill (Y_T) can be determined as follows:

$$Y_T = \frac{SP - PP}{PP} \times \frac{365}{n}$$

where

$$SP = \text{selling price}$$
$$PP = \text{purchase price}$$
$$n = \text{number of days of the investment (holding period)}$$

An investor purchases a T-bill with a 6-month (182-day) maturity and a $10,000 par value for $9,800. If this T-bill is held until maturity, its yield is:

$$Y_T = \frac{\$10,000 - \$9,800}{\$9,800} \times \frac{365}{182}$$
$$= 4.09\%$$

WEB

https://fred.stlouisfed
.org/categories
Go to the section on
interest rates to review
Treasury bill rates over
time.

Suppose the investor plans to sell the T-bill after 120 days and forecasts a selling price of $9,950 at that time. The expected annualized yield based on this forecast is

$$Y_T = \frac{\$9,950 - \$9,800}{\$9,800} \times \frac{365}{120}$$
$$= 4.65\%$$

The higher the forecasted selling price, the higher the expected annualized yield. ●

Treasury Bill Discount   Some business periodicals quote the T-bill discount along with the T-bill yield. The T-bill discount represents the percentage discount of the purchase price from par value (par) for newly issued T-bills, and is computed as follows:

$$\text{T-bill discount} = \frac{Par - PP}{Par} \times \frac{360}{n}$$

Note that the discount formula uses a 360-day year versus the 365-day year used in the yield calculation.

If a newly issued 6-month (182-day) T-bill with a par value of $10,000 is purchased for $9,800, the T-bill discount is

$$Y_T = \frac{\$10,000 - \$9,800}{\$10,000} \times \frac{360}{182}$$
$$= 3.95\%$$

●

For a newly issued T-bill that is held to maturity, the T-bill yield will always be higher than the discount. This difference occurs because the purchase price is the denominator of the yield equation, whereas the par value is the denominator of the T-bill discount equation; the par value will always exceed the purchase price of a newly issued T-bill.

6-1b Treasury Bill Auction

The primary T-bill market is an auction. Individual investors can submit bids online for newly issued T-bills at www.treasurydirect.gov.

Financial institutions can submit their bids for T-bills (and other Treasury securities) online using the Treasury Automated Auction Processing System (TAAPS). Individuals and financial institutions can set up an account with the Treasury. Once their account is established, they can select the specific maturity and face value that they desire and submit their bids electronically. Payments to the Treasury are withdrawn electronically from the account, and payments received from the Treasury when the securities mature are deposited electronically into the account.

In the auctions, investors have the option of bidding competitively or noncompetitively. The Treasury has a specified amount of funds that it plans to borrow, which dictates the amount of T-bill bids that it will accept for that maturity. Investors who wish to ensure that their bids will be accepted can use noncompetitive bids, in which they agree to pay whatever price is established at the auction. Noncompetitive bidders are limited to purchasing T-bills with a maximum par value of $5 million per auction. Large corporations, however, typically make competitive bids so that they can purchase larger amounts. Competitive bidders specify the price that they are willing to pay.

After accounting for noncompetitive bids, the Treasury accepts the highest competitive bids first and then works its way down until it has generated the amount of funds from competitive bids that it needs. Any bids below that cutoff point are not accepted. The Treasury applies the lowest accepted bid price to all competitive bids that are accepted and to all noncompetitive bids. Thus, the price paid by competitive and noncompetitive bidders reflects the lowest price of the competitive bids. Competitive bids are still submitted because, as noted earlier, many bidders want to purchase more T-bills than the maximum that can be purchased on a noncompetitive basis.

At each auction, the prices paid for six-month T-bills are significantly lower than the prices paid for three-month T-bills, because the investment term is longer. The lower price results in a higher unannualized yield that compensates investors for their longer-term investment.

The results of the weekly auctions of 13-week and 26-week T-bills are summarized in the financial media each Tuesday and provided online at the Treasury Direct website. Some of the more commonly reported statistics are the dollar amount of applications and Treasury securities sold, the average price of the accepted competitive bids, and the coupon equivalent (annualized yield) for investors who paid the average price.

WEB

www.treasurydirect.gov
Results of recent
Treasury bill auctions.

6-1c **Commercial Paper**

Commercial paper is a short-term debt instrument issued only by well-known, creditworthy firms; it is typically unsecured. Most commonly, these securities are issued to provide liquidity or to finance a firm's investment in inventory and accounts receivable. The issuance of commercial paper is an alternative to short-term bank loans. Some large firms prefer to issue commercial paper rather than borrow from a bank because it is usually a cheaper source of funds. Nevertheless, even large creditworthy firms that are able to issue commercial paper usually obtain some short-term loans from commercial banks so as to maintain a business relationship with them. Financial institutions such as finance companies and bank holding companies are major issuers of commercial paper.

Placement of Commercial Paper   Some firms place commercial paper directly with investors. Other firms rely on commercial paper dealers to sell their commercial paper at a transaction cost of about one-eighth of 1 percent of the face value. This transaction cost is generally less than it would cost to establish a department within the firm to place commercial paper directly. If companies issue commercial paper frequently, however, they may reduce expenses by creating such an in-house department. Most nonfinancial companies use commercial paper dealers rather than in-house resources to place their commercial paper. Their liquidity needs, and therefore their commercial paper issues, are cyclical, meaning that they use an in-house, direct placement department only a few times during the year. Finance companies typically maintain an in-house department because they borrow more frequently using this method.

Although the secondary market for commercial paper is very limited, it is sometimes possible to sell the paper back to the dealer who initially helped to place it. However, in most cases, investors hold commercial paper until maturity.

Denominations of Commercial Paper The minimum denomination of commercial paper is usually $100,000, and typical denominations are in multiples of $1 million. Maturities are normally between 20 and 45 days but can be as short as 1 day or as long as 270 days. The 270-day maximum is due to a Securities and Exchange Commission ruling that paper with a maturity exceeding 270 days must be registered.

Common Investors in Commercial Paper Because of the high minimum denomination, individual investors rarely purchase commercial paper directly. Instead, they may invest in it indirectly by investing in money market funds that have pooled the funds of many individuals. Money market funds are major investors in commercial paper.

Credit Risk of Commercial Paper Although commercial paper is issued by creditworthy firms, all corporations are susceptible to business failure, so commercial paper is subject to credit risk. The risk of default is affected by the issuer's financial condition and cash flow. The annualized commercial paper rate commonly contains a very small risk premium (such as 0.3 percent or smaller) above the T-bill rate to reflect the slight degree of default.

During periods of heightened uncertainty about the economy, investors tend to shift from commercial paper to Treasury securities. As a result of this so-called flight to quality, commercial paper must offer a larger risk premium to attract investors.

Credit Risk Ratings of Commercial Paper Investors can attempt to assess the probability that commercial paper will default by monitoring the issuer's financial condition. Some investors rely heavily on credit ratings to assess the credit risk of commercial paper. These ratings are assigned by rating agencies such as Moody's Investors Service, Standard & Poor's Corporation, and Fitch Ratings, as shown in Exhibit 6.2. The rating serves as an indicator of the potential risk of default.

A money market fund can invest only in commercial paper that has a top-tier or second-tier rating, and second-tier paper cannot represent more than 5 percent of the fund's assets. Thus, corporations can more easily place commercial paper that is assigned a top-tier rating. Some commercial paper (called **junk commercial paper**) is rated low or not rated at all.

Asset-Backed Commercial Paper Some commercial paper is backed by assets of the issuer. However, the issuers of asset-backed commercial paper tend to have more risk of default than the well-known firms that can successfully issue unsecured commercial paper, and the value of the assets used as collateral may be questionable. Therefore, the yields offered on asset-backed commercial paper are often higher than the yields offered on unsecured commercial paper.

WEB

www.federalreserve
.gov/releases/cp/about
.htm
Provides valuable
information about
commercial paper.

Exhibit 6.2 Possible Ratings Assigned to Commercial Paper

	MOODY'S	STANDARD & POOR'S	FITCH
Highest	P1	A1	F1
High	P2	A2	F2
Medium	P3	A3	F3
Low	NP	B or C	F4
Default	NP	D	F5

Some issuers of asset-backed commercial paper obtain credit guarantees from a sponsoring institution in the event that they cannot cover their payments on commercial paper. This practice allows them to more easily sell their commercial paper to investors.

Issuers of commercial paper typically maintain backup lines of credit in case they cannot roll over (reissue) commercial paper at a reasonable rate because, for example, their assigned rating has been lowered. A backup line of credit provided by a commercial bank gives the company the right (but not the obligation) to borrow a specified maximum amount of funds over a specified period of time. The fee for the credit line can be a direct percentage (for example, 0.5 percent) of the total accessible credit, or it can take the form of required compensating balances (for example, 10 percent of the credit line).

Yield from Investing in Commercial Paper

Like T-bills, commercial paper does not pay interest and is priced at a discount from par value. At a given point in time, the yield on commercial paper is slightly higher than the yield on a T-bill with the same maturity because commercial paper carries some credit risk and is less liquid. The nominal return to investors who retain the paper until maturity is the difference between the price paid for the paper and the par value. Thus, the yield received by a commercial paper investor can be determined in a manner similar to the T-bill yield, although a 360-day year is normally used.

EXAMPLE

If an investor purchases 30-day commercial paper with a par value of $1,000,000 for a price of $996,000, and holds the commercial paper until maturity, the annualized yield (Y_{cp}) is

$$Y_{cp} = \frac{\$1,000,000 - \$996,000}{\$996,000} \times \frac{360}{30}$$

$$= 4.82\%$$

●

WEB

https://fred.stlouisfed
.org/categories/120
Provides information
on current commercial
paper rates as well as a
database of commercial
paper rates over time.

When a firm plans to issue commercial paper, the price (and hence the yield) to investors is uncertain. In turn, the cost of borrowing funds is uncertain until the paper is issued. When firms sell their commercial paper at a lower (higher) price than projected, their cost of raising funds will be higher (lower) than they initially anticipated.

Ignoring transaction costs, the cost of borrowing with commercial paper is equal to the yield earned by investors holding the paper until maturity. The cost of borrowing can be adjusted for transaction costs (charged by the commercial paper dealers) by subtracting the nominal transaction fees from the price received.

Commercial Paper Yield Curve

The commercial paper yield curve represents the yield offered on commercial paper at various maturities, based on the assumption that the paper is held to maturity. This curve is typically established for a maturity range from 0 to 90 days, as most commercial paper has a maturity within that range.

The same factors that affect the Treasury yield curve affect the commercial paper yield curve, but they are applied to very short-term horizons. In particular, expectations regarding the interest rate over the next few months can influence the commercial paper yield curve.

Commercial Paper Rate over Time

The rate (or yield) offered on newly issued commercial paper (90-day maturity, top rated) over time is provided in Exhibit 6.3.

Credit Risk of Commercial Paper Following Lehman's Default

The perceived credit risk of commercial paper played an important role in the credit crisis in 2008. Lehman Brothers, a large securities firm, relied on commercial paper as a permanent source of financing. As its outstanding issues of commercial paper came due, it would issue more paper and use the proceeds to pay off the paper that had reached

Exhibit 6.3 Commercial Paper Rate over Time

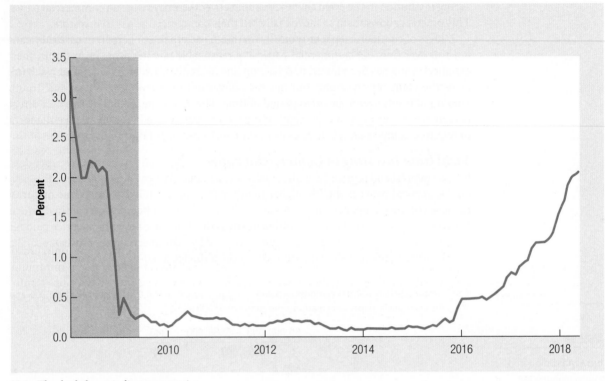

Note: *The shaded area indicates a recession.*
Source: *Federal Reserve.*

maturity. Lehman was heavily invested in mortgage-backed securities and used these securities as collateral when issuing commercial paper to borrow funds. However, when the housing market crashed and the value of mortgage-backed securities declined in 2008, institutional investors were no longer willing to purchase Lehman's commercial paper because they questioned the value of the collateral. Because Lehman could not obtain new funding, it was unable to pay off its existing debt. When Lehman filed for bankruptcy in September 2008, it defaulted on hundreds of millions of dollars of commercial paper that it had issued. Consequently, investors became concerned that commercial paper issued by other financial institutions might also be backed by assets with questionable quality.

Some issuers of asset-backed commercial paper obtained credit guarantees from a sponsoring institution so that they could more easily sell their commercial paper. Normally, credit guarantees would alleviate concerns about credit risk, but during the credit crisis, the financial institutions providing credit guarantees for issuers of commercial paper were highly exposed to credit risk because of concerns about their own holdings of mortgages and other risky assets. A credit guarantee is only as good as the credit of the guarantor. Suddenly, institutional investors such as money market funds began to realize that investing in asset-backed commercial paper exposed them to default risk. As these institutional investors cut back on their investments in commercial paper in an effort to avoid this risk, the financial institutions that relied on commercial paper for their financing could no longer obtain the funds that they needed.

The credit crisis illustrates how problems in one debt security market (for example, mortgage-backed securities) can be contagious, having detrimental impacts on other debt markets (such as the commercial paper market). During the credit crisis, the federal government became concerned about systemic risk and feared that the adverse effects triggered in the market for mortgage-backed securities might spread to all types of financial markets and financial institutions. In November 2008, the Federal Reserve began to purchase commercial paper issued by highly rated firms. The Fed usually does not participate as an investor in the commercial paper market, but this new form of participation was intended to restore activity and, in turn, increase liquidity in the commercial paper market.

Nevertheless, the commercial paper market has not completely recovered since the credit crisis. As shown in Exhibit 6.4, the amount of commercial paper outstanding reached a high of about $2.2 trillion in 2007, but now is less than $1.2 trillion. Furthermore, investors are requiring that asset-backed commercial paper be secured with safer securities (such as Treasury securities) rather than mortgage-backed securities.

6-1d Negotiable Certificates of Deposit

Negotiable certificates of deposit (NCDs) are certificates issued by large commercial banks and other depository institutions as a short-term source of funds. The minimum denomination is $100,000, although a $1 million denomination is more common. Nonfinancial corporations often purchase NCDs. Although NCD denominations are typically too large for individual investors, they are sometimes purchased by money market funds that have pooled individual investors' funds. Thus, money market funds allow individuals to be indirect investors in NCDs, creating a more active NCD market.

Exhibit 6.4   Value of Commercial Paper Outstanding over Time

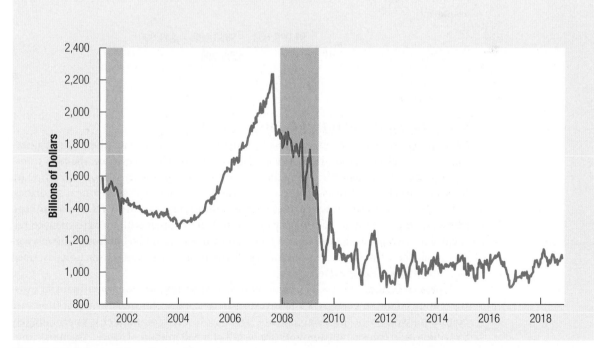

Note: The shaded areas represent recessions.
Source: Federal Reserve.

Maturities on NCDs typically range from two weeks to one year. A secondary market for NCDs exists, providing investors with some liquidity. However, institutions prefer not to have their newly issued NCDs compete with their previously issued NCDs being resold in the secondary market. An oversupply of NCDs for sale could force institutions to sell their newly issued NCDs at a lower price.

Placement of NCDs   Some issuers place their NCDs directly; others use a third-party institution that specializes in placing NCDs. Another alternative is to sell NCDs to securities dealers, which in turn resell them. A portion of unusually large issues is commonly sold to NCD dealers. In most cases, however, NCDs can be sold to investors directly at a higher price.

Yield from Investing in NCDs   Negotiable certificates of deposit provide a return in the form of interest along with the difference between the price at which the NCD is redeemed (or sold in the secondary market) and the purchase price. Given that an institution issues an NCD at par value, the annualized yield that it will pay is the annualized interest rate on the NCD. If investors purchase this NCD and hold it until maturity, their annualized yield is the interest rate. However, the annualized yield can differ from the annualized interest rate for investors who either purchase or sell the NCD in the secondary market instead of holding it from inception until maturity.

Negotiable certificates of deposit must offer a slightly higher yield than T-bills with the same maturity to compensate for their lower liquidity and safety levels. The premiums are generally higher during recessionary periods, reflecting the market's perception of the financial system's safety.

EXAMPLE

An investor purchased an NCD a year ago in the secondary market for $990,000. He redeems it today upon maturity and receives $1,000,000. He also receives interest of $40,000. His annualized yield (Y_{NCD}) on this investment is

$$Y_{NCD} = \frac{\$1,000,000 - \$990,000 + \$40,000}{\$990,000}$$
$$= 5.05\%$$

●

6-1e **Repurchase Agreements**

With a repurchase agreement (or repo), one party sells securities to another with an agreement to repurchase the securities at a specified date and price. In essence, the repo transaction represents a loan backed by the securities. If the borrower defaults on the loan, the lender has claim to the securities. Most repo transactions use government securities, although some involve other securities such as commercial paper or NCDs. A **reverse repo** refers to the purchase of securities by one party from another with an agreement to sell them. Thus, a repo and a reverse repo refer to the same transaction but from different perspectives. These two terms are sometimes used interchangeably, so a transaction described as a repo may actually be a reverse repo.

Financial institutions, such as banks and savings institutions, and nonfinancial institutions are common borrowers and investors in repos, whereas money market funds are common investors in these agreements. The size of the repo market is approximately $5 trillion, and transaction amounts are usually for $10 million or more. The most common maturities are from 1 to 15 days and for 1, 3, and 6 months. A secondary market for repos does not exist.

Some firms in need of funds will set the maturity on a repo to be the minimum time period for which they need temporary financing. If they still need funds when the repo is ready to mature, they will borrow additional funds through new repos and then use these funds to fulfill their obligation on the maturing repos.

Repurchase Agreement Transactions   Repo transactions are negotiated through a telecommunications network. Dealers and repo brokers act as financial intermediaries to create repos for firms with deficient or excess funds, receiving a commission for their services.

When the borrowing firm can find a counterparty to the repo transaction, it avoids the transaction fee involved in having a securities dealer find the counterparty. Some companies that commonly engage in repo transactions have an in-house department for finding counterparties and executing the transactions. A company that borrows through repos may, from time to time, serve as the lender. That is, it may purchase the securities and agree to sell them back in the near future. Because the cash flow of any large company changes on a daily basis, it is not unusual for a firm to act as an investor one day (when it has excess funds) and as a borrower the next (when it has a cash shortage).

Impact of the Credit Crisis   During the credit crisis of 2008, as the values of mortgage securities declined, financial institutions participating in the housing market became exposed to more risk. Consequently, many financial institutions that relied on the repo market for funding were not able to obtain funds. Investors grew more concerned about the securities that were posted as collateral. Bear Stearns, a large securities firm, relied heavily on repos for funding and used mortgage securities as collateral. During this era, however, the valuation of these types of securities was subject to much uncertainty because of the credit crisis. When investors were unwilling to provide funding, Bear Stearns could not obtain sufficient financing. It avoided bankruptcy only with the aid of the federal government.

The lesson from the credit crisis is that repo market funding requires collateral that is trusted by investors. When economic conditions weaken, some securities may not serve as adequate collateral.

Estimating the Yield on Repurchase Agreements   The repo rate is determined as the difference between the initial selling price of the securities and the agreed-on repurchase price, annualized to a 360-day year.

EXAMPLE An investor initially purchased securities at a price (PP) of $9,920,000 while agreeing to sell them back at a price (SP) of $10,000,000 at the end of a 90-day period. The yield (or repo rate) on this repurchase agreement is

$$\text{Repo rate} = \frac{\$10,000,000 - \$9,920,000}{\$9,920,000} \times \frac{360}{90}$$
$$= 3.23\%$$

6-1f Federal Funds

The federal funds market enables depository institutions to lend or borrow short-term funds from each other at the **federal funds rate**, the rate charged on federal funds transactions. This rate is influenced by the supply of and demand for funds in the federal funds market. Commercial banks are the most active participants in the federal funds market.

The Federal Reserve adjusts the amount of funds in depository institutions as a means to influence the federal funds rate (as explained in Chapter 4) and several other short-term interest rates. Financial market participants view changes in the federal funds rate as an indicator of potential changes in other money market rates.

The federal funds rate is normally slightly higher than the T-bill rate at any given time. A lender in the federal funds market is subject to credit risk, since it is possible that the financial institution borrowing the funds could default on the loan.

Federal Funds Market Transactions   Federal funds brokers serve as intermediaries in the market, matching up financial institutions that wish to sell (lend) funds with those that wish to purchase (borrow) them. The brokers receive a commission for their service. The transactions are negotiated through a telecommunications network that links federal funds brokers with participating institutions. Most loan transactions are for $5 million or more and usually have a maturity of one to seven days (although the loans may often be extended by the lender if the borrower requests more time to pay it back). If the loan is for just one day, it will likely be based on an oral agreement between the parties, especially if the institutions commonly do business with each other. The interbank loan volume outstanding now exceeds $200 billion.

6-1g Banker's Acceptances

A **banker's acceptance** indicates that a bank accepts responsibility for a future payment. Banker's acceptances are commonly used for international trade transactions. An exporter that is sending goods to an importer whose credit rating is not known, for example, will often prefer that a bank act as a guarantor. The bank facilitates such a transaction by stamping ACCEPTED on a draft, which obligates payment at a specified point in time. In turn, the importer will pay the bank what is owed to the exporter along with a fee to the bank for guaranteeing the payment.

Secondary Market for Banker's Acceptances   Exporters can hold a banker's acceptance until the date at which payment is to be made, but they frequently sell the acceptance before then at a discount to obtain cash immediately. The investor who purchases the acceptance then receives the payment guaranteed by the bank in the future.

Because acceptances are often discounted and sold by the exporting firm prior to maturity, an active secondary market for these instruments exists. Dealers match up companies that wish to sell acceptances with other companies that wish to purchase them. A dealer's bid price is less than its ask price, which creates the spread (that is, the dealer's reward for doing business). The spread is normally between one-eighth and seven-eighths of 1 percent.

Return on Banker's Acceptances   The investor's return on a banker's acceptance, like that on commercial paper, is derived from the difference between the discounted price paid for the acceptance and the amount to be received in the future. Maturities on banker's acceptances typically range from 30 to 270 days. Because there is a possibility that a bank will default on payment, investors are exposed to a slight degree of credit risk; they deserve a return above the T-bill yield to compensate for this risk.

Steps Involved in Banker's Acceptances   The sequence of steps involved in a banker's acceptance is illustrated in Exhibit 6.5. To understand these steps, consider the example of a U.S. importer of Japanese goods. First, the importer places a purchase order for the goods (Step 1). If the Japanese exporter is unfamiliar with the U.S. importer, it may demand payment before delivery of goods, which the U.S. importer may be unwilling to make. A compromise can be reached by creating a banker's acceptance. The importer asks its bank to issue a **letter of credit (L/C)** on its behalf (Step 2). This L/C represents a commitment by that bank to back the payment owed to the Japanese exporter. The L/C is

Exhibit 6.5   Sequence of Steps in the Creation of a Banker's Acceptance

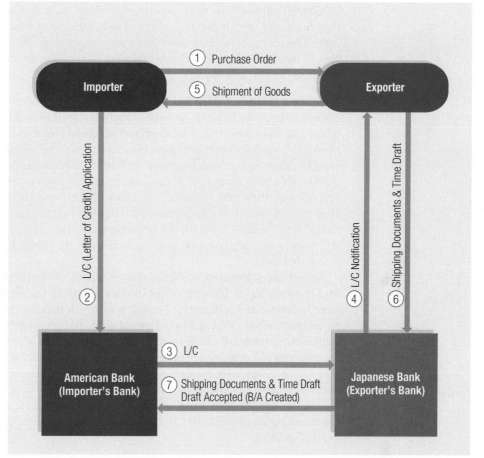

presented to the exporter's bank (Step 3), which informs the exporter that the L/C has been received (Step 4). The exporter then sends the goods to the importer (Step 5) and sends the shipping documents to its bank (Step 6), which passes them along to the importer's bank (Step 7). At this point, the banker's acceptance (B/A) is created, which obligates the importer's bank to make payment to the holder of the banker's acceptance at a specified future date. The banker's acceptance may subsequently be sold to a money market investor at a discount. Potential purchasers of such acceptances are short-term investors. When the acceptance matures, the importer pays its bank, which in turn pays the money market investor who presents the acceptance.

The creation of a banker's acceptance allows the importer to receive goods from an exporter without sending immediate payment. The selling of the acceptance creates financing for the exporter.

Even though banker's acceptances are often created to facilitate international transactions, they are not limited to money market investors with international experience. Investors who purchase acceptances are more concerned with the credit of the bank that guarantees payment than with the credit of the exporter or importer. For this reason, the credit risk on a banker's acceptance is somewhat similar to that of NCDs issued by commercial banks. At the same time, because it has the backing not only of the bank but also of the importing firm, a banker's acceptance may be perceived as having slightly less credit risk than an NCD.

6-1h Summary of Money Market Securities

Exhibit 6.6 summarizes the various types of money market securities. When such securities are issued to obtain funds, the type of securities issued depends on whether the issuer is the Treasury, a depository institution, or a corporation. When investors decide which type of money market securities to invest in, their choice depends on the desired return and liquidity characteristics.

Pricing of Money Market Securities The prices of money market securities change in response to a change in the required rate of return, which itself is influenced by the risk-free interest rate and the perceived credit risk over time. Exhibit 6.7 identifies the underlying forces that can affect the short-term risk-free interest rate (the T-bill rate) and the risk premium and, therefore, influence the required return and prices of money market securities over time. If short-term interest rates increase, the required rate of return on existing money market securities will increase and their prices will decrease. However, this so-called interest rate risk is limited, because money market securities have a short term to maturity. Even if interest rates rise, the existing money market securities will mature soon anyway, so investors can reinvest the proceeds at the prevailing interest rate at that time.

Nevertheless, investors in money market securities closely monitor economic indicators that may signal future changes in the strength of the economy. Some of the more heavily scrutinized indicators of economic growth include employment, gross domestic product, retail sales, industrial production, and consumer confidence. A favorable movement in these indicators tends to create expectations of increased economic growth, which could place upward pressure on money market interest rates (including the risk-free rate for short-term maturities) and downward pressure on prices of money market securities. Investors also keep an eye on indicators of inflation, such as the consumer price index and the producer price index. An increase in these indexes may create expectations of higher interest rates and place downward pressure on prices of existing money market securities.

Exhibit 6.6 Summary of Commonly Issued Money Market Securities

SECURITY	ISSUED BY	COMMON INVESTORS	COMMON MATURITIES	SECONDARY MARKET ACTIVITY
Treasury bills	Federal government	Households, firms, and financial institutions	13 weeks, 26 weeks, 1 year	High
Negotiable certificates of deposit (NCDs)	Large banks and savings institutions	Firms	2 weeks to 1 year	Moderate
Commercial paper	Bank holding companies, finance companies, and other companies	Firms	1 day to 270 days	Low
Banker's acceptances	Banks (exporting firms can sell the acceptances at a discount to obtain funds)	Firms	30 days to 270 days	High
Federal funds	Depository institutions	Depository institutions	1 day to 7 days	Nonexistent
Repurchase agreements	Firms and financial institutions	Firms and financial institutions	1 day to 15 days	Nonexistent

Exhibit 6.7   Framework for Pricing Money Market Securities

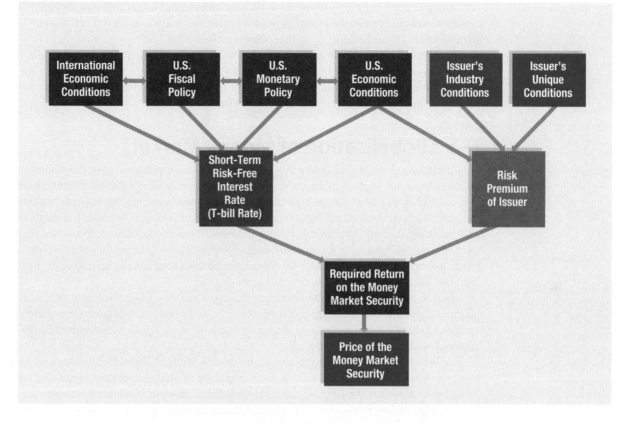

6-2 Institutional Use of Money Markets

Exhibit 6.8 summarizes the institutional use of money market. Financial institutions purchase money market securities in order to earn a return while maintaining adequate liquidity.

Exhibit 6.8   Institutional Use of Money Markets

TYPE OF FINANCIAL INSTITUTION	PARTICIPATION IN THE MONEY MARKETS
Commercial banks and savings institutions	• Bank holding companies issue commercial paper. • Some banks and savings institutions issue NCDs, borrow or lend funds in the federal funds market, engage in repurchase agreements, and purchase T-bills. • Commercial banks create banker's acceptances. • Commercial banks provide backup lines of credit to corporations that issue commercial paper.
Finance companies	• Issue large amounts of commercial paper.
Money market mutual funds	• Use proceeds from shares sold to invest in T-bills, commercial paper, NCDs, repurchase agreements, and banker's acceptances.
Insurance companies	• May maintain a portion of their investment portfolio as money market securities for liquidity.
Pension funds	• May maintain a portion of their investment portfolio as money market securities that may be liquidated when portfolio managers desire to increase their investment in bonds or stocks.

Some financial institutions issue their own money market instruments to obtain cash. For example, depository institutions issue NCDs, and bank holding companies and finance companies issue commercial paper. Depository institutions also obtain funds through the use of repurchase agreements or in the federal funds market.

Many money market transactions involve two financial institutions. For example, a federal funds transaction involves two depository institutions. Money market funds commonly purchase NCDs from banks and savings institutions. Repurchase agreements are frequently negotiated between two commercial banks.

6-3 Globalization of Money Markets

As international trade and financing have grown, money markets have developed in Europe, Asia, and South America. Corporations commonly accept foreign currencies as revenue if they will need those currencies to pay for imports in the future. Because a corporation may not need to use funds at the time it receives them, it deposits the funds in an interesting-earning account until they are needed. Meanwhile, other corporations may need funds denominated in foreign currencies and may wish to borrow those funds from a bank. International banks facilitate the international money markets by accepting deposits and providing loans in a wide variety of currencies.

The flow of funds between countries has increased as a result of tax differences among countries, speculation on exchange rate movements, and a reduction in government barriers that were previously imposed on foreign investment in securities. Consequently, international markets are well integrated.

The money market interest rates in each country are influenced by the demand for short-term funds by borrowers, relative to the supply of available short-term funds that are provided by savers. If the demand for short-term funds denominated in a particular currency is high relative to the short-term funds that are available in that currency, the money market interest rates will be relatively high in that country. Conversely, if the demand for short-term funds in that currency is low relative to the supply of short-term funds available, the money market interest rates in that country will be relatively low.

The money market interest rate paid by corporations that borrow short-term funds in a particular country is slightly higher than the rate paid by the national government in the same country; the higher rate reflects the premium to compensate investors for the increased credit risk of corporate borrowers. There may also be an additional premium to compensate for less liquidity of short-term securities issued by corporations.

While money market interest rates vary among countries, they tend to move in the same direction over time. The interest rates of several European countries are the same as a result of the conversion of their currencies to the euro.

6-3a International Interbank Market

Some international banks periodically have an excess of funds beyond the amount that other corporations want to borrow. Other international banks may be short of funds because their client corporations want to borrow more funds than the banks have available. An international interbank market facilitates the transfer of funds from banks with excess funds to those with deficient funds. This market is similar to the federal funds market in the United States, but it operates on a worldwide basis and conducts transactions in a wide variety of currencies. Some of the transactions are direct from one bank to another, whereas others are channeled through large banks that serve as intermediaries between the lending bank and the borrowing bank. Historically, international banks in London carried out many of these transactions.

The rate charged for a loan from one bank to another in the international interbank market is the London Interbank Offer Rate (LIBOR), which is similar to the federal funds rate in the United States. Several banks report the interest rate that they offer in the interbank market, and their rates may vary slightly. The LIBOR is the average of the reported rates at a given point in time. It varies among currencies, but usually aligns with the prevailing money market rates in a specific currency. It also varies over time in response to changes in money market rates in a particular currency, which are driven by changes in the demand and supply conditions for short-term money in that currency. The term LIBOR is still frequently used, even though many international interbank transactions do not pass through London.

ETHICS

LIBOR Scandal   In 2012, some banks that periodically report the interest rate they offer in the interbank market falsely reported their rates. These banks had some investments or loan positions whose performance depended on the prevailing LIBOR. For example, if banks provide loans with rates that are readjusted periodically in accordance with LIBOR, they may benefit from inflating the reported rate they charge on interbank loans in an effort to push LIBOR higher. Indeed, some banks were charged with colluding to manipulate LIBOR in an attempt to boost their trading profits.

6-3b **Eurodollar Securities**

As corporations outside the United States (especially in Europe) have increasingly engaged in international trade transactions in U.S. dollars, U.S. dollar deposits in non-U.S. banks have grown. These dollar deposits in Europe are referred to as **Eurodollars**. Several types of money market securities utilize Eurodollars.

Eurodollar CDs   **Eurodollar certificates of deposit** are large, dollar-denominated deposits (such as $1 million) accepted by banks in Europe. Eurodollar CD volume has grown substantially over time, because the U.S. dollar is used as a medium of exchange in a significant portion of international trade and investment transactions. Some firms overseas receive U.S. dollars as payment for exports and invest in Eurodollar CDs. Because these firms may need dollars to pay for future imports, they retain dollar-denominated deposits rather than convert dollars to their home currency.

In the so-called **Eurodollar market**, banks channel the deposited funds to other firms that need to borrow them in the form of Eurodollar loans. These deposit and loan transactions in Eurodollars typically amount to $1 million or more per transaction, so only governments and large corporations participate in this market. Because the transaction amounts are large, investors in the market can avoid some costs associated with the continuous small transactions that occur in retail-oriented markets.

A secondary market for Eurodollar CDs exists, allowing the initial investors to liquidate their investments if necessary. The growth in Eurodollar volume has made the secondary market more active.

Investors in fixed-rate Eurodollar CDs are adversely affected by rising market interest rates, whereas issuers of these CDs are adversely affected by declining rates. To deal with this interest rate risk, **Eurodollar floating-rate CDs (FRCDs)** have been used in recent years. With these securities, the rate is adjusted periodically to the LIBOR. As with other floating-rate instruments, the rate on FRCDs ensures that the borrower's cost and the investor's return reflect prevailing market interest rates.

Euronotes Short-term **Euronotes** are short-term securities issued in bearer form with common maturities of one, three, and six months. Typical investors in Euronotes often include the Eurobanks (banks that accept large deposits and make large loans in foreign currencies) that are hired to place the paper. These Euronotes are sometimes underwritten in a manner that guarantees the issuer a specific price.

Euro-Commercial Paper **Euro-commercial paper (Euro-CP)** is issued without the backing of a banking syndicate. Maturities can be tailored to satisfy investors. Dealers that place commercial paper have created a secondary market by purchasing existing Euro-CP before maturity.

The Euro-CP rate is typically between 50 and 100 basis points (a basis point is one hundredth of 1 percent) above LIBOR. Thus, if LIBOR is 5 percent, the Euro-CP rate would typically be between 5.5 and 6 percent. Euro-CP is sold by dealers at a transaction cost ranging from 5 to 10 basis points of the face value.

6-3c **Performance of Foreign Money Market Securities**

The performance of an investment in a foreign money market security is measured by the **effective yield** (that is, the yield adjusted for the exchange rate), which is a function of two factors: (1) the yield earned on the money market security in the foreign currency and (2) the exchange rate effect. The yield earned on the foreign money market security (Y_f) is

$$Y_f = \frac{SP_f - PP_f}{PP_f}$$

where

SP_f = selling price of the foreign money market security in the foreign currency

PP_f = purchase price of the foreign money market security in the foreign currency

The exchange rate effect (denoted as $\%\Delta S$) measures the percentage change in the spot exchange rate (in dollars) from the time the foreign currency was obtained to invest in the foreign money market security until the time the security was sold and the foreign currency was converted into the investor's home currency. Thus, the effective yield is

$$Y_e = (1 + Y_f) \times (1 + \%\Delta S) - 1$$

EXAMPLE

A U.S. investor obtains Mexican pesos when the peso is worth $0.12 and invests in a one-year money market security that provides a yield (in pesos) of 9 percent. At the end of one year, the investor converts the proceeds from the investment back to dollars at the prevailing spot rate of $0.1296 per peso. In this example, the peso increased in value by 8 percent. The effective yield earned by the investor is

$$Y_e = (1 + Y_f) \times (1 + \%\Delta S) - 1$$
$$= (1.09) \times (1.08) - 1$$
$$= 17.72\%$$

●

The effective yield exceeds the yield quoted on the foreign currency whenever the currency denominating the foreign investment increases in value over the investment horizon. However, such an investment is subject to the risk that the currency will depreciate over time. In the previous example, if the peso had depreciated by 8 percent, the effective yield on the investment would have been

$$Y_e = (1 + Y_f) \times (1 + \%\Delta S) - 1$$
$$= (1.09) \times (0.92) - 1$$
$$= 0.28\%$$

U.S. investors have sometimes experienced a negative effective yield in periods when the foreign currency denominating their foreign money market investments depreciated substantially.

Summary

- The main money market securities are Treasury bills, commercial paper, NCDs, repurchase agreements, federal funds, and banker's acceptances. These securities vary according to the issuer and, in turn, their perceived degree of credit risk can vary. They also have different degrees of liquidity. For all these reasons, the quoted yields at any given point in time will vary among money market securities.

- Financial institutions manage their liquidity by participating in money markets. They may issue money market securities such as commercial paper when they experience cash shortages and need to boost liquidity. They can also sell holdings of money market securities to obtain cash.

- Interest rates vary among countries. Some investors are attracted to high interest rates in foreign countries, which cause funds to flow to those countries. Consequently, money markets have become globally integrated. Investments in foreign money market securities are subject to exchange rate risk because the foreign currency denominating the securities could depreciate over time.

Point/Counterpoint

Should Firms Invest in Money Market Securities?

Point   No. Firms are supposed to use money in a manner that generates an adequate return to shareholders. Money market securities provide a return that is less than that required by shareholders. Thus, firms should not use shareholders' funds to invest in money market securities. If firms need liquidity, they can rely on the money markets for short-term borrowing.

Counterpoint   Yes. Firms need money markets for liquidity. If they do not hold any money market securities, they will frequently be forced to borrow to cover unanticipated cash needs. The lenders may charge higher risk premiums when lending so frequently to these firms.

Who Is Correct?   Use the Internet to learn more about this issue and then formulate your own opinion.

Questions and Applications

1. **Primary Market** Explain how the Treasury uses the primary market to obtain adequate funding for the U.S. government.

2. **T-Bill Auction** How can investors using the primary T-bill market be assured that their bid will be accepted?

Why do large corporations typically make competitive bids rather than noncompetitive bids for T-bills?

3. **Secondary Market for T-Bills** Describe the activity in the secondary T-bill market. How can this degree of activity benefit investors in T-bills? Why

might a financial institution sometimes consider T-bills as a potential source of funds?

4.   **Commercial Paper** Who issues commercial paper? Which types of financial institutions issue commercial paper? Why do some firms create a department that can directly place commercial paper? Which criteria affect the decision to create such a department?

5.   **Commercial Paper Ratings** Why do ratings agencies assign ratings to commercial paper?

6.   **Commercial Paper Rates** Explain how investors' preferences for commercial paper change during a recession. How would this reaction affect the difference between commercial paper rates and T-bill rates during recessionary periods?

7.   **Negotiable CDs** How can small investors participate in investments in negotiable certificates of deposits (NCDs)?

8.   **Repurchase Agreements** Based on what you know about repurchase agreements, would you expect them to have a lower or higher annualized yield than commercial paper? Why?

9.   **Banker's Acceptances** Explain how each of the following would use banker's acceptances: (a) exporting firms, (b) importing firms, (c) commercial banks, and (d) investors.

10.   **Foreign Money Market Yield** Explain how the yield on a foreign money market security would be affected if the foreign currency denominating that security declined to a significant degree.

11.   **Motive to Issue Commercial Paper** The maximum maturity of commercial paper is 270 days. Why would a firm issue commercial paper instead of longer-term securities, even if it needs funds for a long period of time?

12.   **Risk and Return of Commercial Paper** You have the choice of investing in top-rated commercial paper or commercial paper that has a lower risk rating. How do you think the risk and return performances of the two investments differ?

13.   **Commercial Paper Yield Curve** How do you think the shape of the yield curve for commercial paper and other money market instruments compares to the yield curve for Treasury securities? Explain your logic.

Advanced Questions

14.   **Influence of Money Market Activity on Working Capital** Assume that interest rates for most maturities are unusually high. Also assume that the net working capital (defined as current assets minus current liabilities) levels of many corporations are relatively low in this period. Explain how the money markets play a role in the relationship between the interest rates and the level of net working capital.

15.   **Applying Term Structure Theories to Commercial Paper** Apply the term structure of interest rate theories that were discussed in Chapter 3 to explain the shape of the existing commercial paper yield curve.

16.   **How Money Market Rates May Respond to Prevailing Conditions** How have money market rates changed since the beginning of the semester? Consider the current economic conditions. Do you think money market rates will increase or decrease during the semester? Offer some logic to support your answer.

17.   **Impact of Lehman Brothers Failure** Explain how the bankruptcy of Lehman Brothers (a large securities firm) reduced the liquidity of the commercial paper market.

18.   **Bear Stearns and the Repo Market** Explain the lesson to be learned about the repo market based on the experience of Bear Stearns.

19.   **Impact of Credit Crisis on Liquidity** Explain why the credit crisis affected the ability of financial institutions to access short-term financing in the money markets.

20.   **Impact of Credit Crisis on Risk Premiums** Explain how the credit crisis affected the credit risk premium in the commercial paper market.

21.   **Systemic Risk** Explain how systemic risk is related to the commercial paper market. That is, why did problems in the market for mortgage-backed securities affect the commercial paper market?

22.   **Commercial Paper Credit Guarantees** Explain why investors that provided guarantees on commercial paper were exposed to so much risk during the credit crisis.

Critical Thinking Question

Money Market Funding during a Credit Crisis Many financial institutions borrow heavily in the money markets using mortgages and mortgage-backed securities as collateral. Write a short essay about the lessons of the credit crisis for the deficit units and the surplus units that participate in the money markets, Should money markets be regulated to a greater degree to ensure proper collateral in money markets?

Interpreting Financial News

Interpret the following statements made by Wall Street analysts and portfolio managers.

a. "Money markets are not used to get rich, but to avoid being poor."
b. "Until conditions are more favorable, investors are staying on the sidelines."
c. "My portfolio is overinvested in stocks because of the low money market rates."

Managing in Financial Markets

Money Market Portfolio Dilemma   As the treasurer of a corporation, one of your jobs is to maintain investments in liquid securities such as Treasury securities and commercial paper. Your goal is to earn as high a return as possible but without taking much of a risk.

a. The yield curve is currently upward sloping, such that 10-year Treasury bonds have an annualized yield 3 percentage points above the annualized yield of 3-month T-bills. Should you consider using some of your funds to invest in 10-year Treasury securities?

b. Assume that your firm has substantially more cash than it would possibly need for any liquidity problems. Your boss suggests that you consider investing the excess funds in some money market securities that have a higher return than short-term Treasury securities, such as negotiable certificates of deposit (NCDs). Even though NCDs are less liquid, this would not cause a problem if your firm has more funds than it needs. Given the situation, which use of the excess funds would benefit the firm the most?

c. Assume that commercial paper is currently offering an annualized yield of 7.5 percent, while Treasury securities are offering an annualized yield of 7 percent. Economic conditions have been stable, and you expect conditions to be very favorable over the next six months. Given this situation, would you prefer to hold T-bills or a diversified portfolio of commercial paper issued by various corporations?

d. Assume that commercial paper typically offers a premium of 0.5 percent above the T-bill rate. Given that your firm typically maintains about $10 million in liquid funds, how much extra will you generate per year by investing in commercial paper versus T-bills? Is this extra return worth the risk that the commercial paper could default?

Problems

1. T-Bill Yield Assume an investor purchased a 6-month T-bill with a $10,000 par value for $9,000 and sold it 90 days later for $9,100. What is the yield?

2. T-Bill Discount Newly issued three-month T-bills with a par value of $10,000 sold for $9,700. Compute the T-bill discount.

3. Commercial Paper Yield Assume an investor purchased six-month commercial paper with a face value of $1 million for $940,000. What is the yield?

4. Repurchase Agreement Stanford Corporation arranged a repurchase agreement in which it purchased securities for $4.9 million and will sell the securities back for $5 million in 40 days. What is the yield (or repo rate) to Stanford Corporation?

5. T-Bill Yield You paid $98,000 for a $100,000 T-bill maturing in 120 days. If you hold it until maturity, what is the T-bill yield? What is the T-bill discount?

6. T-Bill Yield The Treasury is selling 91-day T-bills with a face value of $10,000 for $9,900. If the investor holds them until maturity, calculate the yield.

7. Required Rate of Return A money market security that has a par value of $10,000 sells for $8,816.60. Given that the security has a maturity of two years, what is the investor's required rate of return?

8. Effective Yield A U.S. investor obtains British pounds when the pound is worth $1.50 and invests in a one-year money market security that provides a yield of 5 percent (in pounds). At the end of one year, the investor converts the proceeds from the investment back to dollars at the prevailing spot rate of $1.52 per pound. Calculate the effective yield.

9. T-Bill Yield

a. Determine how the annualized yield of a T-bill would be affected if the purchase price were lower. Explain the logic of this relationship.

b. Determine how the annualized yield of a T-bill would be affected if the selling price were lower. Explain the logic of this relationship.

c. Determine how the annualized yield of a T-bill would be affected if the number of days were reduced, holding the purchase price and selling price constant. Explain the logic of this relationship.

10. Return on NCDs Phil purchased an NCD a year ago in the secondary market for $980,000. The NCD matures today at a price of $1 million, and Phil received $45,000 in interest. What is Phil's return on the NCD?

Flow of Funds Exercise

Financing in the Money Markets

Recall that Carson Company has obtained substantial loans from finance companies and commercial banks. The interest rate on the loans is tied to market interest rates and is adjusted every six months. Carson has a credit line with a bank in case it suddenly needs to obtain funds for a temporary period. It previously purchased Treasury securities that it could sell if it experiences any liquidity problems. If the economy continues to be strong, Carson may need to increase its production capacity by about 50 percent over the next few years to satisfy demand. It is concerned about a possible slowing of the economy because of potential Fed actions to reduce inflation. It needs funding to cover payments for supplies. It is also considering issuing stock or bonds to raise funds in the next year.

a. The prevailing commercial paper rate on paper issued by large publicly traded firms is lower than the rate Carson would pay when using a line of credit. Do you think that Carson could issue commercial paper at this prevailing market rate?

b. Should Carson obtain funds to cover payments for supplies by selling its holdings of Treasury securities or by using its credit line? Which alternative has a lower cost? Explain.

Internet/Excel Exercises

1. Go to https://fred.stlouisfed.org/categories. Under "Money, Banking, & Finance," select "Interest rates." Compare the yield offered on a T-bill with the yield offered by another money market security with a similar maturity. What is the difference in yields? Why do you think the yields differ?

2. How has the risk premium on a specific risky money market security (versus the T-bill) changed since one year ago? Is the change due to a change in economic conditions? Explain.

3. Using the same website, retrieve interest rate data at the beginning of the last 20 quarters for the three-month T-bill and another money market security and place the data in two columns of an Excel spreadsheet. Derive the change in interest rates for both money market securities on a quarterly basis. Apply regression analysis in which the quarterly change in the interest rate of the risky money market security is the dependent variable and the quarterly change in the T-bill rate is the independent variable (see Appendix B for more information about using regression analysis). Is there a positive and significant relationship between the interest rate movements? Explain.

WSJ Exercise

Assessing Yield Differentials of Money Market Securities

Use the "Money Rates" section of *The Wall Street Journal* to determine the 30-day yield (annualized) of commercial paper, certificates of deposit, banker's acceptances, and T-bills. Which of these securities has the highest yield? Why? Which of these securities has the lowest yield? Why?

Online Articles with Real-World Examples

Find a recent practical article available online that describes a real-world example regarding a specific financial institution or financial market that reinforces one or more concepts covered in this chapter. If your class has an online component, your professor may ask you to post your summary of the article there and provide a link to the article so that other students can access it. If your class is live, your professor may ask you to summarize your application of the article in class. Your professor may assign specific students to complete this assignment or may allow any students to do the assignment on a volunteer basis.

For recent online articles and real-world examples related to this chapter, consider using the following search terms (be sure to include the prevailing year as a search term to ensure that the online articles are recent):

1. Treasury bill auction
2. commercial paper AND offering
3. commercial paper AND rating
4. repurchase agreement AND financing
5. money market AND yield
6. commercial paper AND risk
7. institutional investors AND money market
8. banker's acceptance AND yield
9. [name of a specific financial institution] AND repurchase agreement
10. [name of a specific financial institution] AND commercial paper

7

Bond Markets

CHAPTER OBJECTIVES

The specific objectives of this chapter are to:

■ Provide a background on bonds.

■ Describe the different types of bonds and their characteristics.

■ Explain how bond markets have become globally integrated.

■ Describe other types of long-term debt securities.

WEB

finance.yahoo.com /bonds
Summary of bond market activity and analysis of bond market conditions.

From this chapter through Chapter 12, the focus is on capital market securities. These chapters are distinctly different from the previous chapter on money market securities, in that they employ a long-term (rather than a short-term) perspective. This chapter and Chapter 8 focus on bond markets, which facilitate the flow of long-term debt from surplus units to deficit units.

7-1 Background on Bonds

Bonds are long-term debt securities that are issued by government agencies or corporations. Most bonds have maturities of between 10 and 30 years. The issuer of a bond is obligated to pay interest (or coupon) payments periodically (such as annually or semiannually) and the par value (principal) at maturity. An issuer must be able to show that its future cash flows will be sufficient to enable it to make its coupon and principal payments to bondholders. Investors will consider buying bonds for which the repayment is questionable only if the expected return from investing in the bonds is sufficient to compensate for the risk.

Bonds are often classified according to the type of issuer. Treasury bonds are issued by the U.S. Treasury, federal agency bonds are issued by federal agencies, municipal bonds are issued by state and local governments, and corporate bonds are issued by corporations.

Bonds are issued in the primary market through a telecommunications network. They are **registered**, meaning that the issuer is required to maintain records of who owns the bonds so that coupon payments can automatically be sent to the owners. A financial institution makes the coupon payments by reducing the issuer's account and crediting the bond owner's account.

Exhibit 7.1 shows how bond markets facilitate the flow of funds. The U.S. Treasury issues bonds and uses the proceeds to support deficit spending on government programs. Federal agencies issue bonds and use the proceeds to buy mortgages that are originated by financial institutions. In this way, they indirectly finance purchases of homes. Corporations issue bonds and use the proceeds to expand their operations. Overall, by allowing the U.S. government, federal agencies, and corporations to increase their expenditures, bond markets finance economic growth.

Exhibit 7.1 How Bond Markets Facilitate the Flow of Funds

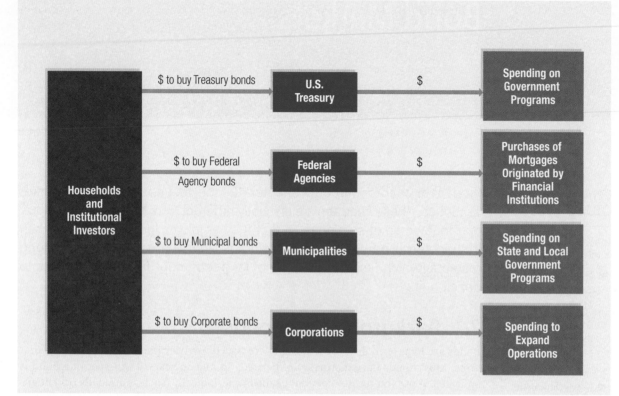

7-1a **Institutional Participation in Bond Markets**

All types of financial institutions participate in the bond markets, as summarized in Exhibit 7.2. Commercial banks, savings institutions, and finance companies commonly issue bonds to raise capital to support their operations. Commercial banks, savings institutions, bond mutual funds, insurance companies, and pension funds are major investors in the bond market. Financial institutions dominate the bond market: They purchase a large proportion of all bonds issued.

Exhibit 7.2 Participation of Financial Institutions in Bond Markets

FINANCIAL INSTITUTION	PARTICIPATION IN BOND MARKETS
Commercial banks and savings and loan associations (S&Ls)	• Purchase bonds for their asset portfolio. • Sometimes place municipal bonds for municipalities. • Sometimes issue bonds as a source of secondary capital.
Finance companies	• Commonly issue bonds as a source of long-term funds.
Mutual funds	• Use funds received from the sale of shares to purchase bonds. Some bond mutual funds specialize in particular types of bonds, whereas others invest in all types.
Brokerage firms	• Facilitate bond trading by matching up buyers and sellers of bonds in the secondary market.
Investment banking firms	• Place newly issued bonds for governments and corporations. They may place the bonds and assume the risk of market price uncertainty or place the bonds on a best-efforts basis; in the latter case, they do not guarantee a price for the issuer.
Insurance companies	• Purchase bonds for their asset portfolio.
Pension funds	• Purchase bonds for their asset portfolio.

7-1b **Bond Yields**

The yield on a bond depends on whether it is viewed from the perspective of the issuer of the bond, which is obligated to make payments on the bond until maturity, or from the perspective of the investors who purchase the bond.

Yield from the Issuer's Perspective   The issuer's cost of financing with bonds is commonly measured by the **yield to maturity**, which reflects the annualized yield that is paid by the issuer over the life of the bond. The yield to maturity is the annualized discount rate that equates the future coupon and principal payments to the initial proceeds received from the bond offering. It is based on the assumption that coupon payments received can be reinvested at the same yield.

EXAMPLE

Consider an investor who can purchase bonds with 10 years until maturity, a par value of $1,000, and an 8 percent annualized coupon rate for $936. The yield to maturity on these bonds can be determined by using a financial calculator as follows:

INPUT	10	936	80	1000		
Function Key	N	PV	PMT	FV	CPT	I
Answer						9%

Notice that the yield paid to investors consists of two components: (1) a set of coupon payments and (2) the difference between the par value that the issuer must pay to investors at maturity and the price it received when selling the bonds. In this example and in most cases, the biggest component of the yield to maturity is the set of coupon payments.

The yield to maturity does not include the transaction costs associated with issuing the bonds. When those transaction costs are considered, the issuer's actual cost of borrowing is slightly higher than the yield to maturity. ●

Yield from the Investor's Perspective   An investor who invests in a bond when it is issued and holds it until maturity will earn the yield to maturity. Yet many investors do not hold a bond to maturity, instead focusing on their *holding period return*, or the return from their investment over a particular holding period. If they hold the bond for a very short time period (such as less than one year), they may estimate their holding period return as the sum of the coupon payments plus the difference between the selling price and the purchase price of the bond, as a percentage of the purchase price. For relatively long holding periods, a better approximation of the holding period yield is the annualized discount rate that equates the payments received to the initial investment.

Because the selling price to be received by investors is uncertain if they do not hold the bond to maturity, their holding period yield is uncertain at the time they purchase the bond. Consequently, an investment in bonds is subject to the risk that the holding period return will be less than expected. The valuation and return of bonds from the investor's perspective are discussed in more detail in Chapter 8.

Treasury Bond Yields over Time   Like most U.S. interest rates, Treasury bond yields change over time in accordance with the demand for and supply of loanable funds (as explained in Chapter 2). Exhibit 7.3 shows how Treasury bond yields have changed since 2000. Since the credit crisis of 2008–2009, the Federal Reserve has attempted to keep Treasury bond yields and all other interest rates low in an effort to encourage borrowing and spending, and stimulate the U.S. economy.

Exhibit 7.3   Treasury Bond Yields over Time (10-Year Maturity)

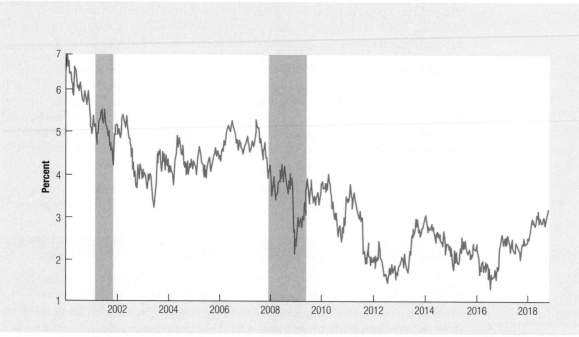

Note: Shaded areas indicate recessions.
Source: Federal Reserve.

7-2 Treasury and Federal Agency Bonds

The U.S. government, like many other national governments, commonly spends more money than it receives from taxes. Under these conditions, it needs to borrow funds to cover the difference between what it wants to spend versus what it receives. To facilitate its fiscal policy, the U.S. Treasury issues Treasury notes and Treasury bonds to finance federal government expenditures. The Treasury pays a yield to investors that reflects the risk-free rate, as it is presumed that the Treasury will not default on its payments. Because Treasury notes and bonds are free from credit (default) risk, they enable the Treasury to borrow funds at a relatively low cost. At some point, however, additional borrowing by the U.S. government might potentially cause investors to worry about the Treasury's ability to cover its debt payments.

WEB

www.treasurydirect.gov
Details about Treasury
bonds.

The minimum denomination for Treasury notes and bonds is now $100. The key difference between a note and a bond is that note maturities are less than 10 years whereas bond maturities are 10 years or more. Since 2006, the Treasury has commonly issued 10-year Treasury bonds and 30-year Treasury bonds to finance the U.S. budget deficit. An active over-the-counter secondary market allows investors to sell Treasury notes or bonds prior to maturity.

Investors in Treasury notes and bonds receive semiannual interest payments from the U.S. Treasury. Although the interest is taxed by the federal government as ordinary income, it is exempt from any state and local taxes. Domestic and foreign firms as well as individuals commonly invest in Treasury notes and bonds.

7-2a Treasury Bond Auctions

The U.S. Treasury obtains long-term funding through Treasury bond offerings, which are conducted through periodic auctions. Treasury bond auctions are typically held in the middle of each quarter. The Treasury announces its plans for an auction, including the date, the amount of funding that it needs, and the maturity of the bonds to be issued. At the time of the auction, financial institutions submit bids for their own accounts or for their clients.

As discussed in Chapter 6, bids can be submitted on a competitive or a noncompetitive basis. Competitive bids specify a price that the bidder is willing to pay and a dollar amount of securities to be purchased. Noncompetitive bids specify only a dollar amount of securities to be purchased (subject to a maximum limit). The Treasury ranks the competitive bids in descending order according to the price bid per $100 of par value. All competitive bids are accepted until the point at which the desired amount of funding is achieved. The Treasury applies the lowest accepted bid price to all accepted competitive bids and all noncompetitive bids. Competitive bids are commonly used because many bidders want to purchase more Treasury bonds than the maximum that can be purchased on a noncompetitive basis.

7-2b Trading Treasury Bonds

Bond dealers serve as intermediaries in the secondary market by matching up buyers and sellers of Treasury bonds, and they also take positions in these bonds. Approximately 2,000 brokers and dealers are registered to trade Treasury securities, but about 20 so-called primary dealers dominate the trading. These dealers make the secondary market for Treasury bonds. They quote a bid price for customers who want to sell existing Treasury bonds to the dealers and an ask price for customers who want to buy existing Treasury bonds from them. The dealers profit from the spread between the bid and ask prices. Because of the large volume of secondary market transactions and the intense competition among bond dealers, the spread is extremely narrow. When the Federal Reserve engages in open market operations, it typically conducts trading with the primary dealers in government securities. The primary dealers also trade Treasury bonds among themselves.

Treasury bonds are registered at the New York Stock Exchange, but the secondary market trading occurs over the counter (through a telecommunications network). The typical daily transaction volume in government securities (including money market securities) for the primary dealers is approximately $570 billion. Although most of this trading volume occurs in the United States, Treasury bonds are also traded worldwide. They are traded in Tokyo from 7:30 P.M. to 3:00 A.M. New York time. The Tokyo and London markets overlap for part of the time, and the London market remains open until 7:30 A.M., when trading begins in New York.

Investors can contact their broker to buy or sell Treasury bonds. The brokerage firms serve as an intermediary between the investors and the bond dealers. Discount brokers usually charge a fee of between $25 and $40 for Treasury bond transactions valued at $10,000. Institutional investors tend to contact the bond dealers directly.

Online Trading Investors can also buy bonds through the Treasury Direct program (www.treasurydirect.gov) and can have the Treasury deduct the amount of their purchase from their bank account. When their Treasury bonds mature, they can reinvest the proceeds into newly issued Treasury bonds.

Online Quotations Treasury bond prices are accessible online at the Markets Data Center (www.wsj.com). This website provides the spread between the bid and the ask (offer) prices for various maturities. Treasury bond yields are accessible online at various websites (for example, www.bloomberg.com and www.finance.yahoo.com). The yields are updated daily and are given for several different maturities.

7-2c Stripped Treasury Bonds

The cash flows of Treasury bonds are commonly transformed (stripped) by securities firms into separate securities, called STRIPS (Separate Trading of Registered Interest and Principal of Securities). In this process, a Treasury bond that makes semiannual interest payments is stripped into several individual securities. One security represents the payment of principal upon maturity; each of the other securities represents payment of interest at the end of a specified period. Consequently, investors can purchase stripped securities that fit their desired investment horizon.

For example, consider a 10-year Treasury bond that pays interest semiannually, for a total of 20 separate interest payments over the life of the bond. If this Treasury bond was stripped, its principal payment would be separated from the interest payments to create a new security that pays only the principal at the end of 10 years. In addition, all 20 interest payments of the Treasury bond would be separated into individual securities, so that one security would provide payment upon its maturity of 6 months, a second security would provide payment upon its maturity of 12 months, a third security would provide payment upon its maturity of 18 months, and so on. Each of the newly formed securities is a zero-coupon security because it provides only one payment that occurs upon its maturity and does not make periodic interest payments.

STRIPS are not issued by the Treasury, but instead are created and sold by various financial institutions. They can be created for any Treasury security. Because they are components of Treasury securities, they are backed by the U.S. government. They do not have to be held until maturity, as there is an active secondary market for these securities. STRIPS have become quite popular over time.

7-2d **Inflation-Indexed Treasury Bonds**

The U.S. Treasury periodically issues inflation-indexed bonds that provide returns tied to the inflation rate. These bonds, which are commonly referred to as TIPS (Treasury Inflation-Protected Securities), enable investors to ensure that the returns on their investments will keep up with the increase in prices over time. The coupon rate offered on TIPS is lower than the rate on typical Treasury bonds, but the principal value is increased by the amount of the U.S. inflation rate (as measured by the percentage increase in the consumer price index) every six months.

EXAMPLE

Consider a 10-year, inflation-indexed bond that has a par value of $10,000 and a coupon rate of 4 percent. Assume that, during the first six months since the bond was issued, the inflation rate (as measured by the consumer price index) was 1 percent, so that the principal of the bond is increased by $100 (0.01 × $10,000). Thus, the coupon payment after six months will be 2 percent (half of the yearly coupon rate) of the new par value, or 0.02 × $10,100 = $202. Assume that the inflation rate over the next six months is 3 percent. Then the principal of the bond is increased by $303 (0.03 × $10,100), which results in a new par value of $10,403. The coupon payment at the end of the year is based on the coupon rate and the new par value, or 0.02 × $10,403 = $208.06. This process is applied every six months over the life of the bond. If prices double over the 10-year period in which the bond exists, the par value of the bond will also double and will be equal to $20,000 at maturity. ●

Inflation-indexed government bonds have become popular in many countries, including Australia and the United Kingdom. They are especially desirable in countries where inflation tends to be high, such as Brazil and Turkey. Inflation-indexed bonds are also popular in the United States. The U.S. Treasury historically focused on TIPS with 10-year maturities but now offers TIPS with 5-year and 30-year maturities as well.

7-2e **Savings Bonds**

Savings bonds are issued by the Treasury, but they can be purchased from many financial institutions. They are attractive to small investors because they can be purchased with as little as $25. Larger denominations are also available. The Series EE savings bond provides a market-based rate of interest, and the Series I savings bond provides a rate of interest that is tied to inflation. The interest accumulates monthly and adds value to the amount received at the time of redemption.

Savings bonds have a 30-year maturity and do not have a secondary market. The Treasury does allow savings bonds issued after February 2003 to be redeemed at any time before maturity after a 12-month period, but a penalty equal to the last three months of interest is assessed for this early redemption.

As is the case with other Treasury securities, the interest income on savings bonds is not subject to state and local taxes but is subject to federal taxes. For federal tax purposes, investors holding savings bonds can report the accumulated interest either on an annual basis or upon bond redemption or maturity.

7-2f **Federal Agency Bonds**

Federal agency bonds are issued by federal agencies. The **Federal National Mortgage Association (Fannie Mae)** and the **Federal Home Loan Mortgage Association (Freddie Mac)** issue bonds and use the proceeds to purchase mortgages in the secondary market. In this way, they channel funds into the mortgage market, thereby ensuring that sufficient financing is available for homeowners who wish to obtain mortgages. Prior to September 2008, these bonds were not backed by the federal government.

ETHICS

During the housing boom in the 2003–2006 period, Fannie Mae and Freddie Mac began to invest heavily in very risky subprime mortgages. This strategy was inconsistent with their traditional conservative strategies, which had enhanced liquidity in the market for high-quality mortgages. The new strategy was partially attributed to a compensation system that rewarded portfolio managers at these agencies for earning very high returns. In their pursuit of mortgages that that could achieve high returns (if the mortgages were repaid), they created a portfolio of mortgages that was exposed to very high risk. In 2007, many subprime mortgages defaulted, which caused losses of more than $14 billion at Fannie Mae and Freddie Mac. Both agencies needed infusions of cash to correct their ailing financial condition, but could not easily obtain new capital. Investors were concerned about their aggressive management strategies, as their stock values had declined by more than 90 percent from the previous year. Institutional investors were reluctant to buy their bonds unless they received a high premium to compensate for the credit risk. After being rescued by the government in 2008, Fannie Mae and Freddie Mac reverted to their more conservative management strategy. Since then, they have fulfilled the more traditional role of providing more liquidity in the market for high-quality mortgages.

7-3 Municipal Bonds

Like the federal government, state and local governments frequently spend more than the revenues they receive. To finance the difference, they issue **municipal bonds**, most of which can be classified as either **general obligation bonds** or **revenue bonds**.

Payments on general obligation bonds are supported by the municipal government's ability to tax, whereas payments on revenue bonds must be generated by revenues of the project (for example, a toll way, toll bridge, or state college dormitory) for which the bonds were issued. Revenue bonds are more common than general obligation bonds. In the United States, more than 44,000 state and local government agencies issue municipal bonds to finance their spending on government projects. The market value of these bonds is almost $4 trillion.

Revenue bonds and general obligation bonds typically promise semiannual interest payments. Such bonds are commonly purchased by financial and nonfinancial institutions as well as individuals. The minimum denomination of municipal bonds is usually $5,000. A secondary market exists for them, although it is less active than the one for Treasury bonds.

Most municipal bonds contain a call provision, which allows the issuer to repurchase the bonds at a specified price before the bonds mature. A municipality may exercise its option to repurchase the bonds if interest rates decline substantially because it can then reissue bonds at the lower interest rate, thereby reducing its cost of financing.

7-3a Credit Risk of Municipal Bonds

Both types of municipal bonds are subject to some degree of credit (default) risk. If a municipality is unable to increase taxes, it could default on general obligation bonds. If it issues revenue bonds and does not generate sufficient revenue, it could default on these bonds.

Municipal bonds have rarely defaulted, and some investors consider them to be safe because they assume that any government agency in the United States can obtain funds to repay its loans. In the last half century, less than 0.1 percent of municipal bonds have defaulted. Nevertheless, several recent high-profile municipal bond defaults should prompt investors to assess the credit risk of any municipal bonds that they consider purchasing. Harrisburg, Pennsylvania, defaulted on bonds in 2010; San Bernardino, California, and Stockton, California, defaulted on bonds in 2012; Jefferson County, Alabama, and Detroit, Michigan, defaulted on bonds in 2013; and Puerto Rico defaulted on bonds in 2016.

Some government agencies have serious budget deficits because of excessive spending and may not be able to repay their loans. For example, the bond defaults of Stockton and Detroit were partially due to their governments having promised generous pensions to government employees without setting aside sufficient funds to cover the future pension payments. The state of California, the city of Chicago, and the state of Illinois are experiencing financial problems because of their massive pension underfunding. The problem of underfunded public pensions is covered in more detail in Chapter 26.

Some investors are concerned that municipalities will file for bankruptcy not as a last resort, but rather as a convenient way to avoid their obligations. That is, they might consider placing the burden on the bondholders rather than correcting their budget deficits with higher taxes or less government spending. Because investors recognize the increased credit risk associated with municipal bonds, they require higher risk premiums as compensation.

State and local governments tend to make very limited disclosures about their financial condition when they issue bonds. Although the issuance of municipal securities is regulated by the respective state government, critics argue that an unbiased regulator would be more appropriate. Better disclosure of financial information by state and local governments could help investors more accurately assess the potential default risk of some municipal bonds before they purchase them.

Ratings of Municipal Bonds Because municipal bonds raise some concerns about their risk of default, investors commonly monitor the ratings of these bonds. Moody's, Standard & Poor's, and Fitch Ratings assign ratings to municipal bonds based on the ability of the issuer to repay the debt. These ratings are important to the issuer because a better rating means investors will require a smaller risk premium, in which case the municipal bonds can be issued at a higher price (lower yield).

Of course, bond ratings can change over time. They can be downgraded if the issuer's financial condition deteriorates. When a rating is downgraded, the price of the bonds in the secondary market decreases, as investors are willing to purchase the bonds only if the price is sufficiently discounted to reflect the increased risk of default.

Insurance against Credit Risk of Municipal Bonds   Some municipal bonds are insured to protect against default. The issuer pays for this protection so that it can issue the bonds at a higher price, which translates into a higher price paid by the investor. As a consequence, investors indirectly bear the cost of the insurance. Also, it is possible that the insurer will default on its obligation of insuring the bonds. If both the municipal bond issuer and the bond insurer default, the investor will incur the loss. For this reason, investors should know which company is insuring the bonds and should assess its financial condition. During the credit crisis, MBIA (the largest insurer of bonds) experienced major losses because it insured many bonds that ultimately defaulted. Although MBIA issued new bonds to boost its capital level, its credit rating was downgraded by rating agencies.

The number of insured municipal bonds has declined substantially since the credit crisis. Whereas about 50 percent of newly issued municipal bonds were insured in 2006, only about 11 percent of newly issued municipal bonds were insured in 2018. This reduction has occurred in part because only a few highly rated insurance companies are willing to insure bonds as a result of the credit crisis. Furthermore, investors may recognize that insured bonds still carry the risk that the insurer will be unable to meet its own obligations if many of the bonds it is insuring default at the same time.

7-3b **Variable-Rate Municipal Bonds**

Variable-rate municipal bonds have a floating interest rate that is based on a benchmark interest rate: The coupon payment adjusts to movements in the benchmark. Some variable-rate municipal bonds can be converted to a fixed rate until maturity under specified conditions. In general, variable-rate municipal bonds attract investors who expect that interest rates will rise. However, there is a risk that interest rates may decline over time, which would cause the coupon payments to decline as well.

7-3c **Tax Advantages of Municipal Bonds**

One of the most attractive features of municipal bonds is that the interest income is usually exempt from federal taxes. In addition, the interest income earned on bonds that are issued by a municipality within a particular state is usually exempt from the income taxes (if any) of that state. Thus, investors who reside in states that impose income taxes can reduce their taxes further by purchasing municipal bonds.

7-3d **Trading and Quotations of Municipal Bonds**

Hundreds of bond dealers operate to accommodate investor requests to buy or sell municipal bonds in the secondary market, although five dealers account for more than half of all the trading volume. Bond dealers can also take positions in municipal bonds.

Investors who do not expect to hold a municipal bond until maturity should consider only bonds that feature active secondary market trading. Many municipal bonds have an inactive secondary market, so it is difficult for investors to know the prevailing market values of these bonds. Although investors do not pay a direct commission on trades, they incur transaction costs in the form of a bid–ask spread on the bonds. This spread can be large, especially for municipal bonds that are rarely traded in the secondary market because it may be difficult for bond dealers to identify willing buyers of these bonds.

Electronic trading of municipal bonds has become very popular and is less expensive than dealing with a traditional broker. Websites such as E*Trade provide access to information on municipal bonds and allow online buying and selling of municipal bonds.

7-3e **Yields Offered on Municipal Bonds**

The yield offered by a municipal bond differs from the yield on a Treasury bond with the same maturity for three reasons. First, the municipal bond must pay a risk premium to compensate for the possibility of default. Second, the municipal bond must pay a slight premium to compensate for being less liquid than Treasury bonds with the same maturity. Third, as mentioned previously, the income earned from a municipal bond is exempt from federal taxes. This tax advantage of municipal bonds more than offsets their two disadvantages and allows municipal bonds to offer a lower yield than Treasury bonds. The yield on municipal securities is commonly 20 to 30 percent less than the yield offered on Treasury securities with similar maturities. Movements in the yield offered on newly issued municipal bonds are highly correlated with movements in the yield offered on newly issued Treasury securities with similar maturities.

7-4 **Corporate Bonds**

Corporate bonds are long-term debt securities issued by corporations that promise the owner coupon payments (interest) on a semiannual basis. The minimum denomination is $1,000, and their maturity is typically between 10 and 30 years. However, Boeing, Chevron, and other corporations have issued 50-year bonds, and Disney, AT&T, and the Coca-Cola Company have even issued 100-year bonds.

The interest paid by the corporation to investors is tax deductible to the corporation, which reduces the cost of financing with bonds. Equity financing does not offer the same tax advantage because it does not involve interest payments. This is a major reason why many corporations rely heavily on bonds to finance their operations. The Tax Cuts and Jobs Act of 2017 somewhat reduced the tax advantage of financing with bonds by setting a maximum on the amount of interest that corporations can deduct, starting in 2018. The deduction for interest is scheduled to be limited further in 2022.

The interest income earned on corporate bonds represents ordinary income to the bondholders, so it is subject to federal taxes and to state taxes, if any. For this reason, corporate bonds do not provide the same tax benefits to bondholders that municipal bonds do.

7-4a **Corporate Bond Offerings**

Corporate bonds can be placed with investors through a public offering or a private placement.

Public Offering Corporations commonly issue bonds through a public offering. A corporation that plans to issue bonds hires a securities firm to underwrite the bonds. The underwriter assesses the market conditions and attempts to determine both the price at which the corporation's bonds can be sold and the appropriate size (dollar amount) of the offering. The goal is to price the bonds high enough to satisfy the issuer, but low enough so that the entire bond offering can be placed. If the offering is too large or the price is too high, there may not be enough investors who are willing to purchase the bonds. In this case, the underwriter will have to lower the price to sell all the bonds. The issuer registers with the Securities and Exchange Commission (SEC) and submits a *prospectus* that explains the planned size of the offering, its updated financial condition (supported by financial statements), and its planned use of the funds. Meanwhile, the underwriter distributes the prospectus to other securities firms that it invites to join a syndicate that will help place the bonds in the market. Once the SEC approves the issue, the underwriting syndicate attempts to place the bonds. A portion of the bonds that are registered can be shelved for up to two years if the issuer wants to defer placing the entire offering at once.

Underwriters typically try to place newly issued corporate bonds with institutional investors (for example, pension funds, bond mutual funds, and insurance companies) because these investors are more likely to purchase large pieces of the offering. Many institutional investors may plan to hold the bonds for a long-term period, but they can be sold to other investors should their plans change.

For some bond offerings, the arrangement between the underwriter and the issuer is a **firm commitment**, whereby the underwriter guarantees the issuer that all bonds will be sold at a specified price. In such a case, the issuer knows the amount of proceeds that it will receive. The underwriter is exposed to the risk if it cannot sell the bonds. Typically, the underwriter will agree to a firm commitment only if it has already received strong indications of interest from institutional investors. Alternatively, the underwriter may agree to a **best efforts** arrangement, in which it attempts to sell the bonds at a specified price, but makes no guarantee to the issuer.

Timing   The yield that corporations pay to investors on the bonds is highly dependent on the market interest rates at the time of the placement. Some corporations attempt to time their bond offerings when market interest rates are low, so that their cost of financing with bonds will be low.

EXAMPLE

Following the credit crisis that began in 2008, interest rates were very low. As business prospects improved, many corporations, such as Apple, Google, Johnson & Johnson, Microsoft, Netflix, and Twitter, were motivated to raise money by issuing bonds. In 2013, Apple engaged in a $17 billion offering, consisting of 10-year bonds at a yield of less than 2.5 percent and 30-year bonds at a yield of less than 4 percent. Google issued 10-year bonds to raise about $3 billion in 2011 at a yield of about 3.7 percent, just 0.6 percent more than the yield on Treasury securities. In 2014, it raised an additional $1 billion at a yield of about 3.3 percent, which was only about .0.6 percent above the yield on Treasury securities with the same maturity. Apple and Google (now called Alphabet) were not desperate for funds at the time of their bond offerings, but capitalized on the low interest rates so that they would have immediate access to funds when expanding their operations. They used the proceeds to make short-term investments in the money markets until they needed the funds to support or expand their operations. ●

Private Placement   Some corporate bonds are privately placed rather than sold in a public offering. A private placement does not have to be registered with the SEC. Small firms that borrow relatively small amounts of funds (such as $30 million) may consider private placements rather than public offerings, as they may be able to find an institutional investor that will purchase the entire offering. Although the issuer does not need to register with the SEC, it must still disclose financial data to convince any prospective purchasers that the bonds will be repaid in a timely manner. The issuer may hire a securities firm to place the bonds: Such firms specialize in identifying institutional investors interested in purchasing privately placed debt.

The institutional investors that commonly purchase a private placement include insurance companies, pension funds, and bond mutual funds. Because privately placed bonds do not have an active secondary market, they tend to be purchased by institutional investors that are willing to invest for long periods of time. The SEC's Rule 144A creates liquidity for privately placed securities by allowing large institutional investors to trade privately placed bonds (and some other securities) with each other even when the securities need not be registered with the SEC.

Credit Risk of Corporate Bonds   Corporate bonds are subject to the risk of default, and the yield paid by corporations that issue bonds contains a risk premium to reflect the credit risk. The general level of defaults on corporate bonds is a function of economic conditions.

When the economy is strong, firms generate higher revenue and are better able to meet their debt payments, so the risk premium is lower. When the economy is weak (as during the credit crisis of 2008), some firms may not generate sufficient revenue to cover their operating and debt expenses. Under these conditions, they are more likely to default on their bonds. Given this elevated risk, investors will require a higher risk premium to invest in the bonds.

The credit risk of corporate bonds is also related to the corporation's degree of financial leverage. When a corporation borrows an excessive amount of funds, it may not generate sufficient revenue to cover its coupon payments along with its other expenses. Investors may be unwilling to purchase the bonds under these conditions, unless they receive a higher risk premium to compensate for the higher credit risk.

Bond Ratings as a Measure of Credit Risk
When corporations issue bonds, they hire rating agencies to rate their bonds. Corporate bonds that receive higher ratings can be placed at higher prices (lower yields) because they are perceived to have lower credit risk. As the preceding example described, Apple and Google were able to issue bonds at a yield almost as low as the yield on Treasury securities.

Some corporations obtain bond ratings to verify that their bonds qualify for at least investment-grade status (that is, a rating of medium quality or above). Commercial banks will only consider investing in bonds that have an investment-grade rating.

A corporate bond's rating may change over time if the issuer's ability to repay the debt changes in response to a change in economic conditions or a change in the corporation's financial leverage. Many investors rely on the rating agencies to detect potential repayment problems on debt. During the credit crisis, however, the rating agencies were slow to downgrade their ratings on some debt securities that ultimately defaulted.

FINANCIAL REFORM

As a result of the Financial Reform Act of 2010, several changes were made to the rating system. The act established the Office of Credit Ratings within the SEC to oversee the credit rating agencies, which were required to establish new internal controls over their operations and to disclose their methodology for determining ratings. When assigning a rating to an issuer of debt, the agencies must consider credible information from sources other than the issuer. The agencies must also disclose the performance of their ratings over time and are held accountable for poor performance. Their ratings analysts are required to pass qualifying exams, and agencies can be sued for issuing credit ratings that they should have known were inaccurate. As a result of these changes, the rating systems have become more transparent overall.

However, the Financial Reform Act did not change the fee structure, whereby debt issuers pay fees to credit rating agencies to have their debt rated. Some critics argue that as long as the agencies are paid by the issuers whose debt they are rating, the potential exists for agencies to inflate those ratings.

Junk Bonds
Corporate bonds that are perceived to have very high risk are referred to as **junk bonds**. The primary investors in junk bonds are mutual funds, life insurance companies, and pension funds. Some bond mutual funds invest only in bonds with high ratings, but more than 100 *high-yield* mutual funds commonly invest in junk bonds. High-yield mutual funds allow individual investors to invest in a diversified portfolio of junk bonds with a small investment. Junk bonds offer high yields that contain a risk premium (spread) to compensate investors for the high risk. Typically, the premium is between 3 and 7 percentage points above Treasury bonds with the same maturity.

Although investors always require a higher *yield* on junk bonds than on other bonds, the premium is more pronounced when the economy is weak because there is a greater likelihood that the issuer will not generate sufficient cash to cover the debt payments. During the credit crisis of 2008–2009, the yields on junk bonds were very high (such as between 15 and 20 percent) because of concerns that these bonds would default. During the credit crisis, junk bonds valued at more than $25 billion defaulted.

Nevertheless, the junk bond market remains popular. In 2017, corporations issued junk bonds valued at more than $300 billion. Many of these firms applied the funds obtained in this way to refinance their operations, because they were able to replace their existing debt that had higher interest rates with debt at lower interest rates (though they still had to pay a high risk premium). Investors may be more willing to purchase junk bonds when it is used for this type of purpose than when it is used to support acquisitions or other types of corporate expansion. In addition, many institutional investors (such as bond mutual funds) have been more willing to invest in junk bonds because the yields on more highly rated bonds are so low.

7-4b Secondary Market for Corporate Bonds

Corporate bonds have a secondary market, so investors who purchase them can sell them to other investors if they prefer not to hold the bonds until maturity. The value of all corporate bonds in the secondary market exceeds $9 trillion. Corporate bonds are listed on an over-the-counter market or on an exchange such as the NYSE American (formerly the American Stock Exchange). More than a thousand bonds are listed on the New York Stock Exchange (NYSE). Corporations whose stocks are listed on the exchange can list their bonds for free.

Dealer Role in Secondary Market The secondary market is served by bond dealers, who can play a broker role by matching up buyers and sellers. Bond dealers also have an inventory of bonds, so they can serve as the counterparty in a bond transaction desired by an investor. For example, if an investor wants to sell bonds that were previously issued by the Coca-Cola Company, bond dealers may execute the deal either by matching the seller with investors who want to buy the bonds or by purchasing the bonds for their own inventories. Dealers commonly handle large transactions, such as those valued at more than $1 million. Information about the trades in the over-the-counter market is provided by the Financial Industry Regulatory Authority's Trade Reporting and Compliance Engine (TRACE). Under rules issued by the Securities and Exchange Commission, dealers must report their transactions to TRACE.

Liquidity in Secondary Market Bonds issued by large, well-known corporations in large volume are liquid because they attract a large number of buyers and sellers in the secondary market. Bonds issued by small corporations in small volume are less liquid because there may be few buyers (or no buyers) for those bonds in some periods. Thus, investors who wish to sell these bonds in the secondary market may have to accept a discounted price to attract buyers. Approximately 95 percent of the trading volume of corporate bonds in the secondary market is attributed to institutional investors.

A company often issues many different bonds with variations in maturity, price, and credit rating. Offering many different bonds allows investors to find a bond issued by a particular company that fits their desired maturity and other preferences. However, such specialized bonds may exhibit reduced liquidity because they may appeal to only a small group of investors. The trading of these bonds will require higher transaction costs, because brokers require more time to execute transactions for investors.

Electronic Bond Networks Electronic bond networks have been established that can match institutional investors that wish to sell some bond holdings or purchase additional bonds in the over-the-counter bond market at a lower transaction cost. Trading platforms have been created by financial institutions such as JPMorgan Chase and Goldman Sachs so that institutional investors can execute bond trades in the secondary market. The institutional investors that wish to purchase bonds can use these platforms to identify bond holdings that are for sale by other institutional investors in the secondary market, and can purchase the bonds electronically, without relying on bond dealers. They pay a small fee (percentage of their transactions) for the use of the trading platforms. However, participation by investors in electronic bond networks is limited, so institutional investors interested in purchasing bonds cannot always find the bonds that they desire.

The NYSE developed an electronic bond trading platform for the bonds sold on its exchange as part of its strategy to increase its presence in the corporate bond market. It allows for greater transparency, as investors have access to real-time data and can more easily monitor the prices and trading volume of corporate bonds.

Types of Orders through Brokers   Individual investors buy or sell corporate bonds through brokers, who communicate the orders to bond dealers. Investors who wish to buy or sell bonds can usually place a **market order**; in this case, the desired transaction will occur at the prevailing market price. Alternatively, they can place a **limit order**; in this case, the transaction will occur only if the price reaches the specified limit. When purchasing bonds, investors use a limit order to specify the maximum limit price they are willing to pay for a bond. When selling bonds, investors use a limit order to specify a minimum limit price at which they are willing to sell their bonds.

Trading Online   Orders to buy and sell corporate bonds are increasingly being placed online at brokerage websites such as www.schwab.com and http://us.etrade.com. The pricing of bonds is more transparent online because investors can easily compare the bid and ask spreads among brokers. This transparency has encouraged some brokers to narrow their spreads so that they do not lose business to competitors. Especially when purchasing or selling less liquid bonds, it can be helpful to check recent transactions on TRACE to determine what the bid and ask spreads have been.

Some online bond brokerage services, such as Fidelity and Vanguard, now charge a commission instead of posting a bid and ask spread, which ensures that investors can easily understand the fee structure. There is also a standard fee for every trade, whereas bid and ask spreads may vary among bonds. For example, the fee may be $2 per bond with a $25 minimum. Thus, an investor who purchases 30 bonds would pay a total fee of $60 (computed as 30 × $2). Online bond brokerage services can execute transactions in Treasury and municipal bonds as well. Their fees are generally lower for Treasury bond transactions than for corporate bond transactions but higher for municipal bond transactions.

7-4c Characteristics of Corporate Bonds

Corporate bonds can be described in terms of several characteristics. The bond **indenture** is a legal document specifying the rights and obligations of both the issuing firm and the bondholders. It is comprehensive (typically several hundred pages in length) and is designed to address all matters related to the bond issue (such as collateral, payment dates, default provisions, and call provisions).

Federal law requires that for each bond issue of significant size, a trustee be appointed to represent the bondholders in all matters concerning the bond issue. The trustee's duties include monitoring the issuing firm's activities to ensure compliance with the terms of the indenture. If the terms are violated, the trustee initiates legal action against the issuing firm and represents the bondholders in that action. Bank trust departments are frequently hired to perform the duties of trustee.

Bonds are not as standardized as stocks. A single corporation may issue more than 50 different bonds with different maturities and payment terms. Some of the characteristics that differentiate one bond from another are identified here.

WEB

www.investinginbonds
.com
This website contains
much useful information
about corporate bonds.

Sinking-Fund Provision

Bond indentures frequently include a **sinking-fund provision**, a requirement that the firm retire a certain amount of the bond issue each year. This provision is considered to be an advantage to the remaining bondholders because it reduces the payments necessary at maturity.

Specific sinking-fund provisions can vary significantly among bond issues. For example, a bond with 20 years until maturity could have a provision to retire 5 percent of the bond issue each year. Alternatively, it could have a requirement to retire 5 percent each year beginning in the fifth year, with the remaining amount to be retired at maturity. The actual mechanics of bond retirement are carried out by the trustee.

Protective Covenants

Bond indentures usually place restrictions on the issuing firm that are designed to protect bondholders from being exposed to increasing risk during the investment period. These so-called protective covenants frequently limit the amount of dividends and corporate officers' salaries that the firm can pay as well as restrict the amount of additional debt the firm can issue. Other financial policies may also be restricted for the firm.

Protective covenants are needed because shareholders and bondholders have different expectations of a firm's management. Shareholders may prefer that managers use a relatively large amount of debt because they can benefit directly from risky managerial decisions that will generate higher returns on investment. In contrast, bondholders simply hope to receive their principal back, with interest. Because they do not share in the excess returns generated by a firm, they would prefer that managerial decisions be conservative. Protective covenants can prevent managers from taking excessive risk, so they cater to the preferences of bondholders. If managers are unwilling to accept some protective covenants, they may not be able to obtain debt financing.

Call Provisions

Most corporate bonds include a provision allowing the firm to call the bonds. A **call provision** usually requires the firm to pay a price above par value when it calls its bonds. The difference between the bond's call price and par value is the **call premium**. Call provisions have two main uses. First, if market interest rates decline after a bond issue has been sold, the firm might end up paying a higher rate of interest than the prevailing rate for a long period of time. Under these circumstances, the firm may consider selling a new issue of bonds with a lower interest rate and using the proceeds to retire the previous issue by calling the old bonds.

EXAMPLE

Four years ago, Mirossa Company issued 10-year bonds that offered a yield of 11 percent. Since then, interest rates have declined, and Mirossa's credit rating has improved. It could issue 10-year bonds today for a yield of 7 percent. The company is sure that it will need funding for the next 10 years. Therefore, it issues new 10-year bonds at a yield of 7 percent and uses some of the proceeds to call (buy back) the bonds issued four years ago. It reduces its cost of financing as a result of calling these bonds. Ten years from today, Mirossa Company will repay the principal on the newly issued bonds. ●

Second, a call provision may be used to retire bonds as required by a sinking-fund provision. Many bonds have two different call prices: a lower price for calling the bonds to meet sinking-fund requirements and a higher price if the bonds are called for any other reason.

Bondholders view a call provision as a disadvantage because it can disrupt their investment plans and reduce their investment returns. As a result, firms must pay slightly higher rates of interest on bonds that are callable, other things being equal.

Bond Collateral   Bonds can be classified according to whether they are secured by collateral and by the nature of that collateral. Usually, the collateral is a mortgage on real property (land and buildings). A **first mortgage bond** has first claim on the specified assets. A **chattel mortgage bond** is secured by personal property.

Bonds unsecured by specific property are called **debentures** (backed only by the general credit of the issuing firm). These bonds are issued by large, financially sound firms whose ability to service the debt is not in question. **Subordinated debentures** have claims against the firm's assets that are junior to the claims of both mortgage bonds and regular debentures. Owners of subordinated debentures receive nothing until the claims of mortgage bondholders, regular debenture owners, and secured short-term creditors have been satisfied. The main purchasers of subordinated debt are pension funds and insurance companies.

Low- and Zero-Coupon Bonds   **Low-coupon bonds** and **zero-coupon bonds** are long-term debt securities that are issued at a deep discount from par value. Investors are taxed annually on the amount of interest earned, even though much or all of the interest will not be received until maturity. The amount of interest taxed is the *amortized discount*. (The gain at maturity is prorated over the life of the bond.) Low- and zero-coupon corporate bonds are purchased mainly for tax-exempt investment accounts (such as pension funds and individual retirement accounts).

To the issuing firm, these bonds have the advantage of requiring low or no cash outflow during their life. Additionally, the firm is permitted to deduct the amortized discount as interest expense for federal income tax purposes, even though it does not pay interest.

WEB

finra-markets
.morningstar.com
/BondCenter
Yields on all types
of bonds for various
maturities.

Variable-Rate Bonds   **Variable-rate bonds** (also called floating-rate bonds) are long-term debt securities with a coupon rate that is periodically adjusted. Most of these bonds tie their coupon rate to the London Interbank Offer Rate (LIBOR), the rate at which banks lend funds to each other on an international basis. The coupon rate is typically adjusted every three months.

Variable-rate bonds tend to be popular near the end of a period of low interest rates. After the credit crisis of 2008, interest rates remained low for a number of years. In 2013, the amount of variable-rate bonds issued was double the amount issued in the previous year. Because many investors believed that interest rates were likely to rise in the future, they were more willing to purchase variable-rate bonds. Coca-Cola, Johnson & Johnson, and Bank of America were among the companies issuing variable-rate bonds at this time.

Convertibility   A **convertible bond** allows investors to exchange the bond for a stated number of shares of the firm's common stock. This conversion feature offers investors the potential for high returns if the price of the firm's common stock rises. For this reason, investors are willing to accept a lower rate of interest on these bonds, which allows the firm to obtain financing at a lower cost. Convertible bonds have been popular in recent years, as they have offered corporations a way to obtain funds at a low cost due to low interest rates, yet they offer some upside potential for investors due to the conversion feature. In a recent year, Twitter raised more than $900 million from issuing convertible bonds.

7-4d How Corporate Bonds Finance Restructuring

Firms can issue corporate bonds to finance the restructuring of their assets and to revise their capital structure. Such restructuring can have a major impact on the firm's degree of financial leverage, the potential return to shareholders, the risk to shareholders, and the risk to bondholders.

Using Bonds to Finance a Leveraged Buyout   A leveraged buyout (LBO) involves the use of debt to purchase shares and take a company private. The proceeds from the debt are used to buy the outstanding shares of stock, so that the firm is owned by a small number of owners. To cover the large debt payments, the owners might sell some of the assets of the firm for cash.

Many firms that engaged in an LBO go public once they have improved their operating performance. They typically use some of the proceeds from the stock issuance to retire a portion of their outstanding debt, thereby reducing their periodic interest payments on the debt. This process is more feasible for firms that can issue shares of stock for high prices: The proceeds will then retire a larger amount of outstanding debt. Firms commonly go public during a period when stock prices are generally high because, under these conditions, they will be able to sell their stock at a higher price.

Using Bonds to Revise the Capital Structure   Corporations commonly issue bonds to revise their capital structure. If managers believe that the company will have sufficient cash flows to cover its debt payments, they may consider using more debt and less equity, which implies a higher degree of financial leverage. Debt is usually perceived to be a cheaper source of capital than equity as long as the corporation can meet its debt payments. Furthermore, a high degree of financial leverage allows the firm's earnings to be distributed to a smaller group of shareholders. In some cases, corporations issue bonds and then use the proceeds to repurchase some of their existing stock, a strategy referred to as a **debt-for-equity swap**.

When corporations use an excessive amount of debt, they may be unable to make their debt payments. Hence they may seek to revise their capital structure by reducing their level of debt. In an equity-for-debt swap, corporations issue stock and use the proceeds to retire existing debt.

7-4e Collateralized Debt Obligations

Corporate bonds are sometimes packaged by commercial banks into collateralized debt obligations (CDOs), in which investors receive the interest or principal payments generated by the debt securities. For example, a CDO might consist of many corporate bonds or loans intended to finance leveraged buyouts. This type of package enables the financial institutions that provided the initial funding to sell their loans in the secondary market; they can then use the proceeds from these sales to support other operations. In addition to corporate debt securities, some CDOs contain other types of debt such as credit card loans, car loans, and commercial or residential mortgages.

Investors who purchase a CDO are essentially investing in a diversified portfolio of debt securities. The CDO is backed (collateralized) by the assets that were purchased with the proceeds from issuing debt. It is segmented into slices ("tranches"), whereby the cash flows derived from the debt securities are prioritized by seniority. Each tranche is rated by a credit rating agency: The most senior tranches may receive a very high credit rating, whereas tranches with lower priority receive lower credit ratings. The investment in a tranche is priced to generate an expected return to investors that compensates them for their risk. Thus, investors who invest in a tranche with a lower priority will earn a higher return, as long as the securities in the tranche ultimately make all the expected payments. However, the investors face the risk that the payments on the bonds or loans will be late or not made at all by the firms that received the financing.

In the 2004–2007 period, investors were willing to buy CDOs without much concern about their risk. This encouraged some securities firms to include higher-risk securities in their CDOs. Furthermore, credit rating agencies collected a fee for rating the CDOs and commonly assigned high ratings to them. Many investors relied heavily on the rating agencies for the assessment of risk. The credit ratings assigned to the CDOs proved to be more favorable than deserved, as many CDOs experienced payment problems after the credit crisis began in 2008.

7-5 Globalization of Bond and Loan Markets

In recent years, financial institutions such as pension funds, insurance companies, and commercial banks have often purchased foreign bonds. For example, the pension funds of ExxonMobil, United Technologies, and IBM frequently invest in foreign bonds with the intention of achieving higher returns for their employees. Many public pension funds also invest in foreign bonds for the same reason. Because of the frequent cross-border investments in bonds, bond markets have become increasingly integrated among countries. In addition, mutual funds containing U.S. securities are accessible to foreign investors.

Furthermore, financial institutions commonly provide large loans to customers in other countries. The globalization process has created a much more integrated market for long-term debt. This integration allows corporations or governments to more easily access funds, but has the potential to allow one country's financial problems to spread to other countries.

7-5a Global Government Debt Markets

One of the most important global markets is the market for government debt. In general, bonds issued by foreign governments (referred to as *sovereign* bonds) are attractive to investors because of the government's ability to meet debt obligations. Even so, some country governments have defaulted on their bonds, including Argentina (1982, 1989, 1990, 2001), Brazil (1986, 1989, 1991), Costa Rica (1989), Russia and other former Soviet republics (1993, 1998), and the former Yugoslavia (1992). Given that sovereign bonds are exposed to credit risk, credit ratings are assigned to them by Moody's and Standard & Poor's.

To the extent that a government borrows from creditors based in other countries, the government's default on debt can impose financial distress on those creditors. For example, if a country's large financial institutions that provided credit are not repaid, they may not be able to repay their own respective bank depositors who provided the institutions with funds. If a country's government that provided credit to another country is not repaid, it may not be able to cover its debt obligations from bonds that it previously issued. Thus, its bondholders could suffer losses. In this way, the globalization of debt might allow a single country's debt crisis to spread globally.

Greek Debt Crisis In the spring of 2010, Greece experienced a credit crisis brought on by weak economic conditions and a large government budget deficit. In May 2010, the other eurozone countries and the International Monetary Fund (IMF) agreed to provide loans to the Greek government totaling 110 billion euros (the equivalent of $120 billion) over a three-year period. As a condition of receiving the loans, the Greek government was required to reduce its budget deficit over time.

Despite this promise, Greece's government continued to spend much more money than it generated from taxes, and in 2012 it needed another bailout. Governments and other creditors in the eurozone provided new loans of about 130 billion euros (the equivalent of $150 billion), with the conditions that Greece institute austerity measures and reduce its spending. Greece did not meet those conditions, however, and in July 2015 it stopped making payments on its loans and announced that it needed 53 billion euros ($60 billion) in additional loans. This request led to many arguments among the eurozone countries. On the one hand, the additional credit could stabilize Greece and, in turn, stabilize the eurozone countries that were exposed to the Greek crisis. On the other hand, the additional credit would increase those countries' exposure to Greece's problems, which might result in greater damage if Greece ultimately defaulted on the loans. Thus, this example illustrates the potential problems that may arise when credit is extended beyond a country's borders.

As of August 2019, Greece's debt level was estimated to be the equivalent of more than $360 billion. Because some European governments served as major creditors for Greece, they were subject to potential credit contagion. A default by Greece on its debt could strain the budgets of other European governments that served as its creditors.

WEB

www.bloomberg.com
Yield curves of major
countries' government
securities.

7-6 Other Types of Long-term Debt Securities

In recent years, other types of long-term debt securities have been created. Some of the more popular types are discussed here.

7-6a Structured Notes

Some firms choose to borrow funds by issuing structured notes. For these notes, the amount of interest and principal to be paid is based on specified market conditions. The amount of the repayment may be tied to a Treasury bond price index or even to a stock index or a particular currency. Sometimes issuers use structured notes to reduce their risk. For example, a structured product may specify that the principal payment will decline if bond prices decline. A bond portfolio manager who needs to borrow funds could partially insulate the portfolio from risk by using structured notes, because the required repayments on the notes would decline if the bond market (and therefore the manager's bond portfolio) performed poorly.

Structured notes became popular in the 1990s, when many participants took positions in the notes in their quest for a high return. One reason for the popularity of structured notes is that some investors may be able to use them to bet indirectly on (or against) a specific market that some restrictions prevent them from betting on directly.

EXAMPLE   The pension fund manager at Cicero Company wants to invest in Brazilian bonds, but the fund has specific restrictions against investing in emerging markets. The restrictions are intended to prevent the manager from taking excessive risk, because she is investing the money that will provide pensions for Cicero's employees when they retire. However, the manager's annual bonus is directly tied to how well the portfolio performs, so she wants to pursue strategies that might generate large returns. She can invest in a structured note issued by a highly rated securities firm that provides large payments when Brazilian bonds perform well. The pension fund's investment holdings will show that it owns a structured product issued by a highly rated securities firm. In this way, the manager circumvents the restrictions and her portfolio has a chance to generate a higher return, although it is also exposed to substantial risk. ●

Risk of Structured Notes   In the early 1990s, the portfolio manager responsible for managing more than $7 billion on behalf of Orange County, California, invested in structured notes that would earn high returns if interest rates declined. The portfolio manager guessed wrong and interest rates increased, which caused the values of the notes to decline substantially. The portfolio manager attempted to make up for the losses by borrowing funds and investing more money in structured notes, but these investments also performed poorly. In 1994, Orange County filed for bankruptcy.

Many other state and local governments also suffered losses because their portfolio managers had invested in structured notes. In essence, the portfolio managers took excessive risks with the state and local government money. These managers benefited directly by receiving substantial bonuses or raises when their investments generated high returns. Their investments were questioned only after they suffered losses.

Given the difficulty of assessing the risk of structured notes, some investors rely on credit ratings for such risk assessment. However, credit ratings of structured notes have not always served as accurate indicators of risk. The structured notes purchased by Orange County were, in fact, rated AAA. Apparently, neither the portfolio manager nor the rating agencies understood the risk of those structured notes. The credit ratings of structured notes have been revised frequently over time, and most of the revisions have been downward. In 2018, Wells Fargo Advisors agreed to pay $4.1 million to settle SEC charges related to its sales of structured notes. The SEC argued that the brokers had failed to disclose all the risks and fees associated with structured notes.

7-6b Exchange-Traded Notes

Exchange-traded notes (ETNs) are debt instruments in which the issuer promises to pay a return based on the performance of a specific debt index after deducting specified fees. The debt typically has a maturity of 10 to 30 years and is not secured by assets, which means that investors are subject to default risk. Issuers of ETNs often include securities firms such as Goldman Sachs and Morgan Stanley. Because ETNs can contain commodities and foreign currencies, they are not legally defined as mutual funds and so are not subject to mutual fund regulations. Therefore, ETNs have more flexibility to use leverage, which means that the funding for the portfolio of debt instruments is enhanced by borrowed funds. This leverage creates a higher potential return for investors in ETNs, but also results in a higher risk. Although leverage magnifies any gain that investors receive, it also exacerbates any loss.

7-6c Auction-Rate Securities

Auction-rate securities have been used since the 1980s as a way for specific borrowers (for example, municipalities and student loan organizations) to borrow for long-term periods while relying on a series of short-term investments by investors. Every 7 to 35 days, the securities can be auctioned off to other investors, and the issuer pays interest based on the new *reset rate* to the winning bidders. The market for auction-rate securities reached $330 billion in 2008. Corporations and individuals with available cash are typical investors in auction-rate securities. Investors can invest for a long-term period or can liquidate their securities to fit their preferred investment horizon. When investors want to sell, the financial institutions that served as intermediaries either repurchase the securities or find other willing buyers.

The auction-rate market suffered in 2008 because some financial institutions were unable to find other buyers and no longer wanted to repurchase the securities. Consequently, when investors wanted to sell their securities at an auction, the financial institutions told them that their investments were frozen and could not be sold for lack of sufficient demand. The values of some of these securities declined substantially, and investors claimed that they had not been informed of the limited liquidity and the risks involved. In response to pressure from the SEC and state regulators, some financial institutions agreed to buy back the securities at face value from individuals who had previously purchased them. These problems occurred after the credit crisis began, when many financial institutions already were holding other types of securities (such as securities backed by subprime mortgages) whose values and liquidity had declined substantially. Although more than $40 billion in auction-rate notes issued before the credit crisis is still outstanding, most auctions fail because of lack of investor interest.

Summary

- Bonds are issued to finance government expenditures, housing, and corporate expenditures. Many financial institutions, such as commercial banks, issue bonds to finance their operations. In addition, most types of financial institutions are major investors in bonds.

- Bonds can be classified in four categories according to the type of issuer: Treasury bonds, federal agency bonds, municipal bonds, and corporate bonds. The issuers of each type of bond are perceived to have different levels of credit risk. In addition, the bonds themselves have different degrees of liquidity and different provisions. Thus, quoted yields at a given point in time vary across bonds.

- Bond yields vary among countries. Investors are attracted to high bond yields in foreign countries,

causing funds to flow to those countries. Consequently, bond markets have become globally integrated.

- Structured notes are long-term debt instruments that allow investors to bet indirectly on or against a specific market that they cannot bet on directly because of restrictions. Exchange-traded notes are debt instruments in which the issuer promises to pay a return based on the performance of a specific debt index after deducting specified fees. Because ETNs are not legally defined as mutual funds, they are not subject to mutual fund regulations. They also have more flexibility to use leverage, which can achieve higher returns for investors but also results in higher risk.

Point/Counterpoint

Should Financial Institutions Invest in Junk Bonds?

Point Yes. Financial institutions have managers who are capable of weighing the risk against the potential return. They can earn a significantly higher return when investing in junk bonds than the return on Treasury bonds. Their shareholders benefit when they increase the return on the portfolio.

Counterpoint No. The financial system is based on trust in financial institutions and confidence that the financial institutions will survive. If financial institutions take on excessive risk, the entire financial system is at risk.

Who Is Correct? Use the Internet to learn more about this issue and then formulate your own opinion.

Questions and Applications

1. **Bond Indenture** What is a bond indenture? What is the function of a trustee with respect to the bond indenture?

2. **Sinking-Fund Provision** Explain the use of a sinking-fund provision. How can it reduce the investor's risk?

3. **Protective Covenants** What are protective covenants? Why are they needed?

4. **Call Provisions** Explain the use of call provisions on bonds. How can a call provision affect the price of a bond?

5. **Bond Collateral** Explain the use of bond collateral, and identify the common types of collateral for bonds.

6. **Debentures** What are debentures? How do they differ from subordinated debentures?

7. **Zero-Coupon Bonds** What are the advantages and disadvantages to a firm that issues low- or zero-coupon bonds?

8. **Variable-Rate Bonds** Are variable-rate bonds attractive to investors who expect interest rates to decrease? Explain. Would a firm that needs to borrow funds consider issuing variable-rate bonds if it expects interest rates to decrease in the future? Explain.

9. **Convertible Bonds** Why can convertible bonds be issued by firms at a higher price than other bonds?

10. **Global Interaction of Bond Yields** If bond yields in Japan rise, how might U.S. bond yields be affected? Why?

11. **Impact of the Credit Crisis on Junk Bonds** Explain how the credit crisis that began in 2008 affected the default rates of junk bonds and the risk premiums offered on newly issued junk bonds.

12. Guidelines for Credit Rating Agencies Explain the guidelines for credit rating agencies that resulted from the Financial Reform Act of 2010.

13. Impact of Greek Debt Crisis Explain the conditions that led to the debt crisis in Greece.

14. Bond Downgrade Explain how the downgrading of bonds for a particular corporation affects the prices of those bonds, the return to investors who currently hold these bonds, and the potential return to other investors who may invest in the bonds in the near future.

Advanced Questions

15. Junk Bonds Merrito, Inc., is a large U.S. firm that issued bonds several years ago. Its bond ratings declined over time and, about a year ago, the bonds were rated in the junk bond classification. Nevertheless, investors continued to buy the bonds in the secondary market because of the attractive yield they offered. Last week, Merrito defaulted on its bonds, and the prices of most other junk bonds declined abruptly on the same day. Explain why news of Merrito's financial problems could cause the prices of junk bonds issued by other firms to decrease, even when those firms had no business relationships with Merrito. Explain why the prices of those junk bonds with less liquidity declined more than those with a high degree of liquidity.

16. Event Risk An insurance company purchased bonds issued by Hartnett Company two years ago. Today, Hartnett Company has begun to issue junk bonds and is using the funds to repurchase most of its existing stock. Why might the market value of those bonds held by the insurance company be affected by this action?

17. Exchange-Traded Notes Explain what exchange-traded notes are and how they are used. Why are they risky?

18. Auction-Rate Securities Explain why the market for auction-rate securities suffered in 2008.

19. Role of the Bond Market Explain how the bond market facilitates a government's fiscal policy. How do you think the bond market could discipline a government and discourage the government from borrowing (and spending) excessively?

Critical Thinking Question

Integration of Bond Markets Write a short essay on the integration of bond markets. Explain why adverse conditions within one bond market (such as a particular country) commonly spread to other bond markets.

Interpreting Financial News

Interpret the following statements made by Wall Street analysts and portfolio managers.

a. "The values of some stocks are dependent on the bond market. When investors are not interested in junk bonds, the values of stocks ripe for leveraged buyouts decline."

b. "The recent practice in which firms use debt to repurchase some of their stock is a good strategy as long as the firms can withstand the stagnant economy."

c. "Although yields among bonds are related, today's rumors of a tax cut caused an increase in the yield on municipal bonds, while the yield on corporate bonds declined."

Managing in Financial Markets

Forecasting Bond Returns As a portfolio manager for an insurance company, you are about to invest funds in one of three possible investments: (1) 10-year coupon bonds issued by the U.S. Treasury, (2) 20-year zero-coupon bonds issued by the Treasury, or (3) one-year Treasury securities. Each possible investment is perceived to have no risk of default. You plan to maintain this investment for a one-year period. The return of each investment over a one-year horizon will be about the same if interest rates do not change over the next year. However, you anticipate that the U.S. inflation rate will decline substantially over the next year, while most of the other portfolio managers in the United States expect inflation to increase slightly.

a. If your expectations are correct, how will the return of each investment be affected over the one-year horizon?

b. If your expectations are correct, which of the three investments should have the highest return over the one-year horizon? Why?

c. Offer one reason why you might not select the investment that would have the highest expected return over the one-year investment horizon.

Problems

1. Inflation-Indexed Treasury Bond An inflation-indexed Treasury bond has a par value of $1,000 and a coupon rate of 6 percent. An investor purchases this bond and holds it for one year. During the year, the consumer price index increases by 1 percent every six months. What are the total interest payments that the investor will receive during the year?

2. Inflation-Indexed Treasury Bond Assume that the U.S. economy experienced deflation during the year and that the consumer price index decreased by 1 percent in the first six months of the year and by 2 percent during the second six months of the year. If an investor had purchased inflation-indexed Treasury bonds with a par value of $10,000 and a coupon rate of 5 percent, how much would she have received in interest during the year?

Flow of Funds Exercise

Financing in the Bond Markets

If the economy continues to be strong, Carson Company may need to increase its production capacity by about 50 percent over the next few years to satisfy demand. It would need financing to expand and accommodate the increase in production. Recall that the yield curve is currently upward sloping. Also recall that Carson is concerned about a possible slowing of the economy because of potential Fed actions to reduce inflation. It needs funding to cover payments for supplies. It is also considering issuing stock or bonds to raise funds in the next year.

a. Assume that Carson has two choices to satisfy the increased demand for its products. On the one hand, it could increase production by 10 percent with its existing facilities by obtaining short-term financing to cover the extra production expense and then using a portion of the revenue received to finance this level of production in the future. On the other hand, it could issue bonds and use the proceeds to buy a larger facility that would allow for 50 percent more capacity. Which alternative should Carson select?

b. Carson currently has a large amount of debt, and its assets have already been pledged to back up its existing debt. It does not have additional collateral. At this time, the credit risk premium it would pay is similar in the short-term and long-term debt markets. Does this imply that the cost of financing is the same in both markets?

c. Should Carson consider using a call provision if it issues bonds? Why? Why might Carson decide not to include a call provision on the bonds?

d. If Carson issues bonds, it would be a relatively small bond offering. Should Carson consider a private placement of bonds? Which type of investor might be interested in participating in a private placement? Do you think Carson could offer the same yield on a private placement as it could on a public placement? Explain.

e. Financial institutions such as insurance companies and pension funds commonly purchase bonds. Explain the flow of funds that runs through these financial institutions and ultimately reaches corporations that issue bonds such as Carson Company.

Internet/Excel Exercise

Go to www.wsj.com/us and click on "Rates." Compare the rate of a 10-year Treasury bond to a 10-year municipal bond. Which type of bond would offer you a higher annual yield based on your tax bracket, given that the municipal bond is not subject to federal income taxes? Determine the premium contained in the yield of a 10-year corporate A-rated bond as compared with the 10-year Treasury bonds. Compare that premium to the premium that existed one month ago. Did the premium increase or decrease? Offer an explanation for the change. Is the change attributed to economic conditions?

WSJ Exercise

Impact of Treasury Financing on Bond Prices

The U.S. Treasury periodically issues new bonds to finance the deficit. Review recent issues of *The Wall Street Journal* or check related online news to find a recent article on such financing. Does the article suggest that financial markets are expecting upward pressure on interest rates as a result of the Treasury financing? What happened to prices of existing bonds when the Treasury announced its intentions to issue new bonds?

Online Articles with Real-World Examples

Find a recent practical article available online that describes a real-world example regarding a specific financial institution or financial market that reinforces one or more concepts covered in this chapter.

If your class has an online component, your professor may ask you to post your summary of the article there and provide a link to the article so that other students can access it. If your class is live, your professor may ask you to summarize your application of the article in class. Your professor may assign specific students to complete this assignment or may allow any students to do the assignment on a volunteer basis.

For recent online articles and real-world examples related to this chapter, consider using the following search terms (be sure to include the prevailing year as a search term to ensure that the online articles are recent):

1. Treasury bond AND yield
2. Treasury bond AND return
3. bond AND federal agency
4. stripped Treasury bond
5. inflation-indexed Treasury bond
6. municipal bond AND risk
7. [name of a specific financial institution] AND bond
8. bond AND private placement
9. junk bond AND financing
10. structured notes

8

Bond Valuation and Risk

CHAPTER
OBJECTIVES

The specific objectives
of this chapter are to:

- Explain how bonds
  are priced.

- Identify the factors
  that affect bond
  prices.

- Explain how the
  sensitivity of bond
  prices to interest
  rates depends on
  particular bond
  characteristics.

- Describe common
  strategies used to
  invest in bonds.

- Explain the
  valuation and risk of
  international bonds.

The values of bonds can change substantially over time. Hence, financial institutions that consider buying or selling bonds closely monitor their values.

8-1 Bond Valuation Process

Bonds are debt obligations with long-term maturities that are commonly issued by governments or corporations to obtain long-term funds. They are also purchased by financial institutions that wish to invest funds for long-term periods.

Bond valuation is conceptually similar to the valuation of capital budgeting projects, businesses, or even real estate. The appropriate price reflects the present value of the cash flows to be generated by the bond in the form of periodic interest (or coupon) payments and the principal payment to be provided at maturity. The coupon payment is based on the coupon rate multiplied by the par value of the bond. Thus, a bond with a 9 percent coupon rate and $1,000 par value pays $90 in coupon payments per year. Because these expected cash flows are known, the valuation of bonds is generally perceived to be easier than the valuation of equity securities.

The current price of a bond should be the present value (PV) of its remaining cash flows:

$$PV \text{ of bond} = \frac{C}{(1+k)^1} + \frac{C}{(1+k)^2} + \cdots + \frac{C + \text{Par}}{(1+k)^n}$$

where

C = coupon payment provided in each period

Par = par value

k = required rate of return per period used to discount the bond

n = number of periods to maturity

EXAMPLE Consider a bond that has a par value of $1,000, pays $100 at the end of each year in coupon payments, and has three years remaining until maturity. Assume that the prevailing annualized yield on other bonds with similar characteristics is 12 percent. In this case, the appropriate price of the bond can be determined as follows. The future cash flows to investors who would purchase this bond are $100 in Year 1, $100 in

Exhibit 8.1   Valuation of a Three-Year Bond

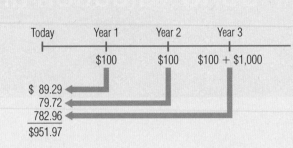

Year 2, and $1,100 (computed as $100 in coupon payments plus $1,000 par value) in Year 3. The appropriate market price of the bond is its present value:

$$PV \text{ of bond} = \frac{\$100}{(1+0.12)^1} + \frac{\$100}{(1+0.12)^2} + \frac{\$1,100}{(1+0.12)^3}$$
$$= \$89.29 + \$79.72 + \$782.96$$
$$= \$951.97$$

This valuation procedure is illustrated in Exhibit 8.1. Because this example assumes that investors require a 12 percent return, k is set equal to 0.12. At the price of $951.97, the bondholders purchasing this bond will receive a 12 percent annualized return. ●

WEB

www.finpipe.com
/bond-valuation
More information on
the process of valuing
bonds.

When using a financial calculator, the present value of the bond in the previous example can be determined as follows (calculator shows PV as a negative value):

INPUT	3	12	100	1000		
Function Key	N	I	PMT	FV	CPT	PV
Answer						951.97

8-1a Impact of the Discount Rate on Bond Valuation

The discount rate selected to compute the present value is critical to accurate valuation of the bond. Exhibit 8.2 shows the wide range of present values that result from using different discount rates for a $10,000 payment in 10 years. The appropriate discount rate for valuing any asset is the yield that could be earned on alternative investments with similar risk and maturity.

Because investors require higher returns on riskier securities, they use higher discount rates to discount the future cash flows of these securities. Consequently, a high-risk security will have a lower value than a low-risk security with the same expected cash flows.

8-1b Impact of the Timing of Payments on Bond Valuation

The market price of a bond is also affected by the timing of the payments made to bondholders. Funds received sooner can be reinvested to earn additional returns. In consequence, a dollar to be received soon has a higher present value than one to be received later. The impact of maturity on the present value of a $10,000 payment is shown in Exhibit 8.3 (assuming that a return of 10 percent could be earned on available funds). The $10,000 payment has a present value of $8,264 if it is to be paid in two years. This implies that if $8,264 were invested today and earned 10 percent annually, it would be worth $10,000 in two years.

Exhibit 8.2   Relationship between Discount Rate and Present Value of $10,000 Payment to Be Received in 10 Years

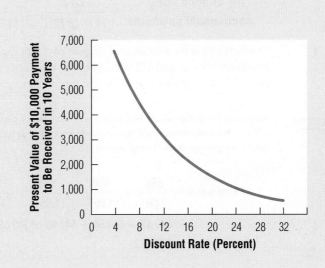

Exhibit 8.3 also shows that a $10,000 payment made 20 years from now has a present value of only $1,486 and that a $10,000 payment made 50 years from now has a present value of only $85 (based on the 10 percent discount rate).

8-1c **Valuation of Bonds with Semiannual Payments**

In reality, most bonds have semiannual payments. The present value of such bonds can be computed as follows. First, the annualized coupon should be split in half, because two payments are made per year. Second, the annual discount rate should be divided by 2 to reflect two 6-month periods per year. Third, the number of periods should be doubled to

Exhibit 8.3   Relationship between Time of Payment and Present Value of Payment

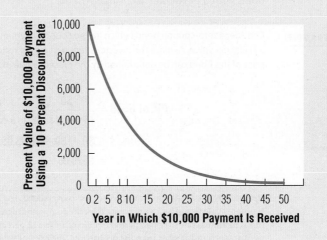

reflect two times the number of annual periods. After these adjustments are incorporated, the present value is determined as follows:

$$\textbf{\textit{PV} of bond with semiannual payments} = \frac{C/2}{[1+(k/2)]^1} + \frac{C/2}{[1+(k/2)]^2} + \cdots + \frac{C/2 + Par}{[1+(k/2)]^{2n}}$$

where $C/2$ is the semiannual coupon payment (half of what the annual coupon payment would have been), and $k/2$ is the periodic discount rate used to discount the bond. The last part of the equation has $2n$ in the denominator's exponent to reflect the doubling of periods.

EXAMPLE

As an example of the valuation of a bond with semiannual payments, consider a bond with $1,000 par value, a 10 percent coupon rate paid semiannually, and three years to maturity. Assuming a 12 percent required return, the present value is computed as follows:

$$\textbf{\textit{PV} of bond} = \frac{\$50}{(1.06)^1} + \frac{\$50}{(1.06)^2} + \frac{\$50}{(1.06)^3} + \frac{\$50}{(1.06)^4} + \frac{\$50}{(1.06)^5} + \frac{\$50 + \$1,000}{(1.06)^6}$$
$$= \$47.17 + \$44.50 + \$41.98 + \$39.60 + \$37.36 + \$740.21$$
$$= \$950.82$$

When using a financial calculator, the present value of the bond in the previous example can be determined as follows (calculator shows PV as a negative value):[1]

INPUT	6	6	50	1000		
Function Key	N	I	PMT	FV	CPT	PV
Answer						950.82

The remaining examples assume annual coupon payments so that we can focus on the concepts presented without concern about adjusting annual payments.

8-1d Relationships among Coupon Rate, Required Return, and Bond Price

Bonds that sell at a price below their par value are called *discount* bonds. The larger the investor's required rate of return relative to the coupon rate, the larger the discount of a bond with a particular par value will be.

EXAMPLE

Consider a zero-coupon bond (which has no coupon payments) with three years remaining to maturity and a $1,000 par value. Assume the investor's required rate of return on the bond is 13 percent. The appropriate price of this bond can be determined by the present value of its future cash flows:

$$\textbf{\textit{PV} of bond} = \frac{\$0}{(1+0.13)^1} + \frac{\$0}{(1+0.13)^2} + \frac{\$1,000}{(1+0.13)^3}$$
$$= \$0 + \$0 + \$693.05$$
$$= \$693.05$$

---

[1]Technically, the semiannual rate of 6 percent is overstated. For a required rate of 12 percent per year, the precise six-month rate would be 5.83 percent. With the compounding effect, which would generate interest on interest, this semiannual rate over two periods would achieve a 12 percent return. Because the approximate semiannual rate of 6 percent is higher than the precise rate, the present value of the bonds is slightly understated.

The very low price of this bond is necessary to generate a 13 percent annualized return to investors. If the bond offered coupon payments, the price would have been higher because those coupon payments would provide part of the return required by investors.

Now consider another bond with a similar par value and maturity that offers a 13 percent coupon rate. The appropriate price of this bond would be

$$PV \text{ of bond} = \frac{\$130}{(1+0.13)^1} + \frac{\$130}{(1+0.13)^2} + \frac{\$1,130}{(1+0.13)^3}$$
$$= \$115.04 + \$101.81 + \$783.15$$
$$= \$1,000$$

Observe that the price of this bond is exactly equal to its par value, as the coupon payments provide the entire compensation required by investors.

Finally, consider a bond with a similar par value and term to maturity that offers a coupon rate of 15 percent, which is greater than the investor's required rate of return. The appropriate price of this bond, as determined by its present value, is

$$PV \text{ of bond} = \frac{\$150}{(1+0.13)^1} + \frac{\$150}{(1+0.13)^2} + \frac{\$1,150}{(1+0.13)^3}$$
$$= \$132.74 + \$117.47 + \$797.01$$
$$= \$1,047.22$$

WEB

finance.yahoo.com
/bonds

Calculates bond returns
and yields.

The price of this bond exceeds its par value because the coupon payments are large enough to offset the high price paid for the bond and still provide a 13 percent annualized return. ●

From the examples provided, the following relationships should now be clear. First, if the coupon rate of a bond is less than the investor's required rate of return, the present value of the bond (and therefore the price of the bond) should be less than the par value. Second, if the coupon rate equals the investor's required rate of return, the price of the bond should be the same as the par value. Finally, if the coupon rate of a bond is greater than the investor's required rate of return, the price of the bond should be great than the par value. These relationships are illustrated in Exhibit 8.4 for a bond with a 10 percent

Exhibit 8.4   Relationship between Required Return and Present Value for a 10 Percent Coupon Bond with Various Maturities

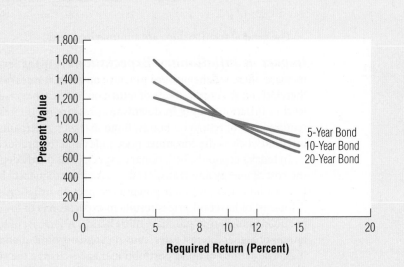

coupon and a par value of $1,000. If investors require a return of 5 percent and desire a 10-year maturity, they will be willing to pay $1,390 for this bond. If they require a return of 10 percent on this same bond, they will be willing to pay $1,000. If they require a 15 percent return, they will be willing to pay only $745. The relationships described here hold for any bond, regardless of its maturity.

8-2 Explaining Bond Price Movements

As explained earlier, the price of a bond should reflect the present value of future cash flows (coupon payments and the par value), based on a required rate of return (k), so that

$$\Delta P_b = f(\Delta k)$$

Because the required rate of return on a bond is primarily determined by the prevailing risk-free rate (R_f), which is the yield on a Treasury bond with the same maturity, and the credit risk premium (RP) on the bond, it follows that the general price movements of bonds can be modeled as

$$\Delta P_b = f(\Delta R_f, \Delta RP)$$

WEB

https://fred.stlouisfed
.org

Data on economic
conditions that affect
bond prices.

Notice how the bond price is affected by a change in either the risk-free rate or the risk premium. An increase in the risk-free rate on bonds results in a higher required rate of return on bonds and, therefore, causes bond prices to decrease. Thus, bond prices are exposed to **interest rate risk**, or the risk that their market value will decline in response to a rise in interest rates. Bonds are also exposed to credit risk: An increase in the credit (default) risk premium also causes investors to require a higher rate of return on bonds and, therefore, causes bond prices to decrease.

The factors that affect the risk-free rate or default risk premiums, and therefore bond prices, are identified next.

8-2a Factors That Affect the Risk-Free Rate

The long-term risk-free rate is driven by inflationary expectations (INF), economic growth (ECON), the money supply (MS), and the budget deficit (DEF):

$$\Delta R_f = f(\underset{+}{\underline{\Delta INF}}, \underset{+}{\underline{\Delta ECON}}, \underset{?}{\underline{\Delta MS}}, \underset{+}{\underline{\Delta DEF}})$$

The general relationships are summarized next.

Impact of Inflationary Expectations   If the level of inflation is expected to increase, there will be upward pressure on interest rates (as explained in Chapter 2) and, therefore, on the required rate of return on bonds. Conversely, a reduction in the expected level of inflation results in downward pressure on interest rates and, therefore, on the required rate of return on bonds. Bond market participants closely monitor indicators of inflation, such as the consumer price index and the producer price index.

In today's economy, inflationary expectations partly depend on oil prices, which affect the cost of energy and transportation. As a consequence, bond portfolio managers must forecast oil prices and their potential impact on inflation so as to forecast interest rates. A forecast of lower oil prices results in expectations of lower interest rates, causing bond portfolio managers to purchase more bonds. A forecast of higher oil prices leads to expectations of higher interest rates, causing bond portfolio managers to sell some of their holdings. The actions of bond portfolio managers change the supply of bonds for sale as well as the demand for bonds in the secondary market, which establishes a new equilibrium price for the bonds.

Inflationary expectations also depend on exchange rate movements. Holding other things equal, inflationary expectations are likely to rise when a weaker dollar is expected because it will increase the prices of imported products. A weaker dollar also prices foreign competitors out of the market, thereby allowing U.S. firms to increase their prices. Thus, U.S. interest rates are expected to rise and bond prices are expected to decrease when the dollar is expected to weaken. Foreign investors anticipating dollar depreciation are less willing to hold U.S. bonds because those bonds' coupon payments will be worth less in their home currency. This could cause an immediate net sale of bonds, placing further downward pressure on bond prices.

Expectations of a strong dollar should have the opposite results. A stronger dollar reduces the prices paid for foreign products, thereby lowering retail prices. In addition, because a stronger dollar makes the prices of foreign products more attractive, domestic firms must maintain low prices to compete effectively. Consequently, expectations of a stronger dollar may encourage bond portfolio managers to purchase more bonds, which places upward pressure on bond prices.

WEB

finance.yahoo.com
/calendar/economic
Calendar of upcoming
announcements of
economic conditions
that may affect bond
prices.

Impact of Economic Growth   Strong economic growth tends to generate upward pressure on interest rates (as explained in Chapter 2), whereas weak economic conditions put downward pressure on rates. Any signals about future economic conditions will affect expectations about future interest rate movements and cause bond markets to react immediately. For example, any economic announcements (such as measurements of economic growth or unemployment) that signal stronger than expected economic growth tend to reduce bond prices. Investors anticipate that interest rates will rise, causing a decline in bond prices. Therefore, they sell bonds, which places immediate downward pressure on bond prices.

Conversely, any economic announcements that signal a weaker than expected economy tend to increase bond prices because investors anticipate that interest rates will decrease and, in turn, cause bond prices to rise. Hence investors buy bonds, which places immediate upward pressure on bond prices. This explains why sudden news of a possible economic recession can cause the bond market to rally. When the credit crisis began in 2008, long-term interest rates declined, which resulted in higher prices for existing Treasury bonds.

Bond market participants closely monitor economic indicators that may signal future changes in the strength of the economy, which in turn may change the risk-free interest rate and the required return from investing in bonds. Some of the more closely monitored indicators of economic growth include employment, gross domestic product, retail sales, industrial production, and consumer confidence.

Impact of Money Supply Growth   When the Federal Reserve increases money supply growth, two reactions are possible (as explained in Chapter 5). First, the increased money supply may result in an increased supply of loanable funds. If the demand schedule (demand curve) for loanable funds is not affected, the increased money supply should place downward pressure on interest rates, causing bond portfolio managers to expect an increase in bond prices and prompting them to purchase bonds based on such expectations.

Second, bond portfolio managers may worry that the high money supply growth could cause higher inflationary expectations, which could lead individuals and firms to borrow and spend more now, before inflation occurs. In this case, the change in borrowing behavior will increase the demand for loanable funds (as a result of inflationary expectations), which may more than offset the effect of the increase in the supply of loanable funds, thereby resulting in higher interest rates and lower bond prices. Such forecasts would encourage immediate sales of long-term bonds.

In response to the credit crisis that began in 2008, the Fed repeatedly increased money supply growth in an effort to reduce interest rates. At that time, economic growth was weak and inflation was low, so investors were not concerned that the high money supply growth would increase inflation. Thus, as the Fed's monetary policy pushed interest rates down, prices of existing bonds increased.

Impact of Budget Deficit   As the annual budget deficit changes, so does the federal government's demand for loanable funds (as explained in Chapter 2). Increased borrowing by the Treasury can result in a higher required return on Treasury bonds. That is, the long-term risk-free rate rises, which results in lower prices on existing bonds with long terms remaining until maturity.

The higher budget deficit leads to the same expected outcome (when other factors are held constant) as occurs in the setting of higher inflationary expectations. In both cases, the amount of funds borrowed increases, which leads to higher interest rates. However, inflationary expectations result in more borrowing by individuals and firms, whereas an increased budget deficit results in more borrowing by the federal government.

8-2b Factors That Affect the Credit (Default) Risk Premium

The general level of credit risk on corporate or municipal bonds can change in response to a change in economic growth (ECON):

$$\Delta RP = f(\Delta ECON)$$

Strong economic growth tends to improve a firm's cash flows and reduce the probability that the firm will default on its debt payments. Conversely, weak economic conditions tend to reduce a firm's cash flows and increase the probability that it will default on its bonds. The credit risk premium is relatively low when economic growth is strong. When the economy is weak, however, the credit risk premium is higher: Investors will provide credit in such periods only if they are compensated for the high degree of credit risk.

EXAMPLE

After the credit crisis began in 2008, the U.S. economy weakened and numerous U.S. companies defaulted on their bonds. In the most notable case, Lehman Brothers (a large securities firm) filed for bankruptcy and subsequently defaulted on its bonds and other debt securities. As a result of the defaults of Lehman Brothers and other firms, investors became more concerned about the credit risk of bonds that corporations issued. Many investors shifted their investments from corporate bonds to Treasury bonds because they wanted to avoid credit risk. Consequently, corporations that needed to borrow long-term funds at this time could issue new bonds only if they were willing to offer a relatively high credit risk premium to compensate investors. ●

Impact of Debt Maturity on the Credit Risk Premium   The credit risk premium tends to be larger for bonds that have longer terms to maturity. Consider an extreme example in which an existing bond issued by a corporation has only one month until maturity. If this corporation is in decent financial condition, it should be capable of completely repaying this debt, because conditions should not change drastically over the next month. By comparison, other bonds issued by this same corporation with 15 years until maturity have a higher risk of default, because the corporation's ability to repay this debt depends on its performance over the next 15 years. Because economic conditions over the next 15 years are very uncertain, so are the corporation's performance and its ability to repay long-term debt over that period.

Impact of Issuer Characteristics on the Credit Risk Premium   A bond's price can also be affected by factors specific to the issuer of the bond, such as a change in its capital structure. If a firm that issues bonds subsequently obtains additional loans, it may be less capable of making its coupon payments, so its credit risk increases. Consequently, investors would now require a higher rate of return if they were to purchase those bonds in the secondary market, which would cause the market value (price) of the bonds to decrease.

8-2c Summary of Factors Affecting Bond Prices

When considering the factors that affect the risk-free rate and the risk premium, the general price movements in bonds can be modeled as follows:

$$\Delta P_b = f(\Delta R_f, \Delta RP)$$
$$= f(\underbrace{\Delta INF}_{-}, \underbrace{\Delta ECON}_{?}, \underbrace{\Delta MS}_{+}, \underbrace{\Delta DEF}_{-})$$

The relationships suggested here assume that other factors are held constant. In the real world, other factors are usually changing, which makes it difficult to disentangle the precise impact of each factor on bond prices. The effect of economic growth is uncertain: A high level of economic growth can adversely affect bond prices by raising the risk-free rate, but it can favorably affect bond prices by lowering the credit risk premium. To the extent that international conditions affect each of the factors, they also influence bond prices.

Exhibit 8.5 summarizes the underlying forces that can affect the long-term, risk-free interest rate and the credit risk premium, thereby causing the general level of bond prices

Exhibit 8.5   Framework for Explaining Changes in Bond Prices over Time

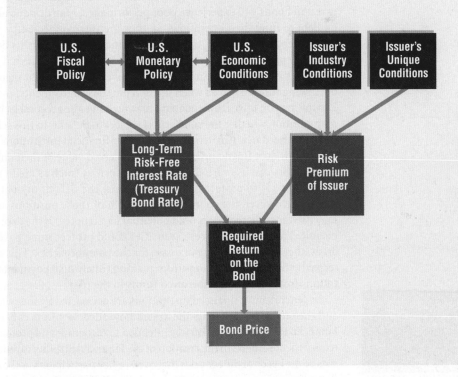

Source: Federal Reserve

to change over time. When pricing Treasury bonds, investors focus on the factors that affect the long-term, risk-free interest rate because the credit risk premium is not applicable. Thus, for a given maturity, the primary difference in the required return of a risky bond (such as a corporate bond) and a Treasury bond is the credit risk premium, which is influenced by economic and industry conditions.

If the bond market is efficient, then bond prices should fully reflect all available public information. In turn, any new information about a firm that changes its perceived ability to repay its bonds will have an immediate effect on the price of its existing bonds.

8-2d Implications for Financial Institutions

Many financial institutions, such as insurance companies, pension funds, and bond mutual funds, maintain large holdings of bonds. The values of their bond portfolios are susceptible to changes in the various factors, described in this section, that affect bond prices. Any factors that lead to higher interest rates tend to reduce the market values of financial institution assets and, therefore, their valuations. Conversely, any factors that lead to lower interest rates tend to increase the market values of financial institution assets and, therefore, their valuations. Many financial institutions attempt to adjust the size of their bond portfolio according to their expectations about future interest rates. When they expect interest rates to rise, they sell bonds and use the proceeds to purchase short-term securities that are less sensitive to interest rate movements. If they anticipate that the risk premiums of risky bonds will increase, they shift their investments toward relatively safe bonds that exhibit less credit risk.

Systemic Risk   Financial institutions that participate in bond markets could be exposed to **systemic risk**, meaning the potential collapse of the entire market or financial system (systemic risk should not be confused with "systematic risk," discussed in Chapter 11). When specific conditions cause a higher risk-free rate and a very high risk premium, they adversely affect the prices of most bonds. Under these conditions, all financial institutions that heavily invest in bonds will experience poor performance. Many financial institutions rely heavily on debt to fund their operations, so they are interconnected by virtue of financing each other's debt positions. If a financial institution cannot repay its debt, then this may create cash flow problems for all the financial institutions from which it borrowed funds.

Some financial institutions use their investments in debt securities as collateral when borrowing funds (such as when using repurchase agreements, as discussed in Chapter 6). During a credit crisis, this collateral may no longer be acceptable, because potential lenders may question whether the collateral is subject to default. In this scenario, financial institutions that need new financing to repay other financial institutions may no longer be able to obtain new debt financing because the perceived value of their collateral has deteriorated.

Creditors can use various derivative securities (such as credit default swaps, described in Chapter 15) to protect themselves against the default of debt securities that they are holding. However, the counterparty in each of those positions serves as the insurer and may itself incur large losses (and potential bankruptcy) if the debt securities that it insures default. Thus, although these securities could protect some participants during a credit crisis, they can result in major losses for the counterparties. This may prevent those counterparty financial institutions from making timely debt payments to other financial institutions from which they borrowed funds in the past.

In general, most financial institutions are connected by the relationships just described, and the credit crisis of 2008 illustrated how adverse effects can spread among them. The Financial Reform Act of 2010 was intended to recognize and protect against this type of systemic risk. It resulted in the creation of the Financial Stability Oversight Council, which consists of the heads of the agencies that oversee key participants in the debt markets and in debt derivatives (insuring against debt default), including the housing industry, securities trading,

FINANCIAL REFORM

depository institutions, mutual funds, and insurance companies. This council is responsible for identifying risks in the U.S. financial system and for making regulatory recommendations to reduce such risks. The council has designated a number of large banks and other financial institutions, including insurance companies, as "systemically important." Such institutions are subject to additional regulation to reduce the risks that they may present.

8-3 Sensitivity of Bond Prices to Interest Rate Movements

The sensitivity of a bond's price to interest rate movements is a function of the bond's characteristics. Investors can measure the sensitivity of their bonds' prices to interest rate movements, which will indicate the potential damage to their bond holdings in response to an increase in interest rates (and therefore in the required rate of return on bonds). Two common methods for assessing the sensitivity of bonds to a change in the required rate of return on bonds are (1) bond price elasticity and (2) duration. In this section, each of these methods is described in turn.

8-3a Bond Price Elasticity

The sensitivity of bond prices (P_b), to changes in the required rate of return (k) is commonly measured by the **bond price elasticity** (P_b^e), which is estimated as

$$P_b^e = \frac{\text{percentage change in } P_b}{\text{percentage change in } k}$$

Exhibit 8.6 compares the price sensitivity of 10-year bonds with a $1,000 par value and four different coupon rates: 0 percent, 5 percent, 10 percent, and 15 percent. Initially, the required rate of return (k) on the bonds is assumed to be 10 percent. The price of each bond

Exhibit 8.6   Sensitivity of 10-Year Bonds with Different Coupon Rates to Interest Rate Changes

(1) BONDS WITH A COUPON RATE OF:	(2) INITIAL PRICE OF BONDS WHEN $k = 10\%$	(3) PRICE OF BONDS WHEN $k = 8\%$	(4) = [(3) − (2)]/(2) PERCENTAGE CHANGE IN BOND PRICE	(5) PERCENTAGE CHANGE IN k	(6) = (4)/(5) BOND PRICE ELASTICITY (P_b^e)
EFFECTS OF A DECLINE IN THE REQUIRED RATE OF RETURN					
0%	$386	$463	+19.9%	−20.0%	−0.995
5	693	799	+15.3	−20.0	−0.765
10	1,000	1,134	+13.4	−20.0	−0.670
15	1,307	1,470	+12.5	−20.0	−0.625

(1) BONDS WITH A COUPON RATE OF:	(2) INITIAL PRICE OF BONDS WHEN $k = 10\%$	(3) PRICE OF BONDS WHEN $k = 12\%$	(4) = [(3) − (2)]/(2) PERCENTAGE CHANGE IN BOND PRICE	(5) PERCENTAGE CHANGE IN k	(6) = (4)/(5) BOND PRICE ELASTICITY (P_b^e)
EFFECTS OF AN INCREASE IN THE REQUIRED RATE OF RETURN					
0%	$386	$322	−16.6%	+20.0%	−0.830
5	693	605	−12.7	+20.0	−0.635
10	1,000	887	−11.3	+20.0	−0.565
15	1,307	1,170	−10.5	+20.0	−0.525

is therefore the present value of its future cash flows, discounted at 10 percent. The initial price of each bond is shown in Column 2. The top panel shows the effect of a decline in interest rates that reduces the investor's required return to 8 percent. Column 3 shows the prices of the bonds based on an 8 percent required return. Column 4 shows the percentage change in the price of each bond resulting from the interest rate movements. The bottom panel shows the effect of an increase in interest rates that increases the investor's required return to 12 percent.

The price elasticity for each bond is estimated in Exhibit 8.6 according to the assumed change in the required rate of return. Notice that the price sensitivity of any particular bond is greater for declining interest rates than for rising interest rates. The bond price elasticity is negative in all cases, reflecting the inverse relationship between interest rate movements and bond price movements.

Influence of Coupon Rate on Bond Price Sensitivity
A zero-coupon bond, which pays all of its proceeds to the investor at maturity, is most sensitive to changes in the required rate of return because the adjusted discount rate is applied to one lump sum in the distant future. Conversely, the price of a bond that pays all its yield in the form of coupon payments is less sensitive to changes in the required rate of return because the adjusted discount rate is applied to some payments that occur in the near future as well as some payments made in the distant future. The adjustment in the present value of such payments in the near future due to a change in the required rate of return is not as pronounced as an adjustment in the present value of payments in the distant future.

Exhibit 8.6 confirms that the prices of zero- or low-coupon bonds are more sensitive to changes in the required rate of return than prices of bonds with relatively high coupon rates. As shown in the exhibit, when the required rate of return declines from 10 percent to 8 percent, the price of the zero-coupon bonds rises from $386 to $463. Thus, the bond price elasticity is

$$P_b^e = \frac{(\$463 - \$386)/\$386}{(8\% - 10\%)/10\%}$$
$$= \frac{+19.9\%}{-20\%}$$
$$= -0.995$$

This implies that, for each 1 percent change in interest rates, zero-coupon bonds change by 0.995 percent in the opposite direction. Column 6 in Exhibit 8.6 shows that the price elasticities of the higher-coupon bonds are considerably lower than the price elasticity of the zero-coupon bond.

Financial institutions commonly restructure their bond portfolios to contain higher-coupon bonds when they are more concerned about a possible increase in interest rates (and therefore an increase in the required rate of return). Conversely, they restructure their portfolios to contain low- or zero-coupon bonds when they expect a decline in interest rates and wish to capitalize on their expectations by holding bonds that are price-sensitive.

Influence of Maturity on Bond Price Sensitivity
As interest rates (and therefore required rates of return) decrease, long-term bond prices (as measured by their present value) increase by a greater degree than short-term bond prices because the long-term bonds will continue to offer the same coupon rate over a longer period of time than the short-term bonds. Of course, if interest rates increase, prices of the long-term bonds will decline by a greater degree.

8-3b Duration

An alternative measure of bond price sensitivity is the bond's duration, which is a measurement of the life of the bond on a present value basis. The longer a bond's duration, the greater its sensitivity to interest rate changes is. A commonly used measure of a bond's duration (DUR) is

$$
DUR = \frac{\sum_{t=1}^{n} \dfrac{C_t(t)}{(1+k)^t}}{\sum_{t=1}^{n} \dfrac{C_t}{(1+k)^t}}
$$

WEB

www.fidelity.com
/learning-center
Search for "bond
duration" to find an
article on this topic.

where

C_t = coupon or principal payment generated by the bond

t = time at which the payments are provided

k = bond's yield to maturity (reflects investors' required rate of return)

The numerator of the duration formula represents the present value of future payments weighted by the time interval until the payments occur. The longer the intervals until payments are made, the larger the numerator and the duration are. The denominator of the duration formula represents the discounted future cash flows resulting from the bond, which is the present value of the bond.

EXAMPLE

The duration of a bond with $1,000 par value and a 7 percent coupon rate, three years remaining to maturity, and a 9 percent yield to maturity is calculated as

$$
DUR = \frac{\dfrac{\$70(1)}{(1.09)^1} + \dfrac{\$70(2)}{(1.09)^2} + \dfrac{\$1,070(3)}{(1.09)^3}}{\dfrac{\$70}{(1.09)^1} + \dfrac{\$70}{(1.09)^2} + \dfrac{\$1,070}{(1.09)^3}}
$$

$$
= 2.8 \text{ years}
$$

By comparison, the duration of a zero-coupon bond with a similar par value and yield to maturity is

$$
DUR = \frac{\dfrac{\$1,000(3)}{(1.09)^3}}{\dfrac{\$1,000}{(1.09)^3}}
$$

$$
= 3 \text{ years}
$$

The duration of a zero-coupon bond is always equal to the bond's term to maturity. The duration of any coupon bond is always less than the bond's term to maturity because some of the payments occur at intervals prior to maturity. ●

Duration of a Portfolio   Bond portfolio managers commonly attempt to *immunize* their portfolio by taking steps intended to insulate its value from the effects of interest rate movements. A first step in this process is to determine the sensitivity of their portfolio to such movements. Once the duration of each individual bond is measured, the bond portfolio's duration (DUR_p) can be estimated as

$$DUR_p = \sum_{j=1}^{m} w_j DUR_j$$

where

m = number of bonds in the portfolio

w_j = bond j's market value as a percentage of the portfolio market value

DUR_j = bond j's duration

In other words, the duration of a bond portfolio is the weighted average of bond durations, with the weights based on the bonds' relative market value. Financial institutions concerned with interest rate risk may compare their asset duration to their liability duration. A positive difference means that the market value of the institution's assets is more rate-sensitive than the market value of its liabilities. Thus, during a period of rising interest rates, the market value of the assets would be reduced by a greater degree than that of the liabilities. The institution's real net worth (market value of net worth) would therefore decrease.

Modified Duration   The duration measurement of a bond or a bond portfolio can be modified to estimate the impact of a change in the prevailing bond yields on bond prices. The modified duration (denoted as DUR^*) is estimated as

$$DUR^* = \frac{DUR}{(1 + k)}$$

where k denotes the prevailing yield on bonds.

The modified duration can be used to estimate the percentage change in the bond's price in response to a change of 1 percentage point in the prevailing bond yields. For example, assume that Bond X has a duration of 8 years and Bond Y has a duration of 12 years. Assuming that the prevailing bond yield is 10 percent, the modified duration is estimated for each bond as follows:

Bond X	Bond Y
$DUR^* = \dfrac{8}{(1 + 0.10)}$	$DUR^* = \dfrac{12}{(1 + 0.10)}$
$= 7.27$ years	$= 10.9$ years

Given the inverse relationship between the change in bond yields and the response in bond prices, the estimate of modified duration should be applied such that the bond price moves in the opposite direction from the change in bond yields. According to the modified duration estimates, a 1 percentage point increase in bond yields (from 10 percent to 11 percent) would lead to a 7.27 percent decline in the price of Bond X and to a 10.9 percent decline in the price of Bond Y. A 0.5 percentage point increase in yields (from 10 percent to 10.5 percent) would lead to a 3.635 percent decline in the price of Bond X (computed as 7.27×0.5) and a 5.45 percent decline in the price of Bond Y (10.9×0.5). The percentage increase in bond prices in response to a decrease in bond yields is estimated in the same manner.

The percentage change in a bond's price in response to a change in yield can be expressed more directly with a simple equation:

$$\%\Delta P_b = -\text{DUR}^* \times \Delta y$$

where

$$\%\Delta P_b = \text{percentage change in the bond's price}$$

$$\Delta y = \text{change in yield}$$

This equation is simply a mathematical expression of the relationship discussed in the preceding paragraphs. For example, the percentage change in price for Bond X for an increase in yield of 0.2 percentage point would be

$$\%\Delta P_b = -7.27 \times 0.002$$

$$= -1.45\%$$

Thus, according to the modified duration estimate, if interest rates rise by 0.2 percentage point, the price of Bond X will drop by 1.45 percent. Similarly, if interest rates decrease by 0.2 percentage point, the price of Bond X will increase by 1.45 percent.

Estimation Errors from Using Modified Duration   If investors rely strictly on modified duration to estimate the percentage change in the price of a bond, they will tend to overestimate the price decline associated with an increase in rates and to underestimate the price increase associated with a decrease in rates.

EXAMPLE
Consider a bond with a 10 percent coupon that pays interest annually and has 20 years to maturity. If the required rate of return is 10 percent (the same as the coupon rate), the value of the bond is $1,000. Based on the formula provided earlier, this bond's modified duration is 8.514 years. If investors anticipate that bond yields will increase by 1 percentage point (to 11 percent), they can estimate the percentage change in the bond's price to be

$$\%\Delta P_b = -8.514 \times 0.01$$

$$= -0.08514 \text{ or } -8.514\%$$

If bond yields rise by 1 percentage point as expected, the price (present value) of the bond would now be $920.37. (Verify this new price by using the time value function on your financial calculator.) The new price reflects a decline of 7.96 percent [calculated as ($920.37 − $1,000) ÷ $1,000]. The decline in price is less pronounced than was estimated in the previous equation. The difference between the estimated percentage change in price (8.514 percent) and the actual percentage change in price (7.96 percent) is due to convexity (discussed next). ●

Bond Convexity   A more complete formula to estimate the percentage change in price in response to a change in yield will incorporate the property of convexity as well as modified duration.

The estimated modified duration suggests a linear relationship in the response of the bond price to a change in bond yields. This is shown by the straight line in Exhibit 8.7. For a given 1 percentage point change in bond yields from our initially assumed bond yield of 10 percent, the modified duration predicts a specific change in bond price. However, the actual response of the bond's price to a change in bond yields is convex, as indicated by the shape of the red curve in Exhibit 8.7. Notice that if the bond yield (horizontal axis) changes slightly from the initial level of 10 percent, the difference between the expected

Exhibit 8.7 Relationship between Bond Yields and Prices

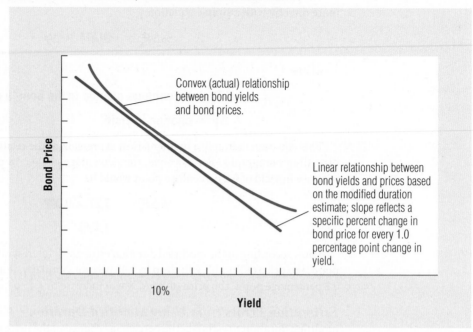

bond price adjustment according to the modified duration estimate (the straight line in Exhibit 8.7) and the bond's actual price adjustment (the convex curve in Exhibit 8.7) is small. For relatively large changes in the bond yield, however, the bond price adjustment as estimated by modified duration is less accurate. The larger the change in the bond yield, the larger the error from estimating the change in bond price in response to the change in yield is.

Because a bond's price change in response to a change in yields is positively related to the maturity of the bond, convexity is also more pronounced for bonds with a long maturity. The prices of low- or zero-coupon bonds are more sensitive to changes in yields. Similarly, bond convexity is more pronounced for bonds with low (or no) coupon rates.

8-4 Bond Investment Strategies

Many investors value bonds and assess their risk when managing investments. Some investors, such as bond portfolio managers of financial institutions, follow a specific strategy for investing in bonds. A few of the more commonly used strategies are described here.

8-4a Matching Strategy

Some investors create a bond portfolio that will generate periodic income to match their expected periodic expenses. For example, an individual investor may invest in a bond portfolio that will provide sufficient income to cover periodic expenses after retirement. Alternatively, a pension fund may invest in a bond portfolio that will provide employees with a fixed periodic income after retirement. The matching strategy involves estimating future cash outflows and then developing a bond portfolio that can generate sufficient coupon or principal payments to cover those outflows.

WEB

https://fred.stlouisfed
.org
Assess the yield of
30-year Treasury bonds
over the last 24 months.

8-4b **Laddered Strategy**

With a laddered strategy, funds are evenly allocated to bonds in each of several differ-ent maturity classes. For example, an institutional investor might create a bond portfolio with one-fourth of the funds invested in bonds with five years until maturity, one-fourth invested in 10-year bonds, one-fourth in 15-year bonds, and one-fourth in 20-year bonds. In 5 years, when the bonds that had 5 years until maturity are redeemed, the proceeds can be used to buy 20-year bonds. Because all the other bonds in the portfolio will have 5 years less until maturity than they had when the portfolio was created, a new investment in 20-year bonds achieves the same maturity structure that existed when the portfolio was created.

The laddered strategy has many variations, but in general it achieves diversified maturi-ties and, therefore, different sensitivities to interest rate risk. Nevertheless, because most bonds are adversely affected by rising interest rates, diversification of maturities in the bond portfolio does not eliminate interest rate risk.

8-4c **Barbell Strategy**

With the barbell strategy, funds are allocated to bonds with a short term to maturity as well as to bonds with a long term to maturity. The bonds with the short term to maturity pro-vide liquidity if the investor needs to sell bonds quickly to obtain cash. The bonds with the long term to maturity tend to have a higher yield to maturity than the bonds with shorter terms to maturity. Thus, this strategy allocates some funds to achieving a relatively high return and other funds to covering liquidity needs.

8-4d **Interest Rate Strategy**

With the interest rate strategy, funds are allocated in a manner that capitalizes on interest rate forecasts. This strategy requires frequent adjustments in the bond portfolio to reflect the prevailing interest rate forecast.

EXAMPLE

Consider a bond portfolio with funds initially allocated equally across various bond maturities. If recent economic events result in an expectation of higher interest rates, the bond portfolio will be revised to con-centrate on bonds with short terms to maturity. Because these bonds are the least sensitive to interest rate movements, they will limit the potential adverse effects on the bond portfolio's value. The sales of all the intermediate-term and long-term bonds will result in significant commissions paid to brokers.

Now assume that after a few weeks, new economic conditions result in an expectation that interest rates will decline in the future. Again the bond portfolio will be restructured, but now it will concentrate on long-term bonds. If interest rates decline as expected, this type of bond portfolio will be most sensitive to that interest rate movement and will experience the largest increase in value. ●

Although investors who believe that they can accurately forecast interest rate move-ments may perceive this type of strategy to be a rational approach, it is difficult for even the most sophisticated investors to consistently forecast future interest rate movements. If investors guess wrong, their portfolio will likely perform worse than if they had used a passive strategy of investing in bonds with a wide variety of maturities.

8-5 **Valuation and Risk of International Bonds**

The value of an international bond represents the present value of future cash flows to be received by the bond's local investors. Bond yields vary among countries, because each yield represents the long-term, risk-free rate for the local country (assuming that the gov-ernment is perceived to be free from default risk). Although the yields on newly issued government bonds vary among countries, they tend to move in the same direction.

The value of government bonds changes over time in response to changes in the risk-free interest rate of the currency denominating the bond and in response to changes in the perceived credit risk of the bond. Because these two factors affect the market price of the bond, they also affect the return on the bond to investors over a particular holding period. An additional factor that affects the return to investors from another country is exchange rate risk. The influence of each of these factors is described next.

8-5a Influence of Foreign Interest Rate Movements

WEB

www.bloomberg.com
/markets
Yields of government
securities from major
countries.

As the risk-free interest rate of a currency changes, the rate of return required by investors in that country changes as well. In turn, the present value of a bond denominated in that currency changes. A reduction in the risk-free interest rate of the foreign currency will result in a lower required rate of return by investors who use that currency to invest, which results in a higher value for bonds denominated in that currency. Conversely, an increase in the risk-free rate of that currency results in a lower value for bonds denominated in that currency.

8-5b Influence of Credit Risk

An increase in credit (default) risk causes a higher required rate of return on the bond and lowers its present value, whereas a reduction in risk causes a lower required rate of return on the bond and increases its present value. Thus, investors who are concerned about a possible increase in the credit risk of an international bond will monitor economic and political conditions in the relevant country that could affect this risk.

8-5c Influence of Exchange Rate Fluctuations

Changes in the value of the foreign currency denominating a bond affect the U.S. dollar cash flows generated from the bond, thereby influencing the return to U.S. investors who invested in it. Consider a U.S. financial institution's purchase of bonds issued in the United Kingdom with a par value of £2 million, a 10 percent coupon rate (payable at the end of each year), currently priced at par value, and with six years remaining until maturity. Exhibit 8.8 shows how the dollar cash flows generated from this investment will differ under three scenarios. The cash flows in the last year also account for the principal payment. The sensitivity of dollar cash flows to the British pound's value is obvious.

Exhibit 8.8   Dollar Cash Flows Generated from a Foreign Bond under Three Scenarios

SCENARIO I (STABLE POUND)	YEAR 1	YEAR 2	YEAR 3	YEAR 4	YEAR 5	YEAR 6
Forecasted value of pound	$1.50	$1.50	$1.50	$1.50	$1.50	$1.50
Forecasted dollar cash flows	$300,000	$300,000	$300,000	$300,000	$300,000	$3,300,000
SCENARIO II (WEAK POUND)						
Forecasted value of pound	$1.48	$1.46	$1.44	$1.40	$1.36	$1.30
Forecasted dollar cash flows	$296,000	$292,000	$288,000	$280,000	$272,000	$2,860,000
SCENARIO III (STRONG POUND)						
Forecasted value of pound	$1.53	$1.56	$1.60	$1.63	$1.66	$1.70
Forecasted dollar cash flows	$306,000	$312,000	$320,000	$326,000	$332,000	$3,740,000

From the perspective of the investing institution, the most attractive foreign bonds offer a high coupon rate and are denominated in a currency that becomes stronger over the investment horizon. Although the coupon rates of some bonds are fixed, the future value of any foreign currency is uncertain. As a consequence, there is a risk that the currency will depreciate and more than offset any coupon rate advantage.

8-5d International Bond Diversification

When investors attempt to capitalize on investments in foreign bonds that have higher interest rates than they can obtain locally, they may diversify their foreign bond holdings among countries to reduce their exposure to different types of risk, as explained next.

Reduction of Interest Rate Risk   Institutional investors diversify their bond portfolios internationally to reduce their exposure to interest rate risk. If all bonds in a portfolio are from a single country, their values will all be systematically affected by interest rate movements in that country. International diversification of bonds reduces the sensitivity of the overall bond portfolio to any single country's interest rate movements.

Reduction of Credit Risk   Another key reason for international diversification to reduce credit (default) risk. Investment in bonds issued by corporations from a single country can expose investors to a relatively high degree of credit risk. The credit risk of corporations is strongly affected by economic conditions, so shifts in credit risk will likely be systematically related to the country's economic conditions. Because economic cycles differ across countries, there is less chance of a systematic increase in the credit risk of internationally diversified bonds. During the credit crisis of 2008–2009, however, there was a perception of higher credit risk (and therefore lower value) for most corporate bonds regardless of the issuer's country.

Reduction of Exchange Rate Risk   Financial institutions may attempt to reduce their exchange rate risk by diversifying among foreign securities denominated in various foreign currencies. In this way, a smaller proportion of their foreign security holdings are exposed to the depreciation of any particular foreign currency. Because the movements of many foreign currency values within one continent are highly correlated, a U.S. investor would reduce exchange rate risk only slightly when diversifying among securities. This is especially true in Europe, where many of the countries have adopted the euro as their home currency. Hence many U.S. financial institutions commonly attempt to purchase securities across continents rather than within a single continent.

International Integration of Credit Risk   Changes in the general credit risk level of loans in one country may affect the level of credit risk in other countries, because country economies are correlated. When one country experiences weak economic conditions, the credit risk of its firms may increase, making it difficult for them to repay loans that they have obtained from financial institutions in other countries. Similarly, if the country's consumers reduce their demand for foreign products, firms in other countries may be adversely affected and be unable to repay their loans to creditors in their own country. Thus, an increase in credit risk in one country may be transmitted to another country, a process that is sometimes referred to as credit contagion.

Summary

- The value of a debt security (such as bonds) is the present value of future cash flows generated by that security, using a discount rate that reflects the investor's required rate of return. As market interest rates rise, the investor's required rate of return increases. The discounted value of bond payments declines when the higher discount rate is applied. Thus, the present value of a bond declines, which forces the bond price to decline.

- Bond prices are affected by the factors that influence interest rate movements, including economic growth, the money supply, oil prices, and the dollar. Bond prices are also affected by a change in credit risk.

- Investors commonly measure the sensitivity of their bond holdings to potential changes in the required rate of return. Two methods used for this purpose are bond price elasticity and duration. Other things being equal, the longer a bond's time to maturity, the more sensitive its price is to interest rate movements.

Prices of bonds with relatively low coupon payments are also more sensitive to interest rate movements.

- Common investment strategies used to invest in bonds are the matching strategy, laddered strategy, barbell strategy, and interest rate strategy. The matching strategy focuses on generating income from the bond portfolio that can cover anticipated expenses. The laddered strategy and barbell strategy are designed to cover liquidity needs while also trying to achieve decent returns. The interest rate strategy is useful for investors who believe that they can predict interest rate movements; these investors shift their funds into long-term bonds when they believe interest rates will decline.

- Foreign bonds may offer higher returns, but they are exposed to exchange rate risk and may also be subject to credit risk. International financial markets are highly integrated, so adverse conditions that cause high credit risk in one country may spread to other countries through credit contagion.

Point/Counterpoint

Does Governance of Firms Affect the Prices of Their Bonds?

Point No. Bond prices are primarily determined by interest rate movements, so they are not affected by the governance of firms that issued the bonds.

Counterpoint Yes. Bond prices reflect the risk of default. Firms with more effective governance may be

able to reduce their default risk, thereby increasing the price of their bonds.

Who Is Correct? Use the Internet to learn more about this issue and then formulate your own opinion.

Questions and Applications

1. **Bond Investment Decision** Based on your forecast of interest rates, would you recommend that investors purchase bonds today? Explain.

2. **How Interest Rates Affect Bond Prices** Explain the impact of a decline in interest rates on:

a. An investor's required rate of return.
b. The present value of existing bonds.
c. The prices of existing bonds.

3. **Relevance of Bond Price Movements** Why is the relationship between interest rates and bond prices important to financial institutions?

4. **Source of Bond Price Movements** Determine the direction of bond prices over the last year and explain the reason for it.

5. **Exposure to Bond Price Movements** How would a financial institution with a large bond portfolio be affected by falling interest rates? Would it be affected to a greater extent than a financial institution with a greater concentration of bonds (and fewer short-term securities)? Explain.

6. **Comparison of Bonds to Mortgages** Since fixed-rate mortgages and bonds have similar payment flows, how is a financial institution with a large

portfolio of fixed-rate mortgages affected by rising interest rates? Explain.

7.   Coupon Rates If a bond's coupon rate is greater than the investor's required rate of return on the bond, would the bond's price be greater than or less than its par value? Explain.

8.   Bond Price Sensitivity Is the price of a long-term bond or the price of a short-term security more sensitive to a change in interest rates? Why?

9.   Required Return on Bonds Why does the required rate of return for a particular bond change over time?

10.   Inflation Effects Assume that inflation is expected to decline in the near future. How could this affect future bond prices? Would you recommend that financial institutions increase or decrease their concentration in long-term bonds based on this expectation? Explain.

11.   Bond Price Elasticity Explain the concept of bond price elasticity. Would bond price elasticity suggest a higher price sensitivity for zero-coupon bonds or high-coupon bonds that are offering the same yield to maturity? Why? What does this suggest about the market value volatility of mutual funds containing zero-coupon Treasury bonds versus high-coupon Treasury bonds?

12.   Economic Effects on Bond Prices An analyst recently suggested that there will be a major economic expansion that will favorably affect the prices of high-rated, fixed-rate bonds because the credit risk of bonds will decline as corporations improve their performance. Assuming that the economic expansion occurs, do you agree with the analyst's conclusion? Explain.

13.   Impact of War When tensions rise or a war erupts in the Middle East, bond prices in many countries tend to decline. What is the link between problems in the Middle East and bond prices? Would you expect bond prices to decline more in Japan or in the United Kingdom as a result of the crisis? (The answer is tied to how interest rates may change in those countries.) Explain.

14.   Bond Price Sensitivity Explain how bond prices may be affected by money supply growth, oil prices, and economic growth.

15.   Impact of Oil Prices Assume that oil-producing countries have agreed to reduce their oil production

by 30 percent. How would bond prices be affected by this announcement? Explain.

16.   Impact of Economic Conditions Assume that breaking news causes bond portfolio managers to suddenly expect much higher economic growth. How might bond prices be affected by this expectation? Explain. Now assume that breaking news causes bond portfolio managers to suddenly anticipate a recession. How might bond prices be affected? Explain.

Advanced Questions

17.   Impact of the Fed on Bond Prices Assume that bond market participants suddenly expect the Fed to substantially increase the money supply.

a. Assuming no threat of inflation, how would this expectation affect bond prices?
b. Assuming that inflation may result, how would bond prices be affected?
c. Given your answers to (a) and (b), explain why expectations of the Fed's increase in the money supply may sometimes cause bond market participants to disagree about how bond prices will be affected.

18.   Impact of a Weak Dollar on Bond Prices The value of the dollar is monitored by bond market participants over time.

a. Explain why expectations of a weak dollar could reduce bond prices in the United States.
b. On some occasions, news of the dollar's weakening has not had any impact on the bond markets. Assuming that no other information offsets the weakening dollar, explain why the bond markets may not have responded to the dollar's decline.

19.   International Bonds A U.S. insurance company purchased British 20-year Treasury bonds instead of U.S. 20-year Treasury bonds because the coupon rate was 2 percentage points higher on the British bonds. Assume that the insurance company sold the bonds after five years. Its yield over the five-year period was substantially less than the yield it would have received on the U.S. bonds over the same five-year period. Assume that the U.S. insurance company had hedged its exchange rate exposure. Given that the lower yield was not because of default risk or exchange rate risk, explain how the British bonds could have generated a lower yield than the U.S. bonds. (Assume that either type of bond could have been purchased at the par value.)

20. International Bonds The pension fund manager of Utterback (a U.S. firm) purchased German 20-year Treasury bonds instead of U.S. 20-year Treasury bonds. The coupon rate was 2 percentage points lower on the German bonds. Assume that the manager sold the bonds after five years. The yield over the five-year period was substantially more than the yield the manager would have received on the U.S. bonds over the same five-year period. Explain how the German bonds could have generated a higher yield than the U.S. bonds for the manager, even if the exchange rate was stable over this five-year period. (Assume that the price of either bond was initially equal to its respective par value.) Be specific.

21. Implications of a Shift in the Yield Curve Assume that the yield curve experiences a sudden shift such that the new yield curve is higher and more steeply sloped today than it was yesterday. If a firm issues new bonds today, would its bonds sell for higher or lower prices than if it had issued the bonds yesterday? Explain.

22. How Bond Prices May Respond to Prevailing Conditions Consider the prevailing conditions for inflation (including oil prices), the economy, the budget deficit, and the Fed's monetary policy that could affect interest rates. Based on these conditions, do you think bond prices will increase or decrease during this semester? Offer some logic to support your answer. Which factor do you think will have the biggest impact on bond prices?

23. Interaction between Bond and Money Markets Assume that you maintain bonds and money market securities in your portfolio, and you suddenly believe that long-term interest rates will rise substantially tomorrow (even though the market does not share your view) while short-term interest rates will remain the same.

a. How would you rebalance your portfolio between bonds and money market securities?
b. If other market participants suddenly recognize that long-term interest rates will rise tomorrow and they respond in the same manner as you do, explain how the demand for these securities (bonds and money market securities), the supply of these securities for sale, and the prices and yields of these securities will be affected.
c. Assume that the yield curve is flat today. Explain how the slope of the yield curve will change tomorrow in response to the market activity.

24. Impact of the Credit Crisis on Risk Premiums Explain how the prices of bonds were affected by a change in the risk-free rate during the credit crisis that began in 2008. Explain how bond prices were affected by a change in the credit risk premium during this period.

25. Systemic Risk Explain why systemic risk is a source of concern in the bond and other debt markets. Also explain how the Financial Reform Act of 2010 was intended to reduce systemic risk.

26. Link between Market Uncertainty and Bond Yields When stock market volatility is high, corporate bond yields tend to increase. Which market forces cause the increase in corporate bond yields under these conditions?

27. Fed's Impact on Credit Risk The Fed's open market operations can change the money supply, which can affect the risk-free rate offered on bonds. Why might the Fed's policy also affect the risk premium on corporate bonds?

28. Contagion Effects Explain why a credit crisis in one country may be transmitted to other countries.

Critical Thinking Question

Impact of Credit Crisis on Bond Markets The credit crisis was caused by the mortgage market, yet it had a serious impact on bond markets. Write a short essay on how the bond market was affected, and offer your opinion on how the bond market could attempt to insulate itself from a credit crisis in the future.

Interpreting Financial News

Interpret the following statements made by Wall Street analysts and portfolio managers.

a. "Given the recent uncertainty about future interest rates, investors are fleeing from zero-coupon bonds."
b. "Catrell Insurance Company invests heavily in bonds, and its stock price increased substantially today in response to the Fed's signal that it plans to reduce interest rates."
c. "Bond markets declined when the Treasury flooded the market with its new bond offering."

Managing in Financial Markets

Bond Investment Dilemma As an investor, you plan to invest your funds in long-term bonds. You have $100,000 to invest. You may purchase highly rated municipal bonds at par with a coupon rate of 6 percent; you have a choice of a maturity of 10 years or 20 years. Alternatively, you could purchase highly rated corporate bonds at par with a coupon rate of 8 percent; these bonds also are offered with maturities of 10 years or 20 years. You do not expect to need the funds for five years. At the end of the fifth year, you will definitely sell the bonds because you will need to make a large purchase at that time.

a. What is the annual interest you would earn (before taxes) on the municipal bond? On the corporate bond?
b. Assume that you are in the 20 percent tax bracket. If the level of credit risk and the liquidity for the

municipal and corporate bonds are the same, would you invest in the municipal bonds or the corporate bonds? Why?
c. Assume that you expect all yields paid on newly issued notes and bonds (regardless of maturity) to decrease by a total of 4 percentage points over the next two years and to increase by a total of 2 percentage points over the following three years. Would you select the 10-year maturity or the 20-year maturity for the type of bond you plan to purchase? Why?

Problems

1. Bond Valuation Assume the following information for an existing bond that provides annual coupon payments:

Par value = $1,000

Coupon rate = 11 percent

Maturity = 4 years

Required rate of return by investors = 11 percent

a. What is the present value of the bond?
b. If the required rate of return by investors was 14 percent instead of 11 percent, what would be the present value of the bond?
c. If the required rate of return by investors was 9 percent, what would be the present value of the bond?

2. Valuing a Zero-Coupon Bond Assume the following information for existing zero-coupon bonds:

Par value = $100,000

Maturity = 3 years

Required rate of return by investors = 12 percent

How much should investors be willing to pay for these bonds?

3. Valuing a Zero-Coupon Bond Assume that you require a 14 percent return on a zero-coupon bond with a par value of $1,000 and six years to maturity. What is the price you should be willing to pay for this bond?

4. Bond Value Sensitivity to Exchange Rates and Interest Rates Cardinal Company, a U.S.-based insurance company, considers purchasing bonds

denominated in Canadian dollars, with a maturity of six years, a par value of C$50 million, and a coupon rate of 12 percent. Cardinal can purchase the bonds at par. The current exchange rate of the Canadian dollar is $0.80. Cardinal expects that the required return by Canadian investors on these bonds four years from now will be 9 percent. If Cardinal purchases the bonds, it will sell them in the Canadian secondary market four years from now. It forecasts the exchange rates as follows:

YEAR	EXCHANGE RATE OF C$	YEAR	EXCHANGE RATE OF C$
1	$0.80	4	$0.72
2	0.77	5	0.68
3	0.74	6	0.66

a. Refer to earlier examples in this chapter to determine the expected U.S. dollar cash flows to Cardinal over the next four years.
b. Does Cardinal expect to be favorably or adversely affected by the interest rate risk? Explain.
c. Does Cardinal expect to be favorably or adversely affected by exchange rate risk? Explain.

5. Predicting Bond Values (Use the chapter appendix to answer this problem.) Bulldog Bank has just purchased bonds for $106 million that have a par value of $100 million, three years remaining to maturity, and an annual coupon rate of 14 percent. It expects the required rate of return on these bonds to be 12 percent one year from now.

a. At what price could Bulldog Bank sell these bonds one year from now?
b. What is the expected annualized yield on the bonds over the next year, assuming they are to be sold in one year?

6. **Predicting Bond Values** (Use the chapter appendix to answer this problem.) Sun Devil Savings has just purchased bonds for $38 million that have a par value of $40 million, five years remaining to maturity, and a coupon rate of 12 percent. It expects the required rate of return on these bonds to be 10 percent two years from now.

a. At what price could Sun Devil Savings sell these bonds two years from now?
b. What is the expected annualized yield on the bonds over the next two years, assuming they are to be sold in two years?
c. If the anticipated required rate of return of 10 percent in two years is overestimated, how would the actual selling price differ from the forecasted price? How would the actual annualized yield over the next two years differ from the forecasted yield?

7. **Predicting Bond Values** (Use the chapter appendix to answer this problem.) Spartan Insurance Company plans to purchase bonds today that have four years remaining to maturity, a par value of $60 million, and a coupon rate of 10 percent. Spartan expects that in three years, the required rate of return on these bonds by investors in the market will be 9 percent. It plans to sell the bonds at that time. What is the expected price it will sell the bonds for in three years?

8. **Bond Yields** (Use the chapter appendix to answer this problem.) Hankla Company plans to purchase either (1) zero-coupon bonds that have 10 years to maturity, a par value of $100 million, and a purchase price of $40 million or (2) bonds with similar default risk that have five years to maturity, a 9 percent coupon rate, a par value of $40 million, and a purchase price of $40 million. Hankla can invest $40 million for five years. Assume that the market's required return in five years is forecasted to be 11 percent. Which alternative would offer Hankla a higher expected return (or yield) over the five-year investment horizon?

9. **Predicting Bond Values** (Use the chapter appendix to answer this problem.) The portfolio manager of Ludwig Company has excess cash that is to be invested for four years. He can purchase either (1) four-year Treasury notes that offer a 9 percent yield or (2) new 20-year Treasury bonds for $2.9 million that offer a par value of $3 million and an 11 percent coupon rate with annual payments. The manager expects that the required return on these same 20-year bonds will be 12 percent four years from now.

a. What is the forecasted market value of the 20-year bonds in four years?
b. Which investment is expected to provide a higher yield over the four-year period?

10. **Predicting Bond Portfolio Value** (Use the chapter appendix to answer this problem.) Ash Investment Company manages a broad portfolio with this composition:

	PAR VALUE	PRESENT MARKET VALUE	YEARS REMAIN-ING TO MATURITY
Zero-coupon bonds	$200,000,000	$63,720,000	12
8% Treasury bonds	300,000,000	290,000,000	8
11% corporate bonds	400,000,000	380,000,000	10
		$733,720,000	

Ash expects that in four years, investors in the market will require an 8 percent return on the zero-coupon bonds, a 7 percent return on the Treasury bonds, and a 9 percent return on corporate bonds. Estimate the market value of the bond portfolio four years from now.

11. **Valuing a Zero-Coupon Bond**

a. A zero-coupon bond with a par value of $1,000 matures in 10 years. At what price would this bond provide a yield to maturity that matches the current market rate of 8 percent?
b. What happens to the price of this bond if interest rates fall to 6 percent?
c. Given the changes in the price of the bond and the interest rate described in part (b), calculate the bond price elasticity.

12. **Bond Valuation** You are interested in buying a $1,000 par value bond with 10 years to maturity and an 8 percent coupon rate that is paid semiannually. How much should you be willing to pay for the bond if the investor's required rate of return is 10 percent?

13. **Predicting Bond Values** You are interested in a bond that pays an annual coupon of 4 percent, has a yield to maturity of 6 percent, and has 13 years to maturity. If interest rates remain unchanged, at what price would you expect this bond to be selling eight years from now? Ten years from now?

14. **Sensitivity of Bond Values**

a. How would the present value (and therefore the market value) of a bond be affected if the coupon payments are smaller and other factors remain constant?

b. How would the present value (and therefore the market value) of a bond be affected if the required rate of return is smaller and other factors remain constant?

15. **Bond Elasticity** Determine how the bond elasticity would be affected if the bond price changed by a larger amount, holding the change in the required rate of return constant.

16. **Bond Duration** Determine how the duration of a bond would be affected if the coupons were extended over additional time periods.

17. **Bond Duration** A bond has a duration of five years and a yield to maturity of 9 percent. If the yield to maturity changes to 10 percent, what should be the percentage price change of the bond?

18. **Bond Convexity** Describe how bond convexity affects the theoretical linear price–yield relationship of bonds. What are the implications of bond convexity for estimating changes in bond prices?

Flow of Funds Exercise

Interest Rate Expectations, Economic Growth, and Bond Financing

If the economy continues to be strong, Carson Company may need to increase its production capacity by approximately 50 percent over the next few years to satisfy demand. It would need financing to expand and accommodate this increase in production. Recall that the yield curve is currently upward sloping. Also recall that Carson is concerned about a possible slowing of the economy because of potential Fed actions to reduce inflation. The company needs funding to cover payments for supplies. It is also considering issuing stock or bonds to raise funds in the next year.

a. At a recent meeting, the chief executive officer (CEO) stated his view that the economy will remain strong, as the Fed's monetary policy is not likely to have a major impact on interest rates. For this reason, he wants to expand the business to benefit from the expected increase in demand for Carson's products. The next step would be to determine how to finance the expansion. The chief financial officer (CFO) stated

that if Carson Company needs to obtain long-term funds, issuing fixed-rate bonds would be an ideal strategy at this point in time because she expects that the Fed's monetary policy to reduce inflation will cause long-term interest rates to rise. If the CFO is correct about future interest rates, what does this suggest about future economic growth, the future demand for Carson's products, and the need to issue bonds?

b. If you were involved in the meeting described here, what do you think needs to be resolved before deciding to expand the business?

c. At the meeting described here, the CEO stated: "The decision to expand should not be dictated by whether interest rates are going to increase. Bonds should be issued only if the potential increase in interest rates is attributed to a strong demand for loanable funds rather than the Fed's reduction in the supply of loanable funds." What does this statement mean?

Internet/Excel Exercises

Go to www.giddy.org/db/corpspreads.htm. The spreads given there are listed in the form of basis points (100 basis points = 1 percent) above the Treasury security with the same maturity.

1. First determine the difference between the AAA and CCC spreads. This indicates how much more of a yield is required on CCC-rated bonds versus AAA-rated bonds. Next, determine the difference

between AAA and BBB spreads. Then determine the difference between BBB and CCC spreads. Is the difference larger between the AAA and BBB or the BBB and CCC spreads? What does this tell you about the perceived risk of the bonds in these rating categories?

2. Compare the AAA spread for a short-term maturity (such as two years) versus a long-term maturity (such as 10 years). Is the spread larger for the short-term or the long-term maturity? Offer an explanation for your findings.

3. Next, compare the CCC spread for a short-term maturity (such as two years) and a long-term maturity (such as 10 years). Is the spread larger for the short-term or the long-term maturity? Offer an explanation for your findings. Notice that the difference in spreads for a given rating level among maturities varies with the rating level that you assess. Offer an explanation for this relationship.

Online Articles with Real-World Examples

Find a recent practical article available online that describes a real-world example regarding a specific financial institution or financial market that reinforces one or more concepts covered in this chapter.

If your class has an online component, your professor may ask you to post your summary of the article there and provide a link to the article so that other students can access it. If your class is live, your professor may ask you to summarize your application of the article in class. Your professor may assign specific students to complete this assignment or may allow any students to do the assignment on a volunteer basis.

For recent online articles and real-world examples related to this chapter, consider using the following search terms (be sure to include the prevailing year as a search term to ensure that the online articles are recent):

1. bond AND valuation
2. bond prices AND economic growth
3. bond prices AND inflation
4. bond prices AND money supply
5. bond prices AND budget deficit
6. bond AND duration
7. bond AND performance
8. bond AND strategy
9. international bonds AND exchange rate
10. international bonds AND credit risk

Appendix 8

Forecasting Bond Prices and Yields

Forecasting Bond Prices

To illustrate how a financial institution can assess the potential impact of interest rate movements on its bond holdings, assume that Laker Bank recently purchased Treasury bonds in the secondary market with a total par value of $80 million. The bonds will mature in five years and have an annual coupon rate of 5 percent. Laker wants to forecast the market value of these bonds two years from now because it may sell the bonds at that time. Therefore, it must forecast the investor's required rate of return as of two years from now, and then use that as the discount rate to determine the present value of the bonds' cash flows over the final three years of their life. The computed present value in two years will represent the forecasted price two years from now.

Assume the investor's required rate of return two years from now is expected to be 4 percent. This rate will be used to discount the periodic cash flows over the remaining three years.

Forecasting Bond Yields

The yield to maturity can be determined by solving for the discount rate at which the present value of future payments (coupon payments and par value) to the bondholder would equal the bond's current price. Calculators and bond tables are available to determine the yield to maturity.

If bonds are held to maturity, the yield is known. However, if they are sold prior to maturity, the yield is not known until the time of sale. Investors can, however, attempt to forecast the yield, by using the forecasted required rate of return to forecast the market value (and therefore the selling price) of the bonds. This selling price can then be incorporated into the cash flow estimates to determine the discount rate at which the present value of cash flows equals the investor's initial purchase price.

Financial institutions that forecast bond yields must first forecast interest rates for the point in time when they plan to sell their bonds. These forecasted rates can be used along with information about the securities to predict the required rate of return that will exist for the securities of concern. The predicted required rate of return is applied to cash flows beyond the time of sale to forecast the market value (selling price) of the bonds at the time of sale. The forecasted selling price is then incorporated into the estimations of cash flows over the investment horizon. Finally, the yield on the bonds is determined by solving for the discount rate that equates these cash flows to the initial purchase price. The accuracy of the forecasted yield depends on the accuracy of the forecasted selling price of the bonds, which in turn depends on the accuracy of the forecasted required rate of return for the time of the sale.

Forecasting Bond Portfolio Values

Financial institutions can quantitatively measure the impact of possible interest rate movements on the market value of their bond portfolio by separately assessing the impact on each type of bond and then consolidating the individual impacts.

The key variable in forecasting the bond portfolio's market value is the anticipated required return for each type of bond. In addition, as economic conditions change, the required returns of some risky securities could change even if the general level of interest rates remains stable.

Forecasting Bond Portfolio Returns

Financial institutions measure their overall bond portfolio returns in various ways. One approach is to account for coupon payments as well as the change in market value over the holding period of concern. The market value at the beginning of the holding period is perceived as the initial investment. The market value at the end of that period is perceived as the price at which the bonds would have been sold. Even if the bonds are retained, the measurement of return requires an estimated market value at the end of the period. Finally, the coupon payments must be taken into account.

A bond portfolio's return is measured the same way as an individual bond's return. Mathematically, the bond portfolio return can be determined by solving for k in the following equation:

$$MVP = \sum_{t=1}^{n} \frac{C_t}{(1+k)^t} + \frac{MVP_n}{(1+k)^n}$$

where

MVP = today's market value of the bond portfolio

C_t = coupon payments received at the end of period t

MVP_n = market value of the bond portfolio at the end of the investment period of concern

k = discount rate that equates the present value of coupon payments and the future portfolio market value to today's portfolio market value

A financial institution can input forecasted required returns for each type of bond into a software program, then let the computer determine projections of the bond portfolio's future market value and its return over a specified investment horizon.

9
Mortgage Markets

CHAPTER OBJECTIVES

The specific objectives of this chapter are to:

- Provide background information on mortgages.

- Describe the common types of residential mortgages.

- Explain the valuation and risk of mortgages.

- Explain mortgage-backed securities.

- Explain how mortgage problems led to the 2008–2009 credit crisis.

WEB

www.mba.org
News regarding the mortgage markets.

Mortgages are securities used to finance real estate purchases; they are originated by various financial institutions, such as savings institutions and mortgage companies. A secondary mortgage market accommodates originators of mortgages that desire to sell their mortgages prior to maturity. The mortgage markets serve individuals or firms that need long-term funds to purchase real estate. They also serve financial institutions that wish to act as creditors by lending long-term funds for real estate purchases.

9-1 Background on Mortgages

A mortgage is a form of debt created to finance investment in real estate. This debt is secured by the property; thus, if the property owner does not meet the payment obligations, the creditor can seize the property. Financial institutions such as savings institutions and mortgage companies serve as intermediaries by originating mortgages. They consider mortgage applications and assess the creditworthiness of the applicants.

The mortgage represents the difference between the down payment and the amount to be paid for the property. The mortgage contract specifies the mortgage rate, the maturity, and the collateral that backs the loan. The originator charges an origination fee when providing a mortgage. In addition, if it uses its own funds to finance the property, it will earn profit from the difference between the mortgage rate that it charges and the rate that it paid to obtain the funds. Most mortgages have a maturity of 30 years, but 15-year maturities are also available.

9-1a How Mortgage Markets Facilitate the Flow of Funds

Exhibit 9.1 illustrates the means by which mortgage markets facilitate the flow of funds. Financial intermediaries originate mortgages and finance purchases of homes. These financial intermediaries obtain their funding from household deposits as well as by selling some of the mortgages that they originate directly to institutional investors in the secondary market. These funds are then used to finance more purchases of homes, condominiums, and commercial property. Overall, mortgage markets allow households and corporations to increase their purchases of homes, condominiums, and commercial property, thereby supporting economic growth.

Institutional Use of Mortgage Markets   Mortgage companies, savings institutions, and commercial banks all act as financial intermediaries that originate mortgages. Mortgage companies tend to sell their mortgages in the secondary market, although they may

Exhibit 9.1   How Mortgage Markets Facilitate the Flow of Funds

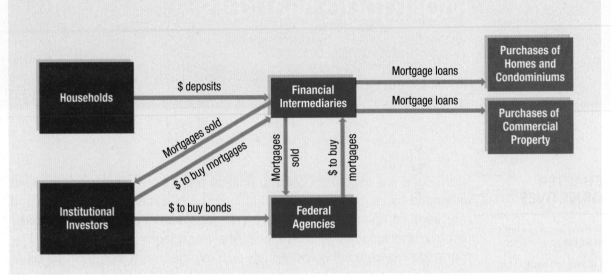

continue to process payments for the mortgages that they originated. Thus, their income is generated from origination and processing fees, and not from financing the mortgages over a long-term period. Savings institutions and commercial banks commonly originate residential mortgages. Commercial banks also originate mortgages for corporations that purchase commercial property. Savings institutions and commercial banks typically use the funds they receive from household deposits to provide mortgage financing, but they also sell some of their mortgages in the secondary market.

In the secondary market, mortgages may be purchased by savings institutions, commercial banks, insurance companies, pension funds, and some types of mutual funds. Exhibit 9.2 summarizes the participation by financial institutions in the mortgage market.

Exhibit 9.2   Institutional Use of Mortgage Markets

TYPE OF FINANCIAL INSTITUTION	INSTITUTION PARTICIPATION IN MORTGAGE MARKETS
Commercial banks and savings institutions	• Originate and service commercial and residential mortgages and maintain mortgages within their investment portfolios. • Bundle packages of mortgages and sell mortgage-backed securities representing the packages of mortgages. • Purchase mortgage-based securities.
Credit unions and finance companies	• Originate mortgages and maintain mortgages within their investment portfolios.
Mortgage companies	• Originate mortgages and sell them in the secondary market.
Mutual funds	• May sell shares and use the proceeds to construct portfolios of mortgage-backed securities.
Securities firms	• Bundle packages of mortgages and sell mortgage-backed securities representing the packages of mortgages. • Offer instruments to help institutional investors in mortgages hedge against interest rate risk.
Insurance companies	• Commonly purchase mortgages or mortgage-backed securities in the secondary market.

the financial institution's profit margin on ARMs could be affected by interest rate fluctuations. Nevertheless, this interest rate risk is significantly less than that of fixed-rate mortgages.

9-2c Graduated-Payment Mortgages

A **graduated-payment mortgage (GPM)** allows the borrower to make small payments initially on the mortgage; the payments increase on a graduated basis over the first 5 to 10 years of the loan and then level off. This type of mortgage is tailored to families who anticipate higher income (and thus the ability to make larger monthly mortgage payments) as time passes. In a sense, they are delaying part of their mortgage payment.

9-2d Growing-Equity Mortgages

A **growing-equity mortgage** is similar to a GPM in that the monthly payments are initially low and increase over time. Unlike the GPM, however, the payments never level off but continue to increase (typically by about 4 percent per year) throughout the life of the loan. With such an accelerated payment schedule, the entire mortgage may be paid off in 15 years or less.

9-2e Second Mortgages

A **second mortgage** can be used in conjunction with the primary or first mortgage. Some financial institutions may limit the amount of the first mortgage based on the borrower's income. Other financial institutions may then offer a second mortgage with a maturity shorter than that of the first mortgage. In addition, the interest rate on the second mortgage is higher because its priority claim against the property (in the event of default) is behind that of the first mortgage. The higher interest rate reflects the greater compensation required as a result of the higher risk incurred by the provider of the second mortgage.

Sellers of homes sometimes offer buyers a second mortgage. This practice is especially common when the old mortgage is assumable and the selling price of the home is much higher than the remaining balance on the first mortgage. By offering a second mortgage, the seller can make the house more affordable and therefore more marketable. The seller and the buyer negotiate specific interest rate and maturity terms.

WEB

www.hsh.com
Detailed information
about mortgage
financing.

9-2f Shared-Appreciation Mortgages

A **shared-appreciation mortgage** allows a home purchaser to obtain a mortgage at a below-market interest rate. In return, the lender providing the attractive loan rate will share in the price appreciation of the home. The precise percentage of appreciation allocated to the lender is negotiated at the origination of the mortgage.

9-2g Balloon-Payment Mortgages

A **balloon-payment mortgage** requires only interest payments for a three- to five-year period. At the end of this period, the borrower must pay the full amount of the principal (the balloon payment). Because no principal payments are made until maturity, the monthly payments are lower. Realistically, though, most borrowers have not saved enough funds to pay off the mortgage in three to five years, so the balloon payment in effect forces them to request a new mortgage. Therefore, they are subject to the risk that mortgage rates will be higher at the time they refinance the mortgage. Because of the restrictions placed on the use of balloon-payment mortgages by individuals, this type of mortgage is now most commonly used for commercial property.

9-3 Valuation of Mortgages

Because mortgages are commonly sold in the secondary market, they are continually valued by institutional investors. The market price (P_M) of a mortgage should equal the present value of its future cash flows:

$$P_M = \sum_{t=1}^{n} \frac{C + \text{Prin}}{(1 + k)^t}$$

where C denotes the interest payment (similar to a coupon payment on bonds), Prin is the principal payment made each period, and k is the required rate of return by investors. As with bonds, the market value of a mortgage is equal to the present value of the future cash flows to be received by the investor. Unlike bonds, however, the periodic cash flows commonly include a payment of principal along with an interest payment.

The required rate of return on a mortgage is primarily determined by the existing risk-free rate for the same maturity. Nevertheless, other factors such as credit risk and lack of liquidity will cause the required return on many mortgages to exceed the risk-free rate. The difference between the 30-year mortgage rate and the 30-year Treasury bond rate, for example, is due mainly to credit risk. Thus, it tends to increase during periods when the economy is weak, such as during the credit crisis of 2008.

Because the required rate of return on a fixed-rate mortgage is primarily driven by the prevailing risk-free rate (R_f) and the risk premium (RP), the change in the value (and hence in the market price P_M) of a mortgage can be modeled as follows:

$$\Delta P_M = f(\underline{\Delta R_f}, \underline{\Delta RP})$$

An increase in either the risk-free rate or the risk premium on a fixed-rate mortgage results in a higher required rate of return when investing in the mortgage, which causes the mortgage price to decrease.

Given the uncertainty inherent the factors that influence mortgage prices, future mortgage prices (and therefore returns) are uncertain. The uncertainty that financial institutions face when investing in mortgages is due to credit risk, interest rate risk, and prepayment risk, as explained next.

9-3a Credit Risk

Credit (default) risk represents the size and likelihood of a loss that investors will experience if borrowers make late payments or even default on their loans. Consequently, investors must weigh the higher potential return from investing in mortgages against the exposure to risk (that the actual return could be lower than the expected return). The probability that a borrower will default is influenced both by economic conditions and by the characteristics that lenders consider when assessing a borrower's creditworthiness (level of equity invested by the borrower, the borrower's debt-to-income ratio, and the borrower's credit score).

Hedging Credit Risk with Credit Default Swaps Financial institutions that invest funds in mortgages can hedge their exposure by purchasing a **credit default swap (CDS)**, which is a privately negotiated contract that protects investors against the risk of default on particular debt securities such as mortgages. These swaps, which were created in the mid-1990s, have become a popular way for financial institutions to hedge the default risk on their holdings of mortgages or other debt securities.

A CDS is a form of insurance. The buyer of the CDS provides quarterly payments (similar to insurance premiums that are paid on other forms of insurance) to the seller. In the event that the debt securities default, the buyer of the CDS stops making payments to the seller of the CDS. In addition, the seller of the CDS is obligated to provide a payment (typically the face value of the defaulted debt) to the buyer of the CDS. In this case, the seller of the CDS takes possession of the debt securities that defaulted.

The obvious downside of buying CDSs to hedge the holdings of debt securities is the cost involved. If the annual cost is 2 percent of the value of the security, that cost might fully offset the yield differential between those debt securities and Treasury (risk-free) securities that have a similar maturity. In this case, the investor could just invest in Treasury securities to achieve the same return.

Pricing of Credit Default Swaps Credit default swaps are priced to reflect the likelihood of default. Like most forms of insurance, the annual cost to a buyer of a CDS is positively related to the likelihood of a bad outcome. For a given face value of debt securities to be insured against default, the quarterly payments by the buyer to the seller are higher if the likelihood of default is higher. Put another way, sellers are only willing to sell CDSs on riskier debt securities if they receive large enough payments to reflect their exposure to possible default of the debt securities.

The pricing of CDSs that cover a particular portfolio of debt securities can change over time, based on conditions that can affect the likelihood of default of the portfolio. During the credit crisis, the default rate on mortgages increased substantially. Consequently, buyers could purchase CDSs to protect a portfolio of mortgages during the credit crisis only if they paid a higher price.

Selling Credit Default Swaps Some financial institutions are motivated to sell CDS contracts if they believe that the underlying debt securities will not default, just as insurance companies are willing to sell flood insurance if they believe a flood is very unlikely. If the borrowers do not default on the underlying debt securities, the seller receives payments over time from the buyer, without having to make any payments.

9-3b **Interest Rate Risk**

Financial institutions that hold mortgages are subject to interest rate risk because the values of mortgages tend to decline in response to an increase in interest rates. Mortgages are long-term loans, but are commonly financed by some financial institutions with short-term deposits, so the investment in mortgages may create high exposure to interest rate risk. Such mortgages can also generate high returns when interest rates fall, but the mortgage holders' potential gains are limited because borrowers tend to refinance (obtain new mortgages at the lower interest rate and prepay their mortgages) when interest rates decline.

When investors hold fixed-rate mortgages until maturity, they do not experience a loss due to a change in interest rates. However, holding fixed-rate mortgages to maturity can create a so-called opportunity cost, based on the returns that the investors might have earned if they had invested in other securities. For example, if interest rates rise consistently from the time when fixed-rate mortgages are purchased until they mature, investors who hold the mortgages to maturity give up the higher return that they would have earned if they had simply invested in money market securities over the same period.

Financial institutions can limit their exposure to interest rate risk by selling mortgages shortly after originating them. However, even institutions that use this strategy are partially exposed to interest rate risk. As a financial institution originates a pool of mortgages, it may commit to a specific fixed rate on some of the mortgages. The mortgages are stored in a *mortgage pipeline* until the institution has a sufficient pool of mortgages to sell. By the time the complete pool of mortgages is originated and sold, interest rates may have risen. In this case, the value of the mortgages in the pool may have declined by the time the pool is sold.

Another way financial institutions can limit interest rate risk is by offering adjustable-rate residential mortgages. Alternatively, they could invest in fixed-rate mortgages that have a short time remaining until maturity. However, this conservative strategy may reduce the potential gains that could have been earned.

9-3c **Prepayment Risk**

Prepayment risk is the risk that a borrower may prepay the mortgage in response to a decline in interest rates. This type of risk is distinguished from interest rate risk to emphasize that even if investors in mortgages do not need to liquidate the mortgages, they are still susceptible to the risk that the mortgages they hold will be paid off. In this case, the investor receives a payment to retire the mortgage and must then reinvest those funds at the prevailing (lower) interest rate. Thus, the interest rate on the new investment will be lower than the rate that would have been received on the retired mortgages.

Because of prepayments, financial institutions that invest in fixed-rate mortgages may experience only limited benefits during periods when interest rates decline. Although these mortgages offer attractive yields compared to the prevailing low interest rates, they are commonly retired as a result of refinancing. Financial institutions can insulate against prepayment risk in the same manner that they limit exposure to interest rate risk: They can sell loans shortly after originating them or invest in adjustable-rate mortgages.

9-4 Mortgage-Backed Securities

As an alternative to selling their mortgages outright, financial institutions can engage in **securitization**, or the pooling and repackaging of loans into securities called **mortgage-backed securities (MBS)** or **pass-through securities**. These securities are then sold to investors, who become the owners of the loans represented by those securities.

9-4a **The Securitization Process**

To securitize mortgages, a financial institution such as a securities firm or commercial bank combines individual mortgages into packages. When several small mortgage loans are packaged together, they become more attractive to the large institutional investors (such as commercial banks, savings institutions, and insurance companies) that focus on large transactions.

The financial institution that packages the mortgages contracts with (pays a fee to) a rating agency to rate each package in terms of its exposure to risk of default. It then sells MBS that represent a particular package of mortgages. Many institutional investors rely on the credit rating assigned by the credit rating agency rather than assess the credit (default) risk of the underlying mortgages on their own.

After the MBS are sold, the financial institution that issued the MBS receives interest and principal payments on the mortgages; it transfers (passes through) the payments to the investors that purchased the securities. The financial institution deducts a fee for servicing these mortgages. In this way, the securitization of mortgages allows mortgage companies to create mortgages even if they do not have the funds to finance the mortgages themselves. They can easily sell the mortgages to a financial institution that is willing to securitize them.

9-4b Types of Mortgage-Backed Securities

Five of the more common types of mortgage-backed securities are the following:

- GNMA (Ginnie Mae) mortgage-backed securities
- Private-label pass-through securities
- FNMA (Fannie Mae) mortgage-backed securities
- FHLMA (Freddie Mac) participation certificates
- Collateralized mortgage obligations (CMOs)

Each type is described in turn.

GNMA Mortgage-Backed Securities   The Government National Mortgage Association (called GNMA, or Ginnie Mae) was created in 1968 as a corporation that is wholly owned by the federal government. When mortgages are backed by FHA and VA mortgages, Ginnie Mae guarantees timely payment of principal and interest to the investors that purchase these securities. To qualify for Ginnie Mae guarantees, the mortgages must satisfy specific guidelines. In particular, they must finance the purchase of single-family homes and are restricted to a maximum dollar amount (that changes over time), as they are intended to serve low- and moderate-income homeowners. The financial institutions that originate mortgages with the Ginnie Mae guarantee can more easily sell the mortgages in the secondary market, because institutional investors do not have to worry about credit risk. The result is a more active secondary market for mortgages.

WEB

http://mtgprofessor
.com/secondary_
markets.htm
Detailed information on
the secondary mortgage
markets.

Private-Label Pass-Through Securities   Private-label pass-through securities are similar to Ginnie Mae mortgage-backed securities except that they are backed by conventional mortgages rather than FHA or VA mortgages. The mortgages backing the securities are insured through private insurance companies.

FNMA (Fannie Mae) Mortgage-Backed Securities   The Federal National Mortgage Association (FNMA, or Fannie Mae) was created by the government in 1938 to develop a more liquid secondary market for mortgages. In 1968, it was converted into a public company, owned by shareholders. Fannie Mae issues long-term debt securities to institutional investors and uses the funds to purchase mortgages in the secondary market. In essence, Fannie Mae channels funds from institutional investors to financial institutions that desire to sell their mortgages. These financial institutions may continue to service the mortgages, earning a fee for this service. The payments are channeled through to the purchasers of MBS, which may be collateralized by conventional or federally insured mortgages.

FHLMA (Freddie Mac) Participation Certificates   The Federal Home Loan Mortgage Association (FHLMA, or Freddie Mac) was chartered as a corporation by the federal government in 1970 to ensure that sufficient funds flow into the mortgage market. In 1989, it was converted into a public company, owned by shareholders. It sells **participation certificates (PCs)** and uses the proceeds to finance the origination of conventional mortgages from financial institutions. This provides another outlet for financial institutions that desire to sell their conventional mortgages in the secondary market.

Both Fannie Mae and Freddie Mac enhance liquidity in the mortgage market, as illustrated in Exhibit 9.5. The proceeds received from selling securities are channeled to purchase mortgages in the secondary market from mortgage originators. Financial institutions can originate more mortgages because they are not forced to finance the mortgages on their own. Because the mortgage market is more liquid, mortgage rates are more competitive and housing is more affordable for some homeowners.

Exhibit 9.5 How Fannie Mae and Freddie Mac Enhance Liquidity in the Mortgage Market

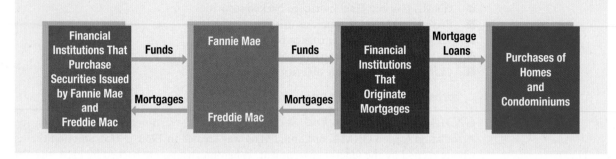

Collateralized Mortgage Obligations **Collateralized mortgage obligations (CMOs)** represent a type of MBS in which the underlying mortgages are segmented into tranches (classes), according to their maturity. The cash flows provided by each tranche are typically structured in a sequential manner, so that the timing of the cash flows generated by a particular tranche is relatively predictable. The first tranche has the quickest payback. Any repaid principal is initially sent to owners of the first-tranche CMOs until the total principal amount representing that tranche is fully repaid. Then any subsequent principal payments are sent to owners of the second-tranche CMOs until the total principal amount representing that tranche is fully repaid. This process continues until principal payments are made to owners of the last-tranche CMOs. Issues of CMOs typically have from three to ten tranches.

Sometimes CMOs are segmented into *interest-only* (IO) and *principal-only* (PO) tranches. Investors in interest-only CMOs receive only interest payments that are paid on the underlying mortgages. When mortgages are prepaid, the interest payments on the underlying mortgages are terminated, as are the payments to investors in interest-only CMOs. For example, mortgage prepayments may cut off the interest rate payments on the CMO after a few years, even though these payments were initially expected to last five years or more. Consequently, investors in these CMOs could lose 50 percent or more of their initial investment. The relatively high yields offered on interest-only CMOs are attributable to their high degree of risk.

Because investors in the principal-only CMO receive principal payments only, they generally receive payments further into the future. Even though the payments to these investors represent principal, the maturity is uncertain due to possible prepayment of the underlying mortgages.

Some mortgages are sold through a **collateralized debt obligation (CDO)**, which is a package of debt securities backed by collateral that is sold to investors. A CDO differs from a CMO in that it also contains other, nonmortgage types of debt securities (e.g., automobile loans and credit card loans).

Like CMOs, CDOs can be separated into tranches based on risk. On average, MBS represent about 45 percent of a CDO, but that percentage may be as low as zero or as high as 90 percent. The mortgages that are included in CDOs are commonly subprime mortgages. When economic conditions weaken, more mortgage defaults occur, in which case the riskiest tranches of a CDO may suffer major losses. Even highly rated tranches are subject to losses in such periods.

When CMO and CDO values deteriorate, financial institutions have more difficulty selling mortgages that they originate because investors are no longer willing to invest in them. Thus, the activity in the CMO and CDO market influences the volume of funds available to finance new mortgages.

9-4c Valuation of Mortgage-Backed Securities

The valuation of MBS is difficult because of the limited transparency involved. Unlike for other securities such as stocks and Treasury bonds, there is no centralized reporting system that discloses details on the trading of MBS in the secondary market The only participants who know the price of the securities that were traded are the buyer and the seller. Given the lack of a centralized reporting system, a financial institution may overpay when buying MBS.

Reliance on Ratings to Assess Value   When deciding whether to purchase MBS, institutional investors may rely on rating agencies (Moody's, Standard & Poor's, or Fitch) rather than attempt to conduct their own valuation. An agency is hired by the issuer of the securities to assign ratings to the MBS that it plans to sell. The financial institutions that create MBS pay a fee to rating agencies to assign a rating to their MBS. Many institutional investors will not purchase MBS unless they have a high rating. However, many of the MBS that were highly rated still suffered major losses during the credit crisis that began in 2008.

Fair Value of Mortgage-Backed Securities   When financial institutions believe that they will incur a loss on MBS (or any other long-term assets), they are expected to "write down" the value to reflect the true market value (also called the "fair value"). In doing so, they may attempt to rely on prices of MBS that are traded in the secondary market to determine the market value of the MBS they are holding. However, MBS can vary substantially in terms of risk, such that MBS at a particular financial institution may warrant a much higher (or lower) valuation than those recently traded in the secondary market. Furthermore, when the secondary market for MBS is not active (such as during the credit crisis, when investors were no longer willing to buy them), insufficient market information is available to estimate a market value.

9-5 Credit Crisis

In 2003–2006, low interest rates and favorable economic conditions stimulated buyers' demand for new homes. The market values of homes increased substantially, and many institutional investors invested their funds in mortgages or mortgage-backed securities. Home builders responded to the favorable housing conditions by building more homes. Furthermore, many lenders were so confident that home prices would continue to rise that they reduced the down payment (equity investment) that they required from home buyers. These lenders believed that, even if the home buyers defaulted on the loan, the home's value would serve as sufficient collateral.

In 2006, some prospective buyers became less willing to purchase homes because of the abrupt increase in home prices that occurred during 2005. Suddenly, the demand for new homes was less than the supply of new and existing homes for sale, and housing prices declined. When interest rates increased in 2006, existing homeowners with adjustable-rate mortgages found it more difficult to make their mortgage payments. In addition, mortgage companies had previously offered mortgages with low initial rates for the first few years. Now these "teaser rates" were expiring on homes that were recently purchased, so that their owners also faced higher mortgage payments. As a result of all these factors, mortgage defaults increased. Because the market values of homes had declined substantially in some areas, the collateral backing many mortgages was not sufficient to cover the entire mortgage amount. Even some mortgages that were insured against default by private insurers defaulted because some insurers did not have adequate funds to cover their obligations.

As economic conditions weakened further, the number of mortgage defaults continued to increase. By June 2008, 9 percent of all homeowners in the United States were either behind on their mortgage payments or in foreclosure. The default rate for subprime mortgages was much higher than that for prime mortgages. In 2008, approximately 25 percent of all outstanding subprime mortgages had late payments of at least 30 days, versus fewer than 5 percent of prime mortgages. In addition, approximately 10 percent of outstanding subprime mortgages were subject to foreclosure in 2008, versus fewer than 3 percent of prime mortgages. Some mortgages that were supposed to be backed by insurance were not. Furthermore, some private insurers that had insured mortgages went bankrupt, which exposed the institutional investors holding the mortgages to major losses.

ETHICS

9-5a Impact of the Credit Crisis on Fannie Mae and Freddie Mac

Fannie Mae and Freddie Mac were chartered by the federal government to issue securities to the public and use the proceeds to purchase mortgages. In aggregate, they sometimes issued debt securities valued at $20 billion in a single week. In 2008, they also held or guaranteed payments on approximately $5 trillion in mortgages or mortgage-backed securities, which represented roughly half of the total in the market.

Both companies were publicly traded. Most importantly, the compensation of their executives was tied to the companies' performance, which caused them to pursue very risky management strategies. They had invested heavily in subprime mortgages in an attempt to achieve higher returns on their investments than if they invested in safer mortgages. As of 2007, Fannie Mae held about $47 billion in subprime mortgages and securities backed by these mortgages, while Freddie Mac held about $124 billion in such securities. In essence, Fannie Mae and Freddie Mac were no longer just providing liquidity to the mortgage market, but were becoming key participants in the market for risky subprime mortgages. Their size and their connection with the government caused many investors to believe that the government would bail them out if they experienced serious financial problems because they were too big to fail. This is a classic example of a *moral hazard* problem, which occurs when a person or institution does not have to bear the full consequences of its behavior and therefore takes on more risk than it otherwise would. In this case, the executives took risks so that they would benefit if their gambles paid off, with the expectation that the government (taxpayers) would likely bail them out if the gambles failed.

By 2008, many subprime mortgages had defaulted, so Fannie Mae and Freddie Mac were left with properties (the collateral) that had a market value substantially below the amount owed on the mortgages that they held. In August 2008, these companies reported losses of more than $14 billion over the previous year. At that time, they held approximately $84 billion in capital, which represented less than 2 percent of all the mortgages that they held. This was a very small cushion to cover possible losses on their mortgages, especially given their risky investment strategies.

Funding Problems Because of their poor financial performance in the summer of 2008, Fannie Mae and Freddie Mac were incapable of raising capital to improve their financial position or to continue their role of supporting the housing market. Their stock values had declined by more than 90 percent from the previous year. As a consequence, they could not raise the capital they needed by selling more shares of stock because the sales would not generate sufficient funds.

Issuing debt securities to raise funds was also no longer a feasible solution. Historically, Fannie Mae and Freddie Mac were able to obtain funds at almost the same rate as the Treasury, because investors viewed them as having no credit risk. However, after their losses were revealed in the summer of 2008, Fannie Mae and Freddie Mac were forced to pay a risk premium of 2.5 percent for their debt securities above the rate on Treasury securities with a similar maturity to compensate for their high level of risk. At this point, their cost of funds was about as high as the return they could earn on high-quality mortgages. This added to their incentive to invest in subprime mortgages so that they could generate higher returns, but it increased their exposure to credit risk.

Rescue of Fannie Mae and Freddie Mac
In September 2008, the U.S. government stepped in to take over the management of Fannie Mae and Freddie Mac before they generated more losses and placed more pressure on the fragile financial system. The Federal Housing Finance Agency (FHFA) placed the two companies into conservatorship and became responsible for managing them until they were determined to be financially healthy. The CEOs of both companies were removed. Meanwhile, the Treasury agreed to provide whatever funding would be necessary to cushion losses from the mortgage defaults. In return, the Treasury received $1 billion of preferred stock in each of the two companies.

The U.S. government's rescue of Fannie Mae and Freddie Mac removed the risk that their debt securities might default and, therefore, increased the values of these debt securities. It allowed Fannie Mae and Freddie Mac to more easily obtain funds by issuing debt securities at a low cost, so that they could purchase high-quality mortgages, thereby ensuring a more liquid secondary market for the mortgages. In short, the government's rescue forced Fannie Mae and Freddie Mac to perform the role that they were intended to perform when they were first created.

9-5b Impact of the Credit Crisis on Exposed Financial Institutions

Many large financial institutions had heavy exposure to mortgages and were adversely affected by the credit crisis. Notable examples are summarized here.

Impact on Bear Stearns
Bear Stearns was a large securities firm that served as a financial intermediary for MBS and also invested heavily in mortgages. It borrowed heavily to finance its operations. The firm used some of its mortgage securities as collateral when borrowing short-term funds, but its funding was cut off during the credit crisis because prospective creditors questioned the quality of the mortgages that served as collateral. The U.S. government was concerned about the potential failure of Bear Stearns because of its involvement with many other counterparties on financial transactions. If Bear Stearns failed, many counterparties would not receive payments from Bear Stearns, which could have caused additional problems in the financial system. In March 2008, the U.S. government orchestrated the acquisition of Bear Stearns by JPMorgan Chase, and provided financial support to facilitate the acquisition.

Impact on Lehman Brothers
Lehman Brothers was another large securities firm that was heavily invested in mortgages and commercial real estate; like Bear Stearns, it borrowed heavily to finance its operations. In 2007, it was the fourth largest securities firm in the United States and was ranked at the top of *Fortune* magazine's list of "Most Admired

Securities Firms." While Lehman Brothers' focus on mortgages and use of financial leverage allowed it to generate very high returns during the housing boom in the 2002–2005 period, it was highly exposed to the weakened housing market conditions in 2007.

ETHICS

In the first months of 2008, Lehman Brothers was still reporting positive earnings. In June 2008, however, it reported a quarterly loss of almost $3 billion, which was primarily due to its write-downs (reductions in market value) of $4.1 billion of its holdings of mortgages and related securities. In September 2008, the company posted a quarterly loss of almost $4 billion, which was primarily due to the write-downs of $5.6 billion in its holdings of mortgages and related securities. It filed for bankruptcy five days after disclosing this loss, which shocked the financial markets. Had Lehman Brothers accurately disclosed its weakened financial condition earlier, its board of directors, key managers, or large institutional shareholders might have had time to offer possible restructuring solutions before it was too late.

ETHICS

Impact on AIG   American International Group (AIG) was a huge seller of CDS contracts that offered financial institutions (buyers of the CDS contracts) protection against mortgage defaults in the 2004–2008 period. At the time, it was the largest insurance company in the world. By 2008, the face value of the securities that AIG had insured by selling CDS contracts was more than $400 billion.

Insurance companies like AIG rely on diversification when providing insurance. For example, when an insurer sells fire insurance, it knows that an adverse outcome (a fire) that causes a payment under one fire insurance policy normally will not cause adverse outcomes for its other fire insurance policies. However, when AIG sold many CDS contracts on mortgage defaults, and the housing market crashed, the adverse outcome (mortgage default) occurred for many of the CDS contracts that AIG had sold, which required AIG to make large payments to the buyers of those CDS contracts. It appears that AIG focused on trying to maximize quarterly payments from the buyers of CDS contracts, without proper regard for its exposure to a single economic event (decline in housing prices) that could affect its entire portfolio of CDS contracts on mortgages or related securities.

Many of the mortgages and related securities that were covered by CDS contracts declined substantially in value, which forced AIG to write down the market value of its positions in CDS contracts. In the first three quarters of 2008, the company reported earnings losses totaling more than $17 billion.

By September 2008, regulators were concerned that AIG could fail due to its excessive exposure to mortgage defaults. The insurance provided by a CDS contract is only as good as the seller (insurer), which must pay the buyer if defaults occur. If AIG failed, it would not be able to cover the payments that it owed on CDS contracts purchased by financial institutions to insure their mortgage holdings, and some of those financial institutions could fail in turn because AIG could not meet its payment obligations.

One day after Lehman Brothers filed for bankruptcy, the U.S. government took control of AIG. The Federal Reserve Bank of New York and the U.S. Treasury injected approximately $130 billion into AIG by purchasing shares and making loans to AIG during 2008 and 2009, and became the majority owner with an 80 percent stake in the company.

9-5c Systemic Risk Due to the Credit Crisis

The impact of the credit crisis extended far beyond the homeowners who lost their homes and the financial institutions that lost money on their mortgage investments. Insurance companies that provided mortgage insurance so that homeowners could obtain a mortgage incurred large expenses from many foreclosures, because the property collateral was worth less than the amount owed on the mortgage. In this way, the problems of the mortgage sector spread to the insurance industry.

As mortgages defaulted in 2008, the valuations of MBS weakened. Consequently, financial institutions were no longer able to use MBS as collateral when borrowing funds from lenders. The lenders could not trust that the MBS would constitute adequate collateral if the financial institutions that had borrowed funds were unable to repay their loans. As a result, many financial institutions with large investments in MBS in 2008 were no longer able to access sufficient funds to support their operations. Moreover, they could not sell their MBS in the secondary market to obtain cash unless they were willing to accept heavily discounted prices for those securities.

Individual investors whose investments were pooled (by mutual funds, hedge funds, and pension funds) and then used to purchase MBS also experienced losses. Investors who had purchased stocks of financial institutions such as Bear Stearns, Lehman Brothers, or many others that had large holdings of mortgages experienced major losses (between 50 and 100 percent) on their stock positions.

Several financial institutions failed, and many employees of financial institutions lost their jobs. Home builders went bankrupt, and many employees in the construction industry lost their jobs, too. The losses on investments and the layoffs contributed to a weaker economy, which made the crisis worse.

International Systemic Risk   Although much of the credit crisis originated in and affected the United States, the problems proved contagious to international financial markets as well. Financial institutions in other countries (e.g., the United Kingdom) had offered subprime loans, and they also experienced high delinquency and default rates. In addition, some financial institutions based in foreign countries had routinely purchased subprime mortgages that originated in the United States. Many institutional investors in Asia and Europe had purchased MBS and CDOs that contained subprime mortgages originated in the United States. For example, UBS (a large Swiss bank) incurred a loss of $3.5 billion from its positions in MBS. Such problems contributed to weaker economies around the world.

9-5d Who Is to Blame for the Credit Crisis?

The credit crisis illustrated some important problems in the mortgage markets. Various participants in the mortgage financing process were subjected to criticism, as explained next.

ETHICS

Mortgage Originators   The mortgage companies and other financial institutions that originate mortgages are supposed to assess the creditworthiness of prospective homeowners. During the housing boom in the 2003–2005 period, however, some mortgage originators aggressively sought new business without exercising adequate control over quality. In some cases, they approved loans without even verifying the prospective buyer's income. Moreover, as described earlier, they reduced the required down payment because they incorrectly presumed that the market values of homes would always serve as sufficient collateral in the event of default.

Many mortgage companies that initiated the mortgages were not concerned about the possible default risk, as they knew the mortgage would be financed by other investors through the securitization process. Many individuals involved in the origination process were paid commissions based on the dollar value of the mortgages they created, which led to very aggressive strategies to create new mortgages.

ETHICS

Credit Rating Agencies   As described earlier, the mortgage-backed securities that are issued by securities firms and financial institutions are assigned credit ratings by credit rating agencies. Those rating agencies, which are paid by the issuers of mortgage-backed securities to rate those securities, were criticized for being too lenient during the run-up to the credit crisis. Mortgage-backed securities were commonly rated AAA even though they represented risky mortgages. Some ratings were based on an assessment of the average level of risk of the underlying mortgages, a method that ignored information about the risk of some of the individual mortgages. Thus, an MBS could receive a high rating even though a significant percentage of its individual mortgages were very risky.

By 2010, a large proportion of the MBS that were issued in 2006 and backed by subprime mortgages either were in default or ultimately were downgraded to the lowest level by the credit rating agencies. Because those downgrades commonly occurred after payments had already been delayed, many investors who purchased those MBS might argue that the certification process by the credit rating agencies was not effective.

According to the Securities and Exchange Commission, many MBS were overrated. Rating agencies were motivated to assign a high rating because the issuing firms could more easily sell highly rated MBS and would be more likely to hire the same agencies to rate future MBS. A credit rating agency typically receives a fee of $300,000 to $500,000 from the issuer for rating a package of mortgages, so a rating agency that assigned more honest (and lower) ratings stood to lose substantial fees if financial institutions hired rating agencies with more liberal standards to rate their next issues of MBS.

Publicized results of investigations of credit rating agencies documented that some analysts at credit rating agencies apparently understood that their ratings were flawed. For example, a manager at one agency sent an e-mail to his coworkers saying that assigning high ratings to MBS was like building a house of cards that would inevitably fall. An e-mail message from another rating agency's analyst stated that the rating model used by the agency to assess risk did not capture even half of the risk involved.

The credit ratings of MBS come with a disclaimer in small print noting that investors should not rely on the credit rating to make investment decisions. Nevertheless, investors who suffered major losses on their MBS investments during the credit crisis might well ask why credit rating agencies were hired to assign ratings if their role was not to determine the risk of the MBS.

ETHICS

Financial Institutions That Packaged the MBS   Securities firms, commercial banks, and other financial institutions that packaged the MBS could have verified the credit ratings assigned by the credit rating agencies by making their own assessment of the risks involved. After all, such financial institutions have considerable experience in assessing credit quality. Nevertheless, during the credit crisis, they relied on the high ratings assigned by the rating agencies, or presumed that households would continue to make their mortgage payments, or simply assumed that the real estate would serve as adequate collateral if households could not make payments.

ETHICS

Institutional Investors That Purchased MBS   Many financial institutions pooled the funds that they received from individual investors and used the proceeds to invest in MBS. These institutions could have conducted their own assessment of the credit quality of the MBS, since they also have experience in assessing credit quality. Once again, however, they relied heavily on the ratings assigned to MBS by credit rating agencies without undertaking an independent due diligence assessment.

Fannie Mae and Freddie Mac were major institutional investors in mortgages and should have been able to assess the risk of the mortgages that they were purchasing. They also could have avoided purchasing mortgages that were assigned weak ratings, or that required very little information from mortgage applicants. By being willing to purchase so many of the risky mortgages that were originated during this era, Fannie Mae and Freddie Mac encouraged the mortgage originators to keep creating risky mortgages. They also encouraged home builders to keep building homes, because prospective buyers of new homes were readily able to obtain financing, even if they could not actually afford the homes.

ETHICS

Financial Institutions That Insured MBS   Mortgage-backed securities that contained insured mortgages provided a slightly lower return to investors (to reflect the fee paid to insurers) but were perceived to be safe and were easier to sell to investors. Yet, as MBS defaults accelerated, some insurance companies found that the mortgages they insured were fraudulent because of inaccurate information about the home buyers. Thus, the financial institution that originated the mortgage either did not verify the information disclosed by many home buyers or withheld some information, causing the mortgage contracts to be fraudulent.

ETHICS

Speculators in Credit Default Swaps   Although CDS contracts were often purchased by financial institutions to protect (or hedge) against a possible decline in valuations of mortgages held, they were also commonly purchased in 2006 and 2007 by institutions that were betting on the potential demise of specific mortgages. For example, some financial institutions believed that the MBS containing subprime mortgages were much riskier than perceived by credit rating agencies and other institutional investors. They were able to purchase CDS contracts from other financial institutions (sellers of CDS contracts) at a low price because those sellers presumed, incorrectly, that the MBS would not default. Thus, many of the buyers of CDS contracts on MBS were not holding any mortgages in MBS that they needed to hedge, but instead were simply betting that subprime mortgages within the MBS would default. By purchasing CDS contracts, they were "insured" against the defaults on specific pools of mortgages even though they did not hold the mortgages that defaulted.

Some CDS contracts were purchased as a speculative strategy by the same financial institutions that also had departments investing heavily in MBS. A large financial institution might have a large mortgage department on one floor where mortgage traders were purchasing MBS due to their favorable expectations about the housing market, and a trading desk on another floor where traders were buying CDS contracts to capitalize on their own expectations that MBS would default. Although all the traders are attempting to generate large returns for their financial institution, and therefore earn large annual bonuses for themselves, each department had its own agenda and perspective.

Speculators in CDSs were criticized for capitalizing on the collapse of the mortgage market. Yet those speculators might counter that the housing bubble was caused by the mortgage originators, credit rating agencies, and financial institutions, and that their own actions simply corrected for the overvaluation of home prices. Moreover, if the sellers of CDS contracts had been less eager to do business (generate insurance premiums) in this market and had more accurately priced the premiums to reflect the risk that they assumed when selling the contracts, the speculators would not have been so willing to take the other side of the CDS contracts.

ETHICS

Conclusion about Blame   The question of who is to blame for the credit crisis has been debated for many years. All targets of blame shared one common characteristic— managerial decisions that were driven by incentives for personal gain such as additional compensation and bonuses.

9-5e Government Programs Implemented in Response to the Crisis

In an effort to stimulate the market for homes and mortgages and reduce the number of foreclosures, the U.S. government implemented various programs. The Housing and Economic Recovery Act of 2008 enabled some homeowners to keep their existing homes, thereby reducing the excess supply of homes for sale in the market. The financial institutions were allowed to create a new mortgage that was no more than 90 percent of the current appraised home value. Because the mortgage value exceeded the home value for many of the qualified homeowners, financial institutions that volunteered for the program essentially forgave a portion of the previous mortgage loan when creating a new mortgage.

Other programs promoted "short sale" transactions in which the lender allowed homeowners to sell the home for less than was owed on the existing mortgage. After an appraisal, the lender informed the homeowner of the price it was willing to accept on the home. Lenders involved in this program did not recover the full amount owed on the mortgage, but they minimized their losses by avoiding the costly foreclosure process, and the homeowners reduced the potential damage to their credit score.

Government Programs to Bail Out Financial Institutions As the credit crisis intensified, many investors became unwilling to invest in MBS because of the risk of continued defaults. Thus, financial institutions that had large holdings of MBS could not easily sell them in the secondary market. The Emergency Economic Stabilization Act of 2008 (also referred to as the Bailout Act) enabled the Treasury to inject $700 billion into the financial system and improve the liquidity of these financial institutions. A key part of the act was the Troubled Asset Relief Program (TARP), which allowed the Treasury to inject capital into large banks by purchasing the banks' preferred stock, thereby cushioning them against expected loan losses. In addition, the Treasury purchased MBS from financial institutions to provide them with more cash. A key challenge of this activity was determining the proper price at which the securities should be purchased, since the secondary market for the securities was not sufficiently active to determine appropriate market prices.

FINANCIAL REFORM

ETHICS

9-5f Financial Reform Act of 2010

In July 2010, the Financial Reform Act (formally called the Dodd–Frank Wall Street Reform and Consumer Protection Act) was implemented; one of its main goals was to ensure stability in the financial system. This act mandated that financial institutions granting mortgages must verify the income, job status, and credit history of mortgage applicants before they approved mortgage applications. The goal was to tighten the looser standards that had been instrumental in creating the credit crisis of 2008.

The Financial Reform Act called for the creation of the Financial Stability Oversight Council to identify risks within the financial system and to make regulatory recommendations that could reduce those risks. The council's 10 members are the heads of agencies that regulate key components of the financial system, including the housing industry, securities trading, depository institutions, mutual funds, and insurance companies.

The Financial Reform Act also requires financial institutions that sell mortgage-backed securities to retain 5 percent of the portfolio unless the portfolio meets specific standards that reflect low risk. This provision forces financial institutions to maintain a stake in the mortgage portfolios that they sell. Moreover, the act requires more disclosure regarding the quality of the underlying assets when mortgage-backed securities are sold.

ETHICS

Finally, the Financial Reform Act established new rules intended to ensure that credit rating agencies provide unbiased assessments when rating MBS. Specifically, the credit rating agencies are required to publicly disclose data on the assumptions they used to derive each credit rating. In addition, the agencies are required to provide an annual report about their internal controls used to ensure an unbiased process of rating securities.

Summary

- Residential mortgages can be characterized by whether they are prime or subprime, whether they are federally insured, the type of interest rate used (fixed or adjustable), and the maturity. Quoted interest rates on mortgages vary at a given point in time, depending on these characteristics.

- Various types of residential mortgages are available, including fixed-rate mortgages, adjustable-rate mortgages, graduated-payment mortgages, growing-equity mortgages, second mortgages, and shared-appreciation mortgages.

- The valuation of a mortgage is the present value of its expected future cash flows, discounted at a discount rate that reflects the uncertainty surrounding the cash flows. A mortgage is subject to credit risk, interest rate risk, and prepayment risk.

- Mortgage-backed securities (MBS) represent packages of mortgages; the payments on those mortgages are passed through to investors. Ginnie Mae provides a guarantee of payments on mortgages that meet specific criteria, and these mortgages can be easily packaged and sold. Fannie Mae and Freddie Mac issue debt securities and purchase mortgages in the secondary market.

- Mortgages were provided without adequate qualification standards (including allowing very low down payments) during the 2003–2006 period. When a glut in the housing market caused a drastic decline in home prices, the market values of many homes fell below the amounts owed on their mortgages. Many homeowners defaulted on their mortgages, which led to a credit crisis in 2008–2009. The U.S. government used various strategies to revive the U.S. mortgage market, including an emergency housing recovery act, the rescue of Fannie Mae and Freddie Mac, and a bailout of financial institutions that had heavy investments in mortgages and mortgage-backed securities.

Point/Counterpoint

Is the Trading of Mortgages Similar to the Trading of Corporate Bonds?

Point   Yes. In both cases, the issuer's ability to repay the debt is based on income. Both types of debt securities are highly influenced by interest rate movements.

Counterpoint   No. The assessment of corporate bonds requires an analysis of the financial statements of the firms that issued the bonds. The assessment of mortgages requires an understanding of the structure of the mortgage market (MBS, CMOs, or something else).

Who Is Correct?   Use the Internet to learn more about this issue and then formulate your own opinion.

Questions and Applications

1. **FHA Mortgages** Distinguish between FHA and conventional mortgages.

2. **Mortgage Rates and Risk** What is the general relationship between mortgage rates and long-term government security rates? Explain how mortgage lenders can be affected by interest rate movements. Also explain how they can insulate themselves against interest rate movements.

3. **ARMs** How does the initial rate on adjustable-rate mortgages (ARMs) differ from the rate on fixed-rate mortgages? Why? Explain how caps on ARMs can affect a financial institution's exposure to interest rate risk.

4. **Mortgage Maturities** Why is the 15-year mortgage attractive to homeowners? Is the interest rate risk to the financial institution higher for a 15-year mortgage or a 30-year mortgage? Why?

5. **Balloon-Payment Mortgage** Explain the use of a balloon-payment mortgage. Why might a financial institution prefer to offer this type of mortgage?

6. **Graduated-Payment Mortgage** Describe the graduated-payment mortgage. What type of homeowners would prefer this type of mortgage?

7. **Growing-Equity Mortgage** Describe the growing-equity mortgage. How does it differ from a graduated-payment mortgage?

8.   **Second Mortgages** Why are second mortgages offered by some home sellers?

9.   **Shared-Appreciation Mortgage** Describe the shared-appreciation mortgage.

10.   **Exposure to Interest Rate Movements** Mortgage lenders with fixed-rate mortgages should benefit when interest rates decline, yet research has shown that this favorable impact is dampened. By what?

11.   **Mortgage Valuation** Describe the factors that affect mortgage prices.

12.   **Selling Mortgages** Explain why some financial institutions prefer to sell the mortgages they originate.

13.   **Secondary Market** Compare the secondary market activity for mortgages to the activity for other capital market instruments (such as stocks and bonds). Provide a general explanation for the difference in the activity level.

14.   **Financing Mortgages** What types of financial institutions finance residential mortgages? What type of financial institution finances the majority of commercial mortgages?

15.   **Mortgage Companies** Explain how a mortgage company's degree of exposure to interest rate risk differs from that of other financial institutions.

Advanced Questions

16.   **Mortgage-Backed Securities** Describe how mortgage-backed securities (MBS) are used.

17.   **CMOS** Describe how collateralized mortgage obligations (CMOs) are used, and explain why they have been popular.

18.   **Maturities of MBS** Explain how the maturity of mortgage-backed securities can be affected by interest rate movements.

19.   **Response of Secondary Mortgage Prices to Prevailing Conditions** Consider current conditions that could affect interest rates, including inflation (including oil prices), the economy, the budget deficit, and the Fed's monetary policy. Based on the prevailing conditions, do you think the values of mortgages that are sold in the secondary market will increase or decrease during this semester? Offer some logic to support your answer. Which factor do you think will have the biggest impact on the values of existing mortgages?

20.   **CDOs** Explain collateralized debt obligations (CDOs).

21.   **Motives for Offering Subprime Mortgages** Describe the characteristics of subprime mortgages. Why were mortgage companies aggressively offering subprime mortgages before the credit crisis?

22.   **Subprime versus Prime Mortgages** How did the repayment of subprime mortgages compare to repayment of prime mortgages during the credit crisis?

23.   **MBS Transparency** Explain the problems that arise in valuing mortgage-backed securities.

24.   **Contagion Effects of Credit Crisis** Explain how the credit crisis adversely affected many other people and institutions beyond homeowners and mortgage companies.

25.   **Blame for Credit Crisis** Many investors that purchased mortgage-backed securities just before the credit crisis believed that they were misled because these securities were riskier than they thought. Who was at fault?

26.   **Avoiding Another Credit Crisis** Do you think that the U.S. financial system will be able to avoid another credit crisis in the future?

27.   **Role of Credit Ratings in Mortgage Market** Explain the role of credit rating agencies in facilitating the flow of funds from investors to the mortgage market (through mortgage-backed securities).

28.   **Fannie and Freddie Problems** Explain why Fannie Mae and Freddie Mac experienced mortgage problems during the credit crisis.

29.   **Rescue of Fannie and Freddie** Explain why the rescue of Fannie Mae and Freddie Mac during the credit crisis improved the ability of mortgage companies to originate mortgages.

30.   **U.S. Treasury Bailout Plan** The U.S. Treasury attempted to resolve the credit crisis by establishing a plan to buy mortgage-backed securities held by financial institutions. Explain how the plan could improve the situation for MBS.

31.   **Assessing the Risk of MBS** Why do you think it is difficult for investors to assess the financial condition of a financial institution that has purchased a large amount of mortgage-backed securities?

32. Mortgage Information during the Credit Crisis Explain why mortgage originators have been criticized for their behavior during the credit crisis. Should other participants in the mortgage securitization process have recognized the lack of complete disclosure in mortgages?

33. Short Sales Explain how short sales work in the mortgage markets. Are short sales fair to homeowners? Are they fair to mortgage lenders?

34. Government Intervention in Mortgage Markets The U.S. government intervened to resolve problems in the mortgage markets during the credit crisis. Summarize the advantages and disadvantages of the government intervention during the credit crisis. Should the government intervene when mortgage market conditions are very weak?

35. Financial Reform Act and Credit Ratings of MBS Explain how the Financial Reform Act of 2010 attempted to prevent biased ratings of mortgage-backed securities by credit rating agencies.

Critical Thinking Question

Regulation in Mortgage Markets   Many critics argue that greed in the mortgage markets caused the credit crisis. Yet many market advocates suggest that greed is good, as the thirst for profits by firms that participate in mortgage markets allows for economic growth. Write a short essay on how regulations can allow for greed while also ensuring proper transparency in the mortgage markets so that another credit crisis does not occur.

Interpreting Financial News

Interpret the following comments made by Wall Street analysts and portfolio managers.

a. "If interest rates continue to decline, the interest-only CMOs will take a hit."
b. "Estimating the proper value of CMOs is like estimating the proper value of a baseball player; the proper value is much easier to assess five years later."
c. "When purchasing principal-only CMOs, be ready for a bumpy ride."

Managing in Financial Markets

CMO Investment Dilemma   As a manager of a savings institution, you must decide whether to invest in collateralized mortgage obligations (CMOs). You can purchase interest-only (IO) or principal-only (PO) classes. You anticipate that economic conditions will weaken in the future and that government spending (and therefore government demand for funds) will decrease.

a. Given your expectations, would IOs or POs be a better investment?
b. Given the situation, is there any reason why you might not purchase the class of CMOs that you selected in the previous question?
c. Your boss suggests that the value of CMOs at any point in time should be the present value of their future payments. He says that since a CMO represents mortgages, its valuation should be simple. Why is your boss wrong?

Problem

Amortization

Use an amortization table (go to www.bankrate.com and click on "amortization calculator" under "Mortgages" or use another online source) that determines the monthly mortgage payment based on a specific interest rate and principal with a 15-year maturity and then for a 30-year maturity. Is the monthly payment for the 15-year maturity twice the amount for the 30-year maturity or less than twice the amount? Explain.

Flow of Funds Exercise

Mortgage Financing

Carson Company currently has a mortgage on its office building through a savings institution. It is attempting to determine whether it should convert its mortgage from an adjustable rate to a fixed rate. Recall that the yield curve is currently upward sloping. Also recall that Carson is concerned about a possible slowing of the economy because of potential Fed actions to reduce inflation. The fixed rate that it would pay if it refinances is higher than the prevailing short-term rate but lower than the rate it would pay from issuing bonds.

a. What macroeconomic factors could affect interest rates and, therefore, the company's mortgage refinancing decision?

b. If Carson refinances its mortgage, it also must decide on the size of a down payment. If it uses more funds for a larger down payment, it will need to borrow more funds to finance its expansion. Should Carson make a minimum down payment or a larger down payment if it refinances the mortgage? Why?

c. Who is indirectly providing the money that is used by companies such as Carson to purchase office buildings? That is, what is the source of the money that the savings institutions channel into mortgages?

Internet/Excel Exercise

Assess a mortgage payment schedule (go to www .mortgagecalculator.org and select "Amortization Calculator" under "Financial Calcs" or use another online source). Assume a loan amount of $120,000, an interest rate of 7.4 percent, and a 30-year maturity. Given this information, what is the monthly payment? In the first month, how much of the monthly payment is interest and how much is principal? What is the outstanding balance after the first year? In the last month of payment, how much of the monthly payment is interest and how much is principal? Why is there such a difference in the composition of the principal versus interest payment over time?

WSJ Exercise

Explaining Mortgage Rate Premiums

Review the "Corporate Borrowing Rates and Yields" table in a recent issue of *The Wall Street Journal* to determine the Treasury bond yield. How do these rates compare to the Fannie Mae yield quoted in the *Journal's* "Borrowing Benchmarks" section? Why do you think there is a difference between the Fannie Mae rate and Treasury bond yields?

Online Articles with Real-World Examples

Find a recent practical article available online that describes a real-world example regarding a specific financial institution or financial market that reinforces one or more concepts covered in this chapter.

If your class has an online component, your professor may ask you to post your summary of the article there and provide a link to the article so that other students can access it. If your class is live, your professor may ask you to summarize your application of the article in class. Your professor may assign specific students to complete this assignment or may allow any students to do the assignment on a volunteer basis.

For recent online articles and real-world examples related to this chapter, consider using the following search terms (be sure to include the prevailing year as a search term to ensure that the online articles are recent):

1. subprime mortgages AND risk
2. adjustable-rate mortgage AND risk
3. balloon-payment mortgage AND risk
4. mortgage AND credit risk
5. mortgage AND prepayment risk
6. [name of a specific financial institution] AND mortgage
7. credit crisis AND mortgage
8. mortgage-backed securities AND default
9. credit crisis AND Fannie Mae
10. credit crisis AND Freddie Mac

PART 3 INTEGRATIVE PROBLEM

Asset Allocation

This problem requires an understanding of how economic conditions influence interest rates and security prices (Chapters 6–9).

As a personal financial planner, one of your tasks is to prescribe the allocation of available funds across money market securities, bonds, and mortgages. Your philosophy is to take positions in securities that will benefit most from your forecasted changes in economic conditions. As a result of a recent event in Singapore, you expect that in the next month investors in Singapore will reduce their investment in U.S. Treasury securities and shift most of their funds into Singapore securities. You expect that this shift in funds will persist for at least a few years. You believe this single event will have a major effect on economic factors in the United States, such as interest rates, exchange rates, and economic growth in the next month. Because the prices of securities in the United States are affected by these economic factors, you must determine how to revise your prescribed allocation of funds across securities.

Questions

1. How will U.S. interest rates be directly affected by the event (holding other factors equal)?

2. How will economic growth in the United States be affected by the event? How might this influence the values of securities?

3. Assume that day-to-day exchange rate movements are dictated primarily by the flow of funds between countries, especially international bond and money market transactions. How will exchange rates be affected by possible changes in the international flow of funds that are caused by the event?

4. Using your answer to question 1 only, explain how prices of U.S. money market securities, bonds, and mortgages will be affected.

5. Now use your answer to question 2 along with your answer to question 1 to assess the impact on security prices. Would prices of risky securities be affected more or less than those of risk-free securities with a similar maturity? Why?

6. Assume that, for diversification purposes, you prescribe that at least 20 percent of an investor's funds should be allocated to money market securities, 20 percent to bonds, and 20 percent to mortgages. This allows you to allocate freely the remaining 40 percent across those same securities. Based on all the information you have

about the event, prescribe the proper allocation of funds across the three types of U.S. securities. (Assume that the entire investment will be concentrated in U.S. securities.) Defend your prescription.

7. Would you recommend high-risk or low-risk money market securities? Would you recommend high-risk or low-risk bonds? Why?

8. Assume that you would consider recommending that as much as 20 percent of the funds be invested in foreign debt securities. Revise your prescription to include foreign securities if you desire (identify the type of security and the country).

9. Suppose that, instead of reducing the supply of loanable funds in the United States, the event in Singapore increased demand for them. Would your assessment of future interest rates be different? What about your general assessment of economic conditions? What about your general assessment of bond prices?

PART 4
Equity Markets

Equity markets facilitate the flow of funds from individual or institutional investors to corporations. Thus, they enable corporations to finance their investments in new or expanded business ventures. They also facilitate the flow of funds between investors. Chapter 10 describes stock offerings and explains how participants in the stock market monitor firms that have publicly traded stock. Chapter 11 explains the valuation of stocks, describes investment strategies involving stocks, and indicates how a stock's performance is measured. Chapter 12 describes the stock market microstructure and explains how orders are placed and executed on stock exchanges.

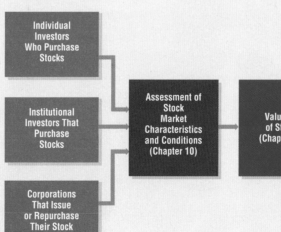

Individual Investors Who Purchase Stocks

Institutional Investors That Purchase Stocks

Corporations That Issue or Repurchase Their Stock

Assessment of Stock Market Characteristics and Conditions (Chapter 10)

Valuation of Stocks (Chapter 11)

Execution of Stock Transactions (Chapter 12)

10

Stock Offerings and Investor Monitoring

Stock markets facilitate equity investment into firms and the transfer of equity investments between investors.

10-1 Private Equity

When a firm is created, its founders typically invest their own money in the business. The founders may also invite family or friends to invest equity in the business. These funds are referred to as private equity because the business is privately held and the owners cannot sell their shares to the public. Like debt, equity can help a firm finance its business expansion, but providers of equity become part owners of the firm, whereas lenders that offer debt financing to a firm do not.

Young businesses that need some debt financing from financial institutions are better able to obtain loans if they have substantial equity invested, because they are in a stronger financial position to repay their debt. Over time, businesses may retain a large portion of their earnings and reinvest it to support expansion. This practice serves as another means of building equity in the firm.

10-1a Financing by Venture Capital Funds

Private firms that need a large equity investment but are not yet in a position to go public (that is, sell shares to the public) may attempt to obtain funding from a venture capital (VC) fund. A VC fund receives money from wealthy investors and from pension funds that are willing to maintain the investment for a long-term period, such as 5 or 10 years. These investors are not allowed to withdraw their money before a specified deadline. A VC fund uses the money that it receives from its investors to purchase minority stakes in selected private companies that need funding. The VC market brings together the private businesses that need equity funding and the VC funds that can provide funding.

Many private companies need equity financing because they have already borrowed the maximum amount of money allowed by banks or other creditors to pursue their business plan. Some of these companies might consider an initial public offering (IPO) in the future, but are presently not large enough to pursue that option. Furthermore, some private companies do not have the long history of stable business performance that would enable them to raise money from a large number of investors in an IPO. Prominent technology firms that relied on VC funding before conducting an IPO include Apple, Facebook, Microsoft, Oracle, and Twitter.

During the period from 2007 until its IPO in 2013, Twitter needed funds to expand its operations. It turned to VC funds and obtained at least $2 million in 2007, $20 million in 2008, and $30 million in 2009. With a proven track record and much potential, it attracted about $800 million in venture capital in 2010 and another $300 million in 2011. Some of its VC funding sources included Benchmark Capital, Union Square Ventures, Charles River Ventures, Marc Andreessen (cofounder of Netscape Communications), and Jeff Bezos (founder of Amazon). Twitter's venture capital funding allowed it to pursue major expansion before it engaged in an IPO in November 2013. Its IPO raised more than $1.8 billion in additional funds. ●

Business Proposals Intended to Attract Venture Capital

Venture capital conferences allow for interactions between firms that need private equity funding and VC funds that have funds to invest. Each firm makes a brief presentation about why its business project will be successful and generate high returns to the VC fund if it receives equity funding. Alternatively, any firm may submit proposals directly to individual VC funds. If a VC fund identifies a proposal that it believes has much potential, it may arrange a meeting with the firm's owners and request more detailed information. Most proposals are rejected, however, because VC funds recognize that the majority of new businesses ultimately fail.

Terms of a Venture Capital Deal

When a VC fund decides to invest in a business, it typically invests an amount such as $5 million or $10 million in exchange for a minority stake in that business. The fund sets out clear requirements that the business must meet to receive the funding, such as providing detailed periodic financial reports.

When a VC fund invests in a firm, the fund's managers have an incentive to ensure that the business performs well. To ensure that the company is following a promising path, the VC fund managers may serve as advisers to the business. They may also insist on having a seat on the board of directors so that they can influence the firm's future progress. The VC fund often provides its funding in stages based on various conditions that the firm must satisfy. In this way, the VC fund's total investment is aligned with the firm's ability to meet specified financial goals.

During its early years, Facebook, which incorporated in 2004, needed funds to support its business operations. Facebook's CEO Mark Zuckerberg met with Peter Thiel (cofounder of PayPal) about possible funding for Facebook. Thiel agreed to invest $500,000 in Facebook for an equity stake of about 10 percent, and was also invited to join Facebook's board of directors. In April 2005, Accel Partners (a VC firm) invested about $13 million in Facebook and was allowed to have a representative serve on the board of directors. Facebook received about $27 million from other venture capitalists in April 2006 and continued to accept equity investments from venture capitalists over time. Facebook's access to venture capital enabled it to pursue its long-term growth objectives without having to worry about a quick repayment to the venture capitalists. After Facebook's IPO in 2012, Thiel sold much of his equity stake for more than $1 billion. ●

Exit Strategy of VC Funds

A VC fund typically plans to exit from its original investment in about four to seven years. One common exit strategy is to sell the equity stake to the public after the business engages in a public stock offering. Many VC funds sell their shares of the businesses in which they invest during the first 6 to 24 months after the business goes public. Alternatively, the VC fund may cash out if the company is acquired by another firm: Such an acquirer purchases all of the company's shares, including those owned by the VC fund. Thus, the VC fund commonly serves as a bridge for financing the business until it either goes public or is acquired.

When VC funds invest wisely, they can achieve very high returns on their investment.

Sequoia Capital is a VC fund that has provided venture capital financing to many firms in the tech sector during their early stages of development, including Apple, Google, Oracle, and Yahoo. During the 2011–2013 period, Sequoia Capital invested approximately $60 million in WhatsApp for an ownership stake estimated to be about 20 percent. WhatsApp benefited because it was able to more fully develop its business with the funds provided by Sequoia Capital. In February 2014, WhatsApp was acquired by Facebook, and Sequoia Capital earned more than $3 billion from its investment. Ultimately, Sequoia's return may have been more than 50 times its investment. ●

Examples like Sequoia Capital's tremendous return from its investment in WhatsApp provide motivation for the creation of new VC funds. However, investing in VC funds also entails much risk. Many young firms with good business ideas fail for many reasons, which can result in losses of 100 percent of the investment provided by VC funds.

Performance of VC Funds The performance of VC funds tends to vary over time. In periods when stock prices are low, valuations of private companies are low, and VC funds can invest their money more wisely in those companies. However, when stock prices are high, valuations of private companies are high, and VC funds may pay too much when investing in companies.

The performance of VC funds is also influenced by the amount of investment received from investors. In some periods, VC funds may receive more funds from investors than they can invest wisely, especially when economic conditions have been favorable and prevailing valuations of companies are high. Under these conditions, VC funds are more likely to compete with each other when they invest in companies, and the bidding may cause them to pay a higher premium for a stake in an especially promising company. Conversely, when VC funds have less money available to invest, they can focus only on the most desirable investments. Under these conditions, they are less likely to pay too much when investing in companies.

10-1b Financing by Private Equity Funds

Private companies that need private equity may also consider private equity funds, which receive investments from institutional investors (such as pension funds and insurance companies) and invest the funds in businesses. With these funds, some restrictions are placed on the minimum amount of funds that can be invested by an investor (such as $1 million) and the amount of time that the funds must be invested before the investor can withdraw them (such as five years). Unlike VC funds, private equity funds purchase a majority stake in a business or even the entire company. Consequently, their investment in a business is usually much larger than the typical investment by a VC fund. By purchasing a majority stake or the entire business, the private equity fund can take full control of the management of the companies it targets. Its managers typically take a percentage of the profits they earn from their investments in return for managing the fund. The private equity fund also charges its investors an annual fee (such as 2 percent of the fund's asset value) for managing the fund.

Use of Financial Leverage by Private Equity Funds In addition to using the funds that they receive from institutional investors, private equity firms borrow heavily to finance their investments. This practice enables them to purchase larger companies or to buy more businesses with a given level of equity. Their use of financial leverage also magnifies the return that they earn on their equity investment. However, if they incur a loss on their investment, the loss will be also magnified because of their high degree of financial leverage.

Because of their heavy reliance on financial leverage, private equity funds tend to invest more money in companies when they can easily obtain debt in financial markets. During the financial crisis of 2008–2009, private equity firms had very limited access to new debt sources, because potential creditors were less willing to provide credit to them.

Strategy of Private Equity Funds   Private equity firms look for companies that are undervalued and mismanaged (in their opinion), because they can more easily achieve a high return on their investment when buying weak firms that they can improve. Because they commonly purchase a majority stake or all of a business, they have control over the company and can restructure the business as they wish in an attempt to improve its performance. Private equity funds tend to sell their stake in the business after several years, sometimes by taking the company public once its performance has improved.

Some critics (including some unions) suggest that private equity firms destroy firms by laying off employees. Private equity firms might counter that the businesses they target are overstaffed and inefficient, and that the firms need to be restructured if they are to survive.

Exit Strategy of Private Equity Funds   Private equity funds can sell their stake in a private business in the same way that VC funds do. If the business conducts an IPO, the private equity fund can cash out by selling its ownership to new investors. Alternatively, it can sell the business to another company.

Performance of Private Equity Funds   If private equity funds are able to improve businesses to a significant extent, they should be able to sell their stakes to new investors or to other firms for a much higher price than they paid for those businesses. The performance of private equity firms tends to vary over time. Like VC funds, private equity funds invest their funds more wisely in companies when stock prices (and therefore valuations of private businesses) are generally low. However, if they invest in private businesses when valuations are very high, they may be subject to large losses (if stock market conditions and valuations of businesses deteriorate) even if they can improve their target company's operations. Private equity funds may be especially prone to making bad investments when they receive large amounts of funds from investors and pursue more investments than are feasible.

10-1c **Financing by Crowdfunding**

In addition to obtaining funds from VC and private equity firms, new companies today have the option of trying to raise funds from a large number of investors through a process called "crowdfunding" over the Internet. Crowdfunding has become an increasingly important way for small businesses to raise funds since Congress passed the Jumpstart Our Business Startups Act (JOBS Act) in 2012. The purpose of the act was to encourage funding of small businesses by easing securities regulations and making it easier for them to use crowdfunding. Since 2012, the Securities and Exchange Commission (SEC) has issued new regulations pursuant to the JOBS Act that make it easier for small investors to invest in new companies. Whereas only investors with a significant net worth were able to invest in startups under the original regulations, now investors with incomes of less than $100,000 can invest $2,000 or 5 percent of their income, whichever is larger; investors who make more than $100,000 can invest up to 10 percent of their income.

To engage in crowdfunding, the founders of a company provide information about their business or project on an Internet platform. Investors then can invest their funds in the projects of their choice. Hundreds of websites now provide crowdfunding platforms of various types. Some, such as Crowdfunder and Indiegogo, provide equity funding, and investors receive shares in the company. Others, such as Kickstarter, specialize in creative projects such as art or music projects. On these platforms, investors who provide funding receive tangible rewards such as tickets to a performance or an item produced by the business seeking funding; they do not receive equity in the company.

Many startup companies today use a variety of funding sources. They may start with crowdfunding, and if that is successful and the business grows, they may turn to VC funds.

EXAMPLE

In 2012, the virtual reality headset maker Oculus Rift raised $2.4 million from 9,500 people on Kickstarter. The business grew, and in 2013 Oculus Rift raised almost $100 million from several venture capitalists including Marc Andreessen, who also invested in Twitter as described earlier. In 2014, Facebook acquired Oculus Rift for $2 billion. ●

Although billions of dollars have been raised worldwide through crowdfunding and some startups have had very successful campaigns, many companies fail to obtain all the funding they seek. Similarly, although some investors have received large returns from their crowdfunding investments, many others have not received any returns at all or have found that it can be difficult to sell their shares, especially if the company never becomes large enough to have an IPO. In addition, companies that rely on crowdfunding may disclose very limited information to these investors. For all these reasons, investing through crowdfunding can be very risky.

10-2 Public Equity

The founders of many firms dream of issuing stock to the public ("going public") someday so that they can obtain a large amount of equity financing to support the firm's growth or pay off some of their debt. They may also hope to "cash out" by selling their own original equity investment to others.

10-2a Ownership and Voting Rights

When a firm engages in a public offering, it issues (sells) many shares of stock in the primary market in exchange for cash. This endeavor changes the firm's ownership structure by increasing the number of owners. A public offering of stock can appeal to many individual investors who want to become shareholders so that they can earn a good return on their investment if the firm performs well. They may also receive dividends on a quarterly basis from the firms in which they invest. However, investors who purchase shares of stock are also susceptible to large losses, as the stock values of even the most respected firms have declined substantially in some periods.

Common Stock   The ownership of **common stock** entitles shareholders to a number of rights. Usually, only the owners of common stock are permitted to vote on certain key matters concerning the firm, such as the election of the board of directors, authorization to issue new shares of common stock, approval of amendments to the corporate charter, and adoption of bylaws. Many investors assign their vote to management through the use of a *proxy*, and many other shareholders do not bother to vote. As a result, management typically receives the majority of the votes and can elect its own candidates as directors.

Preferred Stock   Preferred stock represents an equity interest in a firm that usually does not allow for significant voting rights. Preferred shareholders technically share the ownership of the firm with common shareholders and, therefore, are compensated only when earnings have been generated. Thus, if the firm does not have sufficient earnings from which to pay the preferred stock dividends, it may omit the dividend without fear of being forced into bankruptcy. A cumulative provision on most preferred stock prevents dividends from being paid on common stock until all preferred stock dividends (both current and those previously omitted) have been paid. The owners of preferred stock rarely participate in the profits of the firm beyond the stated fixed annual dividend; instead, all profits above those needed to pay dividends on preferred stock belong to the owners of common stock. The firm may use the profits to pay dividends to the common shareholders or reinvest the funds to finance future expansion.

Because it can forgo paying the dividends on preferred stock, a firm assumes less risk when it issues this type of stock than when it issues corporate bonds. However, a firm that omits preferred stock dividends may be unable to raise new capital until the forgone dividends have been paid, because investors will be reluctant to make new investments in a firm that is unable to compensate its existing sources of capital.

From a cost perspective, preferred stock is a less desirable source of capital for a firm than bonds. Because a firm is not legally required to pay preferred stock dividends, it must entice investors to assume the risk involved by offering higher dividends. In addition, preferred stock dividends are technically compensation to owners of the firm. Therefore, the dividends paid are not a tax-deductible expense to the firm, whereas interest paid on bonds is tax deductible up to a certain maximum. Because preferred stock normally has no maturity, it represents a permanent source of financing.

10-2b How Stock Markets Facilitate Corporate Financing

Exhibit 10.1 illustrates the means by which stock markets facilitate corporate financing in the primary equity market. The stock markets are like other financial markets in that they link surplus units (that have excess funds) with deficit units (that need funds). Individual investors participate in stock offerings by corporations by purchasing stocks directly or by investing in shares of stock mutual funds, which then use the proceeds to invest in stocks.

The investment by individuals in a large corporation commonly exceeds 50 percent of the total equity. Each individual's investment is typically small, however, so that ownership is scattered among numerous individual shareholders.

Institutional investors such as pension funds and insurance companies also participate in stock offerings of corporations by purchasing stocks directly. The massive growth in the stock market has enabled many corporations to expand to a much greater degree and has allowed investors to share in the profitability of corporations.

10-2c Participation of Financial Institutions in Stock Markets

Exhibit 10.2 summarizes the various types of financial institutions that participate in the stock markets. Because some financial institutions hold large amounts of stock, their collective sales or purchases of stocks can significantly affect stock market prices.

Exhibit 10.1   How Stock Markets Facilitate Corporate Financing

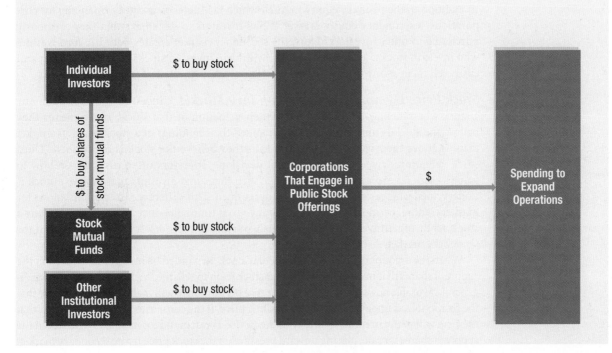

Exhibit 10.2   Institutional Use of Stock Markets

TYPE OF FINANCIAL INSTITUTION	PARTICIPATION IN STOCK MARKETS
Commercial banks	• Issue stock to boost their capital base. • Manage trust funds that usually contain stocks.
Stock-owned savings institutions	• Issue stock to boost their capital base.
Savings banks	• Invest in stocks for their investment portfolios.
Finance companies	• Issue stock to boost their capital base.
Stock mutual funds	• Use the proceeds from selling shares to individual investors to invest in stocks.
Securities firms	• Issue stock to boost their capital base. • Place new issues of stock. • Offer advice to corporations that consider acquiring the stock of other companies. • Execute buy and sell stock transactions of investors.
Insurance companies	• Issue stock to boost their capital base. • Invest a large proportion of their premiums in the stock market.
Pension funds	• Invest a large proportion of pension fund contributions in the stock market.

In addition to participating in stock markets by investing funds, financial institutions sometimes issue their own stock as a means of raising funds. Many stock market transactions involve two financial institutions. For example, an insurance company may purchase the newly issued stock of a commercial bank.

10-2d **Secondary Market for Stocks**

In addition to the primary equity market, which facilitates new equity financing for corporations, a secondary equity market allows investors to sell stocks that they previously purchased to other investors. Thus, the secondary market creates liquidity for investors who invest in stocks. Many investors are willing to invest in stocks only because they can easily sell them at any time.

Stock Price Dynamics in the Secondary Market Investors may decide to buy a stock when its market price is below their valuation of that stock, which means they believe the stock is undervalued. They may sell their holdings of a stock when its market price is above their valuation, which means they believe the stock is overvalued. Thus, stock valuation drives their investment decisions. Investors often disagree on how to value a stock (as explained in Chapter 11), such that some investors may believe a stock is undervalued whereas others believe it is overvalued. This difference in opinions allows for market trading, because it means that at any given time some investors will want to buy a stock, while other investors who previously purchased the stock will want to sell it in the secondary market.

When the amount of shares of a particular stock demanded by investors differs from the supply of shares that investors holding that stock want to sell, the stock's price will change. In general, favorable news about a firm's expected performance will make investors believe that the firm's stock is undervalued at its prevailing price. If the consensus among investors is that the firm will perform more favorably in the future, the demand for its shares will exceed the supply of shares for sale, placing upward pressure on the stock price in the secondary market.

Conversely, unfavorable news about a firm's expected performance will make investors believe that the firm's stock is overvalued at its prevailing price. If the consensus among investors is that the firm will perform worse than expected going forward, the demand for its shares will be less than the supply of shares for sale, placing downward pressure on the stock price in the secondary market.

10-3 **Initial Public Offerings**

When a corporation first decides to issue stock to the public in an effort to raise funds, it engages in an initial public offering. An IPO is used not only to obtain new funding but also to offer some founders and VC funds a way to cash out their investment. A typical IPO is for at least $50 million, as this is the minimum size needed to ensure adequate liquidity in the secondary market if investors wish to sell their shares. In recent years, however, the size of IPOs has tended to increase. Approximately half of the IPOs in 2018 were for firms in the $100 million to $500 million range, and 9 percent were for firm valued at more than $1 billion. Public companies are required to comply with many rules (such as periodic reporting of their financial condition to the public), which can be expensive, which is another reason why only firms that are sufficiently large should consider an IPO.

IPOs tend to occur more frequently during bullish stock markets, when investors are more interested in purchasing new stocks. Prices of stocks tend to be higher in these periods, and issuing firms attempt to capitalize on such prices to obtain more funds through their stock offerings.

10-3a **Process of Going Public**

Because private firms typically are not well known to investors, when those firms engage in an IPO, they must provide detailed information about their operations and their financial condition to attract investors. A firm planning an IPO usually hires a securities firm that serves as the lead underwriter for the IPO. The lead underwriter is involved in the development of the prospectus, the organization of the road show, and the pricing and placement of the shares.

Developing a Prospectus

A few months before the IPO, the issuing firm (with the help of the lead underwriter) develops a prospectus and files it with the SEC. This prospectus contains detailed information about the firm and includes financial statements and a discussion of the risks involved. It is intended to provide potential investors with the information they need to decide whether to invest in the firm. Within about 30 days, the SEC will assess the prospectus and determine whether it contains all the necessary information. In many cases, before approving the prospectus, the SEC asks the firm to provide more information about its financial condition.

The 2012 JOBS Act loosened the reporting requirements for smaller firms about to go public. This act created a new category called emerging growth companies (EGCs) for companies with less than $1 billion in annual gross revenue. An EGC can file a confidential draft registration statement with the SEC for review, is required to provide only two years of audited financial statements instead of three years, and may delay complying with certain independent audit and internal control rules.

Once the firm has complied with all of the SEC's requirements and recommendations, it can begin to promote the IPO. The underwriter will organize a road show, in which the firm's managers travel to major cities around the country to make presentations to stock analysts and potential investors. The managers describe the firm's products or service, discuss its prospects, and answer questions. The goal is to arouse interest in the IPO so that investors will be eager to buy the shares when they become available. A road show typically lasts for one or two weeks.

Pricing and Bookbuilding

Before the road show, the firm and its underwriters will have begun to consider the price at which the firm's stock will be offered to the public. The firm may rely on the lead underwriter to determine the so-called offer price, which is based on the valuation of the firm. Businesses are commonly assigned a valuation that reflects the present value of their future cash flows. The lead underwriter may forecast future cash flows of an IPO firm based on the firm's recent earnings. However, many firms have experienced negative earnings before going public. Their ability to sell shares at a high price is heavily influenced by the expected growth in their revenue and earnings over time. The growth estimates are based on the company's business model as well as on its employees, management style, creativity, reputation, and competition. Nevertheless, it is difficult to forecast growth in revenues or earnings of a young firm at the time it engages in an IPO.

Given the uncertainty about an IPO firm's proper valuation, the lead underwriter often relies on a bookbuilding process to gauge the demand for the firm's shares at the time of the IPO. It elicits feedback from institutional investors on how many shares of the IPO stock they would be willing to buy at various possible offer prices. Based on the findings from this process, the underwriter can estimate the offer price at which it would be able to sell the number of shares that the firm wants to issue at the time of the IPO.

Because so much uncertainty surrounds the valuation of a firm engaging in an IPO, even the large institutional investors that commonly invest in IPO stocks may develop very different valuations of an IPO stock. Such disparity in opinions can cause wild swings in the stock price on the day of the IPO.

EXAMPLE

When LinkedIn went public in May 2011, its offer price was set at $45 per share, which reflected a valuation of about $4.25 billion. Some investors considered this valuation to be excessive because the offer price was about 283 times LinkedIn's recent annual earnings per share (EPS). Furthermore, the offer price was about 46 times LinkedIn's forecasted EPS for the following year. Yet by the end of the trading day of its IPO, LinkedIn's stock price had risen to $94.25, more than twice the offer price. Overall, the market valuation of LinkedIn increased from $4.25 billion to about $9 billion in less than eight hours. Investors who purchased shares at the offer price in the morning saw their investment more than double in value within a single day.

When the market opened on the following day, the opening stock price for LinkedIn was $83. Overnight the stock valuation had declined by about 12 percent, which reflected a decline in the market valuation of more than $1 billion.

In 2017, the IPO for Snapchat had an offer price of $17 per share. The stock price was about $24 per share at the end of the first day, representing a gain of about 44 percent above the offer price and a market valuation of $33 billion. ●

When the market price rises substantially on the day of the IPO, as in the preceding examples, several interpretations of this event are possible. For instance, perhaps the offer price was set too low. Some issuing firms may be concerned that they "left money on the table" because they might have sold the shares at a much higher offer price. The amount of proceeds that the firm receives from the IPO is based on the price at which it sells the new shares. If the offer price is $46 per share, that is what the firm receives, even if the market price of the shares rises to $94 later in the day. The underwriter might counter that the lower offer price was appropriate because it ensured that all the shares would be sold at the offering. If the stock price rises over time (which means that the IPO investors benefit from their investment), the issuing firm may more easily engage in another stock offering in the future because it has gained investors' trust.

Another interpretation of the price increase is that the securities firm underwriting the IPO set a lower offer price to provide institutional investors with special favors, thereby attracting other business from those investors. To the extent that the shares were essentially discounted from their appropriate price, the proceeds that the issuing firm receives from the IPO are less than it deserves. The underwriter might point out that if the offer price had been set higher, institutional investors might not have participated in the IPO, and all the shares might not have been sold.

In some countries, an auction process is used for IPOs and investors pay whatever they bid for the shares. The top bidder's order is accommodated first, followed by the next highest bidder, and so on, until all shares are issued. The issuer can set a minimum price at which the bidding must occur for shares to be issued. This process prevents the underwriter from setting the offer price at a level that is intended to please specific institutional investors.

Allocation of IPO Shares

The lead underwriter may rely on a group (called a *syndicate*) of other securities firms to participate in the underwriting process and share the fees to be received for the underwriting. Each underwriter in the syndicate contacts institutional investors and informs them of the offering. Most of the shares are sold to institutional investors rather than individual investors, as it is more convenient for the underwriting syndicate to sell shares in large blocks. Brokerage firms may receive a very small portion (such as 2 percent) of the IPO shares, which they can sell to their individual investors. Perhaps not surprisingly, they usually give priority to their biggest customers.

Transaction Costs

The transaction cost to the issuing firm is usually 7 percent of the funds raised. For example, an IPO of $50 million would result in a transaction cost of $3.5 million ($0.07 \times \$50$ million). In addition, the issuer incurs other costs, such as the cost of assessing whether to go public, compiling data for the prospectus, and ensuring that the prospectus is properly written. It also incurs fees from hiring legal or financial advisers during this process. As a consequence, the total cost of engaging in an IPO may be close to 10 percent of the total offering.

10-3b Underwriter Efforts to Ensure Price Stability

The lead underwriter's performance can be partially measured by the movement in the IPO firm's share price following the IPO. If investors quickly sell the stock that they purchased during the IPO in the secondary market, there will be downward pressure on the stock's price. If most stocks placed by a particular underwriter perform poorly after the IPO, institutional investors may no longer want to purchase shares sold by that underwriter. Therefore, underwriters may purchase shares in the secondary market shortly after the IPO or take other steps to attempt to stabilize the stock's price.

Underwriter Efforts to Prevent Flipping   Some investors who know about the unusually high initial returns on many IPOs attempt to purchase the stock at the offer price and sell the stock shortly afterward. This strategy is referred to as *flipping*. Investors who engage in flipping have no intention of investing in the firm over the long run and are simply interested in capitalizing on the initial return that occurs for many IPOs. If many institutional investors flip their shares, the market price of the stock may decline shortly after the IPO. Thus, underwriters are concerned that flipping might place excessive downward pressure on the stock's price.

To discourage flipping, some securities firms make more shares of future IPOs available to institutional investors that retain shares for a relatively long period of time. The securities firms may also prevent institutional investors that engage in flipping from participating in any subsequent IPOs that they underwrite.

Overallotment Option   For many IPOs, the lead underwriter has an overallotment option, which allows it to allocate an additional 15 percent of the firm's shares for a period of up to 30 days after the IPO. Twitter's IPO was initially planned for 70 million shares, but its lead underwriter was allowed to sell an additional 10.5 million shares (15 percent of the original plan). Many issuers do not mind issuing additional shares at the time of their IPO if they can do so without causing a decline in the stock price, and if they can make good use of the extra cash that they will receive.

The overallotment option gives the lead underwriter the right to purchase those extra shares from the issuing firm at the IPO offer price. The underwriter then issues the additional shares to investors at the offer price, so it does not gain or lose from issuing the shares, but earns a commission on the extra shares that are sold. The underwriter monitors the stock price over the next several days. If the market price of the stock falls below the offer price, the underwriter commonly purchases all or a portion of the extra shares for sale in an attempt to stabilize the stock price.

EXAMPLE   Bluecrest Securities Company is the lead underwriter for Zuber Company's IPO. The planned allocation is 40 million Zuber Company shares. Bluecrest has an overallotment option that allows it to sell an additional 15 percent of Zuber shares, or 6 million more shares than planned. If Zuber's stock trades at prices above the offer price shortly after the IPO, Bluecrest will exercise its overallotment option and obtain the additional 6 million shares from Zuber so that it can deliver the extra shares to the investors that purchased them. The IPO will result in a total of 46 million shares distributed to investors.

If Zuber's stock price declines shortly after the IPO, Bluecrest will buy back the extra 6 million shares that it sold in the market. In this case, the IPO will result in a total of 40 million shares distributed to investors because the 6 million shares from the overallotment option will be bought back.

Bluecrest's purchase of 6 million Zuber shares in the market offsets the 6 million shares that it initially oversold. Thus, Bluecrest does not become an investor in shares when taking this action. ●

In recent years, the lead underwriters exercised their overallotment option in more than half of all IPOs.

Lockup The lead underwriter attempts to ensure stability in the stock's price after the offering by requiring a lockup provision, which prevents the original owners of the firm and the VC firms from selling their shares for a specified period (usually six months from the date of the IPO). The purpose of the lockup provision is to prevent downward pressure that could occur if the original owners or VC firms immediately sold their shares in the secondary market.

WEB

www.nasdaq.com
/markets/ipos/
Information about IPOs,
including a schedule of
planned IPOs.

In reality, the lockup provision simply defers the possible excess supply of shares sold in the secondary market. When the lockup period expires, the number of shares for sale in the secondary market may increase abruptly, in which case the share price typically declines significantly. In fact, some investors who are allowed to sell their shares before the lockup expiration date now recognize this effect and sell their IPO shares just before that date. Consequently, the stock price begins to decline shortly before the expiration date.

10-3c Facebook's IPO

On May 18, 2012, Facebook engaged in an IPO and raised about $16 billion with its offering. Because of its popularity, Facebook's IPO attracted much attention. It had 33 securities firms that served as underwriters by selling the shares to investors. These underwriters earned fees totaling approximately $176 million for their services. The offer price for Facebook's stock on the IPO date was $38. The stock price initially increased, but then declined later in the day. Based on the offer price, Facebook's market value was about $104 billion at that time, larger than almost all other firms in the United States.

On the day of Facebook's IPO, nearly 571 million shares were traded, and the stock closed at $38.23, just 23 cents above the offer price. Nevertheless, some traders experienced substantial profits or losses because of wild gyrations in the stock price on the first day. Some institutional traders reportedly lost more than $100 million on this single day of trading.

Facebook's opening price of $38 per share reflected a multiple of about 100 times its annual earnings per share at the time. By comparison, Apple's price–earnings ratio at that time was about 14. Facebook's extremely high stock price could be justified only if its earnings would grow much faster than those of Apple and other companies. For Facebook's earnings to grow at this rate, its customer base would have to expand substantially across the world. Some analysts argued that Facebook would have difficulty achieving such aggressive growth because some countries already had local firms that provided a similar service. Using more conservative growth assumptions, they estimated that Facebook's value was about $20 per share, consistent with the price three months after the IPO. Yet by 2015, Facebook's stock price exceeded $100 per share. Given this increase, investors may argue that Facebook was not really overvalued at the time of its IPO.

10-3d Abuses in the IPO Market

Initial public offerings may be subject to several abuses. Some of the more common abuses are described in this section.

ETHICS

Spinning Spinning occurs when the underwriter allocates shares from an IPO to corporate executives who may be considering an IPO or to another business requiring the help of a securities firm. The underwriter hopes that the executives will remember the favor and hire the securities firm in the future.

ETHICS

Laddering   When there is substantial demand for an IPO, some brokers engage in *laddering*, whereby they encourage investors to place first-day bids for the shares that are above the offer price. This helps to build upward price momentum. Some investors may be willing to participate to ensure that the broker will reserve some shares of the next hot IPO for them.

ETHICS

Excessive Commission   Some brokers have charged excessive commissions when demand was high for an IPO. Investors were willing to pay the price because they could usually recover the cost from the return on the first day. Because the underwriter set an offer price significantly below the market price that would occur by the end of the first day of trading, investors were willing to accommodate the brokers. The gain to the brokers was a loss to the issuing firm, however, because its proceeds were less than they would have been if the offer price had been set higher.

ETHICS

Distorted Financial Statements   When firms engage in an IPO, their valuation is highly dependent on the financial statements that they provide to investors. If these statements exaggerate a firm's revenues and earnings, investors may overestimate its value and be willing to pay a higher offer price for its shares. As a result, the firm receives more funds at the time of the IPO than it deserves at the expense of the investors who buy the shares.

EXAMPLE

On November 4, 2011, Groupon went public at an offer price of $20. Its stock price quickly jumped from $20 to about $31 (a 55 percent return) on the first day of the IPO, before then declining. Critics voiced concerns that Groupon was understating its expenses and, therefore, exaggerating its earnings. In its first year as a public company, Groupon frequently made corrections to its financial statements. It then acknowledged that its internal controls were weak. By November 2012, its stock price had declined to about $3 per share, which represented an 85 percent loss from its offer price at the time of the IPO. An employee who owned shares before the IPO was able to sell 1,000 shares for $20,000 at the time of the IPO, but an investor who purchased those 1,000 shares for $20,000 at the time of the IPO would have received only about $3,000 from selling those shares one year later. ●

10-3e Long-Term Performance Following IPOs

Many firms (such as Apple and Google) have demonstrated long-term strong performance following their IPOs. Those success stories tend to receive more attention than the many other IPOs whose long-term performance is weak. Considerable evidence shows that, on average, IPOs perform poorly over a period of a year or longer. Thus, from a long-term perspective, many IPOs are overpriced at the time of the issue. This is especially true from the perspective of individual investors who cannot obtain shares at the offer price, but instead buy shares later on the first day of the IPO at a price much higher than the offer price.

The generally poor long-term performance of IPOs may occur for several different reasons. First, investors (especially individual investors) tend to be excessively optimistic about a business going public and may be willing to buy shares at any price. The weak long-term performance may be partially attributed to a gradual decline in the stock price toward a more rational valuation once the hype wears off.

Second, the poor performance may be caused by the firm's managers. Sometimes they may spend excessively and waste some of the funds received from the IPO by making bad investments.

Third, some firms may have exaggerated their earnings at the time of the IPO in an effort to maximize the price at which the shares could be sold. The managers are not able to inflate the earnings continuously over time. In fact, the effort to shift earnings into the quarter just before the IPO may cause relatively low earnings in the following quarters. Consequently, the stock price may decline in response to lower reported earnings after the IPO. As a related explanation, many firms try to conduct their IPOs when conditions are very favorable and their earnings are peaking; subsequently, their earnings and stock price drift downward during the following quarters.

10-4 Stock Offerings and Repurchases

Even after a firm has gone public, it may issue more stock or repurchase some of the stock that it previously issued. These actions are explained next.

10-4a Secondary Stock Offerings

A firm may need to raise additional equity to support its growth or to expand its operations. A **secondary stock offering** is a new stock offering by a specific firm whose stock is already publicly traded. Some firms have engaged in several secondary offerings to support their expansion. A firm that wants to engage in a secondary stock offering must file the offering with the SEC. It will likely hire a securities firm to advise it on the number of shares it can sell, to help develop the prospectus submitted to the SEC, and to place the new shares with investors.

Because there is already a market price for the stock of a firm that engages in a secondary offering, the firm hopes that it can issue shares at the existing market price. But given that a secondary offering may involve millions of shares, there may not be sufficient demand by investors at the prevailing market price. In this case, the underwriter will have to reduce the price so that it can sell all of the new shares. Many secondary offerings cause the market price for the firm's stock to decline by 1 to 4 percent on the day of the offering, which reflects the new price at which the increased supply of shares in the market is equal to the demand for those shares. Because of the potential for a decline in the equilibrium price of all of its shares, a firm considering a secondary stock offering commonly monitors stock market movements. It prefers to issue new stock when the market price of its outstanding shares is relatively high and when the general outlook for the firm is favorable. Under these conditions, it can issue new shares at a relatively high price, which will generate more funds for a given number of shares issued.

Corporations sometimes direct their sales of stock toward a particular group, such as their existing shareholders, by giving them preemptive rights (first priority) to purchase the new stock. By placing newly issued stock with existing shareholders, the firm avoids diluting its ownership. Preemptive rights are exercised by purchasing new shares during the subscription period (which normally lasts a month or less) at the price specified by the rights. Alternatively, the rights can be sold to someone else.

Shelf Registration Corporations can publicly place securities without the time lag often caused by registering with the SEC. With a so-called shelf registration, a corporation can fulfill SEC requirements as many as two years before issuing new securities. The registration statement contains financing plans over the upcoming two years. The securities are, in a sense, shelved until the firm needs to issue them. Shelf registrations allow firms quick access to funds without repeatedly being slowed by the registration process. Thus, corporations anticipating unfavorable conditions can quickly lock in their financing costs. Although this is beneficial to the issuing corporation, potential purchasers must realize that the information disclosed in the registration is not continually updated and, therefore, may not accurately reflect the firm's status over the shelf-registration period.

10-4b **Stock Repurchases**

Corporate managers have information about the firm's future prospects that is not known by the firm's investors, knowledge that is often referred to as *asymmetric information*. When corporate managers believe that their firm's stock is undervalued, they can use the firm's excess cash to repurchase a portion of its shares in the market at a relatively low price based on their valuation of what the shares are really worth. Firms tend to repurchase some of their shares when share prices are at very low levels.

In general, studies have found that stock prices increase when stock repurchase are announced, which implies that investors interpret the announcement as signaling management's perception that the shares are undervalued. Investors respond favorably to this signal.

10-5 **Stock Exchanges**

Any shares of stock that have been issued as a result of an IPO or a secondary offering can be traded by investors in the secondary market. In the United States, stock trading between investors occurs on the organized stock exchanges and the over-the-counter (OTC) market.

10-5a **Organized Exchanges**

An **organized exchange** is a securities marketplace where buyers and sellers regularly trade securities in the secondary market. Although there are several organized stock exchanges in the United States, the New York Stock Exchange (NYSE), which is owned by Intercontinental Exchange (ICE), and the Nasdaq (National Association of Securities Dealers Association) are by far the largest. Almost all trading on both the NYSE and the Nasdaq is conducted electronically.

Approximately 2,400 companies are listed on the NYSE, and together they have a market capitalization of more than $21 trillion. Nearly 3,300 companies are listed on the Nasdaq, and they have a combined market capitalization of approximately $11 trillion. The Nasdaq's market capitalization is roughly half as large as the NYSE's market capitalization even though it lists more companies, because many of the Nasdaq's companies are relatively small firms. However, the Nasdaq also includes some very large companies such as Apple and Intel. Several billion shares are generally traded on both exchanges every day. For some firms, more than 100 million shares are traded on a daily basis.

The NYSE has two broad types of members: floor brokers and designated market makers. **Floor brokers** are either commission brokers or independent brokers. **Commission brokers** are employed by brokerage firms and execute orders for clients. **Independent brokers** trade for their own account and are not employed by any particular brokerage firm. However, they sometimes handle the overflow for brokerage firms and handle orders for brokerage firms that do not employ full-time brokers. The fee that independent brokers receive depends on the size and liquidity of the order they trade.

Designated market makers (DMMs; previously referred to as specialists) match orders of buyers and sellers. In addition, they can buy or sell stock for their own account, thereby creating more liquidity for the stock. They are required to maintain an orderly market by accommodating orders requested by investors. At a given point in time, the price at which they are willing to sell a stock is higher than the price at which they are willing to purchase the stock. This difference reflects the spread, which compensates them for the service that they provide. Even under weak economic conditions when stock prices are declining, DMMs are supposed to stand ready to accommodate sell orders, but they set the prices at which they are willing to sell or buy the stock. They are likely to buy a large amount of stock only under adverse economic conditions at a discounted price to reflect their risk of taking this position (the uncertainty surrounding the price at which they will be able to sell that stock to other investors over time). In addition, such adverse economic conditions will likely cause them to widen the spread between the prices at which they would be willing to sell the stock versus buy the stock. There is one DMM for each listed stock on the NYSE. Many DMMs are employees of large financial firms such as Barclays PLC and IMC Financial Markets.

The Nasdaq has market makers who perform functions similar to those of the DMMs. However, each Nasdaq market maker is generally responsible for maintaining liquidity and orderly trading in approximately 14 companies.

Listing Requirements   The NYSE and the Nasdaq charge an initial fee to firms that wish to have their stock listed, with this fee depending on the size of the firm. Corporations must meet specific requirements to have their stock listed, such as a minimum number of shares outstanding and a minimum level of earnings, cash flow, and revenue over a recent period. The fee for listing on the Nasdaq is considerably less than the NYSE's fee, and the Nasdaq's requirements are less stringent. In recent years, several major companies including PepsiCo have moved from the NYSE to the Nasdaq. Such companies cite the cost savings as a major reason for the move.

10-5b Over-the-Counter Market

Stocks not listed on the organized exchanges are traded in the OTC market. Like the organized exchanges, the OTC market facilitates secondary market transactions. Unlike the organized exchanges, the OTC market does not have a trading floor. Instead, the buy and sell orders are completed through a telecommunications network. Because there is no trading floor, it is not necessary to buy a seat to trade on this exchange; however, it is necessary to register with the SEC.

OTC Bulletin Board   The OTC Bulletin Board (OTC BB) lists stocks that have a price below $1 per share, which are sometimes referred to as *penny stocks*. Many of these stocks were once traded on the Nasdaq but no longer meet that exchange's requirements. Penny stocks are less liquid than those traded on exchanges because there is an extremely limited amount of trading. They are typically traded only by individual investors. Institutional investors tend to focus on more liquid stocks that can be easily sold in the secondary market at any time.

OTC Markets Group   The OTC Markets Group has three segments where even smaller stocks are traded: OTCQX, OTCQB, and Pink (formerly known as the Pink Sheets). Financial data on these stocks are very limited, if available at all. Companies listed on the OTCQX must undergo a qualitative review to be listed and must be registered with the SEC. Companies listed on the OTCQB must certify that the information they provide is up-to-date, whereas those listed on Pink do not have to meet any financial standards or register with the SEC. Some of the stocks listed on these markets have very little trading volume and may not be traded at all for several weeks.

10-5c Extended Trading Sessions

The NYSE and Nasdaq market offer extended trading sessions beyond normal trading hours. A late trading session enables investors to buy or sell stocks after the market closes, and an early morning session (sometimes referred to as a *pre-market* session) enables them to buy or sell stocks just before the market opens on the following day. Beyond the sessions offered by the exchanges, some electronic communication networks (ECNs) allow for trading at any time. Because many announcements about firms are made after normal trading hours, investors can attempt to take advantage of this information before the market opens the next day.

Market liquidity during the extended trading sessions is limited compared to that during the day session. For example, the total trading volume of a widely traded stock at night may be only 5 percent (or less) of its trading volume during the day. Some stocks are rarely traded at all during the night. Consequently, a large trade is more likely to jolt the stock price during an extended trading session because a large price adjustment may be necessary to entice other investors to take the opposite position. Some investors attempt to take advantage of unusual stock price movements during extended trading sessions, but in doing so they expose themselves to the risk that the market price will not adjust in the anticipated manner.

10-5d Stock Quotations Provided by Exchanges

WEB

www.nasdaq.com
U.S. stock quotes and charts.

The trading of stocks between investors in the secondary market can cause any stock's price to change. Investors can monitor stock price quotations both in real time and historically at financial websites. Although the format varies, most quotations provide similar information. Stock prices are always quoted on a per-share basis, as in the example of Zikard Company (a hypothetical company) in Exhibit 10.3. This exhibit is intended to supplement the following discussion of other information in stock quotations.

52-Week Price Range   The stock's highest price (Hi in Exhibit 10.3) and lowest price (Lo) over the previous 52 weeks are commonly listed. The high and low prices indicate the range for the stock's price over the last year. Some investors use this range as an indicator of how much the stock price fluctuates.

Notice that Zikard's 52-week high price was $121.88 and its low price was $80.06 per share. The low price is about 34 percent below the high price, which indicates a wide range of values over the last year.

Symbol   Each stock has a specific symbol that is used to identify the firm. This symbol may be used to communicate trade orders to brokers. Ticker tapes at brokerage firms or on financial news television shows use the symbol to identify each firm. Each symbol is usually composed of two to four letters. Zikard's ticker symbol is ZIK. Nike's symbol is NKE, Facebook's symbol is FB, and Twitter's symbol is TWTR.

Exhibit 10.3   Example of Stock Price Quotations

YTD % CHANGE	HI	LO	STOCK	SYM	DIV	YLD%	PE	VOL 100s	LAST	NET CHG
+10.3	121.88	80.06	ZIKARD CO.	ZIK	.56	.6	20	71979	93.77	+1.06
Year to-date percentage change in stock price	Highest price of the stock in this year	Lowest price of the stock in this year	Name of stock	Stock symbol	Annual dividend paid per year	Dividend yield, which represents the annual dividend as a percentage of the prevailing stock price	Price–earnings ratio based on the prevailing stock price	Trading volume during the previous trading Day	Closing stock price	Change in the stock price from the close on the day before

Dividend   The annual dividend (Div) shows the dividends distributed to stockholders over the last year on a per-share basis. Zikard's dividend is $0.56 per share, which indicates an average of $0.14 per share for each quarter. The annual dollar amount of dividends paid can be determined by multiplying the dividends per share by the number of shares outstanding.

Dividend Yield   Stock quotations usually show the dividend yield (Yld), which is the annual dividend per share as a percentage of the stock's prevailing or closing price (under Last in the exhibit). Zikard's annual dividend is $0.56 per share and its prevailing stock price is $93.77, so its dividend yield is

$$\text{Dividend yield} = \frac{\text{Dividends paid per share}}{\text{Prevailing stock price}}$$
$$= \frac{\$0.56}{\$93.77}$$
$$= 0.60\%$$

Some firms attempt to provide a fairly stable dividend yield over time, but other firms do not.

Price–Earnings Ratio   Most stock quotations include the stock's price–earnings (PE) ratio, which represents the prevailing stock price per share divided by the firm's earnings per share (earnings divided by number of existing shares of stock) generated over the last year. Zikard's PE ratio of 20 in Exhibit 10.3 is derived by dividing its stock price of $93.77 by the previous year's earnings. Price–earnings ratios are closely monitored by some investors who believe that a low PE ratio (relative to other firms in the same industry) signals that the stock is undervalued in terms of the company's earnings.

Volume   Stock quotations also usually include the volume (referred to as "Vol" or "Sales") of shares traded on the previous day. The volume is normally quoted in hundreds of shares. It is not unusual for several million shares of a large firm's stock to be traded on a single day. Exhibit 10.3 shows that more than 7 million shares of ZIK stock were traded. Some financial media also show the percentage change in the volume of trading from the previous day.

WEB

www.bloomberg.com
/markets/stocks
Quotations on various
U.S. and world stock
market indexes.

Closing Price Quotations   Stock quotations show the closing price ("Last") on that trading day or on the previous trading day if the quotation is being checked during trading hours. In addition, the change in the price ("Net Chg") is typically provided and indicates the increase or decrease in the stock price from the closing price on the day before.

10-5e Stock Index Quotations

Stock indexes serve as performance indicators of specific stock exchanges or of particular subsets of the market. These indexes allow investors to compare the performance of individual stocks with more general market indicators. Some of the more closely monitored indexes are identified next.

Dow Jones Industrial Average   The Dow Jones Industrial Average (DJIA) is a price-weighted average of stock prices of 30 large U.S. firms. ExxonMobil, IBM, and the Coca-Cola Company are among the stocks included in the index. Because the DJIA is based on only 30 large stocks, it is not always an accurate indicator of the overall market or (especially) of smaller stocks.

Standard & Poor's 500   The Standard & Poor's (S&P) 500 index is a value-weighted index of stock prices of 500 large U.S. firms. Because this index contains such a large number of stocks, it is more representative of the U.S. stock market than the DJIA. However, because the S&P 500 index focuses on large stocks, it does not serve as a useful indicator for stock prices of smaller firms.

Wilshire 5000 Total Market Index   The Wilshire 5000 Total Market Index was created in 1974 to reflect the values of 5,000 U.S. stocks, although the number of stocks included has changed over the years. Since this indicator's inception, some of the firms originally included the index have been acquired, so the Wilshire index now represents about 3,500 stocks. The Wilshire 5000 is widely quoted in financial media and closely monitored by the Federal Reserve and many financial institutions.

New York Stock Exchange Indexes   The NYSE provides quotations on indexes that it has created. The *Composite Index* is the average of all stocks traded on the NYSE. It is an excellent indicator of the general performance of stocks traded on the NYSE. However, because these stocks represent mostly large firms, the Composite Index is not an appropriate measure of small stock performance. In addition to the Composite Index, the NYSE provides indexes for various sectors such as energy, healthcare, financial, and industrial. These indexes are commonly used as benchmarks for comparing an individual firm or portfolio to its respective sector. Although the indexes are positively correlated, substantial differences may occur in their movements during some periods.

Nasdaq Stock Indexes   The Nasdaq website provides quotations on indexes of stocks traded on the Nasdaq. These indexes are useful indicators of small stock performance because many small stocks are traded on that exchange.

10-5f Private Stock Exchanges

Prior to undertaking an IPO, some private firms list their shares on a private stock exchange. In such a forum, employees or owners who own shares of these firms can sell their shares to other investors. Nasdaq Private Market and SharesPost are examples of private stock exchanges that facilitate the sale of private firm shares. The main advantage of a private stock exchange is that it allows owners of a private firm to obtain cash. The owners can sell some of their shares to investors in exchange for cash. In addition, the private stock exchange allows investors to become part owners of privately held firms. Many of these firms may ultimately engage in IPOs, so investors could wait to purchase shares. However, if investors can invest in private firms, they may be able to obtain shares at a lower price. In addition, they may not have access to purchasing shares at the time of the IPO, because most IPOs give priority to the large institutional investors.

To purchase shares through a private exchange, investors need to register with the exchange and prove that they meet certain income (such as about $200,000 per year) and net worth (such as at least $1 million) requirements. A problem with investing through a private exchange is that the information disclosed by firms listed on the exchanges may be less than is required when firms go public. The limited information could cause some investors to make bad investment decisions. Investors are at a disadvantage when estimating the proper value of the shares because they do not have all the information that the owners have. In addition, shares of private firms are relatively illiquid, as the trading volume in a private stock market is very limited.

10-6 Monitoring Publicly Traded Companies

A publicly traded firm's managers serve as agents for shareholders by making decisions that are supposed to maximize the stock's price. The separation of ownership (by shareholders) and control (by managers) can result in agency problems because of conflicting interests. Managers may be tempted to make decisions such as paying themselves high salaries or hiring excessive workers that serve their own personal interests rather than the interests of shareholders. If they serve their own interests, they will not maximize the stock's price.

Many institutional investors own millions of shares of a single firm and, therefore, have an incentive to ensure that managers serve the shareholders' interests. The easiest way for shareholders to monitor the firm is to monitor changes in its value (as measured by its share price) over time. Because the share price is continuously available, shareholders can quickly detect any abrupt changes in the value of the firm. In addition, publicly traded firms are required to provide financial statements that disclose their financial condition to the public, so investors can monitor these statements as well.

Investors rely on the board of directors of each firm to ensure that its managers make decisions that enhance the firm's performance and maximize the stock price. A firm's board of directors is responsible for supervising its business.. Directors are also responsible for monitoring operations and making sure that the firm complies with financial reporting laws and ethical guidelines. They should also ensure that the firm has an effective system for internal control and reporting.

10-6a Role of Analysts

Securities firms often employ analysts who are assigned to monitor a small set of publicly traded firms. These analysts communicate with the high-level managers of the firms that they cover. They publicize their opinion of the companies that they monitor for investors by assigning a rating (or recommendation) to the firm's stock such as Strong Buy, Buy, Hold, or Sell.

Although analysts can provide useful information for investors, they may face a conflict of interest because their firms may provide advisory services for the companies that the analysts rate. In that situation, an analyst may feel pressure to assign a high rating to a firm that is likely to hire the analyst's company for advisory services. Perhaps as a result, many analysts tend to use a liberal rating system when rating stocks. In consequence, their effectiveness in detecting ineffective management of publicly traded firms is limited.

Stock Exchange Rules   In the 2002–2004 period, U.S. stock exchanges imposed new rules in an attempt to prevent some obvious conflicts of interest faced by analysts. First, analysts cannot be supervised by the division that provides advisory services, and their compensation cannot be based on the amount of advisory business they generate. This rule is intended to encourage analysts to provide more unbiased ratings of stocks. Second, securities firms must disclose summaries of their analysts' ratings for all the firms that they rate so that investors can determine whether the ratings are excessively optimistic.

10-6b Sarbanes-Oxley Act

To the extent that managers of firms can manipulate the financial statements, they may be able to hide information from investors. Some public companies have used unusual accounting methods to embellish their financial performance. Moreover, although financial statements have to be audited, the auditors are hired by the public companies and recognize that they may be rehired periodically as long as they approve the financial statements.

ETHICS

WEB

www.marketwatch.com
/tools/stockresearch
/updown
List of stocks that
were upgraded or
downgraded by
analysts.

ETHICS

ETHICS

The Sarbanes-Oxley Act was enacted in 2002 to ensure more accurate disclosure of financial information to investors, thereby allowing investors to more effectively monitor the financial condition of firms. This act requires firms to establish an internal control process to improve their reporting. It also attempts to prevent potential conflicts of interest that could occur when firms have their financial statements audited by a public accounting firm. For example, the Sarbanes-Oxley Act prevents a public accounting firm from auditing a client firm whose chief executive officer (CEO) or other executives were employed by the accounting firm within one year prior to the audit. In addition, it prevents the members of a firm's audit committee from receiving consulting or advising fees or other compensation from the firm beyond that earned from serving on the board. This provision prevents a firm from providing excessive compensation to the members of an audit committee as a means of paying them off so that they do not closely oversee the audit. In addition, the act requires that a firm's CEO and chief financial officer (CFO) certify that the audited financial statements are accurate, which makes the CFO and CEO accountable for their veracity. The act specifies major fines or imprisonment for employees who mislead investors or hide evidence.

Although the Sarbanes-Oxley Act has improved transparency, investors still have limited financial information about publicly traded firms, which can cause errors in valuations.

EXAMPLE

Lehman Brothers was ranked at the top in *Barron's* annual survey of corporate performance for large companies. In 2007, *Fortune* magazine put Lehman Brothers at the top of its list of "Most Admired Securities Firms." In March 2007, the value of Lehman's stock was about $40 billion. Yet in September 2008, when Lehman filed for bankruptcy, its stock was worthless. How does a company lose $40 billion in value in 18 months? Some critics would argue that the reported market value of the firm's assets was exaggerated, so its value should never have been as high as $40 billion. ●

Cost of Being Public   Establishing a process that satisfies the Sarbanes-Oxley provisions can be very costly. For many firms, the cost of adhering to the guidelines of the act exceeds $1 million per year. Facing this fact, many small, publicly traded firms decided to revert back to private ownership in the wake of the act's implementation. These firms perceived that they would have a higher value if they were private, rather than publicly held, because they could eliminate the substantial reporting costs required of publicly traded firms.

10-6c Shareholder Activism

If shareholders are displeased with the way that managers are managing a firm, they have three general choices. The first is to do nothing and retain their shares in the hope that management's actions will ultimately lead to strong stock price performance. The second choice is to sell the stock. This choice is often pursued by shareholders who do not believe that they can change the firm's management or do not wish to spend the time and money needed to bring about change. This third choice is to engage in shareholder activism. Some of the more common types of shareholder activism are examined here.

Communication with the Firm   Shareholders can communicate their concerns to other investors in an effort to place more pressure on the firm's managers or its board members. Institutional investors frequently communicate with high-level corporate managers and have opportunities to offer their concerns about the firm's operations. The business's managers may be willing to consider changes suggested by a large institutional investor because they do not want such investors to sell their holdings of the firm's stock.

The California Public Employees' Retirement System (CALPERS) manages the pensions for employees of the state of California and frequently invests considerable money in stocks of publicly traded firms. When CALPERS believes that the firms in which it has invested are not being managed properly, it may communicate its concerns to the firms and often proposes solutions. It might even request a seat on the board of directors, or ask that the firm replace one of the board members with an outside investor. In response, some of the firms adjust their management to accommodate CALPERS.

CALPERS periodically announces a list of firms that it believes have serious agency problems. These firms may have been unwilling to respond to CALPERS's concerns about their management style. ●

Firms are especially responsive when institutional investors communicate as a team. Institutional Shareholder Services (ISS), which is owned by Genstar Capital, organizes institutional shareholders to push for a common cause. After receiving feedback from institutional investors about a particular firm, ISS organizes a conference call with high-ranking executives of the firm so that it can obtain information from the firm. It then announces the time of the conference call to investors and allows them to listen in on the call. The questions during this call focus on institutional shareholders' concerns about the firm's management. Unlike earnings conference calls, which are controlled by firms, ISS runs the conference call. Common questions asked by ISS include the following:

■ Why is your CEO also the chair of the board?
■ Why is your executive compensation much higher than the industry norm?
■ What is your process for nominating new board members?

Transcripts of the conference calls are available shortly after they conclude.

Proxy Contest   Shareholders may also engage in proxy contests in an attempt to change the composition of the board. A more formal effort than communicating with the firm, this action is usually considered only if the firm ignores an informal request for a change in the board (through communication with the board). If the dissident shareholders gain enough votes, they can elect one or more directors who share their views. In this case, shareholders are truly exercising their control.

Institutional Shareholder Services may recommend that shareholders vote a certain way on specific proxy issues. As a result of these more organized efforts, institutional shareholders can exert greater influence over management decisions. At some firms, they have succeeded in implementing changes that can enhance shareholder value, such as the following:

■ Limiting severance pay for executives who are fired.
■ Revising the voting guidelines on the firm's executive compensation policy.
■ Requiring more transparent reporting of financial information.
■ Imposing ceilings on the CEO's salary and bonus.
■ Allowing for an annual election of all directors so that ineffective directors can be quickly removed from the board.

ETHICS

Shareholder Lawsuits   Investors may sue the board if they believe that the directors are not fulfilling their responsibilities to shareholders. This action is intended to force the board to make decisions that are aligned with the shareholders' interests. Lawsuits are often filed when corporations make restructuring decisions that some shareholders believe will reduce the stock's value.

At some firms, the boards have been negligent in representing the shareholders. Nevertheless, because business performance is subject to uncertainty, directors cannot be held responsible every time a key business decision has an unsatisfactory outcome.

When directors are sued, the court typically focuses on whether the directors' decisions were reasonable, not on whether they increased the firm's profitability. Thus, from the court's perspective, the directors' decision-making process is more relevant than the actual outcome.

10-6d Limited Power of Governance

Although much attention has been given in financial markets to how managers are subject to increased governance, some evidence indicates that this governance is not very effective. Numerous examples can be cited of executives who continue to receive extremely high compensation even when their firm's performance is quite weak. In spite of the Sarbanes-Oxley Act, shareholder activism, proxy contests, and shareholder lawsuits, some firms continue to have severe agency problems.

10-7 Market for Corporate Control

When corporate managers notice that another firm in the same industry has a low stock price as a result of poor management, they may attempt to acquire that firm. They may try to purchase the business at a low price and then improve its management so that they can increase the value of the business. In addition, the combination of the two firms may reduce redundancy in some operations and allow for synergistic benefits. In this way, the managers of the acquiring firm may earn a higher return than if they used their funds for some other type of expansion. In essence, weak businesses are subject to a takeover by more efficient corporations, leaving them open to the "market for corporate control." Therefore, if a firm's stock price is relatively low because of bad management, it may become an attractive target for other corporations.

A firm may especially benefit from acquisitions when its own stock price has risen. It can use its stock as currency to acquire the shares of a target by exchanging some of its own shares for the target's shares. Some critics claim that acquisitions of inefficient firms typically lead to layoffs and are unfair to employees. The counterargument suggests that, without the market for corporate control, firms would be allowed to be inefficient, which is unfair to the shareholders who invested in them. Managers recognize that if their poorly performing business is taken over, they may lose their jobs. When they face this personal risk, the market for corporate control can encourage managers to make decisions that maximize the stock's value so that they can better avoid takeovers.

In general, studies have found that in the market for corporate control, the share prices of target firms react positively but that the share prices of acquiring firms are not favorably affected. Some evidence indicates that firms engaging in acquisitions do not eliminate inefficient operations after the acquisitions, perhaps because of the low morale that would result from layoffs. In addition, an acquiring firm commonly has to pay a very large premium, such as 20 to 40 percent above the publicly traded target firm's prevailing stock price, to gain control of the target firm. It is difficult to achieve sufficient benefits from such an acquisition to offset the very large cost incurred by the acquiring firm.

10-7a Use of LBOs to Achieve Corporate Control

The market for corporate control is enhanced by the use of leveraged buyouts (LBOs), which are acquisitions that require substantial amounts of borrowed funds. That is, the acquisition requires a substantial amount of financial leverage. Some so-called buyout firms identify poorly managed firms, acquire them (mostly with the use of borrowed funds), improve their management, and then sell them at a higher price than they paid. Alternatively, a group of managers who work for the firm may believe that they can restructure the firm's operations to improve cash flows. These managers may attempt an LBO in the hope that they can improve the firm's performance.

The use of debt to retire a company's stock creates a highly leveraged capital structure. One favorable aspect of such a revised capital structure is that the ownership of the firm is typically reduced to a small group of people, who may be managers of the firm. Agency costs should be reduced when managers' interests are more closely aligned with those of the firm, as occurs in such a case. However, the firm may potentially experience cash flow problems over time because of the high periodic debt payments that result from the high degree of financial leverage. A firm financed in this way has a high potential return but is also risky.

Some firms that engage in LBOs issue new stock after improving the firm's performance, a process is referred to as a reverse leveraged buyout (reverse LBO). Whereas an LBO may be used to purchase all the stock of a firm that has not achieved its full potential (causing its stock to be priced low), a reverse LBO is normally desirable when the stock can be sold at a high price. In essence, the owners hope to issue new stock at a much higher price than they paid when undertaking the LBO.

10-7b **Barriers to the Market for Corporate Control**

The power of corporate control to eliminate agency problems is limited by barriers that can make it more costly for a potential acquiring firm to acquire another firm whose managers are not serving the firm's shareholders. Some of the more common barriers to corporate control are identified next.

Antitakeover Amendments   Some firms have added antitakeover amendments to their corporate charter. For example, an amendment may require that at least two-thirds of the shareholder votes approve a takeover before the firm can be acquired. Antitakeover amendments are supposed to protect shareholders against an acquisition that will ultimately reduce the value of their investment in the firm, but it also could be argued that shareholders are adversely affected by antitakeover amendments.

Poison Pills   Poison pills are special rights awarded to shareholders or specific managers on the occurrence of specified events. They can be enacted by a firm's board of directors without the approval of shareholders. Sometimes a target enacts a poison pill to defend against takeover attempts. For example, a poison pill might give all shareholders the right to be allocated an additional 30 percent of shares (based on their existing share holdings) without cost whenever a potential acquirer attempts to acquire the firm. The poison pill makes it more expensive and more difficult for a potential acquiring firm to acquire the target.

Golden Parachutes   A golden parachute specifies compensation to managers in the event that they lose their jobs or control of the firm. For example, all managers might have the right to receive 100,000 shares of the firm's stock whenever the firm is acquired. It can be argued that a golden parachute protects managers so that they may be more willing to make decisions that will enhance shareholder wealth over the long run, even though those decisions may adversely affect the stock price in the short run.

Golden parachutes can discourage takeover attempts by increasing the cost of the acquisition. To the extent that this (or any) defense against takeovers is effective, it may allow managers of some firms to be protected while serving their own interests rather than shareholder interests.

10-8 Globalization of Stock Markets

Stock markets are becoming globalized in the sense that barriers between countries have been removed or reduced. Firms in need of funds can now tap foreign markets, and investors can purchase foreign stocks. In recent years, many firms have obtained funds from foreign markets through international stock offerings. This strategy may represent an effort by a firm to enhance its global image. Another motive is that, because the issuing firm is tapping a larger pool of potential investors, it can more easily place the entire issue of new stock.

10-8a Privatization

In recent decades, the governments of many countries have allowed privatization, or the sale of government-owned firms to individuals. Some of these businesses are so large that the local stock markets cannot digest the stock offerings. Consequently, investors from various countries have invested in the privatized businesses.

10-8b Emerging Stock Markets

Emerging markets enable foreign firms to raise large amounts of capital by issuing stock. These markets also provide a means for investors from the United States and other countries to invest their funds. Some emerging stock markets are relatively new and small, and they may not be as efficient as the U.S. stock market. Hence some stocks could be undervalued, which may attract investors to these markets.

However, stock markets in some developing countries are still subject to certain limitations. First, non-U.S. regulatory agencies may make little effort to ensure that the financial information offered by stock issuers is correct. In addition, the smaller markets might be especially susceptible to manipulation by large traders. Furthermore, insider trading (trading based on information about a firm that is not disclosed to the public) is more prevalent in many foreign markets because rules against it are not enforced. In general, large institutional investors and insiders based in the foreign markets may have some advantages.

Although international stocks may generate high returns in some periods, they may also exhibit high risk. Indeed, some emerging stock markets are referred to as "casinos" because of the wide variations in prices that sometimes occur. Large price swings are common because of two notable characteristics of emerging markets. First, for stocks with very limited trading activity, large trades can jolt the equilibrium price. Second, valid financial information about firms is sometimes lacking, causing investors to trade according to rumors. Trading patterns based on continual rumors are more volatile than trading patterns based on factual data.

10-8c Variation in Characteristics across Stock Markets

The volume of trading activity in each stock market is influenced by legal and other characteristics of the country in which it operates. Shareholder rights vary among countries, and shareholders in some countries have more voting power and can exert a stronger influence on corporate management.

The legal protection of shareholders also varies substantially among countries. Shareholders in some countries can more effectively sue publicly traded firms if their executives or directors commit financial fraud. In general, common law countries such as the United States, Canada, and the United Kingdom allow for more legal protection than civil law countries such as France and Italy.

The government's enforcement of securities laws also varies among countries. If a country has laws to protect shareholders but does not enforce those laws, shareholders are not protected as a practical matter. Some countries tend to have less corporate corruption than others; in these countries, shareholders are less exposed to major losses due to corruption.

Finally, the degree of financial information that must be provided by public companies varies among countries. This variation may reflect the accounting laws set by the government for public companies or the reporting rules enforced by local stock exchanges. Shareholders are less susceptible to losses due to a lack of information if public companies are required to be more transparent in their financial reporting.

10-8d Methods Used to Invest in Foreign Stocks

Investors can obtain foreign stocks by purchasing shares directly, purchasing American depository receipts (ADRs), investing in international mutual funds, and purchasing exchange-traded funds (ETFs). Each of these methods is explained in turn.

Direct Purchases   Investors can easily invest in stocks of foreign companies that are listed on the local stock exchanges. Foreign stocks not listed on local stock exchanges can be purchased through some brokerage firms. Since foreign stocks listed on local stock exchanges are denominated in the local currency, the returns to U.S. investors investing in foreign stocks are influenced by the movement of the foreign currency against the dollar over the investment horizon. If the foreign currency appreciates (increases in value) against the dollar, that will boost the return to U.S. investors. Conversely, if the foreign currency depreciates (decreases in value) against the dollar, that will reduce the return to U.S. investors.

American Depository Receipts   An alternative means of investing in foreign stocks is by purchasing American depository receipts (ADRs), which represent shares of non-U.S. stock. Many non-U.S. companies establish ADRs in order to develop name recognition or raise funds in the United States. More than 2,000 ADRs representing shares of stocks from more than 70 countries trade on U.S. stock markets, most of them on the NYSE or the Nasdaq.

American depository receipts are attractive to U.S. investors for several reasons. First, they are closely followed by U.S. investment analysts. Second, companies represented by ADRs are required by the SEC to file financial statements that are consistent with Generally Accepted Accounting Principles used in the United States. In contrast, these statements may not be available for other non-U.S. companies. Third, reliable quotes on ADR prices are consistently available, with existing currency values factored in to translate the price into dollars.

One disadvantage of ADRs is that the selection of investments is somewhat limited. Also, some ADRs are less liquid than many U.S. stocks.

International Mutual Funds   Another way to invest in foreign stocks is to purchase shares of international mutual funds (IMFs), which are portfolios of international stocks created and managed by various financial institutions. In this way, individuals can diversify across international stocks by investing in a single IMF. Some IMFs focus on a specific foreign country, whereas others contain stocks across several countries or even several continents. The shares of an IMF that are sold in the United States are denominated in dollars. Since the foreign stocks within the IMF are denominated in non-dollar currencies, the returns on IMFs earned by U.S. investors are influenced by the change in the foreign currency's value against the dollar over the investment horizon.

International Exchange-Traded Funds   Exchange-traded funds are passive funds that track a specific index. International ETFs represent international stock indexes, and they have become popular in recent years. By investing in an international ETF, investors can invest in a specific index representing a foreign country's stock market. An ETF trades like a stock: It is listed on an exchange, and its value changes in response to trading activity. Although ETFs are denominated in dollars, the net asset value of an international ETF is determined by translating the foreign currency value of the foreign securities into dollars.

A major difference between ETFs and IMFs is that IMFs are managed, whereas ETFs simply represent an index. If investors prefer that the portfolio be rebalanced by portfolio managers over time, they may prefer an IMF. However, ETFs have lower expenses because they avoid the cost of active portfolio management.

The shares of international ETFs that are sold in the United States are denominated in dollars. Since the foreign stocks represented by the ETFs are denominated in non-dollar currencies, the returns earned by U.S. investors in international ETFs are influenced by the change in the foreign currency's value against the dollar over the investment horizon.

WEB

finance.yahoo.com
/world-indices
Provides quotations on
various stock market
indexes around the
world.

Summary

- When businesses are created, they typically rely on private equity along with borrowed funds. Some private businesses that expand attempt to obtain additional private equity funding from venture capital firms. When venture capital firms provide financing, they usually attempt to pull their cash out in four to seven years.

- Many large companies rely on funding from investors obtained by issuing stock to the public. Stock market participants include individual investors as well as institutional investors such as stock mutual funds, pension funds, and insurance companies.

- An initial public offering (IPO) is a first-time offering of shares by a specific firm to the public. Many firms undertake IPOs to obtain funding for additional expansion and to give the founders and venture capital funds a way to cash out their investments. A firm that engages in an IPO must develop a prospectus that is filed with the SEC, and it typically uses a road show to promote its offering. The firm hires an underwriter to help with the prospectus and road show and to place the shares with investors.

- A secondary stock offering is an offering of shares by a firm that already has publicly traded stock.

- Firms engage in secondary offerings when they need more equity funding to support additional expansion.

- Publicly traded firms are monitored in various ways. Analysts monitor firms so that they can assign a rating to their stock. Investors that purchase stock of firms monitor performance and may use shareholder activism to ensure that managers make decisions that are beneficial to the firm's shareholders.

- The market for corporate control allows firms to acquire control over businesses that they hope to improve by replacing managers or revising operations.

- Many U.S. firms issue shares in foreign countries as well as in the United States, so that they can spread their shares among a larger set of investors and possibly enhance the firm's global name recognition. Global stock exchanges facilitate the trading of stocks around the world. U.S. investors can invest in foreign stocks by making direct purchases on foreign stock exchanges, purchasing American depository receipts, investing in international mutual funds, and investing in international exchange-traded funds.

Point/Counterpoint

Should a Stock Exchange Enforce Some Governance Standards on the Firms Listed on the Exchange?

Point   No. Governance is the responsibility of the firms, not the stock exchange. The stock exchange should simply ensure that the trading rules of the exchange are enforced and should not intervene in the firms' governance issues.

Counterpoint   Yes. By enforcing governance standards such as requiring a listed firm to have a majority of outside members on its board of directors, a stock exchange can enhance its own credibility.

Who Is Correct?   Use the Internet to learn more about this issue and then formulate your own opinion.

Questions and Applications

1. **Shareholder Rights** Explain the rights of common stockholders that are not available to other individuals.

2. **Stock Offerings** What is the danger of issuing too much stock? What is the role of the securities firm that serves as the underwriter, and how can it ensure that the firm does not issue too much stock?

3. **IPOs** Why do firms engage in IPOs? What is the amount of the fees that the lead underwriter and its syndicate charge a firm that is going public? Why are there many IPOs in some periods and few IPOs in other periods?

4. **Venture Capital** Explain the difference between obtaining funds from a venture capital firm and engaging in an IPO. Explain how the IPO may serve as a means by which the venture capital firm can cash out.

5. **Prospectus and Road Show** Explain the use of a prospectus developed before an IPO. Why does a firm do a road show before its IPO? What factors influence the offer price of stock at the time of the IPO?

6. **Bookbuilding** Describe the process of bookbuilding. Why is bookbuilding sometimes criticized as a means of setting the offer price?

7. **Lockups** Describe a lockup provision and explain why it might be required by the lead underwriter.

8. **Initial Return** What is the meaning of an initial return for an IPO?

9. **Flipping** What does it mean to "flip" shares? Why would investors want to flip shares?

10. **Performance of IPOs** How do IPOs perform over the long run?

11. **Asymmetric Information** Discuss the concept of asymmetric information. Explain why it may motivate firms to repurchase some of their stock.

12. **Stock Repurchases** Explain why the stock price of a firm may rise when the firm announces that it is repurchasing its shares.

13. **Corporate Control** Describe how the interaction between buyers and sellers affects the market value of a firm, and explain how that value can subject a firm to the market for corporate control.

14. **ADRs** Explain how ADRs enable U.S. investors to become part owners of foreign companies.

15. **NYSE** Explain why stocks traded on the New York Stock Exchange generally exhibit less risk than stocks that are traded on other exchanges.

16. **Role of Organized Exchanges** Are organized stock exchanges used to place newly issued stock? Explain.

Advanced Questions

17. **Role of IMFs** How have international mutual funds (IMFs) increased the international integration of capital markets among countries?

18. **Spinning and Laddering** Describe spinning and laddering in the IPO market. How do you think these actions influence the price of a newly issued stock? Who is adversely affected as a result of these actions?

19. **Impact of Accounting Irregularities** How do you think accounting irregularities affect the pricing of corporate stock in general? From an investor's viewpoint, how do you think the information used to price stocks changes in response to accounting irregularities?

20. Impact of Sarbanes-Oxley Act Briefly describe the provisions of the Sarbanes-Oxley Act. Discuss how this act affects the monitoring performed by shareholders.

21. IPO Dilemma Denton Company plans to engage in an IPO and will issue 4 million shares of stock. It is hoping to sell the shares for an offer price of $14. It hires a securities firm, which suggests that the offer price for the stock should be $12 per share to ensure that all the shares can easily be sold. Explain the dilemma for Denton Company. What is the advantage of following the securities firm's advice? What is the disadvantage? Is the securities firm's incentive to place the shares aligned with that of Denton Company?

22. Variation in Investor Protection among Countries Explain how shareholder protection varies among countries. Explain how enforcement of securities laws varies among countries. Why do these characteristics affect the valuations of stocks?

23. International ETFs Describe international ETFs, and explain how ETFs are exposed to exchange rate risk. How do you think an investor decides whether to purchase an ETF representing Japan, Spain, or some other country?

24. VC Fund Participation and Exit Strategy Explain how venture capital (VC) funds finance private businesses as well as how they exit from their participation in a firm.

25. Dilemma of Stock Analysts Explain the dilemma of stock analysts who work for securities firms and assign ratings to large corporations. Why might they prefer not to assign low ratings to weak but large corporations?

26. Limitations of an IPO Businesses valued at less than $50 million or so rarely go public. Explain the limitations to such businesses if they did go public.

27. Private Equity Funds Explain the incentive for private equity funds to invest in a firm and improve its operations.

28. VCs and Lockup Expiration Following IPOs Venture capital firms commonly attempt to cash out as soon as possible following IPOs. Describe the likely effect that would have on the stock price at the time of lockup expiration. Would the effect be different for a firm that relied more heavily on VC firms than on other investors for its funds?

29. Impact of SOX on Going Private Explain why some public firms decided to go private in response to the passage of the Sarbanes-Oxley (SOX) Act.

30. Pricing Facebook's IPO Stock Price Describe the dilemma of securities firms that served as underwriters for Facebook's IPOs, when attempting to satisfy Facebook and the institutional investors that invested in Facebook's stock. Do you think that those securities firms satisfied Facebook or the investors in the IPO? Explain.

31. Private Stock Market What are some possible disadvantages to investors who invest in stocks listed on a private stock market?

32. Use of Financial Leverage by Private Equity Funds Explain why private equity funds use a very high degree of financial leverage and how this affects their risk and potential return on investment.

33. Overallotment Option in IPOs Explain how underwriters use the overallotment option in IPOs.

34. Designated Market Maker on NYSE Describe the role of the designated market maker on the New York Stock Exchange.

Critical Thinking Question

Valuations of IPOs Write a short essay explaining why there is so much uncertainty surrounding the valuation of a firm that engages in an IPO. Why do you think some investors overvalue firms at the time of their IPO?

Interpreting Financial News

Interpret the following statements made by Wall Street analysts and portfolio managers.

a. "The recent wave of IPOs is an attempt by many small firms to capitalize on the recent run-up in stock prices."
b. "IPOs transfer wealth from unsophisticated investors to large institutional investors who get in at the offer price and get out quickly."
c. "Firms must be more accountable to the market when making decisions because they are subject to indirect control by institutional investors."

Managing in Financial Markets

Investing in an IPO As a portfolio manager of a financial institution, you are invited to numerous road shows at which firms that are going public promote themselves and the lead underwriter invites you to invest in the IPO. Beyond any specific information about the firm, what other information would you need to decide whether to invest in the upcoming IPO?

Problem

Dividend Yield

Over the last year, Calzone Corporation paid a quarterly dividend of $0.10 in each of the four quarters. The current stock price of Calzone Corporation is $39.78. What is the dividend yield for Calzone stock?

Flow of Funds Exercise

Contemplating an Initial Public Offering

If the economy continues to be strong, Carson Company may need to increase its production capacity by about 50 percent over the next few years to satisfy demand. It would need financing to expand and accommodate this increase in production. Recall that the yield curve is currently upward sloping. Also recall that Carson is concerned about a possible slowing of the economy because of potential Fed actions to reduce inflation. It is considering issuing stock or bonds to raise funds in the next year.

a. If Carson issued stock now, it would have the flexibility to obtain more debt and would also be able to reduce its cost of financing with debt. Why?

b. Why would an IPO result in heightened concerns in financial markets about Carson Company's potential agency problems?

c. Explain why institutional investors, such as mutual funds and pension funds, that invest in stock for long-term periods (at least a year or two) might prefer to invest in IPOs rather than purchase other stocks that have been publicly traded for several years.

d. Given that institutional investors such as insurance companies, pension funds, and mutual funds are the major investors in IPOs, explain the flow of funds that results from an IPO. That is, what is the original source of the money that is channeled through the institutional investors and provided to the firm going public?

Internet/Excel Exercises

Go to www.nasdaq.com/markets/ipos and find an IPO that is scheduled for the near future. Review the deal information about this IPO.

1. What is the offer amount? How much are total expenses? How much are total expenses as a percentage of the deal amount? How many shares are issued? How long is the lockup period?

2. Review some additional IPOs that are scheduled. What is the range for the offer amount? What is the range for the lockup period length?

WSJ Exercise

Assessing Stock Market Movements

Review a recent issue of *The Wall Street Journal*. Indicate whether the market prices increased or decreased, and explain what caused the market's movement.

Online Articles with Real-World Examples

Find a recent practical article available online that describes a real-world example regarding a specific financial institution or financial market that reinforces one or more concepts covered in this chapter.

If your class has an online component, your professor may ask you to post your summary of the article there and provide a link to the article so that other students can access it. If your class is live, your professor may ask you to summarize your application of the article in class. Your professor may assign specific students to complete this assignment or may allow any students to do the assignment on a volunteer basis.

For recent online articles and real-world examples related to this chapter, consider using the following search terms (be sure to include the prevailing year as a search term to ensure that the online articles are recent):

1. private equity AND investment
2. venture capital AND investment
3. initial public offering
4. plans to go public
5. stock repurchase
6. stock offering
7. stock listing AND exchange
8. extended trading session AND stock
9. stock AND analyst
10. stock AND shareholder activism

11
Stock Valuation and Risk

CHAPTER OBJECTIVES

The specific objectives of this chapter are to:
- Explain methods of valuing stocks.
- Explain how to determine the required rate of return on stocks.
- Identify the factors that affect stock prices.
- Explain how to measure the risk of stocks.
- Explain common methods of measuring risk-adjusted stock performance.
- Explain the concept of stock market efficiency.
- Discuss foreign stock valuation and performance.

Because stock values change continuously, so do stock prices. Institutional and individual investors constantly value stocks so that they can capitalize on expected changes in stock prices.

11-1 Stock Valuation Methods

Investors conduct valuations of stocks when making their investment decisions. They consider investing in undervalued stocks and selling their holdings of stocks that they consider to be overvalued. Many different methods may be used to value stocks. **Fundamental analysis** relies on fundamental financial characteristics (such as earnings) of the firm and its corresponding industry that are expected to influence stock values. **Technical analysis** relies on stock price trends to determine stock values. Our focus in this chapter is on fundamental analysis. Investors who rely on fundamental analysis commonly use the price–earnings method, the dividend discount model, or the free cash flow model to value stocks. Each of these methods is described in turn.

11-1a Price–Earnings Method

A relatively simple method of valuing a stock is to apply the mean price–earnings (PE) ratio (based on expected earnings rather than recent earnings) of all publicly traded competitors in the respective industry to the firm's expected earnings for the next year.

EXAMPLE

Consider a firm that is expected to generate earnings of $3 per share next year. If the mean ratio of share price to expected earnings of competitors in the same industry is 15, then the valuation of the firm's shares is

$$\text{Valuation per share} = \text{Expected earnings of firm per share} \times \text{Mean industry PE ratio}$$
$$= \$3 \times 15$$
$$= \$45$$

●

WEB

finance.yahoo.com
Type in the ticker symbol to obtain financial data, including earnings forecasts, for a stock.

The logic of this method is that future earnings are an important determinant of a firm's value. Although earnings beyond the next year are also relevant, this method implicitly assumes that the growth in earnings for the specific firm in future years will be similar to that of the industry.

Reasons for Different Valuations   The PE method has several variations, which can result in different valuations. For example, investors may use different forecasts for the firm's earnings or the mean industry earnings over the next year. The previous year's earnings are often used as a base for forecasting future earnings, but recent earnings do not always yield an accurate forecast.

Limitations of the PE Method   The PE method may result in an inaccurate valuation of a firm if errors are made in forecasting the firm's future earnings.

EXAMPLE

Firms in a cyclical industry, such as heavy equipment manufacturing, generally have very low or even negative earnings during recessions. Their earnings tend to increase dramatically when the economy is strong. Caterpillar is an example of a company whose earnings usually decline substantially when the economy is weak and few building projects are undertaken; as soon as the economy improves, its earnings increase. Thus, relying on the previous year's earnings to forecast future earnings for a cyclical company may not be very useful if the economy is expected to become weaker or stronger in the future. In contrast, the earnings of a consumer goods company such as Procter & Gamble generally do not vary as much because people continue to buy basic consumer goods even when the economy is weak.

Using previous earnings may not be useful for valuing a firm that is restructuring its operations. To try to improve its performance through restructuring, the firm may close some plants, eliminate divisions, and lay off employees, all of which may be costly. In consequence, the firm's earnings may be low or negative temporarily due to the restructuring, so this would not serve as a useful method for valuing the company. ●

Another limitation with the PE method for valuing firms is that some firms may use creative accounting methods to exaggerate their earnings in a particular period, but be unable to sustain that earnings level in the future. Furthermore, investors may disagree on the proper measure of earnings. Some investors prefer to use operating earnings or exclude some unusually high expenses that result from one-time events.

Investors may also disagree on which firms represent the industry norm that should be used when applying the price–earnings ratio to a firm's earnings. Some investors rely on a narrow industry composite composed of firms that are similar (in terms of size, lines of business, and so on) to the firm being valued; other investors prefer a broader industry composite. Consequently, even if investors agree on a firm's forecasted earnings, they may still derive different values for that firm as a result of applying different price–earnings ratios. Even if investors agree on the firms to include in the industry composite, they may disagree on how to weight each firm.

An additional limitation in using the PE method is that stock buybacks (repurchases) by firms can distort a firm's earnings and, in turn, distort a valuation derived from those earnings. Stock buybacks complicate the stock valuation process because they reduce the number of shares outstanding and increase earnings per share even when the company's total earnings have not increased.

EXAMPLE

Assume that a firm has 10 million shares of stock outstanding and has total earnings of $100 million for the year. Thus, its earnings per share are $10. If the firm initiates a buyback program and repurchases 1 million shares of stock, its earnings are still $100 million, but its earnings per share increase to $11.11 because the firm now has only 9 million shares of stock outstanding. In this way, using reported earnings per share without adjusting for stock buybacks can lead to inaccurate valuations. ●

11-1b Dividend Discount Model

One of the first models used for pricing stocks was developed by John B. Williams in 1931. This model is still applicable today. Williams stated that the price of a stock should reflect the present value of the stock's future dividends, or

$$\text{Price} = \sum_{t=1}^{\infty} \frac{D_t}{(1 + k)^t}$$

where

$$t = \text{period}$$
$$D_t = \text{dividend in period } t$$
$$k = \text{discount rate}$$

The model can account for uncertainty by allowing D_t to be revised in response to revised expectations about a firm's cash flows or by allowing k to be revised in response to changes in the required rate of return by investors.

EXAMPLE

To illustrate how the dividend discount model can be used to value a stock, consider a stock that is expected to pay a dividend of $7 per share annually forever. This constant dividend represents a perpetuity, or an annuity that lasts forever. Hence the present value of the cash flows (dividend payments) to investors in this example is the present value of a perpetuity. Assuming that the required rate of return (k) on the stock of concern is 14 percent, the present value (PV) of the future dividends is

$$PV \text{ of stock} = D/k$$
$$= \$7/0.14$$
$$= \$50 \text{ per share}$$ ●

WEB

www.investopedia
.com/terms/t
/fundamentalanalysis
.asp
A discussion of
fundamental analysis
and various valuation
methods.

Unfortunately, the valuation of most stocks is not this simple because their dividends are not expected to remain constant forever. If the dividend is expected to grow at a constant rate, however, the stock can be valued by applying the constant-growth dividend discount model:

$$PV \text{ of stock} = D_1/(k - g)$$

where D_1 is the expected dividend per share to be paid over the next year, k is the required rate of return by investors, and g is the rate at which the dividend is expected to grow. For example, if a stock is expected to provide a dividend of $7 per share next year, the dividend is expected to increase by 4 percent per year, and the required rate of return is 14 percent, the stock can be valued as

$$PV \text{ of stock} = \$7/(0.14 - 0.04)$$
$$= \$70 \text{ per share}$$

Relationship with PE Ratio for Valuing Firms   The dividend discount model and the PE ratio might seem to be unrelated, given that the dividend discount model is highly dependent on the required rate of return and the growth rate, whereas the PE ratio is driven by the mean multiple of competitors' stock prices relative to their earnings expectations and by the earnings expectations of the firm being valued. Yet the PE multiple is influenced by the required rate of return on stocks of competitors and the expected growth rate of competitor firms. When using the PE ratio for valuation, the investor implicitly assumes that the required rate of return and the growth rate for the firm being valued are similar to those of its competitors. When the required rate of return on competitor firms is relatively high, the PE multiple will be relatively low, which results in a relatively low valuation of the firm for its level of expected earnings. When the competitors' growth rate is relatively high, the PE multiple will be relatively high, which results in a relatively high valuation of the firm for its level of expected earnings. Thus, an inverse relationship between the required rate of return and the firm's value exists when either the PE method or the dividend discount model is applied. In addition, there is a positive relationship between a firm's growth rate and its value when applying either method.

Limitations of the Dividend Discount Model　　The dividend discount model may result in an inaccurate valuation of a firm if errors are made in estimating the dividend to be paid over the next year or in estimating the growth rate or the required rate of return by investors. The limitations of this model are more pronounced when valuing firms that retain most of their earnings, rather than distributing them as dividends, because the model relies on the dividend as the base for applying the growth rate. For example, many smaller publicly traded firms that are attempting to grow retain all earnings to support growth; for this reason, they are not expected to pay any dividends.

11-1c Adjusted Dividend Discount Model

The dividend discount model can be adapted to assess the value of any firm, even those firms that retain most or all of their earnings. From the investor's perspective, the value of the stock is equal to (1) the present value of the future dividends to be received over the investment horizon *plus* (2) the present value of the forecasted price at which the stock will be sold at the end of the investment horizon. To forecast this sales price, investors must estimate the firm's earnings per share (after removing any nonrecurring effects) in the year that they plan to sell the stock. This estimate is derived by applying an annual growth rate to the prevailing annual earnings per share. Then the estimate can be used to derive the expected price per share at which the stock can be sold.

EXAMPLE　　Assume that a firm currently has earnings of $12 per share. Future earnings can be forecast by applying the expected annual growth rate to the firm's existing earnings (E):

$$\text{Forecasted earnings in } n \text{ years} = E(1 + g)^n$$

where g is the expected growth rate of earnings and n is the number of years until the stock is to be sold.

If investors anticipate that the earnings per share will grow by 2 percent annually and expect to sell the firm's stock in three years, the earnings per share in three years are forecast to be

$$\text{Earnings in three years} = \$12 \times (1 + 0.02)^3$$
$$= \$12 \times 1.0612$$
$$= \$12.73$$

The forecasted earnings per share can be multiplied by the PE ratio of the firm's industry to forecast the future stock price. For example, if the mean PE ratio of all other firms in the same industry is 6, the stock price in three years can be forecast as follows:

$$\text{Stock price in three years} = \text{Earnings in three years} \times \text{PE ratio of industry}$$
$$= \$12.73 \times 6$$
$$= \$76.38$$

This forecasted stock price can be used along with expected dividends and the investor's required rate of return to value the stock today. If the firm is expected to pay a dividend of $4 per share over the next three years and if the investor's required rate of return is 14 percent, then the present value of expected cash flows to be received by the investor is

$$PV = \$4/(1.14)^1 + \$4/(1.14)^2 + \$4/(1.14)^3 + \$76.38/(1.14)^3$$
$$= \$3.51 + \$3.08 + \$2.70 + \$51.55$$
$$= \$60.84 \qquad \bullet$$

In this example, the present value of the cash flows is based on (1) the present value of dividends to be received over the three-year investment horizon, which is $9.29 per share ($3.51 + $3.08 + $2.70), and (2) the present value of the forecasted price at which the stock can be sold at the end of the three-year investment horizon, which is $51.55 per share.

Limitations of the Adjusted Dividend Discount Model   This model may result in an inaccurate valuation if the investor errs in deriving the present value of dividends over the investment horizon or the present value of the forecasted price at which the stock can be sold at the end of the investment horizon. Because the required rate of return affects both of these factors, using the wrong required rate of return will lead to inaccurate valuations. Methods for determining the required rate of return are discussed later in this chapter.

11-1d Free Cash Flow Model

For firms that do not pay dividends, a more suitable valuation may be the free cash flow model, which is based on the present value of future cash flows. It involves three steps. First, estimate the free cash flows that will result from operations. Second, subtract existing liabilities to determine the value of the firm. Third, divide the value of the firm by the number of shares to derive a value per share.

Limitations   A key limitation of this model is the difficulty in obtaining an accurate estimate of the free cash flow per period. One possibility is to start with forecasted earnings and then add a forecast of the firm's noncash expenses and capital investment and working capital investment required to support the growth in the forecasted earnings. However, as explained earlier, obtaining accurate earnings forecasts can be difficult.

11-2 Required Rate of Return on Stocks

When investors attempt to value a firm based on discounted cash flows, they must determine the required rate of return by investors who invest in that stock. Investors require a return that reflects the risk-free interest rate plus a risk premium. Although investors generally require a higher return on firms that exhibit more risk, there is not complete agreement on the ideal measure of risk or the way risk should be used to derive the required rate of return.

11-2a Capital Asset Pricing Model

The capital asset pricing model (CAPM) is sometimes used to estimate the required rate of return for any firm with publicly traded stock. The CAPM is based on the premise that the only important risk for a firm is **systematic risk**, or the risk that results from exposure to general stock market movements. This model is not concerned with so-called unsystematic risk, which is specific to an individual firm, because investors can avoid that type of risk by holding diversified portfolios. With this approach to investing, any particular adverse condition (such as a labor strike) affecting one particular firm in an investor's stock portfolio should be offset in a given period by some favorable condition affecting another particular firm in the portfolio. In contrast, the systematic impact of general stock market movements on stocks in the portfolio cannot be diversified away because most of the stocks would be adversely affected by a general market decline.

The CAPM suggests that the return of a stock (R_j) is influenced by the prevailing risk-free rate (R_f), the market return (R_m), and the beta (B_j), as follows:

$$R_j = R_f + B_j(R_m - R_f)$$

where B_j is the covariance between R_j and R_m, which reflects the asset's sensitivity to general stock market movements. The CAPM implies that, given a specific R_f and R_m, investors will require a higher return on a stock that has a higher beta. A higher beta implies a higher covariance between the stock's returns and market returns, which reflects a greater sensitivity of the stock's return to general stock market movements.

Estimating the Market Risk Premium The yield on newly issued Treasury bonds is commonly used as a proxy for the risk-free rate. The term within parentheses in the previous equation is the market risk premium: the return of the market in excess of the risk-free rate. Historical data for 30 or more years can be used to determine the average market risk premium over time, which serves as an estimate of the market risk premium that will exist in the future. Note, however, that the market risk premium may be higher in some periods than in others.

During the financial crisis that began in 2008, much uncertainty arose regarding the valuations of stocks in general. Some investors were willing to maintain investments in the stock market only if the market risk premium was sufficiently high to compensate them for the risk of investing in the stock market. Put simply, prices of all stocks in the market had to be sufficiently discounted to offer sufficient upside potential to attract these investors.

In contrast, when stock market conditions are very favorable, investors may not be as concerned about the risk of the stock market in general. In these periods, investors do not require such a large market risk premium, as they do not fear that the market is susceptible to a major decline. ●

Estimating the Firm's Beta A stock's beta is typically measured by applying regression analysis to determine the sensitivity of the asset's return to the market return based on monthly or quarterly data over the last four years or so. The stock's return is the dependent variable, and the market's return (as measured by the Standard & Poor's [S&P] 500 index or some other suitable proxy) is the independent variable over those same periods. A computer spreadsheet package such as Excel can be used to run the regression analysis. This analysis focuses specifically on estimating the slope coefficient, which represents the estimate of each stock's beta (see Appendix B for more information on using regression analysis). If the slope coefficient of an individual stock is estimated to be 1.2, this means that, for a given return in the market, the stock's expected return is 1.2 times that amount.

Estimated betas for most stocks are reported on financial websites and by investment services such as *Value Line*, and betas can be computed by the individual investor who understands how to apply regression analysis. Because a stock's sensitivity to market conditions may change over time in response to changes in the firm's operating characteristics, the stock's beta may also change over time.

Application of the CAPM Given the risk-free rate as well as estimates of the firm's beta and the market risk premium, it is possible to estimate the required rate of return from investing in the firm's stock.

index and producer price index) and of government borrowing (such as the budget deficit and the volume of funds borrowed at upcoming Treasury bond auctions) also affect the risk-free rate, thereby influencing the required return of investors. In general, whenever these indicators signal that interest rates may go higher, they place upward pressure on the required rate of return by investors and downward pressure on a firm's value.

In addition, it is common practice to estimate expected future cash flows when deriving a firm's value, and these cash flows are influenced by economic conditions, industry conditions, and firm-specific conditions. Exhibit 11.2 provides an overview of what stock market participants monitor when attempting to anticipate future stock price movements.

11-3f Gaining an Edge in the Valuation Process

Many market participants seek what Wall Street refers to as "an edge," which is an information advantage (private information) over other investors. Institutional investors that possess an edge should be able to outperform other investors, which may enable their portfolio managers to charge high fees or to justify taking a large share of the profits generated by the portfolios. Analysts within securities firms who have an edge can offer valuable insights to their favored institutional investor clients, which will likely create stronger relationships with those investors. The securities firms will then be rewarded by receiving more requests from institutional investors to execute stock trades, which generates larger commission revenue.

ETHICS   *Information Leakages*   Before 2000, firms commonly disclosed information about changes in their expected quarterly earnings to analysts a day or two before they announced this information to the public. Such actions might have been intended to strengthen relationships with analysts, so that the analysts would assign higher ratings to the firms when making stock recommendations. Some analysts who received the private information passed it on to their favored institutional investor clients, and these clients traded on the information before the rest of the market was aware of the information. Consequently, they were a step ahead of the market because of the leakage of relevant information.

In 2000, the Securities and Exchange Commission (SEC) issued Regulation Fair Disclosure (FD), which was intended to prevent such leakages of information. Under this regulation, when firms disclose material information to any person (including an analyst), they must disclose it to the general public at the same time so that no one has an information advantage over anyone else. For example, if managers believe that their firm's quarterly earnings will be higher than they initially predicted, they can no longer disclose this information to certain analysts before announcing the information to the public. Thus, Regulation FD ended analysts' information advantage. Analysts still attempt to gain an advantage by preparing valuations of companies so that those stocks will appeal to institutional investors, but they have to rely more heavily on their own skills rather than on access to private information.

ETHICS   *Reliance on Expert Networks*   Many institutional investors commonly attempt to obtain private information by hiring experts in the field as consultants. These expert networks can be especially valuable when investors are conducting valuations of tech firms because there is a high degree of asymmetric information between these firms and the investment community. A single technological innovation can have a major impact on a tech firm's valuation, and investors have an incentive to try to obtain private information about a firm that other investors do not have. The proper valuation of these firms is highly influenced by their intellectual property (such as patents), which can change abruptly over time. For example, an institutional investor might hire a doctor to conduct a clinical trial of a new drug developed by a publicly traded biotechnology firm. Although the drug would have to win the approval of the Food and Drug Administration (FDA) to be marketed, the doctor's clinical trial would enable the institutional investor to learn more about the likely success or failure of the drug before the FDA issued its decision. Thus, the investor would be one step ahead of the market in knowing about a drug that could have a large impact on the drug developer's value.

These kinds of experts are not supposed to provide inside information to an institutional investor that is not available to the market, yet institutional investors are unlikely to hire experts for general insight that is available from public information. In some cases, experts might have special insight about a firm or an industry that they can offer institutional investors without having inside information. For example, experts may have a sense that a biotech company's experimental drugs will be successful because of their knowledge about the quality of the company's research and development. In this sense, the experts' insight can be beneficial to institutional investors even when they lack access to the company's private information.

ETHICS

In many other cases, experts' opinions really are influenced by their knowledge of material inside information, and they pass that inside information on in exchange for their consulting fee. For example, scientists who were involved in clinical trials of experimental drugs have been hired by investment firms for their scientific insight and passed on confidential information about the results of those trials to the securities firms that hired them. Such actions may allow the securities firms to purchase the stock of the company (or provide more-accurate recommendations about this company to their favored investor clients) if the information is favorable before the news is publicly disclosed. Some experts have been paid as much as $1,000 per hour for their insight on particular companies. Critics have attacked these cozy relationships, suggesting that the institutional investors are only willing to hire such experts if they can obtain inside information. In recent years, the U.S. government has prosecuted many cases in which so-called experts provided inside information to institutional investors.

Some market participants might argue that the use of inside information should be allowed because it expedites the process by which stock prices account for all (including nonpublic) information. However, precisely because inside information is not public, it gives some investors an unfair advantage over others. If the use of inside information were legal, investors who do not have access to it might avoid the stock market, because they would be at a disadvantage relative to the investors who have such information.

11-4 Stock Risk

A stock's risk reflects the uncertainty about its future returns, which may be less than expected. Several sources of uncertainty may cause the future returns of a stock, and the company's valuation, to be different than otherwise expected. First, economic factors, such as economic growth, that affect a firm's future cash flows (or the future growth rate of cash flows) are uncertain. Second, the firm's management policies (such as its planned acquisitions) that affect its future cash flows are uncertain. As a result of these kinds of uncertainty, the estimates of future cash flows vary among investors. Even the discount rate used for discounting cash flows may vary among investors. Consequently, valuations vary among investors.

The cash flows of some firms are somewhat stable and easier to predict in the future and, therefore, are more predictable. The stock prices of these firms should be more stable as well. For other firms, their cash flows are unstable and difficult to predict. The degree of disagreement about the valuation among investors is much larger for these types of firms. Furthermore, new information about economic conditions or the firm's operations can cause pronounced adjustments in the perceived valuations of these firms. Consequently, these firms are perceived to exhibit more risk.

The return from investing in stock over a particular period is measured as

$$R = \frac{(SP - INV) + D}{INV}$$

where

$$INV = \text{initial investment}$$
$$D = \text{dividend}$$
$$SP = \text{selling price of the stock}$$

The main source of uncertainty is the price at which the stock will be sold. Dividends tend to be much more stable than stock prices are. Dividends contribute to the immediate return received by investors but reduce the amount of earnings reinvested by the firm, which limits its potential growth.

The risk associated with a stock can be measured by using its price volatility, its beta, and the value-at-risk method. Each of these is discussed in turn.

11-4a Volatility of a Stock

A stock's volatility serves as a measure of risk because it may indicate the degree of uncertainty surrounding the stock's future returns. This volatility is often referred to as *total risk* because it reflects movements in stock prices for any reason, not just movements attributable to stock market movements.

Using Standard Deviation to Forecast Stock Price Volatility   One way to forecast stock price volatility is by using a historical period to derive a stock's standard deviation of periodic (such as daily, monthly, or quarterly) returns, and then using that estimate as the forecast over the future. Assuming that stock returns are normally distributed, there is a 68 percent probability that the stock's returns will be within 1 standard deviation of the expected outcome and a 95 percent probability that they will be within 2 standard deviations. A higher standard deviation reflects wider dispersion in the stock's returns over time. Although a stock price's level of volatility may change over time, this method can be useful when there is no obvious trend in volatility.

Using Volatility Patterns to Forecast Stock Price Volatility   A second method for forecasting stock price volatility is to use volatility patterns in previous periods.

EXAMPLE

The standard deviation of daily stock returns is determined for each of the last three months. Then, a time-series trend of these standard deviation levels is used to form an estimate for the standard deviation of daily stock returns over the next month. This method differs from the historical method in that it uses information beyond that contained in the previous month. For example, the forecast for September might be based on the following weighting scheme: 50 percent of the standard deviation in the most recent month (August) plus 30 percent of the standard deviation in the month before that (July) plus 20 percent of the standard deviation in the month before that (June). ●

Usually, the weights and the number of previous periods (lags) that were most accurate (that is, had the lowest forecast error) in previous periods are used. However, various economic and political factors can cause stock price volatility to change abruptly, so even a sophisticated time-series model does not necessarily generate accurate forecasts of stock price volatility.

Using Implied Volatility to Forecast Stock Price Volatility   A third method for forecasting stock price volatility is to derive the stock's implied standard deviation (ISD) from the stock option pricing model (options are discussed in detail in Chapter 14). The premium on a call option for a stock depends on various factors, including the stock's volatility as anticipated by investors. By considering the actual call option premium paid by investors for a specific stock along with the values of all other factors that affect the premium, it is possible to derive the anticipated volatility of that stock.

Forecasting Stock Price Volatility of the Stock Market

Market participants who want to forecast volatility of the stock market in general can monitor the CBOE Volatility Index (VIX), which is calculated by the Chicago Board Options Exchange (CBOE) from stock options on the S&P 500 stock index. At a given point in time, the VIX measures investors' expectation of the stock market volatility over the next 30 days. Some investors refer to the VIX as an indicator of stock market fear. If conditions occur that cause investors to expect more uncertainty surrounding stock prices over the next 30 days, this means that investors would require a higher premium to sell call options (as explained in Chapter 14). As the option premium on options representing the S&P 500 index increases, the VIX will increase. Conversely, if conditions in the stock market are expected to be more stable over the next 30 days, the premium on call options would decline and the VIX would decline.

Although it would be impossible to survey all market participants to obtain their view of stock market volatility, the movements in the premiums of options on the S&P 500 index are commonly used to derive an estimate of expected stock market volatility. Because the VIX simply measures the expectations of investors in general, it will not necessarily provide a perfectly accurate forecast of the stock market volatility over the next 30 days. Nevertheless, many investors believe that it is a useful indicator of expected stock market volatility.

Exhibit 11.3 shows movements in the VIX level over time. Notice how it increased during the credit crisis in 2008, when there was much uncertainty about the U.S. economy and about stock valuations in general. During the 2012–2018 period, economic conditions stabilized, stock market conditions stabilized, and the VIX level declined substantially.

When the VIX rises sharply, stock prices tend to decline, as the conditions that cause more stock market fear also cause investors to sell their stocks, which results in lower stock prices. Conversely, when the VIX declines abruptly, stock prices tend to rise, as the conditions that make investors believe that stock prices will be more stable also encourage investors to purchase stocks, which results in higher stock prices.

Volatility of a Stock Portfolio

Participants in the stock market tend to invest in a portfolio of stocks rather than a single stock, so they are more concerned with the risk of a portfolio than with the risk of an individual stock. A portfolio's volatility depends on the volatility of the individual stocks in the portfolio, on the correlations between returns of the stocks in the portfolio, and on the proportion of total funds invested in each stock.

The volatility of returns of a two-stock portfolio can be measured by its standard deviation:

$$\sigma_p = \sqrt{w_i^2 \sigma_i^2 + w_j^2 \sigma_j^2 + 2w_i w_j \sigma_i \sigma_j \text{CORR}_{ij}}$$

where

w_i = **proportion of funds invested in the ith stock**

w_j = **proportion of funds invested in the jth stock**

σ_i = **standard deviation of returns of the ith stock**

σ_j = **standard deviation of returns of the jth stock**

CORR_{ij} = **correlation coefficient between the ith and jth stocks**

Exhibit 11.3   Implied Volatility Index for U.S. Stocks Based on the CBOE Volatility Index

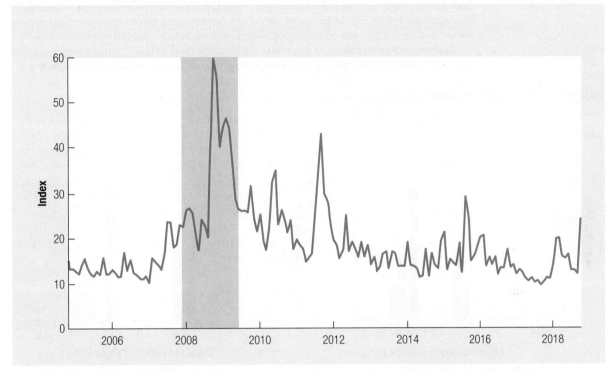

The shaded area represents recession.

Source: Chicago Board Options Exchange, CBOE Volatility Index: VIX [VIXCLS], retrieved from FRED, Federal Reserve Bank of St. Louis; https://fred.stlouisfed.org/series/VIXCLS, October 29, 2018.

For portfolios containing more securities, the formula for the portfolio standard deviation contains the standard deviation of each stock and the correlation coefficients between all pairs of stocks in the portfolio, weighted by the proportion of funds invested in each stock. The equation for a two-stock portfolio is sufficient to demonstrate that, when other factors are held constant, a stock portfolio has more volatility when its individual stock volatilities are high and when its individual stock returns are highly correlated. As an extreme example, if the returns of the stocks are all perfectly positively correlated (correlation coefficients = 1.0), the portfolio will have a relatively high degree of volatility because all stocks will experience peaks or troughs simultaneously. Conversely, a stock portfolio containing some stocks with low or negative correlation will have less volatility because the stocks will not experience peaks and troughs at the same time. Some offsetting effects will occur, smoothing the returns of the portfolio over time.

Because the volatilities and correlations of a portfolio's individual stocks can change over time, so, too, can the volatility of the portfolio. A forecast of the portfolio's volatility can be derived from forecasts of its components: the volatility levels of individual stocks contained in the portfolio and the pairwise correlation coefficients between stocks, weighted by the proportional investment in each stock.

11-4b Beta of a Stock

As explained earlier, a stock's beta measures the sensitivity of its returns to market returns. This measure of risk is used by many investors who have a diversified portfolio of stocks and believe that this strategy diversifies away the unsystematic risk of the portfolio (because favorable firm-specific characteristics will offset unfavorable firm-specific characteristics).

EXAMPLE   Exhibit 11.4 shows how the probability distribution of a stock's returns depends on its beta. At one extreme, Stock A (with a very low beta) is less responsive to market movements in either direction, so its possible returns range only from −4.8 percent under poor market conditions to 6 percent under the most favorable market conditions. At the other extreme, Stock D (with a very high beta) has possible returns that range from −11.2 percent under poor market conditions to 14 percent under the most favorable market conditions. This stock is perceived to be risky because it experiences large losses when stock market conditions decline. ●

Exhibit 11.4   How Beta Influences Probability Distributions

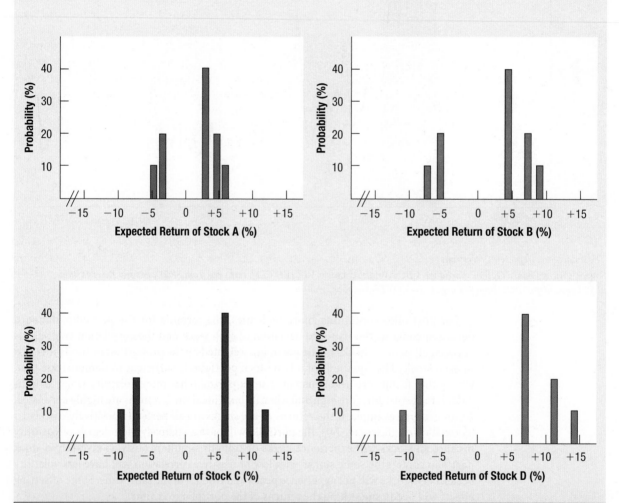

PROBABILITY	R_m	STOCK A'S EXPECTED RETURNS, $E(R)$, if $B_j = 0.6$	STOCK B'S EXPECTED RETURNS, $E(R)$, if $B_j = 0.9$	STOCK C'S EXPECTED RETURNS, $E(R)$, if $B_j = 1.2$	STOCK D'S EXPECTED RETURNS, $E(R)$, if $B_j = 1.4$
10%	−8%	−4.8%	−7.2%	−9.6%	−11.2%
20	−6	−3.6	−5.4	−7.2	−8.4
40	5	3	4.5	6	7
20	8	4.8	7.2	9.6	11.2
10	10	6	9	12	14

Beta of a Stock Portfolio   Portfolio risk can be measured based on the betas of the component stocks weighted by the proportional investment in each stock:

$$\beta_p = \sum w_i \beta_i$$

That is, the portfolio beta is a weighted average of the betas of the stocks that make up the portfolio, where the weights reflect the proportion of funds invested in each stock. This equation makes intuitive sense, because it simply suggests that a portfolio consisting of high-beta stocks will have a relatively high beta. Such a portfolio usually performs poorly relative to other stock portfolios in a period when the market return is negative.

The beta of each individual stock may be forecast in a subjective manner; for example, a portfolio manager may forecast that a stock's beta will increase from its existing level of 0.8 to 0.9 because the firm has initiated a more aggressive growth strategy. Alternatively, the manager can assess a set of historical periods to determine whether there is a trend in the beta over those periods and then apply this trend.

The beta of a stock and its volatility are typically related. High-beta stocks are expected to be relatively volatile because they are more sensitive to market returns over time. Likewise, low-beta stocks are expected to be less volatile because they are less responsive to market returns.

11-4c **Value at Risk**

Value at risk is a measurement that estimates the largest expected loss in a particular investment position for a specified confidence level. It is intended to warn investors about the potential maximum loss that could occur. If the investors are uncomfortable with the potential loss that could occur in a day or a week, they can revise their investment portfolio to make it less risky.

The value-at-risk measurement focuses on the pessimistic portion of the probability distribution of returns from the investment of concern. For example, a portfolio manager might use a confidence level of 90 percent, which estimates the maximum daily expected loss for a stock on 90 percent of the trading days over an upcoming period. The higher the level of confidence desired, the larger the maximum expected loss that could occur for a given type of investment is. That is, one may expect that the daily loss from holding a particular stock will be no worse than −5 percent when using a 90 percent confidence level, but as much as −8 percent when using a 99 percent confidence level. In essence, the more confidence investors have that the actual loss will be no greater than the expected maximum loss, the further they will move into the left tail of the probability distribution.

Application of Value at Risk to a Stock   A common method for applying value at risk is to measure the stock's standard deviation of daily returns over the previous period and then apply it to derive boundaries for a specific confidence level.

EXAMPLE

Assume that the standard deviation of daily returns for a particular stock in a recent historical period is 2 percent. Also assume that the 95 percent confidence level is desired to estimate the maximum one-day loss. If the daily returns are normally distributed, the lower boundary (the left tail of the probability distribution) is approximately 1.65 standard deviations away from the expected outcome. Assume that the expected daily return of the stock is 0.02 percent. The lower boundary can be estimated as

$$0.02\% - [1.65 \times (2\%)] = -3.28\%$$

The expected daily return of 0.02 percent may reflect subjective information, or it could be the average daily return during the recent historical period assessed. The lower boundary for a given confidence level can easily be derived for any expected daily return. For example, if the expected daily return is 0.04 percent, the lower boundary is

$$0.04\% - [1.65 \times (2\%)] = -3.26\%$$ •

Deriving the Maximum Dollar Loss

Once the maximum percentage one-day loss for a given confidence level is determined, that value can be applied to derive the maximum dollar one-day loss of a particular investment.

EXAMPLE

In the preceding example, the maximum percentage one-day loss of a particular stock was estimated to be −3.26 percent. If an investor has a $20 million investment in that stock, the maximum dollar one-day loss can be determined by applying the maximum percentage loss to the value of the investment. Hence the maximum one-day loss in dollars is estimated to be

$$(-3.26\%) \times \$20,000,000 = -\$652,000$$ •

Value at Risk Applied to a Stock Portfolio

The value-at-risk method is used to measure the risk of a stock portfolio in the same manner that it is applied to measure the risk of one stock. The standard deviation of daily returns for the stock portfolio can be derived from a recent historical period. If the daily returns of the stock portfolio are normally distributed, the lower boundary (the left tail of the probability distribution) is approximately 1.65 standard deviations away from the expected outcome.

Adjusting the Investment Horizon Desired

An investor who wants to assess the maximum loss over a weekly instead of daily investment horizon can apply the value-at-risk method to a series of weekly (instead of daily) historical stock returns.

Limitations of the Value-at-Risk Method

A common criticism of using historical periods to measure value at risk is that portfolio managers may rely on a relatively calm historical period when assessing possible future risk. If, for example, the distribution of returns has been narrow because the economy was unusually stable in the previous period, this approach may underestimate the maximum loss expected in a future period (when the economy is not as stable). In the language of portfolio managers, the distribution of possible returns used to estimate value at risk may have short tails (edge of the distribution), whereas the distribution of returns over the future period may have long tails. This implies that the actual loss of a portfolio in the future may be more pronounced than the expected maximum loss that is estimated from historical data.

11-5 Measuring Risk-Adjusted Stock Performance

The performance of a stock or a stock portfolio over a particular period can be measured by its excess return (return above the risk-free rate) for that period divided by its risk. Two common methods of measuring performance are the Sharpe index and the Treynor index. Both indexes measure the excess return above the risk-free rate per unit of risk. However, the indexes differ in the proxy used for risk.

11-5a Sharpe Index

If volatility (variability)of stock returns is deemed an appropriate measure of risk, a stock's risk-adjusted returns over a period can be determined by the reward-to-variability ratio (also called the **Sharpe index**):

$$\text{Sharpe index} = \frac{\overline{R} - \overline{R}_f}{\sigma}$$

where

$$\overline{R} = \text{average return on the stock}$$
$$\overline{R}_f = \text{average risk-free rate}$$
$$\sigma = \text{standard deviation of the stock's return}$$

If a stock's average return is less than the average risk-free rate, the Sharpe index for that stock will be negative. The higher the stock's mean return relative to the mean risk-free rate, and the lower the standard deviation, the higher the Sharpe index will be.

EXAMPLE

Assume the following information for two stocks over a three-year period:

- Average monthly return for Sooner stock = 1.2 percent
- Average monthly return for Longhorn stock = 1.0 percent
- Average annualized risk-free rate = 0.3 percent
- Standard deviation of Sooner's monthly stock returns = 2.0 percent
- Standard deviation of Longhorn's monthly stock returns = 1.4 percent

Then

$$\text{Sharpe index for Sooner stock} = \frac{1.2\% - 0.3\%}{2.0\%}$$
$$= .45$$
$$\text{Sharpe index for Longhorn stock} = \frac{1.0\% - 0.3\%}{1.4\%}$$
$$= .50$$

Even though Sooner stock had a higher average percentage return, Longhorn stock had a higher performance based on the Sharpe ratio because of its lower risk. ●

11-5b Treynor Index

If beta is thought to be the most appropriate measure of risk, a stock's risk-adjusted returns over a period can be determined by the Treynor index, computed as

$$\text{Treynor index} = \frac{\overline{R} - \overline{R}_f}{B}$$

where B is the stock's beta. Like the Sharpe index, the Treynor index is negative for a stock whose average return is less than the average risk-free rate. The Treynor index differs from the Sharpe index only in that it uses beta rather than the standard deviation as a proxy for the stock's risk.

EXAMPLE   Using the information provided in the preceding example on Sooner stock and Longhorn stock, and assuming that Sooner's stock beta is 1.1 and Longhorn's beta is 1.0, the Treynor index is computed for each stock as follows:

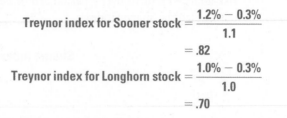

$$\text{Treynor index for Sooner stock} = \frac{1.2\% - 0.3\%}{1.1}$$
$$= .82$$
$$\text{Treynor index for Longhorn stock} = \frac{1.0\% - 0.3\%}{1.0}$$
$$= .70$$

Based on the Treynor index, the Sooner stock experienced higher performance than did the Longhorn stock. ●

These examples for the Sharpe and Treynor indexes show that results from comparing two investments may depend on the index (and therefore the risk proxy) that is used when conducting the comparison.

11-6 Stock Market Efficiency

If stock markets are efficient, the prices of stocks at any point in time should fully reflect all available information. As investors attempt to capitalize on new information that is not already accounted for, stock prices should adjust immediately. Although investors commonly overreact or underreact to information, this does not mean that markets are inefficient unless the reaction is biased (that is, consistently overreacting or underreacting). Investors who can recognize such bias will be able to earn abnormally high risk-adjusted returns.

11-6a Forms of Stock Market Efficiency

Efficient stock markets can be classified into three forms: weak, semistrong, and strong.

Weak-Form Efficiency   **Weak-form efficiency** suggests that security prices reflect all market-related information, such as historical security price movements and the volume of securities trades. If the stock market is weak-form efficient, investors will not be able to earn abnormal returns on a trading strategy that is based solely on past price movements.

Semistrong-Form Efficiency   **Semistrong-form efficiency** suggests that security prices fully reflect all public information. The difference between public information and market-related information is that public information also includes announcements by firms, economic news or events, and political news or events. Market-related information is a subset of public information. Therefore, if semistrong-form efficiency holds, weak-form efficiency must also hold. Nevertheless, weak-form efficiency may hold even though semistrong-form efficiency does not. In this case, investors could earn abnormal returns by using the relevant information that was not immediately accounted for by the market.

Strong-Form Efficiency   **Strong-form efficiency** suggests that security prices fully reflect all information, including private or inside information. If strong-form efficiency holds, semistrong-form efficiency must hold as well. If inside information leads to abnormal returns, semistrong-form efficiency could hold even though strong-form efficiency does not.

Inside information gives insiders (such as some employees or board members) an unfair advantage over other investors. For example, if employees of a firm are aware of favorable news about the firm that has not yet been disclosed to the public, they may consider purchasing shares or advising their friends to purchase the firm's shares. Although such actions are illegal, they do occur and can create market inefficiencies.

11-6b **Tests of the Efficient Market Hypothesis**
Tests of market efficiency are segmented into three categories, as discussed next.

Test of Weak-Form Efficiency Weak-form efficiency has been tested by searching for a nonrandom pattern in security prices. If the future change in price is related to recent changes, historical price movements could be used to earn abnormal returns. In general, studies have found that historical price changes are independent over time. This means that historical information is already reflected by today's price and cannot be used to earn abnormal profits. Even when some dependence was detected, the transaction costs offset any excess return earned.

Some evidence indicates that stocks have performed better in certain time periods. First, as mentioned earlier, small stocks have performed unusually well in the month of January (the "January effect"). Second, stocks have historically performed better on Fridays than on Mondays (the "weekend effect"). Third, stocks have historically performed well on the trading days just before holidays (the "holiday effect"). To the extent that a given pattern continues and can be used by investors to earn abnormal returns, market inefficiencies exist. In most cases, there is no clear evidence that such patterns persist once they are recognized by the investment community.

One could use the number of market corrections to evaluate stock market inefficiency. During the twentieth century, there were more than 100 days on which the market (as measured by the Dow Jones Industrial Average) declined by 10 percent or more. On more than 300 days, the market declined by more than 5 percent. These abrupt declines frequently followed a market run-up, which suggests that the run-up might have been excessive. In other words, a market correction was necessary to counteract the excessive run-up.

Test of Semistrong-Form Efficiency Semistrong-form efficiency has been tested by assessing how security returns adjust to particular announcements. Some announcements are specific to a firm, such as a dividend increase, an acquisition, or a stock split. Other announcements are related to the economy, such as a decrease in the federal funds rate. In general, security prices have been shown to immediately adjust to reflect the information from these kinds of announcements. Hence the securities were not consistently overvalued or undervalued, so abnormal returns could not consistently be achieved. This is especially true when transaction costs are taken into account. This evidence supports semistrong efficiency.

Test of Strong-Form Efficiency Tests of strong-form efficiency are difficult to perform because the inside information used is not publicly available and cannot be properly tested. Nevertheless, many forms of insider trading could easily result in abnormally high returns. For example, evidence clearly shows that share prices of target firms rise substantially when their acquisition is announced. If insiders purchased stock of targets prior to other investors, they would normally achieve abnormally high returns. Insiders are discouraged from using this information because it is illegal, not because markets are strong-form efficient.

11-7 Foreign Stock Valuation and Performance

Some of the key concepts in this chapter can be adjusted so that they apply on a global basis, as explained next.

11-7a Valuation of Foreign Stocks

Foreign stocks can be valued by using the price–earnings method or the dividend discount model with an adjustment to reflect international conditions.

Price–Earnings Method   The expected earnings per share of the foreign firm are multiplied by the appropriate PE ratio (based on the firm's risk and local industry) to determine the appropriate price of the firm's stock. Although it is easy to use, this method is subject to some limitations when valuing foreign stocks. The PE ratio for a given industry may change continuously in some foreign markets, especially when the industry consists of just a few firms, which makes it difficult to determine what ratio should be applied to a specific foreign firm. In addition, the PE ratio for any particular industry may need to be adjusted for the firm's country because reported earnings can be influenced by national accounting guidelines and tax laws.

Furthermore, even if U.S. investors are comfortable with their estimate of the proper PE ratio, the value derived by this method is denominated in the local foreign currency (because the estimated earnings are denominated in that currency). Therefore, U.S. investors must also consider exchange rate effects. Even if the stock is undervalued in the foreign country, it may not generate a reasonable return for U.S. investors if the foreign currency depreciates against the dollar.

Dividend Discount Model   The dividend discount model can be applied to the valuation of foreign stocks by discounting the stream of expected dividends while adjusting to account for expected exchange rate movements. Foreign stocks pay dividends in the currency of their denomination. Thus, the cash flow per period to U.S. investors is the dividend (denominated in the foreign currency) multiplied by the value of that foreign currency in dollars. An expected appreciation of the currency denominating the foreign stocks will result in higher expected dollar cash flows and a higher present value. The dividend can normally be forecast with more accuracy than can the value of the foreign currency. Because of exchange rate uncertainty, the value of foreign stock from a U.S. investor's perspective is subject to more uncertainty than is the value of that stock from a local investor's perspective.

11-7b International Market Efficiency

Some foreign markets are likely to be inefficient because of the relatively small number of analysts and portfolio managers who monitor stocks in those markets. It is easier to find undervalued stocks when a smaller number of market participants monitor the market.

Research has documented that some foreign markets are inefficient, as demonstrated by slow price responses to new information (for example, earnings announcements) about specific firms. Such inefficiencies are more common in smaller foreign stock markets. Some emerging stock markets are relatively new and small, so they are unlikely to be as efficient as the U.S. stock market. Hence some stocks may be undervalued, a possibility that has attracted investors to these markets.

Yet precisely because some of these markets are small, they may be susceptible to manipulation by large traders. Furthermore, insider trading is more prevalent in many foreign markets because rules against it are not enforced. In general, large institutional investors and insiders based in the foreign markets may have some advantages.

11-7c **Measuring Performance from Investing in Foreign Stocks**

The returns from investing in foreign stocks are most properly measured in terms of the investor's objectives. For example, if portfolio managers are assigned to select stocks in Europe, their performance should be compared to that of a European index measured in U.S. dollars. In this way, the performance measurement controls for general market and exchange rate movements in the region where the portfolio manager has been assigned to invest funds. Thus, if the entire European market experiences poor performance over a particular quarter, or if the main European currency (the euro) depreciates against the dollar over the period, the portfolio managers assigned to Europe are not automatically penalized. Conversely, if the entire European market experiences strong performance over a particular quarter or the euro appreciates against the dollar, those managers are not automatically rewarded. Instead, the performance of portfolio managers is measured relative to the general market conditions of the region to which they are assigned.

11-7d **Performance from Global Diversification**

A substantial amount of research has demonstrated that investors in stocks can benefit by diversifying their stock portfolios internationally. Most stocks are strongly influenced by the country in which the firm is located (although some firms are more vulnerable to local economic conditions than others).

Because a stock market partially reflects the current and/or forecasted state of its country's economy, and because all economies generally do not move in tandem, particular stocks of the various markets are not highly correlated. This contrasts with the case of a purely domestic portfolio (for example, one consisting entirely of U.S. stocks), in which most stocks often move in the same direction and by a similar magnitude.

Nevertheless, stock price movements among international stock markets are correlated to some degree because some underlying economic factors reflecting the world's general financial condition may systematically affect all markets. In general, correlations between stock indexes have been higher in recent years than they were several years ago. One reason for the increased correlations is the increased integration of business between countries. The more extensive intercountry trade flows and capital flows that occur under this condition mean that each country has more influence on other countries. In particular, many European countries have become more integrated because of the movement to standardize regulations throughout Europe and the use of a single currency (the euro) to facilitate trade between countries. If economies continue to become more integrated, the benefits of international stock diversification will be reduced.

Diversification among Emerging Stock Markets   Emerging markets provide an alternative outlet in which investors from the United States and other countries can invest their funds. The potential economic growth rate in such markets is relatively high. In addition, investors may achieve extra diversification benefits from investing in emerging markets because their respective economies may not move in tandem with those of the more developed countries. Hence the correlation between these stocks and those of other countries is low, so investors can reduce risk by including some stocks from these markets in their portfolios.

Notably, however, emerging market stocks tend to exhibit a high degree of volatility, which partially offsets the advantage of their low correlations with stocks of other countries. Stocks in emerging markets are more exposed to major government turnovers and other forms of political risk. They also expose U.S. investors to a high degree of exchange rate risk because the local currencies involved are typically volatile.

Summary

- Stocks are commonly valued using the price–earnings (PE) method, the dividend discount model, or the free cash flow model. The PE method applies the industry PE ratio to the firm's earnings to derive its value. The dividend discount model estimates the value as the present value of expected future dividends. The free cash flow model is based on the present value of future cash flows.

- When applying the free cash flow model to value a stock, a required rate of return must be estimated. One method of estimating the required rate of return is to apply the capital asset pricing model, in which the required return depends on the risk-free interest rate and the firm's beta.

- Stock prices are affected by those factors that affect future cash flows or the required rate of return by investors. Economic conditions, market conditions, and firm-specific conditions can all affect a firm's cash flows or the required rate of return.

- The risk of a stock is measured by its volatility, beta, or value-at-risk estimate. The Sharpe index and the Treynor index are common methods of measuring risk-adjusted stock performance.

- Stock market efficiency implies that stock prices will reflect all available information. Weak-form efficiency suggests that security prices will reflect all trade-related information, such as historical security price movements and the volume of securities trades. Semistrong-form efficiency suggests that security prices will fully reflect all public information. Strong-form efficiency suggests that security prices will fully reflect all information, including private or insider information. Evidence supports the validity of weak-form efficiency to a degree, but less support exists for semistrong-form and strong-form efficiency.

- Investors may benefit by diversifying internationally. Foreign stocks can be valued by using the PE method or the dividend discount method with adjustments to reflect conditions in the firm's country and the exchange rate.

Point/Counterpoint

Is the Stock Market Efficient?

Point   Yes. Investors fully incorporate all available information when trading stocks. Thus, the prices of stocks fully reflect all information.

Counterpoint   No. The high degree of stock price volatility offers evidence of how much disagreement there is among stock prices. The fact that many stocks declined by more than 40 percent over a few months in some periods suggests that stock prices are not always properly valued to reflect available information.

Who Is Correct?   Use the Internet to learn more about this issue and then formulate your own opinion.

Questions and Applications

1. Price–Earnings Model Explain the use of the price–earnings ratio for valuing a stock. Why might investors derive different valuations for a stock when using the PE method? Why might investors derive an inaccurate valuation of a firm when using the PE method?

2. Dividend Discount Model Describe the dividend discount valuation model. What are some limitations when using this model?

3. Impact of Economic Growth Explain how economic growth affects the valuation of a stock.

4. Impact of Interest Rates How are the interest rate, the required rate of return on a stock, and the valuation of a stock related?

5. Impact of Inflation Assume that the expected inflation rate has just been revised upward by the market. Would that change affect the return required by investors who invest in stocks? Explain.

6. Impact of Exchange Rates Explain how the value of the dollar affects stock valuations.

7. Investor Sentiment Explain why investor sentiment can affect stock prices.

8. January Effect Describe the January effect.

9. Earnings Surprises How do earnings surprises affect valuations of stocks?

10. Impact of Takeover Rumors Why can expectations of an acquisition affect the value of the target's stock?

11. Emerging Markets What are the risks of investing in stocks in emerging markets?

12. Stock Volatility during the Credit Crisis Explain how stock volatility changed during the credit crisis of 2008–2009.

13. Stock Portfolio Volatility Identify the factors that affect a stock portfolio's volatility and explain their effects.

14. Beta Explain how to estimate the beta of a stock. Explain why beta serves as a measure of the stock's risk.

15. *Wall Street* In the movie *Wall Street*, Bud Fox is a broker who conducts trades for Gordon Gekko's firm. Gekko purchases shares of firms that he believes are undervalued. Various scenes in the movie offer excellent examples of concepts discussed in this chapter.

a. Bud Fox comments to Gordon Gekko that a firm's breakup value is twice its market price. What is Bud suggesting in this statement? How would employees of the firm respond to Bud's statement?
b. When Bud informs Gekko that another investor, Mr. Wildman, is secretly planning to acquire a target firm in Pennsylvania, Gekko tells Bud to buy a large amount of this stock. Why?
c. Gekko says, "Wonder why fund managers can't beat the S&P 500? Because they are sheep." What is Gekko's point? How does it relate to market efficiency?

16. Market Efficiency Explain the difference between weak-form, semistrong-form, and strong-form efficiency. Which of these forms of efficiency is most difficult to test? Which is most likely to be refuted? Explain how to test weak-form efficiency in the stock market.

17. Market Efficiency A consulting firm was hired to determine whether a particular trading strategy could generate abnormal returns. The strategy involved taking positions based on recent historical movements in stock prices. The strategy did not achieve abnormal returns. Consequently, the consulting firm concluded that the stock market is weak-form efficient. Do you agree? Explain.

Advanced Questions

18. Value at Risk Describe the value-at-risk method for measuring risk.

19. Implied Volatility Explain the meaning and use of implied volatility.

20. Leveraged Buyout At the time that a management group of RJR Nabisco initially considered engaging in a leveraged buyout, RJR's stock price was less than $70 per share. Ultimately, RJR was acquired by the firm Kohlberg Kravis Roberts (KKR) for about $108 per share. Does the large discrepancy between the stock price before an acquisition was considered and after the acquisition mean that RJR's price was initially undervalued? If so, does this imply that the market was inefficient?

21. How Stock Prices May Respond to Prevailing Conditions Consider the prevailing conditions that could affect the demand for stocks, including inflation, the economy, the budget deficit, the Fed's monetary policy, political conditions, and the general mood of investors. Based on these conditions, do you think stock prices will increase or decrease during this semester? Offer some logic to support your answer. Which factor do you think will have the biggest impact on stock prices?

22. Application of the CAPM to Stock Pricing Explain (using intuition instead of math) why stock prices may decrease in response to a higher risk-free rate according to the CAPM. Explain (using intuition instead of math) why stock prices may increase in this situation even though the risk-free rate increases.

23. Impact of SOX on Stock Valuations Use a stock valuation framework to explain why the Sarbanes-Oxley Act (SOX) could improve the valuation of a stock. Why might SOX cause a reduction in the valuation of a stock? (See the chapter appendix.)

24. Interpretation of VIX Explain why participants in the stock market monitor the VIX. What does a decline in the VIX imply about a change in expected volatility by market participants?

Critical Thinking Question

Credit Crisis versus Equity Crisis The credit crisis that occurred in 2008–2009 could also be called an equity crisis due to systemic risk. Write a short essay to explain the impact of the credit markets on the equity markets during the crisis.

Interpreting Financial News

Interpret the following statements made by Wall Street analysts and portfolio managers.

a. "The stock market's recent climb has been driven by falling interest rates."

b. "Future stock prices are dependent on the Fed's policy meeting next week."

c. "Given the recent climb in stocks that cannot be explained by fundamentals, a correction is inevitable."

Managing in Financial Markets

Stock Portfolio Dilemma   As an investment manager, you frequently make decisions about investing in stocks versus other types of investments and about types of stocks to purchase.

a. You have noticed that investors tend to invest more heavily in stocks after interest rates have declined. You are considering this strategy as well. Is it rational to invest more heavily in stocks once interest rates have declined?

b. Assume that you are about to select a specific stock that will perform well in response to an expected run-up in the stock market. You are very confident that the stock market will perform well in the near future. Recently, a friend recommended that you consider purchasing stock of a specific firm because it had decent earnings over the last few years, it has a low beta (reflecting a low degree of systematic risk), and its beta is expected to remain low. You usually rely on beta as a measurement of a firm's systematic risk. Should you seriously consider buying that stock? Explain.

c. You are considering an investment in an initial public offering by Marx Company, which has performed very well recently, according to its financial statements. The firm will use some of the proceeds from selling stock to pay off some of its bank loans. How can you apply stock valuation models to estimate this firm's value when its stock is not yet publicly traded? Once you estimate the value of the firm, how can you use this information to determine whether to invest in it? What are some limitations in estimating the value of this firm?

d. In the past, your boss assessed your performance based on the actual return on the portfolio of U.S. stocks that you manage. For each quarter in which your portfolio generated an annualized return of at least 20 percent, you received a bonus. Now your boss wants you to develop a method for measuring your performance in managing the portfolio. Offer a method that accurately measures your performance.

e. Assume that you were also asked to manage a portfolio of European stocks. How would your method for measuring your performance in managing this portfolio differ from the method you devised for the U.S. stock portfolio in the previous question?

Problems

1. Risk-Adjusted Return Measurements Assume the following information over a five-year period:

- Average risk-free rate = 6 percent
- Average return for Crane stock = 11 percent
- Average return for Load stock = 14 percent
- Standard deviation of Crane stock returns = 2 percent
- Standard deviation of Load stock returns = 4 percent
- Beta of Crane stock = 0.8
- Beta of Load stock = 1.1

Determine which stock has higher risk-adjusted returns according to the Sharpe index. Which stock has higher risk-adjusted returns according to the Treynor index? Show your work.

2. Measuring Expected Return Assume Mess stock has a beta of 1.2. If the risk-free rate is 7 percent and the market return is 10 percent, what is the expected return of Mess stock?

3. Using the PE Method You discovered that Olmsted stock is expected to generate earnings of $4.38 per share this year and that the mean PE ratio for its industry is 27.195. Use the PE valuation method to determine the value of Olmsted shares.

4. Using the Dividend Discount Model Suppose that you are interested in buying the stock of a company that has a policy of paying a $6 per share dividend every year. Assuming no changes in the firm's policies, what is the value of a share of stock if the required rate of return is 11 percent?

5. Using the Dividend Discount Model Micro, Inc., will pay a dividend of $2.30 per share next year. If the company plans to increase its dividend by 9 percent per year indefinitely, and you require a 12 percent return on your investment, what should you pay for the company's stock?

6. Using the Dividend Discount Model Suppose you know that a company *just paid* an annual dividend of $1.75 per share on its stock and that the dividend will continue to grow at a rate of 8 percent per year. If the required return on this stock is 10 percent, what is the current share price?

7. Deriving the Required Rate of Return The next expected annual dividend for Sun, Inc., will be $1.20 per share, and analysts expect the dividend to grow at an annual rate of 7 percent indefinitely. If Sun stock currently sells for $22 per share, what is the required rate of return?

8. Deriving the Required Rate of Return A share of common stock currently sells for $110. Current dividends are $8 per share annually and are expected to grow at 6 percent per year indefinitely. What is the rate of return required by investors in the stock?

9. Deriving the Required Rate of Return A stock has a beta of 2.2, the risk-free rate is 6 percent, and the expected return on the market is 12 percent. Using the CAPM, what would you expect the required rate of return on this stock to be? What is the market risk premium?

10. Deriving a Stock's Beta You are considering investing in a stock that has an expected return of 13 percent. If the risk-free rate is 5 percent and the market risk premium is 7 percent, what is the beta of this stock?

11. Measuring Stock Returns Suppose you bought a stock at the beginning of the year for $76.50. During the year, the stock paid a dividend of $0.70 per share and had an ending share price of $99.25. What is the total percentage return from investing in that stock over the year?

12. Measuring the Portfolio Beta Assume the following information:

- Beta of Stock D = 1.31
- Beta of Stock E = 0.85
- Beta of Stock F = 0.94

If you invest 40 percent of your money in Stock D, 30 percent in Stock E, and 30 percent in Stock F, what is your portfolio's beta?

13. Measuring the Portfolio Beta Using the information from Problem 12, suppose that you instead decide to invest $20,000 in Stock D, $30,000 in Stock E, and $50,000 in Stock F. What is the beta of your portfolio now?

14. Value at risk Assume that the standard deviation of daily returns for a particular stock in a recent historical period is 1.8 percent. Assume that the expected daily return of the stock is 0.01 percent. Estimate the maximum possible one-day loss based on a 95 percent confidence level.

15. Value at Risk Assume that in the previous problem, an investor has invested $10 million in the stock of concern. Estimate the maximum dollar one-day loss based on a 95 percent confidence level.

16. Dividend Model Relationships

a. When computing the price of a stock with the dividend discount model, how would the price be affected if the required rate of return is increased? Explain the logic of this relationship.

b. When computing the price of a stock using the constant-growth dividend discount model, how would the price be affected if the growth rate is reduced? Explain the logic of this relationship.

17. CAPM Relationships

a. When using the CAPM, how would the required rate of return on a stock be affected if the risk-free rate were lower?

b. When using the CAPM, how would the required rate of return on a stock be affected if the market return were lower?

c. When using the CAPM, how would the required rate of return on a stock be affected if the beta were higher?

18. Value at Risk

a. How is the maximum expected loss on a stock affected by an increase in the volatility (standard deviation), based on a 95 percent confidence interval?

b. Determine how the maximum expected loss on a stock would be affected by an increase in the expected return of the stock, based on a 95 percent confidence interval.

Flow of Funds Exercise

Valuing Stocks

Recall that if the economy continues to be strong, Carson Company may need to increase its production capacity by approximately 50 percent over the next few years to satisfy demand for its products. It would need financing to expand and accommodate this increase in production. The yield curve is currently upward sloping, and Carson is concerned about a possible slowing of the economy because of potential Fed actions to reduce inflation. The company is also considering issuing stock or bonds to raise funds in the next year. If Carson goes public, it might even consider using its stock as a means of acquiring some target firms. It would also consider engaging in a secondary offering at a future point in time if the IPO is successful and if its growth continues over time. It would also change its compensation system so that most of its managers would receive about 30 percent of their compensation in shares of Carson stock and the remainder as salary.

a. At the present time, the price–earnings ratio (stock price per share divided by earnings per share) of other firms in Carson's industry is relatively low but should rise in the future. Why might this information affect the time at which Carson issues its stock?

b. Assume that Carson Company believes that issuing stock is an efficient means of circumventing the potential for high interest rates. Even if long-term interest rates have increased by the time it issues stock, Carson thinks that it would be insulated from the effects of this increase by issuing stock instead of bonds. Is this view correct?

c. Carson Company recognizes the importance of a high stock price at the time it engages in an IPO (if it goes public). But why would its stock price be important to Carson Company even after the IPO?

d. If Carson Company goes public, it may be able to motivate its managers by granting them stock as part of their compensation. Explain why the stock may motivate managers to perform well. Then explain why the use of stock as compensation may motivate them to focus on short-term goals even though they are supposed to focus on maximizing shareholder wealth over the long run. How can a firm provide stock as a motivational tool, yet prevent its managers from adopting a short-term focus?

Internet/Excel Exercises

1. Go to finance.yahoo.com/most-active. Compare the performance of the Dow, Nasdaq, and S&P 500 indexes. Click on each of these indexes and describe the trend for that index since January. Which index has had the best performance?

2. Go to finance.yahoo.com and search for INTC (the symbol for Intel Corporation). Then go to the top of the stock price chart and retrieve the end-of-month stock price of Intel over the last 12 months. Record this information on an Excel spreadsheet and estimate the standard deviation of the stock's price movements. (See Appendix B for guidance on how to estimate the standard deviation of a stock's price movements.) Repeat the process for Oracle Corporation (its symbol is ORCL). Which stock does your analysis show to be riskier? Assume that the expected return on Intel stock and Oracle stock is 0 percent for the next month. Use the value-at-risk method to determine the maximum expected loss of Intel and Oracle for the next month, based on a 95 percent confidence level.

WSJ Exercise

Reviewing Abrupt Shifts in Stock Valuation

Review Section C of a recent issue of *The Wall Street Journal*. Notice that the stocks with the largest one-day gains and losses are shown. Do an Internet search for news about the stock with the biggest gain. What is the reason for the gain? Repeat the exercise for the stock with the biggest loss.

Online Articles with Real-World Examples

Find a recent practical article available online that describes a real-world example regarding a specific financial institution or financial market that reinforces one or more concepts covered in this chapter.

If your class has an online component, your professor may ask you to post your summary of the article there and provide a link to the article so that other students can access it. If your class is live, your professor may ask you to summarize your application of the article in class. Your professor may assign specific students to complete this assignment or may allow any students to do the assignment on a volunteer basis.

For recent online articles and real-world examples related to this chapter, consider using the following search terms (be sure to include the prevailing year as a search term to ensure that the online articles are recent):

1. stock AND valuation
2. price–earnings AND valuation
3. free cash flow AND valuation
4. stock AND investor sentiment
5. stock AND risk
6. stock valuation AND uncertainty
7. stock valuation AND beta
8. stock AND value at risk
9. stock AND volatility
10. stock market AND efficient

Appendix 11

The Link between Accounting and Stock Valuation

In a publicly traded firm, the managers who run the firm are separate from the investors who own it. Managers are hired to serve as agents of the corporation and are expected to serve the interests of the firm's shareholders by making decisions that maximize the value of the firm. The firm's management is required to provide substantial information about the firm's financial condition and performance, which shareholders and other investors then use to monitor management and to value the firm. For example, if investors use the price–earnings method to derive a valuation, they would rely on the firm's reported earnings. If they use the dividend discount model, they may derive an expected growth rate from recently reported earnings or revenue figures. If they use the adjusted dividend discount model, they may rely on financial statements to estimate future cash flows.

If firms provide inaccurate financial information, investors will derive inaccurate valuations and money will flow to the wrong sources in the stock markets. In addition, inaccurate financial information creates more risk for stocks because investors must worry about the uncertainty surrounding the reported financial statement numbers. If financial statement data are questionable, stock values may decline whenever investors recognize that the earnings or some other proxy used to estimate cash flows is overstated. Investors will require a higher rate of return to hold stocks subject to downside risk because of distorted accounting. In this way, deceptive accounting practices disrupt the stock market and increase the cost of capital raised by issuing stock.

To ensure that managers serve shareholder interests, firms commonly tie managerial compensation to the stock price. For example, managers may be granted stock options that allow them to buy the firm's stock at a specified price over a specified time period (such as the next five years). In this way, the managers benefit directly from a high stock price just like other shareholders and, in theory, should make decisions that result in a high stock price.

Unfortunately, some managers recognize that it may be easier to increase their stock's price by manipulating the financial statements than by improving the firm's operations. When the firm's reported earnings are inflated, investors will likely overestimate the value of its stock, regardless of the method they use to value stocks.

Managers may be tempted to temporarily inflate reported earnings because doing so may temporarily inflate the stock's price. If no limits are imposed on the stock options granted, managers may be able to exercise their options (buying the stock at the price specified in the option contracts) during this period of a temporarily inflated price and immediately sell the stock in the secondary market. In this way, they can capitalize on the inflated stock price before other investors realize that the earnings and stock price are inflated.

Problems with Creative Accounting

Managers would not be able to manipulate a firm's financial information if accounting rules did not allow them to be creative. The accounting for a firm's financial statement items is guided by Generally Accepted Accounting Principles (GAAP) set by the Financial Accounting Standards Board (FASB). However, these guidelines allow for substantial flexibility in accounting, which means that there is no standard formula for converting accounting numbers into cash flows. The accounting confusion is compounded by the desire of some managers to inflate their firm's earnings in particular periods when they wish to sell their holdings of the firm's stock. Specifically, the accounting can inflate revenue in a particular period without inflating expenses or defer the reporting of some expenses until a future quarter. Investors who do not recognize that some of the accounting numbers are distorted may overestimate the value of the firm.

Creative accounting can also be used to distort expenses. When a firm discontinues one of its business projects, it commonly records this termination as a write-off, or a one-time charge against earnings. Investors tend to ignore write-offs when estimating future expenses because they do not expect them to occur again. Some firms, however, shift a portion of their normal operating expenses into the write-off even though those expenses will occur again in the future. Investors who do not recognize this accounting gimmick will underestimate the future expenses.

As a classic example of shifting expenses, WorldCom attempted to write off more than $7 billion following its acquisition of MCI in 1998. When the Securities and Exchange Commission (SEC) questioned this accounting, WorldCom changed the amount to about $3 billion. If it had succeeded in including the extra $4 billion in the write-off, WorldCom could have reduced its reported operating expenses by $4 billion. Thus, investors who trusted WorldCom's income statement would have underestimated its future expenses by about $4 billion per year and, in turn, would have grossly overestimated the value of the stock.

When firms go beyond the loose accounting guidelines, the SEC may require them to restate their earnings and provide a corrected set of financial statements. The SEC has forced hundreds of firms to restate their earnings in recent years, but the investors who lost money because they trusted a firm's distorted accounting were not reimbursed.

Governance of Accounting

Several types of governance can be used to attempt to prevent firms from using distorted accounting, as explained next.

Auditing

Firms are required to hire auditors to audit their financial statements and verify that these statements comply with the accounting guidelines. As a practical matter, however, the auditors rely on these firms for their future business. Many large firms pay auditors more than $1 million per year for their auditing services as well as for non-auditing services. Thus, auditors may be tempted to sign off on distorted accounting so that they will be rehired by their clients in the future. If the auditors uphold proper standards that force their clients to revise their reported earnings, they may not be hired again. The temptation to sign off on creative accounting used by client firms is especially strong given the subjectivity allowed by the accounting rules. Auditors may be more willing to sign off on financial statements that are somewhat confusing but that do not directly violate accounting rules.

Board of Directors

A firm's board of directors is expected to represent the firm's shareholders. These directors oversee the firm's financial reporting process and should attempt to ensure that the financial information provided by the firm is accurate. Unfortunately, some boards have not forced managers to accurately disclose the firm's financial condition. A board can be ineffective if it is run by insiders who are the same managers that the board is supposed to monitor. Board members who are managers of the firm (insiders) are less likely to scrutinize the firm's management. In recent years, many firms have increased the proportion of independent board members (outsiders), who are not supposed to be subject to pressure from the firm's executives. Nevertheless, even some independent board members have strong ties to the firm's executives or receive substantial consulting income beyond their compensation for serving on the board. In such a case, they may be willing to overlook distorted accounting or other unethical behavior so as to maintain their existing income stream from the firm.

Several proposals have been made to try to increase the independence of board members. For example, the Commission on Public Trust and Private Enterprise has recommended that corporations consider separating the offices of chair of the board and CEO, and that the board chair should be an independent director.

Compensation of Board Members   Some boards are ineffective because of the way the board members are compensated. If board members receive stock options from the firm as compensation, those options' value is tied to the firm's stock price. Consequently, some board members may be tempted to ignore their oversight duties because they may benefit from selling their shares of the stock (received as compensation) while the price is temporarily inflated. Meanwhile, shareholders who hold their stock for a longer time period will be adversely affected once the market recognizes that the financial statements are distorted.

Board members are more likely to serve the long-term interests of shareholders if they are compensated in a manner that encourages them to maximize the long-term value of the firm. If they are provided with stock that they cannot sell for a long time, they are more likely to focus on improving the firm's long-term outlook.

Several regulations have been issued to address the potential abuses resulting from granting stock options to managers and board members. In 2003, the SEC ruled that corporations listed on the New York Stock Exchange (NYSE) or the Nasdaq market must have shareholder approval before giving executives company stock or options. The rules were drafted and approved by the NYSE and Nasdaq. In addition, FASB now requires that corporations expense their executive stock options on their income statements. This increases transparency in financial reporting and might improve corporate governance.

Board's Independent Audit Committee   Some board members may serve on an independent audit committee that is responsible for monitoring the firm's auditor. This committee is expected to ensure that the audit is completed without conflicts of interest so that the auditors will provide an unbiased audit. Some committees have not prevented distorted audits, however, either because they did not recognize the conflicts of interest or because they were unwilling to acknowledge them.

Role of Credit Rating Agencies

Investors may also rely on credit rating agencies such as Standard & Poor's and Moody's to assess a firm's risk level. These agencies do not always detect a firm's financial problems in advance because they typically focus on assessing a firm's risk level based on the financial statements provided; they do not seek to determine whether the financial statements are accurate. The agencies may simply assume that the financial statements are accurate because they were verified by an auditor.

Role of the Market for Corporate Control

In the market for corporate control, firms that perform poorly should be acquired and reorganized by other more efficient firms (called raiders). The raiders have an incentive to seek out inefficient firms because they can buy them at a low price (reflecting their poor performance) and remove their inefficient management. Nevertheless, the market for corporate control does not necessarily prevent faulty accounting. First, raiders may not be able to identify firms that inflated their earnings. Second, firms that have inflated their earnings are probably overvalued, and raiders will not want to acquire them at their inflated price. Third, an acquisition involves substantial costs of integrating businesses, and these costs may offset any potential benefits.

The Enron Scandal

A notorious example of the use of creative accounting occurred at Enron Corporation. Enron was formed in 1985 from the merger of two natural gas pipeline companies. It grew relatively slowly until the 1990s, when the deregulation of the utilities industry presented new opportunities. Enron began to expand in several directions. It acquired power plants in the United States and also expanded internationally, acquiring a power distributor in Brazil, a power plant in India, and a water company in the United Kingdom, among others. Perhaps most importantly, it took advantage of the newly deregulated environment to pioneer the trading of natural gas and electricity. Soon it had branched out beyond simple energy trading to trade such instruments as weather derivatives. In 1999, it introduced Enron Online, an Internet-based trading platform that gave the company the appeal of an "Internet stock" at a time when such stocks were highly desired. The company introduced online trading of metals, wood products, and even broadband capacity as well as energy. By 2000, Enron was the seventh largest firm (in terms of gross revenues) in the United States.

Most investors were caught by surprise when Enron began to experience financial problems in October 2001 and then filed for bankruptcy on December 2, 2001. At the time, it was the largest U.S. firm to go bankrupt. In retrospect, Enron's stock may have been overvalued for many years, but some investors and creditors were fooled by its financial statements. The Enron fiasco received much publicity because it demonstrated how a firm could manipulate its financial statements, and therefore manipulate its valuation, in spite of various controls designed to prevent that type of behavior. This section offers some insight into why investors' valuations and risk assessments of Enron were so poor.

Enron's Letter to Its Shareholders

If investors trusted the claims made by Enron in its annual report, it is understandable that they would value the stock highly. The letter to shareholders in Enron's 2000 annual report included the following statements:

■ "Enron's performance in 2000 was a success by any measure, as we continued to outdistance the competition and solidify our leadership in each of our businesses.

- Enron has built unique and strong businesses that have limitless opportunities for growth.
- At a minimum, we see our market opportunities company-wide tripling over the next five years.
- Enron is laser-focused on earnings per share, and we expect to continue strong performance.
- Enron is increasing earnings per share and continuing our strong return to shareholders.
- The company's total return to shareholders was 89% in 2000, compared with a −9% return by the S&P 500.
- The 10-year return to Enron shareholders was 1,415%, compared with 383% for the S&P 500.
- We plan to . . . create significant shareholder value for our shareholders."

Enron's Stock Valuation

The valuation of a firm is usually developed by using the firm's financial statements to derive cash flows and to derive a required rate of return that is used to discount those cash flows. Enron's valuation was excessive because of various irregularities in its financial statements.

Estimating Cash Flows   Because Enron's earnings were distorted, the estimates of its cash flows derived from those earnings were also distorted. Moreover, Enron's earnings were manipulated to create the perception of consistent earnings growth, which tempted investors to apply a high growth rate when estimating future cash flows.

Estimating the Required Rate of Return   Investors can derive a required rate of return as the prevailing long-term, risk-free interest rate plus the firm's risk premium. The risk premium can be measured by the firm's existing degree of financial leverage, its ability to cover interest payments with operating earnings, and its sensitivity to market movements.

Until the accounting distortions were publicized, Enron's risk was underestimated. The company concealed much of its debt by keeping it off its consolidated financial statements, as will be explained shortly. Consequently, investors who estimated Enron's sensitivity to market movements using historical data were unable to detect Enron's potential for failure. As a result, they used a lower risk premium than was appropriate. In essence, the financial statements caused investors both to overestimate Enron's future cash flows and to underestimate its risk. Both effects led to a superficially high stock price.

Applying Market Multiples   Given the difficulty of estimating cash flows and the required rate of return, some investors may have tried to value Enron's stock by using market multiples. Determining the appropriate PE multiple for Enron was also difficult, however, because its reported earnings did not represent its real earnings.

Another problem with applying the industry PE method to Enron was the difficulty of identifying the proper industry. One of the company's main businesses was trading various types of energy derivative contracts. Yet Enron did not want to be known as a trading company because the valuations of companies (for example, securities firms) that engage in trading are generally lower for a given level of earnings per share.

Motives of Enron's Management

Enron's problems can also be traced to its management. Managers, of course, are expected to maximize the value of the firm's stock. Like many firms, Enron granted stock options to some of its managers as a means of motivating them to make decisions that would maximize the value of its stock. However, Enron's management seemed to focus more on creating the perception of strong business performance than on improving the firm's actual performance. By manipulating the financial statements, Enron consistently met its earnings forecasts and increased its earnings over 20 consecutive quarters leading up to 2001. In this way, it created a false sense of security about its performance, thereby increasing the demand for its stock. This resulted in a superficially high stock price over a period in which some managers sold their stock holdings. Twenty-nine Enron executives or board members sold their holdings of Enron stock for more than $1 billion in total before the stock price plummeted.

Internal Monitoring   Some firms use internal monitoring to ensure some degree of control over managers and encourage them to make decisions that benefit shareholders. Unfortunately, Enron's internal monitoring was also susceptible to manipulation. For example, managers were periodically required to measure the market value of various energy contracts that the company held. Because there was not an active market for some of these contracts, the prevailing valuations of the contracts were arbitrary. Managers used estimates that resulted in favorable valuations, which in turn led to a higher level of reported performance and higher managerial compensation.

Monitoring by the Board of Directors   Board members serve as representatives of the firm's shareholders and are responsible for ensuring that the managers serve shareholder interests. In fact, board members are commonly compensated with stock so that they have an incentive to ensure that the stock price is maximized. In the case of Enron, some board members followed executives in selling their shares while the stock price was superficially high.

Enron's Financial Statement Manipulation

Some of the methods that Enron used to report its financial conditions were inconsistent with accounting guidelines. Other methods were within the rules but were misleading. Consequently, many investors invested in Enron without recognizing the financial problems that were hidden from the financial statements. Some of these investors lost most or all of their investments.

Accounting for Partnerships   One method by which Enron manipulated its financial statements involved the transfer of assets to partnerships it owned, called special-purpose entities (SPEs). The company found outside investors to invest at least 3 percent of each partnership's capital. Under accounting guidelines, a partnership with this minimum level of investment from an outside investor does not have to be classified as a subsidiary. Because Enron did not classify its SPEs as subsidiaries, it was not required to include any financial information about them in its consolidated financial statements. For this reason, none of the debt incurred by the SPEs appeared on Enron's consolidated financial statements. Because most investors focused on the consolidated financial statements, they did not detect Enron's financial problems.

In addition, whenever Enron created a partnership that would buy one of its business segments, it booked a gain on its consolidated financial statements from the sale of the asset to the partnership. In contrast, losses from a partnership were booked on the partnership's financial statements. Thus, Enron was booking gains from its partnerships on its consolidated financial statements while hiding its losses.

On November 8, 2001, Enron announced that it was restating its earnings for the previous five years because three of its partnerships should have been included in the consolidated financial statements. This announcement confirmed the suspicion of some investors that the company's previous earnings figures were exaggerated. Enron's previously reported earnings were reduced by about $600 million over the preceding five years, but the correction came too late for many investors who had purchased Enron stock when the reported earnings (and share price) were much higher.

Financing of Partnerships   Enron's partnerships were financed by various creditors, such as banks. The loans were supposed to be paid off either from the cash flow generated by the assets transferred to the partnership or from the ultimate sale of the assets. When the partnerships performed poorly, they could not cover their debt payments. In some cases, Enron backed the debt with its stock. But as its stock price plummeted, this collateral no longer covered the debt, setting in motion the downward spiral that ultimately led to the company's bankruptcy.

Arthur Andersen's Audit

Investors and creditors commonly presume that financial statements used to value a firm are accurate when they have been audited by an independent accounting firm. In reality, the auditor and the firm do not always have an arm's-length relationship. The accounting firm that conducts an audit is paid for the audit and recognizes the potential annuity from repeating this audit every year. Moreover, accounting firms that provide auditing services also provide consulting services. Enron hired Arthur Andersen both to serve as its auditor and to provide substantial consulting services. In 2000, Arthur Andersen received $25 million in auditing fees from Enron and an additional $27 million in consulting fees.

Although Arthur Andersen was supposed to be completely independent, the auditing firm recognized that if it did not sign off on Enron's audits it would lose this lucrative audit and consulting business. Furthermore, the annual bonus that an accounting firm pays to its employees assigned to audit a client may be partially based on their billable hours, which would have been reduced if the firm's relationship with such a large client were severed.

Oversight by Investment Analysts

Even if financial statements are contrived, some investors may presume that investment analysts will detect discrepancies. Yet if analysts simply accept a financial statement without questioning its accuracy, they will fail to serve as a control mechanism. The difficulties that analysts faced in interpreting Enron's financial statements are highlighted by a humorous list created by some Enron employees of why the company restructured its operations so frequently. Reason number 7 was "Because the basic business model is to keep the outside investment analysts so confused that they will not be able to figure out that we do not know what we are doing." The humor now escapes some analysts, as well as most creditors and investors.

Another problem is that, like the supposedly independent auditors who hope to generate more business for their accounting firm, investment analysts may encounter a conflict of interest when they attempt to rate firms. As explained in Chapter 10, analysts employed by securities firms have been criticized for assigning high ratings to firms they cover so that their employer may later receive some consulting business from those firms.

As an example of what can happen to analysts who are "too critical," consider the experience of an analyst at BNP Paribus who downgraded Enron in August 2001, a few months before the company's financial problems became public. At the time, BNP Paribus was providing some consulting services for Enron. Shortly after his downgrade of Enron, the analyst was demoted and then fired. To the extent that many other analysts were subjected to a similar conflict of interest, it may explain why they did not downgrade Enron until after its financial problems were publicized. Even if analysts had detected financial problems at Enron, they might have been reluctant to lower their rating.

Market for Corporate Control

As explained earlier, if a firm's managers are running a firm into the ground, a raider has an incentive to purchase that firm at a low price and improve it so that someday it can be sold for a much higher price. Yet this theory presumes that a firm's stock price properly reflects its actual business performance. If the firm's financial statements reflect strong performance, a raider may not realize that the firm is experiencing financial problems. Moreover, even if the raider is able to detect the problems, it will not be willing to pursue a firm whose value is overpriced by the market because of its contrived financial statements.

When Enron's stock price was high, few raiders could have afforded to acquire it. Once the stock price plummeted, Dynegy considered acquiring Enron. Dynegy quickly backed off, however, even though the stock price had fallen 90 percent from its high. Dynegy was concerned about problems it found when trying to reconcile Enron's financial statements.

Monitoring by Creditors

Enron relied heavily on creditors for its financing. Because Enron's consolidated financial statements showed a superficially high level of earnings and a low level of debt, it had easy access to credit from a wide variety of creditors. Enron maintained a low cost of capital by using contrived statements that concealed its risk. Its balance sheet showed debt of $13 billion, but by some accounts the true amount was closer to $20 billion. The hidden debt concealed Enron's actual degree of financial leverage.

Bank of America and JPMorgan Chase each had exposure estimated at $500 million. Many other banks had exposure estimated at more than $100 million. They would not have provided so much credit if they had fully understood Enron's financial situation.

Even the debt rating agencies had difficulty understanding Enron's financial situation. On October 16, 2001, Enron announced $2 billion in write-offs that would reduce its earnings. At this time, Standard & Poor's affirmed Enron's rating of BBB+ and stated that Enron's balance sheet should improve in the future. Over the next 45 days, S&P became more aware of Enron's financial condition and lowered its rating to junk status.

Many of Enron's creditors attempted to sue Enron once it became clear that the financial statements were misrepresented. By that time, Enron's value was depleted because its price had already fallen to less than $1 per share.

Prevention of Accounting Fraud

In response to the accounting fraud at Enron and other firms, regulators attempted to ensure more accurate financial disclosure by firms. Stock exchanges have instituted new regulations for listed firms. The SEC has been given more resources and power to monitor financial reporting. Perhaps the most important regulatory changes occurred as a result of the Sarbanes-Oxley Act of 2002. Some of the act's more important provisions are summarized in Chapter 10.

Alleged Accounting Fraud at Lehman Brothers

Despite the Sarbanes-Oxley Act, cases of accounting irregularities continue to surface. For example, the financial statements of Lehman Brothers did not fully disclose that company's level of debt prior to its bankruptcy filing in September 2008. An external bankruptcy report on Lehman in March 2010 concluded that Lehman manipulated its accounting to reduce its degree of reported financial leverage so that it would receive higher credit ratings. During the 2001–2008 period, Lehman employed an accounting procedure called "Repo 105," whereby it engaged in repurchase transactions that would temporarily delete up to

$50 billion of its debt just before the time to report its financial position. The report also suggested that Lehman inflated the value of its real estate investments and did not properly adjust its controls to deal with its increased exposure to risk.

Discussion Questions

The following discussion questions focus on the use of financial statements in the valuation of firms.

1.   Should an accounting firm be prohibited from providing both auditing and consulting services to the same client? Explain your answer. If an accounting firm is allowed to offer only one service, could there still be conflicts of interest due to referrals (and finder's fees)?

2.   Should members of Congress be allowed to enact laws on accounting and financial matters while receiving donations from related lobbying groups?

3.   What alternative sources of information about a firm should investors rely on if they cannot rely on financial statements?

4.   Should investors have confidence in ratings by analysts who are affiliated with securities firms that provide consulting services to firms? Explain.

5.   Does an analyst employed by a securities firm to rate firms face a conflict of interest? If so, can the conflict be resolved?

6.   How might a firm's board of directors discourage its managers from attempting to manipulate financial statements to create a temporarily high stock price?

7.   How can the compensation of a firm's board of directors be structured so that board members will not be tempted to allow accounting or other managerial decisions that could cause a superficially high price over a short period?

12
Market Microstructure and Strategies

CHAPTER OBJECTIVES

The specific objectives of this chapter are to:

- Describe the common types of stock transactions.

- Explain how stock transactions are executed.

- Describe high frequency trading.

- Describe the regulation of stock transactions.

- Explain how barriers to international stock transactions have been reduced.

Recently, much attention has been given to market microstructure, which is the process by which securities such as stocks are traded. For a stock market to function properly, a structure is needed to facilitate the placing of orders, speed the execution of the trades ordered, and provide equal access to information for all investors.

12-1 Stock Market Transactions

Some of the more common stock market transactions desired by investors are market and limit orders, margin trades, and short sales. Each of these types of transactions is discussed next.

12-1a Placing an Order

To place an order to buy or sell a specific stock, an investor contacts a brokerage firm. Brokerage firms serve as financial intermediaries between buyers and sellers of stock in the secondary market. They receive orders from customers and then pass those orders on to the exchange through a telecommunications network. The orders are frequently executed a few seconds later. Full-service brokers offer advice to customers on which stocks to buy or sell; discount brokers just execute the transactions desired by customers. The larger the transaction amount, the lower the percentage charged by many brokers is. Some discount brokers charge a fixed price per trade, such as $10 to $30 for any trade that involves fewer than 500 shares.

The broker may provide a *bid* quote if the investor wants to sell a stock or an *ask* quote if the investor wants to buy a stock. The investor communicates the order to the broker by specifying (1) the name of the stock, (2) whether to buy or sell that stock, (3) the number of shares to be bought or sold, and (4) whether the order is a market or a limit order. A **market order** to buy or sell a stock means to execute the transaction at the best possible price. A **limit order** differs from a market order in that a limit is placed on the price at which a stock can be purchased or sold.

EXAMPLE

Creo stock is currently selling for $55 per share. If an investor places a market order to purchase (or sell) the stock, the transaction will be executed at the prevailing price at the time the transaction takes place. For example, the price may have risen to $55.25 per share or declined to $54.75 by the time the transaction occurs.

Alternatively, the investor could place a limit order to purchase Creo stock only at a price of $54.50 or less. Such a limit order can be placed for the day only or for a longer period. Other investors who wish to sell Creo stock may place limit orders to sell the stock only if it can be sold for $55.25 or more. The advantage of a limit order is that it may enable an investor to obtain the stock at a lower price. The disadvantage is that there is no guarantee the market price will ever reach the limit price established by the investor. ●

Stop-Loss Order   A stop-loss order is a particular type of limit order. In this case, the investor specifies a selling price that is below the current market price of the stock. When the stock price drops to the specified level, the stop-loss order becomes a market order. If the stock price does not reach the specified minimum, the stop-loss order will not be executed. Investors generally place stop-loss orders either to protect gains or to limit losses.

EXAMPLE

Paul bought 100 shares of Bostner Corporation one year ago at a price of $50 per share. Today, Bostner stock trades for $60 per share. Paul believes that Bostner stock has additional upside potential and does not want to liquidate his position. Nonetheless, he would like to make sure that he realizes at least a 10 percent gain from the stock transaction. He therefore places a stop-loss order with a price of $55. If the stock price drops to $55, the stop-loss order will convert to a market order and Paul will receive the prevailing market price at that time, which will be about $55. If Paul receives exactly $55, his gain from the transaction would be 100 shares × ($55 − $50) = $500. If the price of Bostner stock continues to increase, the stop-loss order will never be executed. ●

Stop-Buy Order   A **stop-buy order** is another type of limit order. In this case, the investor specifies a purchase price that is above the current market price. When the stock price rises to the specified level, the stop-buy order becomes a market order. If the stock price does not reach the specified maximum, the stop-buy order will not be executed.

EXAMPLE

Karen would like to invest in the stock of Quan Company, but only if she sees some evidence that stock market participants are demanding that stock. The stock is currently priced at $12. Karen places a stop-buy order at $14 per share, so if demand for Quan stock is sufficient to push the price to $14, she will purchase the stock. If the price remains below $14, her order will not be executed. ●

Placing an Order Online   Many Internet brokers accept orders online, provide real-time quotes, and provide access to information about stocks. Some of the more popular online brokerage firms include TD Ameritrade (www.tdameritrade.com), Charles Schwab (www.schwab.com), and E*Trade (www.etrade.com).

Some online brokerage services offer zero-commission trades for investors who maintain a certain amount of funds in their brokerage accounts. Brokerage firms can still profit from these no-commission trades because they can use the funds in the accounts to earn a higher return than they pay the investors as interest.

12-1b Margin Trading

When investors place an order, they may consider purchasing the stock on margin, meaning that they make the purchase using funds borrowed from their broker along with their own cash. In such a case, the Federal Reserve imposes **margin requirements**, which represent the minimum proportion of funds that must be covered with cash. This limits the proportion of funds that may be borrowed from the brokerage firm to make the investment. Margin requirements were first imposed in 1934, following a period of volatile market swings, to discourage excessive speculation and ensure greater stability. Currently, an investor must provide cash for at least 50 percent of an investment. Margin requirements are intended to ensure that investors can cover their position if the value of their investment declines over time. With margin requirements, a major decline in stock prices is less likely to cause defaults on loans from brokers and, therefore, will be less damaging to the financial system.

To purchase stock on margin, investors establish an account (called a **margin account**) with their broker. Their initial deposit of cash is referred to as the **initial margin**. To meet the Federal Reserve's requirements, the initial margin must be at least 50 percent of the total investment (although some brokerage firms impose a higher minimum). The brokerage firm then provides financing for the remainder of the stock investment, and the stock serves as collateral for the loan to the investor.

Over time, the market value of the stock will change. Investors are subject to a **maintenance margin**, which is the minimum proportion of equity that an investor must maintain in the account as a proportion of the market value of the stock. The investor's equity position represents what the stock is worth to the investor after paying off the loan from the broker. The New York Stock Exchange (NYSE) and the Financial Industry Regulatory Authority (FINRA) have set the minimum maintenance margin at 25 percent, but some brokerage firms require a higher minimum. If the investor's equity position falls below the maintenance margin, the investor will receive a **margin call** from the brokerage firm and will have to deposit cash to the account to boost the equity.

EXAMPLE

Five days ago, Trish purchased 100 shares of Rimax stock at $60 per share through Ohio Brokerage Firm; thus, the shares were valued at $6,000. Ohio Brokerage required an initial margin of 50 percent. Trish used $3,000 cash as her equity investment and borrowed the remaining $3,000 from Ohio Brokerage to purchase the stock. Ohio Brokerage requires a maintenance margin of 30 percent.

Two days later, the price of Rimax stock declined to $50 per share, so the total value of Trish's shares was $5,000. Because Trish still owed the brokerage firm $3,000, her equity position was equal to $2,000 (computed as the $5,000 market value of the stock minus the $3,000 owed to the broker). This equity position represented 40 percent of the market value of the stock (computed as $2,000/$5,000), which was still above the maintenance margin of 30 percent.

Today, the stock price declined to $40 per share, so the market value of Trish's Rimax stock is $4,000. Now Trish's equity position is $1,000 (computed as $4,000 minus $3,000). This position represents 25 percent of the market value of the stock (computed as $1,000/$4,000), which is below the 30 percent maintenance margin required by Ohio Brokerage. Consequently, Trish receives a margin call from Ohio Brokerage, telling her that she must deposit sufficient cash to her account to raise her equity position to at least 30 percent of the market value of the stock. ●

WEB

www.bloomberg.com
Discloses today's return
for stocks contained in
major stock indexes.

Margin Calls   Because of the potential for margin calls, a large volume of margin lending exposes the stock markets to the potential for crisis. A major downturn in the market could result in many margin calls, some of which may force investors to sell their stock holdings if they do not have the cash to increase their maintenance margin. Such selling can cause stock prices to decline, resulting in more sales of stocks, continued downward pressure on stock prices, and additional margin calls. When the stock market plummeted during the credit crisis of 2008, investors who did not have cash available to respond to margin calls sold their stock, putting additional downward pressure on stock prices.

Impact on Returns   The return on a stock is affected by the proportion of the investment that is from borrowed funds. Over short-term periods, the return (R) on stocks purchased on margin can be estimated as follows:

$$R = \frac{SP - INV - LOAN + D}{INV}$$

where

$$SP = \text{selling price of stock}$$

$$INV = \text{initial investment by investor, not including borrowed funds}$$

$$LOAN = \text{loan payments on borrowed funds, including principal and interest}$$

$$D = \text{dividend payments}$$

EXAMPLE

Consider a stock priced at $40 that pays an annual dividend of $1 per share. An investor purchases the stock on margin, paying $20 per share and borrowing the remainder from the brokerage firm at 10 percent annual interest. If, after one year, the stock is sold at a price of $60 per share, the return on the stock is

$$R = \frac{\$60 - \$20 - \$22 + \$1}{\$20}$$

$$= \frac{\$19}{\$20}$$

$$= 95\%$$

In this example, the stock return (including the dividend) would have been 52.5 percent if the investor had used only personal funds rather than borrowing funds. This illustrates how the use of borrowed funds can magnify the returns on an investment.

Of course, losses are also magnified when borrowed funds are used to invest in stocks. Assume that the investor in this example sells the stock at a price of $30 per share (instead of $60) at the end of the year. If the investor did not use any borrowed funds when purchasing the stock for $40 per share at the beginning of the year, the return on this investment would be

$$R = \frac{\$30 - \$40 - \$0 + \$1}{\$40}$$

$$= -22.5\%$$

However, if the investor had purchased the stock on margin at the beginning of the year, paying $20 per share and borrowing the remainder from the brokerage firm at 10 percent annual interest, the return over the year would be

$$R = \frac{\$30 - \$20 - \$22 + \$1}{\$20}$$

$$= -55\%$$

●

As these examples illustrate, purchasing stock on margin not only increases the potential return from investing in stock but also magnifies the potential losses.

12-1c Short Selling

In a **short sale**, investors place an order to sell a stock that they do not own. They sell a stock short (or "short the stock") when they anticipate that its price will decline. When they sell short, investors essentially borrow the stock from another investor and ultimately have to return that stock to the investor from whom they borrowed it. The short-sellers borrow the stock through a brokerage firm, which facilitates the process. The investors who own the stock are not affected when their shares are borrowed; in fact, they are not even aware of it.

If the price of the stock declines by the time the short-sellers purchase it in the market (to return the stock to the investor from whom they borrowed it), the short-sellers earn the difference between the price at which they initially sold the stock and the price they paid to obtain the stock. Short-sellers must make payments to the investor from whom the stock was borrowed to cover the dividend payments that the investor would have received if the stock had not been borrowed. After subtracting any dividend payments made, the short-seller's profit is the difference between the original selling price and the price paid for the stock.

EXAMPLE On May 5, the market value of Vizer Company stock was $70 per share. Ed conducted an analysis of Vizer stock and concluded that the price should be much lower. He called his broker and placed an order to sell 100 shares of Vizer stock. Because he did not have shares of Vizer to sell, this transaction was a short sale. Vizer stock does not pay dividends, so Ed did not have to cover dividend payments for the stock that his brokerage firm borrowed and sold for him. The sale of the stock resulted in proceeds of $7,000, which was placed in his account at the brokerage firm. Over the next two months, the price of Vizer stock declined. On July 18, Ed placed an order through his brokerage firm to purchase 100 shares of Vizer stock and offset his short position. The market value at the time was $60, so he paid $6,000 for the shares. Thus, Ed earned $1,000 from his short position. (Note that this example ignores transaction costs associated with the short sale.) ●

The risk of a short sale is that the stock price may increase over time, forcing the short-seller to pay a higher price for the stock than the price at which it was initially sold. In the previous example, if the price of Vizer stock had increased after Ed created the short position, his purchase price would have been higher than his selling price. In this case, Ed would have incurred a loss on the short position.

Measuring the Short Position of a Stock   One measure of the degree of short positions for a stock is the ratio of the number of shares that are currently sold short divided by the total number of shares outstanding. For many stocks, this measure is between 0.5 and 2 percent. A higher percentage (such as 3 percent) suggests a large amount of short positions in the market, which implies that a relatively large number of investors expect the stock's price to decline.

Some financial websites disclose the short interest ratio, which is the number of shares of a stock that are currently sold short divided by the average daily trading volume of that stock over a recent period. The higher the ratio, the higher the level of short sales is. A short interest ratio of 2 for a particular stock indicates that the number of shares currently sold short is two times the number of shares traded per day, on average. A short interest ratio of 20 or higher reflects an unusually high level of short sales, indicating that many investors believe that the stock price is currently overvalued. Some stocks have had short interest ratios exceeding 100 at certain times.

The short interest ratio is also measured for the market as a whole to determine the level of short sales for the market overall. A high short interest ratio for the market indicates a high level of short-selling activity in the market. The largest short positions are periodically disclosed in *The Wall Street Journal* and on some financial websites. For each firm with a large short position, the number of shares sold short is disclosed, along with the corresponding number of shares sold short a month earlier. The change in the overall short position by investors from the previous month is also shown.

Using a Stop-Buy Order to Offset Short Selling   Investors who have established a short position commonly use a stop-buy order to limit their losses.

EXAMPLE A year ago, Mary sold short 200 shares of Patronum Corporation stock for $70 per share. Patronum's stock currently trades for $80 per share. Consequently, Mary currently has an unrealized loss on the short sale, but she believes that the price of Patronum stock will drop below $70 in the near future. She is unwilling to accept a loss of more than $15 per share on the transaction, so she places a stop-buy order for 200 shares with a specified purchase price of $85 per share. If Patronum stock increases to $85 per share, the stop-buy order becomes a market order, and Mary will pay approximately $85 per share. If Patronum stock does not increase to $85 per share, the stop-buy order will never be executed. ●

Concerns about Short Selling

When the credit crisis intensified in 2008, hedge funds and other investors took large short positions on many stocks, especially those of financial institutions. Some critics argued that these large short sales placed additional downward pressure on prices and created paranoia in the stock market. Such fear could make stock prices decline to a greater degree, which would be beneficial to the short-sellers.

EXAMPLE Just after the failure of the securities firm Lehman Brothers in September 2008, rumors suggested that Morgan Stanley (another securities firm) was unable to obtain financing and was about to fail. During the three-day period of September 15–17, 2008, the number of Morgan Stanley shares sold short increased from fewer than 5 million shares to approximately 39 million shares. Many of these short sales may have been attributable to this unfounded rumor. During this three-day period, the stock price of Morgan Stanley declined by one-third. One might argue that much of this decline in the stock price was due to the massive short selling, which was likely triggered by the rumor. ●

Restrictions on Short Selling

Following the massive short sales of Morgan Stanley, the Securities and Exchange Commission (SEC) temporarily protected more than 800 firms from short sales. For the most part, the protected firms were financial institutions and other companies that were exposed to the credit crisis; the SEC was attempting to limit the adverse effect that short sales might have on the stock prices of these firms. The SEC also mandated that traders had to borrow the stock before they could execute a short sale. In some cases, traders were using loopholes in the short sale rules to short stock without borrowing it. The SEC delegated authority to the stock exchanges to identify other firms that should be protected from short sales. Some other countries, including Australia, Taiwan, and the Netherlands, subsequently instituted their own short-selling regulations.

Many critics argued that these restrictions did not affect the general behavior of the speculators who were engaging in short sales. Some short-sellers were focused on financial institutions that had very little equity and used mostly borrowed funds (financial leverage) to generate large returns on their equity. These short-sellers might argue that the stock prices of the target financial institutions were declining not because of the short selling, but rather because regulators failed to ensure that these institutions would have sufficient capital backing their business. Furthermore, even though short sales were banned, speculators have other methods (for example, put options) of betting against a stock that might place downward pressure on a stock's price. In October 2008, the ban on short selling was eliminated in the United States because regulators determined that it was not stabilizing stock values.

However, the SEC imposed other restrictions on short selling. In October 2008, it required that short-sellers borrow and deliver the shares to the buyers within three days. This rule was important because brokerage firms were frequently allowing speculators to engage in naked shorting, in which they sold a stock short without first borrowing the stock. Through this practice, speculators were able to take larger short positions than would have been possible if they had to first borrow the shares that they were selling, which resulted in more downward pressure on the stock's prices. This new rule was a stronger version of an SEC rule implemented to prevent naked short selling in 2005 (called Regulation SHO), which applied only to specific stocks and was not strictly enforced.

The SEC also implemented a new version of the uptick rule, which had been eliminated in 2007. This rule prohibits speculators from taking a short position in stocks that have declined at least 10 percent for the day, except when the most recent trade results in an increase in the stock price. This rule is intended to prevent short selling in response to a stock's continuous downward price momentum.

WEB

www.nyse.com
Information about how trading is conducted on the NYSE.

12-2 How Stock Transactions are Executed

Transactions on the stock exchanges and the Nasdaq are facilitated by floor brokers and market makers.

12-2a Floor Brokers

Floor brokers work from the floor of a stock exchange, where they execute orders for their firm's clients. The floor brokers carry powerful tablet computers, which they use to communicate with clients and execute orders.

EXAMPLE
_____

Bryan Adams calls his broker at Zepellin Securities, where he has a brokerage account, and requests the purchase of 1,000 shares of stock in Clapton, Inc., which is traded on the NYSE. Because this is a small order (fewer than 100,000 shares), the broker at Zepellin will probably enter the order in the NYSE's electronic trading platform, which will match Bryan's order to purchase Clapton stock with another investor's order to sell Clapton shares. Alternatively, the broker could communicate this information to the NYSE trading floor. Other floor brokers who have orders to sell Clapton stock will either communicate their willingness to accept the bid or signal the "ask" price at which they would be willing to sell the shares. If the floor brokers can agree on a price, a transaction is executed. The transaction is recorded and transmitted to the tape display. Bryan will likely receive a message from the broker indicating that the trade was executed, and must then provide payment to his brokerage firm. ●

12-2b Market Makers

Designated market makers (DMMs; previously referred to as "specialists") can serve a broker function by matching up buy and sell orders on the NYSE, thereby facilitating trading on this exchange. They gain from accommodating these orders because their bid and ask prices differ. In addition, they take positions in specific stocks. In the past, DMMs' role was described as "making a market" in particular stocks: "Making a market" implies that they stand ready to buy or sell certain stocks even if no other investors are willing to participate. However, that does not mean they are offsetting all orders by taking the opposite side of every transaction. In fact, most transactions on the NYSE are executed electronically and do not require participation by market makers.

Transactions in the Nasdaq market are also facilitated by market makers. They benefit from the difference (spread) between the bid and ask prices and can also take positions in stocks. Some market makers make a market in a few stocks, whereas others make a market for many stocks. Notably, stocks that are more actively traded tend to have a larger number of market makers.

Market makers take positions to capitalize on the discrepancy between the prevailing stock price and their own valuation of the stock. When many uninformed investors take buy or sell positions that push a stock's price away from its fundamental value, the stock price is distorted as a result of the "noise" caused by the uninformed investors (called **noise traders**). Market makers may take the opposite position of the uninformed investors, so that they stand to benefit if their expectations are correct.

Brokers choose the route by which an order is executed, which means that they determine whether the order will be filled by a specific market maker. The spread quoted for a given stock may vary among market makers. Therefore, the manner in which the trade is routed by the broker can affect the size of the spread. Some market makers compensate brokers for orders routed to them. So, while a brokerage firm may charge a customer only $10 for a trade, it may also receive a payment from the market maker. The market maker may use a wider spread so that it can offer such a payment to the broker. The point is that some customers may pay only $10 for a buy order to be executed, but the order is executed at a price that is relatively high because the market maker charged a large spread. Customers should attempt to compare not only the fee that brokers charge for a trade, but also the spread that is quoted by the market maker selected by the brokerage firm. Investors do not have direct control over the routing process, but they can at least select a broker that uses their preferred type of process. The market is not sufficiently transparent for the routing process to be monitored, but technology may soon allow customers to more easily monitor the routing and the quoted spreads.

12-2c The Spread on Stock Transactions

When investors place an order, they are quoted an ask price, or the price that the broker is asking for that stock. There is also a bid price, or the price at which the broker would purchase the stock. The *spread* is the difference between the ask price and the bid price, and it is commonly measured as a percentage of the ask price.

EXAMPLE   Boletto Company stock is quoted by a broker as bid $39.80, ask $40.00. The bid–ask spread is

$$\text{Spread} = \frac{\$40.00 - \$39.80}{\$40.00}$$
$$= 0.5\%$$

This spread of 0.5 percent implies that if investors purchased the stock and then immediately sold it back before market prices changed, they would incur a cost of 0.5 percent of their investment for the round-trip transaction. ●

The transaction cost due to the spread is separate from the commission charged by the broker. The spread has declined substantially over time in response to more efficient methods of executing orders and increased competition from electronic communications networks. The spread is influenced by the following factors:

$$\text{Spread} = f(\underset{+}{\underbrace{\text{Order costs}}}, \underset{+}{\underbrace{\text{Inventory costs}}}, \underset{-}{\underbrace{\text{Competition}}}, \underset{-}{\underbrace{\text{Volume}}}, \underset{+}{\underbrace{\text{Risk}}})$$

Order Costs   Order costs are the costs of processing orders, including clearing costs and the costs of recording transactions.

Inventory Costs   Inventory costs include the cost of maintaining an inventory of a particular stock. An opportunity cost arises because the funds could have been used for some other purpose. If interest rates are relatively high, the opportunity cost of holding an inventory should be relatively high. The higher the inventory costs, the larger the spread that will be established to cover these costs.

Competition   For stocks traded on the NYSE or the Nasdaq market, having multiple market makers promotes competition. When more market makers are competing to sell a particular stock, the spread is likely to be smaller.

Volume   Stocks that are more liquid have less chance of experiencing an abrupt change in price, and stocks that have a large trading volume are more liquid because a sufficient number of buyers and sellers are available for those stocks at any time. This liquidity makes it easier to sell a stock at any point in time, which in turn reduces the risk of a sudden decline in the stock's price.

Risk   If the firm represented by a stock has relatively risky operations, its stock price is normally more volatile. Thus, a market maker is subject to more risk when holding inventory in this type of stock and, therefore, will set a higher spread.

At any particular moment, the spread can vary among stocks. Those who make a market for a particular stock are exposed to the risk that the stock's price could change abruptly in the secondary market and reduce the value of their position in that stock. Consequently, any factors that affect this type of risk to a stock's market maker can affect the spread of that stock.

12-2d Electronic Communication Networks

Electronic communication networks (ECNs) are automated systems for disclosing and sometimes executing stock trades. The SEC requires that any quote provided by a market maker be made available to all market participants. This requirement eliminated the practice of providing more favorable quotes exclusively to proprietary clients. It also resulted in significantly lower spreads between quoted bid and ask prices. Electronic communication networks are appealing to investors because they may allow for more efficient execution of trades.

Some ECNs focus on market orders; that is, they receive these orders and route them through various networks searching for the best price. Other ECNs receive limit orders, which they electronically match up with other orders that are still not fulfilled. Exhibit 12.1 shows an example of an ECN book at a given moment in time. The book lists the limit buy orders and limit sell orders that are currently not fulfilled. When a new limit order matches an existing order, the transaction is immediately executed, and the matching order is removed from the book. If the new limit order cannot immediately be matched to an existing order on the ECN book, it is added to the book.

EXAMPLE

Assume that the ECN book shown in Exhibit 12.1 is the book for a particular stock and that a new limit order is placed to sell 300 shares of that stock at a price of no less than $32.68. This order can be matched by the order to buy 300 shares at a bid price of $32.68. Upon the execution of this trade, the order on the ECN book to buy 300 shares at a bid price of $32.68 is removed. Now assume that a new limit order is placed to purchase 1,400 shares at a price of no more than $32.80. This order is matched up with the order to sell 400 shares at an ask price of $32.78 and the order to sell 1,000 shares at $32.80. Those orders are then removed from the ECN book because they have been fulfilled. ●

Exhibit 12.1   Example of an ECN Book at a Given Point in Time

BID OR ASK?	SHARES	PRICE
Bid	500	$32.50
Bid	300	$32.50
Bid	400	$32.56
Bid	1,000	$32.60
Bid	400	$32.64
Bid	1,200	$32.64
Bid	300	$32.68
Ask	400	$32.78
Ask	1,000	$32.80
Ask	300	$32.84
Ask	500	$32.84
Ask	600	$32.88

To improve execution of orders, both the NYSE and Nasdaq have acquired companies that developed ECNs.

Interaction between Direct Access Brokers and ECNs   A direct access broker is a trading platform on a computer website that allows investors to trade stocks without the use of a broker. The website itself serves as the broker and interacts with ECNs that can execute the trade. Some of the more popular direct access brokers include a division of Charles Schwab (www.schwab.com), Interactive Brokers (www.interactivebrokers.com), and Lightspeed Trading (www.lightspeed.com). Each of these websites offers a variety of trading platforms; some platforms are easier to use and offer less information, whereas others are more complex but provide more information. The direct access broker usually charges a monthly fee for access to a trading platform; the fee is higher for platforms that offer more information.

The advantage of a direct access broker is that investors interested in trading a particular stock can monitor the supply and prices of shares for sale and the demand for shares at various prices on different ECNs. Investors can use this information to determine how stock prices may change in the near future.

The use of direct access brokers and ECNs allows computers to match buyers and sellers without relying on the floor brokers or traders on stock exchanges. Thus, the trend is toward a "floorless" exchange in which all trades are executed in cyberspace and orders are submitted and confirmed through automated systems. As this technology is implemented across countries, it may ultimately create a single global floorless exchange through which investors can easily trade any security in any country by submitting requests from a personal computer.

Dark Pools   Dark pools are platforms that use software to connect buyers and sellers of stocks. They operate like private stock markets that can be used by institutional investors. The "dark pools" stand in contrast to the "lit pools" of the NYSE and the Nasdaq in that the desired trades in dark pools cannot be monitored by others. The ability to trade without having desired orders immediately disclosed to the public can be advantageous for an investor. For example, assume that an investor wants to accumulate a large number of shares of a particular stock. If the investor purchases the shares on a public stock exchange, other investors who see the trades might attempt to buy shares of that stock as well, hoping for a free ride to a bigger profit as the accumulation of shares pushes the stock price up. As they buy shares, the stock price rises, and so does the cost to the original investor. However, if the stock is purchased through a dark pool, the investor can accumulate the shares without the public's knowledge and possibly at a lower cost.

Dark pools also attract other types of traders, such as high frequency traders who use computer algorithms to capitalize on price discrepancies in stocks. Dark pools also offer bid or ask prices that are slightly more favorable for specific institutional traders than those available in the public stock markets.

Dark pools have become quite popular and now execute between 10 and 20 percent of the U.S. stock market volume. Approximately 40 dark pools have registered with the SEC, including CrossFinder (operated by Credit Suisse), Liquidnet, ITG Posit, MS Pool (operated by Morgan Stanley), and Sigma X (operated by Goldman Sachs). Public stock exchanges are losing business as a result of the popularity of dark pools.

One concern associated with dark pools is the risk that they could reduce the transparency in the stock market because the supply and demand for a given stock is fragmented across several markets. The public stock markets such as the NYSE and Nasdaq have criticized dark pools for decreasing transparency in this way, thereby making it more difficult for investors to assess existing demand and supply conditions for a particular stock.

In August 2012, the NYSE initiated a trading program called Retail Liquidity Program. It is similar to a dark pool and allows its members to offer stock price improvements (better prices than the prevailing quotes) for retail customers. The trades are not visible to the public. This program enables the NYSE to be more competitive with the dark pools offered by private stock markets. The Nasdaq market followed suit by developing a similar type of program.

The lack of transparency associated with dark pools is a problem not only for the public stock exchanges, but also for the traders in the dark pools themselves. In 2015, several firms, including UBS, Credit Suisse, and ITG, paid millions of dollars to the SEC to settle charges related to their dark pool operations. Among the charges were allegations that the firms had failed to disclose information to some traders in the dark pools while allowing others to have access to it, or had not revealed that the firms' own affiliates were operating a trading desk within the dark pool. In 2018, the SEC approved new rules that require operators of dark pools to disclose more data and reveal any potential conflicts of interest.

12-3 High Frequency Trading

Many stock transactions are triggered by computers that detect a particular pricing or volume pattern. **High frequency trading (HFT)** represents the use of electronic platforms to execute orders based on an algorithm with programmed instructions. It is used to submit orders frequently and quickly or to cancel existing orders. Securities firms and some institutional investors such as hedge funds commonly engage in HFT, which is also known as automated trading, algorithmic trading, and algo trading.

High frequency trading developed in the early 2000s in response to the creation of high-speed computers and computerized trading. It became very popular in 2010, as the technology allowed for much faster speeds. Today, more than half of all trading volume of stocks in the United States is done through HFT. Such platforms have also become popular in Europe and Asia.

Traders that engage in HFT typically close out their positions on the same day that they are created. Thus, their potential gain (or risk of possible loss) depends on the price volatility of that stock over a single day. They may focus on a widely traded stock whose price tends to fluctuate during the day. In many cases, the stock's closing price may be very close to its opening price on that day, but because the stock price fluctuates so much during the day, high frequency traders can attempt to capitalize on its movements. By trading in large volumes, the traders can earn large profits even when their sell price is just slightly higher than their buy price. Furthermore, they are not tying up their capital. They may use the same capital several times in one day, as they quickly close out each position that they take. The average time from when a position in a stock is taken until it is closed out is a few minutes or less for some high frequency traders.

12-3a Program Trading

One common form of HFT is program trading, which is broadly defined as a computerized response by institutional investors to either buy or sell a large basket of stocks in response to movements in a particular stock index. Although program trading was more narrowly defined by the NYSE in the past, a broad definition is more appropriate today because many variations now exist that are not covered by the narrow definition.

For example, in one form of program trading, numerous stocks that have become "overpriced" (according to a particular model used to value those stocks) are sold. In other words, program trading may involve the sale of a large basket of stocks because a stock index reached an unusually high level, indicating a likely decline in stock prices in the near future. Likewise, a program might call for the purchase of a large basket of stocks because a stock index reached an unusually low level, and those stocks appear to be undervalued (based on a particular model to value that stock index).

Institutional investors establish their own unique program trading strategies. In fact, the trigger that leads one institutional investor to buy a large basket of stocks might lead another to sell a large basket of stocks. The most common program traders are large securities firms, which conduct the trades for their own accounts or for other institutional investors such as pension funds, mutual funds, and insurance companies.

Program trading can be combined with the trading of stock index futures to create **portfolio insurance**. With this strategy, the investor uses futures or options contracts on a stock index. A decline in the market would then result in a gain on the futures or options position, which can offset the reduced market value of the stock portfolio.

12-3b **Bots and Algorithms**

High frequency traders use computerized systems for accessing stock market information and interpreting that information. These systems are commonly referred to as bots (short for robots). The bots are very powerful because they can access public information such as recent stock price movements and existing buy or sell orders that have been submitted by investors. Traders develop algorithms that attempt to interpret existing information about a particular stock's recent price or volume movements (or other information) as a signal of its future price movements. Once the algorithm is implemented, the bot can respond instantaneously as soon as the information it seeks becomes available. The bot is prompted to execute trades as soon as its algorithms recognize specific information that it is seeking. Given the very short time horizon for HFT, interpreting information and executing orders at high speed is critical; indeed, algorithms can carry out these tasks much faster than humans can.

Each institutional investor that uses its own bot has created its own algorithms. These algorithms detect specific information (such as recent trading volume of a specific stock) that triggers the bot to execute a specific transaction (such as a purchase or sale of a specified number of shares of that stock) at a specified price.

EXAMPLE | Vazer Hedge Fund creates the following algorithm: If the price of Glyz Company stock has increased by more than 0.3 percent in the last 8 minutes, and if the trading volume over that interval is at least 30 percent higher than the average trading volume over an 8-minute interval, submit an order to purchase 5,000 shares of Glyz stock at a price that is no higher than the prevailing market price. Then sell the stock 5 minutes later, or sell it even before that point if its price rises by at least 0.1 percent above the purchase price. ●

The ability of each HFT firm to exploit stock pricing patterns or discrepancies depends on the algorithms created by its employees. HFT firms employ many mathematicians, engineers, and computer programmers to develop algorithms that attempt to detect unusual pricing patterns in stock prices that can be exploited. Some algorithms are applied only during a specific period of the day in which a particular stock price pattern is thought to be more consistent, such as during the first hour or the last hour of trading. Nevertheless, previous patterns may not persist in the future, which creates a risk for the HFT firm.

The popularity of HFT has created so much competition that it has become more difficult for traders to develop algorithms that can effectively detect a pattern that can be exploited. Many high frequency traders attempt to stay one step ahead of the competition by constantly revising their algorithms. Some have created special algorithms that attempt to counter other traders' algorithms, leading to battles among the bots called "algo wars."

Vulton Financial Company believes that many other traders are using algorithms that specify the sale of Bluzack Company stock when the stock's price declines by a certain percentage. Those sales could cause a more pronounced price decline than is warranted. Therefore, Vulton attempts to capitalize on this discrepancy by creating an algorithm to purchase Bluzack stock after it has declined by at least a specific percentage in the last 15 minutes. ●

Some algorithms contain randomizers that attempt to disguise a trader's plans for future buy or sell orders by mixing orders to purchase a specific stock with other orders by the same trader to sell shares of that stock. In addition, some algorithms intentionally fake the desire for large trades (canceling them just before they are executed) to mislead the algorithms of other traders into expecting that market forces will be pushing prices of particular stocks higher in the next few minutes. This strategy, referred to as "layering" or "spoofing," can cause competitors to take positions based on false market information inferred from the fake orders. Regulators have occasionally fined high frequency traders for these types of deceptive actions.

The competitive dynamics between high frequency traders (and their respective algorithms) is comparable to that used in various card games in which players bluff to prevent the other players from guessing their positions or plans. Critics may question whether this focus on their opponents causes high frequency traders to ignore the proper valuations of the underlying companies that the stocks represent. Although some institutional investors such as pension funds and mutual funds might assess the potential performance of any particular stock over the next several months or years, the relevant investment horizon of a stock for high frequency traders is only the next few seconds or minutes. Consequently, their main focus is not the long-term prospects of the underlying companies, but rather their ability to purchase a stock for slightly less than the price at which they will be able to sell it seconds or minutes later.

12-3c Impact of High Frequency Trading on Stock Volatility

High frequency trading (including program trading) may cause share prices to reach a new equilibrium more rapidly. To the extent that this trading quickly corrects for price discrepancies, it could smooth stock price movements over time, thereby reducing stock price volatility. On some occasions, however, market stock price conditions appear to have triggered an unusually heavy volume of program trading and other forms of HFT that spooked the stock market and jolted stock prices.

Flash Crash   On May 6, 2010, stock prices declined abruptly in what is now referred to as the "flash crash." Overall, stocks declined by more than 9 percent, on average, before reversing and recovering most of those losses on that same day, when more than 19 billion shares were traded. It appears that the flash crash was triggered by HFT. The computers (bots) of high frequency traders were programmed (with algorithms) to trade stocks based on specific trigger points; for example, they automatically sold shares if a specific stock index (or a specific stock) declined by a certain percentage. These automated sales of shares pushed stock prices lower, which triggered additional sales by other computers that contained similar types of algorithms, and caused a pronounced decline in stock prices.

Some algorithms were designed to sell all of a trader's existing stock positions if the market was experiencing a large loss. Although such algorithms cut the losses for the individual trader, they triggered more pronounced selling among other high frequency traders, which then led to a freefall in stock prices. Ultimately, the stock indexes reached very low levels, which triggered some bots to purchase shares because of their specific algorithms that specified buy orders if stocks became so cheap.

Most of this activity occurred in a 30-minute period on May 6, 2010, the most volatile half hour in the history of the NYSE. This trading activity was especially troubling because it could not be explained or justified by an underlying economic event. That is, there was no major panic among human beings about the existing economic conditions on May 6, 2010, but there was panic based on the interpretations of algorithms contained within the bots. The flash crash aroused concern that if such volatility could occur without a major crisis, it could happen again on any normal day and might be even worse if news of a crisis broke.

Other Breakdowns in Computerized Trading The flash crash is not the only example of a disruption in trading likely caused by HFT. A breakdown in computerized trading on August 1, 2012, caused trading of all Nasdaq stocks to halt for three hours. On January 25, 2013, a minor flash crash occurred when Apple's stock price declined abruptly (causing its market value to decline by approximately $7 billion), before then recovering.

On April 23, 2013, the U.S. stock market's value declined by more than $130 billion following a false media tweet (by a computer hacker) stating that explosions had occurred in the White House. Some critics argued that the extremely quick response of dumping stocks based on the false information was triggered by the computerized systems (bots) that received the media report and contained algorithms specifying sell orders based on that type of information. Such efforts to sell quickly are intended to liquidate stock positions before stock prices decline as other investors sell their shares, but the focus on speed to take positions before other investors do can cause panic in the markets even when the public information disclosed is false.

Concerns about HFT Given traders' heavy reliance on computers to interpret information and to initiate new orders, some critics are concerned that an error in a computer ordering system could cause much panic in financial markets. Furthermore, the coding for a particular institutional investor's bot may be highly dependent on a single computer programmer. The market could potentially be exposed to sabotage if a programmer employed by a high frequency trader becomes upset with the company's management for any reason and changes the coding in a manner that disrupts the trading by the trader's bot. To the extent that such disruptive stock trades are detected by the algorithms of other bots, it could perpetuate the abnormal stock price movements. When stock prices change so abruptly, it is difficult to know if the price changes reflect new relevant information about the stock market or if the prices have deviated from their proper valuations. While there has always been a risk that stock prices could deviate from their proper values, some critics argue that HFT might allow the deviations to become more pronounced before proper corrections occur.

Some algorithms are designed to shut down when the stock market experiences unusually high volatility. However, this could lead to even more instability if some of those algorithms would have recognized that stock prices have declined too much, but are not capable of correcting the stock market's overreaction because they shut down. Even if HFT causes stock price deviations on a given day, one might argue that the prices will soon move back toward their proper valuations. As an extreme example, stock prices declined by 9 percent, on average, in less than 20 minutes during the flash crash in 2010, but rebounded in the following 20 minutes. However, some investors could be devastated by such an event, because if they purchased stocks on margin (with borrowed funds), they could be forced to liquidate their positions when the stock prices declined so as to meet their margin requirements. Since the flash crash, various stock markets have attempted to impose new guidelines that temporarily prevent trading when a stock's price or a market index declines by a particular level over a short interval (such as 5 minutes). These types of regulatory guidelines are described shortly.

ETHICS

12-3d High Frequency Insider Trading

Although HFT may allow the stock market to work more efficiently in some ways, it may also allow some traders with faster trading speed to gain an advantage over other traders. Some traders have used HFT to take advantage of information that they received before other investors did.

EXAMPLE

The Finz financial newspaper conducts a comprehensive survey of biotechnology company executives to determine their views about future economic conditions in that sector. Finz reports the results of the survey each quarter, and many investors use this information when deciding to trade biotechnology stocks. The Wyk Fund agrees to pay Finz $1 million per year to receive the information one hour before the survey is disclosed to the public. If the survey information is generally favorable, the Wyk Fund will use HFT to purchase large volumes of biotechnology stocks before the information is published. Wyk anticipates that once other investors learn of the survey results, they will buy biotechnology stocks, which should push biotechnology stock prices higher within one day. Then Wyk will sell all the shares that it purchased on the following day. ●

Many firms that compile and publish key financial information allow subscribers to pay a fee to receive the information seconds or minutes before it is released to the public. Evidence clearly indicates that when information about particular stocks reaches subscribers before its release to the general public, the trading volumes of those stocks increase abruptly, and their stock prices adjust abruptly before the data become public. The ability to access information even a few seconds before other investors do can be a major advantage as a result of high-speed trading. The SEC has been reviewing this kind of subscriber access and may impose rules to prevent early access to information. But even if rules limit subscriber access to information, some information sources may still sell relevant information illegally to high-speed traders a few seconds or minutes before disclosing it to all other investors.

ETHICS

12-3e High Frequency Front Running

Several financial writers have described how some traders use HFT to gain advantages over others. (For example, see *Dark Pools* by Scott Patterson, Crown Publishing, 2012, and *Flash Boys* by Michael Lewis, W. W. Norton & Company, 2014.) These advantages partially stem from the multiple stock markets in which a particular stock can trade and the differences in speed at which the traders can access trading information and submit orders.

Regulation National Market System (NMS), which was implemented in 2007, requires brokers to seek the best prices for their investors. The creation of private electronic stock markets has introduced many alternative markets where stocks can be purchased or sold. A few of these markets are transparent (similar to the NYSE and Nasdaq), in that recent and desired orders of investors are displayed by electronic data feeds so that other market participants can view them (although some participants may have better access than others). For example, in 2019, the Members Exchange (MEMX) was created to compete with the NYSE and Nasdaq for stock transactions. It is controlled by a group of very large financial institutions, and its goal is to utilize the most up-to-date technology to increase transparency and reduce transaction costs.

Although allowing investors to simultaneously consider multiple markets to accommodate their orders is intended to lead to more competitive pricing of stocks (and lower transaction costs), it can lead to a form of "front running" whereby traders with relatively faster access to specific markets can use another trader's planned orders and cut in front of those orders. When an investor submits an order to various markets, the speed at which it reaches each market depends on the length of the fiber-optic connection path from the investor to the markets. In fact, even if an investor is located near the specific exchanges, the fiber-optic path to them may be much longer than the geographic distance. Because the order usually reaches each market in less than one second, the difference in speeds may seem irrelevant. However, when traders with access to the market orders receive the order first, they may have programmed subsequent trades that can beat that order to some other exchanges. Even though a set of orders might happen within one second, the priority (sequence) in which the orders are received and executed across stock markets can determine the price paid for each order and which orders are executed or not executed.

EXAMPLE

Consider a large institutional investor called SLOWCO that submits a limit order to purchase 1 million shares of stock symbol ZQ at the price of $30. SLOWCO's order arrives first at a dark pool, but another firm called FASTCO pays for special access to information about orders at that dark pool. FASTCO's bot contains algorithms that trigger buy orders at the same price as any large order that is submitted to that dark pool. On noticing the order to purchase stock ZQ, the bot may place a similar order, which may reach an exchange where the stock is being sold for $30 per share or less before SLOWCO's order reaches that market. Here are possible outcomes.

1. FASTCO's order reaches markets faster than SLOWCO's order, so FASTCO's order is completed first (front running). FASTCO's platform may have been programmed to purchase only shares of ZQ stock that could be purchased for less than $30 per share, and to then make those shares available for sale at $30 per share to SLOWCO. In this case, FASTCO profits from acting as an intermediary in the stock market. SLOWCO could have paid less than $30 per share for ZQ stock if its order had reached the market before FASTCO purchased the shares, but it paid $30 per share because its order took longer to reach the market.

2. FASTCO may presume that SLOWCO's large order will push up the price of ZQ stock, so FASTCO's front running may be intended simply to obtain the shares and hold them until after SLOWCO's order causes the market price of ZQ stock to rise. If FASTCO beats SLOWCO to the market where shares are available, it might purchase all shares that are available at $30 per share or less. Many bots have algorithms called "order awareness algos" that are purposely designed to detect large orders (called whales) by mutual funds and then take positions before those orders are executed.

3. FASTCO might already own ZQ stock when it detects that SLOWCO has submitted a large buy order of the stock. FASTCO might have been planning to sell its existing holdings of ZQ stock at $30 per share, but its platform may be programmed to delete sell limit orders of any stock if it detects a sudden large buy order of that stock by another investor. The reasoning is that a large buy order might push the stock price higher, so FASTCO may prefer to defer its sell limit orders until after the price rises. This possibility explains why some large buy orders of a particular stock that reach one market suddenly cause the disappearance of high frequency traders' sell limit orders of that same stock.

Each of these three scenarios would have taken place in less than one second. ●

Because of the advantage of speed in accessing market information and submitting orders, high frequency traders continue searching for ways to shave even one one-hundredth of a second off the time necessary to reach a particular market. Recently, microwave stations have been established to transmit orders to stock markets; this technology might lead to slightly faster order speeds than if the signal is transmitted through a fiber-optic network. Lasers are also being used to relay signals between stock markets. The ultimate goal is to relay signals at the speed of light.

The concerns about front running led to the creation of a new electronic stock exchange called Investors Exchange (IEX) in October 2013. One key rule of this exchange is that it will consider only orders that are not also routed to other exchanges or markets. Information about buy or sell orders is publicized only after trades are executed. The general idea behind this exchange is that the trades executed will be completely transparent. However, IEX might not attract the large trades initiated by many securities firms that are partial owners of other electronic exchanges and prefer that their orders be routed through their own exchanges. Despite this possibility, IEX quickly became very popular. In 2017, it received permission from the SEC to list public companies; in 2018, it listed its first company (Interactive Brokers).

12-3f Impact of High Frequency Trading on Spreads

Many high frequency traders are willing to serve as intermediaries (similar to market makers) by accommodating orders that they believe will ultimately result in profits. For example, they might accommodate a sell order by purchasing the stock if their algorithm senses that this stock's price will rise in the next few seconds or minutes (at which time they could close out their position with another investor). Likewise, they might accommodate a buy order by selling a particular stock if their algorithm senses that this stock's price will decline in the next few seconds or minutes (at which time they could close out their position). Thus, they commonly participate in trades in which they essentially replace market makers. In fact, high frequency traders have taken market share from the market makers because of the large spreads quoted by market makers in the past. These spreads have declined as a result of the participation by high frequency traders.

The market makers might argue that if a large sell order is placed, they could accommodate the entire order all at once at the prevailing market price (albeit at a larger spread). They might buy all the shares at that price and hold those shares in their inventory for weeks or months before selling the shares to other investors. This might help to prevent any downward pressure in price caused by the large sale. Conversely, if an investor's large sell order is accommodated through a series of small transactions carried out by high frequency traders, the stock's price might decline before all the shares are sold. The high frequency traders quickly sell (within the same day) any stock that they are buying, whereas a market maker might hold the stock in its inventory. Thus, even if the investor incurred lower transaction costs from the smaller spread when accommodated by high frequency traders, it may have sold some of its shares for a lower price.

Furthermore, market makers might argue that when market conditions weaken abruptly, the high frequency traders will not necessarily be ready to accommodate any sell orders. In consequence, any form of market panic will not necessarily be stabilized by the high frequency traders' bots, which are driven by algorithms. A counterargument is that any traders (including market makers and high frequency traders) tend to make trades only when the stock price is favorable from their own perspective. Market makers accommodate orders, but only at the price that is acceptable to them. If a market is crashing, they may be willing to purchase stocks that investors want to sell, but only at a low price that reflects the higher level of uncertainty surrounding the price at which they will be able to sell those shares in the future. In a similar manner, high frequency traders will accommodate sell orders of other investors only when the desired selling price is sufficiently low that they expect to ultimately benefit from accommodating the order.

While HFT can reduce transaction costs for investors, front running and other activities of high frequency traders have caused much concern in financial circles. Some critics argue that high frequency traders should register as brokers and should not be allowed to execute some short-term strategies that can disrupt financial markets.

ETHICS

12-4 Regulation of Stock Trading

Regulation of stock markets is necessary to ensure that investors are treated fairly. Without regulation, trading abuses might potentially discourage many investors from participating in the market. Thus, stock trading is regulated both by the individual exchanges and by the SEC. The **Securities Act of 1933** and the **Securities Exchange Act of 1934** were enacted to prevent unfair or unethical trading practices on securities exchanges. As a result of the 1934 act, stock exchanges were empowered and expected to discipline individuals or firms that violate regulations imposed by the exchange.

The NYSE, for example, states that every transaction made at the exchange is under surveillance. The NYSE uses a computerized system to detect unusual trading of any particular stock that is traded on the exchange. It also employs personnel who investigate any abnormal price or trading volume of a particular stock or unusual trading practices of individuals.

In 2002, the NYSE issued a regulation requiring its listed firms to have a majority of independent directors (not employees of the firm) on their respective boards of directors. This requirement was intended to reduce directors' potential conflicts of interests so that they will concentrate on ensuring that the firm's management focuses on maximizing the stock's value for shareholders.

12-4a Circuit Breakers

To promote stability in the markets, stock exchanges can impose circuit breakers, which are restrictions on trading when stock prices or a stock index reaches a specified threshold level. In general, circuit breakers are intended to temporarily stop the trading of stocks in response to a large decline in stock prices within a single day. They may prevent an initial pronounced stock market decline from causing panic selling in the market. See www.nyse.com/markets/nyse/trading-info for more information on circuit breakers.

12-4b Trading Halts

Stock exchanges may also impose trading halts on particular stocks when they believe market participants need more time to receive and absorb material information that could affect the stock's value. For example, they may impose trading halts on stocks that are associated with mergers, earnings reports, lawsuits, and other news. A trading halt does not prevent a stock from experiencing a loss in response to news. Instead, the purpose of the halt is to ensure that market participants have complete information before trading on the news. A trading halt may last for just a few minutes, for several hours, or even for several days. Once the stock exchange believes that the market has complete information, it will allow trading of the stock to resume.

Trading halts are intended to reduce stock price volatility, as the market price is adjusted by market forces in response to news. Such halts can prevent excessive optimism or pessimism about a stock by restricting trading until the news about the firm is completely and widely disseminated to the market. However, some critics believe that the trading halts merely slow the inevitable adjustment in the stock's price to the news. In general, research has found that stock volatility is relatively high after a halt is lifted but that the volatility subsides over the next few days.

12-4c Taxes Imposed on Stock Transactions

For investors below the highest tax bracket, dividends and long-term capital gains are taxed at a maximum of 15 percent for federal taxes, whereas investors in the highest tax bracket pay a tax rate of 20 percent on dividends and long-term capital gains. For all investors, short-term capital gains are taxed at the investor's marginal tax rate on ordinary income. Investors subject to high marginal tax brackets on ordinary income commonly attempt to reduce their taxes by holding their stocks for at least one year. In addition to the federal taxes, many states and a few cities impose an income tax on dividends and capital gains.

12-4d Securities and Exchange Commission

The Securities Act of 1933 and the Securities Exchange Act of 1934 gave the SEC authority to monitor the exchanges and required listed companies to file a registration statement and financial reports with the SEC and the exchanges. In general, the SEC attempts to protect investors by ensuring full disclosure of pertinent information that could affect the values of securities. Some of the more relevant SEC regulations involve the following requirements:

- Firms must publicly disclose all information about themselves that could affect the value of their securities.
- Employees of firms may take positions in their own firm's securities only during periods when they do not know of inside information that will affect the value of the firm once the information becomes public.
- Participants in security markets who facilitate trades must work in a fair and orderly manner.

These regulations are meant to prevent abuses that would give someone an unfair advantage over other investors, thereby reducing the willingness of investors to participate in security markets. The SEC regulations allow all investors to have the same access to public information. Note that the SEC focuses on sufficient disclosure, not on accuracy; it relies on auditors to certify that the financial statements are accurate.

Structure of the SEC   The SEC consists of five commissioners appointed by the president of the United States and confirmed by the U.S. Senate. Each commissioner serves a five-year term. The terms are staggered so that, each year, one commissioner's term ends and a new appointee is added. The president also selects one of the five commissioners to chair the commission.

The commissioners meet to assess whether existing regulations are successfully preventing abuses and to revise the regulations as needed. Specific staff members of the SEC may be assigned to develop a proposal for a new regulation to prevent a particular abuse that is occurring. When the commission adopts new regulations, they are distributed to the public for feedback before final approval. Some of the more important proposals are subject to congressional review before final approval.

Key Divisions of the SEC   The SEC has several important divisions that attempt to ensure a fair and orderly stock market. The Division of Corporation Finance reviews the registration statement filed when a firm goes public, corporate filings for annual and quarterly reports, and proxy statements that involve voting for board members or other corporate issues. The Division of Trading and Markets requires the orderly disclosure of securities trades by various organizations that facilitate the trading of securities.

The Division of Enforcement assesses possible violations of the SEC's regulations and can discipline individuals or firms. An investigation can involve the examination of securities data or transactions, and the SEC has subpoena power to obtain information from specific individuals. When the SEC finds that action is warranted, it may negotiate a settlement with the individuals or firms that are cited for violations, file a case against them in federal court, or even work with law enforcement agencies if the violations involve criminal activity. Such actions are normally intended to prevent the violations from continuing and to discourage other individuals or firms from engaging in illegal securities activities.

ETHICS

SEC Oversight of Corporate Disclosure

In October 2000, the SEC issued Regulation Fair Disclosure (FD), which requires firms to disclose relevant information broadly to investors at the same time. One of the most important results of Regulation FD is that a firm may no longer provide analysts with information that they can use before the market becomes aware of the information.

The firm may disclose the information on its website, through a filing of a document (8-K form) with the SEC, and through a news release. It may hold a conference call with analysts after the news is announced, but is expected to include all material information in the announcement.

Some critics suggest that Regulation FD has caused firms to disclose less information to them and to the public than they did in the past. To ensure that they do not violate this regulation, some firms may offer less information so that no parties have an unfair advantage. In particular, smaller firms find it expensive to issue a press release every time they have relevant information.

ETHICS

SEC Oversight of Insider Trading

Insiders at a publicly traded company (such as managers or board members) sometimes have information about the company that has not yet been publicized. For example, they might know that a company has just obtained a patent that will likely prove very valuable. It is illegal for these individuals to take positions in the stock based on their inside information, because this would give them an unfair advantage over other investors. It is also illegal for insiders to pass the information on to other investors, or for those investors to take positions in the stock based on that information.

Nevertheless, evidence suggests that insider trading occurs quite frequently. Numerous studies have shown that a public company's stock price typically increases a few weeks before an announcement is made that the company will be acquired. Bidders often pay a large premium to buy targets, such as 30 percent or more above the prevailing stock price. Thus, investors who can obtain the stock before the bid is announced can sometimes earn a return of 30 percent or more in just a few weeks. In many cases, the stock price of a public company that is targeted for an acquisition experiences an abnormal increase in stock price a few weeks before the acquisition announcement. Such an abnormal increase in price for many targeted companies suggests that some traders have inside information that the company will be acquired. Such insider trading is not restricted to mergers, but can also occur in advance of many different events that will likely push up the stock price once the information becomes public.

A recent concern is that so-called expert networks may leak information to institutional investors. Some managers or executives of publicly traded companies are hired as consultants ("experts") by a hedge fund to provide the fund with insights about their company. Such a relationship can be completely legitimate if the consultants divulge only information about the company that is already public. Yet some of these consultants are paid more than $100,000 to have phone conversations with the hedge fund. Some regulators have suggested that a hedge fund would be willing to incur such a high expense for information only if it expects to receive inside information from the consultants.

The SEC attempts to prevent investors from trading based on inside information. In October 2009, it (along with other government agencies including the Justice Department and the Federal Bureau of Investigation) charged many defendants connected with the

Galleon Fund (a hedge fund) with trading based on inside information. Over the next three years, more than 60 defendants charged with insider trading (or related charges) either pled guilty or were convicted in the court system.

The Galleon case received special attention because the government effectively used wiretap evidence to prosecute insider trading cases. In addition, the government exposed the illegal activities of some insiders who were hired on the side as consultants or experts by the hedge fund. Furthermore, the penalties imposed on the defendants who were found guilty of insider trading (or related charges) were much more severe than the punishments that had been ordered in previous years.

12-5 Trading International Stocks

Although the international trading of stocks has grown over time, it has been limited by three barriers: transaction costs, information costs, and exchange rate risk. Although exchange rate risk still exists, transaction costs and information costs have been reduced, as explained next.

12-5a Reduction in Transaction Costs

Most countries have their own stock exchanges where the stocks of local, publicly held companies are traded. In recent years, countries have consolidated their exchanges, increasing their efficiency and reducing the transaction costs. Some European stock exchanges use an extensive cross-listing system (called Eurolist) so that investors in a given European country can easily purchase stocks of companies based in other European countries.

Most major international stock exchanges are now fully computerized, so a trading floor is not needed to execute orders. The details of the orders (including the stock's name, the number of shares to be bought or sold, and the price at which the investor is willing to buy or sell) are fed into a computer system. The system matches buyers and sellers, and then sends information confirming the transaction to the financial institution, which informs the investor that the transaction has been completed. When there are many more buy orders than sell orders for a given stock, the computer will not be able to accommodate all orders. Some buyers will then increase the price they are willing to pay for the stock. Thus, the price adjusts in response to the demand (buy orders) for the stock and the supply (sell orders) of the stock for sale, as recorded by the computer system. Furthermore, the Internet allows investors to use their computers to place orders (through the website of a member of the stock exchange), which will then be executed and confirmed by the computer system back through the Internet to the investor.

Thus, all parts of the trading process, from the placement of orders to the confirmations that transactions have been executed, are carried out electronically. The ease of placing orders regardless of the investor's location and the location of the stock exchange will likely increase the volume of international stock transactions in the future.

12-5b Reduction in Information Costs

Information about foreign stocks is now available on the Internet, enabling investors to make more informed decisions without having to purchase information about these stocks. Consequently, investors should be more comfortable assessing foreign stocks. Differences in accounting rules may still limit the degree to which financial data about foreign companies can be interpreted or compared to data about firms in other countries, but some progress has occurred in making accounting standards uniform across countries.

Summary

- Investors engage in various types of stock transactions. They can place an order by phone or online. They can request that a transaction be executed at the prevailing price or only if the stock price reaches a specified level. They can finance a portion of their stock purchase with borrowed funds as a means of increasing the potential return on their investment. They can also sell stocks short.

- Organized stock exchanges such as the NYSE and the Nasdaq facilitate secondary stock market transactions. Members of these exchanges trade stock for their own accounts or for their clients. The exchanges are served by floor brokers and market makers, who execute transactions, although most stock transactions are now executed through a telecommunications network. Electronic communication networks (ECNs) facilitate the execution of orders. ECNs can interact with a trading platform on a website that allows investors to trade stocks without the use of a broker.

- High frequency trading (HFT) entails the use of electronic platforms to execute orders based on an algorithm with programmed instructions. High frequency traders take large positions in stocks and typically close them out on the same day. Bots and algorithms enable traders to place or cancel orders in less than a second in response to information such as recent stock price movements. HFT now accounts for more than half of the trading volume in the United States.

- Stock markets are regulated to ensure that investors are treated fairly. Stock trading is regulated both by the individual exchanges and by the SEC. Many of the regulations are intended to prevent unfair or unethical trading practices on the securities exchanges. In particular, the stock exchanges and the SEC attempt to prevent the use of inside information by investors.

- As various stock markets have removed their barriers to foreign investors, they have become more globally integrated. Transaction costs and information costs have been reduced, making it easier for investors to engage in international stock trading.

Point/Counterpoint

Is a Market Maker Needed?

Point   Yes. A market maker can make a market by serving as the counterparty on a transaction. Without market makers, stock orders might be heavily weighted toward buys or sells, and price movements would be more volatile.

Counterpoint   No. Market makers do not prevent stock prices from declining. A stock that has more selling pressure than buying pressure will experience a decline in price, as it should. The electronic communication networks can serve as the intermediary between buyer and seller.

Who Is Correct?   Use the Internet to learn more about this issue and then formulate your own opinion.

Questions and Applications

1. **Orders** Explain the difference between a market order and a limit order.

2. **Margins** Explain how margin requirements can affect the potential return and risk from investing in a stock. What is the maintenance margin?

3. **Short Selling** Under what conditions might investors consider short selling a specific stock?

4. **Short Selling** Describe the short selling process. Explain the short interest ratio.

5. **Market Makers** Describe the roles of market makers.

6. **ECNs** What are electronic communication networks?

7. **SEC Structure and Role** Briefly describe the structure and role of the Securities and Exchange Commission.

8. **SEC Enforcement** Explain how the Securities and Exchange Commission attempts to prevent violations of SEC regulations.

9. Circuit Breakers Explain how circuit breakers are used to reduce the likelihood of a large stock market crash.

10. Trading Halts Why are trading halts sometimes imposed on particular stocks?

Advanced Questions

11. Regulation FD What are the implications of Regulation FD?

12. Stock Exchange Transaction Costs Explain how foreign stock exchanges have reduced transaction costs.

13. Bid–Ask Spread of Penny Stocks Your friend just told you about a penny stock that he purchased, which increased in price from $0.10 to $0.50 per share. You start investigating penny stocks, and after conducting a large amount of research, you find a stock with a quoted price of $0.05. Upon further investigation, you notice that the ask price for the stock is $0.08 and that the bid price is $0.01. Discuss the possible reasons for this wide bid–ask spread.

14. Ban on Short Selling Why did the SEC impose a temporary ban on short sales of specific stocks in 2008? Do you think a ban on short selling is effective?

15. Dark Pools What are dark pools? How can they help investors accumulate shares without other investors knowing about the trades? Why are dark pools criticized by public stock exchanges? Explain the strategy used by public stock exchanges to compete with dark pools.

16. Inside Information Describe inside information as applied to the trading of stocks. Why is it illegal to trade based on inside information? Describe the evidence that suggests some investors use inside information.

17. Galleon Insider Trading Case Explain how the Galleon Fund case led to stronger enforcement against insider trading.

18. Strategy of HFT Firms Explain the strategy of high frequency trading firms. Describe the typical time horizon of an investment that is relevant to high frequency traders and explain how it varies from the time horizons of other institutional investors.

19. Flash Crash of May 6, 2010 Describe the flash crash of May 6, 2010, and explain why it caused so much concern among investors and regulators.

20. Front Running by High Frequency Traders Explain how some high frequency traders use a form of front running to capitalize on faster access to specific markets.

21. Impact of HFT on Spreads Explain how and why high frequency trading affects spreads.

Critical Thinking Question

Regulation of Insider Trading Some critics argue that insider trading should not be illegal, because it allows market prices to more quickly reflect the inside information. Write a short essay that supports or refutes this opinion.

Interpreting Financial News

Interpret the following statements made by Wall Street analysts and portfolio managers.

a. "Individual investors who purchase stock on margin might as well go to Vegas."

b. "During a major stock market downturn, market makers suddenly are not available."

c. "The trading floor may become extinct due to ECNs."

Managing in Financial Markets

Focus on Heavily Shorted Stocks As a portfolio manager, you commonly take short positions in stocks that have a high short interest ratio. What is the advantage of focusing on these types of firms? What is a possible disadvantage?

Problems

1. Buying on Margin Assume that Vogl stock is priced at $50 per share and pays a dividend of $1 per share. An investor purchases the stock on margin, paying $30 per share and borrowing the remainder from the brokerage firm at 10 percent annualized interest. If, after one year, the stock is sold at a price of $60 per share, what is the return to the investor?

2. Buying on Margin Assume that Duever stock is priced at $80 per share and pays a dividend of $2 per share. An investor purchases the stock on margin, paying $50 per share and borrowing the remainder from the brokerage firm at 12 percent annualized interest. If, after one year, the stock is sold at a price of $90 per share, what is the return to the investor?

3. Buying on Margin Suppose that you buy a stock for $48 by paying $25 and borrowing the remaining $23 from a brokerage firm at 8 percent annualized interest. The stock pays an annual dividend of $0.80 per share, and after one year you are able to sell it for $65. Calculate your return on the stock. Then, calculate the return on the stock if you had used only personal funds to make the purchase. Repeat the problem assuming that only personal funds are used and that you are able to sell the stock at $40 at the end of one year.

4. Buying on Margin How would the return on a stock be affected by a lower initial investment (and higher loan amount)? Explain the relationship between the proportion of funds borrowed and the return.

Flow of Funds Exercise

Shorting Stocks

Recall that if the economy continues to be strong, Carson Company may need to increase its production capacity by approximately 50 percent over the next few years to satisfy demand. It would need financing to expand and accommodate the increase in production. Recall that the yield curve is currently upward sloping. Carson is concerned about a possible slowing of the economy because of potential Fed actions to reduce inflation. It is also considering issuing stock or bonds to raise funds in the next year.

a. In some cases, a stock's price is too high or too low because of asymmetric information (information known by the firm but not by investors). How can Carson attempt to minimize asymmetric information?

b. Carson Company is concerned that if it issues stock, its stock price over time could be adversely affected by certain institutional investors that take large short positions in a stock. When this happens, the stock's price may be undervalued because of the pressure on the price caused by the large short positions. What can Carson do to counter major short positions taken by institutional investors if it really believes that its stock price should be higher? What is the potential risk involved in this strategy?

Internet/Excel Exercises

1. Go to finance.yahoo.com and enter the ticker symbol of the firm of your choice in the search box. Review the statistics provided. What is the average daily trading volume (Avg. Volume)? What is the market capitalization of the firm? What is its price–earnings ratio (PE Ratio)? What is the amount of dividends paid, if any, and what is the dividend yield (Dividend & Yield)? What is the firm's beta?

2. For the same firm, under "Statistics," find its return on assets (ROA) and return on equity (ROE). What is its short ratio?

Online Articles with Real-World Examples

Find a recent practical article available online that describes a real-world example regarding a specific financial institution or financial market that reinforces one or more concepts covered in this chapter.

If your class has an online component, your professor may ask you to post your summary of the article there and provide a link to the article so that other students can access it. If your class is live, your professor may ask you to summarize your application of the article in class. Your professor may assign specific students to complete this assignment or may allow any students to do the assignment on a volunteer basis.

For recent online articles and real-world examples related to this chapter, consider using the following search terms (be sure to include the prevailing year as a search term to ensure that the online articles are recent):

1. stock AND transaction cost
2. stock loss AND margin requirement
3. buying on margin AND risk
4. short selling AND gains
5. short selling AND risk
6. stock AND bid/ask spread
7. stock AND market makers
8. stock AND ECNs
9. stock regulations AND conflict
10. international stock AND transaction cost

PART 4 INTEGRATIVE PROBLEM

Stock Market Analysis

This problem requires an understanding of the different methods for valuing stocks.

As a stock portfolio manager, you spend most of your day searching for stocks that appear to be undervalued. In the last few days, you have received information about two stocks that you are assessing: Olympic stock and Kenner stock. Many stock analysts believe that these stocks are undervalued because their price–earnings ratios are lower than the industry average. Olympic, Inc., has a PE ratio of 6 versus an industry PE ratio of 8. Its stock price declined recently in response to an announcement that its quarterly earnings would be lower than expected because of expenses from recent restructuring. The restructuring is expected to improve Olympic's future performance, but its earnings will take a large one-time hit this quarter.

Kenner Company has a PE ratio of 9 versus a PE ratio of 11 for its industry. Its earnings have been decent in recent years, but it has not kept up with new technology and may lose market share to competitors in the future.

Questions

1. Should you still consider purchasing Olympic stock in light of the analysts' arguments about why it may be undervalued?
2. Should you still consider purchasing Kenner stock in light of the analysts' arguments about why it may be undervalued?
3. Some stock analysts have just predicted that the prices of most stocks will fall because interest rates are expected to increase, which would cause investors to use higher required rates of return when valuing stocks. Based on this logic, the analysts suggested that the present value of future cash flows would decline if interest rates rise. The expected increase in interest rates is due to expectations of a stronger economy, which will result in an increased demand for loanable funds by corporations and individuals. Do you believe that stock prices will decline if the economy strengthens and interest rates rise?

PART 5
Derivative Security Markets

Derivatives are financial contracts whose values are derived from the values of underlying assets. They are widely used to speculate on future expectations or to reduce a security portfolio's risk. The chapters in Part 5 focus on derivative security markets, and each explains how institutional portfolio managers and speculators use them. Many financial market participants simultaneously use all these markets, as is emphasized throughout the chapters.

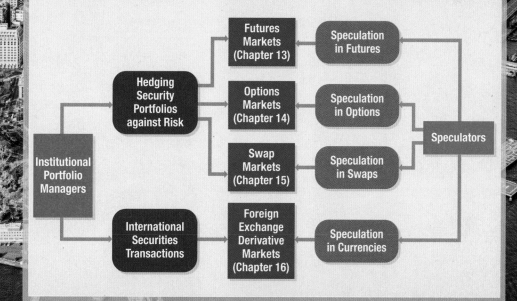

13

Financial Futures Markets

Financial futures markets facilitate the trading of financial futures contracts, which are traded in order to speculate on or hedge against the movement in specific security or commodity prices. These markets are commonly used by financial institutions and other corporations to reduce their risk.

13-1 Background on Financial Futures

A **financial futures contract** is a standardized agreement to deliver or receive a specified amount of a specified financial instrument at a specified price and date. The seller of a financial futures contract delivers the instrument for the specified price, and the buyer of a financial futures contract pays for the financial instrument upon delivery.

13-1a Popular Futures Contracts

Futures contracts are traded on a wide variety of securities and indexes.

Interest Rate Futures   Many of the popular financial futures contracts are on debt securities such as Treasury bills, Treasury notes, Treasury bonds, and Eurodollar CDs. These contracts are referred to as **interest rate futures**. For each type of contract, the settlement dates at which delivery would occur are in March, June, September, and December.

Stock Index Futures   Other financial futures contracts are traded on stock indexes; they are referred to as **stock index futures**. A stock index futures contract allows for the buying and selling of a stock index for a specified price at a specified date. Popular stock index futures contracts are described in Exhibit 13.1.

13-1b Markets for Financial Futures

Markets have been established to facilitate the trading of futures contracts.

Futures Exchanges   Futures exchanges provide an organized marketplace in which standardized futures contracts can be traded. The exchanges clear, settle, and guarantee all transactions. In addition, they ensure that each party's position is sufficiently backed by collateral as the market value of the position changes over time. In this way, any losses that occur are covered, so that counterparties are not adversely affected. Consequently, participants are more willing to trade financial futures contracts on an exchange.

Most financial futures contracts in the United States are traded through the CME Group, which was formed in July 2007 by the merger of the Chicago Board of Trade (CBOT) and

Exhibit 13.1 Stock Index Futures Contracts

TYPE OF STOCK INDEX FUTURES CONTRACT	CONTRACT IS VALUED AS
S&P 500 index	$250 times index
E-Mini S&P 500 index	$50 times index
S&P Midcap 400 index	$100 times index
S&P Small Cap index	$200 times index
Nasdaq 100 index	$100 times index
E-Mini Nasdaq 100 index	$20 times index
E-Mini Russell 2000 index	$50 times index
Russell 2000 index	$500 times index

the Chicago Mercantile Exchange (CME). Most futures contracts are traded electronically on Globex, which is the CME Group's electronic trading platform. Transactions can occur on Globex virtually around the clock (the platform is closed about one hour per day for maintenance) and on weekends.

The operations of financial futures exchanges are regulated by the Commodity Futures Trading Commission (CFTC). The CFTC approves futures contracts before they can be listed by futures exchanges and imposes regulations to prevent unfair trading practices.

WEB

www.cftc.gov
Detailed information on
the CFTC.

Over-the-Counter Market Some specialized futures contracts are sold "over the counter" rather than on an exchange, whereby a financial intermediary (such as a commercial bank or an investment bank) finds a counterparty or serves as the counterparty. These over-the-counter arrangements are more personalized and can be tailored to the specific preferences of the parties involved. Such tailoring is not possible for the more standardized futures contracts sold on the exchanges.

13-1c Purpose of Trading Financial Futures

WEB

www.nfa.futures.org
Information for investors
who wish to trade
futures contracts.

Financial futures are traded either to speculate on prices of securities or to hedge existing exposure to security price movements. **Speculators** in the financial futures markets take positions with the goal of profiting from expected changes in the price of futures contracts over time. They can be classified according to their methods. **Day traders** attempt to capitalize on price movements during a single day; usually, they close out their futures positions on the same day the positions were initiated. By comparison, **position traders** maintain their futures positions for longer periods of time (for weeks or months) and attempt to capitalize on expected price movements over a more extended time horizon.

Hedgers take positions in financial futures in an effort to reduce their exposure to future movements in interest rates or stock prices. Many hedgers who maintain large portfolios of stocks or bonds take a futures position to hedge the risk associated with those securities. Speculators commonly take the opposite position and, therefore, serve as the counterparty on many futures transactions. Thus, speculators provide liquidity to the futures market.

13-1d Institutional Trading of Futures Contracts

WEB

www.cmegroup.com
Offers details about
the products offered
by the CME Group
and also provides price
quotations of the various
futures contracts.

Exhibit 13.2 summarizes how various types of financial institutions participate in the futures markets. Financial institutions generally use futures contracts to reduce risk. Some commercial banks, savings institutions, bond mutual funds, pension funds, and insurance companies trade interest rate futures contracts in an effort to protect themselves against a possible increase in interest rates, thereby insulating their long-term debt securities from

Exhibit 13.2   Institutional Use of Futures Markets

TYPE OF FINANCIAL INSTITUTION	PARTICIPATION IN FUTURES MARKETS
Commercial banks	• Take positions in futures contracts to hedge against interest rate risk.
Savings institutions	• Take positions in futures contracts to hedge against interest rate risk.
Securities firms	• Execute futures transactions for individuals and firms. • Take positions in futures contracts to hedge their own portfolios against stock market or interest rate movements.
Mutual funds	• Take positions in futures contracts to speculate on future stock market or interest rate movements. • Take positions in futures contracts to hedge their portfolios against stock market or interest rate movements.
Pension funds	• Take positions in futures contracts to hedge their portfolios against stock market or interest rate movements.
Insurance companies	• Take positions in futures contracts to hedge their portfolios against stock market or interest rate movements.

interest rate risk. Some stock mutual funds, pension funds, and insurance companies trade stock index futures to partially insulate their respective stock portfolios from adverse movements in the stock market.

13-1e **Trading Process**

To buy or sell futures contracts, customers open accounts at brokerage firms that execute futures transactions. Futures brokers execute the orders requested by their customers and charge fees for this service. They typically provide other personalized services as well, such as research on specific types of futures contracts. Some brokers also allow customers to access their platform for a fee, so that the customers can execute the trades themselves.

Market makers can also execute futures contract transactions for customers. These securities firms have been given authority by the futures exchange to make a market in a particular financial futures product. They quote bid and ask prices for the product to which they are assigned, and may facilitate a buy order for one customer and a sell order for a different customer. The market maker then earns the difference between the bid price and the ask price for such a trade. Market makers can also take positions in futures contracts, and can earn profits when they use their own funds to take such positions. Like any investors, they are subject to the risk of losses on their positions.

Under the futures exchange requirements, a customer must establish a margin deposit with a broker before a transaction can be executed. This initial margin is typically between 5 and 18 percent of a futures contract's full value. Brokers commonly require margin deposits above those required by the exchanges. As the futures contract price changes on a daily basis, its value is "marked to market," or revised to reflect the prevailing conditions. A customer whose contract value moves in an unfavorable direction may receive a margin call from the broker, requiring that additional funds be deposited in the margin account. The margin requirements reduce the risk that customers will later default on their obligations.

Type of Orders   Customers can place either a market order or a limit order. With a market order, the trade is automatically executed at the prevailing price of the futures contract; with a limit order, the trade is executed only if the price is within the limit specified by the customer. For example, a customer may place a limit order to buy a particular futures

WEB

www.bloomberg.com
Today's prices of U.S. bond futures contracts and prices of currency futures contracts.

WEB

www.cmegroup
.com/globex
Information about how investors can engage in electronic trading of futures contracts.

contract if it is priced no higher than a specified price. Similarly, a customer may place an order to sell a futures contract if it is priced no lower than a specified minimum price.

WEB

www.cmegroup.com
Quotations for futures contracts.

Role of the Futures Exchange   The futures exchange facilitates the trading process, but does not itself take buy or sell positions on futures contracts. Instead, the exchange acts as a clearinghouse. A clearinghouse facilitates the trading process by recording all transactions and guaranteeing timely payments. This precludes the need for a purchaser of a futures contract to check the creditworthiness of the contract seller. In fact, purchasers of contracts do not even know who the sellers are, and vice versa. The clearinghouse also supervises the delivery specified by contracts as of the settlement date.

Futures contracts representing debt securities such as bonds result in the delivery of those securities at the settlement date. Futures contracts that represent an index (such as a bond index or stock index) are settled in cash.

13-2 Interest Rate Futures Contracts

Interest rate futures contracts specify a face value of the underlying securities (such as $1,000,000 for T-bill futures and $100,000 for Treasury bond futures), a maturity of the underlying securities, and the settlement date when delivery would occur. There is a minimum price fluctuation (called tick size) for each contract, such as $\frac{1}{32}$ of a point ($1,000), or $31.25 per contract.

Other futures contracts focus on bond indexes; they allow for the buying and selling of a particular bond index for a specified price at a specified date. For financial institutions that trade in municipal bonds, **Municipal Bond Index (MBI) futures** are available. The MBI is based on the **Bond Buyer Index** of 40 actively traded general obligation and revenue bonds. The specific characteristics of MBI futures are shown in Exhibit 13.3.

13-2a Valuing Interest Rate Futures

The price of an interest rate futures contract generally reflects the expected price of the underlying security on the settlement date. In turn, any factors that influence the expected price should influence the current prices of the interest futures contracts. Participants in the Treasury bond futures market closely monitor economic indicators that affect Treasury bond prices, as shown in Exhibit 13.4. Some of the more closely monitored indicators of economic growth include employment, gross domestic product, retail sales, industrial

Exhibit 13.3   Characteristics of Municipal Bond Index Futures

CHARACTERISTICS OF FUTURES CONTRACT	MUNICIPAL BOND INDEX FUTURES
Trading unit	1,000 times the Bond Buyer Municipal Bond Index. A price of 90-00 represents a contract size of $90,000.
Price quotation	In points and thirty-seconds of a point.
Minimum price fluctuation	One thirty-second ($\frac{1}{32}$) of a point, or $31.25 per contract.
Daily trading limits	Three points ($3,000) per contract above or below the previous day's settlement price.
Settlement months	March, June, September, December.
Settlement procedure	Municipal Bond Index futures settle in cash on the last day of trading.

Exhibit 13.4 Framework for Explaining Changes over Time in the Futures Prices of Treasury Bonds and Treasury Bills

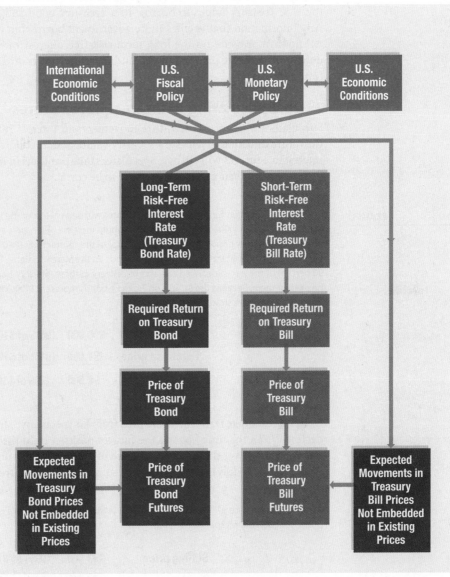

production, and consumer confidence. When indicators signal an increase in economic growth, participants anticipate an increase in interest rates, which places downward pressure on bond prices as well as on Treasury bond futures prices. Conversely, when indicators signal a decrease in economic growth, participants anticipate lower interest rates, which places upward pressure on bond prices as well as on Treasury bond futures.

Participants in the Treasury bond futures market also closely monitor indicators of inflation, such as the consumer price index and the producer price index. In general, an unexpected increase in these indexes tends to create expectations of higher interest rates and places downward pressure on bond prices and, therefore, on Treasury bond futures prices.

Indicators that reflect the amount of long-term financing are also monitored. For example, announcements about the government deficit or the amount of money that the U.S. Treasury hopes to borrow in a Treasury bond auction are closely monitored. Any information that implies more government borrowing than expected tends to signal upward pressure on the long-term risk-free interest rate (the Treasury bond rate), downward pressure on bond prices, and therefore, downward pressure on Treasury bond futures prices.

13-2b Speculating in Interest Rate Futures

Speculators who anticipate future movements in interest rates can likewise anticipate the future direction of Treasury security values and, therefore, predict how valuations of interest rate futures will change. Speculators take positions in interest rate futures that will benefit them if their expectations prove to be correct.

EXAMPLE

In February, Dan Allen forecasts that interest rates will decrease over the next month. If his expectation is correct, the market value of Treasury bonds should increase. Allen calls a broker and purchases a futures contract on Treasury bonds. Assume that the price of the contract was 94-00, which represents 94 percent of the par value, and that the price of Treasury bonds on the March settlement date is 96-00, which represents 96 percent of the par value. Allen can accept delivery of these Treasury bonds and sell them for more than he paid for them. Because the futures on Treasury bonds represent $100,000 of par value, the nominal profit from this speculative strategy is

Selling price	$96,000	(96% of $100,000)
− Purchase price	−94,000	(94% of $100,000)
= Profit	$2,000	(2% of $100,000)

In this example, Dan Allen benefited from his speculative strategy because interest rates declined from the time he took the futures position until the settlement date. If interest rates had risen over this period, the price of Treasury bonds on the settlement date would have declined to less than 94-00, and Allen would have incurred a loss.

EXAMPLE

Assume that the price of Treasury bonds as of the March settlement date is 93-00. In this case, the nominal profit from Dan Allen's speculative strategy is

Selling price	$93,000	(93% of $100,000)
− Purchase price	−94,000	(94% of $100,000)
= Profit	−$1,000	(−1% of $100,000)

Now suppose instead that, in February, Allen had anticipated that interest rates would rise by March. Under these conditions, he would sell a futures contract on Treasury bonds with a March settlement date, obligating him to provide Treasury bonds to the purchaser on that delivery date. If the price of Treasury bonds declined by March, Allen would be able to obtain Treasury bonds at a market price lower than the price at which he was obligated to sell those bonds. ●

Again, there is always the risk that interest rates (and therefore Treasury bond prices) will move contrary to expectations, which would cause speculators to incur a loss on their position in futures contracts.

Exhibit 13.5 Potential Payoffs from Speculating in Financial Futures

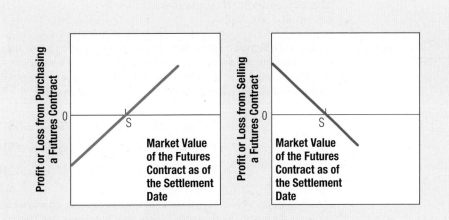

Payoffs from Speculating in Interest Rate Futures   Exhibit 13.5 illustrates the potential payoffs from speculating in futures contracts. The left graph represents a purchaser of futures, and the right graph represents a seller of futures. The "S" on each graph indicates the initial price at which a futures position is created. The horizontal axis represents the market value of the securities in terms of a futures contract as of the delivery date. The maximum possible loss when purchasing futures is the amount to be paid for the securities, but this loss will occur only if the market value of the securities falls to zero. The amount of gain (or loss) to a speculator who initially purchased futures will equal the loss (or gain) to a speculator who initially sold futures on the same date, assuming zero transaction costs.

Impact of Leverage   Because investors commonly use a margin account to take futures positions, the return from speculating in interest rate futures should reflect the degree of financial leverage involved. This return is magnified substantially when considering the relatively small margin maintained by many investors.

EXAMPLE   In the example where Dan Allen earned a profit of $2,000 on a futures contract, the profit represents 2 percent of the underlying contract's par value. Consider that Allen could have taken the interest rate futures position with an initial margin of perhaps $10,000. Under these conditions, the $2,000 profit represents a return of 20 percent over the period of less than two months in which he maintained the futures position.

But just as financial leverage magnifies positive returns, it also magnifies losses. If Allen had an initial margin of $10,000 in the example where he lost $1,000 on a futures contract, he would have lost 10 percent of his investment over the two-month period in which he maintained the futures position. ●

Closing Out the Futures Position   Most buyers or sellers of financial futures contracts do not actually make or accept delivery of the financial instrument; instead, they offset their positions by the settlement date. In the previous example, if Dan Allen did not want to accept delivery of the Treasury bonds at the settlement date, he could have sold a futures contract on Treasury bonds with a March settlement date at any time before that date. Because his second transaction requires him to deliver Treasury bonds at the March settlement date but his initial transaction allows him to receive Treasury bonds at the March settlement date, his obligations net out.

When closing out a futures position, a speculator's gain (or loss) is based on the difference between the price at which a futures contract is sold and the price at which that same type of contract is purchased.

EXAMPLE Suppose Kim Bennett purchased a futures contract on Treasury bonds at a price of 90-00 on October 2. One month later, she sells the same futures contract to close out her position. At this time, the futures contract specifies the price as 92-10, or $92\frac{10}{32}$ percent of the par value. Given that the futures contract on Treasury bonds specifies a par value of $100,000, Bennett's nominal profit is

Selling price	**$92,312**	**($92\frac{10}{32}$ % of $100,000)**
− Purchase price	**−90,000**	**(90.00% of $100,000)**
= Profit	**$2,312**	**($2\frac{10}{32}$ % of $100,000)**

When the initial position is a sale of the futures contract, a purchase of that same type of contract will close out the position. For example, assume that Chris Harper sold Treasury bond futures on October 2 at a price of 90-00 and then took an offsetting position one month later to close out his position. Using the same numbers as before, he will incur a loss of $2,312 (ignoring transaction costs) from closing out his position one month later. Speculators are willing to close out a position at a loss when they expect that a larger loss will occur if the position is not closed out. ●

13-2c Hedging with Interest Rate Futures

Financial institutions can classify their assets and liabilities in terms of the sensitivity of their market value to interest rate movements. The difference between a financial institution's volume of rate-sensitive assets and rate-sensitive liabilities represents its exposure to interest rate risk. Over the long run, an institution may attempt to restructure its assets or liabilities so as to balance its degree of rate sensitivity. However, restructuring the balance sheet takes time. In the short run, the institution may consider using financial futures to hedge its exposure to interest rate movements. A variety of financial institutions use financial futures to hedge their interest rate risk, including mortgage companies, securities dealers, commercial banks, savings institutions, pension funds, and insurance companies.

Using Interest Rate Futures to Create a Short Hedge Financial institutions commonly take a position in interest rate futures to create a short hedge, which is the sale of a futures contract on debt securities or an index that is similar to the institution's assets. The "short" position from the futures contract is taken to hedge the institution's "long" position (in its own assets).

Consider a commercial bank that currently holds a large amount of corporate bonds. Its primary source of funds is short-term deposits. The bank will be adversely affected if interest rates rise in the near future because its liabilities are more rate-sensitive than its assets. Although the bank believes that its bonds are a reasonable long-term investment, it anticipates that interest rates will rise temporarily. Therefore, it hedges against this interest rate risk by selling futures on securities that have characteristics similar to the securities it is holding; the underlying idea is that the futures prices will change in tandem with these securities. One strategy is to sell Treasury bond futures, because the price movements of Treasury bonds are highly correlated with movements in corporate bond prices. This strategy is referred to as *cross hedging*, because the futures contract instrument (Treasury bonds) differs from the securities that are being hedged (corporate bonds).

If interest rates rise as expected, the market value of existing corporate bonds held by the bank will decline. Yet this decline could be offset by the favorable impact of the futures position. The bank locked in the price at which it could sell Treasury bonds. If it can purchase Treasury bonds at a lower price just prior to settlement of the futures contract (because the value of bonds will have decreased), it will then profit after fulfilling its futures contract obligation. Alternatively, it could offset its short position by purchasing futures contracts similar to the type that it sold earlier.

EXAMPLE

Assume that Charlotte Insurance Company plans to obtain cash in six months by selling its Treasury bond holdings for $5 million at that time. It is concerned that interest rates might increase over the next three months, which would reduce the market value of the bonds by the time they are sold. To hedge against this possibility, Charlotte plans to sell Treasury bond futures. It sells 50 Treasury bond futures contracts with a par value of $5 million ($100,000 per contract) for 98-16 (that is, $98\frac{16}{32}$ percent of par value).

Suppose that the actual price of the futures contract declines to 94-16 because of an increase in interest rates. Charlotte can close out its short futures position by purchasing contracts identical to those it has sold. If it purchases 50 Treasury bond futures contracts at the prevailing price of 94-16, its profit on each futures contract will be

Selling price	**$98,500**	**(98.50% of $100,000)**
− Purchase price	**−94,500**	**(94.50% of $100,000)**
= Profit	**$4,000**	**(4.00% of $100,000)**

Charlotte had a position in 50 futures contracts, so its total profit from that position will be $200,000 ($4,000 per contract × 50 contracts). This gain on the futures contract position will help offset the reduced market value of Charlotte's bond holdings. Charlotte also could have earned a gain on its position by purchasing an identical futures contract just before the settlement date.

If interest rates rise by a greater degree over the six-month period, the market value of Charlotte's Treasury bond holdings will decrease further. However, the price of Treasury bond futures contracts will decrease by an even greater degree, creating a larger gain from the short position in Treasury bond futures.

If interest rates decrease over the six-month period, the Treasury futures prices will rise, causing a loss on Charlotte's futures position. That loss will, however, be offset by the increased market value of Charlotte's bond holdings. In this case, the firm would have experienced better overall performance without the hedge. ●

The preceding example presumes that the basis, or the difference between the price of a security and the price of a futures contract, remains the same. In reality, the price of the security may fluctuate more or less than the futures contract used to hedge it. If so, a perfect offset will not result when a given face value amount of securities is hedged with the same face value amount of futures contracts.

Trade-off from Using a Short Hedge

When considering the rising and the declining interest rate scenarios, the advantages and disadvantages of interest rate futures are obvious. Interest rate futures can hedge against both adverse and favorable events. Exhibit 13.6 compares two probability distributions of returns generated by a financial institution whose liabilities are more rate-sensitive than its assets. If the institution hedges its exposure to interest rate risk, its probability distribution of returns is narrower than if it does not hedge. In Exhibit 13.6, the return when hedging would have been higher than the return without hedging if interest rates increased (left side of the graph) but lower if interest rates decreased (right side).

Exhibit 13.6   Comparison of Probability Distributions of Returns; Hedged versus Unhedged Positions

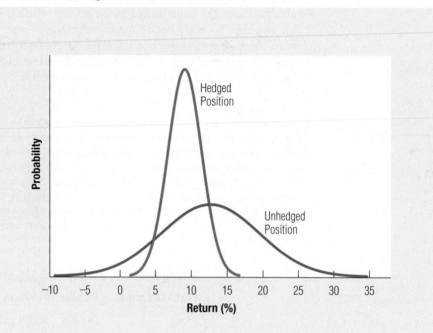

WEB

www.cmegroup.com
Go to the section on
Intraday Data (under
"Data") to review quotes
on interest rate futures.

A financial institution that hedges with interest rate futures is less sensitive to economic events. Thus, financial institutions that frequently use interest rate futures may be able to reduce the variability of their earnings over time, which reflects a lower degree of risk. However, it is virtually impossible to perfectly hedge the sensitivity of all cash flows to interest rate movements.

Using Interest Rate Futures to Create a Long Hedge

Some financial institutions use a **long hedge** to reduce exposure to the possibility of declining interest rates. Consider government securities dealers who plan to purchase long-term bonds in a few months. If the dealers are concerned that prices of these securities will rise before they make their purchases, they may purchase Treasury bond futures contracts. These contracts lock in the price at which Treasury bonds can be purchased, regardless of what happens to market rates prior to actual purchase of the bonds.

Hedging Net Exposure

Because interest rate futures contracts entail transaction costs, they should be used only to hedge **net exposure**, which is the difference between asset and liability positions. Consider a bank that has $300 million in long-term assets and $220 million worth of long-term, fixed-rate liabilities. If interest rates rise, the market value of the long-term assets will decline but the bank will benefit from the fixed rate on the $220 million in long-term liabilities. Thus, the bank's net exposure is only $80 million (assuming that the long-term assets and liabilities are similarly affected by rising interest rates). This financial institution should therefore focus on hedging its net exposure of $80 million by creating a short hedge.

13-3 Stock Index Futures

A futures contract on a stock index is an agreement to purchase or sell an index at a specified price and date. For example, the purchase of an S&P 500 (which represents a composite of 500 large corporations) futures contract obligates the purchaser to purchase the S&P 500 index at a specified settlement date for a specified amount.

The S&P 500 index futures contract is valued as the index times $250, so if the index is valued at 2,700, the contract is valued at 2,700 × $250 = $675,000. E-Mini S&P 500 index futures contracts are available for small investors (the E stands for "electronically"). These contracts are valued at $50 times the index, so if the index is valued at 2,700, the contract is valued at 2,700 × $50 = $135,000.

Stock index futures contracts have settlement dates on the third Friday in March, June, September, and December. The securities underlying the stock index futures contracts are not actually deliverable, so settlement occurs through a cash payment. On the settlement date, the futures contract is valued according to the quoted stock index. The net gain or loss on the stock index futures contract is the difference between the futures price when the initial position was created and the value of the contract as of the settlement date.

Like other financial futures contracts, stock index futures can be closed out before the settlement date by taking an offsetting position. For example, if an S&P 500 futures contract with a December settlement date is purchased in September, this position can be closed out in November by selling an S&P 500 futures contract with the same December settlement date. The net gain or loss on this stock index futures contract is the difference between the futures price when the position was created in September and the futures price when the position was closed out in November.

Recently, sector index futures have been created so that investors can buy or sell an index that reflects a particular sector. These contracts are distinguished from stock index futures in that they represent a component of a stock index, rather than the entire index. Investors who are optimistic about the stock market in general might be more interested in stock index futures, whereas investors who are especially optimistic about one particular sector may be more interested in sector index futures. Sector index futures contracts are available for many different sectors, including consumer goods, energy, financial services, health care, industrial, materials, technology, and utilities.

13-3a Valuing Stock Index Futures

The value of a stock index futures contract is highly correlated with the value of the underlying stock index. However, the value of the stock index futures contract commonly differs from the price of the underlying asset because of some unique features of the stock index futures contract.

EXAMPLE   Consider that an investor can buy either a stock index or a futures contract on the stock index with a settlement date of six months from now. On the one hand, the buyer of the index receives dividends, whereas the buyer of the index futures does not. On the other hand, the buyer of the index must use funds to make that purchase, whereas the buyer of index futures can enter into the futures contract simply by establishing a margin deposit with a relatively small amount of assets (such as Treasury securities), which may generate interest while being used to satisfy margin requirements.

Assume that the index will pay dividends equal to 3 percent over the next six months. Also assume that the purchaser of the index will borrow funds to purchase the index at an interest rate of 2 percent over the six-month period. In this example, the advantage of holding the index (a 3 percent dividend yield) relative to holding a futures contract on the index more than offsets the 2 percent cost of financing the purchase of the index. The *net financing cost* (also called "cost of carry") to the purchaser of the underlying assets (the index) is the 2 percent cost of financing minus the 3 percent yield earned on the assets, or −1 percent. A negative cost of carry indicates that the cost of financing is less than the yield earned from dividends. Therefore, the stock index futures contract should be valued about 1 percent above the underlying stock index so that it is no less desirable to investors than is the stock index itself. ●

In general, the underlying security (or index) tends to change by a much greater degree than the cost of carry, so changes in financial futures prices are primarily attributed to changes in the values of the underlying securities (or indexes).

In some cases, numerous institutional investors may buy or sell index futures instead of selling stocks to prepare for a change in market conditions, and their actions can cause the movement in the index futures price to deviate from the underlying value of the actual stocks that make up the index. The futures can be purchased immediately with a small, up-front payment. Purchasing actual stocks may take longer because of the time needed to select specific stocks, and a larger up-front investment is necessary. Thus, stock index futures may be more responsive to investor expectations about the market than are values of the underlying stock prices.

Indicators of Stock Index Futures Prices   Because stock index futures prices are primarily driven by movements in the corresponding stock indexes, participants in stock index futures monitor indicators that may signal movements in the stock indexes. The economic indicators that signal changes in bond futures prices can also affect stock futures prices, but not necessarily in the same manner. Whereas economic conditions that cause expectations of higher interest rates adversely affect prices of Treasury bonds (and therefore Treasury bond futures), the impact of such expectations on a stock index (and therefore on stock index futures) is not as clear.

13-3b **Speculating in Stock Index Futures**

Stock index futures can be traded to capitalize on expectations about general stock market movements. Speculators who expect the stock market to perform well before the settlement date may consider purchasing S&P 500 index futures. Conversely, participants who expect the stock market to perform poorly before the settlement date may consider selling S&P 500 index futures.

EXAMPLE   Boulder Insurance Company plans to purchase a variety of stocks for its stock portfolio in December, once cash inflows are received. Although the company does not have cash to purchase the stocks immediately, it is anticipating a large jump in stock market prices before December. Given this situation, it decides to purchase S&P 500 index futures. The futures price on the S&P 500 index with a December settlement date is 2,500. The value of an S&P 500 futures contract is $250 times the index. Because the S&P 500 futures price should move with the stock market, it will rise over time if the company's expectations are correct. Assume that the S&P 500 index rises to 2,600 on the settlement date.

In this example, the nominal profit on the S&P 500 index futures is

Selling price	**$650,000**	**(Index value of 2,600 × $250)**
− Purchase price	**−625,000**	**(Index value of 2,500 × $250)**
= Profit	**$25,000**	

By purchasing this futures contract, Boulder was able to capitalize on its expectations even though it did not have sufficient cash to purchase stock. If stock prices had declined over the period of concern, the S&P 500 futures price would have decreased and Boulder would have incurred a loss on its futures position. ●

13-3c Hedging with Stock Index Futures

Stock index futures are also commonly used to hedge the market risk of an existing stock portfolio.

EXAMPLE

Glacier Stock Mutual Fund expects the stock market to decline temporarily, causing a temporary decline in its stock portfolio. The fund could sell its stocks with the intent to repurchase them in the near future, but this would incur excessive transaction costs. A more efficient solution is to sell stock index futures. If the fund's stock portfolio is similar to the S&P 500 index, Glacier can sell futures contracts on that index. If the stock market declines as expected, Glacier will generate a gain when closing out the stock index futures position, which will somewhat offset the loss on its stock portfolio. ●

A hedge based on stock index futures is more effective when the investor's portfolio, such as the S&P 500 index, is diversified. The value of a less diversified stock portfolio will be less correlated with the S&P 500 index, in which case a gain from selling index futures may not completely offset the loss in the portfolio during a market downturn.

Assuming that the stock portfolio moves in tandem with the S&P 500, a full hedge would involve the sale of the amount of futures contracts whose combined underlying value is equal to the market value of the stock portfolio being hedged.

EXAMPLE

Suppose that a portfolio manager has a stock portfolio valued at $5,200,000. In addition, assume the S&P 500 index futures contracts are available for a settlement date one month from now at a level of 2,600, which is about equal to today's index value. The manager could sell S&P 500 futures contracts to hedge the stock portfolio. Because the futures contract is valued at $250 times the index level, the contract will result in a payment of $650,000 at the settlement date. The value of one index futures contract represents one-eighth of the portfolio's value ($650,000/$5,200,000 = $\frac{1}{8}$). Assuming that the stock index moves in tandem with the stock portfolio, the manager would need to sell eight S&P 500 futures contracts to fully hedge the stock portfolio.

For example, if the stock portfolio declines by 5 percent over one month, this reflects a loss of $260,000 (0.05 × $5,200,000 = $260,000). But over this span, the S&P 500 index also should have declined by 5 percent (from 2,600 to 2,470). Thus, one S&P 500 index futures contract that was sold by the manager should result in a gain of $32,500 [(2,600 − 2,470) × $250]. The sale of eight S&P 500 index futures contracts should result in a gain of $260,000, which offsets the loss on the stock portfolio. ●

If the stock market experiences higher prices over the month, the S&P 500 index will rise and create a loss on the futures contract. However, the value of the manager's stock portfolio will have increased to offset the loss.

Hedging a Proportion of the Portfolio   Portfolio managers do not necessarily hedge their entire stock portfolio, because they may wish to be partially exposed in the event that stock prices rise. For instance, the manager in the preceding example could have hedged one-eighth of the stock portfolio's value by selling one S&P 500 futures contract, or one-fourth of the stock portfolio's value by selling two S&P 500 index futures contracts, or one-half of the stock portfolio's value by selling four S&P 500 index futures contracts.

Exhibit 13.7 illustrates the net gain (including the gain on the futures and the gain on the stock portfolio) to the portfolio manager under six possible scenarios for the market return (shown in the first column). If the stock market declines, any degree of hedging is beneficial, but the benefits will be greater if a higher proportion of the portfolio is hedged.

If the stock market performs well, any degree of hedging reduces the net gain, but the reduction will be greater if a higher proportion of the portfolio is hedged. In essence,

Exhibit 13.7 Net Gain (on Stock Portfolio and Short Position in Stock Index Futures) for Different Degrees of Hedging

SCENARIO FOR MARKET RETURN	PROPORTION OF STOCK PORTFOLIO HEDGED			
	0% HEDGED	33% HEDGED	67% HEDGED	100% HEDGED
−20%	−20%	−13.4%	−6.7%	0%
−10%	−10%	−6.7%	−3.35%	0%
−5%	−5%	−3.35%	−1.67%	0%
+5%	+5%	+3.35%	+1.67%	0%
+10%	+10%	+6.7%	+3.35%	0%
+20%	+20%	+13.4%	+6.7%	0%

Note: *Numbers are based on the assumption that the stock portfolio moves in perfect tandem with the market.*

hedging with stock index futures reduces the sensitivity to both unfavorable and favorable market conditions.

Even when the movements in the futures contract value are highly correlated with the value of the portfolio being hedged, the value of the futures contract may change by a higher or lower percentage than the portfolio's market value. If the futures contract value is less volatile than the portfolio value, hedging will require the futures contracts to represent a greater amount of principal. For example, assume that the value of the portfolio moves by 1.25 percent for every percentage point movement in the price of the futures contract. In this case, futures contracts valued at 1.25 times the principal of the portfolio would be needed to fully hedge the portfolio.

13-3d **Dynamic Asset Allocation with Stock Index Futures**

Institutional investors are increasingly using dynamic asset allocation, in which they switch between risky and low-risk investment positions over time in response to changing expectations. This strategy allows managers to increase the exposure of their portfolios when they expect favorable market conditions and to reduce their exposure when they expect unfavorable conditions. When they anticipate favorable market movements, stock portfolio managers can purchase stock index futures, which magnify the effects of market conditions. Conversely, when they anticipate unfavorable market movements, they can sell stock index futures to reduce the effects that market conditions will have on their stock portfolios. Because expectations change frequently, it is not uncommon for portfolio managers to alter their degree of exposure. Stock index futures allow portfolio managers to alter their risk–return position without restructuring their existing stock portfolios. Using dynamic asset allocation in this way avoids the substantial transaction costs that would be associated with frequently restructuring the stock portfolios.

13-3e **Arbitrage with Stock Index Futures**

In some periods, the prices of stock index futures may differ significantly from the prices of the stocks represented by the index. Some securities firms watch for such discrepancies and act as **arbitrageurs** using a strategy known as **index arbitrage**, which involves buying or selling stock index futures while simultaneously taking the opposite position in the stocks represented by the index. Thus, if the index futures contract is priced high relative to the stocks that compose the index, an arbitrageur may purchase the stocks and simultaneously sell stock index futures. Conversely, if the index futures are priced low relative to the stocks represented by the index, an arbitrageur may purchase index futures and simultaneously sell stocks. The arbitrageur can make a profit if the price differential exceeds the transaction costs incurred from trading in both markets.

Index arbitrage does not cause the price discrepancy between the two markets, but instead responds to it. The arbitrageur's ability to detect price discrepancies between the stock and futures markets is enhanced by today's lightning-fast computers.

13-3f Circuit Breakers on Stock Index Futures

As mentioned in Chapter 12, *circuit breakers* are trading restrictions imposed on specific stocks or stock indexes. The CME Group imposes circuit breakers on several stock index futures, including the S&P 500 futures contract.

By prohibiting trading for short time periods when prices decline to specific threshold levels, circuit breakers may allow investors to determine whether circulating rumors are true and to work out credit arrangements if they have received a margin call. If prices are still perceived to be too high when the markets reopen, the prices will decline further. Thus, circuit breakers do not guarantee that prices will turn upward. Nevertheless, they may be able to prevent large declines in prices that would be due to panic selling rather than to fundamental forces.

13-4 Single Stock Futures

A *single* stock futures contract is an agreement to buy or sell a specified number of shares of a specified stock on a specified future date. Single stock futures contracts of U.S. stocks are traded at OneChicago, which is operated by Interactive Brokers, the Chicago Board Options Exchange, and the CME Group. On this exchange, the size of a contract is 100 shares. Investors can buy or sell single stock futures contracts through their broker, and they can be purchased on margin. The orders to buy and sell a specific single stock futures contract are matched electronically. Single stock futures have become increasingly popular, and today are available on more than 1,800 stocks. They are regulated by the Commodity Futures Trading Commission and the Securities and Exchange Commission.

Settlement dates are on the third Friday of the delivery month on a quarterly basis (March, June, September, and December). Investors who expect a particular stock's price to rise over time may consider buying futures on that stock. To obtain a contract to buy March futures on 100 shares of Zorf stock for $5,000 ($50 per share), an investor must submit the $5,000 payment to the clearinghouse on the third Friday in March and will receive shares of Zorf stock on the settlement date. If Zorf stock is valued at $53 at the time of settlement, the investor can sell the stock in the stock market for a gain of $3 per share or $300 for the contract (ignoring commissions). This gain would likely reflect a substantial return on the investment, because the investor had to invest only a small margin (perhaps 20 percent of the contract price) to take a position in futures. If Zorf stock is valued at $46 at the time of settlement, the investor would incur a loss of $4 share, which would reflect a substantial percentage loss on the investment. Thus, single stock futures offer potentially high returns, but also high risk.

Investors who expect a particular stock's price to decline over time can sell futures contracts on that stock. This activity is similar to selling a stock short, except that single stock futures can be sold without borrowing the underlying stock from a broker (as short-sellers must do). To obtain a contract to sell March futures of Zorf stock, an investor must deliver Zorf stock to the clearinghouse on the third Friday in March and will receive the payment specified in the futures contract.

Investors can close out their position at any time by taking the opposite position. Suppose that, shortly after the investor purchased futures on Zorf stock with a March delivery at $50 per share, the stock price declines. Rather than incur the risk that the price could continue to decline, the investor could sell a Zorf futures contract with a March delivery. If this contract specifies a price of $48 per share, the investor's gain will be the difference between the selling price and the buying price, which is $-$2 per share or $-$200 for the contract.

Futures contracts for exchange-traded funds (ETFs, which represent baskets of stocks) are also available. These contracts allow an investor to buy or sell a particular ETF at a specified price at a future point in time. Since many ETFs represent particular sectors or industries, ETF futures provide investors with more ways to speculate or hedge stock movements in various sectors or industries. More information about ETFs is provided in Chapter 23.

13-5 Risk of Trading Futures Contracts

Participants in the futures contracts markets must recognize the various types of risk exhibited by such contracts and other derivative instruments.

13-5a Market Risk

Market risk refers to fluctuations in the value of the instrument as a result of market conditions. Firms that use futures contracts to speculate should be concerned about market risk. If their expectations about future market conditions are wrong, they may suffer losses on their futures contracts. Firms that use futures contracts to hedge are less concerned about market risk because if market conditions cause a loss on their derivative instruments, they should experience a partial offsetting gain on the positions that they were hedging.

13-5b Basis Risk

Basis risk is the risk that the position being hedged by the futures contracts will not be affected in the same manner as the instrument underlying the futures contract. This type of risk applies only to those firms or individuals who are using futures contracts to hedge. The change in the value of the futures contract position may not move in perfect tandem with the change in value of the portfolio that is being hedged, so the hedge might not perfectly offset the risk of the portfolio.

13-5c Liquidity Risk

Liquidity risk refers to potential price distortions due to a lack of liquidity. For example, a firm may purchase a particular bond futures contract to speculate on expectations of rising bond prices. However, when it attempts to close out its position by selling an identical futures contract, it may not find any willing buyers for this type of futures contract at that time. In this case, the firm will have to sell the futures contract at a lower price. Users of futures contracts may reduce their liquidity risk by using only those futures contracts that are widely traded.

13-5d Credit Risk

Credit risk is the risk that a loss will occur because a counterparty defaults on the contract. This type of risk exists for over-the-counter transactions, in which a firm or individual relies on the creditworthiness of a counterparty.

The credit risk of counterparties is not a concern when trading futures and other derivatives on exchanges, because the exchanges usually guarantee that the provisions of the contract will be honored. The financial intermediaries that make the arrangements in the over-the-counter market can take some steps to reduce this type of risk. First, the financial intermediary can require that each party provide some form of collateral to back up its position. Second, the financial intermediary can serve (for a fee) as a guarantor in the event that the counterparty does not fulfill its obligation.

13-5e Prepayment Risk

Prepayment risk refers to the possibility that the assets to be hedged may be prepaid earlier than their designated maturity. Suppose that a commercial bank sells Treasury bond futures in order to hedge its holdings of corporate bonds and that, just after the futures position is created, the bonds are called by the corporation that initially issued them. If interest rates subsequently decline, the bank will incur a loss from its futures position without a corresponding gain from its bond position (because the bonds were called earlier).

As a second example, consider a savings and loan association with large holdings of long-term, fixed-rate mortgages that are mostly financed by short-term funds. It sells Treasury bond futures to hedge against the possibility of rising interest rates; then, after the futures position is established, interest rates decline and homeowners prepay many of the existing mortgages. The savings and loan association will incur a loss from its futures position without a corresponding gain from its fixed-rate mortgage position (because the mortgages were prepaid).

13-5f Operational Risk

Operational risk is the risk of losses as a result of inadequate management or controls. For example, firms that use futures contracts to hedge are exposed to the possibility that the employees responsible for their futures positions do not fully understand how the values of specific futures contracts will respond to market conditions. Furthermore, those employees may take more speculative positions than the firms desire if the firms do not have adequate controls to monitor them.

13-5g Systemic Risk

To the extent that traders of financial futures contracts or other derivative securities are unable to cover their derivative contract obligations in over-the-counter transactions, they could cause financial problems for their respective counterparties. This could expose the futures market to systemic risk, whereby the intertwined relationships among firms may cause one trader's financial problems to be passed on to other traders (if there is not enough collateral backing the contracts).

EXAMPLE

Nexus, Inc., requests several transactions in derivative securities that involve buying futures on Treasury bonds in an over-the-counter market. Bangor Bank accommodates Nexus by taking the opposite side of the transactions. The bank's positions in these contracts also serve as a hedge against its existing exposure to interest rate risk.

As time passes, Nexus experiences financial problems. As interest rates rise and the value of a Treasury bond futures contract declines, Nexus takes a major loss on the futures transactions. Ultimately, because it is unable to fulfill its obligation to buy the Treasury bonds from Bangor Bank at the settlement date, Nexus files for bankruptcy.

Bangor Bank was relying on Nexus's payment to hedge its exposure to interest rate risk. Consequently, Bangor Bank experiences financial problems and cannot make the payments on other over-the-counter derivatives contracts that it has with three other financial institutions. These financial institutions were relying on those funds to cover their own obligations on derivative contracts with several other firms. These firms may then be unable to honor their payment obligations resulting from the derivative contract agreements, causing the adverse effects to spread further. ●

FINANCIAL REFORM

The credit crisis of 2008 and 2009 demonstrated that some financial institutions had high exposure to risk because their derivative security positions were intended to enhance profits rather than to hedge portfolio risk. Since then, regulators have become more aware of the potential for systemic risk to spread throughout futures market participants.

The Financial Reform Act of 2010 resulted in the creation of the Financial Stability Oversight Council, which is responsible for identifying risks to financial stability in the United States and making regulatory recommendations that could reduce any risks to the financial system. The Council consists of 10 members who head regulatory agencies overseeing key components of the financial system (including the CFTC, which regulates financial futures trading).

GLOBAL ASPECTS

13-6 Globalization of Futures Markets

The trading of financial futures also requires the assessment of international financial market conditions. The flow of foreign funds into and out of the United States can affect interest rates and, therefore, the market value of Treasury bonds, corporate bonds, mortgages, and other long-term debt securities. Portfolio managers assess international flows of funds to forecast changes in interest rate movements, which in turn affect the value of their respective portfolios. Even speculators assess international flows of funds to forecast interest rates so that they can determine whether to take short or long futures positions.

13-6a Non-U.S. Participation in U.S. Futures Contracts

Financial futures contracts on U.S. securities are commonly traded by non-U.S. financial institutions that maintain holdings of U.S. securities. These institutions use financial futures to reduce their exposure to movements in the U.S. stock market or interest rates.

13-6b Foreign Stock Index Futures

Foreign stock index futures have been created both for speculating on and for hedging against potential movements in foreign stock markets. Expectations of a strong foreign stock market encourage the purchase of futures contracts on the representative index. Conversely, financial institutions with substantial investments in a particular foreign stock market can hedge against a potential temporary decline in that market by selling foreign stock index futures. Stock index futures contracts that represent some foreign stock markets, such as those in China, Japan, and Brazil, are available through the CME Group. In addition, stock index futures contracts are available in many different countries.

13-6c Currency Futures Contracts

A **currency futures contract** is a standardized agreement to deliver or receive a specified amount of a specified foreign currency at a specified price (exchange rate) and date. The settlement months are March, June, September, and December. Some companies act as hedgers in the currency futures market by purchasing futures on currencies that they will need in the future to cover payables or by selling futures on currencies that they will receive in the future. Speculators in the currency futures market may purchase futures on a foreign currency that they expect to strengthen against the U.S. dollar or sell futures on currencies that they expect to weaken against the U.S. dollar.

Purchasers of currency futures contracts can hold the contract until the settlement date and accept delivery of the foreign currency at that time, or they can close out their long position prior to the settlement date by selling the identical type and number of contracts before then. If they close out their long position, their gain or loss is determined by the difference between the futures price when they created the position and the futures price when they closed out the position. Sellers of currency futures contracts either deliver the foreign currency at the settlement date or close out their position by purchasing an identical type and number of contracts prior to the settlement date.

Summary

- A financial futures contract is a standardized agreement to deliver or receive a specified amount of a specified financial instrument at a specified price and date. Financial institutions such as commercial banks, savings institutions, bond mutual funds, pension funds, and insurance companies trade interest rate futures contracts to hedge their exposure to interest rate risk. Some stock mutual funds, pension funds, and insurance companies trade stock index futures to hedge their exposure to adverse stock market movements.

- An interest rate futures contract locks in the price to be paid for a specified debt instrument. Speculators who expect interest rates to decline can purchase interest rate futures contracts, because the market value of the underlying debt instrument should rise. Speculators who expect interest rates to rise can sell interest rate futures contracts, because the market value of the underlying debt instrument should decrease.

- Financial institutions (or other firms) that desire to hedge against rising interest rates can sell interest rate futures contracts. Financial institutions that desire to hedge against declining interest rates can purchase these contracts. If interest rates move in the anticipated direction, the financial institutions will gain from their futures position, which can partially offset any adverse effects of the interest rate movements on their normal operations.

- Speculators who expect stock prices to increase can purchase stock index futures contracts; speculators who expect stock prices to decrease can sell these contracts. Stock index futures can be sold by financial institutions that expect a temporary decline in stock prices and wish to hedge their stock portfolios.

- A single stock futures contract is an agreement to buy or sell a specified number of shares of a specified stock on a specified future date. The trading of single stock futures is regulated by the Commodity Futures Trading Commission and the Securities and Exchange Commission. Investors who expect a particular stock's price to rise over time may consider buying futures contracts on that stock. Investors who expect a particular stock's price to decline over time can sell futures contracts on that stock. This activity is similar to selling a stock short, but single stock futures can be sold without borrowing the underlying stock from a broker. Investors can close out their position at any time by taking the opposite position.

- Traders in the futures market may be exposed to market risk, basis risk, liquidity risk, credit risk, prepayment risk, and operational risk. The over-the-counter trading of futures contracts and other derivative securities can expose the entire financial system to systemic risk, in that the trading losses of one firm could spread to others if collateral is not sufficient to cover losses. The Financial Reform Act of 2010 resulted in the creation of the Financial Stability Oversight Council, which is responsible for making recommendations that could reduce any risks to the financial system. The Council includes the head of the Commodity Futures Trading Commission, which regulates financial futures trading.

- Financial futures markets have been developed in many countries. Foreign stock index futures have been created for most major stock indexes in international markets. Currency futures contracts have been created both for speculating on and for hedging against movements in various currencies.

Point/Counterpoint

Has the Futures Market Created More Uncertainty for Stocks?

Point Yes. Futures contracts encourage speculation on indexes. Thus, an entire market can be influenced by the trading of speculators.

Counterpoint No. Futures contracts are commonly used to hedge portfolios and, therefore, can reduce the effects of weak market conditions. Moreover, investing in stocks is just as speculative as taking a position in futures markets.

Who Is Correct? Use the Internet to learn more about this issue and then formulate your own opinion.

Questions and Applications

1. **Futures Contracts** Describe the general characteristics of a futures contract. How does a clearinghouse facilitate the trading of financial futures contracts?

2. **Futures Pricing** How does the price of a financial futures contract change as the market price of the security it represents changes? Why?

3. **Hedging with Futures** Explain why some futures contracts may be more suitable than others for hedging exposure to interest rate risk.

4. **Treasury Bond Futures** Will speculators buy or sell Treasury bond futures contracts if they expect interest rates to increase? Explain.

5. **Gains from Purchasing Futures** Explain how purchasers of financial futures contracts can offset their position. How is their gain or loss determined? What is the maximum loss to a purchaser of a futures contract?

6. **Gains from Selling Futures** Explain how sellers of financial futures contracts can offset their position. How is their gain or loss determined?

7. **Hedging with Futures** Assume a financial institution has more rate-sensitive assets than rate-sensitive liabilities. Would it be more likely to be adversely affected by an increase or a decrease in interest rates? Should it purchase or sell interest rate futures contracts in order to hedge its exposure?

8. **Hedging with Futures** Assume a financial institution has more rate-sensitive liabilities than rate-sensitive assets. Would it be more likely to be adversely affected by an increase or a decrease in interest rates? Should it purchase or sell interest rate futures contracts so as to hedge its exposure?

9. **Hedging Decision** Why do some financial institutions remain exposed to interest rate risk, even when they believe that the use of interest rate futures could reduce their exposure?

10. **Long versus Short Hedge** Explain the difference between a long hedge and a short hedge used by financial institutions. When is a long hedge more appropriate than a short hedge?

11. **Impact of Futures Hedge** Explain how the probability distribution of a financial institution's returns is affected when it uses interest rate futures to hedge. What does this imply about its risk?

12. **Cross Hedging** Describe the practice of cross hedging. and explain when this strategy might be used.

13. **Hedging with Bond Futures** How might a savings and loan association use Treasury bond futures to hedge its fixed-rate mortgage portfolio (assuming that its main source of funds is short-term deposits)? Explain how prepayments on mortgages can limit the effectiveness of the hedge.

14. **Stock Index Futures** Describe stock index futures. How could they be used by a financial institution that is anticipating a jump in stock prices but does not yet have sufficient funds to purchase large amounts of stock? Explain why stock index futures may reflect investor expectations about the market more quickly than stock prices.

15. **Selling Stock Index Futures** Why would a pension fund or insurance company consider selling stock index futures?

16. **Systemic Risk** Explain systemic risk as it relates to the futures market. Explain how the Financial Reform Act of 2010 attempted to improve the monitoring of systemic risk in the futures market and other markets.

17. **Circuit Breakers** Explain the use of circuit breakers.

Advanced Questions

18. Hedging with Futures Elon Savings and Loan Association has a large number of 30-year mortgages with floating interest rates that adjust on an annual basis, and obtains most of its funds by issuing five-year certificates of deposit. It uses the yield curve to assess the market's anticipation of future interest rates. Elon believes that expectations of future interest rates are the major force affecting the yield curve. Assume that a downward-sloping yield curve with a steep slope exists. Based on this information, should Elon consider using financial futures as a hedging technique? Explain.

19. Hedging Decision Blue Devil Savings and Loan Association has a large number of 10-year fixed-rate mortgages and obtains most of its funds from short-term deposits. It uses the yield curve to assess the market's anticipation of future interest rates. It believes that expectations of future interest rates are the major force affecting the yield curve. Assume that an upward-sloping yield curve with a steep slope exists. Based on this information, should Blue Devil consider using financial futures as a hedging technique? Explain.

20. How Futures Prices May Respond to Prevailing Conditions Consider the prevailing conditions for inflation (including oil prices), the economy, the budget deficit, and other conditions that could affect the values of futures contracts. Based on these conditions, would you prefer to buy or sell Treasury bond futures at this time? Would you prefer to buy or sell stock index futures at this time? Assume that you would close out your position at the end of this semester. Offer some logic to support your answers. Which factor is most influential for your decision regarding Treasury bond futures and for your decision regarding stock index futures?

21. Use of Interest Rate Futures When Interest Rates Are Low Short-term and long-term interest rates are presently very low. You believe that the Fed will use monetary policy to maintain these interest rates at a very low level. Do you think financial institutions that could be adversely affected by a decline in interest rates would benefit from hedging their exposure with interest rate futures? Explain.

Critical Thinking Question

Stock Index Futures and Systemic Risk Write a short essay explaining how financial futures might reduce systemic risk and how financial futures might increase systemic risk within financial markets.

Interpreting Financial News

Interpret the following statements made by Wall Street analysts and portfolio managers.

a. "The existence of financial futures contracts allows our firm to hedge against temporary market declines without liquidating our portfolios."
b. "Given my confidence in the market, I plan to use stock index futures to increase my exposure to market movements."
c. "We used currency futures to hedge the exchange rate exposure of our international mutual fund focused on German stocks."

Managing in Financial Markets

Managing Portfolios with Futures Contracts As a portfolio manager, you are monitoring previous investments that you made in stocks and bonds of U.S. firms and in stocks and bonds of Japanese firms. Although you plan to keep all of these investments over the long run, you are willing to hedge against adverse effects on your investments that result from economic conditions. You expect that, over the next year, U.S. and Japanese interest rates will decline, the U.S. stock market will perform poorly, the Japanese stock market will perform well, and the Japanese yen (the currency) will depreciate against the dollar.

a. Should you consider taking a position in U.S. bond index futures to hedge your investment in U.S. bonds? Explain.
b. Should you consider taking a position in Japanese bond index futures to hedge your investment in Japanese bonds? Explain.
c. Should you consider taking a position in U.S. stock index futures to hedge your investment in U.S. stocks? Explain.
d. Should you consider taking a position in Japanese stock index futures to hedge your investment in Japanese stocks? (Note: The Japanese stock index is denominated in yen, so it is used to hedge stock movements, not currency movements.)
e. Should you consider taking a position in Japanese yen futures to hedge the exchange rate risk of your investment in Japanese stocks and bonds?

Problems

1. **Profit from T-Bond Futures** Spratt Company purchased Treasury bond futures contracts when the quoted price was 93-50. When this position was closed out, the quoted price was 94-75. Determine the profit or loss per contract, ignoring transaction costs.

2. **Profit from T-Bond Futures** Suerth Investments, Inc., purchased Treasury bond futures contracts when the quoted price was 95-00. When this position was closed out, the quoted price was 93-60. Determine the profit or loss per contract, ignoring transaction costs.

3. **Profit from T-Bond Futures** Toland Company sold Treasury bond futures contracts when the quoted price was 94-00. When this position was closed out, the quoted price was 93-20. Determine the profit or loss per contract, ignoring transaction costs.

4. **Profit from T-Bond Futures** Rude Dynamics, Inc., sold T-bill futures contracts when the quoted price was 93-26. When this position was closed out, the quoted price was 93-90. Determine the profit or loss per contract, ignoring transaction costs.

5. **Profit from T-Bond Futures** Egan Company purchased a futures contract on Treasury bonds that specified a price of 91-00. When the position was closed out, the price of the Treasury bond futures contract was 90-10. Determine the profit or loss, ignoring transaction costs.

6. **Profit from T-Bond Futures** R. C. Clark sold a futures contract on Treasury bonds that specified a price of 92-10. When the position was closed out, the price of the Treasury bond futures contract was 93-00. Determine the profit or loss, ignoring transaction costs.

7. **Profit from Stock Index Futures** Marks Insurance Company sold stock index futures that specified an index of 1,690. When the position was closed out, the index specified by the futures contract was 1,720. Determine the profit or loss, ignoring transaction costs.

Flow of Funds Exercise

Hedging with Futures Contracts

Recall that if the economy continues to be strong, Carson Company may need to increase its production capacity by approximately 50 percent over the next few years to satisfy demand. It would need financing to expand and accommodate the increase in production. Recall that the yield curve is currently upward sloping. Also recall that Carson is concerned about a possible slowing of the economy because of potential Fed actions to reduce inflation. Carson currently relies mostly on commercial loans with floating interest rates for its debt financing.

a. How could Carson use futures contracts to reduce the exposure of its cost of debt to interest rate movements? Be specific about whether it would use a short hedge or a long hedge.

b. Will the hedge that you described in the previous question perfectly offset the increase in debt costs if interest rates increase? Explain what drives the profit from the short hedge, versus what drives the higher cost of debt to Carson, if interest rates increase.

Internet/Excel Exercises

1. Go to www.investing.com and review the charts for the stock index futures on the S&P 500 (under "Indices Futures"). Explain how the price pattern moved recently.

2. Now compare that pattern to the actual trend of the S&P 500, which is provided at the same website (or at other websites such as finance.yahoo.com). Describe the relationship between the movements in S&P 500 futures and movements in the S&P 500 index.

Online Articles with Real-World Examples

Find a recent practical article available online that describes a real-world example regarding a specific financial institution or financial market that reinforces one or more concepts covered in this chapter.

If your class has an online component, your professor may ask you to post your summary of the article there and provide a link to the article so that other students can access it. If your class is live, your professor may ask you to summarize your application of the article in class. Your professor may assign specific students to complete this assignment or may allow any students to do the assignment on a volunteer basis.

For recent online articles and real-world examples related to this chapter, consider using the following search terms (be sure to include the prevailing year as a search term to ensure that the online articles are recent):

1. interest rate futures AND investment
2. interest rate futures AND gains
3. interest rate futures AND losses
4. interest rate futures AND speculators
5. interest rate futures AND hedge
6. stock index futures AND gains
7. stock index futures AND losses
8. stock index futures AND speculators
9. stock index futures AND hedge
10. futures AND risk

14

Option Markets

Speculators can use stock options to benefit from their expectations; financial institutions can use stock options to reduce their risk. Options markets facilitate the trading of stock options.

14-1 Background on Options

Options are classified as *calls* or *puts*. A **call option** grants the owner the right to purchase a specified financial instrument (such as a stock) for a specified price (called the **exercise price** or **strike price**) within a specified period of time.

A call option is said to be **in the money** when the market price of the underlying security exceeds the exercise price, **at the money** when the market price is equal to the exercise price, and **out of the money** when it is below the exercise price.

The second type of option, known as a **put option**, grants the owner the right to sell a specified financial instrument for a specified price within a specified period of time. As with call options, owners pay a premium to obtain put options. They can exercise the options at any time up to the expiration date but are not obligated to do so.

A put option is said to be "in the money" when the market price of the underlying security is below the exercise price, "at the money" when the market price is equal to the exercise price, and "out of the money" when it exceeds the exercise price.

Call and put options specify 100 shares of the stocks to which they are assigned. Premiums paid for call and put options are determined by the participants engaged in trading. The premium for a particular option changes over time as it becomes more or less desirable to traders.

Participants can close out their option positions by making an offsetting transaction. For example, purchasers of an option can offset their positions at any time up to the expiration date by selling an identical option. The gain or loss depends on the premium paid when purchasing the option versus the premium received when selling an identical option. Sellers of options can close out their positions at any time up to the expiration date by purchasing an identical option.

The stock options just described are known as *American-style* stock options. They can be exercised at any time until the expiration date. In contrast, *European-style* stock options can be exercised only just before expiration.

14-1a Comparison of Options and Futures

There are two major differences between purchasing an option and purchasing a futures contract. First, to obtain an option, the purchaser must pay a premium in addition to the price of the financial instrument. Second, the owner of an option can choose to let the option expire on the expiration date without exercising it. Call options grant a right, but not an obligation, to purchase a specified financial instrument. In contrast, buyers of futures contracts are obligated to purchase the financial instrument at a specified date. If the owner of a call option does exercise it, the seller (sometimes called the **writer**) of the option is obligated to provide the specified financial instrument at the price specified by the option contract. Sellers of call options receive an upfront fee (the premium) from the purchaser as compensation.

14-1b Markets Used to Trade Options

The Chicago Board Options Exchange (CBOE), which was created in 1973, is the most important exchange for trading options. It serves as a market for options on more than 2,000 different stocks. The options listed on the CBOE have a standardized format, as will be explained shortly. The standardization of the contracts on the CBOE has proved to be a major advantage because it allows for easy trading of existing contracts (a secondary market). With standardization, the popularity of options has increased, and the options have become more liquid. Because numerous buyers and sellers of the standardized contracts are available, buyers and sellers of a particular option contract can be readily matched.

Options are also traded on the International Securities Exchange, which is owned by the Nasdaq, and on the New York Stock Exchange. In addition, options are traded at the CME Group, which also serves international markets for derivative products (as discussed in Chapter 13). Any particular option contract may be traded on various exchanges, and competition among those exchanges may result in more favorable prices for customers.

At all the exchanges, most option trading is conducted electronically. Many electronic communication networks (ECNs) are programmed to consider all possible trades and execute the order at the best possible price. In addition, market movers can execute option transactions for customers. They earn the difference between the bid price and the ask price for this trade, although this spread has declined significantly in recent years. Market makers also generate profits or losses when they invest their own funds in options.

Some specialized option contracts are sold "over the counter" rather than on an exchange, whereby a financial intermediary (such as a commercial bank or an investment bank) finds a counterparty or serves as the counterparty. These over-the-counter arrangements are more personalized and can be tailored to the specific preferences of the parties involved. Such tailoring is not possible for the more standardized option contracts sold on the exchanges.

Listing Requirements   Each exchange has its own requirements concerning the stocks for which it creates options. One key requirement is a minimum trading volume of the underlying stock, because the volume of options traded on a particular stock will normally be higher if the stock trading volume is high. The decision to list an option is made by each exchange, rather than by the firms represented by the options contracts.

Role of the Options Clearing Corporation   As is the case with a stock transaction, the trading of an option involves a buyer and a seller. The sale of an option imposes specific obligations on the seller under specific conditions. The exchange itself does not take positions in option contracts, but simply provides a market where the options can be bought or sold. The Options Clearing Corporation (OCC) serves as a guarantor on option contracts traded in the United States, which means that the buyer of an option contract does not have to be concerned that the seller will back out of the obligation.

Regulation of Options Trading   Options trading is regulated by the Securities and Exchange Commission and by the various option exchanges. This regulation is intended to ensure fair and orderly trading. For example, it attempts to prevent insider trading (trading based on information that insiders have about their firms and that is not yet disclosed to the public). It also attempts to prevent price fixing that could cause wider bid–ask spreads and impose higher costs on customers.

14-1c **Types of Orders**

As with stocks, an investor can place either a market order or a limit order for an option transaction. A market order will result in the immediate purchase or sale of an option at its prevailing market price. With a limit order, the transaction will occur only if the market price is no higher or lower than the specified price limit. For example, an investor may request the purchase of a specific option only if it can be purchased at or below some specified price. Conversely, an investor may request to sell an option only if it can be sold for some specified limit or more.

Online Trading   Option contracts can also be purchased or sold online. Many online brokerage firms, including E*Trade and TD Ameritrade, facilitate options orders. Online option contract orders are commonly routed to computerized networks on options exchanges, where they are executed.

14-1d **Stock Option Quotations**

Quotations for stock options can be found at financial websites. Exhibit 14.1 provides an example of stock options for Viperon Company stock as of May 1, when the stock was priced at about $45.62 per share. Each row represents a specific option on Viperon stock. The first data column lists the exercise (strike) price, and the second column lists the expiration date. (The expiration date for stock options traded on the CBOE is the Saturday following the third Friday of the specified month.) The third and fourth columns show the volume and the most recently quoted premium of the call option with that exercise price and expiration date. The fifth and sixth columns show the volume and the most recently quoted premium of the put option with that exercise price and expiration date.

Examining the four options illustrates how specific factors affect option premiums. First, comparing Options 1 and 3 (which have the same expiration date) reveals that an option with a higher exercise price has a lower call option premium and a higher put option premium. Comparing Options 2 and 4 then confirms this relationship. Second, comparing Options 1 and 2 (which have the same exercise price) reveals that an option with a longer term to maturity has a higher call option premium and a higher put option premium. Comparing Options 3 and 4 then confirms this relationship.

WEB

www.barchart.com
/options/most-active
/stocks
Summary of the most
actively traded stock
options.

Exhibit 14.1   Viperon Company Stock Option Quotations

	EXERCISE	EXP.	VOLUME	CALL	VOLUME	PUT
Option 1	45	Jun	180	4.50	60	2.75
Option 2	45	Oct	70	5.75	120	3.75
Option 3	50	Jun	360	1.12	40	5.12
Option 4	50	Oct	90	3.50	40	6.50

Exhibit 14.2 Institutional Use of Options Markets

TYPE OF FINANCIAL INSTITUTION	PARTICIPATION IN OPTIONS MARKETS
Commercial banks	• Sometimes offer options to businesses.
Savings institutions	• Sometimes take positions in options on futures contracts to hedge interest rate risk.
Mutual funds	• Stock mutual funds take positions in stock index options to hedge against a possible decline in the prices of stocks in their portfolios. • Stock mutual funds sometimes take speculative positions in stock index options in an attempt to increase their returns. • Bond mutual funds sometimes take positions in options on futures to hedge interest rate risk.
Securities firms	• Serve as brokers by executing stock option transactions for individuals and businesses.
Pension funds	• Take positions in stock index options to hedge against a possible decline in the prices of stocks in their portfolio. • Take positions in options on futures contracts to hedge their bond portfolios against interest rate movements.
Insurance companies	• Take positions in stock index options to hedge against a possible decline in the prices of stocks in their portfolio. • Take positions in options on futures contracts to hedge their bond portfolios against interest rate movements.

14-1e Institutional Use of Options

Exhibit 14.2 summarizes the use of options by various types of financial institutions. Although financial institutions sometimes take options positions for speculative purposes, they more commonly use options for hedging. Specifically, savings institutions and bond mutual funds use options to hedge interest rate risk. Stock mutual funds, insurance companies, and pension funds use stock index options and options on stock index futures to hedge their stock portfolios. Some of the large commercial banks often serve as an intermediary between two parties that take derivative positions in an over-the-counter market.

14-2 Determinants of Stock Option Premiums

Stock option premiums are determined by market forces. Any characteristic of an option that results in many willing buyers but few willing sellers will place upward pressure on the option premium. As a consequence, the option premium must be sufficiently high to equalize the demand by buyers and the supply that sellers are willing to sell. This generalization applies to both call options and put options. The specific characteristics that affect the demand and supply conditions, and therefore affect the stock option premiums, are described next.

14-2a Determinants of Call Option Premiums

Call option premiums are affected primarily by the following factors:

■ The market price of the underlying instrument (relative to the option's exercise price)
■ The volatility of the underlying instrument
■ The time to maturity of the call option

Influence of the Market Price The higher the existing market price of the underlying financial instrument is relative to the exercise price, the higher the call option premium will be, other things being equal. A stock's value has a higher probability of increasing well above the exercise price if it is already close to or above the exercise price. Thus, a purchaser would be willing to pay a higher premium for a call option on such a stock.

The influence of the market price of a stock (relative to the exercise price) on the call option premium can also be understood by comparing stock options with different exercise prices on the same instrument at a given time.

EXAMPLE

Consider the data shown in Exhibit 14.3 for KSR call options quoted on February 25, with a similar expiration date. The stock price of KSR was about $140 at that time. The premium for the call option with the $130 exercise price was almost $10 higher than the premium for the option with the $150 exercise price. This example confirms that a higher premium is required to lock in a lower exercise price on call options. ●

Influence of the Stock's Volatility   The greater the volatility of the underlying stock is, the higher the call option premium will be, other things being equal. If a stock is volatile, there is a higher probability that its price will increase well above the exercise price. Thus, a purchaser would be willing to pay a higher premium for a call option on that stock. For instance, call options on stocks of relatively small companies usually have higher premiums than call options on stocks of large companies because stocks of small companies are typically more volatile.

Influence of the Call Option's Time to Maturity   The longer the call option's time to maturity is, the higher the call option premium will be, other things being equal. A longer time period until expiration allows the owner of the option more time to exercise that option. Given the longer time span, there is a higher probability that the stock's price will move well above the exercise price before the option expires.

The relationship between the time to maturity and the call option premium is illustrated in Exhibit 14.4 for KSR call options quoted on February 25, with a similar exercise price of $135. The premium was $4.50 per share for the call option with a March expiration month versus $7.50 per share for the call option with an April expiration month. The difference reflects the additional time in which the April call option can be exercised.

Exhibit 14.3   Relationship between Exercise Price and Call Option Premium on KSR Stock

EXERCISE PRICE	PREMIUM FOR APRIL EXPIRATION DATE
$130	11.62
135	7.50
140	5.25
145	3.25
150	1.88

Exhibit 14.4   Relationship between Time to Maturity and Call Option Premium on KSR Stock

EXPIRATION DATE	PREMIUM FOR OPTION WITH A $135 EXERCISE PRICE
March	4.50
April	7.50
July	13.25

14-2b **Determinants of Put Option Premiums**

The premium paid on a put option depends on the same factors that affect the premium paid on a call option. However, the direction of influence varies for one of the factors, as explained next.

Influence of the Market Price   The higher the existing market price of the underlying stock is relative to the exercise price, the lower the put option premium will be, all other things being equal. A stock's value has a higher probability of decreasing well below the exercise price if it is already close to or below the exercise price. Thus, a purchaser would be willing to pay a higher premium for a put option on that stock. This influence on the put option premium differs from the influence on the call option premium because, from the perspective of put option purchasers, a *lower* market price is preferable.

The influence of the market price of a stock (relative to the exercise price) on the put option premium can also be understood by comparing options with different exercise prices on the same instrument at a given moment in time. For example, consider the data shown in Exhibit 14.5 for KSR put options with a similar expiration date quoted on February 25. The premium for the put option with the $150 exercise price was more than $9 per share higher than the premium for the option with the $135 exercise price.

Influence of the Stock's Volatility   The greater the volatility of the underlying stock is, the higher the put option premium will be, all other things being equal. This relationship also held for call option premiums. If a stock is volatile, there is a higher probability that its price will deviate far from the exercise price. Thus, a purchaser would be willing to pay a higher premium for a put option on that stock because its market price is more likely to decline well below the option's exercise price by the time the option expires.

Influence of the Put Option's Time to Maturity   The longer the time to maturity is, the higher the put option premium will be, all other things being equal. This relationship also held for call option premiums. A longer time period until expiration allows the owner of the option more time to exercise the option. Thus, there is a higher probability that the stock's price will move well below the exercise price before the option expires.

Exhibit 14.5   Relationship between Exercise Price and Put Option Premium on KSR Stock

EXERCISE PRICE	PREMIUM FOR JUNE EXPIRATION DATE
$130	1.88
135	3.12
140	5.38
145	8.50
150	12.25

Exhibit 14.6   Relationship between Time to Maturity and Put Option Premium on KSR Stock

EXPIRATION DATE	PREMIUM FOR OPTION WITH A $135 EXERCISE PRICE
March	0.50
April	3.12
July	7.25

The relationship between the time to maturity and the put option premium is shown in Exhibit 14.6 for KSR put options with a similar exercise price of $135 quoted on February 25. The premium was $7.25 per share for the put option with a July expiration month versus $0.50 per share for the put option with a March expiration month. This difference reflects the additional time during which the put option with the July expiration date can be exercised.

14-2c How Option Pricing Can Be Used to Derive a Stock's Volatility

The general relationships between the determinants described previously and the option premium are explained in this chapter, but the chapter appendix offers a specific formula that can be applied to estimate the proper price of stock options. Because the anticipated volatility of a stock is not observable, investors can input their own estimate of it when calculating the premium that should be paid for a particular option.

Some investors, when assessing a specific stock's risk, adapt the option-pricing formula to derive an estimate of that stock's anticipated volatility. By plugging in values for the other factors that affect the particular stock option's premium and for the prevailing premium quoted in the market, it becomes possible to derive the stock's anticipated volatility, referred to as the *implied standard deviation* (or *implied volatility*). The implied standard deviation is derived by determining what its value must be, given the quoted option premium and the values of other factors that affect the stock option's premium. Various software packages and calculators are available that can estimate a stock's implied volatility, and implied volatilities for many stocks can be found at financial websites. Such an estimate is of interest to investors because it indicates the market's view of the stock's potential volatility. Some investors may use this estimate as a measure of a stock's risk when they are considering which stocks to purchase.

14-2d Explaining Changes in Option Premiums

Exhibit 14.7 identifies the underlying forces that cause option prices to change over time. Economic conditions and market conditions can cause abrupt changes in the stock price or in the anticipated volatility of the stock price over the time remaining until option expiration. Such changes would have a major impact on the stock option's premium.

EXAMPLE

During the fall of 2008, the credit crisis intensified and stock volatility increased substantially. Consequently, the premiums for options increased as well. Under these conditions, more portfolio managers wanted to hedge their stock positions, but they had to pay a higher premium for put options. Conversely, the sellers of put options recognized that their risk had increased because of the higher volatility and priced the put options accordingly.

In the years after the financial crisis, stock volatility declined. Consequently, the sellers of put options were exposed to a lower level of risk and were more willing to accept a lower premium. ●

Exhibit 14.7 Framework for Changes in Stock Options' Premiums over Time

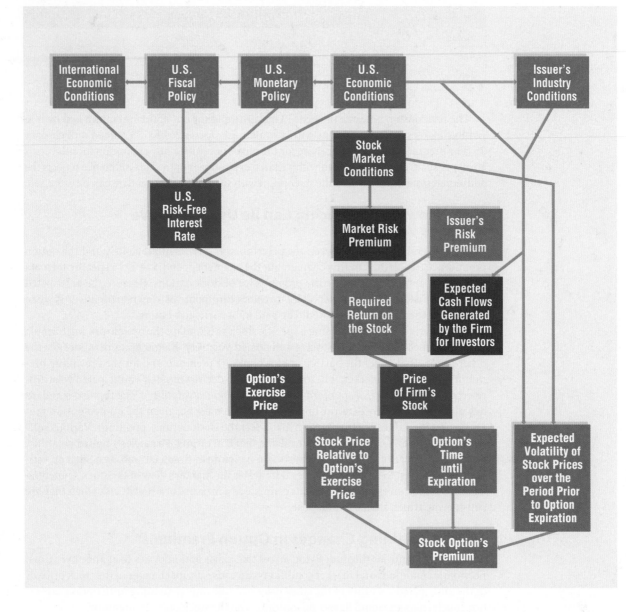

14-3 Speculating with Stock Options

Stock options are frequently traded by investors who are attempting to capitalize on their expectations. When investors purchase an option that does not cover (hedge) their existing investments, the option is labeled "naked" (uncovered). Because speculators trade options to gamble on price movements rather than to hedge existing investments, their positions in options are naked. Whether speculators purchase call options or put options depends on their expectations.

In some cases, speculators borrow a portion of the funds that they use to invest in stock options. The use of borrowed funds can magnify their gains, but it can also magnify their losses. The gains and losses described in this chapter would be more pronounced if the speculators cited in the examples used borrowed funds for a portion of their investment.

14-3a Speculating with Call Options

Investors can use call options to speculate based on their expectation that the price of the underlying stock will increase.

EXAMPLE

Pat Jackson expects Steelco stock to increase from its current price of $113 per share but does not want to tie up her available funds by investing in stocks. She purchases a call option on Steelco with an exercise price of $115 for a premium of $4 per share. Before the option's expiration date, Steelco's price rises to $121. At that time, Jackson exercises her option, purchasing shares at $115 per share. She then immediately sells those shares at the market price of $121 per share. Her net gain on this transaction is measured as follows:

Amount received when selling shares	**$121 per share**
−**Amount paid for shares**	−**$115 per share**
−**Amount paid for the call option**	−**$4 per share**
= **Net gain**	**$2 per share**
	or $200 for one contract

Pat's net gain of $2 per share reflects a return of 50 percent (not annualized). ●

If the price of Steelco stock had not risen to more than $115 before the option's expiration date, Pat would have let the option expire. Her net loss would have been the $4 per share she initially paid for the option, or $400 for one option contract. This example reflects a 100 percent loss, because the entire amount of the investment is lost.

The potential gains or losses from this call option are shown in the left portion of Exhibit 14.8, based on the assumptions that (1) the call option is exercised on the expiration date, if at all, and (2) if the call option is exercised, the shares received are immediately sold. Exhibit 14.8 shows that the maximum loss when purchasing this option is the premium of $4 per share. For stock prices between $115 and $119, the option is exercised, and the purchaser of the call option incurs a net loss of less than $4 per share. The stock price of $119 is the break-even point, because the gain from exercising the option exactly offsets the premium paid for it. At stock prices greater than $119, a net gain is realized.

The right portion of Exhibit 14.8 shows the net gain or loss to a writer of the same call option, assuming that the writer obtains the stock only when the option is exercised. Under

Exhibit 14.8 Potential Gains or Losses on a Call Option: Exercise Price = $115, Premium = $4

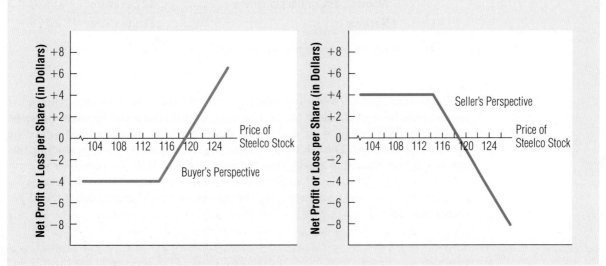

this condition, the call option writer's net gain (loss) is the call option purchaser's net loss (gain), assuming zero transaction costs. The maximum gain to the writer of a call option is the premium received.

Several call options are available for a given stock, and the risk–return potential will vary among them. Assume that three types of call options were available on Steelco stock with a similar expiration date, as described in Exhibit 14.9. The potential gains or losses per unit for each option are also shown in the exhibit, assuming that the option is exercised (if at all) on the expiration date. It is also assumed that if the speculators exercise the call option, they immediately sell the stock. This comparison of different options for a given stock illustrates the various risk–return trade-offs from which speculators can choose.

Purchasers of call options are normally most interested in returns (profit as a percentage of the initial investment) under various scenarios. For this purpose, the data used to create Exhibit 14.9 can be expanded to reflect returns for each possible price per share of the underlying stock, as shown in Exhibit 14.10. For example, at the stock price of $116 shown in the left column, Call Option 1 generates a return of 10 percent ($1 per share profit as a percentage of the $10 premium paid), Call Option 2 generates a loss of about 14 percent ($1 per share loss as a percentage of the $7 premium paid), and Call Option 3 generates a loss of 75 percent ($3 per share loss as a percentage of the $4 premium paid).

14–3b Speculating with Put Options

Investors can use put options to speculate based on their expectation that the price of the underlying stock will decrease.

<table>
<tr><td>EXAMPLE</td><td>A put option on Steelco is available with an exercise price of $110 and a premium of $2. If the price of Steelco stock falls to less than $110, speculators could purchase the stock and then exercise their put options to benefit from the transaction. However, they would need to make at least $2 per share on this transaction to fully recover the premium paid for the option. If the speculators exercise the option when the market price is $104, their net gain is measured as follows:</td></tr>
</table>

Amount received when selling shares	**$110 per share**
− **Amount paid for shares**	−**$104 per share**
− **Amount paid for the put option**	−**$2 per share**
= **Net gain**	**$4 per share**

The net gain here is 200 percent, or twice as much as the amount paid for the put options. ●

The potential gains or losses from the put option described here are shown in the left portion of Exhibit 14.11, based on the assumptions that (1) the put option is exercised on the expiration date, if at all, and (2) the shares would be purchased just before the put option is exercised. The exhibit shows that the maximum loss when purchasing this option is $2 per share. For stock prices between $108 and $110, the purchaser of a put option incurs a net loss of less than $2 per share. The stock price of $108 is the break-even point, because the gain from exercising the put option would exactly offset the $2 per share premium.

Exhibit 14.9   Potential Gains or Losses for Three Call Options (Buyer's Perspective)

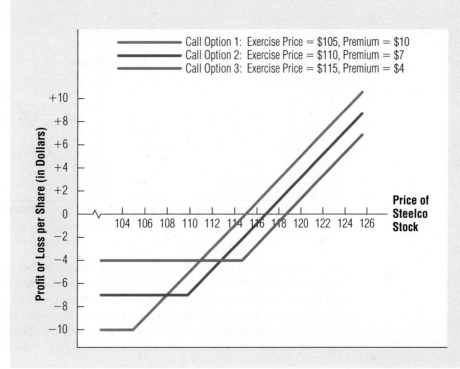

Exhibit 14.10   Potential Returns on Three Different Call Options

PRICE OF STEELCO	OPTION 1: EXERCISE PRICE = $105 PREMIUM = $10		OPTION 2: EXERCISE PRICE = $110 PREMIUM = $7		OPTION 3: EXERCISE PRICE = $115 PREMIUM = $4	
	PROFIT PER UNIT	PERCENTAGE RETURN	PROFIT PER UNIT	PERCENTAGE RETURN	PROFIT PER UNIT	PERCENTAGE RETURN
$104	−$10	−100%	−$7	−100%	−$4	−100%
106	−9	−90	−7	−100	−4	−100
108	−7	−70	−7	−100	−4	−100
110	−5	−50	−7	−100	−4	−100
112	−3	−30	−5	−71	−4	−100
114	−1	−10	−3	−43	−4	−100
116	1	10	−1	−14	−3	−75
118	3	30	1	14	−1	−25
120	5	50	3	43	1	25
122	7	70	5	71	3	75
124	9	90	7	100	5	125
126	11	110	9	129	7	175

Exhibit 14.11   Potential Gains or Losses on a Put Option: Exercise Price = $110, Premium = $2

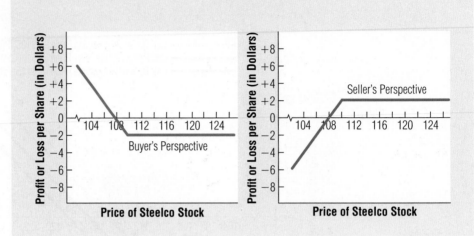

The right portion of Exhibit 14.11 shows the net gain or loss to a writer of the same put option, assuming that the writer sells the stock received when the investor exercises the put option. Under this condition, the put option writer's net gain (loss) is the put option purchaser's net loss (gain), assuming zero transaction costs. The maximum gain to the writer of a put option is the premium received. As with call options, several put options are typically available for a given stock, and the potential gains or losses will vary among them.

14-3c Excessive Risk from Speculation

ETHICS

Speculating in options can be very risky. Financial institutions or other corporations that speculate in options typically have methods in place to closely monitor their risk and to measure their exposure to possible option market conditions. In several cases, however, a financial institution or a corporation incurred a major loss on options positions because of a lack of oversight over its options trading.

EXAMPLE

One of the most famous cases in which a financial institution took excessive risk with stock options involved Barings PLC, an investment bank in the United Kingdom. In 1992, Barings sent Nicholas Leeson to manage the accounting at its Singapore subsidiary called Barings Futures. In Singapore, Leeson began trading derivative contracts on the Singapore International Monetary Exchange as a broker for Barings Futures. He then began to trade for the firm's own account rather than just as a broker, trading options on the Nikkei (Japanese) stock index. At the same time, he continued to serve as the accounting manager for Barings Futures. In this role, Leeson was able to conceal losses on any derivative positions, so the financial reports to Barings PLC showed massive profits.

By January 1995, Leeson's losses had accumulated to more than the equivalent of $300 million. Leeson had periodically required funds to cover margin calls as his positions declined in value. Barings PLC met these funding requests, covering the equivalent of millions of dollars to satisfy the margin calls, yet did not recognize that the margin calls signaled a major problem.

In late February 1995, an accounting clerk at Barings noticed some discrepancies. When Leeson was asked to explain specific accounting entries, he excused himself from the meeting and never returned. He left Singapore that night and faxed his resignation to Barings PLC from Kuala Lumpur, Malaysia. Barings PLC investigated and found that Leeson had accumulated losses totaling more than the equivalent of $1 billion, which caused the firm to become insolvent. Leeson pleaded guilty to charges of fraud, and he was sentenced to prison for six and one-half years. ●

Any firms that use futures or other derivative instruments can draw a few obvious lessons from the Barings collapse. First, firms should closely monitor the trading of derivative contracts by their employees to ensure that derivatives are being used within the firm's guidelines. Second, firms should separate the reporting function from the trading function so that traders cannot conceal trading losses. Third, when firms receive margin calls on their derivative positions, they should recognize that there may be potential losses on their derivative instruments and should closely evaluate those positions. The Barings case was a wake-up call to many firms, which recognized the need to establish guidelines for their employees who take derivative positions and to monitor the actions of these employees more closely.

14-4 Hedging with Stock Options

Call and put options on selected stocks and stock indexes are commonly used for hedging against possible stock price movements. Financial institutions such as mutual funds, insurance companies, and pension funds manage large stock portfolios and are the most common users of options for hedging.

14-4a Hedging with Covered Call Options

Call options on a stock can be used to hedge a position in that stock.

EXAMPLE

Portland Pension Fund owns a substantial amount of Steelco stock. It expects that the stock will perform well in the long run, but it is concerned that the stock may perform poorly over the next few months because of temporary problems Steelco is experiencing. The sale of a call option on Steelco stock can hedge against such a potential loss. This type of option is known as a covered call because the option is covered, or backed, by stocks already owned.

If the market price of Steelco stock rises, the call option will likely be exercised, and Portland will fulfill its obligation by selling its Steelco stock to the purchaser of the call option at the exercise price. Conversely, if the market price of Steelco stock declines, the option will not be exercised. Hence Portland would not have to sell its Steelco stock, and the premium received from selling the call option would represent a gain that could partially offset the decline in the price of the stock. In this case, although the market value of the institution's stock portfolio is adversely affected, that decline is at least partially offset by the premium received from selling the call option.

Assume that Portland Pension Fund purchased Steelco stock at the market price of $112 per share. To hedge against a temporary decline in Steelco's stock price, Portland sells call options on Steelco stock with an exercise price of $110 per share for a premium of $5 per share. Exhibit 14.12 shows the net profit achieved by Portland when using covered call writing under several possible scenarios. For comparison purposes, the profit that Portland would earn if it did not use covered call writing but instead sold the stock on the option's expiration date is also shown (see the diagonal line) for various possible scenarios. The results show how covered call writing can partially offset losses when the stock performs poorly, but can also partially offset gains when the stock performs well. ●

Exhibit 14.12 explains the profit or loss per share from covered call writing. At any price greater than $110 per share as of the expiration date, the call option would be exercised, so Portland would have to sell its holdings of Steelco stock at the exercise price of $110 per share to the purchaser of the call option. The net gain to Portland would be $3 per share, determined as the premium of $5 per share (received when writing the option) minus the $2 per share difference between the price paid for the Steelco stock and the price at which the stock is sold. Comparing the profit or loss per scenarios with and without covered call writing, it is clear that while covered call writing limits the upside potential return on stocks, it also reduces the risk associated with a decline in their market values.

Exhibit 14.12 Risk–Return Trade-off from Covered Call Writing

EXPLANATION OF PROFIT PER SHARE FROM COVERED CALL WRITING								
MARKET PRICE OF STEELCO AS OF THE EXPIRATION DATE	PRICE AT WHICH PORTLAND PENSION FUND SELLS STEELCO STOCK		PREMIUM RECEIVED FROM WRITING THE CALL OPTION		PRICE PAID FOR STEELCO STOCK		PROFIT OR LOSS PER SHARE	
$104	$104	+	$5	−	$112	=	−$3	
105	105	+	5	−	112	=	−2	
106	106	+	5	−	112	=	−1	
107	107	+	5	−	112	=	0	
108	108	+	5	−	112	=	1	
109	109	+	5	−	112	=	2	
110	110	+	5	−	112	=	3	
111	110	+	5	−	112	=	3	
112	110	+	5	−	112	=	3	
113	110	+	5	−	112	=	3	
114	110	+	5	−	112	=	3	
115	110	+	5	−	112	=	3	
116	110	+	5	−	112	=	3	
117	110	+	5	−	112	=	3	
118	110	+	5	−	112	=	3	
119	110	+	5	−	112	=	3	
120	110	+	5	−	112	=	3	

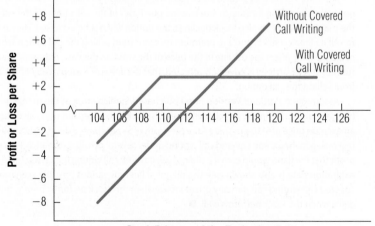

Stock Price as of the Expiration Date

14-4b Hedging with Put Options

Investors may also use put options on to hedge stock positions.

EXAMPLE Reconsider the example in which Portland Pension Fund was concerned about a possible temporary decline in the price of Steelco stock. Portland could hedge against a temporary decline in Steelco's stock price by purchasing put options on that stock. In the event that Steelco's stock price declines, Portland would likely generate a gain on its option position, which would help offset the reduction in the stock's price. If Steelco's stock price does not decline, Portland would not exercise its put option. ●

Hedging with LEAPs **Long-term equity anticipations (LEAPs)** are options that have longer terms to expiration, usually between two and three years from the initial listing date. These options are available for some large capitalization stocks, and they may be a more effective hedge over a longer-term period than using options with shorter terms to expiration. The transaction costs for hedging over a long period are lower than the costs of continually repurchasing short-term put options each time the options expire or are exercised. Furthermore, the costs of continually repurchasing put options are uncertain, whereas the costs of purchasing a put option on a long-term index option are known immediately.

14-5 Options on ETFs and Stock Indexes

Options are also traded on exchange-traded funds (ETFs) and stock indexes. Exchange-traded funds are funds that are designed to mimic particular indexes and are traded on an exchange. An ETF option, in turn, provides the right to trade a specified ETF at a specified price by a specified expiration date. Because ETFs are traded like stocks, options on ETFs are traded like options on stocks. Investors who exercise a call option on an ETF will receive delivery of the ETF in their account. Investors who exercise a put option on an ETF will have the ETF transferred from their account to the counterparty on the put option.

A **stock index option** provides the option purchaser with the right to trade a specified stock index at a specified price by a specified expiration date. Call options on stock indexes allow the purchaser the right to purchase the index, and put options on stock indexes allow the purchaser the right to sell the index. If and when the index option is exercised, the cash payment is equal to a specified dollar amount multiplied by the difference between the index level and the exercise price.

Options on stock indexes are similar to options on ETFs, with one major exception: The values of stock indexes change only at the end of each trading day, whereas ETF values can change throughout the day. Therefore, an investor who wants to capitalize on the expected movement of an index within a particular day will trade options on ETFs. An investor who wants to capitalize on the expected movement of an index over a longer period of time (such as a week or several months) can trade options on either ETFs or indexes.

Options on indexes have become popular vehicles for speculating on general movements in the stock market. Speculators who anticipate a sharp increase in stock market prices overall may consider purchasing call options on one of the market indexes. Likewise, speculators who anticipate a stock market decline may consider purchasing put options on these indexes. A sampling of options that are traded on ETFs and on stock indexes is provided in Exhibit 14.13, where SPDR stands for Standard & Poor's Depositary Receipts.

Options on sector indexes also exist, allowing investors the option to buy or sell an index that reflects a particular sector. These contracts are distinguished from stock index options in that they represent a component of a stock index. Investors who are optimistic (or pessimistic) about the stock market in general might be more interested in stock index options, whereas investors who are especially optimistic (or pessimistic) about one particular sector may be more interested in options on a sector index. Options are available for many different sectors, including banking, energy, housing, oil exploration, semiconductors, and utilities.

14-5a Hedging with Stock Index Options

Financial institutions and other firms commonly take positions in options on ETFs or indexes to hedge against market or sector conditions that would adversely affect their asset portfolio or cash flows. The following discussion is based on the use of options on stock indexes, but options on ETFs could be used in the same manner.

Exhibit 14.13 Sampling of ETFs and Indexes on Which Options Are Traded

SELECTED ETFs ON WHICH OPTIONS ARE TRADED	
iShares Nasdaq Biotechnology	iShares Russell 1000 Growth Index Fund
iShares North American Tech	Energy Select Sector SPDR
iShares North American Tech-Software	Financial Select Sector SPDR
iShares Russell 1000 Index Fund	Utilities Select Sector SPDR
iShares Russell 1000 Value Index Fund	Health Care Select Sector SPDR
SELECTED INDEXES ON WHICH OPTIONS ARE TRADED	
Emerging Markets Asia Index	S&P SmallCap 600 Index
Eurotop 100 Index	Nasdaq 100 Index
Mexico Index	Russell 1000 Index
Dow Jones Industrial Average	Russell 1000 Value Index
Dow Jones Transportation Average	Russell 1000 Growth Index
Dow Jones Utilities Average	Russell 2000 Index
S&P 100 Index	Russell Midcap Index
S&P 500 Index	Goldman Sachs Internet Index
Nasdaq Biotechnology Index	

Financial institutions such as insurance companies and pension funds maintain large stock portfolios whose values are driven by general market movements. If the stock portfolio is broad enough, any changes in its value will likely be highly correlated with market movements. For this reason, portfolio managers consider purchasing put options on a stock index to protect against stock market declines. The put options should be purchased on the stock index that most closely mirrors the portfolio to be hedged. If the stock market experiences a severe downturn, the market value of the portfolio will decline. However, the put options on the stock index will generate a gain because the value of the index will be less than the exercise price. The greater the market downturn, the greater the decline in the market value of the portfolio will be, but also the greater the gain that will be realized from holding put options on a stock index. Thus, this offsetting effect minimizes the overall impact on the firm.

If the stock market rises, the put options on the stock index will not be exercised. In this case, the firm will not recover the cost of purchasing the options. This situation is similar to purchasing other forms of insurance and then not using them. Some portfolio managers may still believe the options were worthwhile for temporary protection against downside risk.

Selecting the Degree of Protection When Hedging Because stock index options are available with various exercise prices, portfolio managers can select an exercise price that provides the degree of protection desired. For example, assume that an existing stock index is quite similar to a manager's stock portfolio and that the manager wants to protect against any loss exceeding 5 percent. If the prevailing level of the index is 400, the manager should purchase put options with an exercise price of 380 because that level is 5 percent lower than 400. If the index declines to a level below 380, the manager will exercise the options, and the gain from doing so will partially offset the reduction in the stock portfolio's market value.

This strategy is essentially a form of insurance, where the premium paid for the put option is similar to an insurance premium. Because the index must decline by 5 percent before there is any possibility that the portfolio manager will exercise the option, the option premium is similar to the "deductible" that is typical of insurance policies. If portfolio managers desire to protect against even smaller losses, they can purchase a put option that specifies a higher exercise price on the index, such as 390. To obtain the extra protection, however, they would have to pay a higher premium for the put options. In other words, the cost of the portfolio insurance would be higher because of the smaller "deductible" desired.

Hedging with Long-Term Stock Index Options   Like the LEAPs on specific stocks described earlier, LEAPs on stock indexes can be used to hedge stock portfolios over longer time periods. For example, LEAPs on the S&P 100 and S&P 500 indexes are available, with expiration dates extending at least two years ahead from the initial listing date.

Dynamic Asset Allocation with Stock Index Options   Dynamic asset allocation involves switching between risky and low-risk investment positions over time in response to changing expectations. Some portfolio managers use stock index options as a tool for dynamic asset allocation. For example, when portfolio managers anticipate favorable market conditions, they may decide to purchase call options on a stock index, which will magnify the effects of the market conditions on their investment performance. Essentially, the managers are using stock index options to increase their exposure to stock market conditions. Conversely, when they anticipate unfavorable market movements, they may decide to purchase put options on a stock index to reduce the effects that market conditions will have on their stock portfolios.

In another form of dynamic asset allocation, portfolio managers can sell (write) call options on stock indexes in periods when they expect the stock market to be stable. This strategy does not create a perfect hedge, but it can enhance the portfolio's performance in periods when stock prices are stagnant or declining.

Portfolio managers can adjust the risk–return profile of their investment position by using stock index options rather than restructuring their existing stock portfolios. This form of dynamic asset allocation avoids the substantial transaction costs associated with restructuring those portfolios.

14-5b Using Index Options to Measure the Market's Risk

Just as a stock's implied volatility can be derived from information about options on that stock, a stock index's implied volatility can be derived from information about options on that stock index. The same factors that affect the option premium on a stock affect the option premium on an index. Thus, the premium on an index option is positively related to the expected volatility of the underlying stock index. If investors want to estimate the expected volatility of the stock index, they can use software packages to insert values for the prevailing option premium and all the other factors (except volatility) that affect an option premium. Some financial websites may also provide estimates of implied volatility.

The CBOE Volatility Index (VIX) represents the implied volatility derived from options on the S&P 500 index (an index of 500 large stocks). Many investors closely monitor this index because it indicates the market's anticipated volatility for the market (with the S&P 500 serving as a proxy for the market). The VIX is sometimes referred to as the "fear index" because high values are perceived to reflect a high degree of fear that stock prices could decline.

14-6 Options on Futures Contracts

In recent years, the concept of options has been applied to futures contracts to create options on futures contracts (sometimes referred to as "futures options"). An option on a particular futures contract gives its owner the right, but not the obligation, to purchase or sell that futures contract for a specified price within a specified period of time. Thus, options on futures grant the purchaser the power to take advantage of the futures position if favorable conditions occur, but provide flexibility that allows the purchaser to avoid the futures position (by letting the option expire) if unfavorable conditions come to pass. As with other options, the purchaser of options on futures pays a premium.

Similarly, options are available on stock index futures. They are used for speculating on expected stock market movements or hedging against adverse market conditions. Individuals and financial institutions use them in a manner similar to the way stock index options are used.

Options are also available on interest rate futures, such as Treasury note futures or Treasury bond futures. The settlement dates of the underlying futures contracts are usually a few weeks after the expiration date of the corresponding options contracts.

A call option on interest rate futures grants the option holder the right to purchase a futures contract at a specified price within a specified period of time. A put option on financial futures grants the option holder the right (again, not an obligation) to sell a particular financial futures contract at a specified price within a specified period of time. Because interest rate futures contracts can hedge interest rate risk, options on interest rate futures might be considered by any financial institution that is exposed to that risk, including savings institutions, commercial banks, life insurance companies, and pension funds.

14-6a **Speculating with Options on Futures**

Speculators who anticipate a change in interest rates should also expect a change in bond prices. They could take a position in options on Treasury bond futures to capitalize on their expectations.

Speculation Based on an Expected Decline in Interest Rates   If speculators expect a decline in interest rates, they may consider purchasing a call option on Treasury bond futures. If their expectations are correct, the market value of Treasury bonds will rise, and the price of a Treasury bond futures contract will rise as well. The speculators can exercise their option to purchase futures at the exercise price, which will be lower than the value of the futures contract.

EXAMPLE   Kelly Warden expects interest rates to decline and purchases a call option on Treasury bond futures. The exercise price on Treasury bond futures is 94-32 (94 $\frac{32}{64}$ percent of $100,000, or $94,500). The call option is purchased at a premium of 2-00 (2 percent of $100,000), which equals $2,000. Assume that interest rates do decline and, as a result, the price of the Treasury bond futures contract rises over time to a value of 99-00 ($99,000) shortly before the option's expiration date. At this time, Kelly decides to exercise the option; she closes out the position by selling an identical futures contract (to create an offsetting position) at a higher price than the price at which she purchased the futures. Kelly's net gain from this speculative strategy is

Selling price of T-bond futures	**$99,000**	(99.00% of $100,000)
−Purchase price of T-bond futures	**−$94,500**	(94.50% of $100,000)
−Call option premium paid	**−$2,000**	(2.00% of $100,000)
= Net gain to purchaser of call option on futures	**$2,500**	(2.50% of $100,000)

This net gain of $2,500 represents a return on investment of 125 percent. ●

The seller of the call option will have the opposite position to the buyer. Thus, the gain (or loss) to the buyer will equal the loss (or gain) to the seller of the call option.

<table>
<tr><td>EXAMPLE</td><td>Ellen Rose sold the call option purchased by Kelly Warden in the previous example. Ellen is obligated to purchase and provide the futures contract at the time Kelly exercises the option. Her net gain from this speculative strategy is</td></tr>
</table>

Selling price of T-bond futures	**$94,500**	**(94.50% of $100,000)**
−Purchase price of T-bond futures	**−$99,000**	**(99.00% of $100,000)**
−Call option premium received	**+$2,000**	**(2.00% of $100,000)**
= Net gain to seller of call option on futures	**−$2,500**	**(−2.50% of $100,000)**

In the absence of transaction costs, Ellen's loss is equal to Kelly's gain. If the Treasury bond futures price had remained below the exercise price of 94-32 ($94,500) until the expiration date, the option would not have been exercised. In that case, the net gain from purchasing the call option on Treasury bond futures would have been −$2,000 (the premium paid for the option) and the net gain from selling the call option would have been $2,000. ●

When interest rates decline, the buyers of call options on Treasury bonds may simply sell their previously purchased options just before expiration. If interest rates rise, the options will not be desirable. Then buyers of call options on Treasury bond futures will let their options expire, and their loss will be the premium paid for the call options on futures.

Some speculators who expect interest rates to remain stable or to decrease may be willing to sell a put option on Treasury bond futures. If their expectations are correct, the price of a futures contract will likely rise and the put option will not be exercised. Therefore, sellers of the put option would earn the premium that was paid to them when they sold the option.

Speculation Based on an Expected Increase in Interest Rates
If speculators expect interest rates to increase, they can benefit from purchasing a put option on Treasury bond futures. If their expectations are correct, the market value of Treasury bonds will decline and the price of a Treasury bond futures contract will also decline. The speculators can exercise their option to sell futures at the exercise price, which will be higher than the value of the futures contract. If interest rates decline, the speculators will likely let the options expire, and their loss will be the premium paid for the put options on futures.

Some speculators who anticipate an increase in interest rates may be willing to sell a call option on Treasury bond futures. If their expectations are correct, the price of the futures contract will likely decline, and hence the call option will not be exercised.

14-6b Hedging with Options on Interest Rate Futures

Options on futures contracts are also used to hedge against risk. In particular, financial institutions commonly hedge their bond or mortgage portfolios with options on interest rate futures contracts. The position they take on the options contract is designed to create a gain that can offset a loss on their bond or mortgage portfolio while still allowing some upside potential.

<table>
<tr><td>EXAMPLE</td><td>Emory Savings and Loan Association has a large number of long-term, fixed-rate mortgages that are mainly supported by short-term funds and, therefore, would be adversely affected by rising interest rates. As explained in Chapter 13, sales of Treasury bond futures can partially offset the adverse effect of rising interest rates in such a situation. Recall that if interest rates decline instead, the potential increase in Emory's interest rate spread (difference between interest revenues and expenses) would be partially offset by the loss on the futures contract.</td></tr>
</table>

Exhibit 14.14   Results from Hedging with Put Options on Treasury Bond Futures

	SCENARIO 1:
	• INTEREST RATES RISE
	• T-BOND FUTURES PRICE
	  DECLINES TO 91-00
		SCENARIO 2:
		• INTEREST RATES DECLINE
		• T-BOND FUTURES PRICE
		  INCREASES TO 104-00

Effect on Emory's spread	Spread is reduced.	Spread is increased, but mortgage prepayments may occur.
Effect on T-bond futures price	Futures price decreases.	Futures price increases.
Decision on exercising the put option	Exercise put option.	Do not exercise put option.
Selling price of T-bond futures	$98,000	Not sold
−Purchase price of T-bond futures	−$91,000	Not purchased
−Price paid for put option	−$2,000	−$2,000
= Net gain per option	$5,000	−$2,000

One potential limitation of selling interest rate futures to hedge mortgages is that households may prepay their mortgages. If interest rates decline and most fixed-rate mortgages are prepaid, Emory will incur a loss on the futures position without an offsetting gain on its spread. To protect against this risk, Emory can purchase put options on Treasury bond futures. Suppose that Emory purchases put options on Treasury bond futures with an exercise price of 98-00 ($98,000) for a premium of 2-00 ($2,000) per contract. The initial Treasury bond futures price is 99-00 at the time. First, assume that interest rates rise, causing a decline in the Treasury bond futures price to 91-00. In this scenario, Emory will exercise its right to sell Treasury bond futures and offset its position by purchasing identical futures contracts, thereby generating a net gain of $5,000 per contract, as shown in Exhibit 14.14. Its gain on the futures position helps to offset the reduction in Emory's spread that occurs because of the higher interest rates.

Now consider a second scenario in which interest rates decline, causing the Treasury bond futures price to rise to 104-00. In this scenario, Emory does not exercise the put options on Treasury bond futures because the futures position would result in a loss. ●

This example shows how a put option on futures offers more flexibility than simply selling futures. However, the purchaser must pay a premium for the put option. Financial institutions that wish to hedge against rising interest rate risk should compare the possible outcomes from selling interest rate futures contracts versus purchasing put options on interest rate futures in an effort to hedge interest rate risk.

14-6c Hedging with Options on Stock Index Futures

Financial institutions and other investors commonly hedge their stock portfolios with options on stock index futures contracts. The position they take on the options contract is designed to create a gain that can offset a loss on their stock portfolio while still allowing some upside potential.

14-7 Options as Executive Compensation

Many firms distribute stock options to executives and other managers as a reward for good performance. For example, a manager may receive a salary along with call options on 10,000 shares of stock that have an exercise price above the prevailing price and an expiration date of five years from today. The purpose of awarding options as compensation is to increase the executives' incentive to make decisions that increase the value of the firm's stock, as their compensation from options is tied to the stock price.

However, many option compensation programs do not account for general market conditions. As a consequence, executives who own stock options when general stock market conditions are more favorable may earn high compensation because their firms' stock prices increase substantially during that period, even though the firms perform poorly relative to others in the same industry. Because compensation from holding options is driven more by general stock market conditions than by the firm's relative performance, stock options are not always effective at aligning executives' incentives with actual firm performance.

Another concern with using options as compensation is that executives with substantial options may be tempted to manipulate the stock's price upward in the short term, even though doing so adversely affects the stock price in the long term. For example, they might use accounting methods that defer the reporting of some expenses until next year and accelerate the reporting of some revenue. This approach makes short-term earnings appear favorable, but it reduces earnings in the following period. When these executives believe that the stock price has peaked in the short term, they can exercise their options by selling their shares in the secondary market. Firms can prevent the wrongful use of options by requiring that executives hold them for several years before exercising them.

14-8 Globalization of Options Markets

The globalization of stock markets has resulted in a corresponding need for a globalized market in stock options. Options on stock indexes representing various countries are now available, and options exchanges have been established in numerous countries. U.S. portfolio managers who maintain large holdings of stocks from specific countries are heavily exposed to the conditions of those markets. Rather than liquidate the portfolio of foreign stocks to protect against a possible temporary decline, the managers can purchase put options on the foreign stock index of concern. Portfolio managers residing in these countries can also use this strategy to hedge their stock portfolios.

Portfolio managers desiring to capitalize on expected temporary favorable movements in foreign markets can purchase call options on the corresponding stock indexes. Thus, the existence of options on foreign stock indexes allows portfolio managers to hedge or speculate based on forecasts of foreign market conditions. The trading of options on foreign stock indexes also avoids the transaction costs associated with buying and selling large portfolios of foreign stocks.

14-8a Currency Options Contracts

A **currency call option** provides the right to purchase a specified currency for a specified exercise (strike) price within a specified period of time. Corporations involved in international business transactions use currency call options to hedge future payables. If the exchange rate at the time payables are due exceeds the exercise price, the corporation can exercise its options and purchase the currency at the exercise price. If the prevailing exchange rate is lower than the exercise price, the corporation can purchase the currency at the prevailing exchange rate and let the options expire.

Speculators purchase call options on currencies that they expect to strengthen against the dollar. If the foreign currency strengthens as expected, they can exercise their call options to purchase the currency at the exercise price and then sell the currency at the prevailing exchange rate.

A **currency put option** provides the right to sell a specified currency for a specified exercise price within a specified period of time. Corporations involved in international business transactions may purchase put options to hedge future receivables. If the exchange rate at the time a corporation receives payment in a foreign currency is less than the exercise price, it can exercise its options by selling the currency at that price. In contrast, if the prevailing exchange rate is higher than the exercise price, it can sell the currency at the prevailing exchange rate and let the options expire.

Speculators purchase put options on currencies that they expect to weaken against the dollar. If the foreign currency weakens as expected, the speculators can purchase the currency at the prevailing spot rate and then exercise their put options to sell the currency at the exercise price.

For every buyer of a currency call or put option, there must be a seller (or writer). A writer of a call option is obligated to sell the specified currency at the specified exercise price if the option is exercised. A writer of a put option is obligated to purchase the specified currency at the specified exercise price if the option is exercised. Speculators are inclined to write call options on foreign currencies that they expect to weaken against the dollar or to write put options on those that they expect to strengthen against the dollar. If a currency option expires without being exercised, the writer earns the premium received.

Summary

- Stock options are traded on exchanges, just as many stocks are. Most trading is done electronically. The premium of a call option is influenced by the characteristics of the option and of the underlying stock that can affect the potential gains. In particular, the premium is higher when the market price of the stock is high relative to the exercise price, when the stock's volatility is greater, and when the term until expiration is longer. For put options, the higher the market price of the stock is relative to the exercise price, the lower the premium will be. The volatility of the underlying stock and the term to expiration are related to the put option premium in the same manner as they are to the call option premium.

- Speculators purchase call options on stocks whose prices are expected to rise and purchase put options on stocks whose prices are expected to decrease.

- Financial institutions can hedge against adverse movements in a stock by selling call options on that stock. Alternatively, they can purchase put options on that stock.

- Financial institutions commonly hedge their stock portfolios by purchasing put options on stock indexes. They may also use stock index options as a tool for dynamic asset allocation, thereby increasing their exposure when they have optimistic views about the stock market and reducing their exposure

(buying put options on stock indexes) when they have pessimistic views.

- Speculators purchase call options on interest rate futures contracts when they expect interest rates to decrease. Financial institutions with large holdings of long-term debt securities can hedge against interest rate risk by purchasing put options on interest rate futures. Index options can be used to speculate on movements in stock indexes and require only a small investment. Put options on stock indexes can be purchased to hedge a stock portfolio whose movements are similar to that of the stock index. Investors can use options on stock index futures to speculate on movements in the value of the stock index futures contract. Portfolio managers can purchase put options on stock index futures to hedge portfolios of stocks that move in tandem with the stock index.

- Many firms distribute options to their executives as part of their compensation. The intent is to increase the executives' incentive to make decisions that increase the value of the firm's stock.

- The globalization of stock markets has led to the development of a globalized market in stock options. Currency option contracts allow firms engaged in international business to hedge their future payables or receivables, and speculators use currency options to speculate on movements in currencies.

Point/Counterpoint

If You Were a Major Shareholder of a Publicly Traded Firm, Would You Prefer That Stock Options Be Traded on That Stock?

Point No. Options can be used by investors to speculate, and excessive trading of the options may push the stock price away from its fundamental price.

Counterpoint Yes. Options can be used by investors to temporarily hedge against adverse movements in the stock, so they may reduce the selling pressure on the stock in some periods.

Who Is Correct? Use the Internet to learn more about this issue and then formulate your own opinion.

Questions and Applications

1. **Options versus Futures** Describe the general differences between a call option and a futures contract.

2. **Speculating with Call Options** How do speculators use call options? Describe the conditions under which their strategy would backfire. What is the maximum loss that could occur for a purchaser of a call option?

3. **Speculating with Put Options** How do speculators use put options? Describe the conditions under which their strategy would backfire. What is the maximum loss that could occur for a purchaser of a put option?

4. **Selling Options** Under what conditions would speculators sell a call option? What is the risk to speculators who sell put options?

5. **Factors Affecting Call Option Premiums** Identify the factors affecting the premium paid on a call option. Describe how each factor affects the size of the premium.

6. **Factors Affecting Put Option Premiums** Identify the factors affecting the premium paid on a put option. Describe how each factor affects the size of the premium.

7. **Leverage of Options** How can financial institutions with stock portfolios use stock options when they expect stock prices to rise substantially but do not yet have sufficient funds to purchase more stock?

8. **Hedging with Put Options** Why would a financial institution holding the stock of Hinton Co. consider buying a put option on that stock rather than simply selling it?

9. **Call Options on Futures** Describe a call option on interest rate futures. How does it differ from purchasing a futures contract?

10. **Put Options on Futures** Describe a put option on interest rate futures. How does it differ from selling a futures contract?

Advanced Questions

11. **Hedging Interest Rate Risk** Assume a savings institution has a large amount of fixed-rate mortgages and obtains most of its funds from short-term deposits. How could it use options on financial futures to hedge its exposure to interest rate movements? Would futures or options on futures be more appropriate if the institution is concerned that interest rates will decline, causing a large number of mortgage prepayments?

12. **Hedging Effectiveness** Three savings and loan institutions (S&Ls) have identical balance sheet compositions: a high concentration of short-term deposits that are used to provide long-term, fixed-rate mortgages. The S&Ls took the following positions one year ago:

NAME OF S&L	POSITION
LaCrosse	Sold financial futures
Stevens Point	Purchased put options on interest rate futures
Whitewater	Did not take any position in futures

Assume that interest rates declined consistently over the last year. Which of the three S&Ls would have achieved the best performance based on this information? Explain.

13. Change in Stock Option Premiums Explain how and why the option premiums may change in response to a surprise announcement that the Fed will increase interest rates, even if stock prices are not affected.

14. Speculating with Stock Options The price of Garner stock is $40. There is a call option on Garner stock that is at the money with a premium of $2.00. There is also a put option on Garner stock that is at the money with a premium of $1.80. Why would investors consider writing this call option and this put option? Why would some investors consider buying this call option and this put option?

15. How Stock Index Option Prices May Respond to Prevailing Conditions Consider the prevailing conditions that could affect the demand for stocks, including inflation, the economy, the budget deficit, the Fed's monetary policy, political conditions, and the general mood of investors. Based on these conditions, would you consider purchasing stock index options at this time? Offer some logic to support your answer. Which factor do you think will have the biggest impact on stock index option prices?

16. CBOE Volatility Index How would you interpret a large increase in the CBOE Volatility Index (VIX)? Explain why the VIX increased substantially during the credit crisis that began in 2008.

Critical Thinking Question

Strategy for Investing in the CBOE Volatility Index An investment newsletter suggests that because the prevailing stock market conditions are subject to much uncertainty, investors should purchase call options on the CBOE Volatility Index (VIX). Write a short essay explaining how the valuation of the VIX is influenced by market uncertainty. Also support or refute the advice provided by the newsletter, and offer a strategy for investing in call options on the VIX based on expectations of changes in market uncertainty.

Interpreting Financial News

Interpret the following comments made by Wall Street analysts and portfolio managers.

a. "Our firm took a hit because we wrote put options on stocks just before the stock market crash."

b. "Before hedging our stock portfolio with options on index futures, we search for the index that is most appropriate."

c. "We prefer to use covered call writing to hedge our stock portfolios."

Managing in Financial Markets

Hedging with Stock Options As a stock portfolio manager, you have investments in many U.S. stocks and plan to hold these stocks over a long-term period. However, you are concerned that the stock market may experience a temporary decline over the next three months and that your stock portfolio will probably decline by about the same degree as the market. The following options on a stock index futures contract are available and have an expiration date about three months from now:

EXERCISE PRICE	CALL PREMIUM	PUT PREMIUM
1372	40	24
1428	24	40

The options on the stock index futures contract are priced at $250 times the quoted premium. Currently, the stock index level is 1400. The exercise price of 1372 represents a 2 percent decline from the prevailing index level, and the exercise price of 1428 represents an increase of 2 percent above the prevailing index level.

a. Assume that you want to take an options position to hedge your entire portfolio, which is currently valued at about $700,000. How many index option contracts should you take a position in to hedge your entire portfolio?

b. Assume that you want to create a hedge so that your portfolio will lose no more than 2 percent of its present value. How can you take a position in options on index futures to achieve this goal? What is the cost to you as a result of creating this hedge?

c. Given your expectations of a weak stock market over the next three months, how can you generate some fees from the sale of options on the stock index futures to help cover the cost of purchasing options?

Problems

1. **Writing Call Options** A call option on Illinois stock specifies an exercise price of $38. Today, the stock's price is $40. The premium on the call option is $5. Assume the option will not be exercised until maturity, if at all. Complete the following table.

ASSUMED STOCK PRICE AT THE TIME THE CALL OPTION IS ABOUT TO EXPIRE	NET PROFIT OR LOSS PER SHARE TO BE EARNED BY THE WRITER (SELLER) OF THE CALL OPTION
$37	
39	
41	
43	
45	
48	

2. **Purchasing Call Options** A call option on Michigan stock specifies an exercise price of $55. Today, the stock's price is $54 per share. The premium on the call option is $3. Assume the option will not be exercised until maturity, if at all. Complete the following table for a speculator who purchases the call option.

ASSUMED STOCK PRICE AT THE TIME THE CALL OPTION IS ABOUT TO EXPIRE	NET PROFIT OR LOSS PER SHARE TO BE EARNED BY THE SPECULATOR
$50	
52	
54	
56	
58	
60	
62	

3. **Purchasing Put Options** A put option on Iowa stock specifies an exercise price of $71. Today, the stock's price is $68. The premium on the put option is $8. Assume the option will not be exercised until maturity, if at all. Complete the following table for a speculator who purchases the put option (and currently does not own the stock).

ASSUMED STOCK PRICE AT THE TIME THE PUT OPTION IS ABOUT TO EXPIRE	NET PROFIT OR LOSS PER SHARE TO BE EARNED BY THE SPECULATOR
$60	
64	
68	
70	
72	
74	
76	

4. **Writing Put Options** A put option on Indiana stock specifies an exercise price of $23. Today, the stock's price is $24. The premium on the put option is $3. Assume the option will not be exercised until maturity, if at all. Complete the following table.

ASSUMED STOCK PRICE AT THE TIME THE PUT OPTION IS ABOUT TO EXPIRE	NET PROFIT OR LOSS PER SHARE TO BE EARNED BY THE WRITER (OR SELLER) OF THE PUT OPTION
$20	
21	
22	
23	
24	
25	
26	

5. **Covered Call Strategy**

a. Evanston Insurance, Inc., has purchased shares of Stock E at $50 per share. It will sell the stock in six months. It considers using a strategy of covered call writing to partially hedge its position in this stock. The exercise price is $53, the expiration date is six months, and the premium on the call option is $2. Complete the following table.

POSSIBLE PRICE OF STOCK E IN SIX MONTHS	PROFIT OR LOSS PER SHARE IF A COVERED CALL STRATEGY IS USED	PROFIT OR LOSS PER SHARE IF A COVERED CALL STRATEGY IS NOT USED
$47		
50		
52		
55		
57		
60		

b. Assume that each of the six stock prices in the table's first column has an equal probability of occurring. Compare the probability distribution of the profits (or losses) per share when using covered call writing versus not using it. Would you recommend covered call writing in this situation? Explain.

6. Put Options on Futures Purdue Savings and Loan Association purchased a put option on Treasury bond futures with a September delivery date and an exercise price of 91-16. The put option has a premium of 1-32. Assume that the price of the Treasury bond futures decreases to 88-16. Should Purdue exercise the option or should it let the option expire? What is Purdue's net gain or loss after accounting for the premium paid on the option?

7. Call Options on Futures Wisconsin, Inc., purchased a call option on Treasury bond futures at a premium of 2-00. The exercise price is 92-08. If the price of the Treasury bond futures rises to 93-08, should Wisconsin exercise the call option or should it let the option expire? What is Wisconsin's net gain or loss after accounting for the premium paid on the option?

8. Call Options on Futures DePaul Insurance Company purchased a call option on a stock index futures contract. The option premium is quoted as $6. The exercise price is 1,430. Assume the index on the futures contract reaches 1,440. Should DePaul exercise the call option or should it let the option expire? What is the net gain or loss to DePaul after accounting for the premium paid for the option (assume the value is measured as $250 times the index)?

9. Covered Call Strategy Coral, Inc., has purchased shares of Stock M at $28 per share. Coral will sell the stock in six months. It considers using a strategy of covered call writing to partially hedge its position in this stock. The exercise price is $32, the expiration date is six months, and the premium on the call option is $2.50. Complete the following table.

POSSIBLE PRICE OF STOCK M IN SIX MONTHS	PROFIT OR LOSS PER SHARE IF COVERED CALL STRATEGY IS USED
$25	
28	
33	
36	

10. Hedging with Bond Futures Smart Savings Bank desired to hedge its interest rate risk. It considered two possibilities: (1) sell Treasury bond futures at a price of 94-00 or (2) purchase a put option on Treasury bond futures. At the time, the price of Treasury bond futures was 95-00 and their face value was $100,000. The put option premium was 2-00, and the exercise price was 94-00. Just before the option expired, the Treasury bond futures price was 91-00, and Smart Savings Bank would have exercised the put option at that time, if at all. This is also the time when it would have offset its futures position, if it had sold futures. Determine the net gain to Smart Savings Bank if it had sold Treasury bond futures versus if it had purchased a put option on Treasury bond futures. Which alternative would have been more favorable, based on the situation that occurred?

Flow of Funds Exercise

Hedging with Options Contracts

Carson Company would like to acquire Vinnet, Inc., a publicly traded firm in the same industry. Vinnet's stock price is currently much lower than the prices of other firms in the industry because it operates inefficiently.

Carson believes that it could restructure Vinnet's operations and improve the company's performance. It is about to contact Vinnet to determine whether Vinnet will agree to an acquisition. Carson is somewhat concerned that investors may learn of its plans and buy Vinnet stock in anticipation that Carson will need to pay a high premium (perhaps a 30 percent premium above the prevailing stock price) to complete the acquisition. Carson decides to call a bank about its risk, as the bank has a brokerage subsidiary that can help it hedge with stock options.

a. How can Carson use stock options to reduce its exposure to this risk? Are there any limitations to this strategy, given that Carson will ultimately have to buy most or all of the Vinnet stock if the acquisition occurs?

b. Describe the maximum possible loss that may be directly incurred by Carson as a result of engaging in this strategy.

c. Explain the results of the strategy you offered in the previous question if Vinnet plans to avoid the acquisition attempt by Carson.

Internet/Excel Exercises

1. Go to www.cboe.com and, under "Quotes & Data," select "Delayed Quotes." Insert the ticker symbol for a stock option in which you are interested. Assess the results. Did the premium ("Net") on the call options increase or decrease today? Did the premium on the put options increase or decrease today?

2. Based on the changes in the premium, do you think the underlying stock price increased or decreased? Explain.

Online Articles with Real-World Examples

Find a recent practical article available online that describes a real-world example regarding a specific financial institution or financial market that reinforces one or more concepts covered in this chapter.

If your class has an online component, your professor may ask you to post your summary of the article there and provide a link to the article so that other students can access it. If your class is live, your professor may ask you to summarize your application of the article in class. Your professor may assign specific students to complete this assignment or may allow any students to do the assignment on a volunteer basis.

For recent online articles and real-world examples related to this chapter, consider using the following search terms (be sure to include the prevailing year as a search term to ensure that the online articles are recent):

1. stock options AND profits
2. stock options AND losses
3. stock options AND speculators
4. stock options AND hedge
5. stock option premium AND volatility
6. stock option AND ETFs
7. stock index option
8. LEAPs AND speculate
9. selling stock options AND cover
10. stock options AND compensation

Appendix 14

Option Valuation

The Binomial Pricing Model

The binomial option-pricing model was originally developed by William F. Sharpe. An advantage of the model is that it can be used to price both European-style and American-style options with or without dividends. European options are put or call options that can be exercised only at maturity, whereas American options can be exercised at any time prior to maturity.

Assumptions of the Binomial Pricing Model

The binomial pricing model includes the following assumptions:

1. The continuous random walk underlying the Black–Scholes model can be modeled by a discrete random walk with the following properties:

- The asset price changes only at discrete (non-infinitesimal) time steps.
- At each time step, the asset price may move either up or down; thus, there are only two returns, and these two returns are the same for all time steps.
- The probabilities of moving up and down are known.

2. The world is risk-neutral. This allows the assumption that investors' risk preferences are irrelevant and that investors are risk-neutral. Furthermore, the return from the underlying asset is the risk-free interest rate.

Using the Binomial Pricing Model to Price Call Options

The following example illustrates how the binomial pricing model can be employed to price a call option (that is, to determine a call option premium). To use the model, we need information for three securities: the underlying stock, a risk-free security, and the stock option.

Assume that the price of Gem Corporation stock today is $100. Furthermore, it is estimated that Gem stock will be selling for either $150 or $70 in one year. That is, the stock is expected either to rise by 50 percent or to fall by 30 percent. Also assume that the annual risk-free interest rate on a one-year Treasury bill is 10 percent, compounded continuously, and that a T-bill currently sells for $100. Because interest is continuously compounded, the T-bill will pay interest of $100 \times (e^{10} - 1)$, or $10.52.

Currently, a call option on Gem stock is available with an exercise price of $100 and an expiration date one year from now. Because the call option is an option to buy Gem stock, the option will have a value of $50 if the stock price increases to $150 in one year. If the stock price in one year falls to $70, the call option will have a value of $0. Our objective is to value this call option using the binomial pricing model.

The first step in applying the model to this call option is to recognize that three investments are involved: the stock, a risk-free security, and the call option. Using the information already given, we have the following payoff matrix in one year:

SECURITY	PRICE IF STOCK IS WORTH $150 IN ONE YEAR	PRICE IF STOCK IS WORTH $70 IN ONE YEAR	CURRENT PRICE
Gem stock	$150.00	$70.00	$100.00
Treasury bill	110.52	110.52	100.00
Call option	50.00	0.00	?

The objective of the binomial pricing model is to determine the current price of the call option. The key to understanding the valuation of the call option using the binomial pricing model is that the option's value must be based on a combination of the value of the stock and the T-bill. If this were not the case, arbitrage opportunities would result. Consequently, in either the up or the down state, the payoff of a portfolio consisting of N_s shares of Gem stock and N_b T-bills must be equal to the value of the call option in that state. Using the payoff matrix just given, we derive the following system of two equations:

$$150N_s + 110.52N_b = 50$$
$$70N_s + 110.52N_b = 0$$

Because we are dealing with two linear equations with two unknowns, we can easily solve for the two variables by substitution. Doing so gives the following values for the number of shares and the number of T-bills in the investor's so-called replicating portfolio:

$$N_s = 0.625$$
$$N_b = -0.3959$$

In other words, the payoffs of the call option on Gem stock can be replicated by borrowing $39.59 at the risk-free rate and buying 0.625 share of Gem stock for $62.50 (because one share currently sells for $100). Because the payoff of this replicating portfolio is the same as that for the call, the cost to the investor must be the value of the call. In this case, because $39.59 of the outlay of $62.50 is financed by borrowing, the outlay to the investor is $62.50 − $39.59 = $22.91. Thus, the call option premium must be $22.91.

In equation form, the value of the call option (V_c) can be written as

$$V_c = N_s P_s + N_b P_b$$

Computation of N_s can be simplified somewhat. More specifically,

$$N_s = h = \frac{P_{ou} - P_{od}}{P_{su} - P_{sd}}$$

where

$$P_{ou} = \text{value of the option in the up state}$$
$$P_{od} = \text{value of the option in the down state}$$
$$P_{su} = \text{price of Gem stock in the up state}$$
$$P_{sd} = \text{price of Gem stock in the down state}$$

This value is also referred to as the *hedge ratio* (h).

In this example, the amount borrowed (BOR) is equal to the product of the number of risk-free securities in the replicating portfolio and the price of the risk-free security:

$$N_b P_b = \text{BOR} = PV(hP_{sd} - P_{od})$$

where

$$PV = \text{present value of a continuously compounded sum}$$
$$h = \text{hedge ratio}$$

Thus, the value of the call option can be expressed more simply as

$$V_c = hP_s + \text{BOR}$$

To illustrate why the relationships discussed so far should hold, we assume for the moment that a call option on Gem stock is selling for a premium of $25 (that is, the call option is overpriced). In this case, investors are presented with an arbitrage opportunity to make an instantaneous, riskless profit. In particular, investors could write a call, buy the stock, and borrow at the risk-free rate. Now assume that the call option on Gem stock is selling for a premium of only $20 (that is, the call option is underpriced). Using arbitrage, investors would buy a call, sell the stock short, and invest at the risk-free rate.

Using the Binomial Pricing Model to Price Put Options

Continuing with the example of Gem Corporation, the only item that changes in the payoff matrix when the option is a put option (that is, an option to sell Gem stock) is the value of the option at expiration in the up and down states. If Gem stock is worth $150 in one year, the put option will be worthless; if Gem stock is worth only $70 in one year, the put option will be worth $30. Because the value of the risk-free security is contingent only on the T-bill interest rate, it will be unaffected by the fact that we are now dealing with a put option.

The hedge ratio and the amount borrowed can be determined using the formulas introduced previously. The hedge ratio is

$$h = \frac{0 - 30}{150 - 70} = -0.375$$

The amount borrowed is

$$\text{BOR} = PV[-0.375(70) - 30] = \frac{-56.25}{e^{RT}} = -50.90$$

Therefore, to replicate the put option, the investor would sell short 0.375 Gem share and lend $50.90 at the risk-free rate. Thus, the net amount the investor must put up is $50.90 − $37.50 = $13.40. Accordingly, this is the fair value of the put.

Put-Call Parity

With some mathematical manipulation, the following relationship can be derived between the prices of puts and calls (that have the same exercise price and time to expiration):

$$P_p = P_c + \frac{E}{e^{RT}} - P_s$$

where

P_p = price of a put option

P_c = price of a call option

E = exercise price of the option

e^{RT} = present value operator for a continuously compounded sum, discounted at interest rate R for T years

P_s = price of the stock

Using the example of Gem Corporation,

$$P_p = \$22.91 + \frac{\$100}{e^{0.10}} - \$100 = \$13.39$$

The Black–Scholes Option-Pricing Model for Call Options

In 1973, Black and Scholes devised an option-pricing model that motivated further research into option valuation that continues to this day.

Assumptions of the Black–Scholes Option-Pricing Model

Among the key assumptions underlying the Black–Scholes option-pricing model are the following points:

1. The risk-free rate is known and constant over the life of the option.
2. The probability distribution of stock prices is lognormal.
3. The variability of a stock's return is constant.
4. The option is to be exercised only at maturity, if at all.
5. There are no transaction costs involved in trading options.
6. Tax rates are similar for all participants who trade options.
7. The stock of concern does not pay cash dividends.

The Black–Scholes Partial Differential Equation

The Black–Scholes option-pricing model was one of the first frameworks to introduce the concept of a *riskless hedge*. Assume that an amount π is invested in a risk-free asset, so that the investor earns a return of $r\pi dt$ over a time interval dt. If an appropriately selected portfolio—with a current value of π consisting of a company's stock and an offsetting position in an option on that stock—returns more than $r\pi dt$ over a time interval dt, an investor could conduct arbitrage by borrowing at the risk-free rate and investing in the portfolio. Conversely, if the portfolio returns less than $r\pi dt$, the investor would short the portfolio and invest in the risk-free asset. In either case, the arbitrageur would make a riskless, no-cost, instantaneous profit. Thus, the return on the portfolio and on the riskless asset must be roughly equal.

Using this argument, Black and Scholes developed what has become known as the *Black–Scholes partial differential equation:*

$$\frac{\partial V}{\partial t} + \frac{1}{2}\sigma^2 S^2 \frac{\partial^2 V}{\partial S^2} + rS\frac{\partial V}{\partial S} - rV = 0$$

where

$$V = \text{value of an option}$$
$$S = \text{price of the underlying stock}$$
$$r = \text{risk-free rate of return}$$
$$t = \text{a measure of time}$$
$$\sigma^2 = \text{variance of the underlying stock's price}$$
$$\partial \text{ and } \partial^2 = \text{first- and second-order partial derivatives}$$

The Black–Scholes Option-Pricing Model for European Call Options

To price an option, the partial differential equation is solved for V, the value of the option. Assuming that the risk-free interest rate and stock price volatility are constant, solving the Black–Scholes partial differential equation results in the Black–Scholes formula for European call options:

$$V = SN(d_1) - Ee^{-rT}N(d_2)$$

where

$$V = \text{value of the call option}$$
$$S = \text{stock price}$$
$$N(\cdot) = \text{cumulative distribution function for a standardized normal}$$
$$\text{random variable}$$
$$E = \text{exercise price of the call option}$$
$$e = \text{base } e \text{ antilog} = 2.7183$$
$$r = \text{risk-free rate of return for one year assuming continuous}$$
$$\text{compounding}$$
$$T = \text{time remaining to maturity of the call option, expressed as a}$$
$$\text{fraction of a year}$$

The terms $N(d_1)$ and $N(d_2)$ deserve further elaboration. The term N represents a cumulative probability for a unit normal variable, where

$$d_1 = \frac{\ln(S/E) + \left(r + \frac{1}{2}\sigma^2\right)(T)}{\sigma\sqrt{T}}$$

and

$$d_2 = \frac{\ln(S/E) + \left(r - \frac{1}{2}\sigma^2\right)(T)}{\sigma\sqrt{T}}$$

$$= d_1 - \sigma\sqrt{T}$$

Here $\ln(S/E)$ is the natural logarithm, and σ denotes the standard deviation of the continuously compounded rate of return on the underlying stock.

Using the Black–Scholes Option-Pricing Model to Price a European Call Option

To illustrate how the Black–Scholes equation can be used to price a call option, assume you observe a call option on MPB Corporation stock expiring in six months with an exercise price of $70. Thus, $T = 0.50$ and $E = \$70$. Furthermore, the current price of MPB stock is $72, and the stock has a standard deviation of 0.10. The annual risk-free rate is 7 percent. Solving for d_1 and d_2, we obtain

$$d_1 = \frac{\ln(72/70) + [0.07 + 0.5(0.10)^2](0.5)}{0.10\sqrt{0.5}} = 0.9287$$

$$d_2 = 0.9287 - 0.10\sqrt{0.50} = 0.8580$$

To determine the cumulative probability, use a table that measures the area under the standard normal distribution function (see Exhibit 14A.1). Because d_1 is 0.9287, the cumulative probability from zero to 0.9287 is approximately 0.3235 (from Exhibit 14A.1, using linear interpolation). Because the cumulative probability for a unit normal variable from negative infinity to zero is 0.50, the cumulative probability from negative infinity to 0.9287 is $0.50 + 0.3235 = 0.8235$. For d_2, the cumulative probability from zero to 0.8580 is 0.3042. Therefore, the cumulative probability from negative infinity to 0.8580 is $0.50 + 0.3042 = 0.8042$.

Now that $N(d_1)$ and $N(d_2)$ have been calculated, the call option value can be estimated as follows:

$$V_c = (\$72 \times 0.8235) - \left(\frac{\$70}{e^{0.07 \times 0.50}} \times 0.8045\right) = \$4.91$$

Thus, a call option on MPB stock should sell for a premium of $4.91.

Put–Call Parity

Using the Black–Scholes option-pricing model, the same relationship exists between the price of a call and the price of a put as in the binomial option-pricing model. Thus, we have

$$P_p = P_c + \frac{E}{e^{RT}} - P_s$$

Deriving the Implied Volatility

The example of deriving the value of a call option used an estimate of the stock's standard deviation. In some cases, investors want to derive the market's implied volatility rather than a valuation of the call option. This volatility is referred to as "implied" under these

Exhibit 14A.1   Measuring the Area under the Standard Normal Distribution Function

d	0.00	0.01	0.02	0.03	0.04	0.05	0.06	0.07	0.08	0.09
0.0	0.0000	0.0040	0.0080	0.0120	0.0160	0.0199	0.0239	0.0279	0.0319	0.0359
0.1	0.0398	0.0438	0.0478	0.0517	0.0557	0.0596	0.0636	0.0675	0.0714	0.0753
0.2	0.0793	0.0832	0.0871	0.0910	0.0948	0.0987	0.1026	0.1064	0.1103	0.1141
0.3	0.1179	0.1217	0.1255	0.1293	0.1331	0.1368	0.1406	0.1443	0.1480	0.1517
0.4	0.1554	0.1591	0.1628	0.1664	0.1700	0.1736	0.1772	0.1808	0.1844	0.1879
0.5	0.1915	0.1950	0.1985	0.2019	0.2054	0.2088	0.2123	0.2157	0.2190	0.2224
0.6	0.2257	0.2291	0.2324	0.2357	0.2389	0.2422	0.2454	0.2486	0.2517	0.2549
0.7	0.2580	0.2611	0.2642	0.2673	0.2704	0.2734	0.2764	0.2794	0.2823	0.2852
0.8	0.2881	0.2910	0.2939	0.2967	0.2995	0.3023	0.3051	0.3078	0.3106	0.3133
0.9	0.3159	0.3186	0.3213	0.3238	0.3264	0.3289	0.3315	0.3340	0.3365	0.3389
1.0	0.3413	0.3438	0.3461	0.3485	0.3508	0.3531	0.3554	0.3577	0.3599	0.3621
1.1	0.3643	0.3665	0.3686	0.3708	0.3729	0.3749	0.3770	0.3790	0.3810	0.3830
1.2	0.3849	0.3869	0.3888	0.3907	0.3925	0.3944	0.3962	0.3980	0.3997	0.4015
1.3	0.4032	0.4049	0.4066	0.4082	0.4099	0.4115	0.4131	0.4147	0.4162	0.4177
1.4	0.4192	0.4207	0.4222	0.4236	0.4251	0.4265	0.4279	0.4292	0.4306	0.4319
1.5	0.4332	0.4345	0.4357	0.4370	0.4382	0.4394	0.4406	0.4418	0.4429	0.4441
1.6	0.4452	0.4463	0.4474	0.4484	0.4495	0.4505	0.4515	0.4525	0.4535	0.4545
1.7	0.4554	0.4564	0.4573	0.4582	0.4591	0.4599	0.4608	0.4616	0.4625	0.4633
1.8	0.4641	0.4649	0.4656	0.4664	0.4671	0.4678	0.4686	0.4693	0.4699	0.4706
1.9	0.4713	0.4719	0.4726	0.4732	0.4738	0.4744	0.4750	0.4756	0.4761	0.4767
2.0	0.4773	0.4778	0.4783	0.4788	0.4793	0.4798	0.4803	0.4808	0.4812	0.4817
2.1	0.4821	0.4826	0.4830	0.4834	0.4838	0.4842	0.4846	0.4850	0.4854	0.4857
2.2	0.4861	0.4866	0.4868	0.4871	0.4875	0.4878	0.4881	0.4884	0.4887	0.4890
2.3	0.4893	0.4896	0.4898	0.4901	0.4904	0.4906	0.4909	0.4911	0.4913	0.4916
2.4	0.4918	0.4920	0.4922	0.4925	0.4927	0.4929	0.4931	0.4932	0.4934	0.4936
2.5	0.4938	0.4940	0.4941	0.4943	0.4945	0.4946	0.4948	0.4949	0.4951	0.4952
2.6	0.4953	0.4955	0.4956	0.4957	0.4959	0.4960	0.4961	0.4962	0.4963	0.4964
2.7	0.4965	0.4966	0.4967	0.4968	0.4969	0.4970	0.4971	0.4972	0.4973	0.4974
2.8	0.4974	0.4975	0.4976	0.4977	0.4977	0.4978	0.4979	0.4979	0.4980	0.4981
2.9	0.4981	0.4982	0.4982	0.4982	0.4984	0.4984	0.4985	0.4985	0.4986	0.4986
3.0	0.4987	0.4987	0.4987	0.4988	0.4988	0.4989	0.4989	0.4989	0.4990	0.4990

circumstances because it is not directly observable in the market. The implied volatility can be derived with some software packages by inputting values for the other variables (prevailing stock price, exercise price, option's time to expiration, and interest rate) in the call option-pricing model and also inputting the market premium of the call option. Instead of deriving a value for the call option premium, the prevailing market premium of the call option is used along with these other variables to derive the implied volatility. The software package will also show how the stock's implied volatility is affected by different values of the call option premium. An increase in the market premium of the call option, when other variables have not changed, reflects an increase in the implied volatility.

This relationship can be verified by entering a slightly higher market premium into the software program and checking how the implied volatility changes in response to that increase. The point is that investors can detect changes in the implied volatility of a stock by monitoring how the stock's call option premium changes over short intervals of time.

American versus European Options

American Call Options

An American call option is an option to purchase stock that can be exercised at any time prior to maturity. However, the original Black–Scholes model was developed to price European call options, which are options to purchase stock that can be exercised only at maturity. Naturally, European put options could be directly derived using the put–call parity relationship. Consequently, the question is whether the Black–Scholes equation can be used to price American call options.

In general, early exercise of a call may be justified only if the asset makes a cash payment such as a dividend on a stock. If no dividends are paid during the life of the option, early exercise would be equivalent to buying something earlier than you need it and then giving up the right to decide later whether you really wanted it. However, if it is possible to save a little money in doing so, early purchase/exercise can sometimes be justified. Early exercise is not appropriate every time the firm issues a dividend, but if early exercise is justified, then it should occur just before the stock's ex-dividend date (the date after which a purchaser of the stock is not entitled to the next dividend). This minimizes the amount of time value given up without sacrificing the dividend.

Thus, if there are no dividends on the underlying stock, the Black–Scholes model can be used to price American call options. In contrast, if the underlying stock pays dividends, the Black–Scholes model may not be directly applicable. The binomial option-pricing model can be used to price American call options that pay dividends.

American Put Options

Suppose you purchase a European put option. If the value of the underlying asset goes to zero, then the option has reached its maximum value: It allows you to sell a worthless asset for the exercise price. Yet because the option is European, it cannot be exercised prior to maturity. Its value will simply be the present value of the exercise price, and this value will gradually rise as a function of the time value of money until expiration, when the option will be exercised. In such a situation, you would clearly prefer an American option, so you could exercise it as soon as the asset value goes to zero.

The previous example indicates that there would be a demand for an option that allowed early exercise. It is not necessary, however, for the asset price to go to zero. The European put price must be at least the present value of the exercise price minus the asset price. Clearly, the present value of the exercise price minus the asset price is less than the exercise price minus the asset price, which is the amount that could be claimed by exercising the put option early. Thus, an American put will sell for more than the European put and, in turn, the Black–Scholes option-pricing model cannot be used to price an American put option. There is a point where the right to exercise early is at its maximum value, and at that point the American put would be exercised. Finding that point is difficult, but doing so unlocks the mystery of pricing the American put.

The only surefire way to price the American put option correctly is to use a numerical procedure such as the binomial model. The procedure is similar to partitioning a two-dimensional space of time and the asset price into finer points and then solving either a difference or a differential equation at each time point.

The process starts at expiration and successively works its way back to the present by using the solution at the preceding step. Thus, a closed-form solution does not exist. Instead, American puts can be viewed as an infinite series of compound options (that is, an option on an option). At each point in time, the holder of the put has the right to decide whether to exercise it. A decision not to exercise the put is tantamount to exercising the compound option and obtaining a position in a new compound option, which can be exercised an instant later. The sequence reiterates until the expiration day. This logic can lead to an intuitive but complex mathematical formula that contains an infinite number of terms.

Thus, the holders of American puts face an infinite series of early exercise decisions. Only at an instant before the asset goes ex-dividend do the holders know that they should wait to exercise. Because they know the asset will fall in value an instant later, they might as well wait an instant and benefit from the decline in value.

15
Swap Markets

CHAPTER OBJECTIVES

The specific objectives of this chapter are to:

- Provide background information on interest rate swaps.

- Describe the types of swaps that are available.

- Explain the risks of interest rate swaps.

- Explain how interest rate swaps are priced.

- Identify factors influencing interest rate swap performance.

- Identify other interest rate derivative instruments that are commonly used.

- Explain how credit default swaps are used to reduce credit risk.

- Describe how the swap markets have become globalized.

Many firms have inflow and outflow payments that are not equally sensitive to interest rate patterns. Consequently, they are exposed to interest rate risk. Interest rate swap contracts have been established to reduce these risks. In addition, credit default swap contracts have been established to reduce credit risk.

15-1 Background

An **interest rate swap** is an arrangement whereby one party exchanges one set of interest payments for another. In the most common arrangement, fixed-rate interest payments are exchanged for floating-rate interest payments over time. The provisions of an interest rate swap include the following:

- The **notional principal** value to which the interest rates are applied to determine the interest payments involved
- The fixed interest rate
- The formula and type of index used to determine the floating rate
- The frequency of payments, such as every six months or every year
- The lifetime of the swap

For example, a swap arrangement may involve an exchange of 11 percent fixed-rate payments for floating payments at the prevailing one-year Treasury bill rate plus 1 percent, based on $30 million of notional principal, at the end of each of the next seven years. Other money market rates are sometimes used instead of the T-bill rate to index the interest rate.

Although each participant in the swap agreement owes the other participant at each payment date, the amounts owed are typically netted out so that only the net payment is made. If a firm owes 11 percent of $30 million (the notional principal) but is supposed to receive 10 percent of $30 million on a given payment date, it will send a net payment of 1 percent of the $30 million, or $300,000.

The market for swaps has been facilitated by over-the-counter trading rather than trading on an organized exchange. Given the uniqueness of the provisions in each swap arrangement, swaps are less standardized than other derivative instruments such as futures or options. Thus, over-the-counter arrangements are more appropriate than an exchange for working out the specific provisions of swaps. As discussed later in the chapter, however, under new rules and regulations, swaps are becoming more standardized, and much trading is now being conducted on electronic platforms.

Interest rate swaps became more popular in the early 1980s, when corporations were experiencing the effects of large fluctuations in interest rates. Although some manufacturing companies were exposed to interest rate movements, financial institutions were exposed to a greater degree and became the primary users of interest rate swaps. Initially, only those institutions wishing to swap payments on amounts of $10 million or more engaged in interest rate swaps. More recently, swaps have been conducted involving smaller amounts as well.

The Chicago Mercantile Exchange (CME) offers futures contracts on interest rate swaps. These contracts allow participants to engage in interest rate swaps, but provide the same efficiency and transparency as a futures contract.

15-1a Use of Swaps for Hedging

Financial institutions in the United States, such as savings institutions and commercial banks, traditionally had more interest rate–sensitive liabilities than assets and, therefore, were adversely affected by *increasing* interest rates. Conversely, some financial institutions in other countries, such as some commercial banks in Europe, had access to long-term fixed-rate funding, but used these funds primarily for making floating-rate loans. These institutions were adversely affected by *declining* interest rates.

By engaging in an interest rate swap, both types of financial institutions could reduce their exposure to interest rate risk. Specifically, a U.S. financial institution could send fixed-rate interest payments to a European financial institution in exchange for floating-rate payments. This type of arrangement is illustrated in Exhibit 15.1. In the event of rising interest rates, the U.S. financial institution receives higher interest payments from the floating-rate portion of the swap agreement, which helps offset the rising cost of obtaining deposits. In the event of declining interest rates, the European financial institution provides lower interest payments in the swap arrangement, which helps offset the lower interest payments received on its floating-rate loans.

Exhibit 15.1   Illustration of an Interest Rate Swap

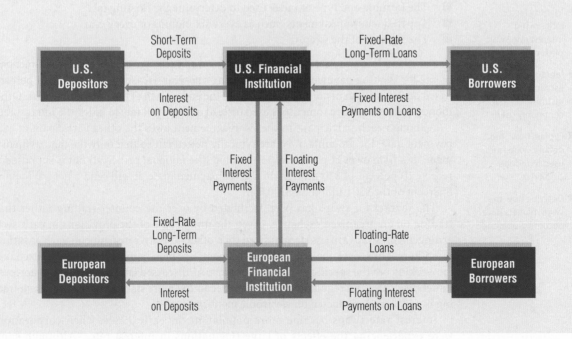

In our example, the U.S. financial institution forgoes the potential benefits from a decline in interest rates, whereas the European financial institution forgoes the potential benefits from an increase in interest rates. The interest rate swap enables each institution to offset any gains or losses that result specifically from interest rate movements. Consequently, although interest rate swaps reduce interest rate risk, they also reduce potential returns. Most financial institutions that anticipate interest rates will move in a favorable direction do not hedge their positions. Instead, interest rate swaps are primarily used by financial institutions that would be adversely affected by an expected movement in interest rates.

A primary reason for the popularity of interest rate swaps is the existence of market imperfections. If the parties involved in a swap could easily access funds from various markets without having to pay a premium, they would not need to engage in swaps. Using our previous example, a U.S. financial institution could access long-term funds directly from the European market and the European institution could access short-term funds directly from U.S. depositors. However, a lack of information about foreign institutions and convenience encourages individual depositors to place deposits locally. Consequently, swaps are necessary for some financial institutions to obtain the maturities or rate sensitivities on funds that they desire.

15-1b Use of Swaps to Accommodate Financing

Some interest rate swaps are combined with other financial transactions such as the issuance of bonds. Corporate borrowers may be able to borrow at a more attractive interest rate when using floating-rate debt than when using fixed-rate debt. Even so, if they want to make fixed payments on their debt, they can swap fixed-rate payments for floating-rate payments and use the floating-rate payments received to cover their coupon payments. Alternatively, some corporations may prefer to borrow at a floating rate but find it advantageous to borrow at a fixed rate. These corporations can issue fixed-rate bonds and then swap floating-rate payments in exchange for fixed-rate payments.

EXAMPLE

Quality Company is a highly rated firm that prefers to borrow at a variable rate. Risky Company is a low-rated firm that prefers to borrow at a fixed rate. These companies would pay the following rates when issuing either variable-rate or fixed-rate Eurobonds:

	FIXED-RATE BOND	VARIABLE-RATE BOND
Quality Company	9%	LIBOR + ½%
Risky Company	10½%	LIBOR + 1%

LIBOR is the London Interbank Offer Rate, or the interest rate charged on loans between European banks, which varies among currencies. For swaps involving U.S. firms, the LIBOR on U.S. dollars would normally be used.

Based on the information given, Quality Company has an advantage when issuing either fixed-rate or variable-rate bonds, but its advantage is greater when issuing fixed-rate bonds. Quality Company could issue fixed-rate bonds while Risky Company issues variable-rate bonds. Quality could then provide variable-rate payments to Risky in exchange for fixed-rate payments.

Assume that Quality negotiated with Risky to provide variable-rate payments at LIBOR plus ½ percent in exchange for fixed-rate payments of 9½ percent. This interest rate swap is shown in Exhibit 15.2. Quality Company benefits because its fixed-rate payments received on the swap exceed the payments owed to its bondholders by ½ percent. Its variable-rate payments to Risky Company are the same as what it would have paid if it had issued variable-rate bonds. Risky is receiving LIBOR plus ½ percent on the swap, which is ½ percent less than what it must pay on its variable-rate bonds. However, it is making fixed payments of 9½ percent, which is 1 percent less than it would have paid if it had issued fixed-rate bonds. Overall, it saves ½ percent per year on financing costs. ●

Exhibit 15.2 Illustration of an Interest Rate Swap to Reconfigure Bond Payments

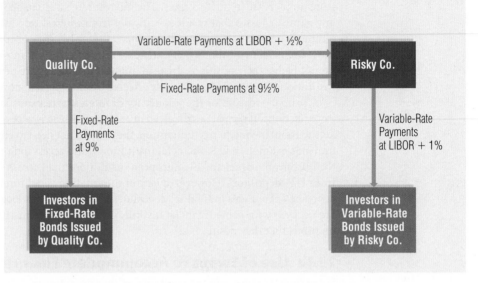

Two limitations of the swaps just described are worth mentioning. First, the process of searching for a suitable swap candidate and negotiating the swap terms entails a cost in time and resources. Second, each swap participant faces the risk that the counterparty could default on payments. For this reason, financial intermediaries may match up participants and sometimes assume the credit (default) risk involved (for a fee).

15-1c Use of Swaps for Speculating

Interest rate swaps are sometimes used by financial institutions and other firms for speculative purposes. For example, a firm may engage in a swap to benefit from its expectations that interest rates will rise even if not all of its operations are exposed to interest rate movements. When the swap is used for speculating rather than for hedging, any loss on the swap positions will not be offset by gains from other operations.

15-1d Participation by Financial Institutions

Financial institutions participate in the swap markets in various ways, as summarized in Exhibit 15.3. Financial institutions such as commercial banks, savings institutions, insurance companies, and pension funds that are exposed to interest rate movements commonly engage in swaps to reduce interest rate risk.

A second way to participate in the swap market is by acting as an intermediary. Some commercial banks and securities firms serve in this capacity by matching up firms and facilitating the swap arrangement. Financial institutions that serve as intermediaries for swaps charge fees for their services. They may even provide credit guarantees (for a fee) to each party in the event that the counterparty does not fulfill its obligation. Under these circumstances, the parties engaged in swap agreements assess the creditworthiness of the intermediary that is backing the swap obligations. For this reason, participants in the swap market prefer intermediaries that have a high credit rating.

A third way to participate is by acting as a dealer in swaps. The financial institution takes the counterparty position in order to serve a client. In such a case, the financial

Exhibit 15.3　Participation of Financial Institutions in Swap Markets

FINANCIAL INSTITUTION	PARTICIPATION IN SWAP MARKETS
Commercial banks	• Engage in swaps to reduce interest rate risk. • Serve as an intermediary by matching up two parties in a swap. • Serve as a dealer by taking the counterparty position to accommodate a party that desires to engage in a swap.
Savings and loan associations and savings banks	• Engage in swaps to reduce interest rate risk.
Finance companies	• Engage in swaps to reduce interest rate risk.
Securities firms	• Serve as an intermediary by matching up two parties in a swap. • Serve as a dealer by taking the counterparty position to accommodate a party that desires to engage in a swap.
Insurance companies	• Engage in swaps to reduce interest rate risk.
Pension funds	• Engage in swaps to reduce interest rate risk.

institution may be exposing itself to interest rate risk unless it has recently taken the opposite position as a counterparty to another swap agreement.

15-2　Types of Swaps

In response to firms' diverse needs, a variety of swaps have been created, including the following:

- Plain vanilla swaps
- Forward swaps
- Callable swaps
- Putable swaps
- Extendable swaps
- Zero-coupon-for-floating swaps
- Rate-capped swaps
- Equity swaps
- Tax advantage swaps.

Most of these swaps can be classified as interest rate swaps because they involve the exchange of interest rate payments. Some types of interest rate swaps are more effective than others at offsetting any unfavorable effects of interest rate movements on the U.S. institution. However, those swaps also offset any favorable effects to a greater degree. Other types of interest rate swaps do not provide as effective a hedge but do allow the institution more flexibility to benefit from favorable interest rate movements.

15-2a　Plain Vanilla Swaps

In a **plain vanilla swap**, sometimes referred to as a fixed-for-floating swap, fixed-rate payments are periodically exchanged for floating-rate payments. The earlier example of the U.S. and European institutions involved this type of swap.

Consider the exchange of payments under different interest rate scenarios in Exhibit 15.4 when using a plain vanilla swap. Although infinite possible interest rate scenarios exist, only two scenarios are considered: (1) a consistent rise in market interest rates and (2) a consistent decline in market interest rates.

Exhibit 15.4   Illustration of a Plain Vanilla (Fixed-for-Floating) Swap

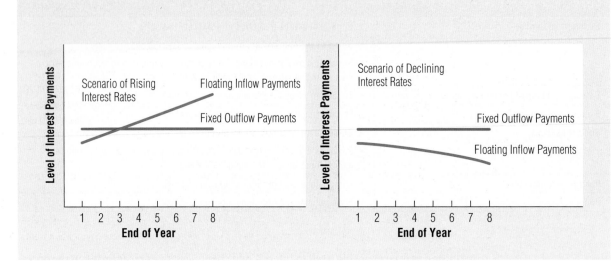

EXAMPLE

The Bank of Orlando has negotiated a plain vanilla swap whereby it will exchange fixed payments of 9 percent for floating payments equal to LIBOR plus 1 percent at the end of each of the next five years. Assume the notional principal is $100 million.

Two scenarios for LIBOR are shown in Exhibit 15.5. The first scenario (in the upper panel of the exhibit) reflects rising U.S. interest rates, which cause LIBOR to increase. The second scenario (in the lower panel) reflects declining U.S. interest rates, which cause LIBOR to decrease. The swap differential derived for each scenario represents the floating interest rate received minus the fixed interest rate paid. The net dollar amount to be transferred as a result of the swap is determined by multiplying the swap differential by the notional principal. ●

Exhibit 15.5   Possible Effects of a Plain Vanilla Swap Agreement (Fixed Rate of 9 Percent in Exchange for Floating Rate of LIBOR + 1 Percent)

	YEAR				
SCENARIO I	1	2	3	4	5
LIBOR	7.0%	7.5%	8.5%	9.5%	10.0%
Floating rate received	8.0%	8.5%	9.5%	10.5%	11.0%
Fixed rate paid	9.0%	9.0%	9.0%	9.0%	9.0%
Swap differential	−1.0%	−0.5%	+0.5%	+1.5%	+2.0%
Net dollar amount received based on notional value of $100 million	−$1,000,000	−$500,000	+$500,000	+$1,500,000	+$2,000,000

	YEAR				
SCENARIO II	1	2	3	4	5
LIBOR	6.5%	6.0%	5.0%	4.5%	4.0%
Floating rate received	7.5%	7.0%	6.0%	5.5%	5.0%
Fixed rate paid	9.0%	9.0%	9.0%	9.0%	9.0%
Swap differential	−1.5%	−2.0%	−3.0%	−3.5%	−4.0%
Net dollar amount received based on notional value of $100 million	−$1,500,000	−$2,000,000	−$3,000,000	−$3,500,000	−$4,000,000

15-2b **Forward Swaps**

A **forward swap** involves an exchange of interest payments that does not begin until a specified future time. It is useful for financial institutions or other firms that expect to be exposed to interest rate risk at some time in the future.

EXAMPLE

Detroit Bank is currently insulated against interest rate risk. Three years from now, it plans to increase its proportion of fixed-rate loans (in response to consumer demand for these loans) and reduce its proportion of floating-rate loans. In order to prevent the adverse effects of rising interest rates after these changes go into effect, Detroit Bank may want to engage in interest rate swaps. It can immediately arrange for a forward swap that will begin three years from now. The forward swap allows Detroit Bank to lock in the terms of the arrangement today even though the swap period is delayed (see Exhibit 15.6).

Although Detroit Bank could have waited before arranging for a swap, it may prefer a forward swap to lock in the terms of the swap arrangement at the prevailing interest rates. If it expects interest rates to be higher three years from now than they are today, and waits until then to negotiate a swap arrangement, the fixed interest rate specified in the arrangement will likely be higher. A forward interest rate swap may allow Detroit Bank to negotiate a fixed rate today that is less than the expected fixed rate on a swap negotiated in the future. Because Detroit Bank will be exchanging fixed-rate payments for floating-rate payments, it wants to minimize the fixed rate used for the swap agreement. ●

The fixed rate negotiated on a forward swap will not necessarily be the same as the fixed rate negotiated on a swap that begins immediately. The pricing conditions on any swap are based on expected interest rates over the swap's lifetime.

Like any interest rate swap, forward swaps involve two parties. Our example of a forward swap involves a U.S. institution that expects interest rates to rise and wants to immediately lock in the fixed rate that it will pay when the swap period begins. The party that takes the opposite position in the forward swap will likely be a firm that will be adversely affected by declining interest rates and expects interest rates to decline. This firm would prefer to lock in the prevailing fixed rate because that rate is expected to be higher than the applicable fixed rate when the swap period begins. This institution will be receiving the fixed interest payments, so it wishes to maximize the fixed rate specified in the swap arrangement.

Exhibit 15.6   Illustration of a Forward Swap

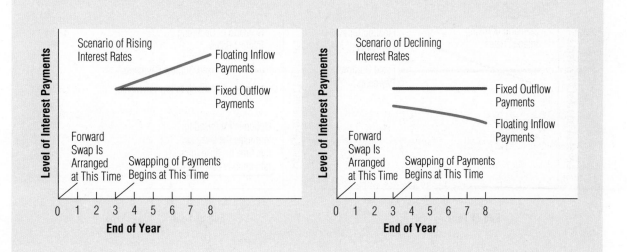

15-2c **Callable Swaps**

Another form of interest rate swaps is **swap options** (or **swaptions**). A **callable swap** gives the party making the fixed payments the right to terminate the swap prior to its maturity. It allows the fixed-rate payer to avoid exchanging future interest payments if it desires.

EXAMPLE Reconsider the U.S. institution that wanted to swap fixed interest payments for floating interest payments to reduce any adverse effects of rising interest rates. If interest rates decline, the interest rate swap arrangement offsets the potential favorable effects on this institution. A callable swap allows the institution to terminate the swap in the event that interest rates decline (see Exhibit 15.7). ●

The disadvantage of a callable swap is that the party given the right to terminate the swap pays a premium that is reflected in a higher fixed interest rate than that party would pay without the call feature. This party may also incur a termination fee in the event that it exercises its right to terminate the swap arrangement.

15-2d **Putable Swaps**

A **putable swap** gives the party making the floating-rate payments the right to terminate the swap. To illustrate, reconsider the European institution that wanted to exchange floating-rate payments for fixed-rate payments to reduce the adverse effects of declining interest rates. If interest rates rise, the interest rate swap arrangement offsets the potential favorable effects on the financial institution. A putable swap allows this institution to terminate the swap in the event that interest rates rise (see Exhibit 15.8). As with callable swaps, the party given the right to terminate the swap pays a premium. For putable swaps, the premium is reflected in a higher floating rate than would be paid without the put feature. The party may also incur a termination fee in the event that it exercises its right to terminate the swap arrangement.

Exhibit 15.7 Illustration of a Callable Swap

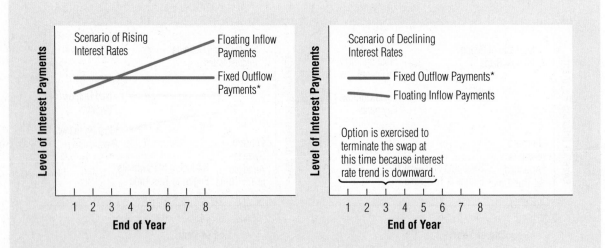

Note that the fixed outflow payments in a callable swap are slightly higher than those in a plain vanilla swap because the payer of the fixed outflow payments incurs the cost for the option to terminate the swap before it matures.

Exhibit 15.8   Illustration of a Putable Swap

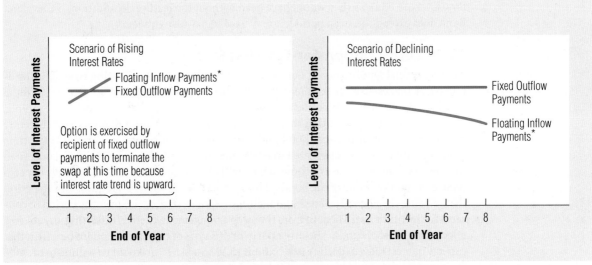

Note that the floating inflow payments in a putable swap are slightly higher than those in a plain vanilla swap because the payer of the floating inflow payments incurs the cost for the option to terminate the swap before it matures.

15-2e Extendable Swaps

An **extendable swap** contains a feature that allows the fixed-for-floating party to extend the swap period.

EXAMPLE

Cleveland Bank negotiates a fixed-for-floating swap for eight years. Assume that interest rates increase over this time period as expected. If Cleveland Bank believes interest rates will continue to rise, it may prefer to extend the swap period (see Exhibit 15.9). Although it could create a new swap, the terms would reflect the current economic conditions. A new swap would typically involve an exchange of fixed payments at the prevailing higher interest rate for floating payments. Cleveland Bank would prefer to extend the previous swap agreement that calls for fixed payments at the lower interest rate that existed at the time the swap was created. It has additional flexibility because of the extendable feature. ●

Exhibit 15.9   Illustration of an Extendable Swap

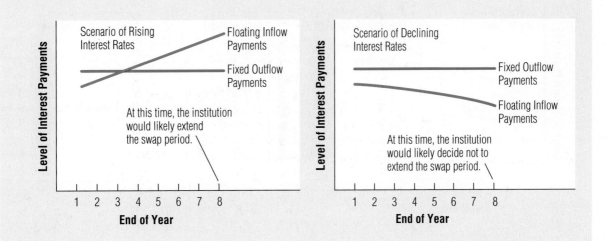

The terms of an extendable swap reflect a price paid for the extendibility feature. That is, the interest rates specified in a swap agreement allowing an extension are not as favorable for Cleveland Bank as they would have been without the feature. In addition, if Cleveland Bank does extend the swap period, it may have to pay an extra fee.

15-2f Zero-Coupon-for-Floating Swaps

Another special type of interest rate swap is the **zero-coupon-for-floating swap**. The fixed-rate payer makes a single payment at the maturity date of the swap agreement, and the floating-rate payer makes periodic payments throughout the swap period. For example, consider a financial institution that primarily attracts short-term deposits and currently has large holdings of zero-coupon bonds that it purchased several years ago. At the time it purchased the bonds, it expected interest rates to decline. Now it has become concerned that interest rates will rise over time, which will not only increase its cost of funds but also reduce the market value of the bonds. This financial institution can request a swap period that matches the maturity of its bond holdings. If interest rates rise over the period of concern, the institution will benefit from the swap arrangement, thereby offsetting any adverse effects on its cost of funds. The other party in this type of transaction might be a firm that expects interest rates to decline (see Exhibit 15.10). Such a firm would be willing to provide floating-rate payments based on this expectation because the payments will decline over time even though the single payment to be received at the end of the swap period is fixed.

15-2g Rate-Capped Swaps

A **rate-capped swap** involves the exchange of fixed-rate payments for floating-rate payments that are capped.

EXAMPLE

Reconsider the example in which the Bank of Orlando arranges to swap fixed payments for floating payments. The counterparty may want to limit its possible payments by setting a cap or ceiling on the interest rate it must pay. The floating-rate payer pays an up-front fee to the fixed-rate payer for this feature.

In this case, the size of the potential floating payments to be received by the Bank of Orlando would now be limited by the cap, which may reduce the effectiveness of the swap in hedging its interest rate

Exhibit 15.10 Illustration of a Zero-Coupon-for-Floating Swap

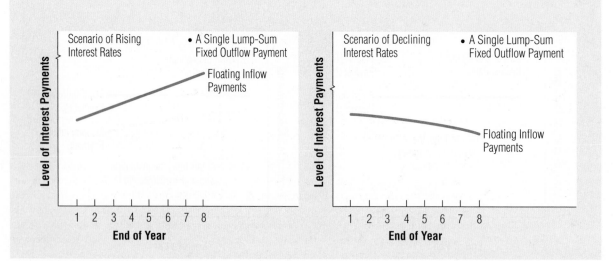

Exhibit 15.11   Illustration of a Rate-Capped Swap

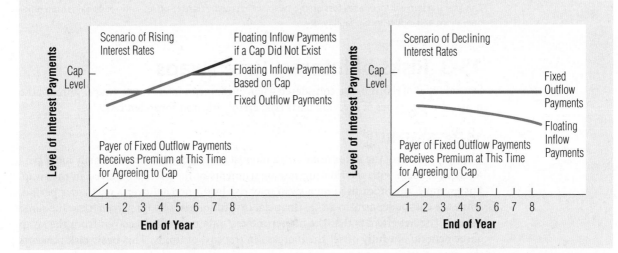

risk. If interest rates rise above the cap, the floating payments received will not move in tandem with the interest that the Bank of Orlando will pay depositors for funds (see Exhibit 15.11). Nevertheless, the Bank of Orlando might believe that interest rates will not exceed a specified level and, therefore, would be willing to allow a cap. Moreover, the Bank of Orlando would receive an up-front fee from the counterparty for allowing this cap. ●

15-2h Equity Swaps

An **equity swap** involves the exchange of interest payments for payments linked to the degree of change in a stock index. For example, using an equity swap arrangement, a company could swap a fixed interest rate of 7 percent in exchange for the rate of appreciation on the S&P 500 index each year over a four-year period. If the stock index appreciates by 9 percent over the year, the differential is 2 percent (9 percent received minus 7 percent paid), which will be multiplied by the notional principal to determine the dollar amount received. If the stock index appreciates by less than 7 percent, the company will have to make a net payment.

An equity swap may be appropriate for portfolio managers of insurance companies or pension funds that are managing stocks and bonds. This type of arrangement would enhance their investment performance in bullish stock market periods without requiring the managers to change their existing allocation of stocks and bonds.

15-2i Tax Advantage Swaps

Some types of swaps involve payments that are not dependent on market interest rates. One example is a tax advantage swap, which firms implement for tax purposes.

EXAMPLE   Columbus, Inc., has expiring tax loss carryforwards from previous years. To utilize the carryforwards before they expire, the firm may engage in a swap that calls for receipt of a large up-front payment with somewhat less favorable terms over time. However, Columbus may realize an immediate gain on the swap with possible losses in future years. The tax loss carryforwards from previous years can be applied to offset any taxes on the immediate gain from the swap. Any future losses realized from future payments due to the swap agreement may be used to offset future gains from other operations.

Meanwhile, Ann Arbor Company expects future losses but will realize large gains from its operations in the current year. It can take a position opposite to that of Columbus. That is, Ann Arbor will arrange for a swap in which it makes an immediate large payment and receives somewhat favorable terms on future payments. This year the firm will incur a tax loss on the swap, which can be used to offset some of its gains from other operations and reduce its tax liability. ●

15-3 Risks of Interest Rate Swaps

Several types of risk must be considered when engaging in interest rate swaps. Three of the more common types of risks are basis risk, credit risk, and sovereign risk.

15-3a Basis Risk

The interest rate of the index used for an interest rate swap will not necessarily move perfectly in tandem with the floating-rate instruments of the parties involved in the swap. For example, the index used on a swap may rise by 0.7 percent over a particular period, while the cost of deposits to a U.S. financial institution rises by 1.0 percent over the same period. The net effect is that the higher interest rate payments received from the swap agreement do not fully offset the increase in the cost of funds. This **basis risk** prevents the interest rate swap from completely eliminating the financial institution's exposure to interest rate risk.

15-3b Credit Risk

One risk when engaging in interest rate swaps is that a firm involved in the swap will not meet its payment obligations. This credit risk is not a deal breaker, however, for the following reasons. As soon as the firm recognizes that it has not received the interest payments it is owed, it will discontinue its payments to the other party. The potential loss is a set of net payments that would have been received (based on the differential in swap rates) over time. In some cases, the financial intermediary that matched up the two parties incurs the credit risk by providing a guarantee for the payments (for a fee). If so, the parties engaged in the swap do not need to be concerned with the credit risk, assuming that the financial intermediary will be able to cover any guarantees promised.

Concerns about a Swap Credit Crisis   The willingness of large banks and securities firms to provide guarantees has increased the popularity of interest rate swaps, but has also raised concerns that widespread adverse effects might occur if any of these intermediaries cannot meet their obligations. If a large bank that has taken numerous swap positions and guaranteed many other swap positions fails, a number of defaults on swap payments could result. These defaults could cause cash flow problems for other swap participants and force them to default on some of their payment obligations on swaps or other financial agreements. In this way, given the global integration of the swap network, defaults by a single large financial intermediary could be transmitted throughout the world. In fact, when American International Group was rescued by the federal government during the credit crisis (as discussed later in this chapter), the potential damage throughout the swap network was cited as a reason for the rescue.

Because of the potential damage that a single shock could cause to ripple throughout the swap network, the Financial Reform Act of 2010 called for numerous changes in the swap markets. In the years since this act was passed, the Commodity Futures Trading Commission and the Securities and Exchange Commission have issued a number of new rules and regulations, which will be discussed later in the chapter in the context of credit default swaps, which played a major role in the credit crisis.

15-3c **Sovereign Risk**

Sovereign risk reflects potential adverse effects resulting from a country's political conditions. Various political conditions could prevent the counterparty from meeting its obligation in the swap agreement. For example, the local government might take over the counterparty and then decide not to meet its payment obligations. Alternatively, the government might impose foreign exchange controls that prohibit the counterparty from making its payments.

Sovereign risk differs from credit risk because it depends on the financial status of the government rather than on the counterparty itself. A counterparty could have very low credit risk but conceivably be perceived as having high sovereign risk because of its home country's government. The counterparty does not have control over some restrictions that may be imposed by its government.

15-4 Pricing Interest Rate Swaps

The setting of specific interest rates for an interest rate swap is referred to as *pricing* the swap. This pricing is influenced by several factors, including prevailing market interest rates, availability of counterparties, and credit and sovereign risk.

15-4a **Prevailing Market Interest Rates**

The fixed interest rate specified in a swap is influenced by supply and demand conditions for funds having the appropriate maturity. For example, a plain vanilla (fixed-for-floating) interest rate swap structured when interest rates are very high would have a much higher fixed interest rate than one structured when interest rates were low. In general, the interest rates specified in a swap agreement reflect the prevailing interest rates at the time of the agreement.

15-4b **Availability of Counterparties**

Swap pricing is also determined by the availability of counterparties. When numerous counterparties are available for a particular desired swap, a party may be able to negotiate a more attractive deal. For example, consider a U.S. financial institution that wants a fixed-for-floating swap. If several European institutions are willing to serve as the counterparty, the U.S. institution may be able to negotiate a slightly lower fixed rate.

The availability of counterparties can change in response to economic conditions. For example, in a period when interest rates are expected to rise, many institutions will want a fixed-for-floating swap, but few institutions will be willing to serve as the counterparty. The fixed rate specified on interest rate swaps will be higher under these conditions than in a period when many financial institutions expect interest rates to decline.

15-4c **Credit and Sovereign Risk**

A party involved in an interest rate swap must assess the probability of default by the counterparty. For example, a firm that desires a fixed-for-floating swap will likely require a lower fixed rate applied to its outflow payments if the credit risk or sovereign risk of the counterparty is high. If a well-respected financial intermediary guarantees payments by the counterparty, however, the fixed rate will be higher.

15-5 Performance of Interest Rate Swaps

Exhibit 15.12 shows how the performance of an interest rate swap is influenced by several underlying forces that affect interest rate movements. The impact of the underlying forces on the performance of an interest rate swap depends on the party's swap position. For example, to the extent that strong economic growth can increase interest rates, that growth will be beneficial for a party that is swapping fixed-rate payments for floating-rate payments but detrimental to a party that is swapping floating-rate payments for fixed-rate payments.

The diagram in Exhibit 15.12 can be adjusted to fit any currency. For an interest rate swap involving an interest rate benchmark denominated in a foreign currency, the economic conditions of that country are the primary forces that determine interest rate movements in that currency and thereby the performance of the interest rate swap.

Because the performance of a particular interest rate swap position is normally influenced by future interest rate movements, participants in the interest rate swap market closely monitor indicators that may affect these movements. Among the more closely watched indicators are indicators of economic growth (employment, gross domestic product), indicators of inflation (consumer price index, producer price index), and indicators of government borrowing (budget deficit, expected volume of funds borrowed at upcoming Treasury bond auctions).

Exhibit 15.12 Framework for Explaining Net Payments Resulting from an Interest Rate Swap

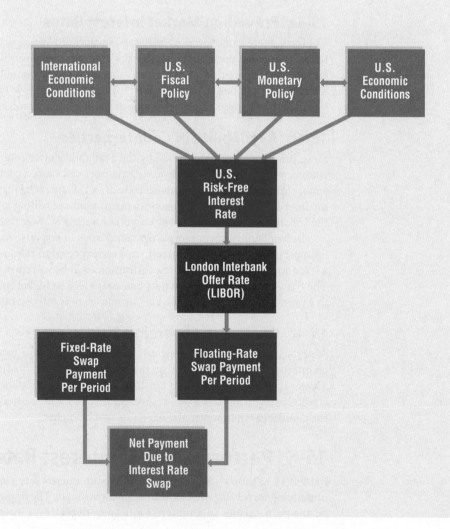

15-6 Interest Rate Caps, Floors, and Collars

In addition to the more traditional forms of interest rate swaps, three other interest rate derivative instruments are commonly used:

■ Interest rate caps
■ Interest rate floors
■ Interest rate collars

These instruments are normally classified separately from interest rate swaps, but they do result in interest payments between participants. Each of these instruments can be used by financial institutions to capitalize on expected interest rate movements or to hedge their interest rate risk.

15-6a Interest Rate Caps

An **interest rate cap** offers payments in periods when a specified interest rate index exceeds a specified ceiling (cap) interest rate. The payments are based on the amount by which the interest rate exceeds the ceiling, multiplied as usual by the notional principal specified in the agreement. The purchaser pays an up-front fee for an interest rate cap, and the lifetime of the cap commonly ranges between three and eight years.

The typical purchaser of an interest rate cap is a financial institution that is adversely affected by rising interest rates. If interest rates rise, the payments received from the interest rate cap agreement will help offset any adverse effects.

The seller of an interest rate cap receives the fee paid by the purchaser and is obligated to provide periodic payments when the prevailing interest rates exceed the ceiling rate specified in the agreement. The typical seller of an interest rate cap is a financial institution that expects interest rates to remain stable or to decline.

Large commercial banks and securities firms serve as dealers for interest rate caps in which they act as the counterparty to the transaction. They also serve as brokers, matching up participants that wish to purchase or sell interest rate caps. They may even guarantee (for a fee) the interest payments that are to be paid to the purchaser of the interest rate cap over time.

EXAMPLE

Assume that Buffalo Savings Bank purchases a five-year cap for a fee of 4 percent of notional principal valued at $60 million (so the fee is $2.4 million) with an interest rate ceiling of 10 percent. The agreement specifies LIBOR as the index used to represent the prevailing market interest rate.

Assume that LIBOR moved over the next five years as shown in Exhibit 15.13. Based on these movements, Buffalo Savings Bank received payments in three of the five years. The amount received by Buffalo in any year is based on the percentage points above the 10 percent ceiling multiplied by the notional principal. For example, in Year 1 the payment is zero because LIBOR was below the ceiling rate. In Year 2, however, LIBOR exceeded the ceiling by 1 percentage point, so Buffalo received a payment of $600,000 (0.01 × $60 million). To the extent that Buffalo's performance is adversely affected by high interest rates, the interest rate cap creates a partial hedge by providing payments to Buffalo that are proportionately related to the interest rate level. The seller of the interest rate cap in this example had the opposite payments of those shown for Buffalo in Exhibit 15.13. ●

Interest rate caps can be devised to meet various risk–return profiles. For example, Buffalo Savings Bank could have purchased an interest rate cap with a ceiling rate of 9 percent that would generate payments whenever interest rates exceeded that ceiling. The bank would have had to pay a higher up-front fee for this interest rate cap, however.

Exhibit 15.13 Illustration of an Interest Rate Cap

		END OF YEAR:				
	0	1	2	3	4	5
LIBOR		6%	11%	13%	12%	7%
Interest rate ceiling		10%	10%	10%	10%	10%
LIBOR's percent above the ceiling		0%	1%	3%	2%	0%
Payments received (based on $60 million of notional principal)		$0	$600,000	$1,800,000	$1,200,000	$0
Fee paid	$2,400,000					

15-6b **Interest Rate Floors**

An **interest rate floor** offers payments in periods when a specified interest rate index falls below a specified floor rate. The payments are based on the amount by which the interest rate falls below the floor rate, which is multiplied by the notional principal specified in the agreement. The purchaser pays an up-front fee for an interest rate floor, and the lifetime of the floor commonly ranges between three and eight years. The interest rate floor can be used to hedge against lower interest rates in the same manner that the interest rate cap hedges against higher interest rates. Any financial institution that purchases an interest rate floor will receive payments if interest rates decline below the floor, and these payments will help offset any adverse interest rate effects.

The seller of an interest rate floor receives the fee paid by the purchaser and is obligated to provide periodic payments when the interest rate on a specified money market instrument falls below the floor rate specified in the agreement. The typical seller of an interest rate floor is a financial institution that expects interest rates to remain stable or to rise. Large commercial banks or securities firms may serve as dealers and/or brokers of interest rate floors, just as they do for interest rate swaps or caps.

EXAMPLE

Assume that Toland Finance Company purchases a five-year interest rate floor for a fee of 4 percent of notional principal valued at $60 million (so the fee is $2.4 million) with an interest rate floor of 8 percent. The agreement specifies LIBOR as the index used to represent the prevailing interest rate.

Assume that LIBOR moved over the next five years as shown in Exhibit 15.14. Based on these movements, Toland received payments in two of the five years. The dollar amount received by Toland in any year is based on the percentage points below the 8 percent floor multiplied by the notional principal. In Year 1, for example, LIBOR was 2 percentage points below the interest rate floor, so Toland received a payment of $1.2 million (0.02 × $60 million). The seller of the interest rate floor in this example had the opposite payments of those shown for Toland in Exhibit 15.14. ●

Exhibit 15.14 Illustration of an Interest Rate Floor

		END OF YEAR:				
	0	1	2	3	4	5
LIBOR		6%	11%	13%	12%	7%
Interest rate floor		8%	8%	8%	8%	8%
LIBOR's percent below the floor		2%	0%	0%	0%	1%
Payments received (based on $60 million of notional principal)		$1,200,000	$0	$0	$0	$600,000
Fee paid	$2,400,000					

15-6c Interest Rate Collars

An **interest rate collar** involves the purchase of an interest rate cap and the simultaneous sale of an interest rate floor. In its simplest form, the up-front fee received from selling the interest rate floor to one party can be used to pay the fee for purchasing the interest rate cap from another party. Any financial institution that desires to hedge against the possibility of rising interest rates can purchase an interest rate collar. The hedge results from the interest rate cap, which will generate payments to the institution if interest rates rise above the interest rate ceiling.

Because the collar also involves the sale of an interest rate floor, the financial institution is obligated to make payments if interest rates decline below the floor. However, if interest rates rise as expected, the rates will remain above the floor and, in turn, the financial institution will not have to make payments.

Assume that Pittsburgh Bank's performance is inversely related to interest rates. It anticipates that interest rates will rise over the next several years and decides to hedge its interest rate risk by purchasing a five-year interest rate collar, with LIBOR as the index used to represent the prevailing interest rate. The interest rate cap specifies a fee of 4 percent of notional principal valued at $60 million (so the fee is $2.4 million) with an interest rate ceiling of 10 percent. The interest rate floor specifies a fee of 4 percent of notional principal valued at $60 million and an interest rate floor of 8 percent.

Assume that LIBOR moved over the next five years as shown in Exhibit 15.15. Based on these movements, the payments received from purchasing the interest rate cap and the payments made from selling the interest rate floor are derived separately over each of the five years.

Because the fee received from selling the interest rate floor was equal to the fee paid for the interest rate cap, the initial fees offset each other. The net payments received by Pittsburgh Bank as a result of purchasing the collar are equal to the payments received from the interest rate cap minus the payments made as a result of the interest rate floor. In the years when interest rates were relatively high, the net payments received by Pittsburgh Bank were positive.

As this example illustrates, when interest rates are high, the collar can generate payments that may offset the adverse effects of the high interest rates on the bank's normal operations. Although the net payments were negative in those years when interest rates were low, the performance of the bank's normal operations should have been strong. Like many other hedging strategies, the interest rate collar reduces the sensitivity of the financial institution's performance to interest rate movements. ●

Exhibit 15.15 Illustration of an Interest Rate Collar (Combined Purchase of an Interest Rate Cap and Sale of an Interest Rate Floor)

		END OF YEAR:				
	0	1	2	3	4	5
Purchase of interest rate cap						
LIBOR		6%	11%	13%	12%	7%
Interest rate ceiling		10%	10%	10%	10%	10%
LIBOR's percent above the ceiling		0%	1%	3%	2%	0%
Payments received		$0	$600,000	$1,800,000	$1,200,000	$0
Fee paid	$2,400,000					
Sale of interest rate floor						
Interest rate floor		8%	8%	8%	8%	8%
LIBOR's percent below the floor		2%	0%	0%	0%	1%
Payments made		$1,200,000	$0	$0	$0	$600,000
Fee received	$2,400,000					
Fee received minus fee paid	$0					
Payments received minus payments made		−$1,200,000	+$600,000	+$1,800,000	+$1,200,000	−$600,000

15-7 Credit Default Swaps

A **credit default swap (CDS)** is a privately negotiated contract that protects investors against the risk of default on particular debt securities. The main participants in the CDS market are commercial banks, insurance companies, hedge funds, and securities firms. The swap involves two parties that have different needs or expectations about the future performance of particular debt securities. The buyer is willing to provide periodic (usually quarterly) payments to the other party, the seller. Thus, the seller receives the payments from the buyer, but is obligated to reimburse the buyer if the securities specified in the swap agreement default. In this case, the seller pays the par value of the securities in exchange for the securities. Alternatively, the securities may be auctioned off by the buyer, in which case the seller must pay the buyer of the CDS the difference between the par value of the securities and the price at which those securities were sold.

The buyer of a CDS is protected if the securities specified in the CDS contract default. Financial institutions purchase CDS contracts to protect their own investments in debt securities against default risk. The seller of a CDS expects that the CDS is unlikely to default. If its expectations come true, it will not have to make a payment and, therefore, benefits from the quarterly payments it receives over the life of the CDS contract.

| EXAMPLE | Last year, Inve Co. purchased bonds (issued by Zykmo Co.) with a par value of $30 million. Since then, Inve has become concerned that the bonds it purchased could default over the next five years. Inve Co. therefore purchases a CDS on these bonds. The CDS refers to Zykmo Co. as the reference entity, because that is the company for which credit protection is purchased. The maximum amount to be paid (notional principal) of this CDS is $30 million. A financial institution is willing to sell the CDS contract for these bonds over the five years for a premium of 2 percent of the value per year, or $0.02 \times \$30$ million = $600,000. Inve Co. will pay $150,000 each quarter to cover the $600,000 premium over one year. If at any time over the next five years Zykmo Co. files for bankruptcy and the bonds become worthless, Inve would not make any additional payments, and the seller of the CDS contract would be obligated to pay Inve Co. $30 million. If, however, the bonds do not default over the next five years (that is, while the CDS contract exists), Inve Co. would make quarterly payments until the bonds reach maturity. In this case, the seller of the CDS contract is not obligated to pay any funds to Inve Co., and it receives $600,000 annually for five years because it was willing to insure the bonds. ● |

This example is simplified in that it focuses on insuring against default of one particular type of bond issued by one firm. When CDS contracts were first created in the 1990s, they were used as a way to protect bond-purchasing investors against default risk. Over time, CDS contracts were adapted to also protect investors that purchased mortgage-backed securities comprising bundles of mortgages.

The maturity of a CDS is typically between 1 and 10 years, but the most common maturity is 5 years. The notional value of the securities represented by a CDS contract is typically between $10 million and $20 million. The CDS contracts are traded over the counter and are not backed by an organized exchange.

15-7a Secondary Market for CDS Contracts

A secondary market for CDS contracts exists in which CDS dealers serve as intermediaries. Some of the major dealers that facilitate secondary market transactions include Goldman Sachs, Citigroup, Bank of America, and Morgan Stanley. The secondary market allows financial institutions participating in a CDS contract to pass on their obligations to other willing parties.

When the securities protected by a CDS contract decline in price because of conditions that increase the likelihood of their default, the seller of the CDS must post a higher level of collateral to back its position. This requirement is intended to ensure that the seller of the CDS does not default on its position.

15-7b Collateral on CDS Contracts

Until recent reforms aimed at increasing transparency, the value of a CDS contract was known only by the dealer serving as intermediary between buyer and seller, and transaction prices were not publicized. Without transparency, dealers might not acknowledge that the market price of a specific CDS contract had changed, especially if their position would force them to post more collateral in response to such a change. Furthermore, if there was not much activity in the secondary market, the valuation of the CDS might be based on the price of the last transaction for that type of CDS that occurred several weeks previously. If the prevailing valuation was inaccurate, the amount of collateral posted might not be sufficient to cover potential losses to a participant. The lack of transparency in CDS pricing caused conflicts regarding the levels of collateral to be held and led to some lawsuits.

15-7c Payments on a Credit Default Swap

Holding maturity and notional value constant, the payments required on a new CDS are positively related to the default risk. For example, a CDS on $10 million of debt securities that have a relatively low likelihood of default may require an annual payment of 1 percent, or $100,000 per year (divided into quarterly payments). A CDS on $10 million of riskier debt securities might require an annual payment of 3 percent, or $300,000 per year. A seller of a CDS requires more compensation to provide protection against default if the likelihood of default is higher.

In periods when economic growth is strong, the payments required on a CDS contract on most securities should be relatively low because the default risk is usually low under these conditions. In contrast, when economic conditions are weak, the payments required on a CDS contract on most securities should be relatively high because the default risk is high.

15-7d How CDS Contracts Affect Debtor–Creditor Negotiations

When a firm encounters financial problems, its creditors attempt to work with the firm to prevent it from going bankrupt. They may be willing to help the debtor firm avoid bankruptcy by accepting a fraction of what they are owed, as they may receive even less if the firm files for bankruptcy. However, if the creditors have purchased a CDS contract, they may benefit more if the debtor firm goes bankrupt because then they will receive payment from the seller of the CDS. Thus, creditors who hold CDS contracts have less incentive to help a debtor firm avoid bankruptcy.

15-7e Impact of the Credit Crisis on the CDS Market

During the housing boom in the 2003–2006 period, many financial institutions accumulated large holdings of mortgage-backed securities (MBS). They were willing to purchase mortgages and MBS because they presumed that households would continue to make their mortgage payments or that home values would remain high enough to provide sufficient collateral to cover the mortgages against defaults. In addition, MBS were presumed to be safe because the rating agencies rated the securities highly even when they contained subprime mortgages.

As the housing market began to weaken in 2006, financial institutions began to purchase CDS contracts as protection against the default of their holdings of MBS. The desire for insurance against the default of these securities contributed to the rapid growth of the CDS market, which represented $2 trillion of notional principal in 2003, $13 trillion in

2006, and $35 trillion in 2009. (To avoid double counting, these values count each contract only once, even though there are two parties involved.) Meanwhile, other financial institutions that believed the MBS were safe served as the counterparties, a position that allowed them to generate periodic income.

Using CDS Contracts to Bet on Mortgage Defaults   Some financial institutions that anticipated a major decline in housing prices purchased CDS contracts on MBS even when they had no exposure to MBS. That is, they were not hedging an existing position, but instead were simply taking a speculative position based on their expectations that many mortgages would default. The cost of their bet was the periodic premium they paid to sellers of the CDS contracts; their potential benefit was the money that they would be owed if the MBS specified by their CDS contracts defaulted before the contract matured.

These speculators realized that not all MBS were the same and that some had a much higher probability of failure. Some speculators targeted MBS that contained subprime mortgages because these mortgages were more likely to default. Speculators could easily find sellers of the CDS contracts they wanted to buy, because many sellers of CDS contracts (wrongly) presumed that any MBS rated highly by the agencies had a low risk of default. In fact, as the housing market collapsed, many MBS defaulted, which generated large profits for the buyers of CDS contracts and major losses for the sellers.

Insufficient Margins on CDS Contracts   During the credit crisis, the sellers of many credit default swaps did not establish a sufficient margin backing the agreement. The debt securities (such as MBS) referenced by these swaps were not standardized, and therefore were not traded on a frequent basis. This low trading activity meant that their market values were outdated and uncertain. Even when the debt securities were likely to default, there was no documented market valuation that could force the seller of the CDS to post a larger margin. By the time the debt securities officially failed, the margin provided by the seller of the CDS covered only a small portion of the payment that the seller owed to the buyer of that swap. Although the underlying debt securities referenced in a CDS were rated by rating agencies, their ratings were not always updated, even when it was obvious that the debt securities were likely to default.

Impact of Lehman Brothers Failure   The securities firm Lehman Brothers was a major participant in the CDS market. When it went bankrupt in September 2008, it did not cover all of its CDS obligations. Thus, many financial institutions that had purchased CDS contracts from Lehman to protect against the default of MBS were not protected once the firm went bankrupt. Because the CDS market was an over-the-counter market at the time, there was little available information about the exposure of financial institutions to CDS contracts. The credit crisis illustrated how protection provided to buyers of a CDS is only as good as the creditworthiness of the CDS seller.

Another lesson of the Lehman Brothers failure was that the U.S. government will not automatically rescue all large financial institutions. Thus, the annual payments necessary to buy new CDS contracts on large financial institutions increased substantially just after the Lehman Brothers failure. Sellers of new CDS contracts required the higher payments because the risk premium on the CDS contracts had increased.

Impact of AIG's Financial Problems   American International Group (AIG), then the world's largest insurance company, frequently sold CDS contracts as a means of generating periodic revenue. By 2008, it was on the sale side of CDS contracts representing approximately $440 billion in debt securities. Many of its CDS contracts obligated AIG to cover risky MBS that represented subprime mortgages. As housing conditions weakened further, rumors circulated that AIG might not be able to cover all the future claims on its

CDS contracts due to defaults. The federal government was concerned that if AIG could not satisfy its obligations, all the financial institutions that had purchased CDS contracts from AIG would lose their protection and might fail. In September 2008, the Federal Reserve injected billions of dollars into AIG because it feared the company's failure would cause major damage to the financial sector. In the following months, the bailout continued. By early 2009, AIG had received $150 billion in government funds.

Problems with CDS Contracts after the Credit Crisis   Even after the credit crisis ended, their positions in CDS contracts resulted in substantial losses for some financial institutions. In 2012, a trader in JPMorgan Chase's London office was investing in credit default swaps as part of the bank's hedging strategy. After suffering losses on his investment, he began to speculate, rather than hedge, and took such large positions selling CDS contracts that counterparties began to refer to him as the "London Whale." Ultimately, his positions resulted in losses of more than $6 billion for JPMorgan Chase, which some of his colleagues tried to hide by assigning false values to his positions in their internal reports. The bank paid nearly $1 billion to U.S. and British regulatory agencies to resolve charges that it lacked sufficient internal controls and misled investors. The "London Whale" case also led to increased calls for reform of the swap markets.

15-7f Reform of CDS Contracts

FINANCIAL REFORM

In the aftermath of the credit crisis, the Financial Reform Act of 2010 mandated substantial reforms of CDS contracts and the swap markets in general. Both the Commodity Futures Trading Commission (CFTC) and the Securities and Exchange Commission (SEC) issued new rules and regulations. The reforms are aimed at increasing the transparency of the swap markets, improving market efficiency, and reducing the systemic risk caused by derivative securities.

First, the rules require all entities that deal in swaps to register as "swap dealers" with the CFTC or the SEC; in addition, firms that are not dealers but take such large positions that they could pose significant risk to counterparties or the U.S. financial system must register as "major swap participants." Swap dealers and major swap participants are subject to increased margin (collateral), record-keeping, and reporting requirements; they must also meet certain minimum capital standards.

Second, the majority of swaps are now traded on electronic platforms known as swap execution facilities, somewhat similar to the electronic trading in the stock and futures markets. As a result of these rules, derivative contracts are becoming more standardized, and their pricing is becoming more transparent.

Third, most swaps are now cleared through a central clearinghouse. Thus, each party in a swap agreement works with a central clearinghouse when settling payments, rather than with the counterparty. This arrangement enhances the safety of the swap market because the centralized clearinghouse can more effectively ensure that any party in a swap agreement continually maintains a sufficient margin to cover future payments to the other party.

Fourth, all swap contracts, whether cleared or uncleared, must be reported to a swap data repository (SDR). The required information includes all of the initial terms of the contract, the buyer and seller, and the notional principal. In addition, if any changes are made in the contract over time, those modifications must be reported to the SDR. One of the problems that arose during the credit crisis was that the authorities lacked information about the full extent of the risk caused by the CDS contracts. The SDRs are intended to enable the CFTC and the SEC to have full information at all times about the swap markets, so that they can take appropriate steps to shore up the financial system if it appears to be at risk. Several SDRs have been established, including one operated by the CME Group and another run by Intercontinental Exchange, which owns the New York Stock Exchange.

Although the new rules reduce the risk associated with the swap markets, participants in the market have voiced concerns that the new reporting, margin, and record-keeping requirements will increase the costs of using swap contracts.

GLOBAL ASPECTS

15-8 Globalization of Swap Markets

The market for interest rate swaps is not restricted to the United States. As mentioned earlier, European financial institutions commonly have the opposite exposure to interest rate risk and, therefore, take swap positions counter to the positions desired by U.S. financial institutions. Manufacturing corporations from various countries that are exposed to interest rate risk also engage in interest rate swaps.

Interest rate swaps are executed in various countries and are denominated in many different currencies. Dollar-denominated interest rate swaps account for approximately half the value of all interest rate swaps outstanding.

Given that swap participants come from various countries, the banks and securities firms that serve as intermediaries have a globalized network of subsidiaries. In this way, they can link participants from various countries. One obvious barrier to the global swap market is the lack of information about participants based in other countries, which means that credit risk concerns may discourage some participants from engaging in swaps. This barrier is reduced when international banks and securities firms that serve as intermediaries are willing to back the payments that are supposed to occur under the provisions of the swap agreement.

Financial institutions from numerous countries also participate in the credit default swap market. Some of them are attempting to protect against the default risk of their investments in bonds issued by governments around the world. Before the credit crisis, some of the most popular CDS contracts were written on bonds issued by the governments of emerging markets such as Brazil, Russia, and Turkey. Because CDS contracts were traded internationally, the credit crisis spread globally as participants began to realize that their counterparties might not be able to fulfill their obligations. Like the United States, the European Union has taken steps to strengthen the regulation of the swap market.

15-8a Currency Swaps

A **currency swap** is an arrangement whereby currencies are exchanged at specified exchange rates and at specified intervals. It is essentially a combination of currency futures contracts, although most futures contracts are not available for periods in the distant future. Currency swaps are commonly used by firms to hedge their exposure to exchange rate fluctuations.

EXAMPLE

Springfield Company is a U.S. firm that expects to receive 2 million British pounds (£) in each of the next four years. Given this inflow of funds, it may want to lock in the exchange rate at which it can sell British pounds over the next four years. A currency swap will specify the exchange rate at which the £2 million can be exchanged in each year. Assume the exchange rate specified by a swap is $1.70 (the spot exchange rate at the time of the swap arrangement), so that Springfield will receive $3.4 million (£2 million × $1.70 per £1.00) in each of the four years. If the firm does not engage in a currency swap, the dollar amount received will depend on the spot exchange rate at the time the pounds are converted to dollars.

The impact of the currency swap is illustrated in Exhibit 15.16. This exhibit also shows the payments that would have been received under two alternative scenarios if the currency swap had not been arranged. Note that the payments received from the swap would have been less favorable than the unhedged strategy if the pound appreciated against the dollar over that period. However, the payments received from the swap would have been more favorable than the unhedged strategy if the pound depreciated against the dollar over that period. The currency swap arrangement reduces the firm's exposure to changes in the pound's value. ●

Exhibit 15.16 Impact of Currency Swaps

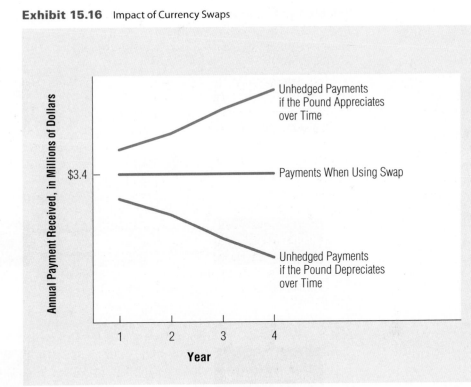

The large commercial banks that serve as financial intermediaries sometimes take positions in currency swaps. That is, they may agree to swap currencies with a firm rather than simply search for a suitable swap candidate.

Like interest rate swaps, currency swaps are available in several variations. Some currency swap arrangements allow one of the parties to have an option to terminate the contract. That party incurs a premium for the option, which is either charged upfront or reflected in the exchange rates specified in the swap arrangement.

Using Currency Swaps to Hedge Bond Payments   Although currency swaps are commonly used to hedge payments on international trade, they may also be used in conjunction with bond issues to hedge foreign cash flows.

EXAMPLE

Philly Company, a U.S. firm, wants to issue a bond denominated in euros (the currency now used in several European countries) because it could make payments with euro inflows to be generated from ongoing operations. Philly, however, is not well known to investors that would consider purchasing euro-denominated bonds. Another firm, Windy Company, wants to issue dollar-denominated bonds because its inflow payments are mostly in dollars, but Windy is not well known to the investors who would purchase these bonds. If Philly is known in the dollar-denominated market and Windy is known in the euro-denominated market, the following transactions are appropriate: Philly can issue dollar-denominated bonds while Windy issues euro-denominated bonds. Philly can exchange euros for dollars to make its bond payments, and Windy will receive euros in exchange for dollars to make its bond payments. This currency swap is illustrated in Exhibit 15.17. ●

Exhibit 15.17   Illustration of a Currency Swap

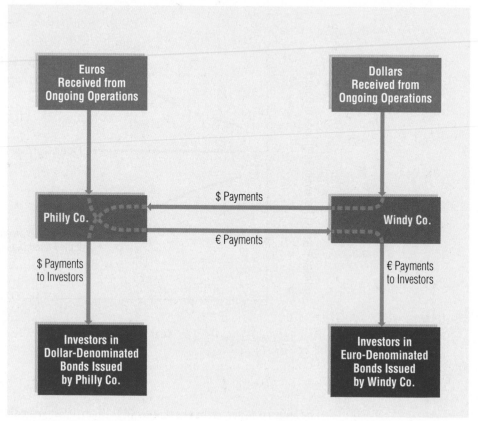

Risk of Currency Swaps   The same types of risk that apply to interest rate swaps may also apply to currency swaps. First, basis risk may arise if the firm cannot obtain a currency swap on the currency to which it is exposed and instead uses a related currency. For example, consider a U.S. firm with cash inflows in British pounds that cannot find a counterparty to enact a swap in pounds. The firm may enact a swap in euros because movements (against the dollar) in the euro and the pound are highly correlated. Specifically, the firm will enact a currency swap to exchange euros for dollars. As it receives pounds, it will convert them to euros and then exchange the euros for dollars as specified by the swap arrangement. The exchange rate between pounds and euros is not constant, however; so basis risk exists.

Currency swaps can also be subject to credit risk, which reflects the possibility that the counterparty may default on its obligation. However, the potential loss in such a case is somewhat limited because one party can stop exchanging its currency if it no longer receives currency from the counterparty.

A third type of risk is sovereign risk, which reflects the possibility that a country may restrict the convertibility of a particular currency. In this case, a party involved in a swap arrangement may not be able to fulfill its obligation because its government prohibits local currency from being converted to another currency. This scenario is less likely in countries that encourage free trade of goods and securities across borders.

Summary

- An interest rate swap allows one party to exchange one set of interest payments for another. Swaps are used for hedging and for speculating.

- In response to firms' needs, various types of swaps have been created, most of which are used to reduce interest rate risk. Some of the more popular types of interest rate swaps are plain vanilla swaps, forward swaps, callable swaps, putable swaps, extendable swaps, rate-capped swaps, and equity swaps. Each type of swap accommodates a particular need of financial institutions or other firms that are exposed to interest rate risk.

- When engaging in interest rate swaps, the participants can be exposed to basis risk, credit risk, and sovereign risk. Basis risk prevents the interest rate swap from completely eliminating the swap user's exposure to interest rate risk. Credit risk reflects the possibility that the counterparty on a swap agreement may not meet its payment obligations. Sovereign risk reflects the possibility that political conditions could prevent the counterparty in a swap agreement from meeting its payment obligations.

- The pricing of interest rate swaps is influenced by the prevailing market interest rates, the availability of counterparties, and the degree of credit and sovereign risk involved.

- The performance of an interest rate swap is influenced by several forces that affect interest rate movements, including economic growth, inflation, and fiscal and monetary policy.

- In addition to the traditional forms of interest rate swaps, three other interest rate derivative instruments are commonly used to hedge interest rate risk: interest rate caps, interest rate floors, and interest rate collars. Interest rate caps offer payments when a specified interest rate index exceeds the interest rate ceiling (cap) and, therefore, can hedge against rising interest rates. Interest rate floors offer payments when a specified interest rate index falls below a specified interest rate floor; they can be used to hedge against declining interest rates. An interest rate collar involves the purchase of an interest rate cap and the simultaneous sale of an interest rate floor; it is used to hedge against rising interest rates.

- Credit default swaps are commonly purchased by financial institutions to protect against default on specific debt securities that they previously purchased. These swaps are sold by financial institutions that are willing to insure against the securities' default. Some financial institutions with major positions in CDS contracts experienced financial problems during the credit crisis of 2008 and were unable to cover their obligations. The credit crisis was intensified by the uncertainty surrounding potential losses of financial institutions that had positions in credit default swaps.

- The interest rate swap market has become globalized in the sense that financial institutions from various countries participate. Interest rate swaps are available in a variety of currencies.

Point/Counterpoint

Should Financial Institutions Engage in Interest Rate Swaps for Speculative Purposes?

Point Yes. They have expertise in forecasting future interest rate movements and can generate gains for their shareholders by taking speculative positions.

Counterpoint No. They should use their main business to generate gains for their shareholders. They should serve as intermediaries for swap transactions only to generate transaction fees or should take a position only to hedge their exposure to interest rate risk.

Who Is Correct? Use the Internet to learn more about this issue and then formulate your own opinion.

Questions and Applications

1. **Hedging with Interest Rate Swaps** Bowling Green Savings & Loan uses short-term deposits to fund fixed-rate mortgages. Explain how Bowling Green can use interest rate swaps to hedge its interest rate risk.

2. **Decision to Hedge with Interest Rate Swaps** Explain the types of cash flow characteristics that would cause a firm to hedge interest rate risk by swapping floating-rate payments for fixed payments. Why would some firms avoid the use of interest rate swaps even when they are highly exposed to interest rate risk?

3.   Role of Securities Firms in Swap Market Describe the possible roles of securities firms in the swap market.

4.   Hedging with Swaps Chelsea Finance Company receives floating inflow payments from its provision of floating-rate loans. Its outflow payments are fixed because of its recent issuance of long-term bonds. Chelsea is concerned that interest rates will decline in the future. Yet it does not want to hedge its interest rate risk because it believes interest rates may increase. Recommend a solution to Chelsea's dilemma.

5.   Basis Risk Comiskey Savings provides fixed-rate mortgages of various maturities, depending on what customers want. It obtains most of its funds from issuing certificates of deposit with maturities ranging from one month to five years. Comiskey has decided to engage in a fixed-for-floating swap to hedge its interest rate risk. Is Comiskey exposed to basis risk?

6.   Fixed-for-Floating Swaps Shea Savings negotiates a fixed-for-floating swap with a reputable firm in South America that has an exceptional credit rating. Shea is very confident that there will not be a default on inflow payments because of the very low credit risk of the South American firm. Do you agree? Explain.

7.   Fixed-for-Floating Swaps North Pier Company entered into a two-year swap agreement, which would provide fixed-rate payments for floating-rate payments. Over the next two years, interest rates declined. Based on these conditions, did North Pier Company benefit from the swap?

8.   Equity Swap Explain how an equity swap could allow Marathon Insurance Company to capitalize on expectations of a strong stock market performance over the next year without altering its existing portfolio mix of stocks and bonds.

9.   Swap Network Explain how the failure of a large commercial bank could cause a worldwide swap credit crisis.

10.   Currency Swaps Markus Company purchases supplies from France once a year. Would Markus be favorably affected if it establishes a currency swap arrangement and the dollar strengthens? What if it establishes a currency swap arrangement and the dollar weakens?

11.   Basis Risk Explain basis risk as it relates to a currency swap.

12.   Sovereign Risk Give an example of how sovereign risk is related to currency swaps.

13.   Use of Interest Rate Swaps Explain why some companies that issue bonds engage in interest rate swaps in financial markets. Why do they not simply issue bonds that require the type of payments (fixed or variable) that they prefer to make?

14.   Use of Currency Swaps Explain why some companies that issue bonds engage in currency swaps. Why do they not simply issue bonds in the currency that they would prefer to use for making payments?

Advanced Questions

15.   Rate-Capped Swaps Bull and Finch Company wants a fixed-for-floating swap. It expects interest rates to rise far above the fixed rate that it would pay and to remain very high until the swap maturity date. Should it consider negotiating for a rate-capped swap with the cap set at 2 percentage points above the fixed rate? Explain.

16.   Forward Swaps Rider Company negotiates a forward swap, to begin two years from now, in which it will swap fixed payments for floating-rate payments. What will be the effect on Rider if interest rates rise substantially over the next two years? That is, would Rider be better off using this forward swap than if it had simply waited two years before negotiating the swap? Explain.

17.   Swap Options Explain the advantage of a swap option to a financial institution that wants to swap fixed payments for floating payments.

18.   Callable Swaps Back Bay Insurance Company negotiated a callable swap involving fixed payments in exchange for floating payments. Assume that interest rates decline consistently up until the swap maturity date. Do you think Back Bay might terminate the swap prior to maturity? Explain.

19.   Credit Default Swaps Credit default swaps were once viewed as a great innovation that could make mortgage markets more stable. However, these swaps have been criticized for making the credit crisis worse. Why?

20.   Credit Default Swap Prices Explain why the failure of Lehman Brothers caused prices on credit default swap contracts to increase.

21. Reform of CDS Contracts Explain how the Financial Reform Act of 2010 and the rules issued to implement it attempted to reduce the risk in the financial system resulting from the use of credit default swaps.

Critical Thinking Question

Credit Default Swaps and the Credit Crisis

A critic recently stated that the creation of credit default swaps caused the credit crisis in the 2008–2009 period. Write a short essay that supports or refutes this statement.

Interpreting Financial News

Interpret the following comments made by Wall Street analysts and portfolio managers.

a. "The swaps market is another Wall Street–developed house of cards."

b. "As a dealer in interest rate swaps, our bank takes various steps to limit our exposure."

c. "The regulation of commercial banks, securities firms, and other financial institutions that participate in the swaps market could create a regulatory war."

Managing in Financial Markets

Assessing the Effects of an Interest Rate Collar

As a manager of a commercial bank, you just purchased a three-year interest rate collar with LIBOR as the interest rate index. The interest rate cap specifies a fee of 2 percent of notional principal (valued at $100 million) and an interest rate ceiling of 9 percent. The interest rate floor specifies a fee of 3 percent of the $100 million notional principal and an interest rate floor of 7 percent. Assume that LIBOR is expected to be 6 percent, 10 percent, and 11 percent (respectively) at the end of each of the next three years.

a. Determine the net fees paid, as well as the expected net payments to be received as a result of purchasing the interest rate collar.

b. Assuming you are very confident that interest rates will rise, should you consider purchasing a callable swap instead of the collar? Explain.

c. Explain the conditions under which your purchase of an interest rate collar could backfire.

Problems

1. Vanilla Swaps Cleveland Insurance Company has just negotiated a three-year plain vanilla swap in which it will exchange fixed payments of 8 percent for floating payments of LIBOR plus 1 percent. The notional principal is $50 million. LIBOR is expected to be 7 percent, 9 percent, and 10 percent (respectively) at the end of each of the next three years.

a. Determine the net dollar amount to be received (or paid) by Cleveland each year.

b. Determine the dollar amount to be received (or paid) by the counterparty on this interest rate swap each year based on the assumed forecasts of LIBOR.

2. Interest Rate Caps Northbrook Bank purchases a four-year cap for a fee of 3 percent of notional principal valued at $100 million, with an interest rate ceiling of 9 percent and LIBOR as the index representing the market interest rate. Assume that LIBOR is expected to be 8 percent, 10 percent, 12 percent, and 13 percent (respectively) at the end of each of the next four years.

a. Determine the initial fee paid, as well as the expected payments to be received by Northbrook if LIBOR moves as forecasted.

b. Determine the dollar amount to be received (or paid) by the seller of the interest rate cap based on the assumed forecasts of LIBOR.

3. Interest Rate Floors Iowa City Bank purchases a three-year interest rate floor for a fee of 2 percent of notional principal valued at $80 million, with an interest rate floor of 6 percent and LIBOR representing the interest rate index. The bank expects LIBOR to be 6 percent, 5 percent, and 4 percent (respectively) at the end of each of the next three years.

a. Determine the initial fee paid, as well as the expected payments to be received by Iowa City if LIBOR moves as forecasted.

b. Determine the dollar amounts to be received (or paid) by the seller of the interest rate floor based on the assumed forecasts of LIBOR.

Flow of Funds Exercise

Hedging with Interest Rate Derivatives

Recall that if the economy continues to be strong, Carson Company may need to increase its production capacity by approximately 50 percent over the next few years to satisfy demand. It would need financing to expand and accommodate the increase in production. Recall that the yield curve is currently upward sloping, and that Carson is concerned about a possible slowing of the economy because of potential Fed actions to reduce inflation. Carson currently relies mostly on commercial loans with floating interest rates for its debt financing. It has contacted Blazo Bank about the use of interest rate derivatives to hedge the risk.

a. How could Carson use interest rate swaps to reduce the exposure of its cost of debt to interest rate movements?

b. What is a possible disadvantage of Carson using the interest rate swap hedge as opposed to no hedge?

c. How could Carson use an interest rate cap to reduce the exposure of its cost of debt to interest rate movements?

d. What is a possible disadvantage of Carson using the interest cap hedge as opposed to no hedge? Explain the trade-off between using an interest rate swap versus an interest rate cap.

Internet/Excel Exercises

1. Go to www.economagic.com/fedbog.htm and review the recent annualized rate for a short-term security (such as the 1-year Treasury rate) versus a long-term security (such as the 10-year Treasury rate). Based on this information, do you think that the market expects interest rates to rise over time? Explain.

2. Assume that you need long-term funds and can borrow at the short-term Treasury rate. Based on the existing interest rates, would you consider engaging in a swap of a floating rate in exchange for a fixed rate? Explain.

WSJ Exercise

Impact of Interest Rates on a Swap Arrangement

Use a recent issue of *The Wall Street Journal* to determine how short-term interest rates have changed over the last year (assess the Treasury yield for a three-month maturity based on the yield curve shown for today versus the yield curve shown for a year ago). The three-month Treasury bill rate at the present time and one year ago are quoted in the Money & Investing section of the *Journal.* Explain whether the interest rate movement would have had a favorable impact on a firm that initiated a fixed-for-floating swap agreement one year ago.

Online Articles with Real-World Examples

Find a recent practical article available online that describes a real-world example regarding a specific financial institution or financial market that reinforces one or more concepts covered in this chapter.

If your class has an online component, your professor may ask you to post your summary of the article there and provide a link to the article so that other students can access it. If your class is live, your professor may ask you to summarize your application of the article in class. Your professor may assign specific students to complete this assignment or may allow any students to do the assignment on a volunteer basis.

For recent online articles and real-world examples related to this chapter, consider using the following search terms (be sure to include the prevailing year as a search term to ensure that the online articles are recent):

1. interest rate swap AND hedge
2. interest rate swap AND losses
3. interest rate swap AND financial institutions
4. interest rate swap AND pricing
5. interest rate swap AND risk
6. credit default swap AND losses
7. credit default swap AND crisis
8. credit default swap AND risk
9. credit default swap AND failure
10. credit default swap AND hedge

16

Foreign Exchange Derivative Markets

CHAPTER OBJECTIVES

The specific objectives of this chapter are to:

■ Provide a background on foreign exchange markets.

■ Explain how various factors affect exchange rates.

■ Explain how to forecast exchange rates.

■ Describe the use of foreign exchange rate derivatives.

■ Explain international arbitrage.

In recent years, various derivative instruments have been created to manage or capitalize on exchange rate movements. These **foreign exchange derivatives** (or "forex" derivatives) include forward contracts, currency futures contracts, currency swaps, and currency options. Foreign exchange derivatives account for approximately half of the daily foreign exchange transaction volume.

The potential benefits from using foreign exchange derivatives depend on the expected exchange rate movements. Given this relationship, it is necessary to understand why exchange rates change over time before exploring the use of foreign exchange derivatives.

16-1 Foreign Exchange Markets and Systems

Foreign exchange markets facilitate international trade and international investment transactions. They enable firms, government agencies, and individuals to sell their currencies in exchange for the currencies they need to execute their international transactions, either immediately (in the spot market) or at a specified future date (in the forward market).

16-1a Spot Market

The spot market facilitates foreign exchange transactions for immediate exchange. It is served by a telecommunications network of foreign exchange intermediaries (typically large commercial banks) that are willing to exchange currencies with the firms, government agencies, and individuals who engage in international transactions. These commercial banks quote a **spot rate** for each currency, representing the exchange rate at which they are willing to sell that specific currency. At any given time, the price at which banks will buy a currency (bid price) is slightly lower than the price at which they will sell it (ask price).

Like the markets for other commodities and securities, the market for foreign currencies is more efficient because of financial intermediaries (commercial banks). Otherwise, individual buyers and sellers of currency would be unable to identify the necessary counterparties to accommodate their needs. Most transactions in the spot market are completed electronically.

EXAMPLE

Raleigh Co. wants to invest in German securities that have a value of 1 million euros (€). It contacts its bank, which quotes a spot rate of €1.00 = $1.17. Raleigh instructs its bank to convert dollars from its bank account into €1,000,000, and send the payment to a German investment company. At the spot rate of $1.17 per euro, Raleigh converts $1,170,000 into €1,000,000 (computed as €1,000,000 × $1.17 = $1,170,000). The bank reduces Raleigh's account balance by $1,170,000, and electronically transmits €1,000,000 to the bank account of the investment company based in Germany. ●

Exchange Rate Quotations   Exchange rate quotations may be either direct or indirect. The **direct exchange rate** specifies the value of a currency in U.S. dollars. For example, the Mexican peso may have a value such as $0.07 while the British pound is valued at $1.25. The **indirect exchange rate** specifies the number of units of a currency equal to a U.S. dollar. It is the reciprocal of the direct exchange rate. Thus, for the direct exchange rate values given here, the indirect exchange rates are about 14.3 Mexican pesos per dollar and 0.80 British pound per dollar. Both direct and indirect exchange rates for most world currencies are available on some financial websites.

Cross-Exchange Rates   Most exchange rate quotation tables express currencies relative to the dollar. In some instances, however, the exchange rate between two nondollar currencies is needed.

EXAMPLE

Suppose that a U.S. firm needs Mexican pesos to buy Mexican goods, but it has just received a large payment in Canadian dollars and wishes to use those funds to pay for the Mexican goods. Thus, it is concerned about the value of the Mexican peso relative to the Canadian dollar. Such a *cross-exchange rate* reflects the amount of one foreign currency per unit of another foreign currency. Cross-exchange rates can be easily determined with the use of foreign exchange quotations. The general formula follows:

$$\frac{\text{Value of 1 unit of Currency A}}{\text{in units of Currency B}} = \frac{\text{Value of Currency A in \$}}{\text{Value of Currency B in \$}}$$

If the peso is worth $0.07 and the Canadian dollar (C$) is worth $0.70, the value of the peso in Canadian dollars is calculated as follows:

$$\text{Value of peso in C\$} = \frac{\text{Value of peso in \$}}{\text{Value of C\$ in \$}} = \frac{\$0.07}{\$0.70} = 0.10$$

Thus, a Mexican peso is worth C$0.10. The exchange rate can also be expressed as the number of pesos equal to one Canadian dollar. This figure can be computed by taking the reciprocal, 0.70/0.07 = 10, which indicates that a Canadian dollar is worth 10 pesos according to the information provided. ●

Cross-exchange rates for most currencies can also be found on some financial websites.

16-1b Forward Market

Instead of exchanging currencies immediately in the spot market, firms, government agencies, or individuals may want to lock in the exchange rate for a transaction to be conducted in the future. They can do this by negotiating a **forward contract** with a commercial bank that allows the purchase or sale of a specified amount of a particular foreign currency at a specified exchange rate on a specified future date. The exchange rate at which one currency can be exchanged for another at a specified future point in time is known as the **forward rate**. The **forward market** facilitates the trading of forward contracts via a telecommunications network. Many of the commercial banks that offer foreign exchange transactions in the spot market also offer forward contracts for widely traded currencies. Forward contracts are discussed in more detail later in the chapter.

16-1c Institutional Use of Foreign Exchange Markets

Exhibit 16.1 summarizes how financial institutions utilize the foreign exchange markets and foreign exchange derivatives. Large commercial banks commonly provide international loans to businesses in foreign countries. In addition, many mutual funds, pension funds, and insurance companies invest in foreign securities. As financial institutions

Exhibit 16.1   Institutional Use of Foreign Exchange Markets

TYPE OF FINANCIAL INSTITUTION	USES OF FOREIGN EXCHANGE MARKETS
Commercial banks	• Serve as financial intermediaries in the foreign exchange market by buying or selling currencies to accommodate customers. • Speculate on foreign currency movements by taking long positions in some currencies and short positions in others. • Provide forward contracts to customers. • Some commercial banks offer currency options to customers; unlike the standardized currency options traded on an exchange, these options can be tailored to a customer's specific needs.
International mutual funds	• Use foreign exchange markets to exchange currencies when reconstructing their portfolios. • Use foreign exchange derivatives to hedge a portion of their exposure.
Brokerage firms and securities firms	• Some brokerage firms and securities firms engage in foreign security transactions for their customers or for their own accounts.
Insurance companies	• Use foreign exchange markets when exchanging currencies for their international operations. • Use foreign exchange markets when purchasing foreign securities for their investment portfolios or when selling foreign securities. • Use foreign exchange derivatives to hedge a portion of their exposure.
Pension funds	• Require foreign exchange of currencies when investing in foreign securities for their stock or bond portfolios. • Use foreign exchange derivatives to hedge a portion of their exposure.

increase their participation in international transactions, they rely more heavily on foreign exchange markets to exchange currencies and on foreign exchange derivatives to hedge their investments in foreign securities.

16-1d Types of Exchange Rate Systems

From 1944 to 1971, the exchange rate at which one currency could be exchanged for another was maintained by governments within 1 percent of a specified rate. This period was known as the **Bretton Woods era** because the agreement establishing the system was negotiated at the Bretton Woods Conference in Bretton Woods, New Hampshire. The manner by which governments were able to control exchange rates is discussed later in the chapter.

By 1971, the U.S. dollar was clearly overvalued. That is, its value was maintained only by central bank intervention. In 1971, an agreement among all major countries (known as the **Smithsonian Agreement**) allowed for devaluation of the dollar. In addition, the Smithsonian Agreement called for a widening of the boundaries from 1 to $2\frac{1}{4}$ percent around each currency's set value. Governments intervened in the foreign exchange markets whenever exchange rates threatened to wander outside these boundaries.

In 1973, the boundaries were eliminated. Since then, the exchange rates of major currencies have been floating without any government-imposed boundaries. A government may still intervene in the foreign exchange markets to influence the market value of its currency, however. A system with no boundaries and in which exchange rates are market determined but still subject to government intervention is called a **dirty float**. By contrast, in a **freely floating system**, the foreign exchange market is totally free from government intervention. Most countries allow their local currency to float but periodically intervene in the foreign exchange market to influence the value of that currency, as will be explained shortly.

Pegged Exchange Rate System   Some countries today use a pegged exchange rate system. For example, Hong Kong has tied the value of its currency (the Hong Kong dollar) to the U.S. dollar since 1983. Thus, its currency's value is fixed relative to the U.S. dollar, which means that its value moves in tandem with the U.S. dollar against other currencies, including other Asian currencies. Technically, its value can change slightly, but its value is restricted to a range within very narrow boundaries, from HK7.75 to HK7.85 per U.S. dollar (so HK1 is restricted to the range from $0.127 to $0.129). Because the Hong Kong dollar is fixed against the U.S. dollar, any currency that appreciates against the U.S. dollar will appreciate against the Hong Kong dollar by roughly the same percentage.

A country that pegs its currency cannot control its local interest rate because its interest rate must be aligned with the interest rate of the currency to which its currency is tied.

EXAMPLE

If Hong Kong lowered its interest rates in an effort to stimulate the local economy, investors based in Hong Kong would then be enticed to exchange Hong Kong dollars for U.S. dollars and invest in the United States, where interest rates are higher. Because the Hong Kong dollar is tied to the U.S. dollar, the investors would be able to change their investment proceeds back to Hong Kong dollars at the end of the investment period without any concern for exchange rate risk.

Therefore, Hong Kong maintains its local interest rate to be equal to the U.S. interest rate plus a slight premium for risk. As the U.S. interest rate changes, Hong Kong's interest rate changes by approximately the same degree and in the same direction. ●

China's currency (the yuan) was pegged to the U.S. dollar until 2005. Many U.S. politicians argued that China was maintaining its currency at a level that was too low, which led to an annual U.S. balance of trade deficit of approximately $200 billion with China. In July 2005, China implemented a new system that allowed the yuan to float within narrow boundaries based on a set of major currencies. This move had only a limited effect on the relative pricing of Chinese and U.S. products, however, and the balance of trade deficit between the two countries remains large.

16-1e **Eurozone Arrangement**

In January 1999, the euro replaced the national currencies of 11 European countries; since then, 8 more countries have converted their home currency to the euro. The 19 countries that now use the euro as their home currency make up the eurozone: Austria, Belgium, Cyprus, Estonia, Finland, France, Germany, Greece, Ireland, Italy, Latvia, Lithuania, Luxembourg, Malta, the Netherlands, Portugal, Slovakia, Slovenia, and Spain. Because all of these countries use the same currency, transactions between them do not require any exchange of currencies. Together, the participating countries produce more than 20 percent of the world's gross domestic product, which exceeds the total production of the United States. Nine European countries are members of the European Union (EU) but do not participate in the euro: Bulgaria, Croatia, Czech Republic, Denmark, Hungary, Poland, Romania, Sweden, and the United Kingdom, although the United Kingdom is negotiating to exit the EU in the near future. These countries continue to use their own home currency.

The countries in Eastern Europe that are members of the EU are eligible to participate in the euro if they meet specific economic goals, including a maximum limit on their budget deficit. Some of these countries peg their currency's value to the euro, so their currency moves in tandem with the euro against other currencies. Under this arrangement, they still have the flexibility to adjust their exchange rate system and can assess how their economy might be affected if they adopted the euro.

Eurozone Monetary Policy   The European Central Bank (ECB) is responsible for setting monetary policy for all countries in the eurozone. The bank's objective is to maintain price stability (control inflation) in these countries, as it believes that price stability is necessary to achieve economic growth. Because the interest rate on the euro is influenced by the eurozone monetary policy, all participating countries have the same risk-free interest rate. Thus, the eurozone monetary policy simultaneously affects the interest rate in all countries that have adopted the euro as their currency. Although a single monetary policy may allow for more consistent economic conditions across countries, it prevents any individual country from solving local economic problems via its own, unique monetary policy. However, the member countries can still apply their own fiscal policies (that is, decisions on taxing and government expenditures).

Eurozone Crisis   During the 2010–2015 period, Greece suffered from a weak economy and a large government budget deficit. Debt rating agencies lowered the country's debt rating substantially, which increased the government's cost of borrowing funds. Portugal and Spain also experienced severe financial problems, and the economies of Italy and Ireland weakened as well. Just as integration among economies within the eurozone can allow one country's stimulus to benefit others, so a given country's weakness can adversely affect others. During the eurozone crisis, institutional investors moved their investments out of the eurozone and into other regions, which placed downward pressure on the euro's exchange rate.

Abandoning the Euro   When a government in the eurozone is unable to obtain sufficient credit to cover its budget deficit, it may need to rely on the ECB for funds. However, when the ECB provides credit to a country, as it did for Greece, it imposes austerity conditions that are intended to help the government resolve its budget deficit problems over time. These conditions may include a reduction in government spending and higher tax rates on citizens. Although these conditions may be necessary to correct the budget deficit, they may further weaken the country's economy.

Some critics have argued that a country's government should abandon the euro rather than accept funding from the ECB, because the austerity conditions imposed by this institution are too harsh. If a country had its own currency, it might be able to devalue the currency to a degree that would increase demand for the country's exports, thereby stimulating its economy. However, a weak home currency is not a perfect cure for a country with debt problems, because it can cause higher inflation. In addition, to repay its debt, the country would have to use the new weak home currency, so larger payments would be required to cover the existing debt.

If a country abandons the euro, it may cause fear that other countries would follow, which could cause the euro's value to collapse. Consequently, multinational corporations (MNCs) and institutional investors may be unwilling to invest funds in the eurozone and might even decide to sell their assets in the eurozone so that they could move their money before the euro weakens.

16-1f **Cryptocurrencies**

Cryptocurrencies are digital or virtual currencies that use encryption techniques to verify fund transfers; they are emerging as a viable means of conducting international transactions. Cryptocurrencies are created and operate independently of national governments, so until recently they have been outside the jurisdiction of central banks and the financial regulations issued by governments. As a result of this independence and the relative anonymity of cryptocurrency transactions, cryptocurrencies have sometimes been used for illegal activities, such as money laundering and tax evasion. Recently, however, some governments have implemented regulations intended to prevent these less desirable uses of cryptocurrencies while still allowing their use for legitimate payments. In contrast, a few countries have banned their use altogether.

Although several cryptocurrencies exist, bitcoins are the most widely used. Bitcoin was established in 2009 as a peer-to-peer payment network that is owned and controlled by its users. Its innovative payment system is known as blockchain technology. When a transaction is conducted in bitcoins, each step in the transaction is recorded in a "public ledger" created by the community of bitcoin users. The ledger forms a long chain of verified transactions in chronological order called "blocks." A validated block cannot be changed, so the blockchain forms a complete and irrevocable record of all transactions. Because of its speed and security, a number of companies are exploring the potential of blockchain technology for other uses besides payments.

Using Bitcoins   To use bitcoins in an international transaction, a firm deposits its own local currency into its account at an online bitcoin exchange or platform. The money is used to purchase bitcoins, which can be either stored in the owner's digital wallet or sent immediately to a recipient in any country where bitcoins are allowed. The recipient then sells the bitcoins on the online platform for its local currency, withdraws the money from its account, and deposits the money into its bank account (the withdrawal of the funds from the platform and their deposit into a bank account would likely take place online). Alternatively, the recipient could keep the bitcoins in its digital wallet and use them to conduct other transactions.

Bitcoins can also be used for small transactions. Consumers can use their digital wallets to send payments around the world by entering the payee's bitcoin address and the amount. Most digital wallets allow the sender to enter the amount in dollars, euros, or other major currencies. The wallet software then converts that amount into bitcoins before transmitting the payment to the payee. Consumers can also use bitcoins to purchase products at some companies, including Overstock and Expedia.

Advantages and Disadvantages of Bitcoins   One major advantage of bitcoins is the speed of transactions, especially international transactions. Bitcoins can be transferred from person to person or from business to business anywhere in the world in 10 minutes, although some platforms require several confirmations, especially for large transactions, which can lengthen the time. In addition, the fees for fund transfers are generally lower than the fees charged by financial institutions for international payments. Several central banks are exploring the possibility of adopting blockchain technology to take advantage of its potential to increase the speed and security of the conventional international payments system.

Another potential advantage of bitcoins is that credit risk is eliminated because the payer must pay upfront by depositing the full payment at the bitcoin platform to obtain bitcoins. Of course, this requirement can also be a disadvantage, because it prevents a firm from making purchases on credit. In addition, bitcoin transactions are irreversible: That can be an advantage in that the seller is assured of payment, but can be a disadvantage if the purchaser is not satisfied with the products. In that case, the purchaser's only recourse is to seek a refund from the seller, because it cannot revoke the payment once it has been entered into the bitcoin ledger.

For an MNC with subsidiaries in several countries around the world, using bitcoins for all of its transactions could eliminate or at least reduce the need to maintain accounts in several different currencies. The firm can make payments in any country where bitcoins are allowed by simply using the bitcoins in its digital wallet. Nevertheless, at the present time, it is unlikely that all of an MNC's suppliers and employees would be willing to accept payments in bitcoins. Thus, the firm would probably have to continue making at least some payments in local currencies.

A major reason that bitcoins may not be accepted in payment is their potential volatility. In 2017, for example, the value of a bitcoin rose from less than $1,000 in January to nearly $20,000 in December; a year later, the value had dropped again to less than $4,000. On some days, the value of a bitcoin has risen or fallen by 10 percent or more in just a short time. Given this volatility, the value of bitcoins in a digital wallet could potentially change dramatically in a matter of hours or even minutes. Consequently, firms that are willing to accept bitcoins may quickly convert them into another currency upon receipt. Similarly, some firms that make payments in bitcoins may purchase the bitcoins only at the time the payment is to be made, rather than maintaining an ongoing supply of bitcoins in a digital wallet. But the parties still incur exchange rate risk during the short time while the bitcoins are being transmitted from the sender to the recipient and converted into the local currency. During some periods, bitcoin's volatility has been so great that the value changed in the short time that a transaction was taking place.

Another problem with retaining a large amount of bitcoins in an account is that the firm has no protection against loss. Deposit insurance is not available for bitcoins. If hackers access a digital wallet and steal the bitcoins, the owner has no recourse against them. In recent years, hackers have stolen millions of dollars' worth of bitcoins from customers' accounts at various bitcoin exchanges.

The Outlook for Bitcoins   Although bitcoins offer several advantages for international transactions, their volatility and the resulting exposure to exchange rate risk, the lack of protection for bitcoin owners, and the potential for illegal activity have hindered their use. Nevertheless, some recent developments may make bitcoins more useful. The CME Group now offers bitcoin futures, which can be used to hedge bitcoin exposure. To date, this futures market has been quite volatile and illiquid. The bitcoin futures are based on the prices of bitcoins at unregulated cryptocurrency exchanges, which has made institutional investors reluctant to enter the futures market, thereby contributing to the lack of liquidity. However, in 2018, Intercontinental Exchange (ICE), the owner of the New York Stock Exchange, announced plans for a new type of bitcoin futures contract and a new global trading network called Bakkt, which it believes will provide more protection for investors. If ICE's plans pan out, the creation of a liquid futures market and the ability to hedge bitcoin exposure may increase the use of bitcoins in international payments.

In another development, exchange-traded funds (ETFs) based on bitcoins and other cryptocurrencies have been proposed as securities that would trade on the New York Stock Exchange or the Nasdaq. In 2018, the SEC rejected all of these proposals, stating that there was too much potential for fraud in the bitcoin market and too great a concern that investors could manipulate prices. Indeed, several recent academic research papers concluded that price manipulation may have influenced the huge increase in the value of bitcoins that occurred in 2017.

Near the end of 2018, however, the SEC agreed to review modified proposals for ETFs based on bitcoins. In doing so, this U.S. agency called for a globally coordinated effort to establish and enforce stability at the online bitcoin exchanges. As noted by the SEC, one of the biggest problems with regulating cryptocurrencies is that all the transactions take place online and the exchanges are based in countries around the world. Thus, regulation enacted by a single country will have little effect, and a global effort will be required to create a safer bitcoin market.

16-2 Factors Affecting Exchange Rates

As the value of a currency adjusts to changes in demand and supply conditions, it moves toward equilibrium. In equilibrium, there is no excess or deficiency of that currency.

EXAMPLE

A large increase in the U.S. demand for European goods and securities will result in an increased demand for euros. Because the demand for euros will then exceed the supply of euros for sale, the foreign exchange dealers (commercial banks) will experience a shortage of euros and will respond by increasing the quoted price of euros. Hence, the euro will appreciate, or increase in value.

Conversely, if European corporations begin to purchase more U.S. goods and European investors purchase more U.S. securities, the opposite forces will occur. There will be an increased sale of euros in exchange for dollars, causing a surplus of euros in the market. The value of the euro will therefore decline until it once again achieves equilibrium. ●

WEB

finance.yahoo.com
/currencies
News of interest to
speculators about
specific currencies that
are frequently traded in
the foreign exchange
market.

In reality, both the demand for euros and the supply of euros for sale can change simultaneously. The adjustment in the exchange rate will depend on the direction and magnitude of these changes.

A currency's supply and demand are influenced by a variety of factors, including (1) differential inflation rates, (2) differential interest rates, and (3) government (central bank) intervention. These factors are discussed next.

16-2a Differential Inflation Rates

Assume an equilibrium situation exists, and consider what will happen to the U.S. demand for euros, and to the supply of euros for sale, if U.S. inflation suddenly becomes much higher than European inflation. The U.S. demand for European goods will increase, reflecting an increased U.S. demand for euros. Conversely, the supply of euros to be sold for dollars will decline as the European desire for U.S. goods decreases. Both forces will place upward pressure on the value of the euro.

Under the reverse situation, in which European inflation suddenly becomes much higher than U.S. inflation, the U.S. demand for euros will decrease while the supply of euros for sale increases, placing downward pressure on the value of the euro.

A well-known theory about the relationship between inflation and exchange rates, referred to as **purchasing power parity (PPP)**, suggests that the exchange rate will, on average, change by a percentage that reflects the inflation differential between the two countries of concern.

EXAMPLE

Assume an initial equilibrium situation in which the British pound's spot rate is $1.30, U.S. inflation is 3 percent, and British inflation is also 3 percent. If U.S. inflation suddenly increases to 5 percent, then, according to PPP, the British pound will appreciate against the dollar by approximately 2 percent. The rationale is that, as a result of the higher U.S. prices, U.S. demand for British goods will increase, thereby placing upward pressure on the pound's value. Once the pound appreciates by 2 percent, the purchasing power of U.S. consumers will be the same whether they purchase U.S. goods or British goods. Although the prices of the U.S. goods will have risen by a higher percentage, the British goods will be just as expensive to U.S. consumers because of the pound's appreciation. Thus, a new equilibrium exchange rate results from the change in U.S. inflation. ●

In reality, exchange rates do not always change as suggested by the PPP theory. Other factors that influence exchange rates (discussed next) can distort the PPP relationship. All these factors must be considered when assessing why an exchange rate has changed. Furthermore, forecasts of future exchange rates must account for the potential direction and magnitude of changes in all factors that affect exchange rates.

16-2b Differential Interest Rates

Interest rate movements affect exchange rates by influencing the capital flows between countries. An increase in interest rates may attract foreign investors, especially if the higher interest rates do not reflect an increase in inflationary expectations.

EXAMPLE

Assume U.S. interest rates suddenly become much higher than European interest rates. U.S. investors' demand for European interest-bearing securities decreases as these securities become less attractive. In contrast, the supply of euros to be sold in exchange for dollars expands as European investors increase their purchases of U.S. interest-bearing securities. Both forces put downward pressure on the euro's value.

Conversely, opposite forces play out when European interest rates exceed U.S. interest rates, resulting in upward pressure on the euro's value. In general, the currency of the country with a higher increase (or smaller decrease) in interest rates is expected to appreciate, other factors held constant. ●

16-2c Central Bank Intervention

Central banks commonly consider adjusting a currency's value to influence economic conditions. For example, the U.S. central bank may wish to weaken the dollar to increase demand for U.S. exports, which can stimulate the economy. However, a weaker dollar can also create U.S. inflation by reducing foreign competition (because it raises the price of foreign goods to U.S. consumers). Alternatively, the U.S. central bank may prefer to strengthen the dollar to intensify foreign competition, which can reduce U.S. inflation.

Direct Intervention   A country's government can intervene in the foreign exchange market to affect a currency's value. Direct intervention occurs when a country's central bank (such as the Federal Reserve Bank for the United States or the European Central Bank for the eurozone countries) sells some of its currency reserves for a different currency.

EXAMPLE

Assume that the Fed and the ECB desire to strengthen the value of the euro against the dollar. They use dollar reserves to purchase euros in the foreign exchange market. In essence, they dump dollars in the foreign exchange market, thereby increasing the demand for euros. ●

Central bank intervention is sometimes used to slow the momentum of adverse exchange rate movements. In addition, the central bank may take steps to discourage institutional investors from assuming large speculative positions that might be intended to manipulate the market value of a currency in their favor.

Indirect Intervention   The Fed can affect the dollar's value indirectly by influencing the factors that determine its value. For example, the Fed can attempt to lower interest rates by increasing the U.S. money supply (assuming that inflationary expectations are not affected). Lower U.S. interest rates tend to discourage foreign investors from investing in U.S. securities, thereby putting downward pressure on the value of the dollar. Alternatively, to boost the dollar's value, the Fed can attempt to increase interest rates by reducing the U.S. money supply. This type of indirect intervention can be an effective means of influencing a currency's value.

When countries experience substantial net outflows of funds (which put severe downward pressure on their currency), they commonly use indirect intervention by raising interest rates to discourage excessive outflows, with the intention of limiting the downward pressure on their currency's value. However, this action adversely affects local borrowers (government agencies, corporations, and consumers) and may weaken the economy.

Indirect Intervention during Currency Crises   Currency crises in Mexico, many Asian countries, Brazil, Russia, and most recently Turkey have led to similar actions by the local government. These crises were often preceded by massive inflows of foreign funds from foreign investors who wanted to capitalize on investment opportunities in the country. When those investors began to fear that the country could experience economic problems, they sold their investments and exchanged the local currency for their own currency. The result is massive sales of the local currency in exchange for other currencies and substantial weakening of the local currency.

The local government has commonly intervened in such cases by raising interest rates in an attempt to encourage foreign investors to keep their money in the country. In some cases, the government has doubled or even tripled the local interest rates. However, foreign investors may still fear that this desperate action will not stop the momentum, so they may scramble to get out of that currency quickly to beat the likely freefall in the local currency's value as other investors also sell the currency. Furthermore, the very high local interest rates increase the cost of borrowing for local firms and discourage them from borrowing to expand. Consequently, the local government's actions tend to slow economic growth.

Turkey is the most recent country to experience these conditions. In August 2018, many of its foreign investors began to move their funds outside of Turkey. The Turkish currency (lira) depreciated by 25 percent against the dollar in just one week. Because some of the Turkish government's debt is denominated in dollars, the weak lira increased the cost of Turkey's debt.

16-3 Forecasting Exchange Rates

The decisions by institutional investors to invest in foreign countries are commonly influenced by their expectations of future exchange rates. They often hedge their exposure if they anticipate a decline in the value of the currency denominating their investments. Alternatively, they may take positions in foreign exchange derivatives to benefit from the expectation that specific currencies will strengthen. For all these activities, market participants need to develop a forecast of specific exchange rates.

WEB

www.x-rates.com
/historical

Historical exchange
rates.

Most forecasting techniques can be classified as one of the following types:

- Technical forecasting
- Fundamental forecasting
- Market-based forecasting
- Mixed forecasting

16-3a Technical Forecasting

Technical forecasting involves the use of historical exchange rate data to predict future values. For example, the fact that a given currency has increased in value over four consecutive days may suggest how the currency will move tomorrow. Sometimes a more complex statistical analysis is applied. For example, a computer program can be developed to detect particular historical trends. In addition, several **time-series models** examine moving averages and allow the forecaster to identify relevant patterns, such as a currency tending to decline in value after a rise in its moving average over three consecutive periods.

If the pattern of currency values over time appears to be random, then technical forecasting is not appropriate. Unless historical trends in exchange rate movements can be identified, examination of past movements will not be useful for indicating future movements.

16-3b Fundamental Forecasting

Fundamental forecasting is based on fundamental relationships between economic variables and exchange rates. Given current values of these variables along with their historical impact on a currency's value, corporations can develop exchange rate projections. For example, high inflation in a given country can lead to depreciation in its currency.

Sometimes, a forecast may be based on a subjective assessment of the degree to which general movements in economic variables in one country may be expected to affect exchange rates. Alternatively, a forecast can be derived from quantitatively measured impacts of factors on exchange rates.

16-3c Market-Based Forecasting

Market-based forecasting, or the process of developing forecasts from market indicators, is usually based on either the spot rate or the forward rate. As the spot rate is derived from the demand for and supply of a currency in the market, it may represent a reasonable expectation of that currency's value in the very near future. The forward rate can also serve as a forecast of the future spot rate, because speculators would take positions in case of a large discrepancy between the forward rate and expectations of the future spot rate.

EXAMPLE

The 30-day forward rate of the British pound is $1.40, and the general expectation of speculators is that the future spot rate of the pound will be $1.45 in 30 days. Hence, speculators might buy pounds 30 days forward at $1.40 and then sell them when received (in 30 days) at the spot rate existing then. If their forecast is correct, they will earn $0.05 ($1.45 − $1.40) per pound. If a large number of speculators implement this strategy, the substantial forward purchases of pounds will cause the forward rate to increase until this speculative demand stops. Thus, the forward rate should move toward the market's general expectation of the future spot rate. In this sense, the forward rate serves as a market-based forecast because it reflects the market's expectation of the spot rate at the end of the forward horizon (in this example, 30 days from now). ●

16-3d Mixed Forecasting

Because no single forecasting technique has been found to be consistently superior to the others, some market participants use a combination of forecasting techniques, known as **mixed forecasting**. Various forecasts for a particular currency value are developed using several forecasting techniques. Each of the techniques used is assigned a weight, with the techniques believed to be more reliable receiving higher weights. Thus, the forecast of the currency will be a weighted average of the various forecasts developed.

16-4 Foreign Exchange Derivatives

Foreign exchange derivatives can be used to speculate on future exchange rate movements or to hedge anticipated cash inflows or outflows in a given foreign currency. As foreign securities markets have become more accessible, institutional investors have increased their international investments, which in turn has increased their exposure to exchange rate risk. Some institutional investors use foreign exchange derivatives to hedge their exposure. The most popular foreign exchange derivatives are forward contracts, currency futures contracts, currency swaps, and currency options contracts.

16-4a Forward Contracts

As described earlier, a forward contract enables a firm to lock in the price to be paid for a foreign currency at a specified date in the future. Thus, forward purchases or sales can hedge the firm's risk that the currency's value may change over time.

EXAMPLE

St. Louis Insurance Company plans to invest about $20 million in Mexican stocks two months from now. Because the Mexican stocks are denominated in pesos, the amount of stock that can be purchased depends on the peso's value at the time of the purchase. If St. Louis Insurance Company is concerned that the peso will appreciate by the time of the purchase, it can buy pesos forward to lock in the exchange rate. ●

A corporation receiving payments denominated in a particular foreign currency in the future can lock in the price at which the currency can be sold by selling that currency forward.

EXAMPLE

The pension fund manager of Gonzaga, Inc., plans to liquidate the fund's holdings of British stocks in six months but anticipates that the British pound will depreciate by that time. The pension fund manager can insulate the future transaction from exchange rate risk by negotiating a forward contract to sell British pounds six months forward. In this way, the British pounds received when the stocks are liquidated can be converted to dollars at the exchange rate specified in the forward contract. ●

Estimating the Forward Premium The forward rate of a currency may sometimes exceed the existing spot rate, so that it represents a premium. At other times, it may be below the spot rate, so that it represents a discount. Forward contracts are sometimes referred to in terms of their percentage premium or discount rather than their actual rate. For example, assume that the spot rate (S) of the Canadian dollar is $0.70 while the 180-day ($n = 180$) forward rate ($FR$) is $0.71. The forward rate premium (p) would be

$$p = \frac{FR - S}{S} \times \frac{360}{n}$$

$$= \frac{\$0.71 - \$0.70}{\$0.70} \times \frac{360}{180}$$

$$= 2.86\%$$

WEB

www.cmegroup.com
Provides information
on currency futures
contracts.

This premium simply reflects the percentage by which the forward rate exceeds the spot rate on an annualized basis.

16-4b Currency Futures Contracts

An alternative to the forward contract is a currency futures contract, which is a standardized contract that specifies an amount of a particular currency to be exchanged on a specified date and at a specified exchange rate. A firm can purchase a futures contract to hedge payables in a foreign currency by locking in the price at which it could purchase that specific currency at a particular point in time. To hedge receivables denominated in a foreign currency, the firm could sell futures, thereby locking in the price at which it could sell that currency. A futures contract represents a standard number of units. Currency futures contracts also have specific maturity (or "settlement") dates from which the firm must choose.

Futures contracts are standardized, whereas forward contracts can specify whatever amount and maturity date the firm desires. Forward contracts have this flexibility because they are negotiated with commercial banks.

16-4c **Currency Swaps**

A currency swap is an agreement that allows one currency to be periodically swapped for another at specified exchange rates. It essentially represents a series of forward contracts. Commercial banks facilitate currency swaps by serving as the intermediary that links two parties with opposite needs. Alternatively, these banks may be willing to take the position counter to that desired by a particular party. In such a case, they expose themselves to exchange rate risk unless the position they have assumed will offset existing exposure.

16-4d **Currency Options Contracts**

Another foreign exchange derivative used for hedging is the currency option. Its primary advantage over forward and futures contracts is its stipulation that the parties have the right, but not the *obligation*, to purchase or sell a particular currency at a specified price within a given period.

A currency call option provides the right to purchase a particular currency at a specified price (called the *exercise price*) within a specified period. This type of option can be used to hedge future cash payments denominated in a foreign currency. If the spot rate remains less than the exercise price, the option will not be exercised because the firm could purchase the foreign currency at a lower cost in the spot market. However, a fee (or a premium) must be paid for options, so hedging with options carries a cost even if the purchaser does not exercise the options.

A put option provides the right to sell a particular currency at a specified price (the exercise price) within a specified period. If the spot rate remains greater than that price, the option will not be exercised because the firm could sell the foreign currency at a higher price in the spot market. In contrast, if the spot rate is less than the exercise price at the time the foreign currency is received, the firm will exercise its put option.

16-4e **Comparing Foreign Exchange Derivatives for Hedging**

When deciding whether to use forward, futures, or options contracts for hedging, a firm should consider the following characteristics of each contract. First, if the firm requires a tailor-made hedge that cannot be matched by existing futures contracts, a forward contract may be preferred. Otherwise, forward and futures contracts should generate somewhat similar results.

The choice between an obligation type of contract (forward or futures) or an options contract depends on the expected trend of the spot rate. If the currency in which payables are denominated appreciates, the firm will benefit more from a futures or forward contract than from a call option contract. The call option contract requires an up-front fee, but it is a wiser choice when the firm is less certain of a currency's future direction. The call option allows the firm both to hedge against possible appreciation and to ignore the contract and instead use the spot market if the currency depreciates. Similarly, put options may be preferred over futures or forward contracts for hedging receivables when future currency movements are especially uncertain, because the firm has the flexibility of letting the options expire if the currencies strengthen.

16-4f **Comparing Foreign Exchange Derivatives for Speculating**

The forward, currency futures, and currency options markets may be used for speculating as well as for hedging. A speculator who expects the Singapore dollar to appreciate could consider any of the following strategies:

1. Purchase Singapore dollars forward; when they are received, sell the Singapore dollars in the spot market.

2. Purchase futures contracts on Singapore dollars; when they are received, sell the Singapore dollars in the spot market.
3. Purchase call options on Singapore dollars; at some point before the expiration date, when the spot rate exceeds the exercise price, exercise the call option and then sell the Singapore dollars received in the spot market.

Conversely, a speculator who expects the Singapore dollar to depreciate could consider any of the following strategies:

1. Sell Singapore dollars forward, and then purchase them in the spot market just before fulfilling the forward obligation.
2. Sell futures contracts on Singapore dollars; purchase Singapore dollars in the spot market just before fulfilling the futures obligation.
3. Purchase put options on Singapore dollars; at some point before the expiration date, when the spot rate is less than the exercise price, purchase Singapore dollars in the spot market and then exercise the put option.

Speculating with Currency Futures   As an example of speculating with currency futures, consider the following information:

- The spot rate of the British pound is $1.56 per pound.
- The price of a futures contract is $1.57 per pound.
- The pound's expected spot rate on the settlement date of the futures contract is $1.63 per pound.

Given that the future spot rate is expected to be higher than the futures price, you could buy currency futures. You would receive pounds on the settlement date for $1.57. If your expectations are correct, you would then sell the pounds for $0.06 more per unit than you paid for them. The risk associated with your speculative strategy, of course, is that the pound may decline rather than increase in value. If it declines to $1.55 by the settlement date, you would have sold the pounds for $0.02 less per unit than you paid.

To account for uncertainty, speculators may develop a probability distribution for the future spot rate as follows:

FUTURE SPOT RATE OF BRITISH POUND	PROBABILITY
$1.50	10%
1.59	20
1.63	50
1.66	20

This probability distribution suggests that four outcomes are possible. For each possible outcome, the anticipated gain or loss can be determined:

POSSIBLE OUTCOME FOR FUTURE SPOT RATE	PROBABILITY	GAIN OR LOSS PER UNIT
$1.50	10%	−$0.07
1.59	20	0.02
1.63	50	0.06
1.66	20	0.09

This analysis measures the probability and potential magnitude of a loss from the speculative strategy.

Exhibit 16.2 Estimating Speculative Gains from Options Using a Probability Distribution

(1) POSSIBLE OUTCOME FOR FUTURE SPOT RATE	(2) PROBABILITY	(3) WILL THE OPTION BE EXERCISED BASED ON THIS OUTCOME?	(4) GAIN PER UNIT FROM EXERCISING OPTION	(5) PREMIUM PAID PER UNIT FOR THE OPTION	(6) NET GAIN OR LOSS PER UNIT
$1.50	10%	No	—	$0.03	−$0.03
1.59	20	Yes	$0.02	0.03	−0.01
1.63	50	Yes	0.06	0.03	0.03
1.66	20	Yes	0.09	0.03	0.06

Speculating with Currency Options   Consider the information from the previous example and assume that a British call option is available with an exercise price of $1.57 and a premium of $0.03 per unit. Recall that your best guess of the future spot rate was $1.63. If your guess is correct, you will earn $0.06 per unit on the difference between what you paid (the exercise price of $1.57) and the price for which you could sell a pound ($1.63). After the premium paid for the option ($0.03 per unit) is deducted, the net gain is $0.03 per unit.

The risk of purchasing this option is that the pound's value might decline over time. If that outcome is realized, you will be unable to exercise the option, and your loss will be the premium paid for it. To assess the risk involved, a probability distribution can be developed. In Exhibit 16.2, the probability distribution from the previous example is applied here. The distribution of net gains from the strategy is shown in the sixth column.

Speculators should always compare the potential gains from currency options and currency futures contracts to determine which type of contract (if any) to trade. Two speculators may potentially have similar expectations about potential gains from both types of foreign exchange derivative contracts, yet prefer different types of contracts because the speculators have different degrees of risk aversion.

16-5 International Arbitrage

Exchange rates and exchange rate derivatives are determined by the market. If they become misaligned, various forms of arbitrage can occur, forcing realignment. Common types of international arbitrage are explained next.

16-5a Locational Arbitrage

Locational arbitrage is the act of capitalizing on a discrepancy between the spot exchange rate at two different locations by purchasing the currency where it is priced low and selling it where it is priced high.

EXAMPLE   The exchange rates for the European euro quoted by two banks differ, as shown in Exhibit 16.3. The ask quote is higher than the bid quote; this difference reflects the transaction costs charged by each bank. Because Baltimore Bank is asking $1.046 for euros and Sacramento Bank is willing to pay (bid) $1.050 for euros, an institution could execute locational arbitrage. That is, it could achieve a risk-free return without tying funds up for any length of time by buying euros at one location (Baltimore Bank) and simultaneously selling them at the other location (Sacramento Bank). ●

Exhibit 16.3 Bank Quotes Used for Locational Arbitrage Example

	BID RATE ON EUROS	ASK RATE ON EUROS
Sacramento Bank	$1.050	$1.056
Baltimore Bank	$1.042	$1.046

As locational arbitrage is executed, Baltimore Bank will begin to raise its ask price on euros in response to the strong demand. In contrast, Sacramento Bank will begin to lower its bid price in response to the excess supply of euros it has recently received. Once Baltimore's ask price is at least as high as Sacramento's bid price, locational arbitrage will no longer be possible. Because some financial institutions (particularly the foreign exchange departments of commercial banks) watch for locational arbitrage opportunities, any discrepancy in exchange rates among locations is quickly eliminated.

16-5b Triangular Arbitrage

If the quoted cross-exchange rate between two foreign currencies is not aligned with the two corresponding exchange rates, a discrepancy exists in the exchange rate quotations. Under this condition, investors can engage in **triangular arbitrage**, which involves buying or selling the currency that is subject to a mispriced cross-exchange rate.

EXAMPLE

If the spot rate is $0.07 for the Mexican peso and $0.70 for the Canadian dollar, the cross-exchange rate should be C$1 = 10 pesos (computed as $0.70/$0.07). Assume that the Canadian dollar/peso exchange rate is quoted as C$1 = 10.3 pesos. In this case, the quote for the Canadian dollar is higher than it should be. An investor could benefit by using U.S. dollars to buy Canadian dollars, using those Canadian dollars to buy pesos, and then using the pesos to buy U.S. dollars. These three transactions would be executed at about the same time, before the exchange rates change. With $1,000, you could buy C$1,428.57 (computed as 1,000 ÷ 0.70), convert those Canadian dollars into 14,714 pesos (computed as 1,428.57 × 10.3), and then convert the pesos into $1,030 (computed as 14,714 × 0.07). Thus, you would have a gain of $30. Of course, the gain would be larger if you engaged in triangular arbitrage using a larger amount of money. ●

Whenever a discrepancy exists in exchange rates, financial institutions with large amounts of money will engage in triangular arbitrage, causing the quoted exchange rates to quickly adjust. The arbitrage transaction of using U.S. dollars to buy Canadian dollars will cause the Canadian dollar to appreciate with respect to the U.S. dollar; the transaction of using Canadian dollars to buy pesos will cause the Canadian dollar to depreciate against the peso; and the transaction of using pesos to buy U.S. dollars will cause the peso to depreciate against the U.S. dollar. Once the cross-exchange rate adjusts to its appropriate level, triangular arbitrage will no longer be feasible. The rates may adjust within a matter of seconds in response to the market forces. Quoted cross-exchange rates usually do not reflect a discrepancy because, if they did, financial institutions would capitalize on the discrepancy until the exchange rates were realigned.

16-5c Covered Interest Arbitrage

The coexistence of international money markets and forward markets creates a special relationship between a forward rate premium and the interest rate differential of two countries, known as **interest rate parity**. This relationship also has implications for currency futures contracts, as they are usually priced in the same way as forward contracts.

According to interest rate parity, the premium on the forward rate can be determined as

$$p = \frac{(1 + i_h)}{(1 + i_f)} - 1$$

where

$$p = \text{forward premium of foreign currency}$$
$$i_h = \text{home country interest rate}$$
$$i_f = \text{foreign interest rate}$$

EXAMPLE

The spot rate of the New Zealand dollar is $0.50, the one-year U.S. interest rate is 9 percent, and the one-year New Zealand interest rate is 6 percent. Under conditions of interest rate parity, the forward premium of the New Zealand dollar will be

$$p = \frac{(1 + 9\%)}{(1 + 6\%)} - 1$$
$$\simeq 2.8\%$$

Thus, the forward rate of the New Zealand dollar will be about $0.514, reflecting a 2.8 percent premium above the spot rate. ●

Examining the equation for interest rate parity reveals that if the interest rate is lower in the foreign country than in the home country, the forward rate of the foreign currency will represent a premium. In the opposite situation, the forward rate will represent a discount.

Interest rate parity suggests that the forward rate premium (or discount) should be about equal to the differential in interest rates between the countries of concern. If this relationship does not hold, market forces should act to restore it. The act of capitalizing on the discrepancy between the forward rate premium and the interest rate differential is called **covered interest arbitrage**.

EXAMPLE

Both the spot rate and the one-year forward rate of the Canadian dollar are $0.80. The Canadian interest rate is 10 percent and the U.S. interest rate is 8 percent. Hence U.S. investors can take advantage of the higher Canadian interest rate, without being exposed to exchange rate risk, by executing covered interest arbitrage. Specifically, they will exchange U.S. dollars for Canadian dollars and invest those funds at the rate of 10 percent. They will simultaneously sell Canadian dollars one year forward. Because they are able to purchase and sell Canadian dollars for the same price, their return is the 10 percent interest earned on their investment. ●

As the U.S. investors demand Canadian dollars in the spot market while selling Canadian dollars forward, they place upward pressure on the spot rate and downward pressure on the one-year forward rate of the Canadian dollar. Thus, the Canadian dollar's forward rate will exhibit a discount. Once the discount becomes large enough, the interest rate advantage in Canada will be offset. In other words, what U.S. investors gain on the higher Canadian interest rate is offset by their need to buy Canadian dollars at a higher (spot) rate than the selling (forward) rate. Then covered interest arbitrage will no longer generate a return that is any higher for U.S. investors than an alternative investment in the United States. Once the forward discount (or premium) offsets the interest rate differential in this manner, interest rate parity exists.

The interest rate parity equation determines the forward discount that the Canadian dollar must exhibit to offset the interest rate differential:

$$p = \frac{(1 + i_h)}{(1 + i_f)} - 1$$
$$= \frac{(1 + 8\%)}{(1 + 10\%)} - 1$$
$$\simeq -1.82\%$$

In this case, if the forward rate is lower than the spot rate by 1.82 percent, the interest rate is offset and covered interest arbitrage would yield a return to U.S. investors similar to the U.S. interest rate.

The existence of interest rate parity prevents investors from earning higher returns from covered interest arbitrage than can be earned in the United States. Nevertheless, international investing may still be feasible if the investing firm does not simultaneously cover in the forward market. Of course, failure to do so usually exposes the firm to exchange rate risk; if the currency denominating the investment depreciates over the investment horizon, the return on the investment is reduced.

Summary

- Exchange rate systems vary in the degree to which a country's central bank controls its currency's exchange rate. Many countries allow their currency to float, yet periodically engage in interventions to control the exchange rate. Some countries use a pegged exchange rate system in which their currency's value is pegged to the U.S. dollar or to another currency. Several European countries have adopted the euro as their currency; a single monetary policy is implemented in those countries.

- Exchange rates are influenced by differential inflation rates, differential interest rates, and central bank intervention. A foreign currency's value is subject to upward pressure when its home country has relatively low inflation or relatively high interest rates. Central banks can place upward pressure on a currency by purchasing that currency in the foreign exchange markets (by exchanging other currencies held in reserve for that currency). Alternatively, they can place downward pressure on a currency by selling that currency in the foreign exchange markets in exchange for other currencies.

- Exchange rates can be forecasted using technical, fundamental, and market-based methods. Each method has its own advantages and limitations.

- Foreign exchange derivatives include forward contracts, currency futures contracts, currency swaps, and currency options contracts. Forward contracts can be purchased to hedge future payables or be sold to hedge future receivables in a foreign currency. Currency futures contracts can be used in a manner similar to forward contracts to hedge payables or receivables in a foreign currency. Currency swaps can be used to lock in the exchange rate of a foreign currency to be received or purchased in the future.

- Currency call (put) options can be purchased to hedge future payables (receivables) in a foreign currency. Currency options offer more flexibility than the other foreign exchange derivatives, but a premium must be paid for them.

- Foreign exchange derivatives can also be used to speculate on expected exchange rate movements. When speculators expect a foreign currency to appreciate, they can lock in the exchange rate at which they may purchase that currency by purchasing forward contracts, futures contracts, or call options on that currency. When speculators expect a currency to depreciate, they can lock in the exchange rate at which they may sell that currency by selling forward contracts or futures contracts on that currency. They could also purchase put options on that currency.

- International arbitrage ensures that foreign exchange market prices are set properly. If exchange rates vary among the banks that serve the foreign exchange market, locational arbitrage will be possible. In such a case, foreign exchange market participants will purchase a currency at the bank with a low quote and sell it to another bank where the quote is higher. If a quoted cross-exchange rate is misaligned with the corresponding exchange rates, triangular arbitrage will be possible; it involves buying or selling the currency that is subject to the mispriced exchange rate. If the interest rate differential is not offset by the forward rate premium (as suggested by interest rate parity), covered interest arbitrage will be possible, as a firm may invest in a foreign currency and simultaneously sell the currency forward. Arbitrage will occur until interest rate parity is restored.

Point Counter-Point

Do Financial Institutions Need to Consider Foreign Exchange Market Conditions When Making Domestic Security Market Decisions?

Point   No. If there is no exchange of currencies, there is no need to monitor the foreign exchange market.

Counter-Point   Yes. Foreign exchange market conditions can affect an economy or an industry and, therefore, affect the valuation of securities. In addition,

the valuation of a firm can be affected by currency movements because of its international business.

Who Is Correct?   Use the Internet to learn more about this issue and then formulate your own opinion on this issue.

Questions and Applications

1. **Exchange Rate Systems** Explain the exchange rate system that existed during the 1950s and 1960s. How did the Smithsonian Agreement in 1971 revise it? How does today's exchange rate system differ from the earlier systems?

2. **Dirty Float** Explain the difference between a freely floating system and a dirty float. Which type is more representative of the U.S. system?

3. **Impact of Quotas** Assume that European countries impose a quota on goods imported from the United States and that the United States does not plan to retaliate. How could this affect the value of the euro? Explain.

4. **Impact of Capital Flows** Assume that stocks in the United Kingdom become very attractive to U.S. investors. How could this affect the value of the British pound? Explain.

5. **Impact of Inflation** Assume that Mexico suddenly experiences high and unexpected inflation. How could this affect the value of the Mexican peso according to purchasing power parity (PPP) theory?

6. **Impact of Economic Conditions** Assume that Switzerland has a very strong economy, putting upward pressure on both its inflation and interest rates. Explain how these conditions could put pressure on the value of the Swiss franc, and determine whether the franc's value will rise or fall.

7. **Central Bank Intervention** The Bank of Japan desires to decrease the value of the Japanese yen against the U.S. dollar. How could it use direct intervention to achieve this goal?

8. **Conditions for Speculation** Explain the conditions under which a speculator would like to invest in

a foreign currency today even when the speculator has no use for that currency in the future.

9. **Risk from Speculating** Seattle Bank just took speculative positions by borrowing Canadian dollars and converting the funds to invest in Australian dollars. Explain a possible future scenario that could adversely affect the bank's performance.

10. **Impact of a Weak Dollar** How does a weak dollar affect U.S. inflation? Explain.

11. **Speculating with Foreign Exchange Derivatives** Explain how U.S. speculators could use foreign exchange derivatives to speculate on the expected appreciation of the Japanese yen.

Advanced Questions

12. **Interaction of Capital Flows and Yield Curve** Assume a horizontal yield curve exists. How do you think the yield curve would be affected if foreign investors in short-term securities and long-term securities suddenly anticipate that the value of the dollar will strengthen? (You may find it helpful to refer to the discussion of the yield curve in Chapter 3.)

13. **Changes in the Euro's Value in Response to Prevailing Conditions** Consider the prevailing conditions for inflation (including oil prices), the economy, interest rates, and any other factors that could affect exchange rates. Based on these conditions, do you think the euro's value will likely appreciate or depreciate against the dollar for the remainder of this semester? Offer some logic to support your answer. Which factor do you think will have the biggest impact on the euro's exchange rate?

14. Obtaining Credit from the European Central Bank What are the consequences for a government in the eurozone when it obtains credit from the ECB?

15. Impact of Abandoning the Euro on Eurozone Conditions. Explain the possible signal that would be transmitted to the market if a country abandoned its use of the euro.

Critical Thinking Question

Central Bank Intervention as a Policy Tool Recently, a government official in Europe stated that the European Central Bank needs to weaken the euro so as to improve the European economy. Write a short essay that explains the logic behind this recommendation, and state whether you believe the strategy would be successful.

Interpreting Financial News

Interpret the following statements made by Wall Street analysts and portfolio managers.

a. "Our use of currency futures has completely changed our risk–return profile."

b. "Our use of currency options resulted in an upgrade in our credit rating."

c. "Our strategy of using forward contracts to hedge backfired on us."

Managing in Financial Markets

Using Forex Derivatives for Hedging You are the manager of a stock portfolio for a financial institution, and approximately 20 percent of your stock portfolio is in British stocks. You expect the British stock market to perform well over the next year, and you plan to sell the stocks one year from now (and will convert the British pounds received to dollars at that time). However, you are concerned that the British pound may depreciate against the dollar over the next year.

a. Explain how you could use a forward contract to hedge the exchange rate risk associated with your position in British stocks.

b. If interest rate parity holds, does this limit the effectiveness of a forward contract as a hedge?

c. Explain how you could use an options contract to hedge the exchange rate risk associated with your position in stocks.

d. Assume that, although you are concerned about the potential decline in the pound's value, you also believe that the pound could appreciate against the dollar over the next year. You would like to benefit from the potential appreciation but also wish to hedge against the possible depreciation. Should you use a forward contract or options contracts to hedge your position? Explain.

Problems

1. Currency Futures Use the following information to determine the probability distribution of per unit gains from selling Mexican peso futures.

- The spot rate of the peso is $0.10.
- The price of peso futures is $0.102 per unit.
- Your expectation of the peso spot rate at maturity of the futures contract is:

POSSIBLE OUTCOME FOR FUTURE SPOT RATE	PROBABILITY
$0.090	10%
0.095	70
0.110	20

2. Currency Call Options Use the following information to determine the probability distribution of net gains per unit from purchasing a call option on British pounds.

- The spot rate of the British pound is $1.45.
- The premium on the British pound option is $0.04 per unit.
- The exercise price of a British pound option is $1.46.
- Your expectation of the British pound spot rate prior to the expiration of the option is:

POSSIBLE OUTCOME FOR FUTURE SPOT RATE	PROBABILITY
$1.48	30%
1.49	40
1.52	30

3. Locational Arbitrage Assume the following exchange rate quotes on British pounds:

	BID	ASK
Orleans Bank	$1.46	$1.47
Kansas Bank	1.48	1.49

Explain how locational arbitrage would occur. Also explain why this arbitrage will realign the exchange rates.

4. Covered Interest Arbitrage Assume the following information:

- British pound spot rate = $1.58
- British pound one-year forward rate = $1.58
- British one-year interest rate = 11 percent
- U.S. one-year interest rate = 9 percent

Explain how U.S. investors could use covered interest arbitrage to lock in a higher yield than 9 percent. What would be their yield? Explain how the spot and forward rates of the pound would change as covered interest arbitrage occurs.

5. Covered Interest Arbitrage Assume the following information:

- Mexican one-year interest rate = 15 percent
- U.S. one-year interest rate = 11 percent

If interest rate parity exists, what would be the forward premium or discount on the Mexican peso's forward rate? Would covered interest arbitrage be more profitable to U.S. investors than investing at home? Explain.

Flow of Funds Exercise

Hedging with Foreign Exchange Derivatives

Carson Company expects that it will receive a large order from the government of Spain. If the order occurs, Carson will be paid approximately 3 million euros. Because all of its expenses are in dollars, Carson would like to hedge this position. Carson has contacted a bank with brokerage subsidiaries that can help it hedge with foreign exchange derivatives.

a. How could Carson use currency futures to hedge its position?
b. What is the risk of hedging with currency futures?
c. How could Carson use currency options to hedge its position?
d. Explain the advantage and disadvantage to Carson of using currency options instead of currency futures.

Internet/Excel Exercises

Use the website www.x-rates.com to assess exchange rates.

1. What is the most recent value of the Australian dollar in terms of U.S. dollars? How many British pounds does a U.S. dollar buy?

2. Click on "Historic Lookup" to review the pound's value over the past year. Offer a possible explanation for the recent movements in the pound's value.

3. What is the most recent value of the Hong Kong dollar in terms of U.S. dollars? Do you notice anything unusual about this value over time? What could explain an exchange rate trend such as this?

WSJ Exercise

Assessing Exchange Rate Movements

Use a recent issue of *The Wall Street Journal* to determine how a particular currency's value has changed against the dollar since the beginning of the year. The "Currencies" table lists the percentage change in many currencies since the beginning of the year.

Online Articles with Real-World Examples

Find a recent practical article available online that describes a real-world example regarding a specific financial institution or financial market that reinforces one or more concepts covered in this chapter. If your class has an online component, your professor may ask you to post your summary of the article there and provide a link to the article so that other students can access it.

If your class is live, your professor may ask you to summarize your application of the article in class. Your professor may assign specific students to complete this assignment or may allow any students to do the assignment on a volunteer basis.

For recent online articles and real-world examples related to this chapter, consider using the following search terms (be sure to include the prevailing year as a search term to ensure that the online articles are recent):

1. foreign exchange AND institutional investors
2. inflation AND exchange rate
3. interest rate AND exchange rate
4. central bank intervention
5. foreign exchange controls
6. currency AND forecasting
7. currency AND forward contract
8. forward contract AND hedge
9. currency futures AND speculate
10. currency options AND hedge

Appendix 16

Currency Option Pricing

Understanding what drives the premiums paid for currency options makes it easier to recognize the various factors that must be monitored when anticipating future movements in currency option premiums. Because participants in the currency options market typically take positions based on their expectations of how the premiums will change over time, they can benefit from understanding how options are priced.

Boundary Conditions

The first step in pricing currency options is to recognize the boundary conditions that force the option premium to be within lower and upper bounds.

Lower Bounds

The lower bound of a call option premium (C) is either zero or the difference between the underlying spot exchange rate (S) and the exercise price (X), whichever is greater:

$$C \geq \max(0,\ S - X)$$

This floor is enforced by arbitrage restrictions. For example, assume that the premium on a British pound call option is $0.01, the spot rate of the pound is $1.62, and the exercise price is $1.60. In this example, the spread $(S - X)$ exceeds the call premium, which would allow for arbitrage. An investor could purchase the call option for $0.01 per unit, immediately exercise the option at $1.60 per pound, and then sell the pounds in the spot market for $1.62 per unit. These actions would generate an immediate profit of $0.01 per unit. Arbitrage would continue until the market forces realigned the spread $(S - X)$ to be less than or equal to the call premium.

The put option premium (P) has a lower bound of either zero or the difference between the exercise price and the underlying spot exchange rate, whichever is greater:

$$P \geq \max(0,\ X - S)$$

This floor is also enforced by arbitrage restrictions. For example, assume that the premium on a British pound put option is $0.02, the spot rate of the pound is $1.60, and the exercise price is $1.63. An investor could purchase the pound put option for $0.02 per unit, purchase pounds in the spot market at $1.60, and immediately exercise the option by selling the pounds at $1.63 per unit to yield a profit of $0.01 per unit. Arbitrage would continue until the market forces realigned the spread $(X - S)$ to be less than or equal to the put premium.

Upper Bounds

The upper bound for a call option premium is the spot exchange rate, S:

$$C \leq S$$

If the call option premium ever exceeds the spot exchange rate, an investor could engage in arbitrage by selling call options for a higher price per unit than the cost of purchasing the underlying currency. Even if those call options were exercised, the investor could pay them off using the currency purchased earlier. The arbitrage profit in this example would be the difference between the amount received when selling the currency (which is the premium) and the cost of purchasing the currency in the spot market. Arbitrage would occur until the call option's premium was less than or equal to the spot rate.

The upper bound for a put option is equal to the option's exercise price, X:

$$P \leq X$$

If the put option premium ever exceeds the exercise price, an investor could engage in arbitrage by selling put options. Even if the put options were exercised, the proceeds received from selling the put options would exceed the price paid (that is, the exercise price) at the time of exercise.

Option premiums lie within these boundaries because the boundaries are enforced by arbitrage.

Application of Pricing Models

Although boundary conditions can be used to determine the possible range for a currency option's premium, they do not precisely indicate the appropriate premium for the option. However, pricing models have been developed to price currency options. Based on information about an option (for example, the exercise price and time to maturity) and about the currency (for example, its spot rate, standard deviation, and interest rate), pricing models can derive the premium on a currency option. Biger and Hull (1983) developed the following currency option-pricing model:

$$C = e^{-R_f^* T} S \cdot N(d_1) - e^{-R_f T} X \cdot N(d_1 - \sigma\sqrt{T})$$

where

$$d_1 = \{[\ln(S/X) + (R_f - R_f^* + (\sigma^2/2))T] / \sigma\sqrt{T}\}$$

C = **price of the currency call option**

S = **underlying spot exchange rate**

X = **exercise price**

R_f = **U.S. risk-free rate of interest**

R_f^* = **foreign risk-free rate of interest**

σ = **instantaneous standard deviation of the return on a holding of foreign currency**

T = **time to option maturity expressed as a fraction of year**

$N(\cdot)$ = **standard normal cumulative distribution function**

This equation is based on the stock option-pricing model (OPM) when allowing for continuous dividends. Because the interest gained from holding a foreign security (R_f^*) is equivalent to a continuously paid dividend on a stock share, this version of the OPM holds completely. The key transformation needed to adapt the stock OPM to value currency options is to substitute exchange rates for stock prices. Thus, the percentage change of exchange rates (like the percentage change of stock prices) is assumed to follow a diffusion process with constant mean and variance.

The model developed by Biger and Hull is sometimes referred to as the European model because it does not account for early exercise of the options.[*] Unlike American currency options, European currency options do not allow for early exercise (that is, before the expiration date). The extra flexibility of American currency options should command a higher premium than that for European currency options with similar characteristics. However, there is not a closed-form model for pricing American currency options. Although various techniques are used to price such options, the European model is commonly applied because it can be just as accurate for American as for European currency options.

Given all other parameters, the currency OPM can be used to impute the standard deviation σ. This implied parameter represents the option's market assessment of currency volatility over the life of the option.

Pricing Currency Put Options According to Put–Call Parity

Given the premium C of a European call option, the premium P for a European put option on the same currency and with the same exercise price X can be derived from put–call parity as follows:

$$P = C + Xe^{-R_f T} - Se^{-R_f^* T}$$

where R_f is the risk-free rate of interest, R_f^* is the foreign risk-free rate of interest, and T is the option's time to maturity expressed as a fraction of the year.

If the actual put option premium is *less* than that suggested by the put–call parity equation just shown, arbitrage is possible. Specifically, an investor could (1) buy the put option, (2) sell the call option, and (3) buy the underlying currency. The purchases would be financed with the proceeds from selling the call option and from borrowing at the rate R_f. Meanwhile, the foreign currency that was purchased can be deposited to earn the foreign rate R_f^*. Regardless of the path of the currency's exchange rate movement over the option's lifetime, the arbitrage will result in a profit. First, if the exchange rate is equal to the exercise price so that each option expires without being exercised (is worthless), the foreign currency can be converted in the spot market to dollars; this amount will exceed the amount required to repay the loan. Second, if the foreign currency appreciates to the point that it exceeds the exercise price, the investor will have a loss when the call option is exercised. Although the put option will expire, the foreign currency can be converted in the spot market to dollars, and this amount will exceed the amount required to repay the loan and the amount of the loss on the call option. Third, if the foreign currency depreciates to the point that it falls below the exercise price, the amount received from selling the put option plus the amount received from converting the foreign currency to dollars will exceed the amount required to repay the loan. Because the arbitrage generates a profit under any exchange rate scenario, it will force an adjustment in the option premiums so that put–call parity is no longer violated.

---

[*]Nahum Biger and John Hull, "The Valuation of Currency Options," *Financial Management* (Spring 1983): 24–28.

If the actual put option premium is *more* than that suggested by put–call parity, arbitrage would again be possible. The arbitrage strategy would be the reverse of that just described for the case when the actual put option premium is less than that suggested by put–call parity. Again, the arbitrage would eventually force an adjustment in option premiums so that put–call parity is no longer violated. Note, however, that the arbitrage applicable in case of a violation of put–call parity on American currency options differs slightly from the arbitrage applicable to European currency options. Even so, the concept still holds that the premium of a currency put option is determined by the premium of a call option on the same currency and with the same exercise price.

PART 5 INTEGRATIVE PROBLEM

Choosing among Derivative Securities

This problem requires an understanding of futures contracts (Chapter 13), options markets (Chapter 14), interest rate swap markets (Chapter 15), and foreign exchange derivative markets (Chapter 16). It also requires an understanding of how economic conditions affect interest rates and security prices.

Assume that the United States has just experienced a mild recession, which sent interest rates to their lowest levels in a decade. The U.S. interest rates appear to be influenced more by changes in the demand for funds than by changes in the supply of U.S. savings, because the savings rate does not change much regardless of economic conditions. The yield curve is currently flat. The federal budget deficit has been reduced lately and is not expected to rise substantially.

The federal government recently decided both to reduce personal tax rates significantly for all tax brackets and to reduce corporate tax rates. The U.S. dollar has just recently weakened. Economies of other countries were somewhat stagnant but have improved in the past quarter. Your assignment is to recommend how various financial institutions should respond to the preceding information.

Questions

1. A savings institution holds 50 percent of its assets as long-term, fixed-rate mortgages. Almost all of its funds are in the form of short-term deposits. Which of the following strategies would be most appropriate for this institution?
   - Use a fixed-for-floating swap.
   - Use a swap of floating payments for fixed payments.
   - Use a put option on interest rate futures contracts.
   - Remain unhedged.

   Defend your recommendation.

2. An insurance company maintains a large portfolio of U.S. stocks. Which of the following would be more appropriate?
   - Sell stock index futures contracts.
   - Remain unhedged.

   Defend your recommendation.

3. A pension fund maintains a large bond portfolio of U.S. bonds. Which of the following would be most appropriate?

   ■ Sell bond index futures.
   ■ Buy bond index futures.
   ■ Remain unhedged.

Defend your recommendation.

4. An international mutual fund sponsored by a U.S. securities firm consists of bonds evenly allocated across the United States and the United Kingdom. One of the portfolio managers has decided to hedge all the assets by selling futures on a popular U.S. bond index. The manager has stated that, because the fund concentrates on risk-free Treasury bonds, the only concern is interest rate risk. Assuming that interest rate risk is the only risk of concern, will the manager's hedging strategy be effective? Why or why not? Does any other risk need to be considered? If so, how would you hedge that risk?

PART 6
Commercial Banking

The chapters in Part 6 focus on commercial banking. Chapter 17 identifies the common sources and uses of funds for commercial banks, and Chapter 18 describes the regulations that are imposed on sources and uses of funds and other banking operations. Chapter 19 explains how banks manage their sources and uses of funds to deal with risk. Chapter 20 explains how commercial bank performance can be measured and monitored to assess previous managerial policies.

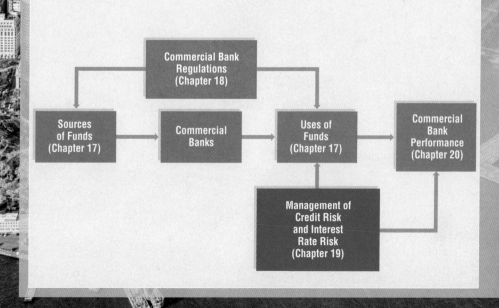

17

Commercial Bank Operations

CHAPTER
OBJECTIVES

The specific objectives
of this chapter are to:

- Describe the
  market structure of
  commercial banks.

- Describe the
  most common
  sources of funds for
  commercial banks.

- Explain the most
  common uses
  of funds for
  commercial banks.

- Describe typical
  off-balance sheet
  activities for
  commercial banks.

- Discuss trends
  in international
  banking.

As measured by total assets, commercial banks are the most important type of financial intermediary. Like other financial intermediaries, they perform the critical function of facilitating the flow of funds from surplus units to deficit units.

17-1 Background on Commercial Banks

Up to this point, this text has focused on the role and functions of financial markets. From this point forward, the emphasis shifts to the role and functions of financial institutions. Recall from Chapter 1 that financial institutions commonly facilitate the flow of funds between surplus units and deficit units. Commercial banks represent a key financial intermediary because they serve all types of surplus and deficit units. They offer deposit accounts with the size and maturity characteristics desired by surplus units. They repackage the funds received from deposits to provide loans and purchase debt securities of the size and maturity desired by deficit units. They have the ability to assess the creditworthiness of deficit units that apply for loans or issue debt securities, so they can limit their exposure to credit (default) risk.

17-1a Bank Market Structure

In 1985, more than 14,000 banks were located in the United States. Today, there are approximately one-third as many banks today as there were in 1985, and consolidation is still occurring. Exhibit 17.1 shows how the number of U.S. banks has declined over time, thereby increasing concentration in the banking industry.

Consolidation among banks has occurred because banks can be more efficient when they expand. In recent decades, these institutions have aggressively pursued growth as a means of capitalizing on economies of scale (lower average costs for larger scales of operations). In the United States, changes in interstate banking regulations implemented in 1994 gave banks more freedom to acquire other banks across state lines, which in turn allowed them to expand across the nation.

In aggregate, commercial banks have assets valued at approximately $17 trillion. The five largest U.S. banks now account for more than 50 percent of bank assets, versus 30 percent in 2001. JPMorgan Chase & Co. is the largest bank in the United States, with about $2.6 trillion in assets; it is followed by Bank of America Corporation, with approximately $2.3 trillion in assets, and Wells Fargo & Company, with some $2 trillion in assets.

Many banks are owned by bank holding companies, which are companies that own at least 10 percent of a bank. The holding company structure allows more flexibility to borrow

Exhibit 17.1 Number of Commercial Banks over Time

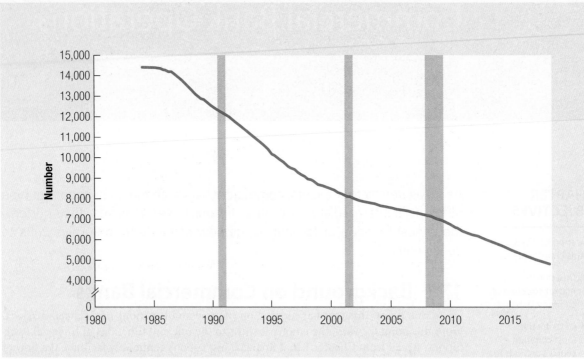

Note: Shaded areas indicate recessions.
Source: Federal Financial Institutions Council.

funds, issue stock, repurchase the company's own stock, and acquire other firms. Bank holding companies may also avoid some state banking regulations.

The operations, management, and regulation of a commercial bank vary with the types of services offered. Therefore, the different types of financial services (such as banking, securities, and insurance) are discussed in separate chapters of this book. This chapter on commercial bank operations applies to independent commercial banks as well as to commercial bank units that are part of a financial conglomerate formed by combining a bank and other financial services firms.

The traditional role of a bank was to serve depositors who want to deposit funds and borrowers who want to borrow funds. Banks charge a higher interest rate on funds loaned out than the interest rate they pay on deposits. The difference in interest between loans and deposits must be sufficient to cover the bank's other expenses (such as salaries) and generate a reasonable profit for the bank's owners. Although banks have become much more sophisticated over time, they continue to serve their traditional role in the financial system.

The primary operations of commercial banks can be most easily identified by reviewing their main sources of funds, their main uses of funds, and the off-balance sheet activities that they provide, as explained in this chapter.

WEB

www.fdic.gov
Statistics on banks'
sources and uses of
funds.

17-2 Banks' Sources of Funds

A review of its balance sheet will reveal how any financial institution (or subsidiary of that institution) obtains funds and uses funds. The institution's reported liabilities and equity indicate its sources of funds, and its reported assets indicate its uses of funds. The major sources of commercial banks' funds are summarized as follows.

Deposit Accounts
1. Transaction deposits
2. Savings deposits
3. Time deposits
4. Money market deposit accounts

Borrowed Funds
1. Federal funds purchased (borrowed)
2. Borrowing from the Federal Reserve banks
3. Repurchase agreements
4. Eurodollar borrowings

Long-Term Sources of Funds
1. Bonds issued by the bank
2. Bank capital

Each source of funds is briefly described in the following subsections.

17-2a **Transaction Deposits**

A **demand deposit account**, or checking account, is offered to customers who desire to write checks against their account or make payments using debit cards. A conventional demand deposit account requires a small minimum balance and pays no interest. From the bank's perspective, demand deposit accounts are classified as transaction accounts that provide a source of funds that can be used until withdrawn by customers (as payments are made with debit cards or checks are written).

Another type of transaction deposit is the **negotiable order of withdrawal (NOW) account**, which pays interest as well as provides checking and debit card services. Because NOW accounts at most financial institutions require a larger minimum balance than some consumers are willing to maintain in a transaction account, traditional demand deposit accounts remain popular.

Electronic Transaction   Most transactions originating from transaction accounts have become much more efficient as a result of electronic banking. Most employees in the United States have direct deposit accounts, which allow their paychecks to be directly deposited in their transaction account (or other accounts). Social Security recipients also have their monthly checks deposited directly in their bank accounts. Online banking enables bank customers to view their bank accounts online, pay bills, make credit card payments, order checks, and transfer funds between accounts.

Bank customers may use automated teller machines (ATMs) to make withdrawals from their transaction accounts, add deposits, check their account balances, and transfer funds. Debit cards allow bank customers to use a card when making purchases, with their bank account being immediately debited to reflect the amount spent. Banks also allow preauthorized debits, in which specific periodic payments are automatically transferred from a customer's bank account to a particular recipient. Preauthorized debits are commonly used to cover recurring monthly expenses such as utility bills, car loan payments, and mortgage payments. Most banks now also offer mobile apps that allow customers to deposit checks through their smartphone, view their accounts, and pay for purchases and have their account debited for the amount.

17-2b Savings Deposits

The traditional savings account is the passbook savings account, which does not permit check writing or the use of a debit card. Passbook savings accounts continue to attract savers with a small amount of funds, as such accounts often have no required minimum balance. Banks also offer various other savings accounts, which require a minimum balance or the payment of a monthly fee. The savings account is usually linked to the customer's checking account, and the customer can transfer funds from one account to the other.

17-2c Time Deposits

Time deposits are deposits that cannot be withdrawn until a specified maturity date. The two most common types of time deposits are certificates of deposit (CDs) and negotiable certificates of deposit.

Certificates of Deposit   A common type of time deposit is a retail certificate of deposit (retail CD), which requires a specified minimum amount of funds to be deposited for a specified period of time. Banks offer a wide variety of CDs to satisfy depositors' needs. Annualized interest rates offered on CDs vary among banks and even among maturity types at a single bank. There is no secondary market for retail CDs. Depositors must leave their funds in the bank until the specified maturity or forgo a portion of their interest as a penalty for early withdrawal of those funds.

The rates offered by CDs are easily accessible on numerous websites. For example, Bankrate (www.bankrate.com) and Bank CD-Rate Scanner (www.bankcd.com) identify the banks that are currently paying the highest interest rates on CDs. Because they can readily access CD rate information online, many depositors invest in CDs at banks far away to earn a higher rate than that offered by local banks. Some banks allow depositors to invest in CDs online by providing a credit card number.

In recent years, some financial institutions have begun to offer CDs with a callable feature (referred to as callable CDs). That is, they can be called by the financial institution, forcing an earlier maturity. For example, a bank could issue a callable CD with a five-year maturity, callable after two years. In two years, the financial institution will likely call the CD if it can obtain funds at a lower rate over the following three years than the rate paid on that CD. Depositors who invest in callable CDs earn a slightly higher interest rate, which compensates them for the risk that the CD may be called.

Negotiable Certificates of Deposit   Another type of time deposit is the **negotiable certificate of deposit (NCD)**, which some large banks offer to their corporate customers. Negotiable CDs are similar to retail CDs in that they have a specified maturity date and require a minimum deposit. Their maturities are typically short term, and their minimum deposit requirement is $100,000. A secondary market for NCDs does exist.

The level of large time deposits is much more volatile than that of small time deposits, because investors with large sums of money frequently shift their funds from place to place in an effort to earn higher rates. Small investors do not have as many options as large investors and, therefore, are less likely to shift their funds in and out of small time deposits.

17-2d Money Market Deposit Accounts

Money market deposit accounts (MMDAs) differ from conventional time deposits in that they do not specify a maturity. From the depositor's point of view, MMDAs are more liquid than retail CDs but offer a lower interest rate. They differ from NOW accounts in that they provide limited check-writing ability (a limited number of transactions is allowed per month), require a larger minimum balance, and offer a higher yield.

17-2e Federal Funds Purchased

The other sources of funds for banks are of nondepository nature. Banks tap these sources when they temporarily need more funds than are being deposited. Some banks use nondepository funds as a permanent source of funds.

One source of nondepository funds is the federal funds market, which allows depository institutions to accommodate the short-term liquidity needs of other financial institutions. Federal funds purchased (or borrowed) represent a liability to the borrowing bank and an asset to the lending bank that sells (or loans) them. Loans in the federal funds market are typically for one to seven days. Such loans can be rolled over so that a series of one-day loans can be made. The intent of federal funds transactions is to correct short-term fund imbalances experienced by banks. A bank may act as a lender of federal funds on one day and as a borrower shortly thereafter, as its fund balance changes on a daily basis.

The interest rate charged in the federal funds market is called the **federal funds rate**. Like other market interest rates, it moves in reaction to changes in demand or supply, or both. If many banks have excess funds and few banks are short of funds, the federal funds rate will be low. Conversely, a high demand by many banks to borrow in the federal funds market combined with a small supply of excess funds available at other banks will result in a higher federal funds rate. The federal funds rate is typically the same for all banks borrowing in the federal funds market, although a financially troubled bank may have to pay a higher rate.

The federal funds rate is quoted on an annualized basis (using a 360-day year), even though the loans are usually for terms of less than one week. This rate is typically close to the yield on a Treasury security with a similar term remaining until maturity.

The federal funds market is typically most active on Wednesday, which is the final day of the particular settlement period for which each bank must maintain a specified volume of reserves required by the Fed. Banks that were short of required reserves, on average, over the period must compensate with additional required reserves before the settlement period ends. Because large banks frequently need temporary funds, they often borrow in the federal funds market.

WEB

www.newyorkfed.org
Click "Data & Statistics"
and then "Federal
Funds Data" to find
information about bank
borrowing in the federal
funds market.

17-2f Borrowing from the Federal Reserve Banks

Another temporary source of funds for banks is the Federal Reserve System, which serves as the U.S. central bank. Along with other bank regulators, the Federal Reserve district banks regulate certain activities of commercial banks. They also provide short-term loans to banks (as well as to some other depository institutions) through the Fed's lending facility, sometimes referred to as the discount window. The interest rate charged on these loans is known as the **primary credit rate**.

Since January 2003, the primary credit rate has been set at a level that exceeds the federal funds rate. This practice is intended to ensure that banks rely on the federal funds market for normal short-term financing and borrow from the Fed only as a last resort.

Loans from the Federal Reserve are short term, commonly with a duration from one day to a few weeks. To ensure that they have a justifiable need for the funds, banks that wish to borrow from the Federal Reserve must first obtain the Fed's approval. As in the federal funds market, loans from the Fed are mainly used to resolve a temporary shortage of funds.

The Federal Reserve's role is intended to be that of a source of funds when banks experience unanticipated shortages of reserves. Frequent borrowing to offset reserve shortages implies that a bank has a permanent (rather than temporary) need for funds and should develop a strategy to obtain a more permanent source of funds by increasing its level of deposits. The Fed may veto continuous borrowing by a bank unless extenuating circumstances exist that would prevent the bank from obtaining temporary financing from other financial institutions.

17-2g Repurchase Agreements

A **repurchase agreement (repo)** represents the sale of securities by one party to another, combined with an agreement to repurchase the securities at a specified date and price. Banks often use a repo as a source of funds when they expect to need funds for just a few days. The bank simply sells some of its government securities (such as Treasury bills) to a corporation with a temporary excess of funds; it then buys those securities back shortly thereafter. The government securities involved in the repo transaction serve as collateral for the corporation providing funds to the bank.

Repurchase agreement transactions occur through a telecommunications network connecting large banks, other corporations, government securities dealers, and federal funds brokers. The federal funds brokers match up firms or dealers that need funds (wish to sell and later repurchase their securities) with those that have excess funds (are willing to purchase securities now and sell them back on a specified date). Transactions are typically in blocks of $1 million. Like the federal funds rate, the yield on repurchase agreements is quoted on an annualized basis (using a 360-day year), even though the loans are for short-term periods. The yield on repurchase agreements is slightly less than the federal funds rate at any given time because the funds loaned out are backed by collateral and, therefore, are less risky.

17-2h Eurodollar Borrowings

If a U.S. bank is in need of short-term funds, it may borrow dollars from banks outside the United States (typically in Europe) that accept dollar-denominated deposits, also called **Eurodollars**. Some foreign banks (or foreign branches of U.S. banks) accept large short-term deposits and make short-term loans in dollars. Because U.S. dollars are widely used as an international medium of exchange, the Eurodollar market is very active.

17-2i Bonds Issued by the Bank

Like other corporations, banks own some fixed assets, such as land, buildings, and equipment. These assets often have an expected life of 20 years or more and are usually financed with such long-term sources as the issuance of bonds. Common purchasers of these bonds are households and various financial institutions, including life insurance companies and pension funds. Banks are less likely to issue bonds compared to most other corporations because they have fewer fixed assets than corporations that use industrial equipment and machinery for production.

17-2j Bank Capital

Bank capital generally represents funds acquired through stock issues or retained earnings. In either case, the bank has no obligation to pay out funds in the future. This characteristic distinguishes bank capital from all the other sources of funds, which represent a future obligation by the bank to pay out funds. Bank capital as defined here represents the equity or net worth of the bank. Capital can be classified as primary or secondary. Primary capital results from issuing common or preferred stock or retaining earnings, whereas secondary capital results from issuing subordinated notes and bonds.

A bank's capital must be sufficient to absorb operating losses in the event that its expenses or losses exceed its revenues, regardless of the reason for those losses. Although long-term bonds are sometimes considered to be secondary capital, they represent a liability to the bank, so they do not appropriately cushion the bank against operating losses.

Although the issuance of new stock increases a bank's capital, it dilutes the bank's ownership, because the proportion of the bank owned by existing shareholders decreases. A bank's reported earnings per share are also reduced when additional shares of stock are issued, unless earnings increase by a greater proportion than the increase in outstanding shares. For these reasons, banks generally avoid issuing new stock unless absolutely necessary.

Bank regulators are concerned that banks might maintain a lower level of capital than they should and, have, therefore imposed capital requirements on them. Because unused capital can be used to absorb losses, a higher level of capital is thought to enhance a bank's safety and may increase the public's confidence in the banking system.

The required level of capital for each bank depends on its risk. Assets with low risk are assigned relatively low weights, whereas assets with high risk are assigned high weights. Bank regulators then set the capital level as a percentage of the risk-weighted assets. As a result of this regulatory scheme, riskier banks are subject to higher capital requirements. The same risk-based capital guidelines used in the United States have been imposed in several other industrialized countries. Additional details are provided in Chapter 18.

17-2k Distribution of Banks' Sources of Funds

Exhibit 17.2 shows the distribution of banks' sources of funds. Deposit accounts make up 76 percent of all bank liabilities. The distribution of sources of funds is influenced by bank size, however. Smaller banks rely more heavily on savings deposits than do larger banks, because small banks concentrate on household savings, which constitute relatively small deposits. Much of this differential is made up in large time deposits (such as NCDs) for very large banks. In addition, the larger banks rely more on short-term borrowings than do small banks. The impact of the differences in the composition of fund sources on bank performance is discussed in Chapter 20.

Exhibit 17.2 Banks' Sources of Funds (as a Proportion of Total Liabilities)

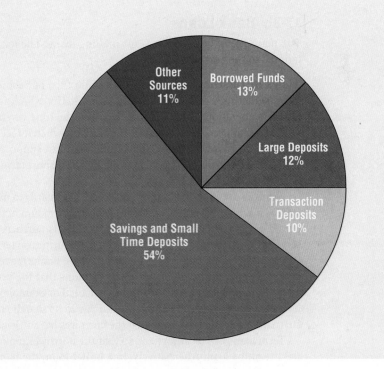

Source: Federal Reserve.

17-3 Banks' Uses of Funds

With the main sources of banks' funds now understood, these institutions' uses of funds can be discussed. Common uses of funds by banks include the following:

- Cash
- Bank loans
- Investment in securities
- Federal funds sold (loaned out)
- Repurchase agreements
- Eurodollar loans
- Fixed assets
- Proprietary trading

17-3a Cash

Banks must hold some cash as reserves to meet the reserve requirements enforced by the Federal Reserve. They also hold cash to maintain some liquidity and to accommodate withdrawal requests by depositors. Because banks do not earn income from cash, they hold only the minimum amount of cash necessary to maintain a sufficient degree of liquidity. Their ability to tap various sources for temporary funds frees banks from being overly concerned with maintaining excess reserves.

Banks hold cash both in their vaults and at their Federal Reserve district bank. Vault cash is useful for accommodating withdrawal requests by customers or for qualifying as required reserves, whereas cash held at the Federal Reserve district banks represents the major portion of required reserves. The Fed mandates that banks maintain required reserves because they provide a means by which the Fed can control the money supply. The amount of required reserves that each bank must maintain depends on the composition of its deposits.

17-3b Bank Loans

The main use of bank funds is for making loans. The loan amount and maturity can be tailored to the borrower's needs.

Types of Business Loans   A common type of business loan is the **working capital loan** (sometimes called a self-liquidating loan), which is designed to support ongoing business operations. There is a lag between the time when a firm needs cash to purchase raw materials used in production and the time when it receives cash inflows from the sales of finished products. A working capital loan can support the business until it generates sufficient cash inflows. These loans are typically short term in duration, but a business may need them on a frequent basis.

Banks also offer **term loans**, which are used primarily to finance the purchase of fixed assets such as machinery. With a term loan, a specified amount of funds is loaned out for a specified period of time and a specified purpose. The assets purchased with the borrowed funds may serve as partial or full collateral on the loan. Maturities on term loans commonly range from 2 to 5 years, but are sometimes as long as 10 years. Banks that offer term loans typically impose protective covenants, which specify conditions that the borrower must meet and that are intended to protect the bank from loan default. For example, a bank may specify a maximum level of dividends that the borrower can pay to its shareholders each year. Such a protective covenant is intended to ensure that the borrower has sufficient cash to repay its loan on time.

Term loans can be amortized so that the borrower makes fixed periodic payments over the life of the loan. Alternatively, in a **bullet loan**, the bank periodically requests interest payments, with the loan principal to be paid off in one lump sum (called a **balloon payment**) at a specified date in the future. Several combinations of these payment methods are also possible. For example, a portion of the loan may be amortized over the life of the loan while the remaining portion is covered with a balloon payment.

As an alternative to providing a term loan, the bank may purchase the assets and lease them to the firm that needs them. This method, known as a **direct lease loan**, may be especially appropriate when the firm wishes to avoid adding more debt to its balance sheet. Because the bank is the owner of the assets, it can depreciate them over time for tax purposes.

A more flexible financing arrangement is the informal line of credit, which allows the business to borrow up to a specified amount within a specified period of time. This sort of financing is useful for firms that may experience a sudden need for funds but do not know precisely when. The interest rate charged on any borrowed funds is typically adjustable in accordance with prevailing market rates. Banks are not legally obligated to provide funds to the business, but they usually honor the arrangement to avoid harming their reputation.

An alternative to the informal line of credit is the **revolving credit loan**, which obligates the bank to offer up to some specified maximum amount of funds over a specified period of time (typically less than five years). Because the bank is committed to provide funds when requested, it typically charges businesses a commitment fee (of about one-half of 1 percent) on any unused funds.

The interest rate charged by banks on business loans is known as the **prime rate**. However, some banks offer a lower rate than the prime rate to their most creditworthy business customers. Banks periodically revise the prime rate in response to changes in market interest rates, which reflect changes in the bank's cost of funds. As a consequence, the prime rate moves in tandem with the Treasury bill rate and other market interest rates. Exhibit 17.3 shows changes in the prime rate since 2004. It increased during the 2004–2006 period when economic conditions were strong, but decreased during the credit crisis of 2008. It was very

Exhibit 17.3   Prime Rate over Time

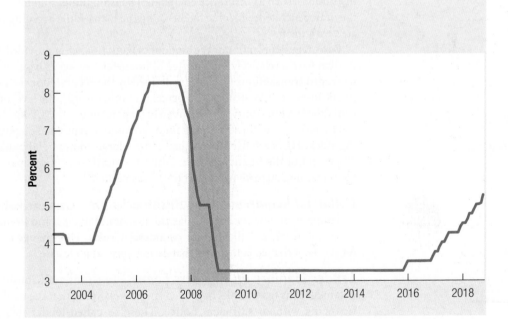

Note: *Shaded area indicates recession.*
Source: *Board of Governors of the Federal Reserve System.*

low during the 2009–2016 period when the United States was recovering from the credit crisis. As the economy strengthened during the 2016–2019 period, the prime rate increased along with many other market interest rates.

Loan Participations

Some large corporations wish to borrow a larger amount of funds than any individual bank is willing to provide. To accommodate this customer, several banks may be willing to pool their available funds in a **loan participation**. The lead bank arranges for the documentation, disbursement, and payment structure of the loan; the other banks supply funds that are channeled to the borrower by the lead bank. The borrower may not even realize that other banks have provided much of the funds. As interest payments are received, the lead bank passes the payments on to the other participants in proportion to the original loan amounts they provided. The lead bank receives fees for servicing the loan in addition to its share of interest payments.

The lead bank is expected to ensure that the borrower repays the loan. It is rarely required to guarantee the interest payments, however, so all participating banks are exposed to credit (default) risk.

Loans Supporting Leveraged Buyouts

Some commercial banks finance leveraged buyouts (LBOs), in which a management group or a business relies mostly on debt to purchase the equity of another business. Firms request LBO financing when they perceive that the market value of certain publicly held shares is too low. Yet because the borrowers are highly leveraged, they may experience cash flow pressure during periods when sales are lower than normal. These firms would like to have access to equity funds, because those funds can serve as a cushion during periods of poor economic conditions. Although the firms prefer not to go public again during such periods, they are at least capable of doing so. Banks financing these firms can, as a condition of any loan, require that the firms reissue stock if they experience cash flow problems.

Some banks originate the loans designed for LBOs and then sell them to other financial institutions, such as insurance companies, pension funds, and foreign banks. In this way, they can generate fee income by servicing the loans while avoiding the credit risk associated with them.

Bank regulators monitor the amount of bank financing provided to corporate borrowers that have a relatively high degree of financial leverage. These loans, known as **highly leveraged transactions (HLTs)**, are defined by the Federal Reserve as credit that results in a debt-to-asset ratio of at least 75 percent. In other words, the level of debt is at least three times the level of equity. Approximately 60 percent of all HLT funds are used to finance LBOs, and some of the remaining funds are used to repurchase a portion of the outstanding stock. HLTs are usually originated by a large commercial bank that provides 10 to 20 percent of the financing itself. Other financial institutions participate by providing the remaining 80 to 90 percent of the funds needed.

Collateral Requirements on Business Loans

Commercial banks are increasingly accepting intangible assets (such as patents, brand names, and licenses to franchises and distributorships) as collateral for commercial loans. This change is especially important for service-oriented companies that do not have tangible assets.

Lender Liability on Business Loans

In recent years, businesses that previously obtained loans from banks have filed lawsuits claiming that the banks terminated further financing without sufficient notice. These so-called lender liability suits have been especially prevalent in the farming, grocery, clothing, and oil industries.

Volume of Business Loans   The volume of business loans provided by commercial banks changes over time in response to economic conditions. When the economy is strong, businesses are more willing to finance expansion. When economic conditions are weak, businesses defer expansion plans and, therefore, do not need as much financing. As an example, economic growth increased during the 2004–2006 period, resulting in a major increase in business loans provided by banks. In contrast, during the credit crisis of 2008–2009, the volume of business loans decreased.

Types of Consumer Loans   Commercial banks may provide individuals with **installment loans** to finance purchases of cars and household products. These loans require the borrowers to make periodic payments over time.

Banks may also provide credit cards to consumers. Credit card holders are assigned a maximum limit based on their income and credit history, and a fixed annual fee may be charged to maintain the account. This service often involves an agreement with VISA or MasterCard. If consumers pay off the balance each month, they usually are not charged interest. Bank rates on credit card balances are sometimes nearly double the rate charged on business loans. State regulators can impose **usury laws** that restrict the maximum rate of interest charged by banks, and these laws may be applied to credit card loans as well.

Assessing the applicant's creditworthiness is much easier for consumer loans than for corporate loans. An individual's cash flow is typically simpler and more predictable than a firm's cash flow. In addition, the average loan amount to an individual is relatively small, warranting a less detailed credit analysis.

Because the interest rate on credit card loans and personal loans is typically much higher than the cost of funds, many commercial banks have pursued these types of loans as a means of increasing their earnings. The most common method of increasing such loans is to use more lenient guidelines when assessing the creditworthiness of potential customers, but doing so creates an obvious trade-off between the potential return and the bank's exposure to credit risk. When commercial banks experience an increase in defaults on credit card loans and other personal loans, they respond by increasing their standards for such loans. This results in a reduced allocation of funds to credit card loans, which also reduces the potential returns of the bank. When the economy weakened during the credit crisis of 2008–2009, for example, many banks raised their standards for credit card loans and reduced the amount of credit that they would extend to consumers. As economic conditions improved after the crisis, commercial banks increased their allocation of funds toward credit card loans.

Real Estate Loans   Banks also provide real estate loans. For residential real estate loans, the maturity on a mortgage is typically 15 to 30 years. The loan is backed by the residence purchased. During the economic expansion in the 2004–2006 period, many banks offered loans to home buyers with questionable credit histories. These *subprime* mortgages were given to home buyers who had relatively lower incomes, high existing debt, or only a small down payment for purchasing a home. Many commercial banks expected to benefit from subprime mortgage loans because they could charge higher up-front fees (such as appraisal fees) and interest rates on the mortgages to compensate for the risk of default. Furthermore, they presumed that home values would continue to rise, such that the residence backing the loan would serve as adequate collateral.

In 2008, however, many borrowers defaulted on their subprime mortgages. Indeed, as of January 2009, about 10 percent of all U.S. homeowners with mortgages were either late on their payments or subject to foreclosure. Banks and other financial institutions were forced to assume ownership of many homes, which led to an excess supply of homes in the housing market. Consequently, the prices of homes declined substantially, which further reduced the collateral value of the homes taken back by the banks. Thus banks that originated mortgages and held them as assets were adversely affected by the credit crisis.

Commercial banks also provide commercial real estate loans, such as loans to build shopping malls and office buildings. The banks commonly retain the commercial real estate loans that they originate as assets. Banks and other financial institutions are likely to use greater diligence in assessing real estate loan applicants when they retain the mortgages that they originate rather than selling them to a third party.

17-3c Investment in Securities

Banks purchase various types of securities. One advantage of investing funds in securities rather than making loans is that the securities tend to be more liquid. In addition, banks can easily invest in securities, whereas more resources are required to assess loan applicants and service loans. However, banks typically expect to generate higher rates of return on funds used to provide loans.

Treasury and Agency Securities   Banks purchase Treasury securities as well as securities issued by agencies of the federal government. Government agency securities can be sold in the secondary market, but this market is not as active as it is for Treasury securities. Federal agency securities are commonly issued by federal agencies, such as the Federal National Mortgage Association (Fannie Mae) and the Federal Home Loan Mortgage Corporation (Freddie Mac). Funds received by the agencies issuing these securities are used to purchase mortgages from various financial institutions. Such securities have maturities that can range from 1 month to 25 years.

The values of the mortgages held by Fannie Mae and Freddie Mac declined in 2008 as a result of the large number of late payments and mortgage defaults during the credit crisis. Consequently, concerns arose that Fannie Mae and Freddie Mac might not be able to cover their debt security payments. In September 2008, the U.S. government took control of Fannie Mae and Freddie Mac, thereby ensuring the safety of the debt securities issued by these agencies.

Corporate and Municipal Bonds   Banks also purchase corporate and municipal bonds. Although corporate bonds are subject to credit risk, they offer a higher return than do Treasury or government agency securities. Municipal bonds exhibit some degree of risk but can also provide an attractive return to banks, especially when their after-tax return is considered. The interest income earned from municipal securities is exempt from federal taxation. Banks purchase only **investment-grade securities**, which are those rated as "medium quality" or higher by rating agencies.

Mortgage-Backed Securities   Banks also commonly purchase mortgage-backed securities (MBS), which represent packages of mortgages. Banks tend to purchase mortgages within a particular "tranche" that is categorized as having relatively low risk. During the credit crisis of 2008–2009, however, many defaults on mortgages occurred within tranches that had been assigned high ratings by rating agencies. Consequently, banks that had invested in MBS experienced losses during the credit crisis. The market value of MBS at any bank is difficult to measure because the MBS are not standardized and the secondary market transactions between parties are not conducted through an organized exchange. Thus two banks could have an equal proportion of their assets classified as MBS, but one bank's MBS may be much riskier than the other bank's MBS.

17-3d Federal Funds Sold

Some banks frequently lend funds to other banks in the federal funds market. The funds sold, or lent out, will be returned (with interest) at the time specified in the loan agreement. The loan period is typically very short, such as a day or a few days. Small banks often act as providers of funds in the federal funds market. If the transaction is executed by a broker, the borrower's cost on a federal funds loan is slightly higher than the lender's return because the broker matching up the two parties charges a transaction fee.

17-3e Repurchase Agreements

Recall that, from the borrower's perspective, a repurchase agreement transaction involves repurchasing the securities it had previously sold. From a lender's perspective, the repo represents a sale of securities that it had previously purchased. Banks can act as the lender (on a repo) by purchasing a corporation's holdings of Treasury securities and then selling them back at a later date. This kind of transaction provides short-term funds to the corporation, and the bank's loan is backed by these securities.

17-3f Eurodollar Loans

Branches of U.S. banks located outside the United States, as well as some foreign-owned banks, provide dollar-denominated loans to corporations and governments. Such Eurodollar loans are common because the dollar is frequently used for international transactions. Eurodollar loans are short term and denominated in large amounts, such as $1 million or more.

17-3g Fixed Assets

Banks must maintain some amount of fixed assets, such as office buildings and land, so that they can conduct their business operations. However, this is not a concern to the bank managers who decide how day-to-day incoming funds will be used. They direct these funds into the other types of assets already identified.

17-3h Proprietary Trading

Banks also engage in proprietary (or "prop") trading, in which they use their own funds to make investments for their own account. For example, banks may have an equity trading desk that takes positions in equity securities as well as a fixed-income desk that takes speculative positions in bonds and other debt securities; they may also have a derivatives trading desk that takes speculative positions in derivative securities. Proprietary trading was a major contributor to the total income generated by commercial banks prior to the credit crisis that began in 2008, when economic conditions were very favorable. The trading desks tended to take on much more risk than traditional bank lending operations involve, and some commercial banks experienced large losses on their proprietary trading during the credit crisis.

Banks also manage investment portfolios in which they pool funds provided by clients and then invest those funds on behalf of the clients. They charge the clients an annual management fee for managing these funds. Banks may own private equity funds, which pool funds provided by wealthy individual and institutional investors, and then invest the funds in businesses. They may charge their investor clients fees for this service and also take a portion of the profits from the funds.

The Financial Reform Act of 2010 (formally called the Dodd-Frank Wall Street Reform and Consumer Protection Act) imposed a limit on the amount of proprietary trading in which banks can engage. This provision is referred to as the Volcker Rule, because it was recommended by Paul Volcker, a previous chair of the Federal Reserve. Final regulations implementing the Volcker Rule went into effect in January 2014, although full compliance with the rule was not required immediately. The rule prevents banks from engaging in short-term trading of derivative securities and some financial instruments, but allows them to continue underwriting, hedging, investing for clients, trading government securities, and other activities unless doing so creates a conflict of interest or poses a risk to the financial system. To comply with the rule, many banks have spun off part of their proprietary trading activities into a separate entity. The Volcker Rule is discussed in more detail in Chapter 18.

17-3i Distribution of Banks' Uses of Funds

Exhibit 17.4 illustrates the distribution of banks' uses of funds. Loans of all types make up approximately 61 percent of bank assets, whereas securities account for approximately 23 percent. The distribution of assets for an individual bank varies with the type of bank. For example, smaller banks tend to have a relatively large amount of household loans and government securities; larger banks have a higher level of business loans (including loans to foreign firms).

The distribution of banks' uses of funds indicates how commercial banks operate. In recent years, however, banks have begun to provide numerous services that are not indicated on their balance sheet. These services differ markedly from banks' traditional operations, which focused mostly on channeling deposited funds into various types of loans and investments.

Exhibit 17.4 Banks' Uses of Funds (as a Proportion of Total Assets)

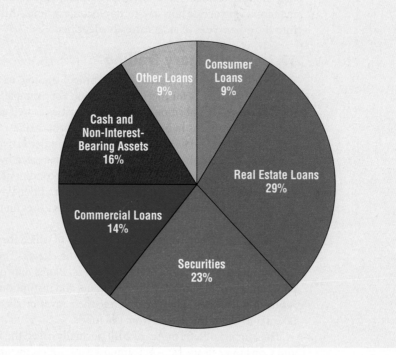

Source: Federal Reserve 2019.

Commercial Bank Balance Sheet   A commercial bank's sources of funds represent its liabilities or equity, and its uses of funds represent its assets. Each commercial bank determines its own composition of liabilities and assets, which determines its specific operations.

EXAMPLE

Exhibit 17.5 shows the balance sheet of Hornet Bank. The bank's assets are shown on the left side of the balance sheet. The second column indicates the dollar amount of each asset, and the third column shows the size of each asset in proportion to total assets to illustrate how Hornet Bank distributes its funds. Hornet's main assets are commercial and consumer loans, in addition to securities. The balance sheet shows the bank's holdings at a particular moment in time, but the bank frequently revises the composition of its assets in response to economic conditions. When the economy is strong and creditworthy businesses want to expand, Hornet Bank will sell some of its holdings of Treasury securities and use the funds to provide more corporate loans.

Hornet Bank's liabilities and stockholders' equity are shown on the right side of the balance sheet. Hornet obtains funds from various types of deposits, and incurs some expenses from all types of deposits. In particular, it must hire employees to serve depositors. The composition of Hornet's liabilities determines its interest expenses. Hornet does not pay interest on demand deposits, but it does pay a relatively high interest rate on large CDs.

Hornet also incurs expenses from managing its assets. Its main expense is the cost of hiring employees to assess the creditworthiness of businesses and households that request loans. In general, Hornet wants to generate enough income from its assets so that it can cover its expenses and provide a reasonable return to its shareholders. Its primary source of income is the interest received on the business loans that it provides. Its capital is shown on the balance sheet as common stock issued and retained earnings. ●

Exhibit 17.5   Balance Sheet of Hornet Bank as of June 30, 2019

ASSETS	DOLLAR AMOUNT (IN MILLIONS)	PROPORTION OF TOTAL ASSETS	LIABILITIES AND STOCKHOLDERS' EQUITY	DOLLAR AMOUNT (IN MILLIONS)	PROPORTION OF TOTAL LIABILITIES AND STOCK-HOLDERS' EQUITY
Cash (includes required reserves)	$50	5%	Demand deposits	$250	25%
Commercial loans	400	40%	NOW accounts	60	6%
Consumer loans	250	25%	Money market deposit accounts	200	20%
Treasury securities	80	8%	Short-term CDs	250	25%
Corporate securities	120	12%	CDs with maturities beyond one year	120	12%
Federal funds sold (lent out)	10	1%	Federal funds purchased (borrowed)	0	0%
Repurchase agreements	20	2%	Long-term debt	30	3%
Eurodollar loans	0	0%			
Fixed assets	70	7%	Common stock issued	50	5%
			Retained earnings	40	4%
TOTAL ASSETS	$1,000	100%	TOTAL LIABILITIES AND STOCKHOLDERS' EQUITY	$1,000	100%

Exhibit 17.6   How Commercial Banks Finance Economic Growth

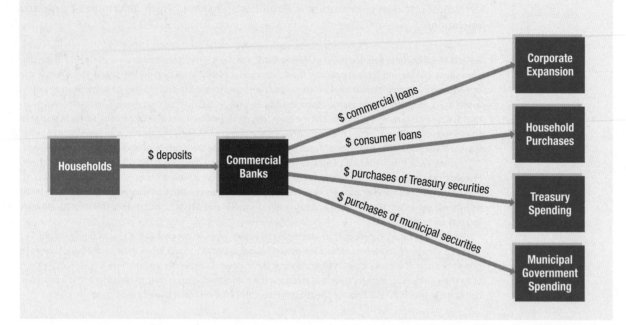

Exhibit 17.6 shows how commercial banks use the key balance sheet items to finance economic growth. They channel funds from their depositors to households, thereby financing household spending. They channel funds from depositors to corporations, thereby financing corporate expansion. They also use some deposits to purchase Treasury and municipal securities, thereby financing spending by the Treasury and municipalities.

17-4 Off-Balance Sheet Activities

Banks commonly engage in off-balance sheet activities, which generate fee income without requiring an investment of funds. However, these activities create a contingent obligation for banks. The following are some of the more popular off-balance sheet activities:

- Loan commitments
- Standby letters of credit
- Forward contracts on currencies
- Interest rate swap contracts
- Credit default swap contracts

17-4a Loan Commitments

A loan commitment is an obligation by a bank to provide a specified loan amount to a particular firm upon the firm's request. The interest rate and purpose of the loan may also be specified. The bank charges a fee for offering the commitment.

One type of loan commitment is a **note issuance facility (NIF)**, in which the bank agrees purchase the commercial paper of a firm if the firm cannot place its paper in the market at an acceptable interest rate. Although banks earn fees for their commitments, they could experience illiquidity if numerous firms request their loans at the same time.

17-4b Standby Letters of Credit

A **standby letter of credit (SLC)** backs a customer's obligation to a third party. If the customer does not meet its obligation, the bank will. The third party may require that the customer obtain an SLC to complete a business transaction. For example, consider a municipality that wants to issue bonds. To ensure that the bonds are easily placed, a bank could provide an SLC that guarantees payment of the interest and principal. In essence, the bank uses its credit rating to enhance the perceived safety of the bonds. In return for the guarantee, the bank charges a fee to the municipality. The bank should be willing to provide the SLC only if the fee received compensates for the possibility that the municipality will default on its obligation.

17-4c Forward Contracts on Currencies

A forward contract on currency is an agreement between a customer and a bank to exchange one currency for another on a particular future date at a specified exchange rate. Banks engage in forward contracts with customers that desire to hedge their exchange rate risk. For example, a U.S. bank may agree to purchase 5 million euros in one year from a firm for $1.10 per euro. The bank may simultaneously find another firm that wishes to exchange 5 million euros for dollars in one year. The bank can serve as an intermediary and accommodate both requests, earning a transaction fee for its services. In doing so, however, it becomes exposed to the risk that one of the parties will default on its obligation.

17-4d Interest Rate Swap Contracts

Banks also serve as intermediaries for interest rate swaps, whereby two parties agree to periodically exchange interest payments on a specified notional amount of principal. Once again, the bank receives a transaction fee for its services. If it guarantees payments to both parties, it becomes exposed to the risk that one of the parties will default on its obligation. If that event occurs, the bank must assume the role of that party and fulfill the obligation to the other party.

Some banks facilitate currency swaps (for a fee) by finding parties with opposite future currency needs and executing a swap agreement. Currency swaps are similar to forward contracts, but they usually involve more distant future dates.

17-4e Credit Default Swap Contracts

Credit default swaps are privately negotiated contracts that protect investors against the risk of default on particular debt securities. Some commercial banks and other financial institutions buy them to protect their own investments in debt securities against default risk; other banks and financial institutions sell them. The banks that sell credit default swaps receive periodic coupon payments for the term of the swap agreement. A typical term of a credit default swap is five years. If there are no defaults on the debt securities, the banks that sold the credit default swaps benefit because they have received periodic payments but were not required to make any payments. However, when there are defaults on the debt securities, the sellers of credit default swaps must make payments to the buyers to cover the damages. In essence, the sellers of credit default swaps are providing insurance against default.

Credit default swaps contracts were widely used to protect against the default risk from investing in mortgage-backed securities. During the credit crisis of 2008, commercial banks that sold these contracts incurred major expenses because of the high frequency of defaults on MBS. Conversely, commercial banks that purchased credit default swap contracts reduced the adverse impact of defaults on MBS (assuming that the counterparty that sold them the swaps did not default on its obligation).

17-5 International Banking

Until historical barriers against interstate banking were largely removed in 1994, some U.S. commercial banks were better able to achieve growth by penetrating foreign markets than by expanding at home. Many U.S. banks have expanded internationally to improve their prospects for growth and to diversify so that their business will not be dependent on a single economy.

17-5a International Expansion

The most common way for U.S. commercial banks to expand internationally is by establishing branches, which are full-service banking offices that can compete directly with other banks located in a particular area. Before establishing foreign branches, a U.S. bank must obtain the approval of the Federal Reserve Board. Among the factors considered by the Fed are the bank's financial condition and experience in international business. Commercial banks may also consider establishing agencies, which can provide loans but cannot accept deposits or provide trust services.

U.S. banks have recently established foreign subsidiaries wherever they expect increased foreign expansion by U.S. firms, such as in Southeast Asia and Eastern Europe. Recently, expansion has also been focused on Latin America. The subsidiaries offer banker's acceptances, foreign exchange services, credit card services, and other household services.

As an example of the diversity in international banking services, Citigroup offers a number of key services to firms around the world, including foreign exchange transactions, forecasting, risk management, cross-border trade finance, acquisition finance, cash management services, and local currency funding. Citigroup serves not only large multinational corporations (for example, Coca-Cola, IBM, and Sony) but also small firms that need international banking services. By spreading itself across the world, Citigroup can typically handle the banking needs of all the subsidiaries of a multinational corporation.

17-5b Impact of the Euro on Global Competition

The use of a single currency in a number of European countries simplifies transactions because the majority of a bank's transactions between those countries are now denominated in euros. Use of the euro also reduces exposure to exchange rate risk, as banks can accept deposits in euros and use euros to lend funds or invest in securities. The use of a single currency throughout many European countries may also encourage firms to engage in bond or stock offerings to support their European business, as the euro can be used to support most of that business. Commercial banks can serve as intermediaries by underwriting and placing the debt or the equity issued by firms.

The single currency makes it easier to achieve economies of scale and to increase the efficiency of banks' internal reporting systems. As banks expand and capitalize on economies of scale, global competition has become more intense. Furthermore, the euro enables businesses in Europe to more easily compare the prices of services offered by banks based in different European countries. This also forces banks to be more competitive.

17-5c International Exposure

As banks attempt to penetrate international markets in an effort to capitalize on opportunities, they become exposed to conditions in those markets. In particular, European countries such as Greece, Portugal, and Spain have experienced weak economies and large budget deficits. The governments of these countries have borrowed substantially from banks to finance their budget deficits, but have also struggled to meet their debt payments. Consequently, banks with large loans to these governments are exposed to the possibility of loan defaults. In addition, banks that penetrated these countries by offering loans to corporations in these countries are subject to possible loan defaults because of the weak economies of these countries.

Summary

- Commercial banks have consolidated over time in an effort to achieve economies of scale and to become more efficient. Today, there are approximately one-third as many U.S. banks as there were in 1985, and consolidation is still occurring. Commercial banks have also acquired many other types of financial services firms in recent years.

- The most common sources of commercial banks' funds are deposit accounts, borrowed funds, and long-term sources of funds. The common types of deposit accounts are transaction deposits, savings deposits, time deposits, and money market deposit accounts. These accounts vary in terms of liquidity (for the depositor) and the interest rates offered. Commercial banks can remedy temporary deficiencies in funds by borrowing from other banks (federal funds market), from the Federal Reserve, or from other sources by issuing short-term securities such as repurchase agreements. When banks need long-term funds to support expansion, they may use retained earnings, issue new stock, or issue new bonds.

- The most common uses of funds by commercial banks are bank loans and investment in securities. Banks can use excess funds by providing loans to other banks or by purchasing short-term securities.

- Banks engage in off-balance sheet activities such as loan commitments, standby letters of credit, forward contracts, and swap contracts. Although these types of activities generate fees for commercial banks, they also reflect commitments by the banks that can expose them to more risk.

- In recent years, many U.S. banks have expanded internationally to improve their prospects for growth and diversify their business, but such expansion may expose banks to more risks if the countries where they expand experience weak economic conditions. The adoption of the euro by many European countries has simplified banking transactions in Europe and made it easier for banks to achieve economies of scale.

Point/Counterpoint

Should Banks Engage in Other Financial Services Besides Banking?

Point   No. Banks should focus on what they do best.

Counterpoint   Yes. Banks should increase their value by engaging in other services. They can appeal to customers who want to have all their financial services provided by one financial institution.

Who Is Correct?   Use the Internet to learn more about this issue and then formulate your own opinion.

Questions and Applications

1. **Bank Balance Sheet** Create a balance sheet for a typical bank, showing its main liabilities (sources of funds) and assets (uses of funds).

2. **Banks' Sources of Funds** What are four major sources of funds for banks? Which alternatives does a bank have if it needs temporary funds? What is the most common reason that banks issue bonds?

3. **CDs** Compare and contrast a retail CD and a negotiable CD.

4. **Money Market Deposit Accounts** How does a money market deposit account differ from other sources of funds for banks?

5. **Federal Funds** Define federal funds, the federal funds market, and the federal funds rate. Who sets the federal funds rate? Why is the federal funds market more active on Wednesday?

6. **Federal Funds Market** Explain how the federal funds market facilitates bank operations.

7. **Borrowing from the Federal Reserve** Describe the process of "borrowing at the Federal Reserve." What rate is charged, and who sets it? Why do banks commonly borrow in the federal funds market rather than through the Federal Reserve?

8. **Repurchase Agreements** How does the yield on a repurchase agreement differ from a loan in the federal funds market? Why?

9. **Bullet Loan** Explain the advantage of a bullet loan.

10. **Banks' Use of Funds** Why do banks invest in securities even though loans typically generate a higher return? Explain how a bank decides the appropriate percentage of funds that should be allocated to each type of asset.

11. **Bank Capital** Explain the dilemma faced by banks when determining the optimal amount of capital to hold. A bank's capital is less than 10 percent of its assets. How do you think this percentage would compare to that of manufacturing corporations? How would you explain this difference?

12. **HLTs** Would you expect a bank to charge a higher rate on a term loan or on a highly leveraged transaction (HLT) loan? Why?

13. **Credit Crisis** Explain how some mortgage operations by some commercial banks (along with other financial institutions) played a major role in instigating the credit crisis that began in 2008.

14. **Bank Use of Credit Default Swaps** Explain how banks use credit default swaps.

Interpreting Financial News

Interpret the following comments made by Wall Street analysts and portfolio managers.

a. "Lower interest rates may reduce the size of banks."
b. "Banks are no longer as limited when competing with other financial institutions for funds targeted for the stock market."
c. "If the demand for loans rises substantially, interest rates will adjust to ensure that commercial banks can accommodate the demand."

Managing in Financial Markets

Managing Sources and Uses of Funds   As a consultant, you have been asked to assess a bank's sources and uses of funds and to offer recommendations on how it can restructure its sources and uses of funds to improve its performance. This bank has traditionally focused on attracting funds by offering certificates of deposit. It offers checking accounts and money market deposit accounts, but it has not advertised these accounts because it has obtained an adequate amount of funds from the CDs. It pays about 3 percentage points more on its CDs than on its MMDAs, but the bank prefers to know the precise length of time it can use the deposited funds. (The CDs have a specified maturity, whereas the MMDAs do not.) This bank's cost of funds has historically been higher than that of most banks, but it has not been concerned because its earnings have been relatively high. The bank's use of funds has historically focused on local real estate loans to build shopping malls and apartment complexes. The real estate loans have provided a very high return over the last several years. However, the demand for real estate in the local area has slowed.

a. Should the bank continue to focus on attracting funds by offering CDs, or should it push its other types of deposits?
b. Should the bank continue to focus on real estate loans? If the bank reduces its real estate loans, where should the funds be allocated?
c. How will the potential return on the bank's uses of funds be affected by your restructuring of the asset portfolio? How will the cost of funds be affected by your restructuring of the bank's liabilities?

Flow of Funds Exercise

Services Provided by Financial Conglomerates

Carson Company is attempting to compare the services offered by different banks, as it would like to have all services provided by one bank.

a. Explain how a bank and its financial service subsidiaries can help Carson Company obtain funding so as to expand its business.

b. Explain how a bank and its financial service subsidiaries can help Carson Company hedge its exposure to risk.

Internet/Excel Exercise

Go to the website of a bank of your choice and list a few services offered by the bank that were mentioned in this chapter. For each service, state whether it reflects an asset (use of funds) or a liability (source of funds) for the bank.

Online Articles with Real-World Examples

Find a recent practical article available online that describes a real-world example regarding a specific financial institution or financial market that reinforces one or more concepts covered in this chapter.

If your class has an online component, your professor may ask you to post your summary of the article there and provide a link to the article so that other students can access it. If your class is live, your professor may ask you to summarize your application of the article in class. Your professor may assign specific students to complete this assignment or may allow any students to do the assignment on a volunteer basis.

For recent online articles and real-world examples related to this chapter, consider using the following search terms (be sure to include the prevailing year as a search term to ensure that the online articles are recent):

1. bank competition
2. [name of specific bank] AND loans
3. [name of specific bank] AND deposits
4. [name of specific bank] AND capital
5. [name of specific bank] AND balance sheet
6. [name of specific bank] AND assets
7. [name of specific bank] AND liabilities
8. bank AND capital
9. bank AND assets
10. bank AND loans

18
Bank Regulation

Because banks rely on funds from depositors, they are subject to regulations that are intended to ensure the safety of the financial system and maintain public confidence in that system. Many of these regulations are intended to prevent banks from taking on excessive risk that could cause them to fail. In particular, regulations are imposed on the types of assets in which banks can invest, and on the minimum amount of capital that banks must maintain. However, bank regulation inevitably involves trade-offs. Some critics suggest that the current level of regulation is excessive and restricts banks from serving their owners. They maintain that banks might be more efficient if they were not so highly regulated. To manage these trade-offs, regulations have been revised over time in response to changing conditions, as regulators seek the optimal level of regulation that will ensure the safety of the banking system, yet also allow banks to be efficient.

Many banking regulations have been removed or reduced over time, which has allowed banks to become more competitive. Because of deregulation, banks have considerable flexibility in the services they offer, the locations where they operate, and the rates they pay depositors for deposits.

In the 2005–2007 period, however, some banks and other financial institutions engaged in excessive risk taking, which was one of the underlying factors leading to the credit crisis in 2008–2009. Many banks failed as a result of the credit crisis, and the government extended subsidies to many other banks to prevent more failures and restore stability to the U.S. financial system. This led to much scrutiny of the regulatory structure and the enactment of new regulations that are intended to still allow for intense competition while preventing bank managers from taking excessive risks. This chapter provides background information on the prevailing regulatory structure, explains how bank regulators attempted to resolve the credit crisis, and describes recent changes in regulations that are intended to prevent another crisis.

WEB

www.federalreserve.gov
Click on "Supervision &
Regulation" to find key
bank regulations at the
website of the Board of
Governors of the Federal
Reserve System.

18-1 Regulatory Structure

The regulatory structure of the banking system in the United States differs dramatically from that of other countries. Because it includes both federal and state regulatory systems, it is often referred to as a dual banking system. More than 4,000 separately owned commercial banks operate in the United States, which are supervised by 3 federal agencies and 50 state agencies.

A charter from either a state government or the federal government is required to open a commercial bank in the United States. A bank that obtains a state charter is referred to as a state bank; a bank that obtains a federal charter is known as a national bank. All national banks are required to be members of the Federal Reserve System (the Fed). The federal charter is issued by the Comptroller of the Currency. An application for a bank charter must be submitted to the proper supervisory agency, should provide evidence of the need for a new bank, and should disclose how the bank will be operated. Regulators determine whether the bank satisfies the general guidelines to qualify for the charter.

State banks may decide whether they wish to be members of the Federal Reserve System. The Fed provides a variety of services for commercial banks and controls the amount of funds within the banking system. Approximately 35 percent of all banks are members of the Federal Reserve. These banks are generally larger than the norm for state banks; their combined deposits represent approximately 70 percent of all bank deposits. Both member and nonmember banks can borrow from the Fed, and both are subject to the Fed's reserve requirements.

18-1a Regulators

National banks are regulated by the Comptroller of the Currency, whereas state banks are regulated by their respective state agency. Banks that are insured by the **Federal Deposit Insurance Corporation (FDIC)** are also regulated by the FDIC. Because all national banks must be members of the Federal Reserve and all Fed member banks must hold FDIC insurance, national banks are, in turn, regulated by the Comptroller of the Currency, the Fed, and the FDIC. By contrast, state banks are regulated by their respective state agency, the Fed (if they are Fed members), and the FDIC. The Comptroller of the Currency is responsible for conducting periodic evaluations of national banks, the FDIC holds the same responsibility for state-chartered banks and savings institutions with less than $50 billion in assets, and the Federal Reserve is responsible for state-chartered banks and savings institutions with more than $50 billion in assets.

18-1b Regulation of Bank Ownership

Commercial banks can be either independently owned or owned by a **bank holding company (BHC)**. Although some multibank holding companies (owning more than one bank) exist, one-bank holding companies are more common. More banks are owned by holding companies than are owned independently.

18-2 Regulation of Bank Operations

Banks are regulated according to how they obtain funds, how they use their funds, and which types of financial services they can offer. Some of the most important regulations are discussed here.

18-2a Regulation of Deposit Insurance

Federal deposit insurance has existed since the FDIC was created in 1933 in response to the bank runs that occurred in the late 1920s and early 1930s. During the Great Depression (1930–1932), more than 5,000 U.S. banks failed, representing more than 20 percent of the existing banks. The initial wave of failures caused depositors at other banks to fear that the failures would spread, so they rushed to withdraw their deposits. These actions actually caused more banks to fail. If deposit insurance had been available, depositors might not have removed their deposits, and some bank failures might have been avoided.

The FDIC preserves public confidence in the U.S. financial system by providing deposit insurance to commercial banks and savings institutions. It is managed by a board of five directors, who are appointed by the president. The FDIC's headquarters are located in Washington, D.C., and it has eight regional offices throughout the United States.

Insurance Limits   The specified amount of deposits per person insured by the FDIC was increased from $100,000 to $250,000 as part of the Emergency Economic Stabilization Act of 2008, which was intended to resolve the liquidity problems of financial institutions and to restore confidence in the banking system. The $250,000 limit was made permanent by the Financial Reform Act of 2010. Large deposit accounts beyond the $250,000 limit are insured only up to this limit. Note that deposits in foreign branches of U.S. banks are *not* insured by the FDIC.

In general, deposit insurance enables depositors to deposit funds under the insured limits in any insured depository institution without the need to assess the institution's financial condition. In addition, the insurance system minimizes bank runs because insured depositors know that their deposits are backed by the U.S. government even if the insured depository institution fails. When a bank fails, insured depositors usually have access to their money within a few days.

Risk-Based Deposit Premiums   Banks insured by the FDIC must pay annual insurance premiums. Until 1991, all banks paid the same rate when obtaining insurance for their depositors. Thus, because the riskiest banks were more likely to fail, their risky behavior was indirectly subsidized by safer banks. This system encouraged some banks to assume more risk because they could still attract deposits from depositors who knew they would be covered regardless of the bank's risk. The act of insured banks taking on more risk because their depositors are protected is an example of a **moral hazard problem**.

To reduce this problem, the Federal Deposit Insurance Corporation Improvement Act (FDICIA) of 1991 phased in a system of risk-based deposit insurance premiums. Consequently, bank insurance premiums are now aligned with the bank's risk, thereby reducing the moral hazard problem.

Deposit Insurance Fund   Before 2006, the Bank Insurance Fund collected premiums and provided insurance for banks, and the Savings Association Insurance Fund collected premiums and provided insurance for savings institutions. In 2006, the two funds were merged into a single fund called the **Deposit Insurance Fund**, which is regulated by the FDIC.

In 2009, the deposit insurance premiums were increased, in response to the FDIC's need to use substantial reserves during the credit crisis to reimburse depositors of failed banks. The range of premiums is now typically between 13 and 53 cents per $100, with most banks paying between 13 and 18 cents. The Deposit Insurance Fund balance is presently about $97 billion. The FDIC also has a large credit line against which it can borrow from the U.S. Treasury.

Bank Deposit Insurance Reserves   The Financial Reform Act of 2010 (also known as the Dodd-Frank Wall Street Reform and Consumer Protection Act) requires that the Deposit Insurance Fund maintain reserves of at least 1.35 percent of total insured bank deposits to ensure that it always has sufficient reserves to cover losses. If the reserves fall below that level, the FDIC is required to develop a restoration plan to boost reserves to that minimum level.

18-2b Regulation of Deposits

Three regulatory acts created more competition for bank deposits over time, as discussed next.

DIDMCA   In 1980, the **Depository Institutions Deregulation and Monetary Control Act (DIDMCA)** was enacted to (1) deregulate the banking (and other depository institutions) industry and (2) improve monetary policy. Because this chapter focuses on regulation and deregulation, only the first goal is discussed here.

The DIDMCA was a major force in deregulating the banking industry and increasing competition among banks. It removed interest rate ceilings on deposits, allowing banks and other depository institutions to make their own decisions about which interest rates to offer for time and savings deposits. In addition, it allowed banks to offer NOW accounts.

Garn-St. Germain Act   Banks and other depository institutions were further deregulated in 1982 as a result of the **Garn-St. Germain Act**. This act was passed at a time when some depository institutions (especially savings institutions) were experiencing severe financial problems. One of its more important provisions permitted depository institutions to offer money market deposit accounts (MMDAs), which have no minimum maturity and no interest ceiling. These accounts allow a maximum of six transactions per month (three by check). They are similar to the traditional accounts offered by **money market mutual funds** (whose main function is to sell shares and pool the funds to purchase short-term securities that offer market-determined rates). Because MMDAs offer savers similar benefits, they allow depository institutions to compete against money market funds in attracting savers' funds.

A second key deregulatory provision of the Garn-St. Germain Act permitted depository institutions (including banks) to acquire failing institutions across geographic boundaries. The intent was to reduce the number of failures that require liquidation, as the chances of finding a potential acquirer for a failing institution improve when geographic barriers are removed. Also, competition was expected to increase because depository institutions previously barred from entering specific geographic areas could now do so by acquiring failing institutions.

Interstate Banking Act   In September 1994, Congress passed the Riegle-Neal Interstate Banking and Branching Efficiency Act, which removed interstate branching restrictions, thereby further increasing the competition among banks for deposits. Nationwide interstate banking enabled banks to grow and achieve **economies of scale**. It also allowed banks in stagnant markets to penetrate other markets where economic conditions were more favorable. Banks in all markets were pressured to become more efficient as a result of the increased competition.

18-2c Regulation of Bank Loans

Because loans represent the key assets of commercial banks, they are regulated to limit a bank's exposure to default risk.

Regulation of Highly Leveraged Transactions   As a result of concerns about the popularity of highly leveraged loans (for supporting leveraged buyouts and other activities), bank regulators now monitor the amount of highly leveraged transactions (HLTs) in which they participate. HLTs are commonly defined as loan transactions in which the borrower has (or will have) a large amount of debt relative to assets. Since the credit crisis of 2008–2009, regulators have tried to discourage banks from engaging in HLTs.

Regulation of Foreign Loans   Regulators also monitor a bank's exposure to loans to entities in foreign countries. Because regulators require banks to report significant exposure to foreign debt, investors and creditors have access to more detailed information about the composition of bank loan portfolios.

Regulation of Loans to a Single Borrower   Banks are restricted to a maximum loan amount of 15 percent of their capital to any single borrower (up to 25 percent if the loan is adequately collateralized). This limit forces banks to diversify their loans to some degree.

Regulation of Loans to Community   Banks are also regulated to ensure that they attempt to accommodate the credit needs of the communities in which they operate. The Community Reinvestment Act (CRA) of 1977 (revised in 1995) requires banks to meet the credit needs of qualified borrowers in their community, including those with low or moderate incomes. The CRA is not intended to force banks to make high-risk loans, but rather seeks to ensure that qualified lower-income borrowers receive the loans that they request. Each bank's performance in this regard is evaluated periodically by its respective regulator.

18-2d Regulation of Bank Investment in Securities

Banks are not allowed to use borrowed or deposited funds to purchase common stock, although they can manage stock portfolios through trust accounts that are owned by individuals. Banks can invest only in bonds that are investment-grade quality. Before the credit crisis, this meant bonds rated Baa or higher by Moody's or BBB or higher by Standard & Poor's. These regulations on bonds are intended to prevent banks from taking excessive risks.

During the credit crisis, the rating agencies were criticized for being too liberal with their ratings. The Financial Reform Act of 2010 changed the rules to require that banks use not only ratings assigned by credit rating agencies, but also other methods to assess the risk of debt securities, including their own assessment of risk. Thus, even if the rating agencies apply liberal ratings, the bank should be able to detect when debt securities are too risky by using its own analysis or other methods to assess risk.

18-2e Regulation of Securities Services

The Banking Act of 1933 (better known as the **Glass-Steagall Act**) separated banking and securities activities. This legislation was prompted by problems that arose after the stock market crash of 1929, when some banks sold some of their poor-quality securities to their trust accounts established for individuals. Some banks also engaged in insider trading: They bought or sold corporate securities based on confidential information provided by firms that had requested loans.

The Glass-Steagall Act prevented any firm that accepted deposits from underwriting stocks and bonds of corporations. The separation of securities activities from banking activities was intended to prevent potential conflicts of interest. For example, if a bank were allowed to underwrite securities, it might advise its corporate customers to purchase these securities and could threaten to cut off future loans if the customers did not oblige.

Financial Services Modernization Act   In 1999, Congress passed the **Financial Services Modernization Act** (also called the **Gramm-Leach-Bliley Act**), which essentially repealed the Glass-Steagall Act. The 1999 act allows affiliations between banks, securities firms, and insurance companies. It also allows bank holding companies to engage in any

WEB

www.federalreserve
.govsupervisionreg.htm
Links to regulations
of securities services
offered by banks.

financial activity through their ownership of subsidiaries. Consequently, a single holding company can engage in traditional banking activities, securities trading, underwriting, and insurance. A bank holding company must be well managed and have sufficient capital before it expands its financial services. The Securities and Exchange Commission regulates any securities products that are created, but the bank subsidiaries that offer the securities products are overseen by bank regulators.

Although many commercial banks had previously pursued securities services, the 1999 act increased the extent to which banks could offer these services. Furthermore, it allowed securities firms and insurance companies to acquire banks. Under the act, commercial banks must have a strong rating in community lending (which indicates that they have actively provided loans in lower-income communities) to pursue additional expansion in securities and other nonbank activities.

Since the passage of the Financial Services Modernization Act, much more consolidation of financial institutions has occurred. Many of the larger financial institutions are able to offer all types of financial services through their various subsidiaries. Because individuals commonly use financial institutions to deposit funds, obtain mortgage loans and consumer loans (such as automobile loans), purchase shares of mutual funds, order stock transactions (brokerage), and purchase insurance, they can obtain all their financial services from a single financial conglomerate. Moreover, because firms commonly use financial institutions to maintain a business checking account, obtain loans, issue stocks or bonds, manage their pension fund, and purchase insurance services, these corporate entities can obtain all of their financial services from a single financial conglomerate.

The Financial Services Modernization Act also provides benefits to financial institutions. By offering more diversified services, financial institutions can reduce their reliance on the demand for any single service that they offer. This diversification may result in less risk for the institution's consolidated business, provided the new services are not subject to a much higher degree of risk than its traditional services.

The individual units of a financial conglomerate may generate some new business simply because they are part of the conglomerate and offer greater convenience to clients who already rely on its other services. Each financial unit's list of existing clients represents a potential source of new clients for the other financial units to pursue.

The consolidation of banks and securities firms continued during the credit crisis in 2008, as some major securities firms (for example, Bear Stearns and Merrill Lynch) were acquired by commercial banks, whereas others (for example, Goldman Sachs and Morgan Stanley) won approval to become bank holding companies. This consolidation improved the stability of the financial system because regulations on bank holding companies are generally more stringent than the regulations on independent securities firms.

18-2f Regulation of Off-Balance Sheet Transactions

Banks offer a variety of off-balance sheet commitments. For example, they provide standby letters of credit to back commercial paper issued by corporations. They also act as the intermediaries on interest rate swaps and usually guarantee payments over the specified period in the event that one of the parties defaults on its payments.

Various off-balance sheet transactions have become popular among banks because they provide fee income to those banks. That is, banks charge a fee for guaranteeing against the default of another party and for facilitating transactions between parties. Off-balance sheet transactions do expose a bank to risk, however. If a severe economic downturn causes many corporations to default on their commercial paper or on payments specified by interest rate swap agreements, the banks that provided guarantees would incur large losses.

Bank exposure to off-balance sheet activities has become a major concern of regulators. The operations of banks could be riskier than their balance sheets indicate because of these transactions. Therefore, the risk-based capital requirements are higher for banks that conduct more off-balance sheet activities. In this way, regulators discourage banks from excessive involvement in such activities.

Regulation of Credit Default Swaps   Credit default swaps are a type of off-balance sheet transaction that became popular during the 2004–2008 period as a means of protecting against the risk of default on bonds and mortgage-backed securities. A swap allows a commercial bank to make periodic payments to a counterparty in return for protection in the event that its holdings of mortgage-backed securities default. Although some commercial banks purchased these swaps as a means of protecting their assets against default, other commercial banks sold them (to provide protection) as a means of generating fee income. By 2008, credit default swaps represented more than $30 trillion of mortgage-backed securities or other types of securities ($60 trillion when counting each contract for both parties).

When commercial banks purchase credit default swaps to protect their assets against possible default, these assets are not subject to capital requirements. If the sellers of the credit default swaps are overexposed, however, they may not be able to provide the protection they promised. Thus the banks that purchased credit default swaps might not be protected if the sellers default. As the credit crisis intensified in 2008 and 2009, regulators became concerned about credit default swaps because of the lack of transparency regarding the exposure of each commercial bank and the credibility of the counterparties on the swaps. They increased their oversight of this market and asked commercial banks to provide more information about their credit default swap positions.

18-2g Regulation of the Accounting Process

Publicly traded banks, like other publicly traded companies, are required to provide financial statements that indicate their recent financial position and performance. The Sarbanes-Oxley (SOX) Act was enacted in 2002 to ensure a more transparent process for reporting on a firm's productivity and financial condition. It was created after the discovery that some publicly traded firms (such as Enron) had inflated their earnings, which caused many investors to pay a much higher price for their stock than was appropriate. The SOX Act requires all firms (including banks) to implement an internal reporting process that can be easily monitored by executives and makes it impossible for executives to pretend that they were unaware of accounting fraud.

Some of the key provisions of the act require banks to improve their internal control processes and to establish a centralized database of information. In addition, executives are now held more accountable for a bank's financial statements; indeed, they must personally verify the accuracy of those statements. Investors may have more confidence in the financial statements because the greater accountability of executives could discourage accounting fraud.

Nevertheless, questionable accounting practices may still occur at banks. Some types of assets do not have a market in which they are actively traded, so banks have some flexibility when valuing these assets. During the credit crisis, many banks assigned values to some types of securities they held that clearly exceeded the proper market values. Consequently, they were able to hide a portion of their losses.

One negative effect of the SOX Act is that publicly traded banks have incurred expenses of more than $1 million per year to comply with its provisions. Such a high expense may encourage smaller publicly traded banks to go private.

18-3 Regulation of Capital

Banks are subject to capital requirements, which force them to maintain a minimum amount of capital (or equity) as a percentage of total assets. They rely on their capital as a cushion against possible losses. The more capital a bank holds, the more easily it can absorb potential losses and the more likely it is to survive. If a bank has insufficient capital to cover losses, it will not be able to cover its expenses and will fail. Therefore, regulators closely monitor bank capital levels.

To account for a bank's size when assessing its capital, regulators closely monitor a bank's **capital ratio**, defined as capital divided by assets. Because a bank's capital requirements depend on the value of its assets, they may differ based on the accounting method used in the valuation process. *Fair value accounting* is used to measure the value of bank assets; that is, a bank is required to periodically "mark its assets to market" so that it can determine the amount of needed capital based on the current market value of the assets.

During the credit crisis, banks reduced their valuations of mortgage-backed securities and mortgage loans. Given a decline in a bank's book value of assets and no associated change in its book value of liabilities, a bank's balance sheet is balanced by reducing its capital. Thus, many banks were required to replenish their capital to meet the capital requirements, and some banks came under extra scrutiny by regulators.

Some bank managers and shareholders would prefer that banks hold a lower level of capital, because a given dollar level of profits represents a higher return on equity if the bank holds less capital. This might allow for managers to receive larger bonuses and shareholders to benefit from higher stock prices during strong economic conditions. Regulators, however, are more interested in the safety of the banking system than in managerial bonuses, and they have increased bank capital requirements in recent years as a means of stabilizing the banking system.

18-3a How Banks Satisfy Capital Requirements

When a bank's capital declines below the amount required by regulators, it can increase its capital ratio in the following ways.

Retaining Earnings   When a bank generates new earnings and retains them rather than distributing them as dividends to shareholders, it boosts its capital. However, it cannot retain earnings if it does not generate earnings. If it incurs losses, its revenue will not be sufficient to cover its expenses, and it will have to use some of its existing capital. Thus losses (negative earnings) result in a lower level of capital. Poorly performing banks cannot rely on retained earnings to boost capital levels because they may not have any new earnings to retain.

Issuing Stock   Banks can boost their capital by issuing stock to the public. However, a bank's capital level declines when its performance is weak; under these conditions, the bank's stock price will probably decrease as well. If the bank has to sell stock when its stock price is very low, it may not receive sufficient funds from its stock offering. During the credit crisis of 2008–2009, bank stock values were very low, so issuing stock was not a viable option at that time. Furthermore, investors may not have much interest in purchasing new shares in a bank that is weak and desperate to build capital because they may reasonably expect the bank to fail.

Reducing Dividends   Banks can increase their capital by reducing their dividends, which enables them to retain a larger amount of any earnings. However, shareholders might interpret a cut in dividends as a signal that the bank is desperate for capital, which could cause its stock price to decline further. The lower stock price could make it more difficult for the bank to issue stock in the future.

Selling Assets   Banks may sometimes sell assets in an effort to improve their capital position. A bank is required to maintain sufficient capital to back assets that are perceived to be risky. If the bank sells those assets, however, it will no longer be required to back them with capital. During the credit crisis, some banks sold assets to improve their capital ratio, but this solution was not ideal because the assets they sold (mortgage-backed securities) were heavily discounted at the time and were expected to increase in value only after the crisis was over.

18-3b Basel I Accord

When regulators of various countries develop capital requirements for their banks, they are commonly guided by the recommendations in the Basel Accord. These guidelines are intended to assist bank regulators in setting their own capital requirements.

In the first Basel Accord (1988, often called Basel I), the central banks of 12 major countries agreed to establish a framework for determining uniform capital requirements. A key provision in the Basel Accord bases the capital requirements on a bank's risk level. Banks with greater risk are required to maintain a higher level of capital, which discourages banks from taking on excessive exposure to credit risk.

Assets are weighted according to risk. Very safe assets such as cash are assigned a zero weight, whereas very risky assets are assigned a 100 percent weight. Because the required capital is set as a percentage of risk-weighted assets, riskier banks are subject to more stringent capital requirements.

WEB

www.federalreserve
.gov/supervisionreg.htm
Click on "Basel
Regulatory Framework"
to find information
about the Basel
framework.

18-3c Basel II Framework

In 2004, a committee of central bank and regulatory authorities of numerous countries (called the Basel Committee on Banking Supervision) created a framework called Basel II, which was added to the Basel Accord. It has two major parts: revising the measurement of credit risk and explicitly accounting for operational risk.

Revising the Measurement of Credit Risk   When banks categorize their assets and assign risk weights to the categories, they take into account possible differences in risk levels of loans within a category. Risk levels may differ if some banks require better collateral to back their loans. In addition, some banks may take positions in derivative securities that can reduce their credit risk, whereas other banks may have positions in derivative securities that increase their credit risk.

A bank's loans that are past due are assigned a higher weight. This adjustment inflates the size of these assets for the purpose of determining minimum capital requirements. Thus banks with more loans that are past due are forced to maintain a higher level of capital (other things being equal).

An alternative method of calculating credit risk, called the internal ratings-based (IRB) approach, allows banks to use their own processes for estimating the probability of default on their loans.

Explicitly Accounting for Operational Risk   The Basel Committee defined operational risk as the risk of losses resulting from inadequate or failed internal processes or systems. They encouraged banks to improve their techniques for controlling operational risk because doing so could reduce failures in the banking system. By imposing higher capital requirements on banks with higher levels of operational risk, Basel II provided an incentive for banks to reduce their operational risk.

The United States, Canada, and countries in the European Union created regulations for their banks that conform to some parts of Basel II. When applying the Basel II guidelines, however, many banks underestimated the probability of loan default during the credit crisis. This motivated the creation of the Basel III framework, described next.

18-3d Basel III Framework

In response to the credit crisis, in 2011 the Basel Committee on Banking Supervision began to develop the Basel III framework, which attempted to correct deficiencies of Basel II. This framework recommended that banks maintain Tier 1 capital (retained earnings and common stock) amounting to at least 6 percent of their total risk-weighted assets. It also recommended a more rigorous process for identifying risk-weighted assets. Prior to Basel III, some assets were assigned a low risk weight based on liberal ratings by rating agencies. Basel III proposed that banks apply scenario analysis to determine how the values of their assets would be affected based on possible adverse economic scenarios.

Basel III also recommended that banks maintain an extra layer of Tier 1 capital (called a capital conservation buffer) of at least 2.5 percent of their risk-weighted assets. Banks that do not maintain this extra layer could be restricted from making dividend payments, repurchasing stock, or granting bonuses to executives.

In addition to the increased capital requirements, Basel III called for banks to maintain increased liquidity so that they can meet short-term demands for cash. The liquidity coverage ratio (LCR) is the ratio of a bank's liquid assets such as cash and Treasury securities to its projected net cash outflows. Some banks that specialize in low-risk loans and have adequate capital might not have adequate liquidity to survive an economic crisis. In the Basel III framework, banks are expected to maintain sufficient liquidity so that they can easily cover their cash needs under adverse conditions. New regulations in the United States require the largest banks and bank holding companies to maintain an LCR slightly more stringent than that identified in Basel III.

18-3e Use of the VaR Method to Determine Capital Levels

To comply with the Basel Accord, banks commonly apply a value-at-risk (VaR) model to assess the risk of their assets and determine how much capital they should hold. The VaR model can be applied in various ways to determine capital requirements. In general, a bank defines the VaR as the estimated potential loss from its trading businesses that could result from adverse movements in market prices. Banks typically use a 99 percent confidence level, meaning that there is a 99 percent chance that the loss on a given day will be more favorable than the VaR estimate. When applied to a daily time horizon, the actual loss from a bank's trading businesses should not exceed the estimated loss by VaR on more than 1 out of every 100 days. Banks estimate the VaR by assessing the probability of specific adverse market events (such as an abrupt change in interest rates) and the sensitivity of responses to those events. Banks with a higher maximum loss (based on a 99 percent confidence interval) are subject to higher capital requirements.

This focus on daily price movements forces banks to monitor their trading positions continuously so that they are immediately aware of any losses. Many banks now have access to the market values of their trading businesses at the end of every day. If banks used a longer-term horizon (such as a month), larger losses might build up before bank executives recognize they have occurred.

Limitations of the VaR Model   The VaR model was generally ineffective at detecting the risk of banks during the credit crisis. Notably, it failed to recognize the degree to which the value of bank assets (such as mortgages or mortgage-backed securities) could decline under adverse conditions. The use of historical data from before 2007 did not capture the risk of mortgages because investments in mortgages during that period had generally resulted in low rates of default. Thus the VaR model was not adequate for predicting the possible estimated losses.

18-3f Stress Tests Used to Determine Capital Levels

Some banks supplement the VaR estimate with their own stress tests.

EXAMPLE

Kenosha Bank wants to estimate the loss that it would incur in response to an extreme adverse market event. First, it identifies an extreme scenario that could occur, such as an increase in interest rates on one day that is at least three standard deviations from the mean daily change in interest rates over the last year. Kenosha Bank then uses this scenario, along with the typical sensitivity of its trading businesses to such a scenario, to estimate the resulting loss in its trading businesses. ●

WEB

www.fdic.gov
Information about specific bank regulations.

Regulatory Stress Tests   As required by the Financial Reform Act of 2010, the Federal Reserve now conducts stress tests on banks with $50 billion or more in assets on an annual basis. Banks that receive low scores must increase their capital levels and may not increase their dividends or engage in stock buybacks.

18-4 How Regulators Monitor Banks

Bank regulators typically conduct an on-site examination of each commercial bank at least once a year. During the examination, regulators assess the bank's compliance with existing regulations and its financial condition. In addition to on-site examinations, regulators periodically monitor commercial banks with computerized monitoring systems that analyze data provided by the banks on a quarterly basis.

18-4a CAMELS Ratings

Regulators monitor banks to detect any serious deficiencies that might develop so that they can correct those deficiencies before the bank fails. The more failures they can prevent, the more confidence the public will have in the banking industry. The evaluation approach described here is used by the FDIC, the Federal Reserve, and the Comptroller of the Currency.

The single most common cause of bank failure is poor management. Unfortunately, no reliable measure of poor management exists. Therefore, the regulators rate banks on the basis of six characteristics that constitute the **CAMELS ratings**, so named for the acronym that identifies the six characteristics:

- Capital adequacy
- Asset quality
- Management
- Earnings
- Liquidity
- Sensitivity

Capital Adequacy   Capital monitoring by regulators was covered in the previous section. It is mentioned again here to emphasize that it is one of the six criteria closely watched by regulators.

Asset Quality   Each bank makes its own decisions as to how deposited funds should be allocated, and these decisions determine its level of credit (default) risk. Regulators therefore evaluate the quality of the bank's assets, including its loans and its securities.

The process of evaluating a bank's assets can be complex. Consider that a bank may have provided 1,000 loans to firms in a variety of industries. Each loan has specific provisions as to how it is secured (if at all) by the borrower's assets. Imagine the task of assigning a rating to this bank's asset quality. Even if all the bank's loan recipients are current on their loan repayments, that fact does not guarantee that the bank's asset quality deserves a high rating. Perhaps the economy was strong during the period of prompt loan repayment, and conditions may weaken in the future. An appropriate examination of the bank's asset portfolio should incorporate the portfolio's exposure to potential events (such as a recession). The reason for the regulatory examination is not to grade past performance but rather to detect any problem that could cause the bank to fail in the future.

Management Each of the characteristics examined by regulators relates to the bank's management. In addition, regulators specifically rate the bank's management based on their administrative skills, ability to comply with existing regulations, and ability to cope with a changing environment. They also assess the bank's internal control systems, which may indicate how easily the bank's management could detect its own financial problems. This evaluation is clearly subjective.

Earnings Although the CAMELS ratings are mostly concerned with risk, earnings are also very important. Banks fail when their earnings become consistently negative. One profitability ratio commonly used to evaluate banks is **return on assets (ROA)**, defined as after-tax earnings divided by assets. In addition to assessing a bank's earnings over time, regulators find it useful to compare the bank's earnings with industry earnings. This allows for an evaluation of the bank relative to its competitors. Regulators may also attempt to assess how a bank's earnings would change if economic conditions change.

Liquidity Regulators may be concerned about banks that frequently obtain funds from outside sources (such as the Federal Reserve or the federal funds market) to cover temporary funding deficiencies, because such ongoing practices might suggest that the deficiencies are not really temporary. Banks that often resort to outside loans to shore up their funding are more likely to experience a liquidity crisis. If other banks that provide short-term funding sense that a bank is experiencing a liquidity problem, they may no longer provide short-term loans, compounding the problem.

Sensitivity Regulators also assess the degree to which a bank might be exposed to adverse financial market conditions. Two banks could be rated similarly in terms of recent earnings, liquidity, and other characteristics, yet one of them may be much more sensitive than the other to financial market conditions. In particular, regulators emphasize a bank's sensitivity to interest rate movements. Many banks have liabilities that are repriced more frequently than their assets and, therefore, are adversely affected by rising interest rates. Banks that are more sensitive to rising interest rates are more likely to experience financial problems.

Deriving a CAMELS Composite Rating Each of the CAMELS characteristics just described is rated on a $1-5$ scale, with 1 being "outstanding" and 5 being "very poor." A composite rating is determined as the mean rating of the six characteristics. Banks with a composite rating of less than 2.0 do not require additional attention. Banks with a composite rating between 2.0 and 3.0 are given extra attention. Banks with a composite rating between 3.0 and 4.0 have serious issues that need to be addressed. Banks with a composite rating between 4.0 and 5.0 require immediate regulatory attention.

Limitations of the CAMELS Rating System   The CAMELS rating system is essentially a screening device. Because so many banks operate in the U.S. market, regulators do not have the resources to closely monitor each bank on a frequent basis. The rating system identifies what are believed to be problem banks. Over time, new banks may be added to the "problem list," some problem banks may improve and be removed from the list, and still others may deteriorate further and ultimately fail.

Although examinations by regulators may help detect problems experienced by some banks in time to save them, many problems still go unnoticed; by the time they are detected, it may be too late to find a remedy. Although an analysis of financial ratios can be useful, the task of assessing a bank is as much an art as a science. Subjective opinion must complement objective measurements to provide the best possible evaluation of a bank.

Any system used to detect financial problems may err in one of two ways: by classifying a bank as safe when it is actually failing, or by classifying a bank as risky when it is actually safe. The first type of mistake is more costly, because some failing banks are not identified in time to help them. To avoid this mistake, bank regulators could lower their benchmark composite rating. If they did, however, many more banks would be added to the problem list and require close supervision, so regulators' limited resources would be spread too thin.

18-4b Corrective Action by Regulators

When a bank is classified as a problem bank, regulators thoroughly investigate the cause of its deterioration. Corrective action is often necessary. For example, regulators may request that a bank boost its capital level or delay its plans to expand. They may also require that additional financial information be provided periodically as part of ongoing monitoring. In addition, regulators have the authority to remove particular officers and directors of a problem bank if doing so would enhance the bank's performance. They even have the authority to take legal action against a problem bank if the bank does not comply with their suggested remedies. Such a drastic measure is rare, however, and would not solve the existing problems of the bank.

18-4c Treatment of Failing Banks

If a failing bank cannot be saved, it will be closed. The FDIC is responsible for the closure of failing banks. In such a case, it must decide whether to liquidate the failed bank's assets or to facilitate the acquisition of that bank by another bank. When liquidating a failed bank, the FDIC draws from its Deposit Insurance Fund to reimburse insured depositors. After reimbursing depositors, the FDIC attempts to sell the failed bank's marketable assets (such as securities and some loans). The cost to the FDIC of closing a failed bank is the difference between the reimbursement to depositors and the proceeds received from selling the failed bank's assets.

Instead of liquidating a failing bank, the FDIC more commonly looks for another bank that is willing to acquire the failing bank. It may provide some financial support to facilitate the acquisition, because the market value of the failed bank's assets is less than its liabilities. The FDIC may also be willing to provide funding if doing so would be less costly than liquidating the failed bank. Whether a failed bank is liquidated or acquired by another bank, it loses its identity.

The number of bank failures is heavily dependent on economic conditions. For example, in 2010, immediately after the credit crisis, 157 banks failed. Since 2015, however, fewer than 10 banks have failed per year.

18-5 Government Actions during the Credit Crisis

The decision of whether to close a failing bank or facilitate its acquisition by another bank can be difficult and is sometimes controversial, especially when the U.S. government engineers an acquisition of the troubled bank in a manner that enables its shareholders to receive at least some payment for their shares (when a failed bank is acquired, shareholders ordinarily lose all of their investment). These issues arose most notably during the credit crisis when several large financial institutions were on the verge of failure. This section presents case studies of three financial institutions that were treated differently by the government during the credit crisis and examines some of the arguments for and against government "rescues" of failing banks.

18-5a Government Rescue of Bear Stearns

Bear Stearns was a very large securities firm that specialized in fixed-income securities such as bonds and mortgages. Although it was not regulated like a bank, it was a major participant in the financial system because of its role as a financial intermediary.

Bear Stearns used a very high level of financial leverage, which magnified its positive returns during the favorable economic conditions in 2004–2006. However, when Bear Stearns began to experience losses in 2007–2008, its financial leverage magnified their adverse impact. The firm had relied heavily on short-term funding to support its operations, but by March 2008, many financial institutions were no longer willing to provide loans because they did not trust the mortgage assets that Bear Stearns used as collateral. Because Bear Stearns could not obtain sufficient funds to support its operations, it suffered a liquidity crisis.

The Federal Reserve provided short-term loans to Bear Stearns to ensure that it had adequate liquidity. When the firm requested longer-term financial support, on Friday, March 14, 2008, the Federal Reserve examined the firm's accounts and found that Bear Stearns was highly exposed to subprime mortgages. The Federal Reserve also discovered a mass of contractual obligations (as a result of credit default swaps and other credit derivatives) between Bear Stearns and other financial institutions. This may have been the first time during the credit crisis that a bank regulator fully realized the extent of the systemic risk in the financial system.

Regulators did not believe that Bear Stearns could survive, but over the weekend they looked for a solution that might lessen the systemic risk. They were aware that on Monday, the financial markets would recognize that Bear Stearns, which was worth approximately $20 billion just 15 months earlier, was failing. Yet the negative market reaction to this news might be less pronounced if market participants believed that the adverse effects would not spread to other financial institutions.

Over the weekend following the examination of Bear Stearns, the Federal Reserve orchestrated the acquisition of the firm by JPMorgan Chase. It gave incentives to Bear Stearns and to JPMorgan Chase to complete the deal by promising financing of as much as $30 billion so that JPMorgan could afford the acquisition. Because JPMorgan was concerned about the real value of some of the assets it was acquiring, the Fed promised to incur the cost if those assets lost value.

This intervention by the Federal Reserve was unprecedented, and some critics questioned whether the Fed (a regulator of commercial banks) should be assisting a securities firm such as Bear Stearns that it did not regulate. Some critics (including Paul Volcker, a previous chair of the Fed) suggested that the rescue of a firm other than a commercial bank should be the responsibility of Congress, rather than the Fed.

The Fed decided that there was no time to allow for congressional deliberations. If it had not intervened during the weekend, the impact across the financial system could have been devastating. Many financial transactions might have been frozen. If Bear Stearns did not meet its obligations to its counterparties (other financial institutions) on its contracts, those institutions might have experienced serious financial problems, which might have led to a string of failures and the destruction of the entire financial system. Thus the main priority of the Federal Reserve at this time was to stabilize the financial system. The Fed was criticized at the time for using government money to rescue a securities firm that it did not even regulate, while many other smaller banks were allowed to fail. But if it had not intervened, it would have been blamed for allowing the failure of Bear Stearns to cause damage throughout the financial system.

18-5b Failure of Lehman Brothers

Lehman Brothers, another large securities firm, also played a major role during the credit crisis. Like Bear Stearns, it was not regulated as a bank, but rather represented a key financial intermediary in the financial system. Lehman was heavily invested in mortgages and commercial real estate, and it earned record profits during the housing boom in 2005–2006. The company was valued at about $60 billion in February 2007. Like Bear Stearns, it relied on a high degree of financial leverage. For every dollar of capital that it owned, it borrowed $40. This financial leverage magnified the firm's gains in the 2005–2007 period, but it also magnified the firm's losses when the housing bubble burst in 2008.

ETHICS

As the mortgage markets began to experience weakness near the end of 2007, Lehman Brothers struggled to obtain financing from financial institutions. In June 2008, it reported a quarterly loss of almost $3 billion, and its stock price quickly plunged by 20 percent. By September 2008, the firm was desperately trying to sell various divisions to raise capital.

The Federal Reserve encouraged financial institutions to consider acquiring divisions of Lehman Brothers, but did not promise any government assistance. Finding buyers for Lehman's divisions was difficult, however, because some financial institutions were already concerned that the firm had used creative accounting to overstate its earnings and understate its debt in 2007 and early 2008.

On September 11, 2008, Moody's Investor Service announced that it planned to cut Lehman's credit rating unless Lehman merged with another financial institution. In turn, Lehman's stock price declined by 42 percent. On Monday, September 15, Lehman announced that it was filing for bankruptcy. At that time, it was the fourth largest securities firm, with assets of about $639 billion, making its bankruptcy the largest in U.S. history. Millions of investors holding Lehman stock lost almost their entire investment. Nearly 26,000 employees at Lehman lost their jobs. Despite announcements by public officials that were intended to calm the financial markets, U.S. stock prices declined by about 4.7 percent on average, making this the worst day for stocks since September 2001. Credit markets froze as many financial institutions stopped providing credit because of concerns about credit risk.

18-5c Government Rescue of AIG

One day after Lehman Brothers filed for bankruptcy, the U.S. government took control of American International Group (AIG), a large insurance company. The U.S. government (through the Federal Reserve and the Treasury) injected approximately $130 billion into AIG by purchasing shares of AIG stock and making loans to the company. Thus the government became the majority owner of the firm, obtaining an 80 percent stake in AIG. The loans that were provided were backed by assets of AIG and its subsidiaries.

The intervention by the Federal Reserve was quite unusual, especially because AIG is an insurance company and is not regulated by the Fed. At the time, however, the government was worried about the adverse impact that AIG's failure would have had on the financial system.

When the government assumed control of the firm, AIG had a very large amount of credit default swap contracts with banks and other financial institutions. Under each contract, AIG insured the bank or other institution against the possibility of default of specific mortgage-backed securities. The counterparty was obligated to make periodic payments (similar to insurance premiums) to AIG for this insurance, so AIG stood to benefit from this arrangement as long as the mortgage-backed securities specified in the contracts did not default.

ETHICS

AIG was very aggressive in insuring against the default of mortgage-backed securities, which may be attributed to the increased compensation garnered by managers who sold a large amount of credit default swaps. As of September 2008, the firm's exposure to credit default swaps exceeded $400 billion. The general idea behind insurance is that if the policies are diversified, the bad events should not spread across all counterparties. For example, not all customers who purchase life insurance policies are likely to die in a short period of time. However, providing insurance against mortgage defaults is different because an adverse event such as a very weak economy could, in fact, prevent many homeowners from making their payments. AIG or its regulators should have recognized that it was heavily exposed to a weak housing market and, therefore, to a high risk that many of its insured mortgages would default.

By September 2008, it was clear that many of the mortgages that were insured by AIG would ultimately default. Once the government became aware of AIG's financial problems, it worried about the high degree of systemic risk created by AIG's contracts. Thus, while many financial institutions attempted to hedge against the default risk of mortgage portfolios with credit default swap contracts, the insurance on those defaults was only as good as the insurer. If AIG failed, there would be no payments to the counterparties on those contracts. As a consequence, many of the financial institutions would experience severe financial problems because the insurance on their mortgage portfolios was not effective. The government decided to rescue AIG, rather than allow it to fail, so that the counterparties to these credit default swap contracts with AIG would have the backing to cover their mortgage defaults.

Why Bail Out AIG But Not Lehman Brothers?

Critics asked why some large financial institutions were bailed out but others were not. At what point does a financial institution become sufficiently large or important that it deserves to be rescued?

Lehman Brothers was a large financial institution with more than $600 billion in assets. Nevertheless, it might have been difficult to find another financial institution willing to acquire the firm without an enormous subsidy from the federal government. Many of the assets held by Lehman Brothers (such as its mortgage-backed securities) were worth substantially less in the market than the book value assigned to them by Lehman.

AIG had more than $1 trillion in assets when it was rescued and, like Lehman, had many obligations to other financial institutions because of its credit default swap arrangements. However, one important difference between AIG and Lehman Brothers was that AIG had various subsidiaries that were financially sound at the time, and the assets in these subsidiaries served as collateral for the loans extended by the federal government to rescue AIG. From the government's perspective, the risk to U.S. taxpayers from the AIG rescue was low. In contrast, Lehman Brothers did not have adequate collateral available, so a large loan from the government could have been very costly to U.S. taxpayers.

18-5d **Argument for Government Rescue**

As described in the preceding sections, the U.S. government's actions during the credit crisis were controversial at the time and have led to an ongoing debate on whether and when the government should attempt to rescue failing financial institutions. If all financial institutions that were weak during the credit crisis had been allowed to fail without any intervention, the FDIC might have had to use all of its reserves to reimburse depositors. To the extent that FDIC intervention can reduce the extent of losses at depository institutions, that action may reduce the cost to the government (and therefore to taxpayers).

How a Rescue Might Reduce Systemic Risk   One of the arguments in favor of a government rescue is that the financial problems of a large bank failure can be contagious to other banks. This so-called systemic risk occurs because of the interconnected transactions involving multiple banks. The rescue of large banks might be necessary to reduce systemic risk in the financial system, as illustrated next.

EXAMPLE

Consider a financial system with only four large banks, all of which make many mortgage loans and invest in mortgage-backed securities. Assume that Bank A sold credit default swaps to Banks B, C, and D; in turn, it receives periodic payments from those banks. It will have to make a large payment to these banks if a particular set of mortgages default.

Now assume that the economy weakens and many mortgages default, including the mortgages referenced by the credit default swap agreements. As a consequence, Bank A now owes a large payment to Banks B, C, and D. But because Bank A incurred losses from its own mortgage portfolio, it cannot follow through on its payment obligation to the other banks. Meanwhile, Banks B, C, and D may have used their credit default swaps positions to hedge their existing mortgage holdings; however, if they do not receive the large payment from Bank A, they will incur losses without any offsetting gains.

If bank regulators do not rescue Bank A, then all four banks may fail because of Bank A's interconnections with the other three banks. However, if bank regulators rescue Bank A, then Bank A can make its payments to Banks B, C, and D, and all banks should survive. Thus a rescue may be necessary to stabilize the financial system. ●

Of course, the real-world financial system is supported not just by a few large banks, but by many different types of financial institutions. Thus the lessons of the preceding example are not restricted to banks, but extend to all types of financial institutions that can engage in those types of transactions. Furthermore, a government rescue of a bank benefits not only bank executives, but also bank employees at all levels. To the extent that a government rescue can stabilize the banking system, it can indirectly stimulate all the sectors that rely on funding from the banking system. This potential benefit was especially relevant during the credit crisis.

18-5e **Argument against Government Rescue**

Critics of government rescues argue that when the federal government rescues a large bank, it sends a message to the banking industry that large banks will not be allowed to fail. Consequently, large banks may take excessive risks without concern about failure. Their managers, who earn higher compensation for contributing to the bank's profits, may engage in very risky strategies because they could benefit personally if those strategies are successful, whereas they can rest assured that the government will provide a bailout if their strategies cause the bank to fail.

Some critics recommend a policy of letting the market work, meaning that no financial institution would ever be bailed out. In this case, managers of a troubled bank would be held accountable for their bad management because their jobs would be terminated in response to the bank's failure. In addition, shareholders would more closely monitor the bank managers to make sure that they do not take excessive risk.

18-6 Government Funding during the Crisis

In response to the failure of Lehman Brothers on September 15, 2008, and the government's takeover of AIG two days later, stock prices continued to decline. The credit markets became paralyzed, as institutional investors were unwilling to lend funds or purchase debt securities. The traditional methods used by bank regulators were not capable of solving the problems faced by financial institutions. Consequently, during the credit crisis, government intervention in the banking industry went beyond the traditional operations of the bank regulatory agencies.

Treasury Secretary Henry Paulson and Federal Reserve Chair Ben Bernanke sent a request to Congress for $700 billion in funding to stabilize the financial markets. Some of the funds would be used by the Treasury to buy illiquid securities that were held at commercial banks. These purchases would inject cash into the banks, which would increase their liquidity and enable them to provide new loans to creditworthy customers. The funding was largely intended to benefit the larger banks that play a major role as intermediaries in financial markets. Funds would also be used to inject more capital into the larger banks so that they could more easily absorb losses incurred during the credit crisis.

Congress initially voted against the bill, because of concerns about bailing out large banks even though many smaller banks had previously been allowed to fail. However, market conditions continued to deteriorate, especially the stock prices of large banks, which declined by more than 50 percent in the month after Lehman's bankruptcy. On October 3, 2008, Congress voted in favor of the bill (called the Emergency Economic Stabilization Act), which allowed the government to inject funds into the banking system by various means.

18-6a Troubled Asset Relief Program (TARP)

One of the most important programs initiated by the government was the Troubled Asset Relief Program (TARP), in which the Treasury injected capital into banks (by purchasing their preferred stock) to provide them with a cushion against their loan losses. TARP was also intended to encourage additional lending by banks and other financial institutions so that qualified firms or individuals could borrow funds. By ensuring that the banks were better capitalized, the government hoped to calm financial market participants' fears about large bank failures that could spread fear throughout the financial system.

On October 13, 2008, Treasury Secretary Paulson presented the CEOs of the nine largest commercial banks with a plan by which the government would inject capital into each bank, making the government a partial owner of the banks. Each bank CEO was asked to agree to sell a specified amount of preferred stock to the Treasury, thereby accepting an infusion of capital. The banks that received these capital injections were required to make dividend payments to the Treasury, but they could repurchase the preferred stock that they had issued to the Treasury (in essence, repaying the funds injected by the Treasury) once their financial position improved.

Some of the CEOs were initially opposed to Paulson's proposal because they did not want to be subjected to government intervention and oversight, but they did not have much choice. The Federal Reserve believed that all of these banks were undercapitalized at the time because of the low quality (high likelihood of default) of some of their loans and investments in debt securities. As a result of this unprecedented strategy of the U.S. government intervening to become a major owner of the largest commercial banks, a total of $125 billion of capital was injected into these banks. For example, by February 2009, the Treasury had a 36 percent ownership stake in Citicorp. By 2011, most of the banks that sold preferred stock to the Treasury had repurchased their stock, thereby ending the partial government ownership.

TARP also involved various other initiatives by the government to inject funds into the financial system. Notably, the Treasury purchased some "toxic" assets that had declined in value, and it even guaranteed against losses of other assets at banks and financial institutions.

In October 2010, TARP stopped extending new funds to banks and other financial institutions. Although the government was subject to some criticism for its intervention in the banking system, it was also praised for restoring the confidence of depositors and investors in the system.

18-6b Protests of Government Funding for Banks

The bailouts during the credit crisis led to the emergence of various groups that opposed the government's actions. In 2009, the Tea Party organized and staged protests throughout the United States. Its members contended that the government was spending excessively, which would lead to larger budget deficits that could potentially weaken the economy further. Their proposed solution was to eliminate the government funding and bailouts of banks as one way of reducing the excessive government spending.

ETHICS

In 2011, the Occupy Wall Street movement was organized and began to stage protests. One of its main criticisms was that the executives of many financial institutions who had allegedly made decisions that caused the crisis were excessively rewarded. For example, the CEO of Lehman Brothers received compensation in excess of $500 million over the 2000–2008 period prior to Lehman's failure. A related criticism was that some financial institutions that received government funding during the crisis continued to pay large bonuses to their executives. Thus the government (taxpayers) appeared to be subsidizing these bonuses.

Some protesters argued that the government should direct more funding to health care, education, and programs to reduce unemployment and help homeowners. This led to the question often associated with Occupy Wall Street protests: "Where's my bailout?"

18-7 Financial Reform Act of 2010

FINANCIAL REFORM

Although many government officials made strenuous efforts to reduce the severity of the credit crisis, concerns remained about how the crisis could have erupted with such little warning. The emergency initiatives taken by the government might not have been necessary if measures had already been in place to prevent such a crisis from occurring.

In July 2010, Congress passed the Financial Reform Act, which was intended to enable regulators to identify and reduce risks in the financial system that might potentially cause another credit crisis. This act contained numerous provisions regarding financial services. The provisions that concern bank regulation are summarized here.

18-7a Mortgage Origination

ETHICS

The Financial Reform Act requires that banks and other financial institutions granting mortgages verify the income, job status, and credit history of mortgage applicants before approving mortgage applications. This provision is intended to prevent applicants from receiving mortgages unless they are creditworthy, which should minimize the possibility of a future credit crisis. It might seem as if banks would naturally take these steps even if not required to do so by law, but before the credit crisis many mortgages were approved for applicants who were clearly not creditworthy.

18-7b **Sales of Mortgage-Backed Securities**

The Financial Reform Act requires that banks and other financial institutions that sell mortgage-backed securities retain 5 percent of the portfolio unless it meets specific standards that reflect low risk. This provision forces financial institutions to maintain a stake in the mortgage portfolios that they sell. The act also requires more disclosure regarding the quality of the underlying assets when mortgage-backed securities are sold.

18-7c **Financial Stability Oversight Council**

The Financial Reform Act created the Financial Stability Oversight Council, which is responsible for identifying risks to financial stability in the United States and making recommendations that regulators can follow to reduce risks to the financial system. The Council can recommend methods to ensure that banks do not rely on regulatory bailouts, which may prevent large financial institutions from being viewed as too big to fail. Furthermore, it can recommend rules such as higher capital requirements for banks that are perceived to be too big and complex, which may prevent these banks from becoming too risky.

The Council consists of 10 members, including the Treasury secretary (who chairs the Council) and the heads of three regulatory agencies that monitor banks: the Federal Reserve, the Comptroller of the Currency, and the Federal Deposit Insurance Corporation. Because systemic risk in the financial system may be caused by financial security transactions that connect banks with other types of financial institutions, the Council also includes the heads of the Securities and Exchange Commission and the Commodities Futures Trading Commission. The remaining members are the heads of the National Credit Union Association, the Federal Housing Finance Agency, and the Consumer Financial Protection Bureau (described shortly), as well as an independent member with insurance experience who is appointed by the president.

18-7d **Orderly Liquidation**

The Financial Reform Act gave specific regulators the authority to determine whether any particular financial institution should be liquidated. This step was intended to expedite the liquidation process and to limit the losses incurred by a failing financial institution. The act calls for the creation of an orderly liquidation fund that can be used to finance the liquidation of any financial institution that is not covered by the FDIC. Shareholders and unsecured creditors are expected to bear most of the losses of failing financial institutions, so they are not covered by this fund. If losses exceed the amount that can be absorbed by shareholders and unsecured creditors, other financial institutions in the corresponding industry are expected to bear the cost of the liquidation. The liquidations are not to be financed by taxpayers.

18-7e **Consumer Financial Protection Bureau**

ETHICS

The Financial Reform Act established the Consumer Financial Protection Bureau, which is responsible for regulating consumer finance products and services offered by commercial banks and other financial institutions, such as online banking, checking accounts, and credit cards. This government agency can set rules to ensure that bank disclosure about financial products is accurate and to prevent deceptive financial practices.

18-7f **Limits on Bank Proprietary Trading**

The Financial Reform Act limits proprietary trading by banks, which occurs when banks use their own funds to invest in stocks, derivative instruments, and other risky investments. This restriction is referred to as the Volcker Rule after Paul Volcker, a previous chair of the Federal Reserve who initially proposed the rule while he was an economic adviser to President Barack Obama in 2010.

The Volcker Rule prohibits banks from sponsoring or holding an ownership interest in a hedge fund or a private equity fund. Banks are allowed to hold securities that are associated with the process of underwriting or market making, but they cannot engage in certain trading activities that could threaten the safety of the bank. The general argument for this rule is that commercial banks should not be making investments in extremely risky projects. If they want to pursue very high returns (and therefore be exposed to very high risk), they should not be part of the banking system, and should not have access to depositor funds or be able to obtain deposit insurance. In other words, if banks want to invest like hedge funds, they should apply to be hedge funds and not commercial banks. To the extent that the Volcker Rule could prevent a major bank from experiencing financial problems, it may prevent government bailouts of banks.

On May 11, 2012, while the Volcker Rule regulations were still being developed, JPMorgan Chase announced a $6.2 billion trading loss at its London subsidiary (incurred by a trader referred to as the "London Whale"). The loss was attributed to proprietary trading. This loss prompted regulators to consider imposing more restrictive provisions that would prevent banks from engaging in any trading in the future. However, because the provisions of the Volcker Rule were vague, experts questioned whether it would have prevented the trading activity that caused the large loss.

18-7g Trading of Derivative Securities

The Financial Reform Act requires that derivative securities be traded through a clearinghouse or exchange, rather than over the counter. This provision should lead to a more standardized structure for margins and collateral as well as more transparency for prices in the market. Consequently, banks that trade these derivatives should be less susceptible to risk that the counterparty posted insufficient collateral.

18-7h Limitations of Regulatory Reform

Ideally, the regulatory structure for the financial system should limit the system's exposure to individual adverse events such as a large bank's failure. Stringent regulations such as high capital requirements can prevent the adverse events that could spread throughout the financial system. However, commercial banks and other financial institutions in the United States are subject to numerous overlapping regulatory agencies, including the Federal Reserve, the FDIC, the Office of the Comptroller of the Currency, the Securities and Exchange Commission, the Commodity Futures Trading Commission, and numerous state agencies. Even if bank regulations were sufficiently powerful to prevent large banks from taking on excessive risk, the banking system is still subject to systemic risk resulting from the entanglements of banks and other types of financial institutions (such as Lehman Brothers and AIG, as discussed earlier) that are not subject to bank regulations.

The complex set of regulators that oversee financial institutions can lead to overlapping and excessive regulation for some types of financial institutions, but very little oversight of other types of financial institutions. In addition, the inconsistent levels of regulation among regulators may motivate some financial institutions to pursue a particular charter that enable them to avoid regulations or allow for easier compliance.

ETHICS   Consolidation of regulatory agencies into a single regulatory structure in the United States would allow for more consistent regulation across financial institutions, more efficiency in regulatory oversight, and a lower total regulatory budget (which is funded by taxpayers). However, reform to allow for a more efficient regulatory structure is unlikely to occur because of political conflicts of interest. Regulatory agencies vigorously protect their turf and resist losing their power (or existence) to another regulator. Some regulators are under the jurisdiction of specific congressional committees, and those committees may also want to protect their turf because it can influence their power and campaign contributions.

18-8 Global Bank Regulations

Although the division of regulatory power between the central bank and other regulators varies among countries, each country has a system for monitoring and regulating commercial banks. Most countries also maintain different guidelines for deposit insurance. The differences in regulatory restrictions may give some banks a competitive advantage in a global banking environment.

Historically, Canadian banks were not as restricted in offering securities services as U.S. banks, which allowed them to control much of the Canadian securities industry. Recently, Canadian banks have also begun to enter the insurance industry.

European banks have also traditionally had much more freedom than U.S. banks in offering securities services such as underwriting corporate securities. Many European banks are allowed to invest in stocks.

Japanese commercial banks have some flexibility in regard to providing investment banking services, but not as much as European banks. Perhaps the most obvious difference between Japanese and U.S. bank regulations is that Japanese banks are allowed to use depositor funds to invest in stocks of corporations. Thus Japanese banks are not only the creditors of firms, but also their shareholders.

18-8a Compliance with Basel III

The Basel III framework for increased capital requirements was intended to provide guidelines for bank regulators around the world. Many countries have taken steps to strengthen their capital requirements in accordance with this framework. Because U.S. banks conduct many transactions with European banks, some concern has arisen that if a large European bank encountered problems (perhaps because of loans to Greece or other countries struggling with large government budget deficits), the U.S. financial system could be affected.

Summary

- The regulatory structure of the U.S. banking system includes both federal and state regulatory systems. Federal regulators include the Federal Reserve, the Office of the Comptroller of the Currency, and the Federal Deposit Insurance Corporation.

- Banks must comply with regulations specifying the deposit insurance they must maintain, their loan composition, the bonds they are allowed to purchase, and the financial services they can offer. In general, regulations on deposits and financial services have been loosened in recent decades to allow for more competition among banks.

- Capital requirements are intended to ensure that banks have a cushion against any losses. These

requirements have become more stringent in recent years; they are adjusted based on risk, such that banks with a higher level of risk are required to maintain a higher level of capital.

- Bank regulators monitor banks by focusing on six criteria: capital, asset quality, management, earnings, liquidity, and sensitivity to financial market conditions. Regulators assign ratings to these criteria to determine whether corrective action is necessary. When a bank is failing, the FDIC or other government agencies consider whether it can be saved.

- During the credit crisis of 2008–2009, many banks as well as Lehman Brothers failed; however, the U.S. government rescued American International

Group (AIG). Unlike Lehman Brothers, AIG had various subsidiaries that were financially sound at the time, and the assets in these subsidiaries served as collateral for the loans extended by the government to rescue AIG.

- The U.S. government injected capital into many banks during the credit crisis to cushion them against massive losses. Although the government argued that this intervention was necessary to protect the financial system, it was controversial and led to protests by different groups.
- In July 2010, the Financial Reform Act was enacted. It set more stringent standards for mortgage applicants, required banks to maintain a stake in the mortgage portfolios that they sell, and established the Consumer Financial Protection Bureau to regulate consumer finance products and services offered by commercial banks and other financial institutions. The Volcker Rule limits proprietary trading by banks.
- All countries have systems for monitoring and regulating banks, but the services that banks are allowed to offer differ considerably among countries. Many countries have taken steps to increase their capital requirements for banks in line with the Basel III recommendations.

Point/Counterpoint

Should Regulators Intervene to Take over Weak Banks?

Point   Yes. Intervention could turn a bank around before weak management results in failure. Bank failures require funding from the FDIC to reimburse depositors up to the deposit insurance limit. This cost could be avoided if the bank's problems are corrected before it fails.

Counterpoint   No. Regulators will not necessarily manage banks any better. Also, this policy would lead to excessive government intervention each time a bank experienced problems. Banks would use a very conservative management approach to avoid intervention, but that approach would not necessarily appeal to their shareholders, who want high returns on their investment.

Who Is Correct?   Use the Internet to learn more about this issue and then formulate your own opinion.

Questions and Applications

1. **Regulation of Bank Sources and Uses of Funds** How are a bank's balance sheet decisions regulated?

2. **Off-Balance Sheet Activities** Provide examples of off-balance sheet activities. Why are regulators concerned about them?

3. **Moral Hazard and the Credit Crisis** Explain why the moral hazard problem received so much attention during the credit crisis.

4. **FDIC Insurance** What led to the establishment of FDIC insurance?

5. **Glass-Steagall Act** Briefly describe the Glass-Steagall Act, and then explain how the related regulations have changed since it was enacted.

6. **DIDMCA** Describe the main provisions of the DIDMCA that relate to deregulation.

7. **CAMELS Ratings** Explain how the CAMELS ratings are used.

8. **Uniform Capital Requirements** Explain how the uniform capital requirements established by the Basel Accord can discourage banks from taking excessive risk.

9. **Value-at-Risk** Explain how the value-at-risk (VaR) method can be used to determine whether a bank has adequate capital.

10. **HLTs** Describe highly leveraged transactions (HLTs), and explain why regulators closely monitor a bank's exposure to HLTs.

11. **Bank Underwriting** Given the higher capital requirements now imposed on them, why might banks be even more interested in underwriting corporate debt issues?

12. **Moral Hazard** Explain the moral hazard problem as it relates to deposit insurance.

13. **Economies of Scale** How do economies of scale in banking relate to the issue of interstate banking?

14. **Contagion Effects** How can the financial problems of one large bank affect the market's risk evaluation of other large banks?

15. **Regulating Bank Failures** Why are bank regulators more concerned about a large bank failure than a small bank failure?

16. **Financial Services Modernization Act** Describe the Financial Services Modernization Act of 1999. Explain how it affected commercial bank operations and changed the competitive landscape among financial institutions.

17. **Impact of SOX on Banks** Explain how the Sarbanes-Oxley Act improved the transparency of banks. Why might the act have a negative impact on some banks?

18. **Conversion of Securities Firms to BHCs** Explain how the conversion of a securities firm to a bank holding company (BHC) structure might reduce its risk.

19. **Capital Requirements during the Credit Crisis** Explain how the accounting method applied to mortgage-backed securities made it more difficult for banks to satisfy capital requirements during the credit crisis of 2008–2009.

20. **Fed Assistance to Bear Stearns** Explain why regulators might argue that the assistance they provided to Bear Stearns during the credit crisis was necessary.

21. **Fed Aid to Nonbanks** Should the Fed have the power to provide assistance to firms, such as Bear Stearns, that are not commercial banks?

22. **Regulation of Credit Default Swaps** Why were bank regulators concerned about credit default swaps during the credit crisis?

23. **Impact of Bank Consolidation on Regulation** Explain how bank regulation can be more effective when there is consolidation of banks and securities firms.

24. **Concerns about Systemic Risk during the Credit Crisis** Explain why the credit crisis caused concerns about systemic risk.

25. **Troubled Asset Relief Program (TARP)** Explain how TARP was expected to help resolve problems during the credit crisis.

26. **Financial Reform Act** Explain how the Financial Reform Act is intended to prevent some problems that contributed to the credit crisis.

27. **Bank Deposit Insurance Reserves** How did the Financial Reform Act of 2010 change the reserve requirements of the FDIC's Deposit Insurance Fund?

28. **Basel III Changes to Capital and Liquidity Requirements** How did Basel III change capital and liquidity requirements for banks?

29. **Regulation of Financial Disclosure** Lehman Brothers continued to report positive earnings throughout the spring of 2008, even though mortgage valuations were clearly declining. Nevertheless, some institutional investors were concerned that Lehman Brothers might have been overstating its earnings in 2007 and early 2008. Explain why more complete and accurate disclosure by banks and other financial institutions may help to resolve financial problems. Could managers' compensation incentives discourage banks from fully disclosing their financial condition? Why or why not?

30. **Regulatory Dilemma Involving AIG** Explain the government's dilemma regarding whether it should rescue American International Group (AIG) during the credit crisis.

31. **Government's Injection of Capital into Large Banks** Describe the U.S. government's efforts to infuse capital into all of the very large banks during the credit crisis.

Critical Thinking Question

Proprietary Trading by Banks   The Volcker Rule is intended to prevent banks from engaging in proprietary trading. Write a short essay offering your opinion on whether banks should be allowed to engage in proprietary trading.

Interpreting Financial News

Interpret the following comments made by Wall Street analysts and portfolio managers.

a. "The FDIC recently subsidized a buyer for a failing bank, which had different effects on FDIC costs than if the FDIC had closed the bank."

b. "Bank of America has pursued the acquisition of many failed banks because it sees potential benefits from these deals."

c. "By allowing a failing bank time to resolve its financial problems, the FDIC imposes an additional tax on taxpayers."

Managing in Financial Markets

Effect of Bank Strategies on Bank Ratings

A bank has asked you to assess various strategies it is considering and explain how they could affect its regulatory review. Regulatory reviews include an assessment of capital, asset quality, management, earnings, liquidity, and sensitivity to financial market conditions. Many types of strategies can result in more favorable regulatory reviews based on some criteria but less favorable reviews based on other criteria. The bank is planning to issue more stock, retain more of its earnings, increase its holdings of Treasury securities, and reduce its business loans. It has historically been rated favorably by regulators, but the bank believes that these strategies will result in an even more favorable regulatory assessment.

a. Which regulatory criteria will be affected by the bank's strategies? How?

b. Do you believe that the strategies planned by the bank will satisfy its shareholders? Is it possible for the bank to use strategies that would satisfy both regulators and shareholders? Explain.

c. Do you believe that the strategies planned by the bank will satisfy the bank's managers? Explain.

Flow of Funds Exercise

Impact of Regulation and Deregulation on Financial Services

Carson Company relies heavily on commercial banks for funding and for some other services.

a. Explain how the services provided by a commercial bank (just the banking services, not the nonbank services) to Carson may be limited because of bank regulation.

b. Explain the types of nonbank services that Carson Company can receive from the subsidiaries of a commercial bank as a result of deregulation.

c. How might Carson Company be affected by the deregulation that allows subsidiaries of a commercial bank to offer nonbank services?

Internet/Excel Exercise

Browse the Failed Bank List at www.fdic.gov/bank/individual/failed/banklist.html. Review the information provided about failed banks, and describe how regulators responded to one recent bank failure listed here.

WSJ Exercise

Impact of Bank Regulations

Using a recent issue of *The Wall Street Journal,* summarize an article that discusses a particular commercial bank regulation that has recently been passed or is currently being considered by regulators. Would this regulation have a favorable or an unfavorable impact on commercial banks? Explain.

Online Articles with Real-World Examples

Find a recent practical article available online that describes a real-world example regarding a specific financial institution or financial market that reinforces one or more concepts covered in this chapter.

If your class has an online component, your professor may ask you to post your summary of the article there and provide a link to the article so that other students can access it. If your class is live, your professor may ask you to summarize your application of the article in class. Your professor may assign specific students to complete this assignment or may allow any students to do the assignment on a volunteer basis.

For recent online articles and real-world examples related to this chapter, consider using the following search terms (be sure to include the prevailing year as a search term to ensure that the online articles are recent):

1. bank AND deposit insurance
2. bank AND moral hazard
3. bank loans AND regulation
4. bank investments AND regulation
5. bank capital AND regulation
6. bank regulator AND rating banks
7. bank regulator AND stress test
8. too big to fail AND conflict
9. bank regulation AND conflict
10. government rescue AND bank

19
Bank Management

CHAPTER OBJECTIVES

The specific objectives of this chapter are to:

■ Describe the underlying goal, strategy, and governance of banks.

■ Explain how banks manage liquidity.

■ Explain how banks manage interest rate risk.

■ Explain how banks manage credit risk.

■ Explain how banks manage market risk.

■ Explain integrated bank management.

■ Discuss how banks manage risk in international operations.

The performance of any commercial bank depends on the management of the bank's assets, liabilities, and capital. Increased competition has made efficient management essential for survival.

19-1 Bank Goals, Strategy, and Governance

The underlying goal of the managerial policies of a bank is to maximize the wealth of the bank's shareholders. To achieve this goal, bank managers should make decisions that maximize the price of the bank's stock. However, bank managers may sometimes make decisions that serve their own goals rather than the preferences of shareholders. For example, if they receive a fixed salary without a bonus, they may prefer to make very conservative decisions that avoid the risk of failure. In this way, they may secure their existing job position for a long-term period. Bank shareholders might prefer that bank managers take some risk to strive for higher returns, which is a common justification for tying bank managers' compensation to a measure of performance such as earnings.

19-1a Aligning Managerial Compensation with Bank Goals

To ensure that managers serve shareholder interests, banks commonly implement compensation programs that provide bonuses to high-level managers whose actions satisfy the bank's goals. For example, managerial compensation may include stock options, which encourage managers to serve shareholders because they are themselves shareholders. However, this type of compensation scheme might also encourage bank managers to focus on increasing the current stock price so that they will receive a large bonus rather than developing long-term projects. To be more effective (in terms of realizing the bank's goals), compensation programs that provide stock options may therefore require managers to hold their stock for several years before selling it. At the same time, compensation programs that award very large bonuses for achieving high earnings may encourage bank managers to take excessive risks. They may be especially willing to take risks if they believe that the government will rescue them if their risky strategies result in large losses.

Thus, when implementing their compensation programs, banks seek to encourage managers to achieve high returns for shareholders, yet simultaneously discourage them from engaging in such risky strategies that they endanger the bank. Banks have been criticized for implementing compensation programs that are overly generous and that do not necessarily align managers' compensation with their long-term performance. Many banks base their compensation programs on the existing compensation programs used by other banks. Correcting deficiencies in compensation programs becomes more difficult when those programs are fairly standard across the industry.

Regulating Managerial Compensation   After the credit crisis in 2008–2009, when many U.S. banks failed and many of the largest banks needed a government bailout, much criticism was targeted at compensation plans that encouraged executives to take excessive risk. In 2010, Congress passed the Financial Reform (Dodd-Frank) Act, which contained several provisions aimed at reducing managerial compensation. Some of its provisions applied to all companies, but others were aimed specifically at banks. The act required that banks report their incentive compensation plans to their regulator, have a governance system in place that would discourage executives from taking excessive risks, and provide at least 50 percent of incentive bonuses over a three-year period to prevent executives from focusing only on the short term. It also mandated "clawbacks" in which executives who received bonuses erroneously because the firm's earnings were miscalculated would have to repay those bonuses.

19-1b Bank Strategy

A bank's strategy involves the management of its sources of funds (liabilities) and its uses of funds (assets). Its managerial decisions will affect its performance, as measured by its income statement, in the following ways. First, a bank's decisions on sources of funds will heavily influence its interest expenses on the income statement. Second, its asset structure will strongly influence its interest revenue on the income statement. The bank's asset structure also affects its expenses; for example, an emphasis on commercial loans will result in a high labor cost for assessing loan applicants.

A bank must also manage the operating risk that results from its general business operations. Specifically, banks face risk related to information (sorting, processing, transmitting through technology), execution of transactions, damaged relationships with clients, legal issues (lawsuits by employees and customers), and regulatory issues (increased costs due to new compliance requirements or penalties due to lack of compliance).

How Financial Markets Facilitate the Bank's Strategy   To implement their strategy, commercial banks rely heavily on the financial markets, as explained in Exhibit 19.1. They rely on the money markets to obtain funds, on the mortgage and bond markets to use some of their funds, and on the futures, options, and swaps markets to hedge their risk (as explained in this chapter).

Exhibit 19.1   Participation of Commercial Banks in Financial Markets

FINANCIAL MARKET	PARTICIPATION BY COMMERCIAL BANKS
Money markets	As banks offer deposits, they must compete with other financial institutions in the money market along with the Treasury to obtain short-term funds. They serve households that wish to invest funds for short-term periods.
Mortgage markets	Some banks offer mortgage loans on homes and commercial property; that is, they provide financing in the mortgage market.
Bond markets	Commercial banks purchase bonds issued by corporations, the U.S. Treasury, and municipalities.
Futures markets	Commercial banks take positions in futures to hedge interest rate risk.
Options markets	Commercial banks take positions in options on futures to hedge interest rate risk.
Swaps markets	Commercial banks engage in interest rate swaps to hedge interest rate risk.

19-1c **Bank Governance by the Board of Directors**

A bank's board of directors oversees the operations of the bank and attempts to ensure that managers' make decisions that are in the best interests of the shareholders. Banks' boards tend to have more directors and a higher percentage of outside directors than do boards of other types of firms. Important functions of bank directors include the following responsibilities:

- Determine a compensation system for the bank's executives.
- Ensure proper disclosure of the bank's financial condition and performance to investors.
- Oversee growth strategies such as acquisitions.
- Oversee policies for changing the capital structure, including decisions to raise capital or to engage in stock repurchases.
- Assess the bank's performance and ensure that corrective action is taken if the performance is weak because of poor management.

Bank directors are liable if they do not fulfill their duties. The Sarbanes-Oxley (SOX) Act, described in Chapter 18, has had a major effect on the monitoring conducted by board members of commercial banks. Recall that this act requires publicly traded firms to implement a more thorough internal control process to ensure more accurate financial reporting to shareholders. As a result of the SOX Act, directors are now held more accountable for their oversight because the internal process requires them to document their assessment and opinion of key decisions made by the bank's executives. Furthermore, directors more frequently hire outside legal and financial advisers to aid in assessing key decisions (such as acquisitions) by bank executives to determine whether the decisions are justified.

Inside versus Outside Directors   Board members who are also managers of the bank (called inside directors) may sometimes face a conflict of interest because their decisions as board members may affect their jobs as managers. Outside directors (directors who are not managers) are generally expected to be more effective at overseeing a bank: They do not face a conflict of interest in serving shareholders.

19-1d **Other Forms of Bank Governance**

In addition to the board of directors, publicly traded banks are subject to potential shareholder activism. In particular, institutional investors holding a relatively large number of shares can attempt to influence the approach taken by the bank's managers. Shareholders may also pursue proxy contests if they want to change the composition of the board, and they can file lawsuits if they believe that the board is not serving shareholder interests.

The market for corporate control serves as an additional form of governance over publicly traded banks, because a bank that performs poorly may be subject to a takeover. To the extent that a bank's management serves its own interests rather than the bank shareholders' interests, the bank's prevailing stock valuation may be low, which could encourage another bank to acquire it. Moreover, bank managers recognize that they could lose their jobs if their poor decision making causes the bank to perform poorly and become vulnerable to a takeover.

19-2 **Managing Liquidity**

Healthy banks tend to have easy access to liquidity. However, banks can experience illiquidity when cash outflows (due to withdrawals by depositors, loans, and other transactions) exceed cash inflows (new deposits, loan repayments, and so on). Banks' liquidity problems are typically preceded by other financial problems such as major defaults on their loans. A bank that is performing poorly has less ability to obtain short-term funds because it may not be able to repay the credit that it desires. Banks can resolve liquidity problems with proper management of their liabilities or their assets.

19-2a **Management of Liabilities**

Banks have access to various forms of borrowing, such as the federal funds market. The decision regarding how to obtain funds depends on the situation. If a bank needs funds for just a few days, an increase in short-term liabilities (from the federal funds market) may be appropriate. However, if the bank needs funds over a longer period, it may consider implementing a policy geared toward increasing deposits or selling liquid assets.

Some banks may borrow frequently by issuing short-term securities such as commercial paper, especially when short-term interest rates are low. They may use this strategy as a form of long-term financing, as the proceeds received from each new issuance of commercial paper are used to repay the principal owed as a result of the previous issuance. However, this strategy is dangerous: If economic conditions deteriorate, causing the bank's loan defaults to increase, then the bank may no longer be able to obtain funds by issuing commercial paper. Some banks have experienced liquidity problems because they were cut off from their short-term funding sources once weak economic conditions caused the assets that they used as collateral to appear risky.

19-2b **Management of Money Market Securities**

Because some assets are more marketable than others, the bank's asset composition can affect its degree of liquidity. At an extreme, banks can ensure sufficient liquidity by using most of their funds to purchase short-term Treasury securities or other money market securities. Banks could easily sell their holdings of these securities at any time to obtain cash. However, they must also be concerned with achieving a reasonable return on their assets, which often conflicts with the liquidity objective. Although short-term Treasury securities are liquid, their yield is low relative to bank loans or investments in other securities. In fact, the return that banks earn on short-term Treasury securities might be lower than the interest rate they pay on deposits. Banks should maintain a level of liquid assets (such as money market securities) that will satisfy their liquidity needs but use their remaining assets to earn a higher return.

19-2c **Management of Loans**

When the secondary market for loans is relatively active, banks can attempt to satisfy their liquidity needs with a higher proportion of loans while striving for higher profitability. However, loans are not as liquid as money market securities. Banks may be unable to sell their loans when economic conditions weaken, because many other banks may be attempting to sell their own loans at the same time, and very few financial institutions will be willing to purchase loans under those conditions.

19-2d **Use of Securitization to Boost Liquidity**

The ability to securitize assets such as automobile and mortgage loans can enhance a bank's liquidity position. The process of securitization commonly involves the sale of assets by the bank to a trustee, who issues securities that are collateralized by the assets. The bank may still service the loans, but the interest and principal payments it receives are passed on to the investors who purchased the securities. Banks are more liquid as a result of securitization because this practice effectively converts future cash flows into immediate cash. In most cases, the process includes a guarantor who, for a fee, guarantees future payments to the investors who purchased the securities. The loans that collateralize the securities usually either exceed the amount of the securities issued or are backed by an additional guarantee from the bank that sells the loans.

Collateralized Loan Obligations   Commercial banks can obtain funds by packaging their commercial loans with those of other financial institutions as collateralized loan obligations (CLOs) and then selling securities that represent ownership of these loans. The banks earn a fee for selling these loans. The pool of loans might be perceived as less risky than a typical individual loan within that pool because the loans were provided to a diversified set of borrowers.

Various classes of securities are issued to investors who invest in the loan pool. For example, one class may consist of BB-rated notes, which offer an interest rate of the LIBOR (London Interbank Offer Rate) plus 3.5 percent. If the corporate borrowers whose loans are in the pool default on their loans, investors in the BB-rated notes will be the first to suffer losses. Another class of securities may consist of BBB-rated notes that offer a slightly lower interest rate. Investors in these notes are slightly less exposed to defaults on the loans. AAA-rated notes offer investors the most protection against loan defaults but provide the lowest interest rate, such as LIBOR plus 0.25 percent. Insurance companies and pension funds commonly invest in CLOs.

19-3 Managing Interest Rate Risk

The performance of a bank is highly influenced by the interest payments earned on its assets relative to the interest paid on its liabilities (deposits). The difference between interest payments received and interest paid is measured by the net interest margin (also known as the *spread*):

$$\text{Net interest margin} = \frac{\text{Interest revenues} - \text{Interest expenses}}{\text{Assets}}$$

Because the rate sensitivity of a bank's liabilities usually does not perfectly match that of the assets, the net interest margin changes over time. The amount and direction of change depend on whether bank assets are more or less rate-sensitive than bank liabilities, the degree of difference in rate sensitivity, and the direction of interest rate movements.

During a period of rising interest rates, a bank's net interest margin will likely decrease if its liabilities are more rate-sensitive than its assets, as illustrated in Exhibit 19.2. Under the opposite scenario, in which market interest rates decrease over time, rates offered on new bank deposits (as well as those earned on new bank loans) will be affected by the decline in interest rates. The deposit rates will typically be more sensitive if their turnover is quicker, as illustrated in Exhibit 19.3.

To manage interest rate risk, a bank measures the risk and then uses its assessment of future interest rates to decide whether and how to hedge the risk. Methods of assessing the risk are described next, followed by a discussion of the hedging decision and methods of reducing interest rate risk.

Exhibit 19.2   Impact of Increasing Interest Rates on a Bank's Net Interest Margin (If the Bank's Liabilities Are More Rate-Sensitive Than Its Assets)

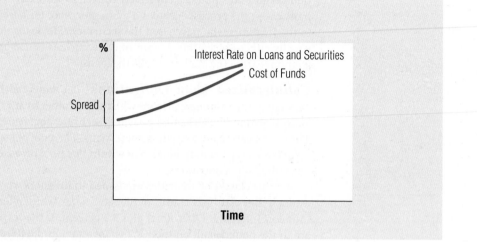

Exhibit 19.3   Impact of Decreasing Interest Rates on a Bank's Net Interest Margin (If the Bank's Liabilities Are More Rate-Sensitive Than Its Assets)

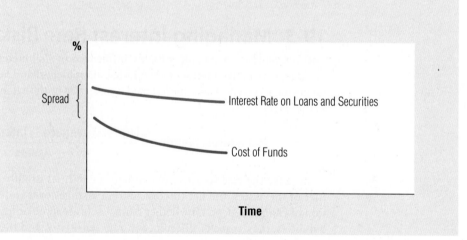

19-3a Methods Used to Assess Interest Rate Risk

No method of measuring interest rate risk is perfect, so commercial banks use a variety of methods to assess their exposure to interest rate movements. The most common methods of measuring interest rate risk are these three approaches:

■   Gap analysis
■   Duration analysis
■   Sensitivity analysis

Gap Analysis   Banks can attempt to determine their interest rate risk by monitoring their **gap** over time, where

$$\text{Gap} = \text{Rate-sensitive assets} - \text{Rate-sensitive liabilities}$$

An alternative formula is the gap ratio, which is measured as the volume of rate-sensitive assets divided by rate-sensitive liabilities. A gap of zero (or a gap ratio of 1.00) indicates that rate-sensitive assets equal rate-sensitive liabilities, so the net interest margin should not be significantly influenced by interest rate fluctuations. A negative gap (or a gap ratio of less than 1.00) indicates that rate-sensitive liabilities exceed rate-sensitive assets. Banks with a negative gap are typically concerned about a potential increase in interest rates, which could reduce their net interest margin.

EXAMPLE   Kansas City (K.C.) Bank had interest revenues of $80 million last year and interest expenses of $35 million. Approximately $400 million of its $1 billion in assets are rate-sensitive, and $700 million of its liabilities are rate-sensitive. K.C. Bank's net interest margin is

$$\text{Net interest margin} = (\$80,000,000 - \$35,000,000) \div \$1,000,000,000$$
$$= 0.045, \text{ or } 4.5\%$$

K.C. Bank's gap is

$$\text{Gap} = \$400,000,000 - \$700,000,000$$
$$= -\$300,000,000$$

and its gap ratio is

$$\text{Gap} = \$400,000,000 \div \$700,000,000$$
$$= 0.5714, \text{ or } 57.14\%$$

Based on the gap analysis, an increase in market interest rates would cause K.C. Bank's net interest margin to decline from its recent level of 4.5 percent. Conversely, a decrease in interest rates would cause its net interest margin to increase to more than 4.5 percent. ●

Many banks classify interest-sensitive assets and liabilities into various categories based on the timing of interest rate adjustments. By considering this schedule, the bank can determine the gap in each category and more accurately assessed its exposure to interest rate risk.

EXAMPLE   Deacon Bank compares the interest rate sensitivity of its assets versus its liabilities as shown in Exhibit 19.4. It has a negative gap in the less-than-1-month maturity range, in the 3-to-6-month range, and in the 6-to-12-month range. Hence, the bank may hedge this gap if it believes that interest rates are rising. ●

Although the gap as described here is an easily applied method for measuring a bank's interest rate risk, it has limitations. Banks must determine which of their liabilities and assets are rate-sensitive. For example, should a Treasury security with a year to maturity be classified as rate-sensitive or rate-insensitive? How short must a maturity be to qualify for the rate-sensitive classification?

Exhibit 19.4   Interest-Sensitive Assets and Liabilities: Illustration of the Gap Measured for Various Maturity Ranges for Deacon Bank

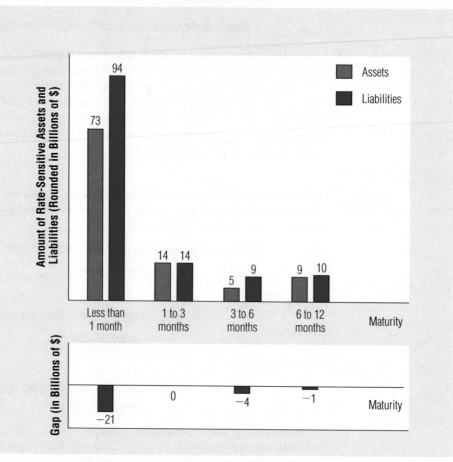

Each bank may have its own classification system. Whatever system is used, there is a possibility that the measurement will be misinterpreted.

EXAMPLE   Spencer Bank obtains much of its funds by issuing CDs with seven-day and one-month maturities as well as through money market deposit accounts (MMDAs). Assume that the bank typically uses these funds to provide loans with a floating rate that is adjusted once per year. These sources and uses of funds will likely be classified as rate-sensitive. Thus the gap will be close to zero, implying that the bank is not exposed to interest rate risk. However, there is a difference in rate sensitivity between the bank's sources and uses of funds: The rates paid by the bank on its sources of funds will change more frequently than the rates earned on its uses of funds. Thus Spencer Bank's net interest margin will likely decline during periods of rising interest rates, but this exposure would not be detected by the gap measurement. ●

Duration Measurement   An alternative approach to assessing interest rate risk is to measure duration. Some assets or liabilities are more rate-sensitive than others, even if the frequency of adjustment and the maturity are the same. For example, a 10-year, zero-coupon bond is more sensitive to interest rate fluctuations than is a 10-year bond that generates coupon payments. Thus the market value of assets in a bank that has invested heavily in zero-coupon bonds will be susceptible to interest rate movements. The duration measurement can capture these different degrees of sensitivity. In recent years, banks and other financial institutions have used the concept of duration to measure the sensitivity of their assets to interest rate movements. Among the various means of measuring an asset's duration, one of the more common options is

$$\text{DUR} = \frac{\sum_{t=1}^{n} \frac{C_t(t)}{(1 + k)^t}}{\sum_{t=1}^{n} \frac{C_t}{(1 + k)^t}}$$

where C_t represents the interest or principal payments of the asset; t is the time at which the payments are provided; and k is the required rate of return on the asset, which reflects the asset's yield to maturity. The duration of each type of bank asset can be determined, and the duration of the asset portfolio is the weighted average (based on the relative proportion invested in each asset) of the durations of the individual assets.

The duration of each type of bank liability can also be estimated, and the duration of the liability portfolio is likewise estimated as the weighted average of the durations of the liabilities. The bank can then estimate its **duration gap**, which is commonly measured as the difference between the weighted duration of the bank's assets and the weighted duration of its liabilities, adjusted for the firm's asset size:

$$\text{DURGAP} = \frac{(\text{DURAS} \times \text{AS})}{\text{AS}} - \frac{(\text{DURLIAB} \times \text{LIAB})}{\text{AS}}$$

$$= \text{DURAS} - \left[\text{DURLIAB} \left(\frac{\text{LIAB}}{\text{AS}} \right) \right]$$

where DURAS is the weighted average duration of the bank's assets, DURLIAB is the weighted average duration of the bank's liabilities, and AS and LIAB represent the market values of the bank's assets and liabilities, respectively. A duration gap of zero suggests that the bank's value should be insensitive to interest rate movements, meaning that the bank is not exposed to interest rate risk. For most banks, the average duration of assets exceeds the average duration of liabilities, so the duration gap is positive. This implies that the market value of the bank's assets is more sensitive to interest rate movements than the value of its liabilities is. So, if interest rates rise, banks with positive duration gaps will be adversely affected. Conversely, if interest rates decline, banks with positive duration gaps will benefit. The larger the duration gap, the more sensitive the bank should be to interest rate movements.

Other things being equal, assets with shorter maturities have shorter durations; also, assets that generate more frequent coupon payments have shorter durations than those that generate less frequent payments. Banks and other financial institutions concerned with interest rate risk use duration to compare the rate sensitivity of their entire asset and liability portfolios. Because duration is especially critical for a savings institution's operations, Chapter 21 gives a numerical example showing the measurement of the duration of a savings institution's entire asset and liability portfolio.

Although duration is a valuable technique for comparing the rate sensitivity of various securities, its capabilities are limited when this method is applied to assets that can be terminated on a moment's notice. For example, consider a bank that offers a fixed-rate, five-year loan that can be paid off early without penalty. If the loan is not paid off early, it is perceived as rate-insensitive. Yet the loan could be terminated at any time over the five-year period. If it is paid off, the bank would reinvest the funds at the prevailing market rate. Thus the funds used to provide the loan *can* be sensitive to interest rate movements, but the degree of sensitivity depends on when the loan is paid off. In general, loan prepayments are more common when market rates decline because borrowers refinance by obtaining lower-rate loans to pay off existing loans. The point here is that the possibility of prepayment makes it impossible to perfectly match the rate sensitivity of assets and liabilities.

Regression Analysis   Gap analysis and duration analysis are based on the bank's balance sheet composition. Alternatively, a bank can assess interest rate risk simply by determining the sensitivity of its performance to interest rate movements over time. Common proxies for performance include return on assets (ROA), return on equity (ROE), and the percentage change in stock price.

To determine how performance is affected by interest rates, regression analysis can be applied to historical data. For example, using an interest rate proxy called i, the S&P 500 stock index as the market, and the bank's stock return (R) as the performance proxy, the following regression model could be used:

$$R = B_0 + B_1 R_m + B_2 i + \mu$$

where R_m is the return on the market; B_0, B_1, and B_2 are regression coefficients; and μ is an error term. The regression coefficient B_2 in this model can also be called the interest rate coefficient because it measures the sensitivity of the bank's performance to interest rate movements. A positive (negative) coefficient suggests that performance is favorably (adversely) affected by rising interest rates. If the interest rate coefficient is not significantly different from zero, the bank's stock returns are likely well insulated from interest rate movements.

Models similar to the one just described have been tested on a portfolio containing all publicly traded banks to determine whether bank stock returns are affected by interest rate movements. The vast majority of this research has found that bank stock returns are inversely related to interest rate movements (that is, the B_2 coefficient is negative and significant). These results can be attributed to the common imbalance between a bank's rate-sensitive liabilities and its assets. Because banks tend to have a negative gap (their liabilities are more rate-sensitive than their assets), rising interest rates reduce bank stock returns. These results are generalized for the banking industry, however; they do not apply to every bank.

Because a bank's assets and liabilities are replaced over time, exposure to interest rate risk must be continually reassessed. As exposure changes, the bank's performance in the face of a particular interest rate pattern will change.

When a bank uses regression analysis to determine its sensitivity to interest rate movements, it may combine this analysis with the value-at-risk (VaR) method to determine how its market value would change in response to specific interest rate movements. The VaR method can be applied by combining a probability distribution of interest rate movements with the interest rate coefficient (measured from the regression analysis) to determine a maximum expected loss due to adverse interest rate movements.

EXAMPLE   After applying the regression model to its monthly data, Dixon Bank determines that its interest rate regression coefficient is −2.4. This implies that, for a 1 percentage point increase in interest rates, the market value of the bank would decline by 2.4 percent. The model also indicates (at the 99 percent confidence level) that the change in the interest rate should not exceed +2.0 percent. For a 2 percentage point increase, the value of Dixon Bank is expected to decline by 4.8 percent (computed as 2.0 percent multiplied by the regression coefficient of −2.4). Thus the maximum expected loss due to interest rate movements (based on a 99 percent confidence level) is a 4.8 percent loss in market value. ●

19-3b **Whether to Hedge Interest Rate Risk**

A bank can consider the measurement of its interest rate risk along with its forecast of interest rate movements to determine whether it should consider hedging that risk. The general conclusions resulting from a bank's analysis of its interest rate risk are presented in Exhibit 19.5. This exhibit shows the three methods commonly used by banks to measure

Exhibit 19.5 Framework for Managing Interest Rate Risk
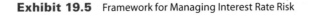

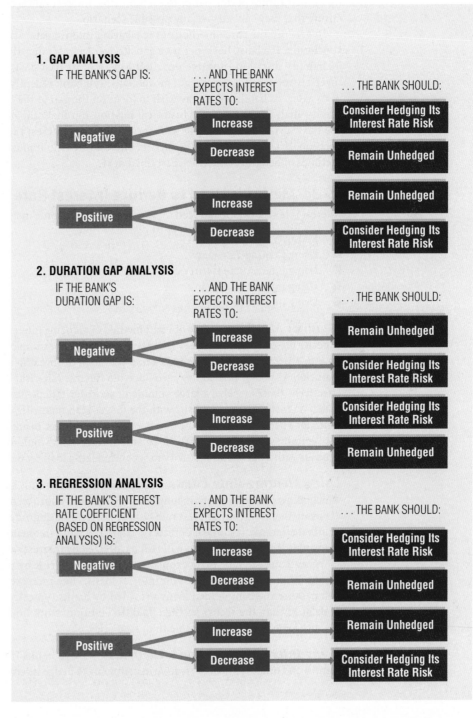

their interest rate risk. Because none of these measures is perfect for all situations, some banks measure interest rate risk using all three methods. Other banks apply just one of the methods.

Using any method along with an interest rate forecast can help a bank determine whether it should consider hedging its interest rate risk. However, because interest rate movements cannot always be accurately forecasted, banks should not be overly aggressive in attempting to capitalize on the expected interest rate. They should assess the sensitivity of their future performance to each possible interest rate scenario that could occur to ensure that they can survive any possible scenario.

In general, the three methods of measuring interest rate risk should lead to a similar conclusion. If a bank has a negative gap, its average asset duration is probably larger than its liability duration (positive duration gap), and its past performance level is probably inversely related to interest rate movements. If a bank recently revised the composition of its assets or liabilities, it may wish to focus on the gap or the duration gap because sensitivity analysis is based on a historical relationship that may no longer exist. Banks can use their analysis of gap along with their forecast of interest rates to make their hedging decision. If a bank decides to reduce its interest rate risk, it must select one of the various methods of hedging, which are described next.

19-3c Methods Used to Reduce Interest Rate Risk

Interest rate risk can be reduced by any of the following means:

- Maturity matching
- Using floating-rate loans
- Using interest rate futures contracts
- Using interest rate swaps
- Using interest rate caps

Maturity Matching   One obvious method of reducing interest rate risk is to match each deposit's maturity with an asset of the same maturity. For example, if the bank receives funds for a one-year CD, it could provide a one-year loan or invest in a security with a one-year maturity. Although this strategy would avoid interest rate risk, it cannot be implemented effectively. Banks receive a large volume of short-term deposits and would not be able to match up maturities on deposits with the longer loan maturities. Borrowers rarely request funds for a period as short as one month or even six months. In addition, the deposit amounts are typically small relative to the loan amounts. A bank would have difficulty combining deposits with a particular maturity to accommodate a loan request with the same maturity.

Using Floating-Rate Loans   An alternative solution is to use floating-rate loans, which allow banks to support long-term assets with short-term deposits without overly exposing themselves to interest rate risk. However, floating-rate loans cannot completely eliminate the risk. If the cost of funds is changing more frequently than the rate on assets, the bank's net interest margin will still be affected by interest rate fluctuations.

When banks reduce their exposure to interest rate risk by replacing long-term securities with more floating-rate commercial loans, they increase their exposure to credit risk because the commercial loans provided by banks typically have a higher frequency of defaults than the securities they hold. In addition, bank liquidity risk would increase because loans are less marketable than securities.

Using Interest Rate Futures Contracts   Large banks frequently use interest rate futures and other types of derivative instruments to hedge interest rate risk. One common method of reducing interest rate risk is to use interest rate futures contracts, which lock in the price at which the specified financial instruments can be purchased or sold on a specified future settlement date. Recall that the sale of a futures contract on Treasury bonds prior to an increase in interest rates will result in a gain, because an identical futures contract can be purchased later at a lower price once interest rates rise. Thus a gain on the Treasury bond futures contracts can offset the adverse effects of higher interest rates on a bank's performance. The size of the bank's position in Treasury bond futures should depend on the size of its asset portfolio, the degree of its exposure to interest rate movements, and its forecasts of future interest rate movements.

Exhibit 19.6 illustrates how the use of financial futures contracts can reduce uncertainty about a bank's net interest margin. The sale of interest rate futures, for example, reduces the potential adverse effect of rising interest rates on the bank's interest expenses, yet also diminishes the potential favorable effect of declining interest rates on the bank's interest expenses. Assuming that the bank initially had more rate-sensitive liabilities, its use of futures would reduce the impact of interest rates on its net interest margin.

Using Interest Rate Swaps   Commercial banks can hedge interest rate risk by engaging in an interest rate swap, which is an arrangement to exchange periodic cash flows based on specified interest rates. A fixed-for-floating swap allows one party to periodically exchange fixed cash flows for cash flows that are based on prevailing market interest rates.

A bank whose liabilities are more rate-sensitive than its assets can swap payments with a fixed interest rate for payments with a variable interest rate over a specified period of time. If interest rates rise, the bank benefits because the payments to be received from the swap will increase while its outflow payments are fixed. This can offset the adverse impact of rising interest rates on the bank's net interest margin.

Exhibit 19.6   Effect of Financial Futures on the Net Interest Margin of Banks That Have More Rate-Sensitive Liabilities Than Assets

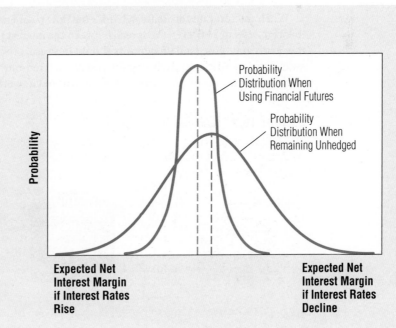

Of course, an interest rate swap requires another party to provide variable-rate payments in exchange for fixed-rate payments. Financial institutions that have more rate-sensitive assets than liabilities may be willing to assume such a position because they could reduce their exposure to interest rate movements in this manner. A financial intermediary is typically needed to match up the two parties that desire an interest rate swap. Some securities firms and large commercial banks are willing to fill this role.

EXAMPLE

Assume that Denver Bank (DB) has large holdings of 11 percent, fixed-rate mortgages. Because most of its sources of funds are sensitive to interest rates, DB desires to swap fixed-rate payments in exchange for variable-rate payments. It informs Colorado Bank of its situation because it knows that this bank commonly engages in swap transactions.

Colorado Bank searches for a client and finds that Brit Eurobank desires to swap variable-rate dollar payments in exchange for fixed dollar payments. Colorado Bank then develops the swap arrangement illustrated in Exhibit 19.7. Denver Bank will swap fixed-rate payments in exchange for variable-rate payments *based on* LIBOR (the rate charged on loans between Eurobanks). Because the variable-rate payments will fluctuate with market conditions, DB's payments received will vary over time. The length of the swap period and the notional amount (the amount to which the interest rates are applied to determine the payments) can be structured to meet the participants' needs.

Colorado Bank, the financial intermediary conducting the swap, charges a fee amounting to 0.1 percent of the notional amount per year. Some financial intermediaries for swaps may serve as the counterparty and exchange the payments desired rather than matching up two parties.

Now assume that the fixed payments are based on a fixed rate of 9 percent. Also assume that LIBOR is initially 7 percent and that DB's cost of funds is 6 percent. Exhibit 19.8 shows how DB's spread is affected by various possible interest rates when unhedged versus when hedged with an interest rate swap. If LIBOR remains at 7 percent, DB's spread would be 5 percent if unhedged and only 3 percent when using a swap. However, if LIBOR increases beyond 9 percent, the spread when using the swap would exceed the unhedged spread because the higher cost of funds causes a lower unhedged spread. The swap arrangement would provide DB with increased payments that offset the higher cost of funds. The advantage of a swap is that it can lock in the spread to be earned on existing assets or at least reduce the possible variability of the spread. ●

When interest rates decrease, a bank's outflow payments would exceed its inflow payments on a swap. However, the spread between the interest rates received on existing fixed-rate loans and those paid on deposits should increase, offsetting the net outflow from the swap. During periods of declining interest rates, fixed-rate loans are often prepaid, which could result in a net outflow from the swap without any offsetting effect.

Exhibit 19.7   Illustration of an Interest Rate Swap

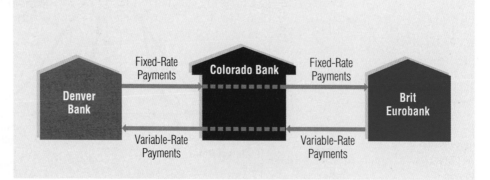

Exhibit 19.8 Comparison of Denver Bank's Spread: Unhedged versus Hedged

	POSSIBLE FUTURE LIBOR RATES					
UNHEDGED STRATEGY	7%	8%	9%	10%	11%	12%
Average rate on existing mortgages	11%	11%	11%	11%	11%	11%
Average cost of deposits	6	7	8	9	10	11
Spread	5	4	3	2	1	0
HEDGING WITH AN INTEREST RATE SWAP						
Fixed interest rate earned on fixed-rate mortgages	11	11	11	11	11	11
Fixed interest rate owed on swap arrangement	9	9	9	9	9	9
Spread on fixed-rate payments	2	2	2	2	2	2
Variable interest rate earned on swap arrangement	7	8	9	10	11	12
Variable interest rate owed on deposits	6	7	8	9	10	11
Spread on variable-rate payments	1	1	1	1	1	1
Combined total spread when using the swap	3	3	3	3	3	3

Using Interest Rate Caps   An alternative method of hedging interest rate risk is an interest rate cap, an agreement (for a fee) to receive payments when the interest rate of a particular security or index rises above a specified level during a specified time period. Various financial intermediaries (such as commercial banks and brokerage firms) offer interest rate caps. During periods of rising interest rates, the cap provides compensation that can offset the reduction in spread during such periods.

19-3d International Interest Rate Risk

When a bank has foreign currency balances, the strategy of matching the overall interest rate sensitivity of assets to that of liabilities will not automatically achieve a low degree of interest rate risk.

EXAMPLE   California Bank has deposits denominated mostly in euros, whereas its floating-rate loans are denominated mostly in dollars. It matches its average deposit maturity with its average loan maturity. However, the difference in currency denominations creates interest rate risk. The deposit and loan rates depend on the interest rate movements of the respective currencies. The performance of California Bank will be adversely affected if the interest rate on the euro increases and the U.S. interest rate decreases. ●

Even though a bank matches the mix of currencies in its assets and its liabilities, it can still be exposed to interest rate risk if the rate sensitivities differ between assets and liabilities for each currency.

EXAMPLE   Oklahoma Bank uses its dollar deposits to make dollar loans and its euro deposits to make euro loans. It has short-term dollar deposits and uses these funds to make long-term dollar loans. It also has medium- and long-term fixed-rate deposits in euros; it uses those funds to make euro loans with adjustable rates. An increase in U.S. interest rates will reduce the spread on Oklahoma Bank's dollar loans versus deposits, because the dollar liabilities are more rate-sensitive than the dollar assets. In addition, a decline in interest rates on the euro will decrease the spread on the euro loans versus deposits, because the euro assets are more rate-sensitive than the euro liabilities. Thus the bank can minimize its exposure to interest rate risk only if the rate sensitivities of assets and liabilities are matched for each currency. ●

WEB

www.fdic.gov
Information about
bank loan and deposit
volume.

19-4 Managing Credit Risk

Most of a bank's funds are used either to make loans or to purchase debt securities. In both cases, the bank acts as a creditor and is subject to credit (default) risk, or the possibility that credit provided by the bank will not be repaid. The types of loans provided and the securities purchased will determine the overall credit risk of the asset portfolio. A bank also can be exposed to credit risk if it serves as a guarantor on interest rate swaps and other derivative contracts for which it is the intermediary.

19-4a Measuring Credit Risk

An important step in managing credit risk is to assess the creditworthiness of prospective borrowers before extending credit. Banks employ credit analysts who review the financial information of corporations applying for loans and evaluate their creditworthiness. The evaluation should indicate the probability of the firm meeting its loan payments so that the bank can decide whether to grant the loan.

Determining the Collateral   When a bank assesses a request for credit, it must decide whether to require collateral that can back the loan in case the borrower is unable to make the payments. For example, if a firm applies for a loan to purchase machinery, the loan agreement may specify that the machinery will serve as collateral. When a bank serves as an intermediary and a guarantor on derivative contracts, it commonly attempts to require collateral such as securities owned by the client.

Determining the Loan Rate   If the bank decides to grant the loan, it can use its evaluation of the firm to determine the appropriate interest rate. Loan applicants deserving of a loan may be rated on a scale of 1 to 5 (with 1 as the highest quality) in terms of their degree of credit risk. The rating dictates the premium that will be added to the base rate. For example, a rating of 5 may dictate a 2 percentage point premium above the prime rate (the basic rate a bank charges on business loans), whereas a rating of 3 may dictate a 1 percentage point premium. By combining the current prime rate with the rating of the potential borrower, the bank can select the appropriate loan rate.

Some high-quality (low-risk) customers are commonly offered loans at rates below the prime rate. This does not necessarily mean that the bank has reduced its spread. Instead, it may imply that the bank has defined the prime rate as representing the appropriate loan rate for borrowers with a moderate risk rating. Thus a discount would be attached to the prime rate when determining the loan rate for borrowers with a superior rating.

Measuring Credit Risk of a Bank Portfolio   The extent of exposure to credit risk for a bank's loan portfolio depends on the types of loans that it provides. When the bank uses a larger proportion of loans for financing credit cards, it increases its exposure to credit risk. A bank's exposure also changes over time in response to economic conditions. As economic conditions weaken, the expected cash flows to be earned by businesses are reduced because their sales will likely decline. Consequently, they are more likely to default on loans. In addition, individuals are more likely to lose their jobs when the economy weakens, which could increase their likelihood of defaulting on loans.

19-4b Trade-Off between Credit Risk and Return

If a bank wants to minimize credit risk, it can use most of its funds to purchase Treasury securities, which are virtually free of credit risk. However, these securities may not generate a much higher yield than the average overall cost of obtaining funds. In fact, some bank sources of funds can be more costly to banks than the yield earned on Treasury securities.

At the other extreme, a bank concerned with maximizing its return could use most of its funds to provide credit card and consumer loans. Although this strategy may allow a bank to achieve a high return, these types of loans experience more defaults than other types of loans. Thus the bank may experience high loan losses, which could offset the high interest payments it received from those loans that were repaid. A bank that pursues the high potential returns associated with credit card loans or other loans that generate relatively high interest payments must accept a high degree of credit risk. Because riskier assets offer higher potential returns, a bank's strategy to increase its ROA will typically entail an increase in the overall credit risk of its asset portfolio. Thus a bank's decision to create a very safe versus a moderate- or high-risk asset portfolio is a function of its risk–return preferences.

Expected Return and Risk of Subprime Mortgage Loans
Many commercial banks aggressively funded subprime mortgage loans in the 2004–2006 period by originating these mortgages or by purchasing mortgage-backed securities that represented subprime mortgages. The banks pursuing this strategy expected that they would earn a relatively high interest rate compared to that available on prime mortgages; they also assumed that the subprime mortgages would have a low default risk because the home served as collateral. They provided many mortgages without requiring much collateral, as they presumed that market values of homes would continue to increase over time. Even after home prices increased substantially, many banks continued to aggressively offer subprime mortgages, driven by the expected return to be earned on this strategy yet blinded to its risk. Perhaps many banks justified their strategy as having to keep up with all the other banks that were using an aggressive strategy and achieving high returns. Furthermore, because bank managerial compensation is commonly tied to the bank's earnings, managers could benefit directly from pursuing aggressive strategies. These risky strategies contributed to the crash in the housing market and the credit crisis in the 2008–2009 period.

19-4c Reducing Credit Risk

Although all consumer and commercial loans exhibit some credit risk, banks can use several methods to reduce this risk.

Industry Diversification of Loans
Banks should diversify their loans to ensure that the majority of their customers are not dependent on a common source of income. For example, a bank in a small farming town that provides consumer loans to farmers and commercial loans to farm equipment manufacturers is highly susceptible to credit risk. If the farmers experience a bad growing season because of poor weather conditions, they may be unable to repay their consumer loans. Furthermore, the farm equipment manufacturers would simultaneously experience a decline in sales and may default on their commercial loans.

When a bank's loans are too heavily concentrated in a specific industry, the bank is exposed to credit risk. To reduce this risk, a bank should attempt to diversify its loans across several industries. Then, if one particular industry experiences weakness (which will lead to loan defaults by firms in that industry), loans provided to other industries will be insulated from that industry's conditions. However, a bank's loan portfolio may still be subject to high credit risk even though its loans are diversified across industries.

International Diversification of Loans
Many banks reduce their exposure to U.S. economic conditions by diversifying their loan portfolio internationally. They use a country risk assessment system to evaluate country characteristics that may influence the ability of a government or corporation to repay its debt. In particular, the country risk

assessment focuses on a country's financial and political conditions. Banks are more likely to invest in countries to which they have assigned a high rating.

Diversifying loans across countries can often reduce the loan portfolio's exposure to any single economy or event. Nevertheless, if diversification across geographic regions means that the bank must accept loan applicants with very high risk, then the bank is defeating its purpose. Furthermore, international diversification does not necessarily avoid some adverse economic conditions that affect most countries.

Selling Loans   Banks can eliminate loans that are causing excessive risk to their loan portfolios by selling them in the secondary market. Most loan sales enable the bank originating the loan to continue servicing it by collecting payments and monitoring the borrower's collateral. However, the bank that originated the loan is no longer funding it, so the loan is removed from the bank's assets. Bank loans are commonly purchased by other banks and financial institutions, such as pension funds, insurance companies, and mutual funds.

Revising the Loan Portfolio in Response to Economic Conditions   Banks continuously assess both the overall composition of their loan portfolios and the economic environment. As economic conditions change, so does the risk of a bank's loan portfolio. A bank is typically more willing to extend loans during strong economic periods because businesses are more likely to meet their loan payments under those conditions. During weak economic periods, the bank will be more cautious and increase its standards, which results in a smaller amount of new loans extended to businesses. Under these conditions, the bank typically increases the credit it extends to the Treasury by purchasing more Treasury securities. Nevertheless, its loan portfolio may still be heavily exposed to economic conditions because some of its existing business loans could default.

19-5 Managing Market Risk

From a bank management perspective, market risk results from changes in the value of securities due to changes in financial market conditions such as interest rate movements, exchange rate movements, and equity prices. As banks pursue new services related to the trading of securities, they have become much more susceptible to market risk. For example, some banks now provide loans to various types of investment funds, which use the borrowed funds to invest in stocks or derivative securities. Thus these loans may not be repaid if the prices of the stocks or derivative securities held by the investment funds decline substantially.

The increase in banks' exposure to market risk is also attributed to their increased participation in the trading of derivative contracts. Many banks now serve as intermediaries between firms that take positions in derivative securities and will be exchanging payments in the future. For some of these transactions, a bank serves as a guarantor to one of the parties if the counterparty in the transaction does not fulfill its payment obligation. If derivative security prices change abruptly and cause several parties involved in these transactions to default, a bank that served as a guarantor could suffer major losses. Furthermore, banks that purchase debt securities issued by foreign countries are subject to abrupt losses resulting from sudden swings in the economic or currency conditions in those countries.

19-5a Measuring Market Risk

Banks commonly measure their exposure to market risk by applying the VaR method, which involves determining the largest possible loss that would occur as a result of changes in market prices based on a specified percentage confidence level. To estimate this loss, the bank first determines an adverse scenario (for example, a 20 percent decline in derivative security prices) that has a 1 percent chance of occurring. Then it estimates the impact of that scenario on its investment or loan positions given the sensitivity of those investments' values to the scenario. All of the losses that would occur from the bank's existing positions are summed to determine the estimated total loss to the bank under this scenario. This estimate reflects the largest possible loss at the 99 percent confidence level, as there is only a 1-in-100 chance that such an unfavorable scenario would occur. By determining its exposure to market risk, the bank can ensure that it has sufficient capital as a cushion against the adverse effects of such an event.

Bank Revisions of Market Risk Measurements   Banks continually revise their estimate of market risk in response to changes in their investment and credit positions and to changes in market conditions. When market prices become more volatile, banks recognize that those prices could change to a greater degree; in turn, they typically increase their estimate of their potential losses due to market conditions.

WEB

www.fdic.gov
Statistical overview
of how banks have
performed in recent
years.

Relationship between a Bank's Market Risk and Interest Rate Risk   A bank's market risk partly depends on its exposure to interest rate risk. Banks give special attention to interest rate risk, because it is often the most important component of market risk. Moreover, many banks assess interest rate risk by itself when evaluating their positions over a longer time horizon. For example, a bank might assess interest rate risk over the next year using the methods described earlier in the chapter. In this case, the bank might use the assessment to alter the maturities on the deposits it attempts to obtain or on its uses of funds. In contrast, banks' assessment of *market* risk tends to focus on a shorter-term horizon, such as the next month. Nevertheless, banks may still use their assessment of market risk to alter their operations, as explained next.

19-5b Methods Used to Reduce Market Risk

If a bank determines that its exposure to market risk is excessive, it can reduce its involvement in the activities that cause the high exposure. For example, the bank could reduce the amount of transactions in which it serves as guarantor for its clients or reduce its investment in foreign debt securities that are subject to adverse events in a specific region. Alternatively, it could attempt to take some trading positions to offset some of its exposure to market risk. It could also sell some of its securities that are heavily exposed to market risk.

19-6 Integrated Bank Management

Banks' management of assets, liabilities, and capital is integrated. A bank's asset growth can be achieved only if it obtains the necessary funds. Furthermore, such growth may require an investment in new technology that will require an accumulation of bank capital. Integration of asset, liability, and capital management ensures that all policies remain consistent with a cohesive set of economic forecasts. An integrated management approach is necessary to manage liquidity risk, interest rate risk, and credit risk.

19-6a Application

Assume that you are hired as a consultant by Atlanta Bank to evaluate its favorable and unfavorable aspects. Atlanta Bank's balance sheet is shown in Exhibit 19.9. A bank's balance

Exhibit 19.9   Balance Sheet of Atlanta Bank (in Millions of Dollars)

ASSETS			LIABILITIES AND CAPITAL		
Required reserves		$400	Demand deposits		$500
Commercial loans			NOW accounts		1,200
Floating-rate	3,000		MMDAs		2,000
Fixed-rate	1,100		CDs		
Total		4,100	Short-term	1,500	
Consumer loans		2,500	From 1 to 5 years	3,800	
Mortgages			Total		5,300
Floating-rate	500		Long-term bonds		200
Fixed-rate	None		CAPITAL		800
Total		500			
Treasury securities					
Short-term	1,000				
Long-term	None				
Total		1,000			
Corporate securities					
High-rated	None				
Medium-rated	1,000				
Total		1,000			
Municipal securities					
High-rated	None				
Medium-rated	None				
Total		None			
Fixed assets		500			
TOTAL ASSETS		$10,000	TOTAL LIABILITIES AND CAPITAL		$10,000

sheet can best be evaluated by converting the actual dollar amounts of the balance-sheet components to percentages of the bank's assets. This conversion facilitates a comparison of the bank to its competitors.

Exhibit 19.10 shows each balance-sheet component as a percentage of total assets for Atlanta Bank (derived from Exhibit 19.9). To the right of each bank percentage is the assumed industry average percentage for a sample of banks with a similar amount of assets. For example, the bank's required reserves are 4 percent of assets (the same as the industry average), its floating-rate commercial loans are 30 percent of assets (versus an industry average of 20 percent), and so on. The same type of comparison is provided for liabilities and capital on the right side of the exhibit. A comparative analysis relative to the industry can indicate the management style of Atlanta Bank.

It is possible to evaluate the potential level of interest revenues, interest expenses, noninterest revenues, and noninterest expenses for Atlanta Bank relative to the industry.

Exhibit 19.10   Comparative Balance Sheet of Atlanta Bank

	ASSETS		LIABILITIES AND CAPITAL		
	PERCENTAGE OF ASSETS FOR ATLANTA BANK	AVERAGE PERCENTAGE FOR INDUSTRY		PERCENTAGE OF TOTAL FOR ATLANTA BANK	AVERAGE PERCENTAGE FOR INDUSTRY
Required reserves	4%	4%	Demand deposits	5%	17%
Commercial loans			NOW accounts	12	8
Floating-rate	30	20	MMDAs	20	20
Fixed-rate	11	11	CDs		
Total	41	31	Short-term	15	35
Consumer loans	25	20	From 1 to 5 years	38	10
Mortgages			Long-term bonds	2	2
Floating-rate	5	7	CAPITAL	8	8
Fixed-rate	0	3			
Total	5	10			
Treasury securities					
Short-term	10	7			
Long-term	0	8			
Total	10	15			
Corporate securities					
High-rated	0	5			
Medium-rated	10	5			
Total	10	10			
Municipal securities					
High-rated	0	3			
Medium-rated	0	2			
Total	0	5			
Fixed assets	5	5			
TOTAL ASSETS	100%	100%	TOTAL LIABILITIES AND CAPITAL	100%	100%

Furthermore, it is possible to assess the bank's exposure to credit risk and interest rate risk as compared to the industry.

Exhibit 19.11 summarizes the evaluation of Atlanta Bank based on the information in Exhibit 19.10. Although its interest expenses are expected to be higher than the industry average, so are its interest revenues. Thus it is difficult to determine whether Atlanta Bank's net interest margin will be above or below the industry average. Because it is more heavily concentrated in risky loans and securities, its credit risk is higher than that of the average bank; however, its interest rate risk is less because of its relatively high concentration of

Exhibit 19.11 Evaluation of Atlanta Bank Based on Its Balance Sheet

	MAIN INFLUENTIAL COMPONENTS	EVALUATION OF ATLANTA BANK RELATIVE TO INDUSTRY
Interest expenses	All liabilities except demand deposits	Higher than the industry average because the bank concentrates more on high-rate deposits than is the norm
Noninterest expenses	Loan volume and checkable deposit volume	Possibly higher than the norm; its checkable deposit volume is less than the norm, but its loan volume is greater than the norm
Interest revenues	Volume and composition of loans and securities	Potentially higher than the industry average because its assets are generally riskier than the norm
Exposure to credit risk	Volume and composition of loans and securities	Higher concentration of loans than the industry average; it has a greater percentage of risky assets than the norm
Exposure to interest rate risk	Maturities on liabilities and assets; use of floating-rate loans	Lower than the industry average; it has more medium-term liabilities, fewer assets with very long maturities, and more floating-rate loans

medium-term CDs and floating-rate loans. A gap measurement of Atlanta Bank can be conducted by first identifying the rate-sensitive liabilities and assets, as follows:

RATE-SENSITIVE ASSETS	AMOUNT (IN MILLIONS)	RATE-SENSITIVE LIABILITIES	AMOUNT (IN MILLIONS)
Floating-rate loans	$3,000	NOW accounts	$1,200
Floating-rate mortgages	500	MMDAs	2,000
Short-term Treasury securities	1,000	Short-term CDs	1,500
Total	$4,500	Total	$4,700

$$\text{Gap} = \$4{,}500 \text{ million} - \$4{,}700 \text{ million}$$
$$= -\$200 \text{ million}$$
$$\text{Gap ratio} = \frac{\$4{,}500 \text{ million}}{\$4{,}700 \text{ million}}$$
$$= 0.957$$

The gap measurements suggest a similar rate sensitivity on both sides of the balance sheet.

The future performance of Atlanta Bank relative to the industry depends on future economic conditions. If interest rates rise, it will be more insulated from that change than other banks; if interest rates fall, other banks will likely benefit to a greater degree. Under strong economic conditions, Atlanta Bank would likely benefit more than other banks because of its aggressive lending approach. Conversely, an economic slowdown could cause more loan defaults, and Atlanta Bank would be more susceptible to possible defaults than other banks. This could be confirmed only if more details were provided (such as a more comprehensive breakdown of the balance sheet).

Management of Bank Capital   An evaluation of Atlanta Bank should also include an assessment of its capital. As is true for all banks, the future performance of Atlanta Bank is influenced by the amount of capital that it holds. It needs to maintain at least the minimum capital ratio required by regulators. However, if Atlanta Bank maintains too much capital, each shareholder will receive a smaller proportion of any distributed earnings. A common measure of the return to the shareholders is the ROE:

$$ROE = \frac{Net\ income}{Equity}$$

where the term *equity* represents the bank's capital. The ROE can be broken down as follows:

$$ROE = ROA \times Leverage\ measure$$
$$\frac{Net\ income}{Equity} = \frac{Net\ income}{Assets} \times \frac{Assets}{Equity}$$

WEB

www.risk.net
Links to risk-related
information in
international banking.

The ratio (assets/equity) is sometimes called the leverage measure because leverage reflects the volume of assets that a firm supports with equity. The greater the leverage measure, the greater the amount of assets that are available per dollar's worth of equity. The preceding breakdown of ROE is useful because it demonstrates how Atlanta Bank's capital can affect its ROE. For a given level of ROA, a higher capital level reduces the bank's leverage measure and, therefore, reduces its ROE.

If Atlanta Bank is holding an excessive amount of capital, it may not need to rely on retained earnings to build its capital, but instead can distribute a high percentage of its earnings to shareholders (as dividends). Thus its capital management is related to its dividend policy. If Atlanta Bank is expanding, it may need more capital to support construction of new buildings, office equipment, and other expenses. In this case, it would need to retain a larger proportion of its earnings to fund its expansion plans.

19-7 Managing Risk of International Operations

Banks that are engaged in international banking face additional types of risk, including exchange rate risk and settlement risk.

19-7a Exchange Rate Risk

When a bank providing a loan requires that the borrower repay in the currency denominating the loan, it may be able to avoid exchange rate risk. However, some international loans contain a clause that allows repayment in a foreign currency, thereby allowing the borrower to avoid exchange rate risk.

In many cases, banks convert available funds (from recent deposits) to whatever currency corporations want to borrow. In this way, they create an asset denominated in that currency, whereas the liability (deposits) is denominated in a different currency. If the liability currency appreciates against the asset currency, then the bank's profit margin is reduced.

All large banks are exposed to exchange rate risk to some degree. They can attempt to hedge this risk in various ways.

EXAMPLE   Cameron Bank, a U.S. bank, converts dollar deposits into a British pound (£) loan for a British corporation, which will pay £50,000 in interest per year. Cameron Bank may attempt to engage in forward contracts to sell £50,000 forward for each date when it will receive those interest payments. That is, it will search for corporations that wish to purchase £50,000 on the dates of concern. ●

In practice, a large bank will not hedge every individual transaction, but instead will net out the exposure and be concerned only with that net exposure. Large banks typically enter into several international transactions on any given day. Some reflect future cash inflows in a particular currency, whereas others involve cash outflows in that currency. The bank's exposure to exchange rate risk is determined by the net cash flow in each currency.

19-7b Settlement Risk

International banks that engage in large currency transactions are exposed not only to exchange rate risk as a result of their different currency positions, but also to settlement risk, or the risk of a loss due to settling their transactions. For example, a bank may send its currency to another bank as part of a transaction agreement, yet it may not receive any currency from the other bank if that bank defaults before sending its payment.

The failure of a single large bank could create more losses if other banks were relying on receivables from the failed bank to make future payables of their own. Consequently, concern arises regarding systemic risk, or the risk that many participants will be unable to meet their obligations because they did not receive payments on obligations due to them.

Summary

- The underlying goal of bank management is to maximize the wealth of the bank's shareholders, which implies maximizing the price of the bank's stock (if the bank is publicly traded). A bank's board of directors needs to monitor bank managers to ensure that managerial decisions serve the best interests of shareholders.
- Banks manage liquidity by maintaining some liquid assets such as short-term securities and ensuring easy access to funds (through the federal funds market).
- Banks measure their sensitivity to interest rate movements so that they can assess their exposure to interest rate risk. Methods of measuring interest rate risk include gap analysis, duration analysis, and measuring the sensitivity of earnings (or stock returns) to interest rate movements. Banks can reduce their interest rate risk by matching the maturities of their assets and liabilities or by using floating-rate loans to create more rate sensitivity in their assets. Alternatively, they can sell financial futures contracts or engage in a swap of fixed-rate payments for floating-rate payments.
- Banks manage credit risk by carefully assessing the borrowers who apply for loans and by limiting the amount of funds they allocate toward risky loans (such as credit card loans). They also diversify their loans across borrowers of different regions and industries so that the loan portfolio is not overly susceptible to financial problems in any single region or industry.
- Banks commonly measure their exposure to market risk by using the value-at-risk method, which determines the largest possible loss that could occur due to changes in market conditions based on a specified confidence level. They can lower their exposure to market risk by changing their investments, taking offsetting trading positions, or reducing involvement in activities that lead to high exposure.
- An evaluation of a bank includes assessment of its exposure to interest rate movements and to credit risk. This assessment can be used along with a forecast of interest rates and economic conditions to forecast the bank's future performance.
- Banks engaged in international banking face exchange rate risk, which can be hedged in various ways, and settlement risk.

Use a regression model in which Montana's stock return is a function of the stock market return and the interest rate. Determine the relationship between the interest rate and Montana's stock return by assessing the regression coefficient applied to the interest rate.

Is the sign of the coefficient positive or negative? What does it suggest about the bank's exposure to interest rate risk? Should Montana Bank be concerned about rising or declining interest rate movements in the future?

Flow of Funds Exercise

Managing Credit Risk

Recall that Carson Company relies heavily on commercial banks for loans. When the company was first established with equity funding from its owners, Carson could easily obtain debt financing because the financing was backed by some of the firm's assets. However, as Carson expanded, it continually relied on extra debt financing, which increased its ratio of debt to equity. Some banks were unwilling to provide more debt financing because of the risk that Carson would not be able to repay additional loans. A few banks were still willing to provide funding, but they required an extra premium to compensate for the risk.

a. Explain the difference in the willingness of banks to provide loans to Carson Company. Why do banks sometimes differ in their conclusions when they are assessing the same information about a firm that wants to borrow funds?

b. Consider the flow of funds for a publicly traded bank that is a key lender to Carson Company. This bank received equity funding from shareholders, which it used to establish its business. It channels bank deposit funds, which are insured by the Federal Deposit Insurance Corporation (FDIC), to provide loans to Carson Company and other firms. The depositors have no idea how the bank uses their funds. Yet the FDIC does not prevent the bank from making risky loans. So who is monitoring the bank? Do you think the bank is taking more risk than its shareholders desire? How does the FDIC discourage the bank from taking too much risk? Why might the bank ignore the FDIC's efforts to discourage excessive risk taking?

Internet/Excel Exercises

1. Assess the services offered by an Internet bank. Describe the types of online services offered by the bank. Do you think this kind of Internet bank offers higher or lower interest rates than a "regular" commercial bank? Why or why not?

2. Go to finance.yahoo.com/, and enter the symbol BK (Bank of New York Mellon Corporation). Click on "5y" just above the stock price trend to review the stock price movements over the last five years. Click on "Chart," then on "Comparison," and then on "S&P 500" to compare the trend for Bank of New York Mellon with the movements in the S&P stock index. Has Bank of New York Mellon Corporation performed better or worse than the index? Offer an explanation for its performance.

3. Go to finance.yahoo.com/, and enter the symbol WFC (Wells Fargo Bank). Retrieve stock price data at the beginning of the last 20 quarters. Then go to http://fred.stlouisfed.org and retrieve interest rate data at the beginning of the last 20 quarters for the three-month Treasury bill. Record the data in an Excel spreadsheet. Derive the quarterly return of Wells Fargo Bank. Derive the quarterly change in the interest rate. Apply regression analysis in which the quarterly return of Wells Fargo Bank is the dependent variable and the quarterly change in the interest rate is the independent variable (see Appendix B for more information about using regression analysis). Is there a positive or negative relationship between the interest rate movement and the return of Wells Fargo Bank stock? Is the relationship significant? Offer an explanation for this relationship.

WSJ Exercise

Bank Management Strategies

Summarize an article in *The Wall Street Journal* that discussed a recent change in managerial strategy by a particular commercial bank. (You may wish to do an Internet search in the online version of *The Wall Street Journal* to identify an article on a commercial bank's change in strategy.) Describe the change in managerial strategy. How will the bank's balance sheet be affected by this change? How will the bank's potential return and risk be affected? What reason does the article give for the bank's decision to change its strategy?

Online Articles with Real-World Examples

Find a recent practical article available online that describes a real-world example regarding a specific financial institution or financial market that reinforces one or more concepts covered in this chapter.

If your class has an online component, your professor may ask you to post your summary of the article there and provide a link to the article so that other students can access it. If your class is live, your professor may ask you to summarize your application of the article in class. Your professor may assign specific students to complete this assignment or may allow any students to do the assignment on a volunteer basis.

For recent online articles and real-world examples related to this chapter, consider using the following search terms (be sure to include the prevailing year as a search term to ensure that the online articles are recent):

1. [name of a specific bank] AND liquidity
2. [name of a specific bank] AND management
3. [name of a specific bank] AND interest rate risk
4. [name of a specific bank] AND credit risk
5. [name of a specific bank] AND strategy
6. bank AND management
7. bank AND strategy
8. bank AND loans
9. bank AND asset management
10. bank AND operations

20-2 Assessing Bank Performance

Exhibit 20.2 illustrates how the general performance of a bank is summarized, based mostly on income statement items. This summary is very basic but still offers much insight about a bank's income, expenses, and its efficiency. Each item in Exhibit 20.2 is measured as a percentage of assets, which allows for easy comparison to other banks or to a set of banks within the same region. Analysts typically compare a bank's performance with that of other banks of the same size. The Federal Reserve provides bank performance summaries for banks in four size classifications: money center banks (the 10 largest banks that serve money centers such as New York), large banks (ranked 11 to 100 in size), medium banks (ranked 101 to 1,000 in size), and small banks (ranked lower than 1,000 in size).

Measuring each item in Exhibit 20.2 as a percentage of assets also allows for an assessment of the bank's performance over time. The measurement of the dollar amount of income and expenses over time could be misleading without controlling for the change in the size (as measured by total assets) of the bank over time. A complete analysis of a bank would require the use of a bank's income statement and balance sheet, but Exhibit 20.2 is sufficient for identifying the key indicators of a bank's performance.

The following discussion examines the items in Exhibit 20.2 in the order they are listed in the exhibit.

20-2a Interest Income and Expenses

Gross interest income (row 1 of Exhibit 20.2) is interest income generated from all assets. It is affected by market rates and the composition of assets held by the bank. Gross interest income tends to increase when interest rates rise, whereas it typically decreases when interest rates decline.

Gross interest income varies among banks of different sizes because of differences in the rates that those banks may charge on particular types of loans. Small banks tend to make more loans to small local businesses, which may allow them to charge higher interest rates than the money center and large banks charge on loans they provide to larger businesses. The rates charged to larger businesses tend to be lower because those businesses generally have more options for obtaining funds than do small local businesses.

Exhibit 20.2   Example of Performance Summary of Canyon Bank 2019

ITEM	2019
1. Gross interest income	5.3%
2. Gross interest expenses	2.3
3. Net interest income	3.0
4. Noninterest income	2.0
5. Loan loss provision	0.6
6. Noninterest expenses	3.0
7. Securities gains (losses)	0.0
8. Income before tax	1.4
9. Taxes	0.4
10. Net income	1.0
11. Cash dividends provided	0.3
12. Retained earnings	0.7

Note: All items in the exhibit are estimated as a proportion of total assets.

Gross interest expenses (row 2 of Exhibit 20.2) represent interest paid on deposits and on other borrowed funds (from the federal funds market). These expenses are affected by market rates and the composition of the bank's liabilities. Gross interest expenses will usually be higher when market interest rates are higher. These expenses will vary among banks depending on how they obtain their deposits. Banks that rely more heavily on NOW accounts, money market deposit accounts, and CDs instead of checking accounts for deposits will incur higher gross interest expenses.

Net interest income (row 3 of Exhibit 20.2) is the difference between gross interest income and gross interest expenses. It is measured as a percentage of assets, commonly referred to as net interest margin. This measure has a major effect on the bank's performance. Banks need to earn more interest income than their interest expenses to cover their other expenses. In general, the net interest margin of all banks is fairly stable over time.

20-2b **Noninterest Income and Expenses**

Noninterest income (row 4 of Exhibit 20.2) results from fees charged on services provided, such as lockbox services, banker's acceptances, cashier's checks, and foreign exchange transactions. Noninterest income is usually higher for larger banks, because they tend to provide more services for which they can charge fees.

The **loan loss provision** (row 5 of Exhibit 20.2) is a means by which a bank can account for anticipated loan losses (defaults) on its income statement, so it offers useful information about the quality of the bank's loans. A loan is not officially in default when the borrower initially misses payments because the bank allows some time for the borrower to catch up on payments. However, a bank recognizes that some of its loans experiencing payment delays will likely default and can allow for a loan loss provision before those loans officially default.

A bank's loan loss provision tends to increase during periods when loan losses are more likely, such as during a recessionary period. The amount of loan losses as a percentage of assets is higher for banks that provide riskier loans, especially when economic conditions weaken. For example, as a result of the credit crisis, the average loan loss provision for banks was 1.95 percent of total assets in 2009, whereas it was only 0.27 percent just two years earlier. The increase was primarily due to mortgage and real estate loan defaults during the credit crisis. The large loan loss provision in 2009 offset the income generated from all other operations of banks in that year. That is, the income of all other operations was needed to cover the losses incurred by banks as a result of the large number of loans that were never repaid.

Noninterest expenses (row 6 of Exhibit 20.2) include salaries, office equipment, and other expenses not related to the payment of interest on deposits. Noninterest expenses depend partially on personnel costs associated with the credit assessment of loan applications, which in turn are affected by the bank's asset composition (proportion of funds allocated to loans). Noninterest expenses also depend on the liability composition because small deposits are more time-consuming to handle compared to large deposits. Banks offering more nontraditional services will incur higher noninterest expenses, although they expect to offset those higher costs with higher noninterest income.

Securities gains (losses) (row 7 of Exhibit 20.2) result from the bank's sale of securities. They are usually negligible for banks in aggregate, although an individual bank's gains or losses can be significant. During the credit crisis, securities losses became more pronounced as banks in general suffered losses on their investments in mortgage-backed securities.

Income before tax (row 8 of Exhibit 20.2) is calculated by summing net interest income, noninterest income, and securities gains, and then subtracting from this sum the provision for loan losses and noninterest expenses.

The key income statement item, according to many analysts, is net income (row 10 of Exhibit 20.2), which accounts for any taxes paid. Therefore, the net income is the focus in the following section.

20-2c Reliance on the Bank's Financial Information

Analysts and investors alike rely heavily on the bank's financial statements to evaluate a bank's performance. Banks have a thorough internal reporting process that they are supposed to follow to ensure accurate reporting. If they are publicly traded, they are required to have their financial statements audited by an independent auditor. Nevertheless, the accounting process used by banks to determine their earnings is still based on subjective decisions. The reporting of a bank's earnings requires managerial judgment about the amount of existing loans that will default. Differences in this assessment can cause two banks with similar loan portfolios to have different earnings. Some banks may use a more conservative accounting approach by allowing for a relatively large loan loss provision to ensure there will be no negative surprises about their loans in the future. In this way, they accept the negative impact of the bad loans on their earnings immediately (in the prevailing quarter) rather than defer the negative impact to a future quarter when the loans default.

In contrast, other banks may understate the likely level of loan losses, which essentially defers the bad news until some future time. When banks increase their loan loss provisions in anticipation of loan defaults, this practice reduces their reported earnings, so they may defer boosting their loan loss provision if they want to temporarily inflate their reported earnings (and therefore their stock price). Because the stock price is partially driven by earnings, the bank may be able to keep its stock price artificially high by understating its loan losses (and, therefore, overstating its earnings). If managers' compensation is tied to the bank's short-term stock price movements or earnings, those executives may be tempted to understate loan losses. Specifically, they might prefer to overstate the reported earnings before they plan to sell some of their stock, so that the stock price will be high when they finally sell the stock.

Bank managers may also prefer to overstate earnings just before issuing new stock, so that the sale of new shares to investors generates a large amount of new funds for the bank. Some banks that are experiencing serious financial problems may prefer to overstate earnings to hide their deficiencies.

The subjectivity in accounting causes a lack of transparency and can create much uncertainty when assessing banks. During weak economic periods, investors may not know whether they can trust that banks have fully acknowledged the reduced valuations of their assets. Thus investors may avoid investing in bank stocks during such periods, which creates even more fear about banks, whether justified or not.

WEB

www.fdic.gov
Financial data provided for individual commercial banks allow their performance to be evaluated. The site also provides a quarterly outlook for the banking industry.

20-3 Evaluation of a Bank's ROA

The net income figure shown in Exhibit 20.2 is measured as a percentage of assets, so it represents the **return on assets (ROA)**. The ROA is influenced by all previously mentioned income statement items and, therefore, by all policies and other factors that affect those items.

Exhibit 20.3 identifies some of the key policy decisions that influence a bank's income statement. It also highlights some factors not controlled by the bank that affect the bank's income statement.

Exhibit 20.3 Influence of Bank Policies and Other Factors on a Bank's Income Statement

INCOME STATEMENT ITEM AS A PERCENTAGE OF ASSETS	BANK POLICY DECISIONS AFFECTING THE INCOME STATEMENT ITEM	UNCONTROLLABLE FACTORS AFFECTING THE INCOME STATEMENT ITEM
(1) Gross interest income	• Composition of assets • Quality of assets • Maturity and rate sensitivity of assets • Loan pricing policy	• Economic conditions • Market interest rate movements
(2) Gross interest expenses	• Composition of liabilities • Maturities and rate sensitivity of liabilities	• Market interest rate movements
(3) Net interest income = (1) − (2)		
(4) Noninterest income	• Service charges • Nontraditional activities	• Regulatory provisions
(5) Noninterest expenses	• Composition of assets • Composition of liabilities • Nontraditional activities • Efficiency of personnel • Costs of office space and equipment • Marketing costs • Other costs	• Inflation
(6) Loan losses	• Composition of assets • Quality of assets • Collection department capabilities	• Economic conditions • Market interest rate movements
(7) Pretax return on assets = (3) + (4) − (5) − (6)		
(8) Taxes	• Tax planning	• Tax laws
(9) After-tax return on assets = (7) − (8)		
(10) Financial leverage, measured here as (assets/equity)	• Capital structure policies	• Capital structure regulations
(11) Return on equity = (9) × (10)		

20-3a Reasons for a Low ROA

Exhibit 20.4 identifies the factors that affect bank performance as measured by ROA and ROE. If a bank's ROA is less than desired, the bank may be incurring excessive interest expenses. Banks typically know what deposit rate is necessary to attract deposits, so they are not likely to pay excessive interest. Yet if all a bank's sources of funds require a market-determined rate, the bank will face relatively high interest expenses. A relatively low ROA could also be due to low interest received on loans and securities because the bank has been overly conservative with its funds or was locked into fixed rates prior to an increase in market interest rates. High interest expenses and/or low interest revenues (on a relative basis) will reduce the net interest margin, thereby reducing ROA.

A relatively low ROA may also result from insufficient noninterest income. Some banks have made a much greater effort than others to offer services that generate fee (noninterest) income.

Exhibit 20.4 Breakdown of Performance Measures

MEASURES OF BANK PERFORMANCE	FINANCIAL CHARACTERISTICS INFLUENCING PERFORMANCE	BANK DECISIONS AFFECTING FINANCIAL CHARACTERISTICS
(1) Return on assets (ROA)	Net interest margin	Deposit rate decisions
		Loan rate decisions
		Loan losses
	Noninterest revenues	Bank services offered
	Noninterest expenses	Overhead requirements
		Efficiency
		Advertising
	Loan losses	Risk level of loans provided
(2) Return on equity (ROE)	ROA	Same as for ROA
	Leverage measure	Capital structure decision

A bank's ROA can be damaged by heavy loan losses. However, if the bank is too conservative in attempting to avoid loan losses, its net interest margin will be low, because of the low interest rates received from very safe loans and investments. Because of the obvious trade-off here, banks generally attempt to tailor their risk–return preferences based on the prevailing economic conditions. For example, they may increase their concentration of relatively risky loans during periods of prosperity, when they can improve their net interest margin without incurring excessive loan losses. Conversely, they may increase their concentration of relatively low-risk (and low-return) investments when economic conditions are less favorable.

A low ROA may also be attributed to excessive noninterest expenses, such as overhead and advertising expenses. Any waste of resources due to inefficiencies can lead to relatively high noninterest expenses.

20-3b **Converting ROA to ROE**

An alternative measure of overall bank performance is ROE. A bank's ROE is affected by the same income statement items that affect ROA but also by the bank's degree of financial leverage:

$$\text{ROE} = \text{ROA} \times \text{Leverage measure}$$

$$\frac{\text{Net income}}{\text{Equity capital}} = \frac{\text{Net income}}{\text{Total assets}} \times \frac{\text{Total assets}}{\text{Equity capital}}$$

The leverage measure is simply the inverse of the capital ratio (when only equity counts as capital). The higher the capital ratio, the lower the leverage measure and the lower the degree of financial leverage will be. For a given positive level of ROA, a bank's ROE will be higher if it has a lower capital ratio and more financial leverage. This relationship explains why managers of banks tend to prefer to use a high degree of financial leverage.

However, when they use a high degree of financial leverage, banks hold less capital to support their assets, which leaves them more exposed to risk. If a bank using a very low level of capital experiences a large loss, the loss could wipe out its remaining capital, causing it to fail.

Exhibit 20.5 shows the average annualized return on equity among banks over time. The ROE was relatively high during the 2005–2007 period when the U.S. economy was

Exhibit 20.5   Average ROE among Banks over Time

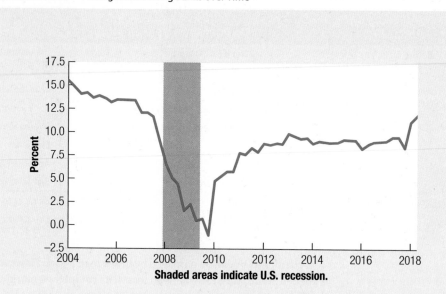

Shaded areas indicate U.S. recession.

Source: Federal Reserve and Federal Financial Institutions Examination Council.

expanding. However, it declined substantially during the credit crisis, even reaching negative levels in 2009, and gradually increased over time as the effects of the crisis subsided.

20-3c Application

Exhibit 20.6 depicts the performance characteristics for Zager Bank and the industry over the last five years. The years in the exhibit are labeled Year 1 through Year 5, where Year 5 has just ended. Because of differences in accounting procedures, the information may not be perfectly comparable. Because Zager Bank is a medium-sized bank, it is compared here to other medium-sized banks.

Zager Bank has used an aggressive management style of providing loans to borrowers that might be viewed as risky given their limited collateral and their cash flow situation. The bank charges high interest rates on these loans because the borrowers do not have alternative lenders. It also charges these borrowers high annual fees after providing its loans. During the strong economic conditions in Years 1 and 2, Zager's strategy was very successful: It achieved a high net interest margin and high noninterest income. The borrowers typically made their loan payments in a timely manner. However, when the economy weakened in Year 3, many of the borrowers who received loans from Zager Bank could not repay them. Furthermore, Zager was not able to extend many new loans because the demand for loans declined.

Although other banks also experienced weak performance when the economy weakened, Zager Bank experienced a more pronounced decline in its performance because it had more loans that were susceptible to default. Exhibit 20.6 shows that net income declined for medium-sized banks in general during Year 3, but it actually turned negative for Zager Bank because of its large loan losses. This example illustrates the risk–return trade-off for

Exhibit 20.6   Comparison of Zager Bank's Expenses and Income to the Industry

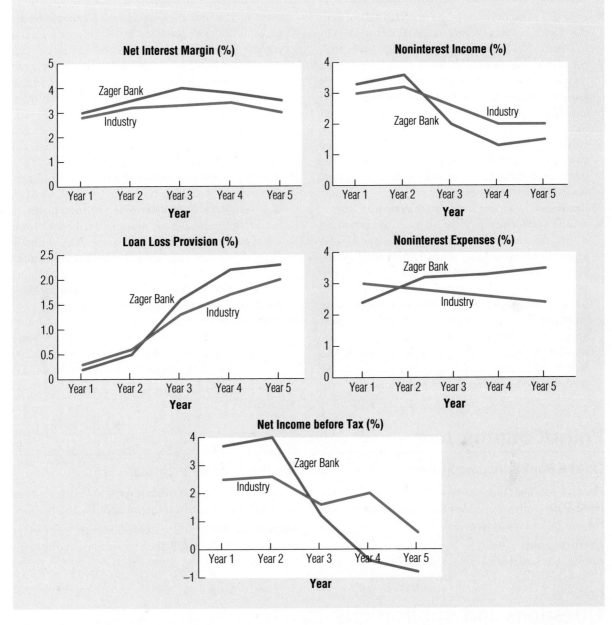

Zager Bank: It was rewarded for its risky strategy when the economy was strong, but it was severely penalized for that strategy when the economy was weak.

Any particular bank will perform a more thorough evaluation of itself than that shown here, including seeking a comprehensive explanation for its performance in recent years. Investors can evaluate any particular bank's performance by conducting an analysis similar to the one described here.

Summary

- A bank's value depends on its expected future cash flows and the rate of return required by investors in that bank. The bank's expected cash flows are influenced by economic growth, interest rate movements, regulatory constraints, and the abilities of the bank's managers. Investors' required rate of return is influenced by the prevailing interest rate (which is affected by other economic conditions) and the risk premium (which is affected by economic growth, regulatory constraints, and the management abilities of the bank). In general, the value of commercial banks is favorably affected by strong economic growth, declining interest rates, and strong management abilities.

- A bank's performance can be evaluated by comparing its income statement items (as a percentage of total assets) to a control group of other banks with a similar size classification. That performance may also be compared to the performance of a control group of banks. Any difference in performance between the bank and the control group typically reflects differences in net interest margin, loan loss provisions, noninterest income, or noninterest expenses. If the bank's net interest margin is relatively low, either it is relying too heavily on deposits with higher interest rates or it is not earning adequate interest on its loans. If the bank consistently has a higher loan loss provision, its loan portfolio may be very risky. If its noninterest income is relatively low, the bank is not providing enough services that generate fee income. If the bank's noninterest expenses are relatively high, its cost of operations is excessive. Other specific details may make the assessment more complex, but the key problems of a bank can usually be detected by following the approach described here.

- A commonly used measure of a bank's overall performance is its return on assets (ROA). The ROA of a bank is partially determined by movements in market interest rates, as many banks benefit from lower interest rates. In addition, the ROA is highly dependent on economic conditions, because banks can extend more loans to creditworthy customers and may also experience a higher demand for their services when economic conditions are strong.

- Another useful measure of a bank's overall performance is its return on equity (ROE). A bank can increase its ROE by increasing its financial leverage, but its leverage is constrained by capital requirements.

Point/Counterpoint

Does a Bank's Income Statement Clearly Indicate the Bank's Performance?

Point   Yes. The bank's income statement can be analyzed to determine its performance and the underlying reasons for its performance.

Counterpoint   No. The bank's income statement can be manipulated because the bank may not fully recognize loan losses (will not write off loans that are likely to default) until a future period.

Who Is Correct?   Use the Internet to learn more about this issue and then formulate your own opinion.

Questions and Applications

1. **Interest Income** How can gross interest income rise while the net interest margin remains somewhat stable for a particular bank?

2. **Impact on Income** If a bank shifts its loan policy to pursue more credit card loans, how will its net interest margin be affected?

3. **Noninterest Income** What has been the trend in noninterest income in recent years? Explain.

4. **Net Interest Margin** How could a bank generate higher income before tax (as a percentage of assets) when its net interest margin has decreased?

5. **Net Interest Income** Suppose the net interest income generated by a bank is equal to 1.5 percent of its assets. Based on past experience, would the bank experience a loss or a gain? Explain.

6. Noninterest Income Why have large money center banks' noninterest income levels typically been higher than those of smaller banks?

7. Bank Leverage What does the assets/equity ratio of a bank indicate?

8. Analysis of a Bank's ROA What are some of the more common reasons why a bank may experience a low ROA?

9. Loan Loss Provisions Explain why the loan loss provisions of most banks could increase in a particular period.

10. Bank Performance during the Credit Crisis Why do you think some banks suffered larger losses than other banks during the credit crisis?

11. Weak Performance What are likely reasons for weak bank performance?

12. Bank Income Statement Assume that SUNY Bank plans to liquidate its Treasury security holdings and use the proceeds for small business loans. Explain how this strategy will affect the different income statement items. Also identify any income statement items for which the effects of this strategy are more difficult to estimate.

Critical Thinking Question

Bank Noninterest Income In recent years, many banks have been relying more heavily on noninterest income as a proportion of their total income. Write a short essay explaining whether banks that rely more heavily on noninterest income will have better or worse performance than banks that rely more heavily on traditional sources of income (such as loans).

Interpreting Financial News

Interpret the following comments made by Wall Street analysts and portfolio managers.

a. "The three most important factors that determine a local bank's bad debt level are the bank's location, location, and location."
b. "The bank's profitability was enhanced by its limited use of capital."
c. "Low risk is not always desirable. Our bank's risk has been too low, given the market conditions. We will restructure operations in a manner to increase risk."

Managing in Financial Markets

Forecasting Bank Performance As a manager of Hawaii Bank, you anticipate the following:

- Loan loss provision at end of year = 1 percent of assets
- Gross interest income over the next year = 9 percent of assets
- Noninterest expenses over the next year = 3 percent of assets
- Noninterest income over the next year = 1 percent of assets
- Gross interest expenses over the next year = 5 percent of assets
- Tax rate on income (both federal and state) = 30 percent
- Capital ratio (capital/assets) at end of year = 5 percent

a. Forecast Hawaii Bank's net interest margin.
b. Forecast Hawaii Bank's earnings before taxes as a percentage of assets.
c. Forecast Hawaii Bank's earnings after taxes as a percentage of assets.
d. Forecast Hawaii Bank's return on equity.
e. Hawaii Bank is considering a shift in its asset structure to reduce its concentration of Treasury bonds and increase its volume of loans to small businesses. Identify each income statement item that would be affected by this strategy, and explain whether the forecast for that item would increase or decrease as a result.

Problem

Assessing Bank Performance

Select a commercial bank whose income statement data are available. Using recent income statement information about that bank, assess its performance. How does the performance of this bank compare to the performance of other banks? Compared with the other banks assessed in this chapter, is its return on equity higher or lower? What is the main reason why its ROE is different from the norm? (Is it due to its interest expenses? Its noninterest income?)

Flow of Funds Exercise

How the Flow of Funds Affects Bank Performance

In recent years, Carson Company has requested the services listed in part (a) from Blazo Financial, a financial conglomerate. These transactions have created a flow of funds between Carson Company and Blazo.

a. Classify each service according to how Blazo benefits from the service.

- Advising on possible targets that Carson may acquire
- Futures contract transactions
- Options contract transactions
- Interest rate derivative transactions
- Loans
- Line of credit
- Purchase of short-term CDs
- Checking account

b. Explain why Blazo's performance from providing these services to Carson Company and other firms will decline if economic growth is reduced.

c. Given the potential impact of slow economic growth on a bank's performance, do you think that commercial banks would prefer that the Fed use a restrictive monetary policy or an expansionary monetary policy?

Internet/Excel Exercises

1. Go to www.suntrust.com and retrieve a recent annual report of SunTrust Bank. Use the income statement to determine SunTrust's performance. Describe SunTrust's performance in recent years.

2. Has SunTrust's ROA increased since the year before? Explain what caused its ROA to change over the last year. Has its net interest margin changed since last year? How has its noninterest income (as a percentage of assets) changed over the last year? How have its noninterest expenses changed over the last year? Did it boost its loan loss provision in the last year? Discuss how SunTrust's recent strategy and economic conditions might explain the changes in these components of its income statement.

WSJ Exercise

Assessing Bank Performance

Using a recent issue of *The Wall Street Journal*, summarize an article that discusses the recent performance of a particular commercial bank. Does the article suggest that the bank's performance was better or worse than the norm? What is the reason given for the performance?

Online Articles with Real-World Examples

Find a recent practical article available online that describes a real-world example regarding a specific financial institution or financial market that reinforces one or more concepts covered in this chapter.

If your class has an online component, your professor may ask you to post your summary of the article there and provide a link to the article so that other students can access it. If your class is live, your professor may ask you to summarize your application of the article in class. Your professor may assign specific students to complete this assignment or may allow any students to do the assignment on a volunteer basis.

For recent online articles and real-world examples related to this chapter, consider using the following search terms (be sure to include the prevailing year as a search term to ensure that the online articles are recent):

1. [name of a specific bank] AND interest income
2. [name of a specific bank] AND interest expense
3. [name of a specific bank] AND loan loss
4. [name of a specific bank] AND net income
5. [name of a specific bank] AND net interest margin
6. [name of a specific bank] AND earnings
7. [name of a specific bank] AND return on equity
8. bank AND income
9. bank AND return on assets
10. bank AND net interest margin

PART 6 INTEGRATIVE PROBLEM

Forecasting Bank Performance

This problem requires an understanding of banks' sources and uses of funds (Chapter 17), bank management (Chapter 19), and bank performance (Chapter 20). It also requires the use of spreadsheet software such as Microsoft Excel. The data provided can be input onto a spreadsheet so that the necessary computations can be completed more easily. A conceptual understanding of commercial banking is needed to interpret the computations.

As an analyst working at a medium-sized commercial bank, you have been asked to forecast next year's performance. In June, you were provided with information about the sources and uses of funds for the upcoming year. The bank's sources of funds for the upcoming year are as follows (where NCDs are negotiable certificates of deposit):

SOURCES OF FUNDS	DOLLAR AMOUNT (IN MILLIONS)	INTEREST RATE TO BE OFFERED
Demand deposits	$5,000	0%
Time deposits	2,000	6%
1-year NCDs	3,000	T-bill rate + 1%
5-year NCDs	2,500	1-year NCD rate + 1%

The bank also has $1 billion in capital.

The bank's uses of funds for the upcoming year are as follows:

USES OF FUNDS	DOLLAR AMOUNT (IN MILLIONS)	INTEREST RATE	LOAN LOSS PERCENTAGE
Loans to small businesses	$4,000	T-bill rate + 6%	2%
Loans to large businesses	2,000	T-bill rate + 4%	1
Consumer loans	3,000	T-bill rate + 7%	4
Treasury bills	1,000	T-bill rate	0
Treasury bonds	1,500	T-bill rate + 2%	0
Corporate bonds	1,100	Treasury bond rate + 2%	0

The bank also has $900 million in fixed assets. The interest rates it charges on loans to small and large businesses are tied to the T-bill rate and will change at the beginning of each new year. The forecasted Treasury bond rate is tied to the future T-bill rate because an upward-sloping yield curve is expected at the beginning of next year. The corporate bond rate is tied to the Treasury bond rate, allowing for a risk premium of 2 percent. Consumer loans will be provided at the beginning of next year, and interest rates will be fixed over the lifetime of the loan. The remaining time to maturity on all assets except T-bills exceeds three years. As the one-year T-bills mature, the funds will be reinvested in new one-year T-bills (all T-bills will be purchased at the beginning of the year).

The bank's loan loss percentage reflects the percentage of bad loans. Assume that no interest will be received on these loans. In addition, assume that this percentage of loans will be accounted for in its loan loss provision (that is, assume that they should be subtracted when determining before-tax income).

The bank has forecast its noninterest revenues to be $200 million and its noninterest expenses to be $740 million. A tax rate of 34 percent can be applied to the before-tax income to estimate after-tax income. The bank has developed the following probability distribution for the one-year T-bill rate at the beginning of next year:

POSSIBLE T-BILL RATE	PROBABILITY
8%	30%
9	50
10	20

Questions

1. Using the information provided, determine the probability distribution of ROA for next year by completing the following table:

INTEREST RATE SCENARIO (POSSIBLE T-BILL RATE)	FORECASTED ROA	PROBABILITY
8%		
9		
10		

2. Will the bank's ROA next year be higher or lower if market interest rates are higher? (Use the T-bill rate as a proxy for market interest rates.) Why?

3. The bank is considering a strategy of attempting to attract an extra $1 billion in funds in the form of one-year negotiable certificates of deposit, which will replace $1 billion of five-year NCDs. Develop the probability distribution of ROA based on this strategy:

INTEREST RATE SCENARIO	FORECASTED ROA BASED ON THE STRATEGY OF INCREASING ONE-YEAR NCDs	PROBABILITY
8%		
9		
10		

4. Is the bank's ROA likely to be higher next year if it uses this strategy of attracting more one-year NCDs?

5. What would be an obvious concern about a strategy of using more one-year NCDs and fewer five-year NCDs beyond the next year?

6. The bank is considering a strategy of using $1 billion to offer additional loans to small businesses instead of purchasing T-bills. Using all the original assumptions provided, determine the probability distribution of ROA (assume that noninterest expenses would not be affected by this change in strategy).

INTEREST RATE SCENARIO (POSSIBLE T-BILL RATE)	FORECASTED ROA IF AN EXTRA $1 BILLION IS USED FOR LOANS TO SMALL BUSINESSES	PROBABILITY
8%		
9		
10		

7. Would the bank's ROA likely be higher or lower over the next year if it allocates the extra funds to small business loans?

8. What is the obvious risk of such a strategy beyond the next year?

9. The previous strategy of attracting more one-year NCDs could affect noninterest expenses and revenues. How would noninterest expenses be affected by this strategy of offering additional loans to small businesses? How would noninterest revenues be affected by this strategy?

10. Now assume that the bank is considering a strategy of increasing its consumer loans by $1 billion instead of using the funds for loans to small businesses. Using this information along with all the original assumptions provided, determine the probability distribution of ROA.

INTEREST RATE SCENARIO (POSSIBLE T-BILL RATE)	POSSIBLE ROA IF AN EXTRA $1 BILLION IS USED FOR CONSUMER LOANS	PROBABILITY
8%		
9		
10		

11. Other than possible changes in the economy that may affect credit risk, what key factor will determine whether this strategy is beneficial beyond one year?

12. Now assume that the bank wants to determine how its forecasted return on equity (ROE) next year would be affected by boosting its capital from $1 billion to $1.2 billion. (The extra capital would not be used to increase interest or noninterest revenues.) Using all the original assumptions provided, complete the following table.

INTEREST RATE SCENARIO (POSSIBLE T-BILL RATE)	FORECASTED ROE IF CAPITAL = $1 BILLION	FORECASTED ROE IF CAPITAL = $1.2 BILLION	PROBABILITY
8%			
9			
10			

Briefly state how the ROE will be affected if the capital level is increased.

PART 7
Nonbank Operations

The chapters in Part 7 cover the key nonbank operations. Each chapter is devoted to a particular type of operation, with a focus on sources of funds, uses of funds, regulations, management, and recent performance. Some of the institutions discussed are independent; others are units (subsidiaries) of financial conglomerates. Each financial institution's interactions with other institutions and its participation in financial markets are also emphasized in these chapters.

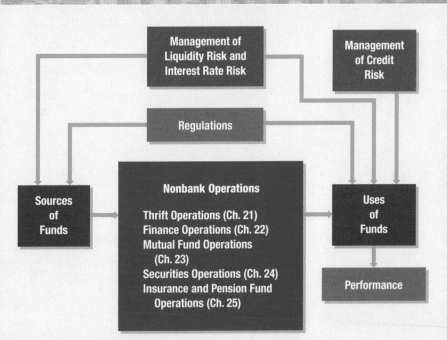

21

Thrift Operations

CHAPTER OBJECTIVES

The specific objectives of this chapter are to:

- Describe the ownership and regulation of savings institutions.

- Identify the key sources and uses of funds for savings institutions.

- Describe the exposure of savings institutions to various types of risk.

- Explain how savings institutions manage interest rate risk.

- Explain the valuation of a savings institution.

- Describe how savings institutions have been exposed to recent crises.

- Provide a background on credit unions, including their main sources and uses of funds.

WEB

https://occ.gov
Background on laws and regulations imposed on savings institutions.

The term *thrift institution* (or *savings institution*) refers to a depository institution that specializes in mortgage lending. These institutions were created to accept deposits and then use much of those funds for mortgage loans, home equity loans, and mortgage-backed securities. Some thrift operations are independent financial institutions, whereas others are units (subsidiaries) of financial conglomerates. Because credit unions are sometimes considered to be thrift institutions, they are also covered in this chapter.

21-1 Background on Savings Institutions

Savings institutions (SIs) include savings banks and savings and loan associations (S&Ls), with S&Ls being the dominant type. Because the two types of thrifts now have very similar sources and uses of funds, the remainder of the chapter focuses on SIs in general. Most SIs are small, with assets of less than $1 billion. SIs can be chartered at the state or federal level.

21-1a Ownership of Savings Institutions

Savings institutions are classified as either stock owned or mutual (owned by depositors). Although most SIs are mutual, many SIs have shifted their ownership structure from depositors to shareholders through what is known as a mutual-to-stock conversion. Such a conversion allows SIs to obtain additional capital by issuing stock.

Beyond having the capability to boost capital, stock-owned institutions provide their owners with greater potential to benefit from their performance. The dividends and/or stock price of a high-performance institution can grow, thereby providing direct benefits to the shareholders. In contrast, the owners (depositors) of a mutual institution do not benefit directly from high performance. Although they have a pro rata claim to the mutual SI's net worth while they maintain deposits there, that claim ends once they close their account.

Because of the difference in owner control, stock-owned institutions are more susceptible to unfriendly takeovers. It is virtually impossible for another firm to take control of a mutual institution, because such an organization's management generally holds all voting rights. From the owners' perspective, the stock-owned institution may seem more desirable because the owners may have more influence on managerial decisions.

When a mutual SI is involved in an acquisition, it first converts to a stock-owned SI. If it is the acquiring firm, it then arranges to purchase the existing stock of the institution to be acquired. Conversely, if it is to be acquired, the SI's stock is purchased by the acquiring institution. This process is often referred to as a **merger-conversion**.

Some SIs have been acquired by commercial banks that wanted to diversify their operations. Even after such an acquisition, the SI may still maintain its operations, albeit under the ownership of the commercial bank. Consolidation and acquisitions have caused the number of mutual and stock SIs to decline consistently over the years: The number of SIs has decreased by more than half over the last 25 years.

Although consolidation among SIs has resulted in a smaller number of institutions, the total assets of SIs in aggregate have increased. The total assets of stock SIs have more than doubled in the last 25 years, whereas the total assets of mutual SIs have remained relatively constant.

21-1b Regulation of Savings Institutions

The current regulatory structure for savings institutions, which was established by the Financial Reform (Dodd-Frank) Act of 2010, involves some overlap among the regulators. The Office of the Comptroller of the Currency supervises mutual SIs and federal SIs. The Federal Reserve regulates the parent holding companies of SIs. The Consumer Financial Protection Bureau supervises larger SIs (with at least $10 billion in assets) to ensure that they comply with federal consumer protection laws. State-chartered SIs are regulated by their respective state. In addition to satisfying their respective regulators, SIs may need to satisfy various guidelines established by the Federal Deposit Insurance Corporation (FDIC).

The Financial Reform Act removed some of the previous advantages of SIs. Holding companies of SIs now have to satisfy the minimum capital standards that are imposed on bank holding companies. Federal SIs have to satisfy the Qualified Thrift Lender Test, which requires that at least 65 percent of the asset portfolio consist of qualified thrift investments such as housing loans, home-equity loans, mortgage-backed securities, small business loans, and credit card loans. Yet SIs are also subject to limits on commercial loans and consumer loans. Since these regulatory changes eliminated some of the advantages of SIs, some SIs have attempted to become commercial banks or credit unions.

Deposit Insurance   Deposit insurance for SIs is provided by the Deposit Insurance Fund (DIF), which is administered by the FDIC. The insurable limit is currently $250,000 per account. The DIF was formed in 2006, as a result of the merger of the **Savings Association Insurance Fund (SAIF)**, which had formerly insured S&Ls, and the Bank Insurance Fund (BIF), which had insured savings banks. The FDIC charges the SIs annual insurance premiums, which are placed in the DIF. If an SI fails, the FDIC uses funds from the DIF to reimburse depositors.

Regulatory Assessment of Savings Institutions   Regulators conduct periodic on-site examinations of SIs using the CAMELS rating system in a manner similar to commercial banks. CAMELS is an acronym for the following characteristics: capital adequacy, asset quality, management, earnings, liquidity, and sensitivity to market conditions. Each SI is assigned a composite CAMELS rating between 1 (best) and 5 (worst). If an SI receives a composite CAMELS rating of 4 or higher, it is classified as a "problem" and receives close attention. Such an SI may also be subject to corrective action by regulators.

Deregulation of Services   In recent years, SIs have been granted more flexibility to diversify the products and services they provide. Many have expanded the scope of their business by merging with other businesses specializing in real estate, insurance, and brokerage services. By offering discount brokerage services and other nontraditional services, an SI can attract customers searching for a one-stop shop.

21-2 Sources and Uses of Funds

Like commercial banks, SIs serve as financial intermediaries, but their sources and uses of funds differ from those of commercial banks.

21-2a Sources of Funds

SIs have three main sources of funds:

- Deposits
- Borrowed funds
- Capital

Deposits   Savings institutions obtain most of their funds from a variety of savings and time deposits, including passbook savings, retail certificates of deposit (CDs), and money market deposit accounts (MMDAs).

Borrowed Funds   When SIs are unable to attract sufficient deposits, they can borrow on a short-term basis from three sources. First, they can borrow from other depository institutions that have excess funds in the federal funds market. The interest rate on funds borrowed in this market is referred to as the federal funds rate.

Second, SIs can borrow through a repurchase agreement (repo). With a repo, an institution sells government securities and makes a commitment to repurchase those securities shortly thereafter. This essentially reflects a short-term loan to the institution that initially sold the securities until the time when it buys the securities back.

Third, SIs can borrow at the Federal Reserve. This approach is not as commonly used as the other alternatives.

Capital   The **capital** (or net worth) of an SI is primarily composed of retained earnings and funds obtained from issuing stock. During periods when SIs are performing well, capital is boosted by additional retained earnings. Capital is commonly used to support ongoing or expanding operations. It also serves as a cushion when SIs experience losses, as happened to many SIs during the credit crisis of 2008–2009.

21-2b Uses of Funds

SIs typically use their funds for the following purposes:

- Cash
- Mortgages
- Mortgage-backed securities
- Other securities
- Consumer and commercial loans
- Other uses

Cash   Savings institutions maintain cash to satisfy the reserve requirements enforced by the Federal Reserve and to accommodate withdrawal requests of depositors. In addition, some SIs hold correspondent cash balances at other financial institutions in return for various services.

Mortgages   Mortgages are the primary asset of SIs. These loans typically have long-term maturities and can usually be prepaid by borrowers. Approximately 90 percent of the mortgages originated by SIs are for homes or multifamily dwellings, with the remaining 10 percent going toward commercial properties.

Mortgages can be sold in the secondary market. Because their market value changes in response to interest rate movements, they are subject to interest rate risk as well as credit (default) risk. To protect against interest rate risk, SIs use a variety of techniques, discussed later in this chapter.

Mortgage-Backed Securities   Some savings institutions purchase mortgage-backed securities. The return on these securities is highly influenced by the default rate on the underlying mortgages. During the 2008–2009 credit crisis, many defaults occurred, and savings institutions that had purchased mortgage-backed securities commonly experienced losses.

Other Securities   Savings institutions invest in securities such as Treasury bonds and corporate bonds. These securities provide liquidity, as they can quickly be sold in the secondary market if funds are needed.

Savings institutions sometimes rely on credit ratings when considering an investment in corporate bonds. However, during the credit crisis, the ratings agencies were criticized for being too liberal with their ratings. The Financial Reform Act of 2010 required that SIs use not only credit ratings assigned by credit rating agencies, but also other methods to assess the risk of debt securities, including their own assessment of risk. Complementing credit ratings with their own analysis should ensure that SIs are less likely to invest in securities with excessive risk.

Consumer and Commercial Loans   Many SIs have increased their consumer and commercial loans. This practice has the benefit of reducing their heavy exposure to mortgage loans. Because consumer and corporate loan maturities closely match their liability maturities, SIs that reduce their fixed-rate mortgage loans in favor of consumer loans reduce their exposure to interest rate risk.

Other Uses of Funds   Savings institutions can provide temporary financing to other institutions through the use of repurchase agreements. In addition, they can lend funds on a short-term basis through the federal funds market. Both methods allow them to efficiently use funds that they will have available for only a short period of time.

21-2c Balance Sheet of Savings Institutions

The sources of funds represent liabilities or equity of an SI, whereas the uses of funds represent assets. Each SI determines its own composition of liabilities and assets, which determines its specific operations.

EXAMPLE

Exhibit 21.1 summarizes the main sources and uses of funds of SIs by showing the balance sheet of Ashland Savings. The assets are shown on the left side of the balance sheet. The second column shows the dollar amount, and the third column shows the size of each asset in proportion to the total assets, to illustrate how Ashland Savings distributes its funds. Ashland's main asset is mortgage loans. Its allocation of assets reflects the average allocation for all SIs. Allocations vary considerably among SIs, however, as some institutions maintain a much larger amount of mortgages than others.

Ashland Savings incurs some expenses from all types of deposits. Specifically, it needs employees to provide service for its depositors and information systems to maintain and process account information. Its composition of liabilities determines its interest expenses, as it must pay a higher interest rate on large CDs than on small savings deposits.

Ashland also incurs expenses from managing its assets. In particular, it requires employees to assess the creditworthiness of the individuals and businesses that request loans. In general, Ashland attempts to generate enough income from its assets to cover its expenses and provide a reasonable return to its shareholders. Its primary source of income is interest received from the mortgage loans that it provides. Its capital is shown on the balance sheet as common stock issued and retained earnings. ●

Exhibit 21.1 Balance Sheet of Ashland Savings as of June 30, 2019

ASSETS	DOLLAR AMOUNT (IN MILLIONS)	PROPORTION OF TOTAL ASSETS	LIABILITIES AND STOCK HOLDERS' EQUITY	DOLLAR AMOUNT (IN MILLIONS)	PROPORTION OF TOTAL LIABILITIES AND STOCKHOLDERS' EQUITY
Cash (includes required reserves)	$60	6%	Savings deposits	$100	10%
Single-family mortgages	500	50%	NOW accounts	50	5%
Multifamily mortgages	50	5%	Money market deposit accounts	300	30%
Other mortgages	40	4%	Short-term CDs	360	36%
Mortgage-backed securities	70	7%	CDs with maturities beyond one year	100	10%
Other securities	100	10%			
Consumer loans	70	7%			
Commercial loans	40	4%			
Fixed assets	70	7%	Common stock issued	50	5%
			Retained earnings	40	4%
TOTAL ASSETS	$1,000	100%	TOTAL LIABILITIES AND STOCK HOLDERS' EQUITY	$1,000	100%

Exhibit 21.2 shows how SIs use the key balance sheet items to finance economic growth. They channel funds from their depositors with surplus funds to other households that purchase homes. They also channel funds to support investments in commercial property. In this way, SIs serve a major role in the development of the housing and commercial property market. They also use some deposits to purchase Treasury and municipal securities, thereby financing spending by the U.S. Treasury and municipalities.

21-2d Interaction with Other Financial Institutions

When SIs obtain and use funds, they commonly interact with other financial institutions, as summarized in Exhibit 21.3. They compete with commercial banks and money market mutual funds to obtain funds, and they compete with commercial banks and finance companies in lending funds. After originating mortgages, they sometimes sell them to insurance companies or other financial institutions in the secondary market. Many SIs have other financial institutions as subsidiaries that provide a variety of services, including consumer finance, trust company, mortgage banking, discount brokerage, and insurance.

21-2e Participation in Financial Markets

To perform their various functions, SIs participate in various financial markets, as summarized in Exhibit 21.4. They rely on mortgage markets when issuing mortgage-backed securities or selling their mortgages in the secondary market. They engage with bond markets when issuing new bonds in the primary market or when buying or selling bonds issued by corporations or government agencies in the secondary market.

Exhibit 21.2 How Savings Institutions Finance Economic Growth

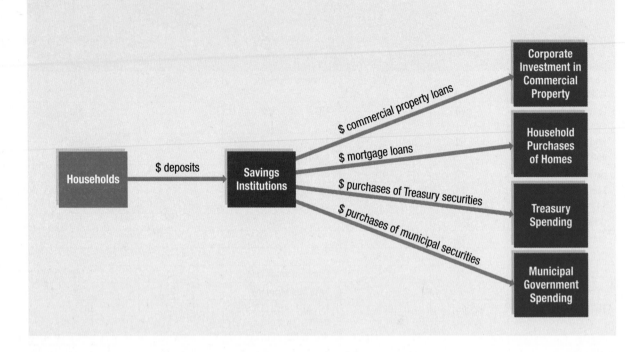

Exhibit 21.3 Interactions between Savings Institutions and Other Financial Institutions

TYPE OF FINANCIAL INSTITUTION	INTERACTION WITH SAVINGS INSTITUTIONS
Commercial banks	• Compete with SIs in attracting deposits, providing consumer loans, and providing commercial loans. • Have merged with SIs in recent years.
Finance companies	• Compete with SIs in providing consumer and commercial loans.
Money market mutual funds	• Compete with SIs in attracting short-term investments from investors.
Investment companies and brokerage firms	• Serve SIs that wish to engage in interest rate swaps and interest rate caps. • Have agreements with SIs to offer brokerage services to their customers.
Insurance companies	• Purchase mortgages from SIs in the secondary market.

Exhibit 21.4 Participation of Savings Institutions in Financial Markets

FINANCIAL MARKET	HOW SAVINGS INSTITUTIONS PARTICIPATE IN THIS MARKET
Money markets	• Compete with other depository institutions for short-term deposits by issuing commercial paper.
Mortgage markets	• Sell mortgages in the secondary market and issue mortgage-backed securities.
Bond markets	• Purchase bonds for their investment portfolios. • Issue bonds to obtain long-term funds.
Futures markets	• Hedge against interest rate movements by taking positions in interest rate futures.
Options markets	• Hedge against interest rate movements by purchasing put options on interest rate futures.
Swap markets	• Hedge against interest rate movements by engaging in interest rate swaps.

21-3 Valuation of a Savings Institution

Savings institutions (or SI operating units that are part of a financial conglomerate) are commonly valued by their managers to monitor the SI's progress over time or by other financial institutions that are considering an acquisition of the SI. The value of an SI can be modeled as the present value of its future cash flows. Thus, the value of an SI should change in response to changes in its expected cash flows in the future and to changes in the rate of return required by investors:

$$\Delta V = f[\underset{+}{\underline{\Delta E(\text{CF})}}, \underset{-}{\underline{\Delta k}}]$$

21-3a Factors That Affect Cash Flows

The change in an SI's expected cash flows may be modeled as

$$\Delta E(\text{CF}) = f(\underset{+}{\underline{\Delta \text{ECON}}}, \underset{-}{\underline{\Delta R_f}}, \underset{?}{\underline{\Delta \text{INDUS}}}, \underset{+}{\underline{\Delta \text{MANAB}}})$$

where ECON represents economic growth, R_f represents the risk-free interest rate, INDUS represents the industry conditions (such as regulations) to which SIs are exposed, and MANAB represents the abilities of the SI's management.

Change in Economic Growth   Economic growth can enhance an SI's cash flows by increasing household demand for consumer or mortgage loans, thereby allowing the SI to provide more loans. In addition, loan defaults are usually reduced in periods of strong economic growth. Furthermore, the demand for other financial services (such as real estate and insurance services) provided by SIs tends to be higher during periods of strong economic growth when households have relatively high levels of disposable income.

Change in the Risk-Free Interest Rate   An SI's cash flows may be inversely related to interest rate movements. First, if the risk-free interest rate decreases, other market rates may also decline, and the result may be a stronger demand for the SI's loans. Second, SIs rely heavily on short-term deposits as a source of funds, and the rates paid on these deposits are typically revised in accordance with other interest rate movements.

The assets (such as consumer loans and fixed-rate mortgage loans) of SIs commonly have fixed rates, so their interest income does not adjust to interest rate movements until those assets reach maturity or are sold. Therefore, when interest rates fall, an SI's cost of obtaining funds declines more steeply than does the interest earned on its loans and investments. An increase in interest rates can reduce the SI's expected cash flows because the interest paid on deposits may increase more than the interest earned on loans and investments.

Change in Industry Conditions   Savings institutions are exposed to industry conditions such as regulatory constraints, technology, and competition. If regulatory constraints are reduced, the expected cash flows of some SIs should increase. For example, when regulators reduced constraints on the services that SIs could offer, some of these institutions were able to provide a broader range of services for their customers. However, a reduction in regulations can cause less efficient SIs to lose market share and, therefore, experience a reduction in cash flows.

WEB

www.fdic.gov
Information about the performance of savings institutions.

Change in Management Abilities   An SI's managers attempt to make internal decisions that will capitalize on the external forces (economic growth, interest rates, regulatory constraints) that the institution cannot control. Thus, the management skills of an SI influence its expected cash flows. For example, skillful managers will recognize whether they need to increase the funds allocated to fixed-rate mortgages based on expectations of future interest rates. They can capitalize on regulatory changes by offering a diversified set of services that accommodate specific customers. They can use technology in a manner that reduces expenses. They may also use derivative securities to alter the potential return and the exposure of the SI to interest rate movements.

21-3b Factors That Affect the Required Rate of Return

The change in the rate of return required by investors who invest in an SI can be modeled as

$$\Delta k = f(\underset{+}{\Delta R_f}, \underset{+}{\Delta RP})$$

where R_f represents the risk-free interest rate and RP represents the risk premium.

An increase in the risk-free rate results in a higher return required by investors. High inflation, economic growth, and a high budget deficit place upward pressure on interest rates, whereas growth of the money supply places downward pressure on interest rates (assuming it does not cause inflation).

Change in the Risk Premium   If the risk premium on an SI rises, so will the rate of return required by investors who invest in the SI. High economic growth results in less risk for an SI because its consumer loans, mortgage loans, and investments in debt securities are less likely to default. By comparison, the effect of industry conditions on SIs can be mixed: A reduction in regulatory constraints on services can reduce the risk of SIs as they diversify their offerings, or it can increase their risk if they engage in new services that are riskier than their traditional services. An improvement in management skills may reduce the perceived risk of the SIs and, in turn, reduce the risk premium.

Exhibit 21.5 provides a framework for valuing an SI based on the preceding discussion. In general, the value of an SI is favorably affected by strong economic growth, a reduction in interest rates, and high-quality management. The sensitivity of an SI's value to these conditions depends on its own characteristics. For example, the value of an SI that emphasizes real estate and insurance services will be more sensitive to regulations that restrict or limit the offering of these services than will the value of an SI that focuses on traditional mortgage lending.

21-4 Exposure to Risk

Like commercial banks, SIs are exposed to liquidity risk, credit risk, and interest rate risk. However, because their sources and uses of funds differ from those of banks, their exposure to risk varies as well.

21-4a Liquidity Risk

Because SIs commonly use short-term liabilities to finance long-term assets, they depend on additional deposits to accommodate withdrawal requests. If new deposits are not sufficient to cover withdrawal requests, an SI can experience liquidity problems. To remedy this situation, SIs can obtain funds through repurchase agreements or borrow funds in

Exhibit 21.5 Framework for Valuing a Savings Institution

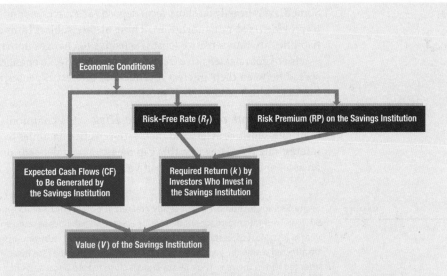

- A stronger economy leads to increased demand for loans (interest income) and other services (noninterest income), fewer loan defaults, and therefore better cash flows for the SI.

- A lower risk-free rate leads to a lower cost of deposits obtained and more favorable valuations of the mortgages held by the SI.

- The valuation is also influenced by industry conditions and the SI's management (not shown in the diagram). These factors affect the risk premium (and therefore the required return by investors) and the expected cash flows for the SI. In particular, regulatory changes can affect the level of competition, thereby influencing the SI's cash flows and risk premium.

the federal funds market. However, these sources of funds will resolve only a short-term deficiency. They will not be appropriate if a longer-term liquidity problem exists.

An alternative way to remedy a problem of insufficient liquidity is to sell assets in exchange for cash. Savings institutions can sell their Treasury securities or even some of their mortgages in the secondary market. Although the sale of assets can boost liquidity, it also reduces the SI's size and possibly its earnings. Therefore, minor liquidity deficiencies are typically resolved by increasing liabilities rather than selling assets.

21-4b **Credit Risk**

Because mortgages represent SIs' primary asset, they are also the main source of their credit risk. Although Federal Housing Authority (FHA) and Veterans Administration (VA) mortgages originated by SIs are insured against credit risk, conventional mortgages are not. Private insurance can usually be obtained for conventional mortgages, but SIs often incur the risk themselves rather than pay for the insurance. If they perform adequate credit analysis of their potential borrowers and geographically diversify their mortgage loans, they should be able to maintain a low degree of credit risk. Many SIs took excessive risks when granting or purchasing mortgages in the 2003–2006 period and suffered the consequences during the credit crisis of 2008–2009, as explained later in this chapter.

21-4c Interest Rate Risk

Some SIs rely heavily on short-term deposits as sources of funds and use most of their funds to provide fixed-rate mortgages. These SIs are subject to interest rate risk because their liabilities are rate-sensitive (cost is sensitive to changes in market interest rates) but their assets are not rate-sensitive (revenue is not sensitive to changes in market rates). Thus, the spread between their interest revenue and interest expenses narrows when interest rates increase, which reduces their profitability.

Measurement of Interest Rate Risk   SIs commonly measure the gap between their rate-sensitive assets and their rate-sensitive liabilities to determine their exposure to interest rate risk. However, this gap measurement depends on the criteria used to classify an asset or a liability as rate-sensitive.

EXAMPLE

Siesta Savings Institution was recently created. It obtains most of its funds from two-year CDs and offers 30-year fixed-rate mortgages. It defines its assets and liabilities as rate-sensitive if they are repriced within a year or less. Most of Siesta's liabilities are initially considered to be rate-insensitive because their rate will not be affected within the year. Its assets are also considered to be rate-insensitive because their rate will not be affected within the year. Thus, Siesta's gap is close to zero because its rate-sensitive assets and liabilities are close to zero, which implies that the institution is not exposed to interest rate risk. Nevertheless, Siesta will be adversely affected by an increase in interest rates because its interest expenses would rise over time but the rate on its mortgage loans is fixed for a long-term period. Thus, the gap measurement is not an accurate indicator of Siesta's exposure to interest rate risk. ●

Given the limitations of the gap measurement, some SIs measure the duration of their respective assets and liabilities to determine the imbalance in the sensitivity of interest revenue versus expenses to interest rate movements.

EXAMPLE

Tucson Savings Institution (TSI) desires to measure the duration of its assets and liabilities. It first needs to classify each balance sheet component into various maturity categories, as shown in Exhibit 21.6. The rates on most adjustable-rate mortgages are adjusted every year, which is why the amounts under the longer-term categories show zero.

The average duration for each asset category is provided below the dollar amount. Some fixed-rate mortgages are classified in the earlier term categories because they are maturing or will be sold soon. The duration for adjustable-rate mortgages is a weighted average of their durations: $0.30(7,000/27,000) + 0.80(15,000/27,000) + 1.9(4,000/27,000) + 2.9(1,000/27,000) = 0.91$.

The durations for fixed-rate mortgages and investment securities were computed in a similar manner. The duration for total assets of 2.76 years is a weighted average of the durations of the individual assets: $0.91(27,000/61,000) + 5.32(20,000/61,000) + 2.65(14,000/61,000) = 2.76$.

A similar procedure is used to estimate the duration of liabilities. NOW accounts and passbook savings have no specified maturity, but their rate is adjusted less frequently than the rate on MMDAs, which is why MMDAs have a shorter duration. The total liability duration is about 0.45.

Thus, TSI's total asset duration is more than six times its liability duration. In other words, its future performance is highly exposed to interest rate movements. Its market value would decrease substantially in response to an increase in interest rates. TSI can reduce its exposure to interest rate risk by reducing the proportion of its assets in the long-duration categories. ●

Financial institutions use computer programs to estimate their asset and liability duration and apply sensitivity analysis to proposed balance sheet adjustments. For example, TSI could determine how its asset and liability duration would change if it engaged in a promotional effort to issue five-year deposits and used the funds to offer adjustable-rate mortgages.

Exhibit 21.6   Duration Schedule for Tucson Savings Institution (Dollar Amounts Are in Thousands)

ASSETS	LESS THAN 6 MONTHS	6 MONTHS TO 1 YEAR	1–3 YEARS	3–5 YEARS	5–10 YEARS	10–20 YEARS	OVER 20 YEARS	TOTAL
Adjustable-rate mortgages	$7,000	$15,000	$4,000	$1,000	$0	$0	$0	$27,000
Amount ($) Average duration (yr)	0.30	0.80	1.90	2.90	0	0	0	0.91
Fixed-rate mortgages								
Amount ($)	500	500	1,000	1,000	2,000	10,000	5,000	20,000
Average duration (yr)	0.25	0.60	1.80	2.60	4.30	5.50	7.60	5.32
Investment securities								
Amount ($)	2,000	3,000	4,000	2,000	1,000	0	2,000	14,000
Average duration (yr)	0.20	0.70	1.70	3.20	5.30	0	8.05	2.65
Total amount ($)	$9,500	$18,500	$9,000	$4,000	$3,000	$10,000	$7,000	$61,000
								Asset duration = 2.76
LIABILITIES								
Fixed-maturity deposits								
Amount ($)	$14,000	$9,000	$2,000	$1,000	$0	$0	$0	$26,000
Average duration (yr)	0.30	0.60	1.80	2.80	0	0	0	0.62
NOW accounts								
Amount ($)	4,000	0	0	0	0	0	0	4,000
Average duration (yr)	0.40	0	0	0	0	0	0	0.40
MMDAs								
Amount ($)	15,000	0	0	0	0	0	0	15,000
Average duration (yr)	0.20	0	0	0	0	0	0	0.20
Passbook accounts								
Amount ($)	13,000	0	0	0	0	0	0	13,000
Average duration (yr)	0.40	0	0	0	0	0	0	0.40
Total amount ($)	$46,000	$9,000	$2,000	$1,000	$0	$0	$0	$58,000
								Liability duration = 0.45

21-5 Management of Interest Rate Risk

Savings institutions can use a variety of methods to manage their interest rate risk, including the following:

- Adjustable-rate mortgages
- Interest rate futures contracts
- Interest rate swaps

21-5a Adjustable-Rate Mortgages

The interest rates on adjustable-rate mortgages (ARMs) are tied to market-determined rates such as the one-year Treasury bill rate and are periodically adjusted in accordance with the formula stated in the ARM contract. A variety of formulas are used. Adjustable-rate mortgages enable SIs to maintain a more stable spread between interest revenue and interest expenses.

Although ARMs reduce the adverse impact of rising interest rates, they also reduce the favorable impact of declining interest rates. Suppose that an SI obtains most of its funds from short-term deposits and uses those funds to provide fixed-rate mortgages. If interest rates decline and the SI does not hedge its exposure to interest rate risk, the spread will increase. If the SI uses ARMs as a hedging strategy, however, the interest on loans will decrease during a period of declining rates, so the spread will not widen.

Although ARMs reduce the risks of SIs, they expose consumers to interest rate risk. While ARMs typically have a maximum cap limiting the increase in interest rates (such as 2 percent per year and 5 percent over the life of the loan), the impact of an upward adjustment in the rate on borrowers' household mortgage payments is still significant. Because some homeowners prefer fixed-rate mortgages, most SIs continue to offer them and, therefore, incur interest rate risk. Thus, other strategies besides the use of ARMs are necessary to reduce this risk.

21-5b Interest Rate Futures Contracts

An interest rate futures contract allows for the purchase of a specific amount of a particular debt security for a specified price at a future point in time. Sellers of futures contracts are obligated to sell the securities for the contract price at the stated future point in time.

Some SIs use Treasury bond futures contracts because the cash flow characteristics of Treasury bonds resemble those of fixed-rate mortgages. Like mortgages, Treasury bonds offer fixed periodic payments, so their market value moves in the opposite direction of interest rate fluctuations. Savings institutions that sell futures contracts on these securities can effectively hedge their fixed-rate mortgages. If interest rates rise, the market value of the securities represented by the futures contract will decrease. The SIs will benefit from the difference between the market value at which they can purchase these securities in the future and the futures price at which they will sell the securities. This difference can offset the reduced spread between their interest revenue and interest expenses during the period of rising interest rates.

21-5c Interest Rate Swaps

WEB

www.fdic.gov
Profiles of individual
savings institutions.

Another strategy for reducing interest rate risk is to pursue interest rate swaps, which allow an SI to swap fixed-rate payments (an outflow) for variable-rate payments (an inflow). The fixed-rate outflow payments can be matched against the fixed-rate mortgages held so that a certain spread can be achieved. In addition, the variable-rate inflows due to the swap can be matched against the variable cost of funds. When interest rates rise, the institution's fixed-rate outflow payments from the swap agreement remain fixed while the variable-rate inflow payments due to the swap increase. This favorable result can partially offset the unfavorable impact of rising interest rates on an SI's spread. However, an interest rate swap also reduces the favorable impact of declining interest rates; that is, inflow interest payments decrease while the outflow interest payments remain the same during a period of declining rates.

21-5d Conclusions about Managing Interest Rate Risk

Although the hedging strategies just described are useful, it is almost impossible to eliminate interest rate risk completely. Notably, the potential prepayment of mortgages cannot be fully accounted for. Homeowners often pay off their mortgages before maturity without much advance notice to the SI. Consequently, SIs do not really know the actual maturity of the mortgages they hold and cannot perfectly match the interest rate sensitivity of their assets and liabilities.

21-6 Exposure of Savings Institutions to Crises

Savings institutions were devastated by the SI crisis during the late 1980s and by the credit crisis in the 2008–2009 period, as explained next.

21-6a Savings Institution Crisis in the Late 1980s

One reason for the SI crisis of the late 1980s was an increase in interest rates. Those SIs that had provided long-term mortgages were adversely affected because the interest they earned on assets remained constant while the interest they paid on liabilities increased. Consequently, their net interest income declined.

In addition, many SIs had been making commercial loans even though they lacked the expertise needed to accurately assess firms' ability to repay their loans. Many loan defaults occurred in the Southwest, where economies were devastated by a decline in oil prices. The ensuing layoffs in the oil industry led to a decline in businesses' revenues. Real estate prices dropped so dramatically that when SIs foreclosed on the bad real estate loans, the property that had served as collateral was worth less than the loans. Although some housing loans defaulted, the major loan losses occurred in commercial real estate, such as office complexes. Some SIs also experienced losses on their investments in junk bonds.

Many SIs experienced a cash flow deficiency as a result of their loan losses, as the inflows from loan repayments were not sufficient to cover depositor withdrawals. Consequently, they were forced to offer higher interest rates on deposits to attract more funds. As depositors became aware of the crisis, they began to withdraw their savings from SIs, which exacerbated the illiquidity problem.

ETHICS

Fraud   Many SIs also experienced financial problems during this period because of various fraudulent activities. In one of the most common types of fraud, managers of SIs used depositors' funds to purchase personal assets, including yachts, artwork, and automobile dealerships. At many SIs, a lack of oversight by executives and by the board of directors allowed some managers to serve their own interests rather than shareholder interests. Many of the problems of the SIs could have been reduced if proper governance had been applied.

Provisions of the FIRREA   To prevent further failures and restore confidence, the Financial Institutions Reform, Recovery, and Enforcement Act (FIRREA) was enacted in 1989. Among other things, the FIRREA increased penalties for officers of SIs and other financial institutions convicted of fraud, raised the capital requirements for SIs, and allowed commercial banks to acquire SIs. In addition, SIs were required to sell off any holdings of junk bonds and prohibited from investing in them in the future.

The Resolution Trust Corporation (RTC) was formed to deal with insolvent SIs. The RTC liquidated the assets of the insolvent SIs and reimbursed depositors or sold the SIs to other financial institutions. By the time the RTC was closed at the end of 1995, it had either liquidated or found a buyer for 747 insolvent SIs. It had also recovered $394 billion by liquidating assets and another $2.4 billion through legal settlements.

Beyond restoring confidence in the SI industry, the FIRREA significantly improved conditions for SIs over the next 15 years. Savings institutions slowly built their capital and sold off risky assets. Nevertheless, many SIs pursued risky strategies again in the 2004–2006 period, which led to high returns when economic conditions were strong, but caused major problems for them during the credit crisis, as described next.

21-6b Credit Crisis of 2008–2009

During the 2003–2006 period of strong economic growth, some SIs used very liberal standards when offering subprime mortgage loans for borrowers who did not qualify for conventional mortgages. Most charged a premium of 3 percentage points or more on subprime mortgage loans over the rate charged on conventional mortgages, along with additional fees at the time the loans were originated. This strategy was based on the presumption that new homeowners who were granted subprime mortgages would be able to afford their mortgage payments.

The interest rates on subprime mortgage loans were commonly fixed for the first two years and then adjusted in line with market interest rates after that. As market interest rates increased in the 2005–2006 period, the required monthly payments on some subprime mortgage borrowers increased, and some homeowners could no longer meet their monthly payments. In addition, home builders continued to build new homes, but the demand for homes suddenly declined, leading to an excess supply of homes for sale. When the economy weakened in the 2008–2009 period, home prices plummeted. At that point, the values of many homes were substantially less than the mortgage balances on those homes—a fact that prompted many mortgage foreclosures. By January 2009, approximately 10 percent of all mortgages were experiencing late payments or were in foreclosure.

Some SIs originated subprime loans and then immediately sold them to institutional investors in the secondary market. These institutions were less exposed to credit risk because they limited their holdings of subprime mortgages. However, those financial firms that focused entirely on subprime mortgages and maintained the mortgages after originating them experienced poor performance in the 2008–2009 period when many borrowers could not cover their mortgage payments. Several subprime lenders went bankrupt. Even the subprime lenders that sold all the mortgages they created were adversely affected by the credit crisis, because once the economy weakened, the level of mortgage originations declined substantially.

Many SIs invested heavily in mortgage-backed securities without recognizing the potential credit risk of these securities. They subsequently incurred losses on these investments because of late payments or defaults on the mortgages represented by these securities. Some SIs sold credit default swap contracts on mortgage-backed securities, which required them to cover damages when some mortgage-backed securities held by other financial institutions defaulted.

In general, the adverse effects of the 2008–2009 credit crisis were very similar to the adverse effects during the savings institution crisis of the late 1980s. In both cases, those SIs that used their funds to make high-risk loans and investments in an attempt to generate very high profits suffered major losses once economic conditions weakened.

ETHICS

Notable Failures during the Credit Crisis   The financial problems of SIs were highlighted by several large failures, including Countrywide Financial (the second largest SI in the United States), IndyMac (the eighth largest SI), and Washington Mutual (the largest SI). Countrywide Financial used a very aggressive strategy of approving subprime mortgage loans of questionable quality. Many of these loans defaulted in 2007. In January 2008, Countrywide Financial was failing and was acquired by Bank of America.

IndyMac suffered major losses on its $32 billion portfolio of mortgages. In July 2008, as rumors circulated about its possible failure, depositors began to withdraw an average of $100 million per day. This created severe liquidity problems for IndyMac, which caused the FDIC to intervene and take it over.

In September 2008, Washington Mutual became the largest depository institution (with assets of $307 billion) ever to fail in the United States. Like IndyMac, Washington Mutual suffered liquidity problems as its depositors began withdrawing funds after hearing rumors about its financial problems. The main reason for Washington Mutual's failure was its heavy investment in mortgages and mortgage-backed securities. The FDIC seized this SI's assets and then sold most of them to JPMorgan Chase. As a result of this acquisition, JPMorgan Chase became the second largest commercial bank in the United States at that time (it is now the largest bank).

21-6c **Reform in Response to the Credit Crisis**

FINANCIAL REFORM

ETHICS

Following the credit crisis, Congress enacted the Financial Reform Act in 2010. This act contained numerous provisions that were intended to stabilize the financial system. It established the regulation of SIs and regulatory structure described earlier in the chapter. Other provisions related to SIs are summarized here.

Mortgage Origination　The Financial Reform Act requires that SIs and other financial institutions granting mortgages verify the income, job status, and credit history of mortgage applicants before approving mortgage applications. This provision is intended to strengthen the standards for obtaining a mortgage, thereby preventing another credit crisis in the future.

Sales of Mortgage-Backed Securities　The Financial Reform Act requires that savings institutions and other financial institutions that sell mortgage-backed securities retain 5 percent of the portfolio unless the portfolio meets specific standards that reflect low risk. This provision forces financial institutions to maintain a stake in the mortgage portfolios that they sell. The act also requires more disclosure regarding the quality of the underlying assets when mortgage-backed securities are sold.

Financial Stability Oversight Council　The Financial Reform Act created the Financial Stability Oversight Council, which is responsible for identifying risks to financial stability in the United States and makes regulatory recommendations to regulators that could reduce systemic risk, which is the risk that the financial problems of SIs or other financial institutions could spread to other members of the financial community. The Council can recommend methods to ensure that depository institutions do not rely on regulatory bailouts and can recommend rules such as higher capital requirements for SIs that are perceived to be too big and complex.

　The Council consists of 10 members, including the Treasury secretary (who chairs the Council) and the heads of the Federal Reserve, Comptroller of the Currency, Federal Deposit Insurance Corporation, National Credit Union Administration (discussed later in the chapter), Securities and Exchange Commission, and Federal Housing Finance Agency.

Orderly Liquidation　The Financial Reform Act gave specific regulators the authority to determine whether any particular financial institution should be liquidated. This expedites the liquidation process and can limit the losses due to a failing financial institution. Shareholders and unsecured creditors are expected to bear most of the losses of failing financial institutions.

Consumer Financial Protection Bureau　The act established the Consumer Financial Protection Bureau, which is responsible for regulating the various consumer finance products and services offered by SIs and other financial institutions, such as online accounts and credit cards. The Bureau can set rules to ensure that SIs disclose accurate information about their financial services and to prevent deceptive financial practices.

Trading of Derivative Securities　The Financial Reform Act requires that derivative securities be traded through a clearinghouse or exchange, rather than over the counter. This allows for a more standardized structure regarding margins and collateral and more transparency of prices in the market. Consequently, SIs that trade these derivatives should be less susceptible to the risk that the counterparty has posted insufficient collateral.

21-7 Credit Unions

WEB

thecommunitybanker
.com/cu_links/
Identifies credit unions
in all states.

Credit unions (CUs) are nonprofit organizations composed of members with a common bond, such as an affiliation with a particular labor union, church, university, or even residential area. Their objective is to serve as an intermediary for those members. Credit unions offer interest on share deposits to members who invest funds. They then channel those funds to members who need loans.

Because of their "common bond" requirement, CUs tend to be much smaller than other depository institutions. Approximately 5,800 CUs operate in the United States. Although the number of CUs now exceeds the number of commercial banks, the total assets of CUs are less than one-tenth the amount of total assets in commercial banks.

21-7a Ownership of Credit Unions

WEB

www.corningcu.org
Information about
services related to
financial planning that
are provided by CUs.

Because CUs do not issue stock, they are technically owned by the depositors. The deposits are called shares, and interest paid on the deposits is called a dividend. Because CUs are nonprofit organizations, their income is not taxed. If CUs accumulate earnings, they can use the earnings either to offer higher rates on deposits or to reduce rates on loans.

Like savings institutions and commercial banks, CUs can be either federally or state chartered. If the state does not offer a charter, a federal charter is necessary. Although a few CUs (such as the Navy Federal CU) have assets of more than $50 billion, most are very small: Approximately 40 percent of them have less than $20 million in assets. Federally chartered CUs are growing at a faster rate than state-chartered CUs, and their total assets are now significantly larger than the aggregate assets of state-chartered CUs.

21-7b Advantages and Disadvantages of Credit Unions

WEB

www.ncua.gov
Provides financial data on
federally chartered CUs.

Because CUs are not taxed, they have an advantage over other types of financial institutions. Credit unions typically offer higher deposit rates, charge lower fees on checking accounts, have lower required minimum balances, and offer lower loan rates than their competitors, yet still achieve a satisfactory level of performance. In addition, their noninterest expenses are relatively low because their offices and furniture are often donated or provided at a very low cost through the affiliation of their members.

Other characteristics of CUs can be less attractive, however. Their employees may not have the incentive to manage operations efficiently. Credit unions may also not have the funds to invest heavily in new technology and may not be able to offer the latest innovations in online and mobile banking. In addition, the "common bond" requirement for membership restricts a given CU from growing beyond the potential size of that particular affiliation and limits the CU's ability to diversify. This is especially true when all members are employees of the same employer. If that employer lays off a number of workers, many members may simultaneously experience financial problems and withdraw their share deposits or default on their loans. This could cause the CU to become illiquid at a time when more members need loans to survive the layoff.

Even when the common bond does not represent a particular employer, many CUs are unable to diversify geographically because all members live in the same area. Thus, an economic slowdown in this area would have an adverse impact on most members. CUs' access to capital is also limited, because they are owned by depositors rather than shareholders and, therefore, cannot issue stock.

To overcome some of these disadvantages as well as to better diversify their services and take greater advantage of economies of scale, CUs increasingly have been merging. Consequently, some CUs now draw their members from a number of employers, organizations, and other affiliations. CUs are also trying to diversify their products by offering other services, such as life insurance, to their members.

21-7c Deposit Insurance for Credit Unions

Approximately 90 percent of CUs are insured by the National Credit Union Share Insurance Fund (NCUSIF), which is administered by the National Credit Union Administration (NCUA). All federally chartered CUs are required to obtain insurance from the NCUSIF. State-chartered CUs are eligible for NCUSIF insurance only if they meet various guidelines. Some states require their CUs to be federally insured; others allow insurance to be offered by alternative insurance agencies.

The CUs typically pay an annual insurance premium of about one-tenth of 1 percent of their share deposits. The NCUSIF sets aside a portion of its funds as reserves to cover expenses resulting from CU failures each year. Given the low number of failures, the reserves are normally adequate to cover these expenses.

21-7d Regulatory Assessment of Credit Unions

Federal CUs are supervised and regulated by the NCUA, whereas state-chartered CUs are regulated by their respective states. The NCUA employs a staff of examiners to monitor CUs each year. The examiners conduct assessments of all federally chartered CUs as well as any state-chartered CUs applying for federal insurance. Each CU completes a semiannual financial report. From this information, the NCUA examiners derive financial ratios that measure the CU's financial condition. The ratios are then compared to an industry norm to detect any significant deviations. Then a summary of the CU, called a Financial Performance Report, is completed to identify any potential problems that deserve special attention in the future.

As part of the assessment, the examiners classify each CU into a specific risk category, ranging from Code 1 (low risk) to Code 5 (high risk). This classification is intended to serve as an early warning system so that CUs that are experiencing problems or are in potential danger can be closely monitored in the future. The criteria used by the NCUA to assess risk are capital adequacy, asset quality, management, earnings, liquidity, and sensitivity to market conditions; those are the same characteristics used by the FDIC to assess commercial banks and savings institutions.

21-7e Credit Union Sources of Funds

Credit union sources of funds can be classified as deposits, borrowed funds, and capital, as explained next.

Deposits   Credit unions obtain most of their funds from share deposits by members. The typical deposit is similar to a passbook savings account deposit at commercial banks or savings institutions, as it has no specified maturity and is insured up to $250,000. Credit unions also offer share certificates, which provide higher rates than share deposits but require the member to invest a minimum amount (such as $500) and have a specified maturity. The share certificates offered by CUs compete against the retail CDs offered by commercial banks and SIs.

In addition to share deposits and certificates, most CUs offer checkable accounts called share drafts. These accounts can pay interest and allow an unlimited amount of checks to be written, but usually require the member to maintain a minimum balance. Share drafts offered by CUs compete against the NOW accounts and MMDAs offered by commercial banks and SIs.

Borrowed Funds If a CU needs funds temporarily, it can borrow from other CUs or from the Central Liquidity Facility (CLF). The CLF acts as a lender for CUs to accommodate seasonal funding and specialized needs or to boost the liquidity of troubled CUs.

Capital Like other depository institutions, CUs maintain capital. Their primary source of capital is retained earnings. In recent years, CUs have boosted their capital, which helps cushion these institutions against any future loan losses. Given that CUs tend to use conservative management, their capital ratio is relatively high compared with other depository institutions.

21-7f Credit Union Uses of Funds

Credit unions use the majority of their funds to make loans to members. These loans finance automobiles, home improvements, and other personal expenses. They are typically secured and carry maturities of five years or less. Some CUs offer long-term mortgage loans, but many prefer to avoid loans with long maturities. In addition to providing loans, CUs purchase government and agency securities to maintain adequate liquidity. The degree to which CUs can offer various products and services is influenced by the type of charter and by their location.

21-7g Exposure of Credit Unions to Risk

Like other depository institutions, CUs are exposed to liquidity risk, credit risk, and interest rate risk. Their balance sheet structure differs from that of other institutions, however, so their exposure to each type of risk also differs.

Liquidity Risk If a CU experiences an unanticipated wave of withdrawals without an offsetting amount of new deposits, it could become illiquid. It can borrow from the CLF to resolve temporary liquidity problems, but if the shortage of funds is expected to continue, the CU must search for a more permanent cure. Other depository institutions have greater ability to boost deposit levels because they can tap various markets. Because the market for a CU is restricted to those consumers who qualify as members, CUs have less ability to generate additional deposits quickly.

Credit Risk Because CUs concentrate on making personal loans to their members, their exposure to credit (default) risk is primarily derived from those loans. Most of their loans are secured, which reduces the loss to CUs in the event of default. Poor economic conditions can have a significant impact on loan defaults. Some CUs will perform much better than others because of more favorable economic conditions in their area. However, even during favorable economic periods, CUs with very lenient loan policies could experience losses. A common concern is that CUs may not conduct a thorough credit analysis of loan applicants; the loans they provide are consumer oriented, however, so an elaborate credit analysis generally is not required.

Although CUs are often viewed as the most conservative of all depository institutions, they were still exposed to the adverse effects of the credit crisis that began in 2008. Some CUs suffered large losses due to late payments or defaults on second mortgages and home-equity loans that they provided. In addition, they experienced some losses on mortgage-backed securities in which they had invested. Although CUs are restricted from investing in risky securities, some of the mortgage-backed securities that they purchased were highly rated at the time of purchase. As housing conditions worsened, the demand for securities backed by mortgages declined and the values of mortgage-backed securities declined as well.

Interest Rate Risk   Loans by CUs to their members typically have short or intermediate maturities, so their asset portfolios are rate-sensitive. Because their sources of funds are also generally rate-sensitive, movements in interest revenues and interest expenses of CUs are highly correlated. The spread between interest revenues and interest expenses remains somewhat stable over time, regardless of how interest rates change. Thus, CUs tend to have less exposure to interest rate risk than savings institutions.

Summary

- Savings institutions are classified as either stock owned or mutual. They are regulated by the Comptroller of the Currency and the Federal Reserve. Their deposits are insured by the Deposit Insurance Fund, which is administered by the Federal Deposit Insurance Corporation.
- The main sources of funds for SIs are deposits and borrowed funds. The main uses of funds for SIs are mortgages, mortgage-backed securities, and other securities.
- The valuation of an SI is a function of its expected cash flows and the rate of return required by its investors. The expected cash flows are influenced by economic growth, interest rate movements, regulatory constraints, and the abilities of the institution's managers. The required rate of return is influenced by the prevailing risk-free rate and the risk premium. The risk premium is lower when economic conditions are strong.
- Savings institutions are exposed to credit risk as a result of their heavy concentration in mortgages, mortgage-backed securities, and other securities. To reduce this risk, they attempt to diversify their investments.

- Savings institutions are highly susceptible to interest rate risk because their asset portfolios are typically less sensitive than their liability portfolios to interest rate movements. They can reduce this risk by using adjustable-rate mortgages instead of fixed-rate mortgages so that the rate sensitivity of their assets is more similar to that of their liabilities. In addition, they can sell interest rate futures contracts, which will generate gains if interest rates increase. Finally, they can engage in interest rate swaps in which they swap fixed rates for floating rates, which will generate gains if interest rates rise.
- In the late 1980s, many SIs made very risky loans and investments and experienced heavy losses from loan defaults, adverse interest rate movements, and fraud. In the 2004–2006 period, many SIs pursued aggressive mortgage lending strategies, which led to major problems during the credit crisis of 2008–2009.
- Credit unions obtain most of their funds from share deposits by members. They use the majority of their funds to make personal loans to members, which means they are exposed to credit risk.

Point/Counterpoint

Can All Savings Institutions Avoid Failure?

Point   Yes. If SIs use conservative management by focusing on adjustable-rate mortgages with limited default risk, they can limit their risk and avoid failure.

Counterpoint   No. Some SIs will be crowded out of the market for high-quality, adjustable-rate mortgages

and will have to take some risk. There are too many SIs, and some that have weaker management will inevitably fail.

Who Is Correct?   Use the Internet to learn more about this issue and then formulate your own opinion.

Questions and Applications

1. SI Sources and Uses of Funds Explain in general terms how savings institutions differ from commercial banks with respect to their sources of funds and uses of funds. Discuss each source of funds for SIs. Identify and discuss the main uses of funds for SIs.

2. Ownership of SIs What are the alternative forms of ownership of a savings institution?

3. Regulation of SIs What criteria do regulators use when examining a savings institution?

4. MMDAs How did the creation of money market deposit accounts influence the overall cost of funds for a savings institution?

5. Offering More Diversified Services Discuss the entrance of savings institutions into the market for consumer and commercial lending. What are the potential risks and rewards of this strategy? Discuss the conflict between diversification and specialization of SIs.

6. Liquidity and Credit Risk Describe the liquidity and credit risk of savings institutions, and discuss how each is managed.

7. ARMs What is an adjustable-rate mortgage (ARM)? Discuss the potential advantages that such mortgages offer a savings institution.

8. Use of Financial Futures Explain how savings institutions could use interest rate futures to reduce interest rate risk.

9. Use of Interest Rate Swaps Explain how savings institutions could use interest rate swaps to reduce interest rate risk. Will SIs that use swaps perform better or worse than those that were unhedged during a period of declining interest rates? Explain.

10. Risk Explain why many savings institutions experience financial problems at the same time.

11. Hedging Interest Rate Movements If market interest rates are expected to decline over time, will a savings institution with rate-sensitive liabilities and a large amount of fixed-rate mortgages perform best by (a) using an interest rate swap, (b) selling financial futures, or (c) remaining unhedged? Explain.

12. Exposure to Interest Rate Risk The following table discloses the interest rate sensitivity of two savings institutions (dollar amounts are in millions).

Based on this information only, which institution's stock price would likely be affected more by a given change in interest rates? Justify your opinion.

| | INTEREST SENSITIVITY PERIOD | | | |
	WITHIN 1 YEAR	FROM 1 TO 5 YEARS	FROM 5 TO 10 YEARS	OVER 10 YEARS
Lawrence S&L				
Interest-earning assets	$8,000	$3,000	$7,000	$3,000
Interest-bearing liabilities	11,000	6,000	2,000	1,000
Manhattan S&L				
Interest-earning assets	1,000	1,000	4,000	3,000
Interest-bearing liabilities	2,000	2,000	1,000	1,000

13. SI Crisis What were some of the more obvious reasons for the savings institution crisis of the late 1980s?

14. FIRREA Explain how the Financial Institutions Reform, Recovery, and Enforcement Act (FIRREA) reduced the perceived risk of savings institutions.

15. Background on CUs Who are the owners of credit unions? Explain the tax status of CUs and the reason for that status. Why are CUs typically smaller than commercial banks or savings institutions?

16. Sources of CU Funds Describe the main source of funds for credit unions. Why might the average cost of funds to CUs be relatively stable even when market interest rates are volatile?

17. Regulation of CUs Who regulates credit unions? What are the regulators' powers? Where do CUs obtain deposit insurance?

18. Risk of CUs Explain how CUs' exposure to liquidity risk differs from that of other financial institutions. Explain why CUs are more insulated from interest rate risk than are some other financial institutions.

19. Advantages and Disadvantages of CUs Identify some advantages of CUs. Identify disadvantages of CUs that relate to their common bond requirement.

20. Impact of the Credit Crisis Explain how the credit crisis in the 2008–2009 period affected some savings institutions. Compare the causes of the credit crisis to the causes of the SI crisis in the late 1980s.

21. Impact of Interest Rates on an SI Explain why savings institutions may benefit when interest rates fall.

22. Impact of Economic Growth on an SI How does high economic growth affect an SI?

Critical Thinking Question

The Future of Thrift Operations Write a short essay on the future of thrift operations. Should savings institutions be merged into the banking industry, or should they remain distinctly different from commercial banks?

Interpreting Financial News

Interpret the following comments made by Wall Street analysts and portfolio managers.

a. "Deposit insurance can fuel a crisis because it allows weak SIs to grow."

b. "Thrifts are no longer so sensitive to interest rate movements, even if their asset and liability compositions have not changed."

c. "Many SIs did not understand that higher returns from subprime mortgages must be weighed against risk."

Managing in Financial Markets

Hedging Interest Rate Risk As a consultant to Boca Savings & Loan Association, you notice that a large portion of its 15-year, fixed-rate mortgages are financed with funds from short-term deposits. You believe that the yield curve is useful in indicating the market's anticipation of future interest rates, and that the yield curve is primarily determined by interest rate expectations. At the present time, Boca has not hedged its interest rate risk. Assume that a steeply upward-sloping yield curve currently exists.

a. Boca asks you to assess its exposure to interest rate risk. Describe how Boca will be affected by rising interest rates and by a decline in interest rates.

b. Given the information about the yield curve, would you advise Boca to hedge its exposure to interest rate risk? Explain.

c. Explain why your advice to Boca might possibly backfire.

Flow of Funds Exercise

Market Participation by Savings Institutions

Rimsa Savings is a savings institution that provided Carson Company with a mortgage for its office building. Rimsa recently offered to refinance the mortgage if Carson Company will change to a fixed-rate loan from an adjustable-rate loan.

a. Explain the interaction between Carson Company and Rimsa Savings.

b. Why is Rimsa willing to allow Carson Company to transfer its interest rate risk to Rimsa? (Assume that there is an upward-sloping yield curve.)

c. If Rimsa maintains the mortgage on the office building purchased by Carson Company, what is the ultimate source of the money that was provided for the office building? If Rimsa sells the mortgage in the secondary market to a pension fund, what is the source that is essentially financing the office building? Why would a pension fund be willing to purchase this mortgage in the secondary market?

Internet/Excel Exercises

1. Assess the recent performance of savings institutions using the website www.fdic.gov/bank /analytical/qbp. Click on "Quarterly Banking Profile." Then select the most recent quarter and click on "Access QBP." Click on "Savings Institution Section," and summarize the general performance of SIs in the last quarter. Repeat this procedure for the seven preceding quarters, and then summarize the general performance of SIs in the last two years.

2. Go to the website of Heritage Financial Corporation (www.hf-wa.com) or another savings institution of your choice. Under "Filings & Financials," click on "Financial Statements" to retrieve recent income statements. Review the SI's recent performance. Has its income as a percentage of assets increased since the year before? Explain what caused this change over the last year. Has the SI's net interest margin changed since last year? How has its noninterest income (as a percentage of assets) changed over the last year? How have its noninterest expenses changed over the last year? How have its loan loss reserves changed in the last year? Discuss how the SI's recent strategy and economic conditions may explain the changes in these components of its income statement.

3. Go to finance.yahoo.com, enter the symbol HFWA (Heritage Financial Corporation), and click on "Chart." Then retrieve stock price data at the beginning of the last 20 quarters. Next, go to https://fred.stlouisfed.org and retrieve interest rate data at the beginning of the last 20 quarters for the three-month Treasury bill. Record the data on an Excel spreadsheet. Derive the quarterly return for Heritage Financial. Derive the quarterly change in the interest rate. Apply regression analysis in which the quarterly return of Heritage Financial is the dependent variable and the quarterly change in the interest rate is the independent variable (see Appendix B for more information about using regression analysis). Is there a positive relationship or a negative relationship between the interest rate movement and the stock return of Heritage Financial? Is the relationship significant? Offer an explanation for this relationship.

WSJ Exercise

Assessing the Performance of Savings Institutions

Using a recent issue of *The Wall Street Journal*, summarize an article that discusses the recent performance of a particular savings institution. Does the article suggest that the SI's performance was better or worse than the norm? What reason is given for the unusual level of performance?

Online Articles with Real-World Examples

Find a recent practical article available online that describes a real-world example regarding a specific financial institution or financial market that reinforces one or more concepts covered in this chapter.

If your class has an online component, your professor may ask you to post your summary of the article there and provide a link to the article so that other students can access it. If your class is live, your professor may ask you to summarize your application of the article in class. Your professor may assign specific students to complete this assignment or may allow any students to do the assignment on a volunteer basis.

For recent online articles and real-world examples related to this chapter, consider using the following search terms (be sure to include the prevailing year as a search term to ensure that the online articles are recent):

1. [name of a specific savings institution] AND interest income

2. [name of a specific savings institution] AND interest expense

3. [name of a specific savings institution] AND loan loss

4. [name of a specific savings institution] AND credit risk

5. [name of a specific savings institution] AND interest rate risk

6. [name of a specific savings institution] AND earnings

7. [name of a specific savings institution] AND operations

8. savings institution AND income

9. savings institution AND return on assets

10. savings institution AND risk

22

Finance Company Operations

The specific objectives
of this chapter are to:

- Describe the main
  types of finance
  companies.

- Identify the main
  sources and uses of
  finance company
  funds.

- Explain how finance
  companies interact
  with other financial
  institutions.

- Identify the factors
  that determine the
  values of finance
  companies.

- Describe how
  finance companies
  are exposed to
  various forms
  of risk.

Finance companies provide short- and intermediate-term credit to consumers and small businesses. Although other financial institutions provide this service, only finance companies specialize in it. Many finance companies operate with a single office; others have hundreds of offices across the United States and even in foreign countries. Consumer finance operations can be conducted by an independent finance company or by a unit (subsidiary) of a financial conglomerate.

22-1 Types of Finance Companies

Today, finance companies have more than $1 trillion in assets. In aggregate, the amount of their business is similar to that of savings institutions. Some finance companies are independently owned; others are subsidiaries of financial institutions or other corporations. For example, General Motors, Ford Motor Company, Wells Fargo, and Capital One all have finance company subsidiaries.

Finance companies are commonly classified according to the specific services that they offer; the various categories are described next. Some finance companies could fit in every category because they offer all types of services.

22-1a Consumer Finance Companies

Consumer finance companies provide financing for customers of retail stores or wholesalers. For example, a consumer finance company may sponsor a credit card for a retailer so that the retailer can offer its own credit card for its customers. This practice means that customers can purchase products from the retailer on credit, which is provided by the finance company.

Most consumer finance companies also provide personal loans directly to individuals to finance purchases of automobiles and other large household items. Some consumer finance companies also provide mortgage loans.

22-1b Business Finance Companies

Business finance companies offer loans to small businesses. For example, they may provide loans to finance inventory costs. The business uses such a loan to purchase materials that are used in the production process. Once the products are manufactured and sold, the business uses the revenue from their sale to pay off the loan. Business finance companies also provide financing in the form of credit cards that are used by a business's employees for travel or for making purchases on behalf of the business.

22-1c Captive Finance Subsidiaries

A captive finance subsidiary (CFS; sometimes called a captive finance company) is a wholly owned subsidiary whose primary purpose is to finance sales or leases of the parent company's products and services, provide wholesale financing to distributors of the parent company's products, and purchase receivables of the parent company. The actual business practices of a CFS typically include various types of financing apart from just the parent company's business. When a CFS is formed, the subsidiary and the parent company draw up an operating agreement containing specific stipulations, such as the type of receivables that qualify for sale to the CFS and the specific services to be provided by the parent.

The motive for creating a CFS can be easily understood by considering the automobile industry. Historically, automobile manufacturers were unable to finance dealers' inventories and had to demand cash from each dealer. Many dealers were unable to sell cars on an installment basis because they needed cash immediately. Banks were the primary source of capital to dealers. However, banks viewed automobiles as luxury items not suitable for bank financing and were unwilling to buy the installment plans created from automobile sales. For this reason, the automobile manufacturers became involved in financing by setting up finance subsidiaries.

Establishing a CFS can offer several advantages. First, a CFS allows a corporation to clearly separate its manufacturing and retailing activities from its financing activities, so that the performance of its segments can be more easily monitored. Second, when lending to a CFS rather than a division of the parent company, the lender does not have to be so concerned about the claims of others. Third, unlike commercial banks, a CFS has no reserve requirements and no legal prohibitions on how it obtains or uses funds.

22-1d Regulation of Finance Companies

Finance company loans are subject to ceiling interest rates and a maximum maturity. These regulations are imposed by the states, so they also vary among states. Because the state-mandated ceiling rates now exceed the market rates by an appreciable amount, they usually do not restrict the rate-setting decisions made by finance companies. State regulations also require finance companies that are planning to expand by establishing branches across state lines to justify how the planned branch would serve the needs of the people in that location.

In addition, finance companies generally have to comply with federal statutes governing equal credit opportunity, proper disclosure, and truth in lending, as well as the Financial Reform Act of 2010's prohibition against deceptive and unfair practices. The Consumer Financial Protection Bureau, which was established by the Financial Reform Act, is responsible for regulating various consumer finance products and services that may be offered by finance companies and other institutions. In addition, it supervises large nonbank finance companies that provide auto loans. The Financial Reform Act also provides that a very large CFS or independent finance company may be designated as systemically important and subjected to additional regulation.

22-2 Sources and Uses of Funds

Finance companies are distinctly different from commercial banks and savings institutions, in that they do not rely heavily on deposits. Their sources and uses of funds are described next.

22-2a Sources of Funds

The main sources of funds for finance companies are as follows:

- Loans from banks
- Commercial paper
- Deposits
- Bonds
- Capital

Loans from Banks   Finance companies commonly borrow from commercial banks and can consistently renew these loans over time. For this reason, bank loans can provide a continual source of funds, although some finance companies use bank loans mainly to accommodate seasonal swings in their business.

Commercial Paper   Although commercial paper is available only for short-term financing, finance companies can continually roll over their issues to create a permanent source of funds. Only the most well-known finance companies have traditionally been able to issue commercial paper to attract funds, because unsecured commercial paper exposes investors to the risk of default. In recent years, as the popularity of secured commercial paper has grown, more finance companies have sought to access funds through this market.

 The best-known finance companies can issue commercial paper through direct placement, thereby avoiding a transaction fee and lowering their cost of funds. Most companies, however, utilize the services of a commercial paper dealer.

Deposits   Under certain conditions, some states allow finance companies to attract funds by offering customer deposit services similar to those provided by depository institutions. Although deposits have not been a major source of funds for finance companies, they may become more widely used where they are legal.

Bonds   Finance companies in need of long-term funds can issue bonds. The decision to issue bonds versus some alternative short-term financing depends on the company's balance sheet structure and its expectations about future interest rates. When the company's assets are less interest rate-sensitive than its liabilities, and when interest rates are expected to increase, bonds can provide long-term financing at a rate that is completely insulated from rising market rates. If the finance company is confident that interest rates will rise, it might consider using the funds obtained from bonds to offer loans with variable interest rates. Conversely, when interest rates decline, finance companies may use more long-term debt to lock in the cost of funds over an extended period of time.

Capital   Finance companies can build their capital base by retaining earnings or by issuing stock. Like other financial institutions, these companies maintain a low level of capital as a percentage of their total assets. Several finance companies have engaged in initial public offerings of stock so that they could expand their businesses.

WEB

www.nfcc.org
More detailed
information about
consumer loans.

22-2b Uses of Funds

Finance companies use funds for the following purposes:

- Consumer loans
- Business loans and leasing
- Real estate loans

 Each use of funds is described in turn.

Consumer Loans Finance companies extend consumer loans in the form of personal loans. One of the most popular types is an automobile loan offered by a finance company that is owned by a car manufacturer. For example, GM Financial finances the purchases and leases of automobiles built by General Motors. Ford Motor Company and Chrysler also have their own finance companies. Subsidiaries of automobile manufacturers may offer unusually low rates to increase automobile sales.

In addition to offering automobile loans, finance companies may offer personal loans for home improvement, mobile homes, and a variety of other personal expenses. These personal loans are often secured by a co-signer or by real property. The maturities on personal loans are typically less than five years.

Some finance companies also offer credit card loans through a particular retailer. For example, a retail store may sell products to customers on credit and then sell the credit contract to a finance company. Customers make payments to the finance company under the terms negotiated with the retail store. The finance company is responsible for the initial credit approval and for processing the credit card payments. The specific arrangement between a finance company and a retailer will vary, however. Under such an arrangement, the retailer can benefit from the finance company's credit allowance through increased sales; the finance company benefits by obtaining increased business. Finance companies increase their customer base in this way and subsequently may offer additional financing for customers who prove to be creditworthy.

The main competition for finance companies in the consumer loan market comes from commercial banks and credit unions. Finance companies have consistently provided more credit to consumers than credit unions have, but they remain a distant second to commercial banks in this market. Recently, savings institutions have also entered this market and are now considered a major competitor.

Business Loans and Leasing In addition to consumer loans, finance companies provide business (commercial) loans. Companies commonly obtain these loans to cover the span from when they purchase raw materials until they generate cash from sales of the finished goods. Although such loans are short term, they may be renewed, as many companies permanently need financing to support their cash cycle. Business loans are often backed by inventory or accounts receivable.

Some finance companies provide loans to support leveraged buyouts (LBOs). These loans are generally riskier than other business loans but offer a higher expected return.

Finance companies commonly act as factors for accounts receivable; that is, they purchase a firm's receivables at a discount and are responsible for processing and collecting the balances of these accounts. With this type of deal, the finance company incurs any losses due to bad debt. Factoring both reduces a business's processing costs and provides short-term financing, as the business receives cash from the finance company earlier than it would have obtained funds from collecting the receivables.

Another way finance companies provide financing is by leasing. For example, they may purchase machinery or equipment and then lease it to businesses that prefer to avoid the additional debt on their balance sheet that purchases would require. Avoiding debt can be important to a business that is already close to its debt capacity and is concerned that taking on additional debt will adversely affect its credit rating.

Real Estate Loans Finance companies offer real estate loans in the form of mortgages on commercial real estate and second mortgages on residential real estate. Second mortgages, which have become increasingly popular, are typically secured and historically have had a relatively low default rate. In the 2003–2006 period, however, some finance companies offered subprime (low-quality) mortgage loans, which resulted in a higher proportion of loan defaults during the credit crisis in 2008.

Summary of Uses of Funds   The particular allocation of a finance company's uses of funds depends on whether the company is focused on business or consumer lending. Some finance companies provide all types of services. Exhibit 22.1 summarizes the sources and uses of funds; it illustrates how finance companies finance economic growth by channeling funds from institutional investors who purchase the securities they issue to households and small businesses that need funds.

22-2c Interaction with Other Financial Institutions

When finance companies obtain or use funds, they interact with other financial institutions, as summarized in Exhibit 22.2. Because of their concentration in consumer lending, finance companies compete with commercial banks, savings institutions, and credit unions. However, those finance companies with subsidiaries that specialize in other financial services also compete with insurance companies and pension plans.

Finance companies utilize various financial markets to manage their operations, as summarized in Exhibit 22.3. For their core business, these companies commonly rely on money markets (commercial paper) and bond markets to obtain funds. Furthermore, the insurance subsidiaries of finance companies often utilize bond and stock markets to invest funds. These subsidiaries may also use futures, options, and swap markets to hedge the risk of their investments.

Exhibit 22.1   How Finance Companies Finance Economic Growth

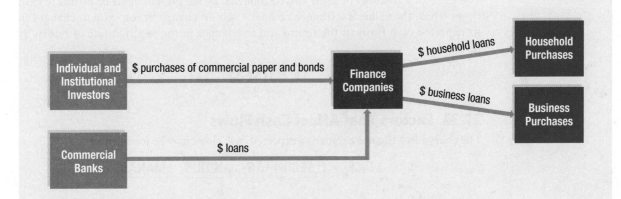

Exhibit 22.2   Interaction between Finance Companies and Other Financial Institutions

TYPE OF FINANCIAL INSTITUTION	INTERACTION WITH FINANCE COMPANIES
Commercial banks and savings institutions	• Compete with finance companies for consumer loan business (including credit cards), commercial loans, and leasing.
Credit unions	• Compete with finance companies for consumer loan business.
Securities firms	• Underwrite bonds that are issued by finance companies.
Pension funds	• Compete with insurance subsidiaries of finance companies that manage pension plans.
Insurance companies	• Compete directly with insurance subsidiaries of finance companies.

Exhibit 22.3 Participation of Finance Companies in Financial Markets

TYPE OF FINANCIAL MARKET	PARTICIPATION BY FINANCE COMPANIES
Money markets	• Finance companies obtain funds by issuing commercial paper.
Bond markets	• Finance companies issue bonds as a method of obtaining long-term funds. • Subsidiaries of finance companies commonly purchase corporate and Treasury bonds.
Mortgage markets	• Finance companies purchase real estate and also provide loans to real estate investors. • Subsidiaries of finance companies commonly purchase mortgages.
Stock markets	• Finance companies issue stock to establish a capital base. • Subsidiaries of finance companies commonly purchase stocks.
Futures markets	• Subsidiaries of finance companies that offer insurance-related services sometimes use futures contracts to reduce the sensitivity of their bond portfolio to interest rate movements. They may also trade stock index futures to reduce the sensitivity of their stock portfolio to stock market movements.
Options markets	• Subsidiaries of finance companies that offer insurance-related services sometimes use options contracts to protect against temporary declines in particular stock holdings.
Swap markets	• Finance companies may engage in interest rate swaps to hedge their exposure to interest rate risk.

22-3 Valuation of a Finance Company

Finance companies (or consumer finance units that are part of a financial conglomerate) are commonly valued by their managers so as to monitor their progress over time or by other financial institutions that are considering an acquisition of the finance company. The value of a finance company can be modeled as the present value of its future cash flows. Thus, the value of a finance company should change in response to changes in its expected cash flows in the future and to changes in the required rate of return by investors:

$$\Delta V = f[\underset{+}{\Delta E(\text{CF})}, \underset{-}{\Delta k}]$$

22-3a Factors That Affect Cash Flows

The change in a finance company's expected cash flows may be modeled as

$$\Delta E(\text{CF}) = f(\underset{+}{\Delta\text{ECON}}, \underset{-}{\Delta R_f}, \underset{?}{\Delta\text{INDUS}}, \underset{+}{\Delta\text{MANAB}})$$

where ECON represents economic growth, R_f represents the risk-free interest rate, INDUS represents industry conditions (such as regulatory constraints), and MANAB represents the abilities of the finance company's management.

Economic Growth   Economic growth can enhance a finance company's cash flows by increasing household demand for consumer loans, thereby allowing the finance company to provide more loans. In addition, loan defaults are usually reduced in periods of strong growth. The valuation of finance companies can be very sensitive to economic conditions because they commonly offer relatively risky loans; in turn, loan repayments are sensitive to economic conditions.

Change in the Risk-Free Interest Rates   A finance company's cash flows may be inversely related to interest rate movements. First, if the risk-free interest rate decreases, other market rates may decline as well. As a result, demand for the finance company's loans may increase.

Second, finance companies rely heavily on short-term funds, and the rates paid on these funds are typically revised in accordance with other interest rate movements. Finance companies' assets (such as consumer loans) commonly have fixed rates, so interest income does not adjust to interest rate movements until those assets reach maturity. Therefore, when interest rates fall, the finance company's cost of obtaining funds declines more than the decline in the interest earned on its loans and investments. An increase in interest rates could reduce the finance company's expected cash flows because the interest paid on its sources of funds increases but the interest earned on its existing loans and investments does not.

Change in Industry Conditions   Industry conditions include regulatory constraints, technology, and competition within the industry. Some finance companies may have a higher valuation if state regulators give them the opportunity to capitalize on economies of scale by expanding throughout the state. However, this practice would result in more competition, in which some finance companies would gain at the expense of others.

Change in Management Abilities   A finance company has control over the composition of its managers and its organizational structure. Its managers attempt to make internal decisions that will capitalize on the external forces (economic growth, interest rates, regulatory constraints) that the institution cannot control. As a consequence, the management skills of a finance company can influence its expected cash flows. In particular, finance companies need skilled managers to analyze the creditworthiness of potential borrowers and assess how future economic conditions may affect their ability to repay their loans.

22-3b Factors That Affect the Required Rate of Return

The required rate of return by investors who invest in a finance company can be modeled as

$$\Delta k = f(\underset{+}{\Delta R_f}, \underset{+}{\Delta RP})$$

where R_f represents the risk-free interest rate and RP represents the risk premium.

The risk-free interest rate is usually expected to be positively related to inflation, economic growth, and the budget deficit level, but inversely related to money supply growth (assuming it does not cause inflation). The risk premium on a finance company is inversely related to economic growth because uncertainty about loan repayments declines when economic conditions are strong. The risk premium is also inversely related to the company's management skills, as more skillful managers may be able to focus on financial services that reduce the finance company's exposure to risk.

Exhibit 22.4 provides a framework for valuing a finance company based on the preceding discussion. In general, the value of a finance company is favorably affected by strong economic growth, a reduction in interest rates, and skilled management. The sensitivity of a finance company's value to these conditions depends on its own characteristics. The higher the risk tolerance reflected in the loans provided by a finance company, the more sensitive its valuation will be to changes in economic growth (and therefore to changes in the ability of borrowers to repay their loans).

Exhibit 22.4 Framework for Valuing a Finance Company

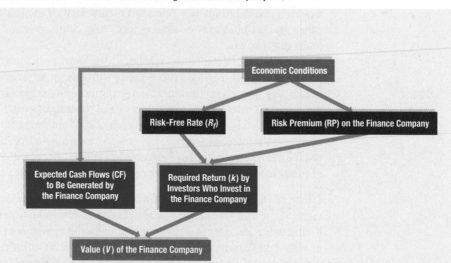

- A stronger economy leads to increased demand for loans (interest income) and other services provided by the finance company (noninterest income), fewer loan defaults, and better cash flows. Economic conditions are especially important for finance companies because the risk that borrowers will default on their loans tends to be higher for them. A weak economy could result in major loan losses.

- The valuation is also influenced by industry conditions and the finance company's management (not shown in the diagram). These factors affect the risk premium (and therefore the required return by investors) and the expected cash flows to be generated by the finance company.

22-4 Exposure of Finance Companies to Risk

Finance companies, like other financial institutions, are exposed to three types of risk:

- Liquidity risk
- Interest rate risk
- Credit risk

Because finance companies' characteristics differ from those of other financial institutions, their degree of exposure to each type of risk differs as well.

22-4a Liquidity Risk

Finance companies generally do not hold many assets that can be easily sold in the secondary market. Thus, if they are in need of funds, they must borrow. Their balance sheet structure does not call for much liquidity, because almost all of their funds come from borrowings rather than deposits. Consequently, these companies are not susceptible to unexpected deposit withdrawals. Overall, finance companies have less liquidity risk compared to other financial institutions.

22-4b Interest Rate Risk

Both the liability and asset maturities of finance companies are short or intermediate term in duration. Therefore, they are not as susceptible to increasing interest rates as those savings institutions that offer fixed-rate mortgage loans. Even so, finance companies can be adversely affected by rising interest rates, because their assets are typically not as rate-sensitive as their liabilities. They can shorten their average asset life or make greater use of adjustable rates if they wish to reduce their interest rate risk.

22-4c Credit Risk

Because the majority of a finance company's funds are allocated as loans to consumers and businesses, credit risk is a major concern. Customers who borrow from finance companies usually exhibit a moderate degree of risk. Although the loan delinquency rate of finance companies is typically higher than that of other lending financial institutions, this higher default level may be more than offset by the higher average rate they charge on their loans. Because their loans entail both relatively high returns and high risk, the performance of finance companies can be quite sensitive to prevailing economic conditions.

Many finance companies provide subprime auto loans, which are made to people with low credit scores and poor credit histories. Like mortgages, auto loans can be securitized, meaning that they are bundled together and sold as a package. Although some critics have expressed concern about the increase in this subprime debt, securitized auto loans tend to receive high ratings. The reasoning is that the credit risk is low because people need their cars to get to work, so they will pay their auto loans even if they cannot afford to make payments on other debt.

22-5 Multinational Finance Companies

Some finance companies are large multinational corporations with subsidiaries in several countries. For example, GM Financial provides auto loan services in North America, Latin America, Europe, and Asia. It provides products and services in local currencies where it does business.

Summary

- Finance companies are classified by type. A consumer finance company provides financing for customers of retail stores or wholesalers, whereas a business finance company offers loans to small businesses. A captive finance subsidiary (CFS) is a wholly owned subsidiary whose primary purpose is to finance sales and leases of the parent company's products and services, provide wholesale financing to distributors of the parent company's products, and purchase receivables of the parent company.

- The main sources of funds for finance companies are loans from banks, sales of commercial paper, bonds, and capital. The main uses of those funds are consumer loans, business loans, leasing, and real estate loans.

- Finance companies compete with depository institutions (such as commercial banks, savings institutions, and credit unions) that provide loans to consumers and businesses. Many finance companies have insurance subsidiaries that compete directly with other insurance subsidiaries.

- Finance companies are valued at the present value of their expected cash flows. Their valuation is highly dependent on economic conditions because qualified borrowers make more requests for loans when economic conditions are favorable. In addition, the loan default rate is usually lower when the economy is strong.

- Finance companies are exposed to credit risk as a result of their consumer loans, business loans, and real estate loans. They are also exposed to liquidity risk because many of their assets are not easily sold in the secondary market. They may also be exposed to interest rate risk.

Point/Counterpoint

Will Finance Companies Be Replaced by Banks?

Point   Yes. Commercial banks specialize in loans and can provide the services that are provided by finance companies. The two types of financial institutions will eventually merge into a single category.

Counterpoint   No. Finance companies and commercial banks tend to target different markets

for loans. Commercial banks will not replace finance companies because they do not serve the same market.

Who Is Correct?   Use the Internet to learn more about this issue and then formulate your own opinion.

Questions and Applications

1. **Exposure to Interest Rate Risk** Is the cost of funds obtained by finance companies very sensitive to market interest rate movements? Explain.

2. **Issuance of Commercial Paper** How are small and medium-sized finance companies able to issue commercial paper? Why do some well-known finance companies directly place their commercial paper?

3. **Finance Company Affiliations** Explain why some finance companies are associated with automobile manufacturers. Why do some of these finance companies offer below-market rates on loans?

4. **Uses of Funds** Describe the major uses of funds by finance companies.

5. **Credit Card Services** Explain how finance companies benefit from offering consumers a credit card.

6. **Leasing Services** Explain how finance companies provide financing through leasing.

7. **Regulation of Finance Companies** Describe the kinds of regulations that are imposed on finance companies.

8. **Liquidity Position** Explain how the liquidity position of finance companies differs from that of depository institutions such as commercial banks.

9. **Exposure to Interest Rate Risk** Explain how the interest rate risk of finance companies differs from that of savings institutions.

10. **Exposure to Credit Risk** Explain how the credit risk of finance companies differs from that of other lending financial institutions.

Critical Thinking Question

The Future of Finance Company Operations
Write a short essay on the future of finance company operations. Should finance companies be merged into

the banking industry, or should they remain distinctly different from commercial banks?

Interpreting Financial News

Interpret the following comments made by Wall Street analysts and portfolio managers.

a. "During a credit crunch, finance companies tend to generate a large amount of business."

b. "Some finance companies took a huge hit as a result of the last recession because they opened their wallets too wide before the recession occurred."

c. "During periods of strong economic growth, finance companies generate unusually high returns without any hint of excessive risk, but their returns are at the mercy of the economy."

Managing in Financial Markets

Managing a Finance Company   As a manager of a finance company, you are attempting to increase the spread between the rate earned on your assets and the rate paid on your liabilities.

a. Assume that you expect interest rates to decline over time. Should you issue bonds or commercial paper to obtain funds?

b. If you expect interest rates to decline, will you benefit more from providing medium-term, fixed-rate loans to consumers or floating-rate loans to businesses?

c. Why would you still maintain some balance between medium-term, fixed-rate loans and floating-rate loans to businesses even if you anticipate that one type of loan will be more profitable under a cycle of declining interest rates?

Flow of Funds Exercise

How Finance Companies Facilitate the Flow of Funds

Carson Company has sometimes relied on debt financing from Fente Finance Company. Fente has been willing to lend money even when most commercial banks have not. Fente obtains funding by issuing commercial paper and focuses mostly on channeling those funds to borrowers.

a. Explain how finance companies are unique by comparing Fente's net interest income, noninterest income, noninterest expenses, and loan losses to those of commercial banks.

b. Explain why Fente performs better than commercial banks in some periods.

c. Describe the flow of funds channeled through finance companies to firms such as Carson Company. What is the original source of the money that is channeled to firms or households that borrow from finance companies?

Internet/Excel Exercises

1. Go to www.onemainfinancial.com. Describe the services offered by OneMain Financial Group.

2. Go to the website of Synchrony Financial (www.synchronycom), which is a large consumer finance company, or select your own consumer finance company. To access income statement information, click on "Investing," then on "Financial Results," and then on "Annual Reports." Review the consumer finance company's recent performance. Has its income as a percentage of assets increased since the year before? Explain what caused this change over the last year. How have its operating expenses changed over the last year? Discuss how the finance company's recent strategy and economic conditions may explain the changes in these components of its income statement.

WSJ Exercise

Finance Company Performance

Using a recent issue of *The Wall Street Journal*, summarize an article that discusses the recent performance of a particular finance company. Does the article suggest that the finance company's performance was better or worse than the norm? What was the reason for the unusual level of performance?

Online Articles with Real-World Examples

Find a recent practical article available online that describes a real-world example regarding a specific financial institution or financial market that reinforces one or more concepts covered in this chapter.

If your class has an online component, your professor may ask you to post your summary of the article there and provide a link to the article so that other students can access it. If your class is live, your professor may ask you to summarize your application of the article in class. Your professor may assign specific students to complete this assignment or may allow any students to do the assignment on a volunteer basis.

For recent online articles and real-world examples related to this chapter, consider using the following search terms (be sure to include the prevailing year as a search term to ensure that the online articles are recent):

1. [name of a specific finance company] AND earnings

2. [name of a specific finance company] AND loans

3. [name of a specific finance company] AND risk

4. [name of a specific finance company] AND net income

5. [name of a specific finance company] AND competition

6. [name of a specific finance company] AND operations

7. [name of a specific finance company] AND return on equity

8. finance company AND income

9. finance company AND return on assets

10. finance company AND risk

23
Mutual Fund Operations

CHAPTER OBJECTIVES

The specific objectives of this chapter are to:

- Provide background information on mutual funds.

- Describe the various types of stock and bond mutual funds.

- Describe key characteristics of money market funds.

- Discuss key characteristics of hedge funds.

- Describe other types of funds.

- Describe the valuation and performance of mutual funds.

WEB

www.bloomberg.com
Information on mutual fund performance.

A **mutual fund** is an investment company that sells shares and uses the proceeds to manage a portfolio of securities. Mutual funds have grown substantially in recent years, and they serve as major suppliers of funds in financial markets.

23-1 Background on Mutual Funds

Mutual funds serve as a key financial intermediary, as summarized in Exhibit 23.1. They sell shares to individual investors and invest the money they receive in a portfolio of securities for the investors. In addition, they accommodate financing needs of corporations by purchasing newly issued stocks and corporate bonds in the primary market. They also accommodate the financing needs of the U.S. Treasury and municipal governments by purchasing newly issued Treasury and municipal bonds in the primary market. Mutual funds also frequently purchase securities in the secondary market, thereby making the securities markets more liquid.

A mutual fund may have holdings of 50 or more securities, yet require a minimum investment of only $250 to $2,500. This low buy-in means that individual investors can invest in a diversified portfolio with just a small investment. In turn, the majority of mutual fund assets are owned by individual investors. Investors who purchase shares of the mutual fund rely on the fund's portfolio managers to make the investment decisions. Mutual funds maintain updated account statements so that shareholders can access their account online to monitor the balance and a record of recent transactions.

Some investment companies offer a family (collection) of many different types of mutual funds so that they can accommodate diverse preferences. Investors can usually transfer money from one mutual fund to another within the same family by accessing their account online. For example, Fidelity manages more than 300 different mutual funds, while Vanguard manages more than 100 different mutual funds.

Mutual funds are sometimes referred to as **open-end funds** because they are open to investors, meaning that they will sell shares to investors at any time. In addition, they allow investors to sell (redeem) the shares back to the fund at any time. Thus, the number of shares of an open-end fund is always changing. Mutual funds also offer various services, such as online access to account information, consolidated account statements, check-writing privileges on some types of funds, and tax information.

The number of mutual funds has grown rapidly over time. Today more than 9,300 different mutual funds operate in the United States, with total assets of more than $19 trillion.

Exhibit 23.1   How Mutual Funds Finance Economic Growth

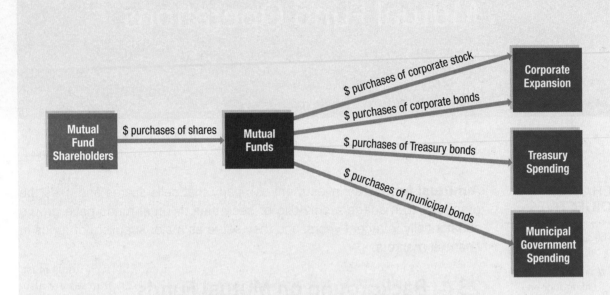

23-1a Pricing Shares of a Mutual Fund

The price per share of a mutual fund is equal to the **net asset value (NAV)** per share, which represents the value of the portfolio (per share) after accounting for expenses incurred from managing the fund. Specifically, the NAV is estimated at the end of each day by first determining the market value of all securities that constitute the mutual fund (any cash is also accounted for). Any interest or dividends accrued in the mutual fund are added to the market value. Then any expenses are subtracted, and the amount is divided by the number of shares of the fund outstanding.

EXAMPLE

Newark Mutual Fund has 20 million shares issued to its investors. It used the proceeds to buy the stocks of 55 different firms. A partial list of its stock holdings is as follows:

NAME OF STOCK	NUMBER OF SHARES	PREVAILING SHARE PRICE	MARKET VALUE
Aztec Co.	10,000	$40	$ 400,000
Caldero, Inc.	20,000	30	600,000
⋮	⋮	⋮	⋮
Zurkin, Inc.	8,000	70	560,000
Total market value of shares today			$500,005,000
+ Interest and dividends received today			+10,000
− Expenses incurred today			−15,000
= Market value of fund			$500,000,000

$$\text{Net asset value} = \text{Market value of fund} \div \text{Number of shares}$$
$$= \$500,000,000 \div 20,000,000$$
$$= \$25 \text{ per share}$$

When a mutual fund pays dividends to its shareholders, its NAV declines by the per-share amount of the dividend payout. The NAV per share of a mutual fund represents the price at which investors can purchase shares or can sell shares back to the mutual fund.

23-1b **Mutual Fund Distributions to Shareholders**

Mutual funds can generate returns to their shareholders in three ways. First, they can pass on any earned income (from dividends or coupon payments) as dividend payments to the shareholders. Second, they can distribute the capital gains resulting from the sale of securities within the fund. A third type of return to shareholders is through mutual fund share price appreciation. As the market value of a fund's security holdings increases, the fund's NAV increases, and the shareholders ultimately benefit when they sell their mutual fund shares.

A mutual fund must distribute at least 90 percent of its taxable income to shareholders if it is to be exempt from taxes on dividends, interest, and capital gains distributed to shareholders. The shareholders are then subject to taxation on these forms of income.

23-1c **Regulation of Mutual Funds**

Mutual funds must adhere to a variety of federal regulations, and all such funds must register with the Securities and Exchange Commission (SEC). Mutual funds are also regulated by state laws, many of which attempt to ensure that investors fully understand the risks.

Information Contained in a Prospectus   Mutual funds are required to provide potential investors with a prospectus that contains information about their objectives, management, and risk. Specifically, the prospectus is required to disclose the following information:

1. The minimum investment required from investors
2. The investment objective of the mutual fund
3. The return on the fund over the past year, the past three years, and the past five years, in comparison to a broad market index
4. The exposure of the mutual fund to various types of risk
5. The services (such as check writing and ability to transfer money online or by telephone) offered by the mutual fund
6. The fees incurred by the mutual fund (such as management fees) that are passed on to the investors
7. Names of the portfolio managers and the length of time that they have been employed by the fund in that position

23-1d **Management of Mutual Funds**

Each mutual fund is managed by one or more portfolio managers, who must focus on achieving the stated investment objective of that fund. These managers, who tend to purchase securities in large blocks, prefer liquid securities that can easily be sold in the secondary market at any time. Because open-end mutual funds allow shareholders to buy shares at any time, their managers stand ready to channel any new cash inflows from investors into new investments.

Portfolio managers may also maintain a small amount of cash for liquidity purposes. If the number of redemptions exceeds the sales of shares at a given point in time, the managers can use this cash to cover the redemptions. If the cash is not sufficient to cover the redemptions, they sell some of their holdings of securities to obtain the cash they need.

Interaction of Mutual Funds with Other Financial Institutions   Mutual funds engage in interactions with other financial institutions, as described in Exhibit 23.2. Mutual funds sometimes purchase stocks or bonds newly issued by financial institutions; in this way, they partially finance the expansion of those institutions. Some mutual funds are owned by commercial banks, in which case bank customers can switch their savings between bank deposits and mutual funds.

Mutual Fund Use of Financial Markets   Each type of mutual fund uses one or more financial markets to manage its portfolio, as described in Exhibit 23.3. Because mutual funds focus on investing in securities, they frequently participate in the securities markets. They also participate in the futures and options markets to hedge against interest

Exhibit 23.2   Interaction between Mutual Funds and Other Financial Institutions

TYPE OF FINANCIAL INSTITUTION	INTERACTION WITH MUTUAL FUNDS
Commercial banks and savings institutions (SIs)	• Money market mutual funds invest in certificates of deposit at banks and SIs, and in commercial paper issued by bank holding companies. • Some commercial banks (such as Citigroup and JPMorgan Chase) have investment company subsidiaries that offer mutual funds. • Some stock and bond mutual funds invest in securities issued by banks and SIs.
Finance companies	• Some money market mutual funds invest in commercial paper issued by finance companies. • Some stock and bond mutual funds invest in stocks and bonds issued by finance companies.
Securities firms	• Mutual funds hire securities firms to execute security transactions for them. • Some mutual funds own a discount brokerage subsidiary that competes with other securities firms for brokerage services.
Insurance companies	• Some stock mutual funds invest in stocks issued by insurance companies. • Some insurance companies have investment company subsidiaries that offer mutual funds. • Some insurance companies invest in mutual funds.
Pension funds	• Pension funds invest in mutual funds, and employer-administered pension funds allow employees to invest in specific mutual funds.

Exhibit 23.3   How Mutual Funds Utilize Financial Markets

TYPE OF MARKET	MUTUAL FUNDS' USE OF THAT MARKET
Money markets	• Money market mutual funds invest in various money market instruments, such as Treasury bills, commercial paper, banker's acceptances, and certificates of deposit.
Bond markets	• Some bond mutual funds invest mostly in bonds issued by the U.S. Treasury or a government agency. Others invest in bonds issued by municipalities or firms. • Foreign bonds are sometimes included in a bond mutual fund portfolio.
Mortgage markets	• Some bond mutual funds invest in bonds issued by the Government National Mortgage Association (GNMA or "Ginnie Mae"), which uses the proceeds to purchase mortgages that were originated by some financial institutions.
Stock markets	• Numerous stock mutual funds purchase stocks with various degrees of risk and potential return.
Futures markets	• Some bond mutual funds periodically attempt to hedge against interest rate risk by taking positions in interest rate futures contracts.
Options markets	• Some stock mutual funds periodically hedge specific stocks by taking positions in stock options. • Some mutual funds take positions in stock options for speculative purposes.
Swap markets	• Some bond mutual funds engage in interest rate swaps to hedge interest rate risk.

rate risk or the risk of adverse stock market conditions. Some mutual funds take speculative positions in futures or options contracts.

23-1e Expenses Incurred by Mutual Fund Shareholders

Mutual funds pass on their expenses to their shareholders. These expenses include compensation to the portfolio managers and other employees, research support, recordkeeping and clerical fees, and marketing fees. Some mutual funds have recently increased their focus on marketing, but more extensive marketing does not necessarily enable a mutual fund to achieve high performance relative to the market or other mutual funds.

Expenses can be compared among mutual funds by measuring the expense ratio, which is equal to the annual expenses per share divided by the fund's NAV. An expense ratio of 2 percent in a given year means that shareholders incur annual expenses reflecting 2 percent of the value of the fund. Many mutual funds have an expense ratio between 0.6 and 1.5 percent. A high expense ratio can have a major impact on the returns generated by a mutual fund for its shareholders over time.

EXAMPLE

WEB

www.sec.gov/fast-answers/answersmffees.htm.html
Detailed information about fees charged by mutual funds to shareholders.

Consider two mutual funds, each of which generates a return on its portfolio of 9.2 percent per year, ignoring expenses. One mutual fund has an expense ratio of 3.2 percent, so its actual return to shareholders is 6 percent per year. The other mutual fund has an expense ratio of 0.2 percent per year (some mutual funds have expense ratios at this level), so its actual return to shareholders is 9 percent per year.

Assume you have $10,000 to invest. Exhibit 23.4 compares the accumulated value of your shares in the two mutual funds over time, assuming that each fund's annual performance remains constant over future years. After five years, the value of the mutual fund with the low expense ratio is approximately 20 percent higher than the value of the mutual fund with the high expense ratio. After 10 years, its value is nearly 40 percent more than the value of the mutual fund with the high expense ratio. After 20 years, its value is 87 percent more. Even though both mutual funds had the same return on investment when ignoring expenses, the returns to shareholders after expenses are very different because of the difference in expenses charged. ●

Exhibit 23.4 How the Accumulated Value Can Be Affected by Expenses (Assume Initial Investment of $10,000 and a Return before Expenses of 9.2 Percent)

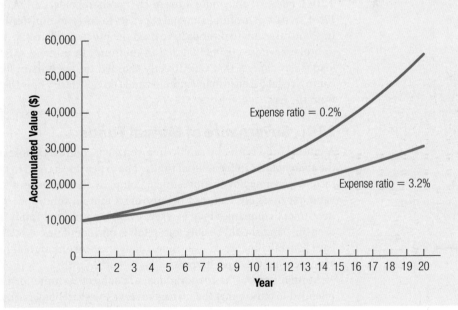

This example illustrates that the higher the expense ratio, the lower the return for a given level of portfolio performance. Mutual funds with lower expense ratios tend to outperform others that have a similar investment objective. That is, funds with higher expenses are generally unable to generate higher returns that could offset those expenses. Because expenses can vary substantially among mutual funds, investors should carefully review the annual expenses of any fund before making an investment.

Sales Charge   Mutual funds may be either **load funds** or **no-load funds**. Load funds are promoted by registered representatives of brokerage firms, who earn a sales charge generally ranging between 3 and 5.75 percent (commonly referred to as a front-end load) when someone invests in the fund. Some investors may believe that this sales charge is worthwhile because the brokerage firm helps determine the type of fund that is appropriate for them. In some cases, front-end load funds offer various discounts that reduce the percentage load for larger investments.

If you invest $10,000 in a load fund and are charged 5 percent, you incur a sales charge of $500 (0.05 × $10,000), so your actual investment in the load fund is $9,500. In other words, on the day you invest in the fund, the value of your holdings is 5 percent less than the amount of funds you initially had available to invest. In contrast, if you invest $10,000 in a no-load fund, you do not incur a sales charge, so your actual investment in the fund is $10,000. ●

Some mutual funds have a **back-end load** (also known as a rear load or reverse load), which is a withdrawal fee charged when the investor withdraws money from the mutual fund. Back-end loads often range between 5 and 6 percent for the first year, but then decline by a certain percentage each subsequent year. Mutual funds with a back-end load may permit investors to withdraw dividends and capital gains at any time without a charge or may allow them to withdraw a specified proportion of the investment each year without incurring a load.

No-load funds are promoted strictly by the mutual fund of concern, thereby avoiding an intermediary. Most investors who feel capable of making their own investment decisions prefer to invest in no-load fund.

12b-1 Fees   Some mutual funds charge shareholders a 12b-1 fee (named for SEC rule 12b-1) as part of the fund's annual expenses to cover administrative or marketing expenses. In some cases, mutual funds have used the proceeds from 12b-1 fees to pay commissions to brokers whose clients invested in the fund. In essence, the fee is substituted for the load (sales charge) that was directly charged to investors in load funds. These fees are controversial because many mutual funds do not clarify how they use the money received from the fees.

23-1f Governance of Mutual Funds

A mutual fund is usually run by an investment company whose owners are different from the shareholders in the mutual funds. The expenses charged to the mutual fund represent income generated by the investment company that manages the mutual fund. Although valid expenses are incurred in running a mutual fund, the expenses charged by some investment companies may be excessive. Many mutual funds have grown substantially over time and should be able to capitalize on economies of scale, yet their expense ratios have generally increased over time. Many investors in mutual funds are not aware of the expenses that they are charged.

Mutual funds, like corporations, are subject to some forms of governance that are intended to ensure that the managers serve the shareholders' interests. Each mutual fund has a board of directors that is supposed to represent the fund's shareholders. The SEC requires that a majority of the directors of a mutual fund board be independent (not employed by the fund). However, an employee of the company can retire and qualify as an independent board member just two years later. In addition, the average annual compensation paid to the board members of large mutual funds exceeds $100,000. Thus, some board members may avoid confronting management about problems if doing so enables them to keep their positions.

Board members of a mutual fund family commonly oversee all funds in the entire family. Consequently, they may concentrate on general issues that are not particular to any one fund and spend a relatively small amount of time on any individual fund within the family. Mutual funds also have a compliance officer who is supposed to ensure that the fund's operations remain in line with its objective and guidelines.

Governance of Corporations by Mutual Funds   Because mutual funds invest large amounts of money in some stocks, they become major shareholders of firms. A mutual fund is often the largest shareholder of many stocks. Portfolio managers of mutual funds that have a large investment in stocks commonly serve on the board of directors of various firms. Even when a fund's managers do not serve on a firm's board, the firm may still attempt to satisfy them so that they do not sell their holdings of the firm's stock.

23-1g Mutual Fund Categories

Mutual funds are typically classified as stock (or equity) mutual funds, bond mutual funds, or money market funds, depending on the types of securities in which they invest. As Exhibit 23.5 shows, based on the market value of assets, stock mutual funds are dominant.

Exhibit 23.5   Composition of Mutual Funds

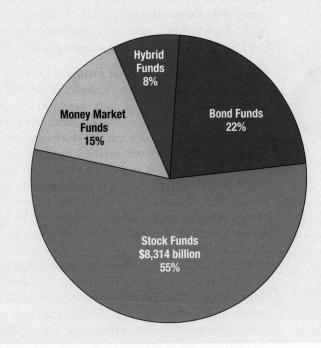

Source: Investment Company Institute.

23-2 Stock and Bond Mutual Funds

Numerous types of stock and bond mutual funds are available, so investors can select a mutual fund that serves their investment objective.

23-2a Types of Stock Mutual Funds

The following stock mutual fund categories are especially popular:

- Growth funds
- Capital appreciation funds
- Growth and income funds
- International and global funds
- Specialty funds
- Index funds
- Multifund funds

Growth Funds   For investors who desire a high return and are willing to accept a moderate degree of risk, **growth funds** are appropriate. These funds are typically composed of stocks of companies that have not fully matured and are expected to grow at a higher than average rate in the future. The primary objective of a growth fund is to achieve an increase in the value of stocks; the fund's managers are less concerned about the generation of steady income.

Capital Appreciation Funds   Also known as aggressive growth funds, **capital appreciation funds** are composed of stocks that have potential for very high growth but may also be unproven. These funds are suited to investors who are willing to risk a possible loss in value.

Growth and Income Funds   Some investors are looking for potential for capital appreciation along with some stability in income. For these investors, a **growth and income fund**, which contains a unique combination of growth stocks, high-dividend stocks, and fixed-income bonds, may be most appropriate.

International and Global Funds   In recent years, awareness of foreign securities has been increasing. Investors historically avoided foreign securities because of the high information and transaction costs associated with purchasing them and monitoring their performance. International mutual funds were created to enable investors to invest in foreign securities without incurring these excessive costs.

The returns on international stock mutual funds are affected not only by foreign companies' stock prices but also by the movements of the currencies that denominate these stocks. As a foreign currency's value strengthens against the U.S. dollar, the value of the foreign stock as measured in U.S. dollars increases. Thus, U.S. investors can benefit not only from higher stock prices but also from a strengthened foreign currency (against the dollar). Of course, they can be adversely affected if the foreign currencies denominating the stocks depreciate.

An alternative to an international mutual fund is a global mutual fund, which includes some U.S. stocks in its portfolio. International and global mutual funds have historically included stocks from several different countries to limit the portfolio's exposure to economic conditions in any single foreign economy.

In recent years, some new international mutual funds have been designed to fully benefit from a particular emerging country or a single continent. Although the potential return from such a strategy is greater, so is the risk, because the entire portfolio value is sensitive to a single economy.

Specialty Funds   Some mutual funds, called **specialty funds**, focus on a group of companies sharing a particular characteristic. For example, industry-specific funds may concentrate on energy, banking, and high-tech stocks. Some funds include only stocks of firms that are likely takeover targets. Other mutual funds specialize in options or other commodities, such as precious metals. Still other mutual funds invest only in socially conscious firms. The risk of specialty funds varies with the particular characteristics of each fund.

Index Funds   Some mutual funds are designed to simply match the performance of an existing stock index. For example, Vanguard offers an **index fund** that is designed to match the S&P 500 index. Index funds are composed of stocks that, in aggregate, are expected to move in line with a specific index. They include many of the same stocks contained in the corresponding index and tend to have very low expenses because they require little portfolio management and execute a relatively small number of transactions.

Index funds have become very popular over time as investors have recognized that most mutual funds do not outperform indexes. Furthermore, investors benefit from these index funds because their expenses are much lower than the expenses of actively managed mutual funds. Some index funds represent specific non-U.S. countries or regions; they may be attractive to investors who wish to invest in a particular foreign market but do not have much knowledge about the specific stocks in that market.

Multifund Funds   A **multifund mutual fund** invests in a portfolio of different mutual funds. It achieves even more diversification than a typical mutual fund because it contains several mutual funds. However, investors incur two types of management expenses: (1) the expenses of managing each individual mutual fund and (2) the expenses of managing the multifund mutual fund. For this reason, the expense ratio of such a mutual fund can be relatively high.

23-2b Types of Bond Mutual Funds

Popular types of bond mutual funds include the following categories:

- Income funds
- Tax-free bond funds
- High-yield junk bond funds
- International and global funds
- Specialty funds

Income Funds   For investors who are mainly concerned with stability of income rather than capital appreciation, **income funds** are appropriate. These funds are usually composed of bonds that offer periodic coupon payments and vary in exposure to risk. Income funds composed of only corporate bonds are susceptible to credit risk, while those composed of only Treasury bonds are not. A third type of income fund contains bonds backed by government agencies, such as the Government National Mortgage Association. Those income funds exhibiting more credit risk will offer a higher potential return, other things being equal.

Tax-Free Bond Funds   Investors in high tax brackets have historically purchased municipal bonds as a way to avoid taxes. Because these bonds are susceptible to default, a diversified portfolio is desirable. Mutual funds containing municipal bonds allow investors in high tax brackets to avoid taxes while maintaining a low degree of credit risk.

High-Yield (Junk) Bond Funds   Investors desiring high returns and willing to incur high risk may consider investing in bond portfolios in which at least two-thirds of the bonds are rated below Baa by Moody's or BBB by Standard & Poor's. Such portfolios are referred to as **high-yield funds** or **junk bond funds**. Typically, the bonds are issued by highly leveraged firms, whose ability to repay the debt is very sensitive to economic conditions.

International and Global Bond Funds   International bond funds contain bonds issued by corporations or governments based in other countries. Global bond funds differ from international bond funds in that they contain U.S. as well as foreign bonds. Global funds may be more appropriate for investors who want a fund that includes U.S. bonds within a diversified portfolio, whereas investors in international bond funds may already have a sufficient investment in U.S. bonds and prefer a fund that focuses entirely on foreign bonds. International and global bond funds provide U.S. investors with an easy way to invest in foreign bonds.

Like bond funds containing only U.S. bonds, international and global bond funds are subject to credit risk based on the financial position of the corporations or governments that issued the bonds. They are also subject to interest rate risk, as the bond prices are inversely related to the interest rate movements in the currency denominating each bond. In addition, these funds are subject to exchange rate risk, as the NAV of the funds is determined by translating the foreign bond holdings to dollars. Thus, when the foreign currency denominating the bonds weakens, the translated dollar value of those bonds will decrease.

Maturity Classifications of Bond Funds   Each type of bond fund may be further segmented according to whether it focuses on long-term or intermediate-term bonds. Intermediate-term bond funds invest in bonds with 5 to 10 years remaining until maturity. In contrast, long-term bond funds typically contain bonds with 15 to 30 years until maturity. The bonds in these funds usually have a higher yield to maturity, but their values are more sensitive to interest rate movements than the bonds in intermediate-term funds. For a given type of bond fund classification (such as income or tax-free bond funds), investors can choose between a fund containing bonds with intermediate-term maturities versus long-term maturities. Investors who expect interest rates to decline would likely prefer a bond fund containing long-term bonds, because that fund would benefit to a greater degree from the interest rate movements.

23-2c Hybrid Funds

Hybrid funds are another category of mutual funds. As their name suggests, they include both stocks and bonds (and sometimes other types of assets as well). Some of the most popular types of hybrid funds are discussed here.

Asset Allocation Funds   Asset allocation funds contain a variety of investments (such as stocks, bonds, and money market securities). The portfolio managers adjust the compositions of these funds in response to expectations. For example, a given asset allocation fund will tend to concentrate more heavily on bonds if interest rates are expected to decline; it will focus on stocks if a strong stock market is expected. These funds may even concentrate on international securities if the portfolio managers forecast favorable economic conditions in foreign countries.

Target Date Funds　Target date funds (also known as life-cycle or age-based funds) are one of the most popular types of hybrid funds. These funds are designed to automatically change the proportions of stocks and bonds as the investor ages. The idea is that younger investors should have a higher proportion of stocks, whereas older investors need income as they retire and therefore should hold a higher proportion of bonds. Consequently, most target date funds are held in retirement accounts such as 401(k) accounts.

Alternative Strategy Funds　After the credit crisis of 2008–2008, when the stock market declined by more than 50 percent, a number of investors looked for mutual funds that might shield them from extreme market volatility. Alternative strategy funds are designed to fulfill that purpose and have become increasingly popular in recent years. These funds use more complex trading strategies than other mutual funds; they hold nontraditional assets, such as global real estate, derivative securities, and commodities. Because alternative strategy funds are designed to have low correlation with the stock market, they are unlikely to perform as well as stock mutual funds when the stock market performs well.

WEB

finance.yahoo.com
/mutualfunds
Links to information
about mutual funds,
including a list of the
top-performing funds.

23-3 Money Market Funds

Money market mutual funds, sometimes called money market funds (MMFs), sell shares to individuals and use the proceeds to invest in money market (short-term) instruments for their investors. They maintain updated account statements so that shareholders can access their account online to monitor the balance and a record of recent transactions. Most MMFs allow check-writing privileges, although they may place restrictions on the number of checks written per month or on the minimum amount of the check.

Because the sponsoring investment company is willing to purchase MMFs back at any time, investors can liquidate their investment whenever they desire. In most years, additional sales of shares exceed redemptions, allowing the companies to build their MMF portfolios by purchasing more securities. When redemptions exceed sales, the company accommodates the amount of excessive redemptions by selling some of the assets contained in the MMF portfolios. If the fund distributes at least 90 percent of its income to its shareholders, the fund itself is exempt from federal taxation.

WEB

www.investor.gov
Under "Introduction
to Investing," click on
"Investment Products"
to find detailed
information about
money market funds.

23-3a Asset Composition of Money Market Funds

Exhibit 23.6 shows the composition of money market fund assets in aggregate. Commercial paper, CDs, and repurchase agreements are the most widely held components. This composition reflects the importance of each type of asset for MMFs overall, rather than representing the typical composition of any particular MMF. Each MMF is usually more concentrated in whatever assets serve its objective.

23-3b Risk of Money Market Funds

Money market funds are generally perceived to be very safe. They have a low level of credit risk because the money market securities in which they invest have low credit risk. Because they invest in instruments with short-term maturities, their market values are not overly sensitive to movements in market interest rates (as are mutual funds containing long-term bonds). Therefore, their exposure to interest rate risk is low. In general, MMFs are normally characterized as having relatively low risk and low expected returns. Many investors maintain a money market fund to serve their liquidity needs, and invest money not needed for liquidity in stock or bond funds.

Exhibit 23.6   Composition of Taxable Money Market Fund Assets in Aggregate

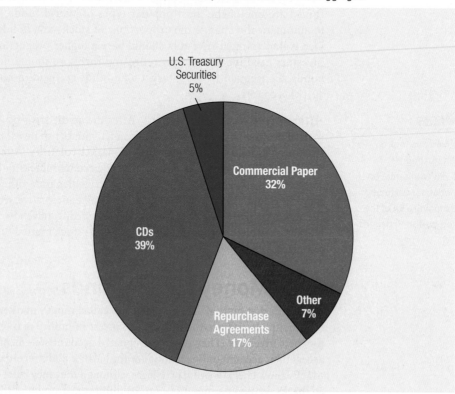

Source: Investment Company Institute, 2019.

23-3c Management of Money Market Funds

The role of MMF portfolio managers is to maintain an asset portfolio that satisfies the underlying objective of a fund. If the managers expect a stronger economy, they may replace maturing risk-free securities (Treasury bills) with more commercial paper or CDs.

Some MMFs have very little flexibility in their composition. For example, some MMFs may as a rule maintain a high percentage of their investment in T-bills to assure investors that they will refrain from investing in risky securities.

Even if managers cannot change the type of money market securities in the portfolio, they can still influence performance by changing the maturities of the securities in which they invest. For example, if managers expect interest rates to increase in the future, they should use funds generated from maturing securities to purchase new securities with shorter maturities.

During the credit crisis of 2008–2009, investors became concerned about the risk of MMFs that invested in commercial paper. Many financial institutions issue commercial paper, and many were struggling during the credit crisis. Some of the commercial paper that Lehman Brothers (a large securities firm) had issued was backed by mortgage-backed securities, which declined in value during the credit crisis. Lehman Brothers went bankrupt in September 2008, which triggered massive withdrawals from MMFs

WEB

www.sec.gov/fast-answers/answershedge
.htm.html
Provides information on hedge funds.

that invested in commercial paper. In one week during September 2008, withdrawals from MMFs exceeded $140 billion.

23-4 Hedge Funds

Hedge funds sell shares to wealthy individuals and financial institutions and use the proceeds to invest in securities. They differ from mutual funds in several ways. First, they require a much larger initial investment (such as $1 million), whereas mutual funds typically allow a minimum investment in the range of $250 to $2,500. Second, many hedge funds are not "open," in the sense that they may not always accept additional investments or accommodate redemption requests unless advance notice is provided. Some hedge funds permit investors to withdraw their investments but require advance notice of 30 days or more. Third, hedge funds may stipulate that investors cannot make withdrawals (redemptions) for several years after their initial investment. This feature is distinctly different from most mutual funds, which allow redemptions at any time. Fourth, hedge funds are subject to minimal regulation. Unlike mutual funds, they are not required to provide extensive information to prospective investors.

Fifth, hedge funds invest in a wide variety of investments to achieve high returns. Thus, unlike mutual funds, they are not restricted in terms of the types of investments that they wish to pursue. Any particular hedge fund might invest in growth stocks, dividend stocks, bonds, and commodities, and might also take short positions in these types of investments as well. For example, consider a hedge fund that believes Chemical Company X is undervalued relative to Chemical Company Y. Rather than just invest in X, the hedge fund may also take a short position in Y. In this way, it is not really focusing its position on the chemical industry in general, but rather is attempting to capitalize on the pricing discrepancy between two firms. This strategy is quite different from that of mutual funds, which are typically restricted from taking short positions.

Hedge funds may also invest in the equity of private companies. Such investments are very illiquid, which would make it difficult for hedge funds to quickly sell these investments. If hedge funds allow frequent redemptions by their investors, they might need to sell illiquid investments at a large discount to obtain cash to satisfy redemptions. However, some hedge funds can afford to pursue illiquid investments because they are allowed to use investor funds for several years before allowing possible redemptions.

In recent years, some hedge funds have purchased businesses that they manage, similar to private equity funds. They either oversee or replace managers to improve the performance of the business, with the goal of ultimately selling the business for a much higher price than they paid. Some hedge funds purchase distressed assets of firms that are in or near bankruptcy.

Many hedge funds were created by owners who were previously successful as mutual fund portfolio managers. They may have created a hedge fund to have a bigger stake in the business or to have more flexibility in their investment decisions. Most hedge funds are organized as limited partnerships. There are at least 11,000 hedge funds in the United States, with a combined market value of approximately $3.5 trillion.

23-4a Hedge Funds' Use of Financial Leverage

Hedge funds commonly use borrowed funds to complement the equity that they receive and invest. This use of financial leverage allows them to make more investments with a given amount of equity and can magnify the returns.

EXAMPLE   Durham Hedge Fund uses $3 of borrowed funds for every $1 of equity that it invests. Therefore, it can obtain $4 of assets for each $1 of equity that it invests. If its investment results in a positive 20 percent return on assets (ROA), this represents a return on its equity (ROE) investment of

$$ROE = ROA \times (Assets/Equity)$$
$$= 20\% \times (4/1)$$
$$= 80\%$$

If Durham Hedge Fund used only equity (no borrowed funds) to invest in assets, its return on equity would have been only 20 percent, the same as its return on assets. The financial leverage in this example allowed the hedge fund to magnify its returns to investors by four times the return on assets. ●

Of course, financial leverage can also magnify negative returns (losses), so it increases the risk to investors.

EXAMPLE   Consider the previous example in which Durham Hedge Fund used $3 of borrowed funds for every $1 of equity that it invests, so that it can obtain $4 of assets for each dollar of equity invested. But now assume that its investment results in a negative 20 percent return on the assets. This represents a return on its equity investment of

$$ROE = ROA \times (Assets/Equity)$$
$$= -20\% \times (4/1)$$
$$= -80\%$$

If this hedge fund had used only equity (no borrowed funds) to invest in assets, its loss would have been only 20 percent. ●

23-4b Hedge Fund Fees

Hedge funds charge a management fee of between 1 and 2 percent of the investment per year. In addition, they charge an incentive fee that is based on the return of the fund. The typical incentive fee is 20 percent of the return.

EXAMPLE   Consider a hedge fund that charges a management fee of 2 percent and an incentive fee of 20 percent of the annual return. In the most recent year, the fund earned a return of 15 percent. The investors in this fund would have paid an incentive fee of 3 percent (computed as 20 percent of the 15 percent return) along with a 2 percent management fee, or a total fee of 5 percent of their total investment. Considering that some index mutual funds have a very small management fee and no incentive fee, this hedge fund would have been a better investment only if its performance exceeded that of index funds by approximately 5 percent in that year. ●

23-4c Hedge Funds' Pursuit of Information

Hedge funds commonly attempt to pursue an information advantage that allows them to make good investments. Yet, the competition among hedge funds and other institutional investors makes it difficult for any hedge fund to access more or better information.

ETHICS   *Hedge Funds' Reliance on Expert Networks*   Hedge funds often hire experts with experience in a particular industry to serve as consultants and offer their insight about the industry or specific firms within that industry. Hedge funds rely heavily on experts for information about stocks in the technology industry, because valuating technology companies is so difficult. An expert might be able to offer critical information that suggests that some technology companies are currently misvalued, which could enable the hedge fund to make investments that capitalize on that information.

If experts have inside information, they are not supposed to provide it when they are hired as consultants. However, there is a fine line between insight derived from public information and insight derived from private information. For example, consider an expert who predicts that the computer industry in general will likely experience an increase in orders over the next month. This general opinion could be derived from private information that the orders for computers at the expert's firm are increasing this month. The U.S. government has charged many experts with disclosing inside information to hedge funds in recent years.

ETHICS

23-4d Short Selling by Hedge Funds

A common strategy used by hedge funds is to take a very large short position in stocks that they believe are overvalued. They recognize that some publicly traded companies may issue misleading financial statements that inflate their reported earnings and, therefore, may inflate their stock prices. Some hedge funds thoroughly investigate such firms, because they can earn very large returns by shorting the stocks of these firms before other investors or regulators or credit agencies recognize that the financial statements are misleading. A hedge fund may even publicly accuse a company of manipulative accounting after it has taken a short position. If many investors believe the hedge fund's claims, they may sell their holdings of the stock, which could drive the stock price down.

EXAMPLE

In April and May of 2008, David Einhorn, president of Greenlight Capital, received a great deal of attention in the financial media when he criticized the lack of financial disclosure by Lehman Brothers, which was one of the largest securities firms at the time. The market valuations of mortgages and mortgage-backed securities had weakened substantially in the first four months of 2008, and Lehman Brothers had heavily invested in these types of assets. Einhorn noted that Lehman had written down only a relatively small amount of these assets, which could cause its earnings to be overstated. Based on his concerns, Einhorn's hedge fund had taken a short position in Lehman Brothers stock. When Einhorn first publicized his concerns, Lehman's stock price was about $40 per share. Lehman Brothers publicly disputed Einhorn's allegations and expressed optimism about its financial position and prospects.

In June 2008, Lehman reported a quarterly loss of $2.8 billion and recognized $4.1 billion in asset write-downs. By then, its stock price had fallen to approximately $30 per share, down about 25 percent in the two months since Einhorn voiced his concerns. Lehman's chief financial officer said that Lehman Brothers would raise $6 billion in new capital that it did not need, but could use to pursue business opportunities. A few days later, Lehman Brothers announced that it was replacing its chief financial officer and its chief operating officer.

Just three months later, Lehman Brothers reported a quarterly loss of $3.9 billion and acknowledged an additional $5.6 billion in asset write-downs. At this time, Lehman's stock price was approximately $7 per share, and its chief executive officer stated that Lehman has been distracted by the public scrutiny but was now on the right track. Five days later, Lehman Brothers filed for bankruptcy.

With the failure of the company, Einhorn's concerns, publicized just four months earlier, were convincingly validated. Furthermore, an independent audit of Lehman Brothers conducted after its bankruptcy verified its lack of financial disclosure. ●

Hedge funds have taken large short positions in once-popular stocks such as Enron, WorldCom, Krispy Kreme, and Groupon while the stocks were highly valued because of inflated earnings. Once the media reported that the financial statements of these firms were being questioned, the prices of these stocks declined, and the hedge funds closed out their positions. The SEC attempts to detect fraudulent financial reporting, but it does not have the resources to closely monitor the financial statements of every publicly traded company. Thus, hedge funds have ample opportunities to detect financial fraud, and in this way they help to trigger stock price corrections.

Some companies that are subjected to these actions claim that hedge funds are manipulating their stock price downward. In contrast, hedge funds would argue that they are just correcting the overpriced stock, which was caused by the company's exaggeration of earnings. If a company is truly performing well and is properly disclosing its financial condition, its valuation should be able to withstand any false allegations, and anyone making false allegations could be charged with fraud. Moreover, any hedge funds that make fraudulent claims should incur losses on their short positions once the company provides sufficient transparency to prove those hedge funds wrong.

ETHICS

Short Selling during the Credit Crisis   During the credit crisis of 2008–2009, hedge funds were accused of making market conditions worse by taking short positions in some of the financial institutions that held subprime mortgages or other mortgage-related securities. The SEC imposed temporary restrictions on short sales of stocks of financial institutions that were highly exposed to subprime mortgages. The hedge funds would likely have justified their short sale strategies by arguing that the financial institutions with heavy exposure to subprime mortgages were overvalued because they had not been fully transparent about their exposure. To the extent that short selling by hedge funds lowers stock prices toward their proper value, the market becomes more efficient.

ETHICS

23-4e Madoff Fund Scandal

Bernard Madoff managed a large and well-respected hedge fund that included various institutions, charities, and wealthy individuals among its investors. The fund reportedly earned favorable returns every year. When some investors wanted to cash out of their investments in December 2008, there was no money available for them. Madoff admitted that he had been periodically using money from new investors to pay off investors who wanted to cash out of the fund. The potential losses to investors were estimated to be as high as $50 billion, making this possibly the biggest financial scandal in U.S. history.

One major lesson from this scandal is that hedge funds deserve closer scrutiny from regulators than they have received in the past. The SEC was alerted several times over the previous nine years to possible irregularities in the Madoff fund, but it failed to detect the fraud.

23-4f Regulatory Reform of Hedge Funds

In July 2010, the Financial Reform Act (also called the Dodd-Frank Act) was enacted; it contained many provisions that were designed to stabilize the financial system. The act mandates that hedge funds managing more than $100 million register with the SEC as investment advisers. These hedge funds must also disclose financial data that can be used by the Financial Stability Oversight Council (created by the Financial Reform Act) to assess systemic risk in the financial system. In addition, the act prevents commercial banks from investing more than 3 percent of their capital in hedge fund institutions, private equity funds, or real estate funds.

23-5 Other Types of Funds

In recent years, several other types of funds have become very popular. These include closed-end funds, exchange-traded funds, venture capital funds, private equity funds, and real estate investment trusts. Each type is described in turn.

23-5a Closed-End Funds

Closed-end funds issue shares and use the proceeds to make investments in stocks or bonds representing a particular sector or country on behalf of their investors. Unlike open-end mutual funds, closed-end funds are closed to new investors after the initial offering of shares. In addition, they do not repurchase (redeem) the shares they sold. Investors who purchased shares of closed-end funds can sell the shares on a stock exchange (in the secondary market), and new investors can purchase the shares on the stock exchange.

Some closed-end funds engage in secondary offerings of new shares and use the proceeds to expand their investment portfolios. In addition, some closed-end funds periodically buy back some of their existing shares on the stock exchange where their shares are listed when they believe that the shares are undervalued.

Approximately 530 closed-end funds operate in the United States. Of these funds, 60 percent invest mainly in bonds or other debt securities, whereas the other 40 percent focus on stocks. The closed-end stock funds represent particular sectors or countries, which enables investors to invest in a portfolio of stocks that reflects a particular sector or country. The total market value of closed-end funds is less than $300 billion, which is much smaller than the total market value of open-end mutual funds.

Unlike open-end funds, closed-end funds can be sold short by investors. This allows investors to capitalize on their expectations that stock prices of a particular sector or country represented by the closed-end fund will decline.

Market Price of Closed-End Funds The market price of a closed-end fund can deviate from the aggregate value of the underlying stocks (measured by net asset value per share). For some closed-end funds, the shares are priced higher than the aggregate value of the respective portfolio. This often occurs when the shares represent stocks of countries that have investment restrictions. Investors from the United States who want to invest in those stocks are willing to pay a premium beyond the market value of the stocks because they cannot easily obtain the stocks otherwise. For many other closed-end funds, the shares are priced at a discount relative to the underlying stocks. This may occur because some of the stocks held by the closed-end funds are illiquid because they represent small firms.

The premium or discount on a closed-end fund can change over time. For example, if a fund's premium increases relative to its NAV (or if its discount is reduced), the return to the fund's shareholders is increased. Some investment strategies focus on investing in closed-end funds that are priced at a large discount from their NAV. This strategy is based on the premise that closed-end funds with large discounts in price are undervalued. Applying this strategy will not always generate high risk-adjusted returns, however, because the market price of some closed-end funds with large discounts could continue to decline over time (their discount could become more pronounced).

23-5b Exchange-Traded Funds

Exchange-traded funds (ETFs) are designed to mimic particular stock indexes and are traded on a stock exchange just like stocks. Unlike an open-end fund, an ETF has a fixed number of shares. ETFs are somewhat similar to open-end mutual funds that invest in a specific stock index, but their shares are traded on an exchange and their share price changes throughout the day. They can be purchased on margin, just like stocks. They are very appealing to institutional investors and individual investors; more than $5 trillion is invested in ETFs. Vanguard, BlackRock, and State Street offer a wide variety of ETFs and dominate the ETF market. Today approximately 2,000 different ETFs are offered in the United States.

Management of ETFs   Because ETFs are intended to mimic a particular index, they differ from most open- and closed-end funds in that they are not actively managed. Some investors may view this as a disadvantage because the ETFs are not trying to outperform an existing index. Yet mutual funds with active management do not necessarily achieve higher returns than benchmarks and could have lower returns. In addition, some investors prefer the lack of active management because the fees are much lower for ETFs. The annual fee on ETFs is, on average, about 0.50 percent.

Some investment companies have recently established actively managed ETFs, which mimic a particular index but allow the manager to increase the level of investment (with borrowed funds) when the manager expects more favorable returns. When the manager expects less favorable returns, no borrowed funds are used. The annual fees of actively managed ETFs are, on average, about 0.70 percent. This rate is higher than the fee for traditional nonmanaged ETFs, but lower than the typical annual fee for open-end mutual funds.

Capital Gains on ETFs   Because ETFs are not actively managed, they usually do not have capital gains and losses that must be distributed to shareholders. Exchange-traded funds have become very popular in recent years because they are an efficient way for investors to invest in a particular stock index.

Liquidity of ETFs   ETFs are more liquid than shares of open-end mutual funds because they can be sold at any moment during trading hours. Conversely, mutual fund shares are sold at the end of the day. This difference can be important for investors who trade shares frequently. However, for investors who hold their investments for long-term periods, this difference may be negligible.

Brokerage Fees When Purchasing ETFs   One disadvantage of ETFs is that each purchase of additional shares must be executed through the exchange where they are traded. Investors incur a brokerage fee from purchasing the shares, just as if they had purchased shares of a stock. This cost is especially important to investors who plan on making frequent additions to their investment in a particular ETF.

Short Sales of ETFs   Like closed-end funds, ETFs can be sold short. In fact, investors more commonly short sell ETFs than closed-end funds as ETFs are more liquid, which makes it easier to execute the short sales. The shares of ETFs sold short represent about 19 percent of all ETF shares. This ratio is about 10 times larger than it is for individual stocks, which is attributed to investors who may more commonly bet on price declines of sectors or countries in aggregate than on individual stocks. In addition, some of the short selling of ETFs is conducted by investors in an effort to hedge a portion of their existing assets. For example, a financial institution that currently holds a very large portfolio of technology stocks may be concerned about the price movements during the next week, although it has confidence in those stocks over the long run. It could take a short position in a technology stock ETF over the next week to hedge its holdings of individual technology stocks.

Popular ETFs   Exchange-traded funds are commonly classified as broad based, sector, or global, depending on the specific index that they mimic. The broad-based funds are the most popular, but both sector and global ETFs have experienced substantial growth in recent years. One popular ETF is the PowerShares QQQ, or Cube (its trading symbol is QQQ), which represents the Nasdaq 100 index of technology firms. Cubes are ideal for investors who believe that technology stocks will perform well but do not want to select individual technology stocks.

even if they are not expected to outperform the market? Explain.

11.   Money Market Funds How do money market funds differ from other types of mutual funds in terms of how they use the money invested by shareholders? Which securities do MMFs invest in most often? How can an MMF accommodate shareholders who wish to sell their shares when the amount of proceeds received from selling new shares is less than the amount needed to cover the withdrawals?

12.   Risk of Money Market Funds Explain the relative risk of the various types of securities in which a money market fund may invest.

13.   Interest Rate Risk of Funds Is the value of a money market fund or a bond fund more susceptible to rising interest rates? Explain.

14.   Diversification among Mutual Funds Explain why diversification across different types of mutual funds is highly recommended.

15.   Impact of Credit Crisis on Hedge Funds Explain why some hedge funds failed as a result of the credit crisis of 2008–2009.

16.   REITs Explain the difference between equity REITs and mortgage REITs. Which type would likely be a better hedge against high inflation? Why?

Advanced Questions

17.   Comparing Management of Open- versus Closed-End Funds Compare the management of a closed-end fund with that of an open-end fund. Given the differences in the funds' characteristics, explain why the management of liquidity is different in the open-end fund as compared with the closed-end fund. Assume that the funds are the same size and have the same goal, to invest in stocks and to earn a very high return. Which portfolio manager do you think will achieve a larger increase in the fund's net asset value? Explain.

18.   Selecting a Type of Mutual Fund Consider the prevailing conditions that could affect the demand for stocks, including inflation, the economy, the budget deficit, the Fed's monetary policy, political conditions, and the general mood of investors. Based on the current conditions, recommend a specific type of stock mutual fund that you think would perform well. Offer some logic to support your recommendation.

19.   Comparing Hedge Funds and Mutual Funds Explain why hedge funds may be able to achieve higher returns for their investors than mutual funds do. Explain why hedge funds and mutual funds may have different risks. When the market is overvalued, why might hedge funds be better able to capitalize on the excessive market optimism than mutual funds can?

20.   How Private Equity Funds Can Improve Business Conditions Money that individual and institutional investors previously invested in stocks is now being invested in private equity funds. Explain why this should result in improved business conditions.

21.   Source of Mutual Fund versus Private Equity Fund Returns Equity mutual funds and private equity funds generate returns for their investors in different ways. Explain this difference. Which type of fund do you think would be better able to capitalize on a weak, publicly traded firm that has ignored all forms of shareholder activism?

22.   Impact of Private Equity Funds on Market Efficiency In recent years, private equity funds have grown substantially. Will the creation of private equity funds increase the semistrong form of market efficiency in the stock market? Explain.

23.   Hedge Funds' Reliance on Expert Networks Explain hedge funds' motivation to rely on expert networks in recent years.

Critical Thinking Question

Hedge Fund Strategy   A critic recently claimed that hedge funds increase market volatility when they publicize (and document) that a public corporation exaggerated its earnings. The critic argued that hedge funds should not be allowed to make such public statements and should not be allowed to take short positions that bet against the firm that is being criticized. Write a short essay that supports or refutes this opinion.

Interpreting Financial News

Interpret the following comments made by Wall Street analysts and portfolio managers.

a. "Just because a mutual fund earned a 20 percent return in one year, that does not mean that investors should rush into it. The fund's performance must be market adjusted."

b. "An international mutual fund's performance is subject to conditions beyond the fund manager's control."

c. "Small mutual funds will need to merge to compete with the major players in terms of efficiency."

Managing in Financial Markets

Investing in Mutual Funds As an individual investor, you are attempting to invest in a well-diversified portfolio of mutual funds so that you will be somewhat insulated from any type of economic shock that may occur.

a. An investment adviser recommends that you buy four different U.S. growth stock funds. Because these funds contain more than 400 different U.S. stocks, the adviser says that you will be well insulated from any economic shocks. Do you agree? Explain.

b. A second investment adviser recommends that you invest in four different mutual funds that are focused on different countries in Europe. The adviser says that you will be completely insulated from U.S. economic conditions and that your portfolio will therefore have low risk. Do you agree? Explain.

c. A third investment adviser recommends that you avoid exposure to the stock markets by investing in four different U.S. bond funds. The adviser says that because bonds make fixed payments, these bond funds have very low risk. Do you agree? Explain.

Flow of Funds Exercise

How Mutual Funds Facilitate the Flow of Funds

Carson Company is considering a private placement of bonds with Venus Mutual Fund.

a. Explain the interaction between Carson and Venus Mutual Fund. How would Venus serve Carson's needs, and how would Carson serve Venus's needs?

b. Why does Carson interact with Venus Mutual Fund instead of trying to obtain the funds directly from individuals who invested in Venus Mutual Fund?

c. Would Venus Mutual Fund serve as a better monitor of Carson Company than the individuals who provided money to the mutual fund? Explain.

Internet/Excel Exercises

1. Assess mutual fund performance using the website finance.yahoo.com/mutualfunds or an alternative financial website. What is the best-performing mutual fund for this year to date (YTD)? What is the net asset value (NAV) of this fund? What is the five-year return on this fund? Do you think mutual fund rankings change frequently? Why or why not?

2. Go to finance.yahoo.com/screener/mutualfund /new. Describe the constraints that you would impose when selecting funds. Impose those constraints on the category, past performance, ratings, and other characteristics, and then allow the screener to identify appropriate mutual funds for you. List one or more mutual funds that satisfied your criteria.

3. Go to finance.yahoo.com and search for MVC (the symbol for the closed-end fund MVC Capital, which invests in U.S. stocks). Click on "5y" just above the stock price trend to review the stock price movements over the last five years. Click on "Chart," then on "Comparison," and select "S&P500" to compare the

trend of MVC's price with the movements in the S&P stock index. Does it appear that MVC's performance is influenced by general stock market movements?

4. Go to finance.yahoo.com and search for DNP (the symbol for the closed-end fund DNP Select Income Fund, which invests in bonds). Retrieve stock price data at the beginning of the last 20 quarters. Then go to fred.stlouisfed.org and retrieve interest rate data at the beginning of the last 20 quarters for the three-month T-bill. Record the data on an Excel spreadsheet. Derive the quarterly return of DNP. Derive the quarterly change in the interest rate. Apply regression analysis in which the quarterly return of DNP is the dependent variable and the quarterly change in the interest rate is the independent variable (see Appendix B for more information about using regression analysis). Is there a positive or a negative relationship between the interest rate movement and the stock return of DNP? Is the relationship significant? Offer an explanation for this relationship.

WSJ Exercise

Performance of Mutual Funds

Using an issue of *The Wall Street Journal*, summarize an article that discusses the recent performance of a specific mutual fund. Has this mutual fund's performance been better or worse than the norm? What reason is given for the particular level of performance?

Online Articles with Real-World Examples

Find a recent practical article available online that describes a real-world example regarding a specific financial institution or financial market that reinforces one or more concepts covered in this chapter.

If your class has an online component, your professor may ask you to post your summary of the article there and provide a link to the article so that other students can access it. If your class is live, your professor may ask you to summarize your application of the article in class. Your professor may assign specific students to complete this assignment or may allow any students to do the assignment on a volunteer basis.

For recent online articles and real-world examples related to this chapter, consider using the following search terms (be sure to include the prevailing year as a search term to ensure that the online articles are recent):

1. [name of a specific mutual fund] AND objective
2. [name of a specific mutual fund] AND expense ratio
3. [name of a specific mutual fund] AND risk
4. [name of a specific mutual fund] AND classification
5. [name of a specific mutual fund] AND management
6. [name of a specific mutual fund] AND performance
7. [name of a specific closed-end fund] AND performance
8. [name of a specific closed-end fund] AND risk
9. [name of a specific money market fund] AND performance
10. [name of a specific exchange-traded fund] AND performance

24
Securities Operations

Securities firms serve as important intermediaries by helping governments and firms raise funds. They also facilitate transactions between investors in the secondary market.

24-1 Functions of Securities Firms

Securities firms perform many different functions. They engage in investment banking services such as facilitating security offerings for corporations and government agencies, the securitization of mortgages, and advisory and financing services for corporations that want to restructure their operations. Securities firms that perform the investment banking functions just listed are sometimes referred to as *investment banks*. Many securities firms also provide brokerage services or engage in proprietary trading.

Some securities firms are independent, but many others are part of a financial conglomerate. Although some securities firms have become part of a bank holding company structure, their securities operations are distinctly different from commercial banking operations, which is why they deserve coverage in a separate chapter.

24-1a Facilitating Stock Offerings

A securities firm acts as an intermediary between a corporation issuing securities and investors by providing the following services:

- Origination
- Underwriting
- Distribution of stock
- Advising
- Private placement of stock

Origination　When a corporation decides to issue stock publicly, it may contact a securities firm. The securities firm can recommend the appropriate amount of stock to issue by estimating the amount of stock that the market can likely absorb without causing a reduction in the stock price. To determine the appropriate price for the newly issued stock, it evaluates the corporation's financial condition. If the corporation has issued stock to the public before, the price at which new stock can be issued should be similar to the prevailing stock price on its outstanding stock.

In the case of an initial public offering (IPO), the company has no stock outstanding; thus, there is no existing market price for the shares. In this scenario, the securities firm will compare the corporation's financial characteristics with those of similar firms in the

603

same industry that have stock outstanding to help determine the proper valuation of the corporation and, therefore, the price at which the stock should be sold.

WEB

www.sec.gov/edgar
.shtml
Information on
upcoming IPOs and
the securities firms
that are involved in the
underwriting process.

The corporation issuing the stock registers with the Securities and Exchange Commission (SEC). All information relevant to the security, as well as the agreement between the issuer and the securities firm, must be provided in the **registration statement**, which is intended to ensure that the issuing corporation discloses accurate information. The required information includes the **prospectus**, which discloses relevant financial data on the firm and provisions applicable to the security. The prospectus can be issued only after the registration is approved, which typically takes 20 to 40 days. SEC approval does not guarantee the quality or safety of the securities to be issued; instead, it simply acknowledges that a firm is disclosing accurate information about itself.

The securities firm, along with the issuing firm, may meet with institutional investors who might be interested in buying some of the new stock that will be issued. In the case of an IPO, representatives of the securities firm and the issuing firm engage in a road show, in which they travel to various cities and meet with institutional investors to discuss the issuing firm's plans for using the funds obtained from the offering.

Underwriting   The original securities firm may form an **underwriting syndicate** by asking other securities firms to underwrite a portion of the stock. In such an arrangement, each participating firm shares in the underwriting fees paid by the issuer. Some of the major securities firms for underwriting include Bank of America's Merrill Lynch division, Goldman Sachs, JPMorgan Chase & Co., and Morgan Stanley.

The term *underwrite* is sometimes wrongly interpreted to mean that the underwriting syndicate guarantees the price at which shares will be sold. In reality, stock offerings usually entail a **best-efforts agreement**, whereby the securities firm does not guarantee a price to the issuing corporation; that is, the issuing corporation bears the risk that the proceeds from the stock offering will be less than it had hoped to raise. When securities firms facilitate IPOs, they attempt to price the stock high enough to satisfy the issuing firm. The higher the average price at which the shares are issued, the greater the proceeds received by the issuing firm will be. If a securities firm prices a stock too high, however, it will not be able to place the entire issue. The reputation of the underwriting syndicate is at stake when it attempts to place the stock of the issuing firm: Other corporations that may issue stock in the future will monitor its ability to place the stock.

Securities firms must also attempt to satisfy the institutional investors that may invest in the IPO. The higher the price that institutional investors pay for the stock being issued, the lower the return that they will earn on their investment when they sell the stock. Underwriting syndicates recognize that other institutional investors monitor stock prices after offerings to determine whether the initial offer price charged by the syndicate was appropriate. If the institutional investors do not earn reasonable returns on their investment, they may not invest in future IPOs. Because securities firms rely on institutional investors to purchase stocks in bulk when placing shares of newly issued stock, they want to maintain a good relationship with them.

Research indicates that securities firms tend to underprice IPOs. That is, institutional investors that invest at the offer price earn high returns, on average, if they retain the investment for a short-term period, such as three months or less. Much of the return occurs within the first few days after the IPO. Consequently, the returns to investors who purchase the shares shortly after the IPO are generally poor.

Distribution of Stock   Once all agreements between the issuing firm, the originating securities firm, and other participating securities firms are complete and the registration is approved by the SEC, the stock may be sold. The prospectus is distributed to all potential purchasers of the stock, and the issue is advertised to the public. In some cases, the issue sells within hours. If the issue does not sell as expected, the underwriting syndicate will likely have to reduce the price to complete the sale. The demand for the stock is somewhat influenced by the sales force involved in selling the stock. Some securities firms participating in a syndicate have brokerage subsidiaries that can sell stock on a retail level. Others may specialize in underwriting but still utilize a group of brokerage firms to sell the newly issued stock. The brokers earn a commission on the amount they sell, but they do not guarantee a specific amount of sales.

When a corporation places stock publicly, it incurs two types of **flotation costs**, or costs of placing the securities. First, it must pay fees to the underwriters who place the stock with investors. Second, it incurs **issue costs** including printing, legal, registration, and accounting expenses. Because these issue costs are not significantly affected by the size of the issue, flotation costs as a percentage of the value of securities issued are lower for larger issues.

Advising   The securities firm acts as an adviser throughout the **origination** stage of the IPO. Even after the stock is issued, the securities firm may continue to provide advice on the timing, amount, and terms of future financing.

Private Placements of Stock   Securities firms are also hired to facilitate private placements of stock. With a **private placement** (or direct placement), an entire stock offering may be placed with a small set of institutional investors and not offered to the general public. Under the SEC's Rule 144A, firms may engage in private placements of stock without filing the extensive registration statement that is required for public placements. Consequently, the issuing firm's costs of reporting are lower than those incurred with a public placement. In addition, the underwriting services are more manageable because it may not be necessary to contract with an underwriting syndicate.

Institutional investors that are willing to hold the stock for a long period of time are prime candidates for participating in a private placement. Because all the stock is held by a small set of institutional investors, no secondary market for the stock will be available. To compensate for this lack of liquidity, institutional investors may expect a higher return on the stock.

24-1b **Facilitating Bond Offerings**
When facilitating a bond offering, a securities firm provides the same five main services as it does for a stock offering.

Origination   The securities firm may suggest a maximum amount of bonds that should be issued based on the issuer's characteristics. The main concern of the institutional investors that will purchase the bonds is the issuer's credit risk. If the issuer already has a high level of outstanding debt, the bonds may not be well received by the market because investors may doubt the issuer's ability to meet the debt payments. Consequently, the bonds will need to offer a relatively high yield to attract investors, which in turn will increase the cost of borrowing to the issuer.

The coupon rate, the maturity, and other provisions of the bonds depend on the characteristics of the issuing firm. The asking price for the bonds is determined by evaluating market prices of existing bonds that are similar in their degree of risk, term to maturity, and other provisions.

Issuers of bonds must register with the SEC. The registration statement contains information about the bonds to be issued, outlines the agreement between the securities firm and the issuer, and includes a prospectus with financial information about the issuer.

Underwriting Bonds   A securities firm may agree to *firm-commitment underwriting*, whereby it guarantees the purchase of the entire bond issue at a specified price. Under these conditions, the issuing firm knows the amount of proceeds it will receive in advance of the bond offering. The securities firm, however, is exposed to the risk that the bond offering will not sell as well as expected, and that it may need to buy some of the bonds itself. For this reason, a securities firm might be willing to make such a commitment only if it has already surveyed institutional investors about the bond offering and is very confident that it will be able to place the entire bond issue at a price equal to or above the price it guaranteed to the issuer. Alternatively, the securities firm and the firm issuing the bonds may agree to *best-efforts underwriting*, whereby the securities firm does not guarantee that it will sell the entire bond issue.

As with stocks, the securities firm may organize an underwriting syndicate of securities firms to participate in placing the bonds. Each securities firm assumes a portion of the risk. Of course, the potential income earned by the original securities firm is reduced with such an arrangement as well.

Distribution of Bonds   Upon SEC approval of the registration, a prospectus is distributed to all potential purchasers of the bonds, and the issue is advertised to the public. The asking price on the bonds is usually set at a level that will ensure the sale of the entire issue. The flotation costs generally range from 0.5 to 3 percent of the value of the bonds issued, a level that can be significantly lower than the flotation costs of issuing stock.

Advising   As with a stock placement, a securities firm that places bonds for issuers may serve as an adviser to the issuer even after the placement is completed. Most issuers of bonds will need to raise long-term funds in the future and will consider the securities firm's advice on the type of securities to issue at that time.

Private Placements of Bonds   If an issuing corporation knows of a potential purchaser for its entire issue, it may be able to sell its securities directly without offering the bonds to the general public (or using the underwriting services of a securities firm). Such a private placement avoids the underwriting fee. In recent years, corporations have been increasingly using private placements. Potential purchasers of securities that are large enough to buy an entire issue include insurance companies, commercial banks, pension funds, and bond mutual funds. Securities can even be privately placed with two or more of these institutions. Private placements of bonds are more common than private placements of stocks.

The price paid for privately placed securities is determined by negotiations between the issuing corporation and the purchaser. Although the securities firm is not needed in such a transaction for underwriting purposes, it may advise the issuing corporation on the appropriate terms of the securities and identify potential purchasers.

A possible disadvantage of a private placement is that the demand may not be as strong as for a publicly placed issue because some institutional investors may not be willing to hold the bonds until maturity. Thus, only a fraction of the market can be targeted. This could force a lower price for the bonds, resulting in a higher cost of financing for the issuing firm.

Overall, securities firms serve as important financial intermediaries between corporations and governments that need funds, and institutional investors that have funds to invest. Exhibit 24.1 illustrates how securities firms help corporations and governments raise funds, thereby facilitating economic growth.

Exhibit 24.1   How Securities Firms Facilitate Economic Growth

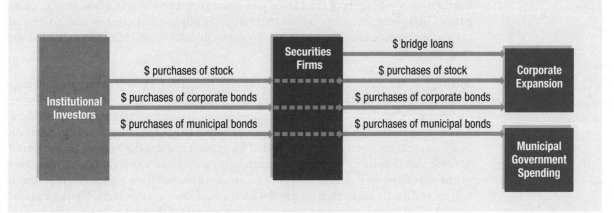

24-1c Securitizing Mortgages

Some securities firms securitize individual mortgages by obtaining them from the financial institutions that originate them, bundling them into packages (in tranches) based on their risk level, hiring a credit rating agency to assign a rating to the packages, and selling the packages to institutional investors. This securitization process is beneficial to the mortgage originators that want to focus on origination or servicing of mortgages, rather than on financing them. Securitization facilitates the sale of smaller mortgage loans that cannot be easily sold in the secondary market on an individual basis. It enables institutional investors such as mutual funds, pension funds, and insurance companies to invest in large bundles of mortgages that have already been assigned a risk rating. Securities firms earn a fee for serving as an intermediary between the mortgage originators and the institutional investors that purchase the packages of mortgages.

They may also package mortgages with other debt securities (such as automobile loans and credit card loans) when engaged in the securitization process.

24-1d Advising Corporations on Restructuring

Securities firms often serve as advisers for corporations that wish to restructure their operations. They conduct a valuation of various existing and potential components of a corporation so that they can recommend how it should restructure its operations. Securities firms commonly suggest that the corporation could benefit from revising its ownership structure by engaging in a carve-out, spinoff, or divestiture, as explained next. For each option, the securities firm can execute the transactions to revise the ownership structure of the corporation, receiving fees for its services in each case.

Carve-out   A securities firm may recommend that a corporation engage in a **carve-out** and then sell part of one of its units to new shareholders through an IPO. Typically, the parent sells about 20 percent of the shares of the new entity, but the new firm has its own management and board of directors. One motive for establishing a carve-out is to raise cash by selling part of a unit that does not fit well with the other businesses run by the parent. Because the new entity will be free to pursue its own line of business without being constrained to fit within the parent's overall operations, the new firm may be valued higher than when it was wholly owned by the parent. Furthermore, managers of the carved-out unit may receive shares of the new stock as part of their compensation, which more directly aligns their interests with those of their shareholders and, therefore, may potentially lead to an increased valuation for the new firm.

Spinoff   Alternatively, a securities firm may recommend that a corporation engage in a **spinoff**, in which the corporation creates a new independent firm from an existing division and distributes shares of stock representing that unit to its existing shareholders. A common motive for establishing a spinoff is that the corporation wants to focus on new areas that have considerable potential for growth and decides to separate out an old division that is unlikely to grow very much in the future. As with a carve-out, managers of the new firm may receive shares of its stock as part of their compensation, which will more directly align their interests with those of their shareholders. Unlike a carve-out, a spinoff simply shifts ownership, so the parent's valuation is lowered because it no longer owns the unit; that is, the unit becomes an independent company. Although a spinoff does not generate new cash for the parent, the combined market value of its stock plus the restructured parent's stock may exceed the pre-spinoff market value of the parent's stock.

Divestiture   A securities firm might sometimes recommend that a corporation engage in a divestiture, in which it sells one or more of its existing units. As with a carve-out or a spinoff, the motive for engaging in divestiture may be that the unit is more valuable when separated from the parent. However, a divestiture differs from a carve-out in that the parent does not retain partial ownership of the unit, but simply sells the entire unit to another company.

Merger   Securities firms commonly serve as advisers on mergers. In such cases, they assess the potential synergies that might result from combining two businesses, and they attempt to determine whether the synergies would be worthwhile for the potential acquirer after considering the premium that the acquirer will likely have to pay to obtain controlling interest in the target firm. Securities firms may suggest that some of a target firm's divisions will not be compatible with the acquirer's business. Thus, after a target firm is acquired, some of its individual divisions may be sold (divested), a process referred to as **asset stripping**.

24-1e Financing for Corporations

When securities firms serve as advisers on mergers, they may also help the acquirer obtain financing. The financing by securities firms may be especially important for acquirers that pursue leveraged buyouts (LBOs). An acquirer may not be able to afford an LBO because of constraints on the amount of funds it can borrow. In such a case, securities firms can help the acquirers issue stock or bonds, as explained earlier. They may also provide a **bridge loan** that serves as temporary financing until the acquirer has access to other funds. Some securities firms may even provide equity financing, whereby they become part owner of the acquired firm.

Exhibit 24.2 illustrates how securities firms participate in an acquisition. Note how many different functions the securities firms may perform for the acquiring firms, all of which generate fees or interest income.

Exhibit 24.2 Participation of Securities Firms in an Acquisition

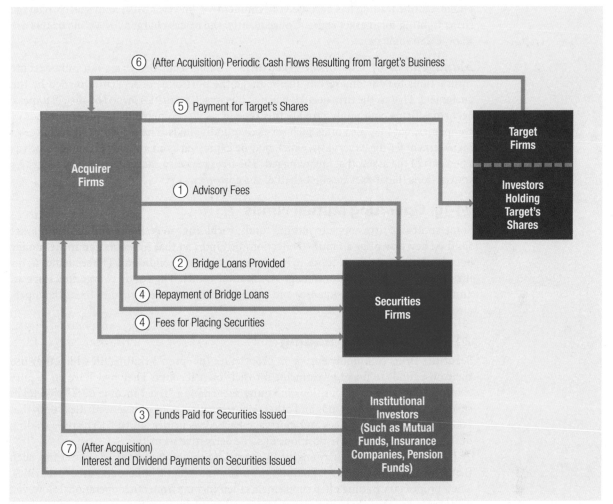

24-1f **Providing Brokerage Services**

Securities firms commonly serve as brokers by executing buy or sell orders desired by their customers. They execute large orders placed by institutional investors, such as an order to purchase 100,000 shares of a specific stock. They also execute orders placed by individuals as well as short-sale transactions for their customers.

Full-Service versus Discount Brokerage Services Brokerage firms can be classified by the services they provide. **Full-service brokerage firms** provide information and personalized advice and execute orders. In contrast, **discount brokerage firms** execute orders only upon request; they do not provide advice. Discount brokers are often unable to maintain long-term relationships with clients because the services they provide are difficult to differentiate from those offered their competitors. The required minimum opening balance for a discount broker is typically in the range of $1,000 to $3,000.

Online Orders Many investors now place orders online rather than calling brokers. Brokerage firms have reduced their costs by implementing online order systems because supporting the online systems is less expensive than having brokers receive the orders by phone. Online trading has become very competitive, however, with numerous brokerage firms fighting for market share. Consequently, the prices charged for online orders are $5 or less in some cases.

Management of Customer Accounts   Some securities firms not only execute transactions for customers, but also manage the portfolios of securities owned by the customers. That is, the firm decides when to buy or sell securities owned by the customers. Securities firms commonly provide this type of service to manage the pension funds of companies, but may also offer such services to individuals. The securities firm charges a management fee for its services, which may be expressed as an annual percentage (such as 1 percent) of the assets that are managed. The firm may also charge fees for any securities transactions that it executes on behalf of the customer.

24-1g Operating Mutual Funds

Some securities firms operate mutual funds, including stock, bond, and money market funds. They may offer a family (collection) of funds, so that investors can move money between different types of funds in response to economic conditions. The securities firms hire portfolio managers to manage the mutual funds. The funds charge investors an annual fee, which covers expenses and provides income to the securities firms that operate the funds.

24-1h Proprietary Trading

Securities firms commonly engage in proprietary (or "prop") trading, in which they use their own funds to make investments for their own account. They may have an "equity trading desk" that takes positions in equity securities, a "fixed-income desk" that takes speculative positions in bonds and other debt securities, a "mortgage securities" desk that takes positions in mortgages and mortgage-backed securities, and a "derivatives trading desk" that takes speculative positions in some derivative securities.

Large securities firms may engage in a very large amount of proprietary trading, such that they maintain very large holdings of stocks, mortgages, bonds, and other securities. Their proprietary trading often supplements their income from other operations. However, some securities firms have experienced financial problems as a result of taking on excessive risk when investing their own funds.

Barings Bank   Barings Bank was established in 1763 and became one of the most prominent financial institutions in England, offering commercial and securities services. In 1995, Nick Leeson, a trader of currencies at Barings' Singapore branch, circumvented trading restrictions and invested much more money than Barings realized. By the time his excessive trading was discovered, Leeson's account had suffered losses of more than $600 million, which wiped out Barings' capital.

Société Générale   In 2008, Société Générale, a large French bank, incurred $7.2 billion in trading losses due to huge unauthorized trades by Jérôme Kerviel, one of its employees. Kerviel's assignment was to take positions in European stock indexes for the company. During 2007, he circumvented the company's computerized controls on the size of the positions that he could take. His supervisors were unaware of the size of his positions.

Bear Stearns   In 2008, the Wall Street securities firm Bear Stearns suffered major losses from investing in mortgage-backed securities. It had relied heavily on borrowed funds (financial leverage) in an effort to magnify its return on investment, but that strategy also meant that its losses were magnified. Once creditors recognized its difficulties, they cut off their credit to the firm, and Bear Stearns suffered liquidity problems. It was ultimately saved from bankruptcy by the U.S. government, as explained later in this chapter.

WEB

www.goldmansachs
.com
Information on
securities firms'
performance and
services.

Lehman Brothers   Lehman Brothers, another Wall Street securities firm, also suffered financial problems due to bad investments in mortgage-backed securities and heavy reliance on borrowed funds. It filed for bankruptcy in September 2008, as explained later in this chapter.

Underlying Cause of Investment Problems   The underlying cause of the problems experienced by each of the four securities firms just described was the huge incentive to take risk. Many employees of securities firms have earned bonuses of more than $1 million in a single year as a result of generating high returns on investment for their securities firms. Thus, they have a strong incentive to pursue investments that may offer high returns, even if the risks are high. The Volcker Rule, which applies to commercial banks and securities firms that have adopted a bank holding company structure, has placed some limits on proprietary trading, as discussed later in this chapter.

24-1i Summary of Services Provided

Exhibit 24.3 summarizes the services commonly provided by securities firms. The proportion of income derived from each type of service in any particular year varies among securities firms. Some firms emphasize investment banking functions such as underwriting and advising, so they generate a higher proportion of income from underwriting and advising fees. Conversely, other firms emphasize brokerage services, so they generate a higher proportion of their income from trading commissions.

Exhibit 24.3   Sources of Income for a Securities Firm

INVESTMENT BANKING SERVICES	
Underwriting	Fees from underwriting stock offerings by firms or underwriting bond offerings by firms and government agencies
Advising	Fees for providing advice to firms about: • Identifying potential targets • Valuing targets • Identifying potential acquirers • Protecting against takeovers
Restructuring	Fees for facilitating: • Mergers • Divestitures • Carve-outs • Spinoffs
BROKERAGE SERVICES	
Management fees	Fees for managing an individual's or a firm's securities portfolio
Trading commissions	Fees for executing securities trades requested by individuals or firms in the secondary market
Margin interest	Interest charged to investors who buy securities on margin
INVESTING ITS OWN FUNDS	
Investing	Profits from investing in securities

Market conditions can also affect the proportion of income earned by a securities firm from particular services. In periods when many companies launch IPOs, securities firms will generate more income from underwriting activities. In periods characterized by a high level of merger activity, securities firms generate more income from advisory services for corporate restructuring.

Some securities firms attempt to diversify their services so that they can capitalize on economies of scope and potentially reduce their exposure if the demand for any particular service is weak. However, demand tends to be highly correlated across services: When market conditions are weak, the volume of IPOs, mergers, securitizations, and secondary market trades is usually low. Under these conditions, securities firms will likely perform poorly.

24-1j Interaction with Other Financial Institutions

As part of providing their financial services, securities firms commonly interact with various types of financial institutions, as summarized in Exhibit 24.4. They offer investment advice and execute security transactions for financial institutions that maintain security portfolios. They also compete against those financial institutions that have brokerage subsidiaries. Furthermore, they compete with some commercial banks that underwrite securities and manage mutual funds. Because securities firms often offer some banking and insurance services and because many insurance companies and commercial banks offer securities services, it is sometimes difficult to distinguish among the various types of financial institutions.

24-1k Participation in Financial Markets

When securities firms provide financial services, they participate in all types of financial markets, as summarized in Exhibit 24.5. They place newly issued securities and execute trades of existing securities for their clients in money markets, mortgage markets, bond markets, and stock markets. In addition, their proprietary trading activity exposes them to fluctuations in stock markets and bond markets.

Exhibit 24.4   Interactions between Securities Firms and Other Financial Institutions

TYPE OF FINANCIAL INSTITUTION	INTERACTIONS WITH SECURITIES FIRMS
Commercial banks and savings institutions	• Compete with securities firms that provide brokerage services. • Compete directly with securities firms to provide merger advisory services.
Mutual funds	• Rely on securities firms to execute trades. • Are sometimes owned by securities firms. • Purchase newly issued securities that are underwritten by securities firms.
Insurance companies	• Receive advice from securities firms on which securities to buy or sell. • Rely on securities firms to execute securities transactions. • Receive advice from securities firms on how to hedge against interest rate risk and market risk. • Purchase stocks and bonds that are underwritten by securities firms. • May compete directly with securities firms to sell mutual funds to investors. • May provide financing for LBOs to securities firms. • May acquire or merge with a securities firm so as to offer more diversified services.
Pension funds	• Receive advice from securities firms on which securities to buy or sell. • Rely on securities firms to execute securities transactions. • Receive advice from securities firms on how to hedge against interest rate risk and market risk. • Purchase newly issued securities that are underwritten by securities firms.

Exhibit 24.5 Participation of Securities Firms in Financial Markets

TYPE OF FINANCIAL MARKET	PARTICIPATION BY SECURITIES FIRMS
Money markets	• Some securities firms have created money market mutual funds, which invest in money market securities. • Securities firms underwrite commercial paper and purchase short-term securities for their own investment portfolios.
Bond markets	• Securities firms underwrite bonds in the primary market, advise clients on bonds to purchase or sell, and serve as brokers for bond transactions in the secondary market. • Some bond mutual funds have been created by securities firms. • Securities firms facilitate mergers, acquisitions, and LBOs by placing bonds for their clients. • Securities firms purchase bonds for their own investment portfolios.
Mortgage markets	• Securities firms underwrite securities that are backed by mortgages for various financial institutions.
Stock markets	• Securities firms underwrite stocks in the primary market, advise clients on which stocks to purchase or sell, and serve as brokers for stock transactions in the secondary market. • Securities firms purchase stocks for their own investment portfolios.
Futures markets	• Securities firms advise large financial institutions on how to hedge their portfolios with financial futures contracts. • Securities firms serve as brokers for financial futures transactions.
Options markets	• Securities firms advise large financial institutions on how to hedge their portfolios with options contracts. • Securities firms serve as brokers for options transactions.
Swap markets	• Some securities firms engage in interest rate swaps to reduce their exposure to interest rate risk. • Many securities firms serve as financial intermediaries in swap markets.

Conflicts of Interest from Participation   When securities firms serve as brokers or as advisers on financial transactions, they are subject to some potential conflicts of interest. In the brokerage business, their fees are likely to depend on the amount of shares traded, which means they would benefit more from recommending that investors change their investments often rather than retain their investments over a long-term period. In the merger advisory business, they would benefit more from advising companies to engage in mergers than they would from advising companies to avoid mergers, because they receive many of their fees only if a merger occurs.

Because securities firms tend to earn larger profits when they execute transactions for their clients, they commonly offer incentives to their employees that are based on (or influenced by) the volume of transactions executed. Consequently, employees have an incentive to generate a large number of transactions, even if that practice does not serve the best interests of the client. In some cases, investor accounts managed by securities firms have had an unusually large number of transactions. Some securities firms have also promoted specific securities to their clients while taking the opposite position (the counterparty) in those transactions.

Situations like these are sometimes the result of a few employees and do not necessarily reflect the culture of the securities firm. However, a securities firm can influence the behavior of its employees by the incentives it uses to set their compensation. Providing employees with a code of principles of ethical behavior is not sufficient to ensure ethical conduct if bonuses are strictly based on the number or dollar amount of transactions that are executed. In the most publicized cases of unethical behavior at securities firms, the employees' actions were motivated by the desire to receive large bonuses.

24-1l **Expanding Functions Internationally**

Most large securities firms have expanded their functions internationally, which offers several possible advantages. First, their international presence allows them to place securities in international markets for corporations or governments. Second, some corporations that are heavily involved with international mergers and acquisitions prefer to receive advice from securities firms that have subsidiaries in all potential markets. Third, institutional investors that invest in foreign securities prefer securities firms that can easily handle such transactions.

Growth in International Joint Ventures In recent years, securities firms have expanded their international business by engaging in joint ventures with foreign securities firms. In this way, they can penetrate foreign markets, yet maintain only a limited stake in each project. Many securities firms have also increased their global presence by facilitating the privatization of government-owned in foreign markets such as Latin America and Eastern Europe.

WEB

www.seclaw.com
/securitiesregulations
Federal rules and
regulations related to
securities firms.

Growth in International Securities Transactions The growth in international securities transactions has created more business for the larger securities firms. For example, many stock offerings are now conducted across numerous countries as some corporations attempt to achieve global name recognition. In addition, an international stock offering can avoid the downward pressure on the stock's price that might occur if the entire issue is sold in the domestic country. Large securities firms facilitate international stock offerings by creating an international syndicate to place the securities in various countries. Those securities firms that have established a global presence receive most of the requests for international stock offerings.

24-2 **Regulation of Securities Firms**

Securities firms are subject to a wide variety of regulations. The SEC plays a key role in regulation by enforcing financial disclosure laws that attempt to ensure that investors who buy or sell securities have access to accurate financial information. In particular, these laws give the SEC the power to require publicly traded companies to provide sufficient financial information to existing or prospective investors. However, securities firms have generally been subject to very limited regulation in terms of how they use their funds.

24-2a **Stock Exchange Regulations**

Stock exchanges impose regulations on securities firms in an effort to prevent unfair or illegal practices, ensure orderly trading, and address customer complaints. The New York Stock Exchange (NYSE) and the Nasdaq market are regulated by the Financial Industry Regulatory Authority (FINRA), which was formed by the merger of the NYSE's regulatory committee and the National Association of Securities Dealers in 2007. FINRA's surveillance department monitors trading patterns and behavior by market makers and floor traders. It also has enforcement divisions that investigate possible violations and can take disciplinary action. FINRA can take legal action as well, and it sometimes works with the SEC to correct cases of market trading abuse.

The SEC tends to establish general guidelines that can affect trading on security exchanges, whereas the specific exchange takes responsibility for the day-to-day regulation of exchange trading. Regulation of trading behavior is necessary to ensure that investors who place orders are properly accommodated. This can establish credibility within the systems used to execute securities transactions.

In addition to the SEC and FINRA, the Federal Reserve Board has some regulatory influence because it determines the credit limits (margin requirements) on securities purchased.

Insurance on Cash and Securities Deposited at Brokerage Firms   The **Securities Investor Protection Corporation (SIPC)** offers insurance on cash and securities deposited at brokerage firms and can liquidate failing brokerage firms. The insurance limit is $500,000, including $250,000 for cash claims. The SIPC uses premiums assessed on brokers that are registered with the SEC to maintain its insurance fund, which currently has a balance of more than $2 billion. In addition to its insurance fund, the SIPC has a $2.5 billion line of credit with the U.S. Treasury. Because the SIPC boosts investor confidence in the securities industry, economic efficiency is increased; in turn, market-related concerns are less likely to trigger a run on deposits of cash and securities at securities firms.

24-2b Regulations That Affect Securities Firms

Several laws and regulations mentioned in previous chapters apply directly or indirectly to securities firms. In addition to the laws and regulations summarized here, the regulations issued after the credit crisis of 2008–2009 apply to securities firms; they are discussed later in the chapter in the context of the credit crisis.

Financial Services Modernization Act   In 1999, Congress enacted the Financial Services Modernization Act, which allows a financial holding company to own subsidiaries that focus on various financial services (such as banking, securities, and insurance services). Firms that adopt this structure are regulated by the Federal Reserve.

By allowing commercial banks, securities firms, and insurance companies to merge and form financial conglomerates, the Financial Services Modernization Act has created a more competitive environment for securities firms. They face more intense competition from commercial banks, which may offer more securities services or even acquire securities firms.

At the same time, the creation of financial conglomerates has offered benefits to securities firms, including cross-listing. When individuals use the brokerage services of a securities firm, that firm may steer them to do their banking with the affiliated commercial bank or to obtain a mortgage with the affiliated savings institution. When firms use the investment banking services of a securities firm, that firm may steer them to do their banking with the affiliated commercial bank. The other types of financial institutions within the conglomerate can reciprocate by steering their customers toward the securities firm. In this way, the bundling of financial services can generate more business for each type of financial institution that is part of the financial conglomerate. However, just as a financial conglomerate can increase market share by pulling business away from other financial institutions, it may lose market share when other financial conglomerates use their bundling of financial services to attract customers.

Regulation FD   In October 2000, the SEC issued Regulation Fair Disclosure (FD), which requires firms to disclose any significant information simultaneously to all market participants. This rule was partially intended to prevent firms from leaking information to analysts who work for securities firms. Before Regulation FD, a firm's chief financial officer could have legally leaked information to an analyst about the firm's earnings or other relevant financial details before announcing this information to the public. Some analysts capitalized on such information by disclosing it to their key clients. Small investors were left out of the loop and, therefore, were at a competitive disadvantage.

As a result of Regulation FD, firms now generally provide their information through news releases or conference calls rather than leaking it to a few analysts. Those analysts who relied on inside information when providing their insight to clients have lost their competitive advantage, whereas those analysts who relied on their own analysis rather than information leaks have gained a competitive edge.

ETHICS

WEB

www.sec.gov
How the SEC monitors
securities trading
activity and enforces
securities laws.

Regulation of Analyst Ratings   In the 2001–2002 period, the process by which analysts rated stocks was widely criticized. Firms recognize that the demand for their stock may be partially dictated by the rating assigned by an analyst. When they need underwriting or advisory services from a securities firm, they are more likely to hire a firm whose analysts rate their stock highly. Securities firms also recognize that they are more likely to attract business from a firm if they give its stock a high rating, regardless of their real opinion of the stock. In the late 1990s and early 2000s, some analysts spent much of their time generating new business, and their compensation was sometimes aligned with the business they brought to the securities firm. Consequently, the analysts were tempted to inflate the ratings they assigned to stocks, and the investors who relied on the ratings to make investment decisions were misled.

In 2002, in an attempt to prevent the obvious conflict of interest, the SEC implemented new rules:

- If a securities firm underwrites an IPO, its analysts cannot promote the stock for the first 40 days after the IPO. Thus, the price of the stock should be driven by factors other than hype provided by the underwriter's analysts in the first 40 days.
- An analyst's compensation cannot be directly aligned with the amount of business that the analyst brings to the securities firm. Analysts cannot be supervised by the investment banking department within the securities firm. This rule is intended to prevent investment bankers from pressuring analysts to provide high rankings of firms in an effort to attract more underwriting business from those firms.
- An analyst's rating must divulge any recent investment banking business provided by the securities firm that assigned the rating.

Regulation of the IPO Market   In the 2001–2003 period, various abuses in the IPO market were highly publicized.

- Some securities firms that served as underwriters on IPOs allocated shares to corporate executives who were considering an IPO for their own firm. Some critics viewed this process, referred to as *spinning,* as an implicit bribe to obtain the future business of the firm.
- Some securities firms that served as underwriters of IPOs encouraged institutional investors to place bids above the offer price on the first day that the shares traded as a condition for being allowed to participate in the next IPO. They also charged excessive commissions to investors in some cases when the demand for the IPO shares was well in excess of the supply.

The SEC investigated cases in which such abuses occurred and imposed fines on some securities firms. In addition, it enacted rules to prevent such abuses from occurring in the future.

To appreciate the effect on risk, consider a new example in which Optima Securities Co. experiences losses on some of its investments in assets such as mortgage-backed securities and has to write down the value of the assets by $50 million (5 percent of their original value) to reflect their prevailing market value. If the firm maintains less than $50 million of equity, it will not have sufficient equity to absorb the loss. Therefore, the value of its liabilities will now exceed the value of its assets, and its creditors may force Optima to file for bankruptcy.

24-5 Impact of the Credit Crisis on Securities Firms

Managers of securities firms are highly rewarded when their decisions generate high returns for their employer. During the housing boom in the 2002–2005 period, they invested heavily in mortgages and mortgage-backed securities. This allowed them to capitalize on the rise in home prices but also increased the securities firms' exposure to the housing market. They may have presumed that home prices would always rise, or at least would not decline.

Securities firms commonly financed their investments by borrowing funds in the money markets, as they would issue commercial paper or repurchase agreements that were collateralized by their assets. To magnify their return on investment, some large securities firms used a high degree of financial leverage, maintaining a debt level that was 20 times their equity (or more). Because they were not subject to bank regulations, they did not have to maintain the same level of capital as commercial banks.

The collapse of home prices in 2008 caused serious financial problems for large securities firms. Various types of debt securities such as mortgages that they had purchased defaulted. As the credit crisis intensified, institutional investors that commonly purchased debt securities became less willing to participate in this market after noticing the higher default rates on credit. Thus, some credit markets became inactive; consequently, the volume of services provided by securities firms declined, and so did the fees they earned. Stock prices plummeted, so firms did not want to issue stock at the prevailing stock prices; in turn, the fees earned by securities firms for facilitating stock offerings declined. Merger volume declined as well, as did the fees earned by securities firms for facilitating merger transactions. In general, the crisis caused a major reduction in securities firms' underwriting income, merger fee income, and brokerage income. Some large securities firms incurred losses that were more pronounced because those firms had used excessive financial leverage to finance their operations. The effects of the crisis on three very large and well-known securities firms are described next.

24-5a Impact of the Crisis on Bear Stearns

Bear Stearns was a large securities firm that served as a key financial intermediary for mortgage-backed securities linked to low-quality (subprime) mortgages, and it also invested in many mortgage-backed securities. As the credit crisis intensified, the value of its mortgage-backed securities declined. In fact, two hedge funds owned by Bear Stearns collapsed because of their heavy investment in subprime mortgage securities. From March 2007 until March 2008, the company wrote down $3 billion of its assets so that their valuation would be closer to the true market value. Although Bear Stearns was involved in diversified services, many of these services (including securitizations, investments in mortgage-backed securities, and the ownership of hedge funds that focused on subprime mortgages) were exposed to risk associated with a potential decline in housing prices.

Liquidity Problems of Bear Stearns   By March 2008, Bear Stearns was suffering from liquidity problems. Some of the financial institutions that had extended loans to the firm in the past were no longer willing to provide funding because they doubted that Bear Stearns would be able to repay the loans. Bear Stearns was not in a position to raise funds with an equity offering because its stock price was slipping and would have fallen further if the company had signaled its need for funding with a secondary stock offering.

On Thursday, March 13, 2008, Bear Stearns secretly notified the Federal Reserve that it was experiencing liquidity problems and would have to file for bankruptcy the next day if it could not obtain funds.

Fed Intervention   The Fed's Board of Governors recognized that the bankruptcy of Bear Stearns could be contagious and create chaos in the financial markets. Because Bear Stearns facilitated various financial transactions for many people and firms, its bankruptcy could cause liquidity problems for all those relying on it to complete the financial transactions in its intermediary role.

On Friday, March 14, 2008, it was announced that JPMorgan Chase (a commercial bank) would offer a loan to Bear Stearns. Rather than calming the markets, however, the announcement validated the suspicion that Bear Stearns lacked adequate liquidity, and its stock price immediately dropped from about $57 to $30.

During the weekend, Fed officials met with executives from Bear Stearns and JPMorgan Chase. Before the financial markets opened on Monday, March 17, 2008, the Fed extended a $30 billion credit line to JPMorgan Chase to help it acquire Bear Stearns. The Fed's role was critical because it would allow JPMorgan Chase to obtain more permanent financing for the acquisition over time. JPMorgan Chase agreed to pay $10 per share, which was about 90 percent less than Bear Stearns's stock price one year earlier.

The Fed also granted JPMorgan Chase an 18-month exemption on the capital requirements that are imposed on commercial banks. This exemption was intended to allow JPMorgan Chase time to absorb Bear Stearns's assets and to sell off high-risk assets that could require a higher capital level.

In addition, the Fed announced that it was willing to provide emergency loans to about 20 primary dealers that served as key financial intermediaries for the large Treasury securities transactions in the secondary market. It also committed to loans of up to $200 billion of Treasury securities to primary dealers for a term of 28 days (rather than overnight) in exchange for other types of securities. These provisions were intended to calm the financial markets.

The Fed's assistance to Bear Stearns offered only limited help to its stockholders; those that had invested in Bear Stearns before its liquidity problems surfaced lost most of their investment. Instead, the major beneficiaries of the Fed's intervention were the creditors that had provided credit to Bear Stearns; if the securities firm had failed and been liquidated, they would probably have received only a small fraction of the credit that they had provided.

Potential Systemic Risk Due to Bear Stearns's Problems   The Fed's assistance to Bear Stearns led to questions about whether there should be a consistent policy for dealing with financial institutions that are deemed "too big to fail." In general, the typical strategy was be to allow the equity value of the failing firm to be dictated by market forces, meaning that equity investors would lose their entire investment. Creditors would have rights to the remaining value of the firm, but in liquidation they would receive only a portion of the funds they had loaned to the firm. The Fed's intervention, however, protected the creditors holding debt securities that were issued by Bear Stearns.

The Fed's justification for its intervention was the high potential for systemic risk, whereby the failure of Bear Stearns could have had adverse effects that spread throughout the financial markets. Because Bear Stearns was a major provider of clearing operations for many types of financial transactions, its failure might have frozen or delayed many transactions, which could have resulted in a liquidity crisis for many individuals and firms that were to receive cash as a result of the transactions. Bear Stearns also served as a counterparty to various types of financial agreements. If it had defaulted on all of its counterparty positions, the financial institutions on the other side of those agreements could have faced liquidity and other problems, creating chaos in the financial markets. In essence, Bear Stearns may have been viewed as "too entangled" (in financial transactions) to fail.

Criticism of the Fed's Assistance to Bear Stearns   Some critics (including Paul Volcker, a previous chair of the Board of Governors of the Fed) questioned whether the Fed should have aided Bear Stearns, because Bear Stearns was a securities firm, not a commercial bank. They suggested that providing assistance to a firm other than a commercial bank should be the responsibility of Congress and not the Fed.

In addition, a rescue can cause a moral hazard problem, meaning that financial institutions may pursue high-risk opportunities to achieve high returns under the assumption that they will be bailed out if their strategies fail. Managers who pursue such strategies may be able to keep their jobs if the firm is rescued before it fails. The Fed's actions also raised the question of what other types of firms might be aided by the Fed rather than Congress.

Some people might counter these arguments by noting that the Fed is in a better position to intervene when a potential bankruptcy could undermine the financial system. Furthermore, the Fed might counter that it needed to act quickly and that waiting for Congress to act would have taken too much time.

24-5b Impact of the Crisis on Merrill Lynch

Like Bear Stearns, Merrill Lynch was a major financial intermediary for mortgage-backed securities. It was heavily concentrated in mortgage originations (through its 2006 acquisition of First Franklin Financial, a large subprime lender), securitizations of mortgages, and investments in mortgage-backed securities. The performance of each of these services was highly exposed to a potential decline in housing prices. Although Merrill Lynch benefited from its participation in the mortgage markets during the housing boom in the 2003–2005 period, it experienced major losses due to write-downs on its mortgage-backed securities in the third and fourth quarters of 2007, and its CEO was fired in October 2007.

ETHICS

Like Bear Stearns, Merrill Lynch relied heavily on short-term funding from the money markets to finance its operations and had a very high degree of financial leverage. In 2008, however, its access to new funding was limited, as both its financial condition and its stock price weakened. On September 15, 2008, Bank of America announced that it was acquiring Merrill Lynch. Bank of America said that the acquisition would give it a well-established brokerage network and would provide Merrill Lynch with the financial support that it needed to clean up its assets. The deal received much media attention because it included provisions for paying bonuses to Merrill Lynch's employees. Although Merrill Lynch had lost approximately $25 billion in 2008, it awarded its employees nearly $3.6 billion in bonuses; 696 Merrill employees received a bonus larger than $1 million. Because Merrill Lynch had received $10 billion in government funds from the Troubled Asset Relief Program (TARP) in 2008, some critics suggested that the government (and therefore the taxpayers) indirectly paid for the bonuses.

Many critics suggested that Bank of America did not properly assess the quality (risk) of Merrill Lynch's assets before the acquisition and, therefore, paid too much for this securities firm. The criticism was especially harsh because Bank of America received $25 billion in TARP funds from the government in 2008 and another $20 billion in TARP funds in January 2009 to help to finance the Merrill Lynch purchase. Thus, the critics argued that the government (and therefore the taxpayers) had subsidized a commercial bank's excessive payment for a securities firm. In 2010, Bank of America repaid the TARP funds, but part of the payment was derived from the proceeds of its large securities offering.

The Federal Reserve was the primary regulator of Bank of America's operations, while the SEC had been the primary regulator of Merrill Lynch. But when Merrill Lynch was acquired by Bank of America, it became subject to oversight by the Federal Reserve.

24-5c Impact of the Crisis on Lehman Brothers

Lehman Brothers, another large securities firm, specialized in underwriting fixed-income securities such as bonds and in asset management for companies and wealthy individuals. In 2006, it was ranked number one in *Barron's* annual survey of corporate performance of large companies. In 2007, it was at the top of *Fortune* magazine's list of "Most Admired Securities Firms." By 2008, it was the fourth largest securities firm in the United States and had become a major participant in the mortgage market. It acquired five mortgage companies so that it could be heavily involved in the origination of mortgages. It packaged mortgages through its securitization process to generate fees; it also invested in some of the mortgage-backed securities that were created from securitization. Yet, like Bear Stearns and Merrill Lynch, Lehman Brothers apparently did not recognize the degree to which its businesses were exposed to a possible decline in housing prices.

Also like Bear Stearns and Merrill Lynch, Lehman Brothers had a relatively high degree of financial leverage. Furthermore, some of its debt was short term, so it could be cut off (not renewed) if creditors sensed that Lehman was experiencing financial problems.

ETHICS

Lehman Brothers' Accounting   Lehman Brothers used an accounting method that made its capital position look stronger than it actually was, because capital was measured in proportion to total assets (which were reduced by the accounting treatment). Thus, its degree of financial leverage was even higher than that reported on its balance sheet. Furthermore, even though the valuations of mortgages across the United States declined rapidly in 2007, Lehman Brothers did not write down the valuations of its holdings of mortgages and mortgage-backed securities to reflect their proper valuations. By deferring the decision to write down these assets, Lehman Brothers inflated its earnings during 2007.

In April and May 2008, highly publicized reports indicated that Lehman Brothers' reported earnings were overstated. Institutional investors asked why the firm did not have more write-downs of its assets, given that the valuations of mortgage-backed securities had declined in recent months. In June 2008, Lehman Brothers reported a loss of $2.8 billion and acknowledged $4.1 billion in asset write-downs. In September 2008, it reported a quarterly loss of $3.9 billion and acknowledged $5.6 billion in asset write-downs (mostly mortgages or related securities). Five days later, the firm filed for bankruptcy.

Some investors suggested that Lehman Brothers did not suddenly experience abrupt declines in the valuations of its assets during the last two quarters of its life, but rather was unwilling to acknowledge the decline in the valuations of its assets during previous quarters. In fact, an independent audit of Lehman Brothers was conducted after its bankruptcy and came to this conclusion. The inflated earnings may explain why the firm was able to pay more than $70 million as compensation to its CEO and more than $5 billion in bonuses to its employees in 2007. Had Lehman Brothers accurately disclosed its weakened financial condition in earlier quarters, its board of directors, key managers, or large institutional shareholders might have had time to look for possible restructuring solutions before it was too late.

One lesson from this example is that despite the Sarbanes-Oxley Act of 2002, it was still possible for financial institutions (and perhaps other companies as well) to use creative accounting in a manner that could misrepresent their financial condition.

Lehman Brothers' Liquidity Problems   From March to September 2008, Lehman Brothers' stock price declined by about 85 percent, and it was unable to raise sufficient funds through a stock offering. In addition, concerns about its creditworthiness prevented it from obtaining credit at a reasonable cost. The growing concerns about Lehman Brothers led some clients to cut their business ties to the firm, which further reduced its cash inflows.

Lehman Brothers' financial problems created a very difficult dilemma for the U.S. government, because it had become so large and played a very important role as a financial intermediary. The Federal Reserve and other government officials were aware that if Lehman Brothers failed, its bankruptcy could create financial problems for many other firms (such as creditors and counterparties on swap agreements) that would not receive payments owed to them. Lehman Brothers itself apparently expected to be rescued by regulators. But no government rescue occurred, and on September 15, 2008, the firm filed for bankruptcy. Perhaps if it had acknowledged its financial problems earlier when the market valuations of its mortgage-related holdings began to decline, it might have been able to find a suitable financial institution to acquire it before its financial problems became overwhelming.

24-5d Impact of the Crisis on Regulatory Reform

Historically, securities firms were subject to looser regulations than those imposed on commercial banks. In particular, securities firms were not subject to capital requirements, leaving them free to use more debt to support their operations. Their higher degree of financial leverage magnified their positive returns, but also magnified their losses. Yet the problems of securities firms such as Bear Stearns, Merrill Lynch, and Lehman Brothers illustrated how the high degree of financial leverage used by securities firms could create excessive risk for the firms and for the financial system as a whole. These problems offer support for the argument that securities firms should be subject to capital requirements just like commercial banks.

Conversion of Securities Firms to BHCs   During the credit crisis, some securities firms were unable to access funds by issuing securities. They did not want to issue stock while their stock prices were weak. In addition, they were unable to issue debt securities because investors were concerned about their financial condition. The lack of funding deepened the financial problems of Bear Stearns and Merrill Lynch before they were acquired and of Lehman Brothers before it went bankrupt. As a result of the consolidation during the credit crisis, Goldman Sachs and Morgan Stanley were the only very large securities firms left standing. They applied to become bank holding companies (BHCs), and the Fed approved the requests in September 2008. This new structure gave the firms more flexibility to obtain financing. Securities firms were allowed to borrow short-term funds from the Federal Reserve during the credit crisis, but their conversion to a BHC structure gave them permanent access to Federal Reserve funding.

A BHC can have commercial banking and securities subsidiaries. The commercial banking subsidiary can accept deposits and perform the functions of commercial banks, such as lending to businesses. It can create some stability for the company overall because it has steady access to deposits that are insured up to a limit. The securities subsidiary performs traditional securities functions such as advising and underwriting securities for client firms. The securities operations are just as important today as they were before the credit crisis, but the main difference is that commercial banks now play a much bigger role in providing brokerage and investment banking services.

Overall, the BHC structure results in a greater degree of regulatory oversight by the Federal Reserve. Consequently, the securities firms may be viewed as safer as a result of their conversion to BHCs.

FINANCIAL REFORM

Financial Reform Act of 2010

The Financial Reform Act of 2010 was enacted following the credit crisis as part of the government's efforts to stabilize the U.S. financial system. Those provisions of the Financial Reform Act that have a direct impact on securities firms are briefly summarized here.

First, the Financial Reform Act mandated that financial institutions granting mortgages verify the income, job status, and credit history of mortgage applicants before approving mortgage applications. Thus, when securities firms serve as intermediaries in the securitization process, the mortgage backing the securities that they sell should be less risky.

Second, the Financial Reform Act requires that securities firms and other financial institutions that sell securities through the securitization process retain 5 percent of the portfolio unless the portfolio meets specific standards that reflect low risk. This provision encourages firms to ensure that the mortgages backing the securities they sell are less risky.

Third, the act created the Financial Stability Oversight Council, which is responsible for identifying risks to financial stability in the United States and makes regulatory recommendations to regulators that could reduce any risks to the financial system. The council can recommend methods to ensure that securities firms and other financial institutions do not rely on regulatory bailouts.

Fourth, the act gave specific regulators the authority to determine that any particular securities firm or other financial institution should be liquidated. This expedites the liquidation process and can limit the losses incurred by a failing financial institution.

Fifth, the act requires that derivative securities be traded through a clearinghouse or exchange rather than over the counter. This allows for a more standardized structure regarding margins and collateral and more transparency of derivative security prices. Consequently, securities firms that trade these derivative securities should be less susceptible to the risk that the counterparty has posted insufficient collateral.

The Volcker Rule

The Financial Reform Act also contained a provision calling for limits on proprietary trading by commercial banks and securities firms that have become BHCs. In 2014, regulators issued final regulations implementing this provision, which is known as the Volcker Rule (after Paul Volcker, the former Fed chair who first proposed it). The Volcker Rule restricts many short-term speculative investments, which formerly were an important part of financial institutions' proprietary trading. As a result, the amount of proprietary trading has declined somewhat, and many of the top traders have left the financial institutions where they worked and have established their own hedge funds.

Summary

- Securities firms facilitate new issues of stock by advising firms on how much stock they can issue, determining the appropriate price for the stock, underwriting the stock, and distributing the stock. They facilitate new issues of bonds in a somewhat similar manner. They also provide advice and financing to corporations pursuing mergers and other restructuring, provide brokerage services, operate mutual funds, and engage in some proprietary trading.

- Many regulations have been imposed on securities firms in an attempt to ensure that no investors have an unfair advantage when conducting transactions in financial markets. Stock exchanges and regulatory authorities impose regulations on securities firms to prevent unfair or illegal practices, ensure orderly trading, and address customer complaints. Several laws and regulations have allowed more competition between securities firms and other financial institutions. Regulations require that corporations disclose any information to the public, which prevents them from leaking information to analysts of securities firms. Rules have been implemented to prevent or discourage analysts from assigning inflated ratings to stocks and to prevent analysts from being compensated by investment bank divisions that seek business from corporate clients.

- The valuation and performance of a securities firm are affected by prevailing economic conditions, interest rate movements, industry conditions including regulation, and the abilities of the firm's management.

- Securities firms are exposed to market risk because their volume of business is larger when stock market conditions are stronger. They are subject to interest rate risk because their underwriting business is sensitive to interest rate movements. They also hold some long-term financial assets whose values decline in response to higher interest rates. In addition, securities firms are subject to credit risk, because they commonly purchase debt securities and provide loans to some of their business clients. The potential damage due to these types of risk is more pronounced for securities firms that use a very high degree of financial leverage.

- As a result of the credit crisis of 2008–2009, several major securities firms experienced financial problems, in part due to their high exposure to credit risk and their high degree of financial leverage. The acquisitions of securities firms by commercial banks and conversion of other securities firms into bank holding companies led to more oversight of security firm operations by the Federal Reserve.

Point/Counterpoint

Should Analysts Be Separated from Securities Firms to Prevent Conflict of Interest?

Point No. Securities firms are known for their ability to analyze companies and value them. Investors may be more comfortable when analysts work within a securities firm because they have access to substantial information.

Counterpoint Yes. Analysts have a conflict of interest because they may be unwilling to offer

negative views about a company that is a client of their securities firm.

Who Is Correct? Use the Internet to learn more about this issue and then formulate your own opinion.

Questions and Applications

1. **Regulation of Securities Activities** Explain the role of the SEC, FINRA, and the stock exchanges in regulating the securities industry.

2. **SIPC** What is the purpose of the SIPC?

3. **Investment Banking Services** How do securities firms facilitate leveraged buyouts? Why are securities firms that are better able to raise funds in the capital

markets preferred by corporations that need advice on proposed acquisitions?

4. **Origination Process** Describe the origination process for corporations that are about to issue new stock.

5. **Underwriting Function** Describe the underwriting function of a securities firm.

6. Best-Efforts Agreement What is a best-efforts agreement?

7. Failure of Lehman Brothers Why did Lehman Brothers experience financial problems during the credit crisis?

8. Direct Placement Describe a direct placement of bonds. What is an advantage of a private placement? What is a disadvantage?

9. International Expansion Explain why securities firms from the United States have expanded into foreign markets.

10. Proprietary Trading Explain the process of proprietary trading by securities firms. How was it affected by the Volcker Rule?

11. Asset Stripping What is asset stripping?

12. Securities Firms' Use of Leverage Explain why securities firms have used a high level of financial leverage in the past. How does such leverage affect their expected return and their risk?

13. Systemic Risk Why was the Federal Reserve concerned about systemic risk due to the financial problems of Bear Stearns?

14. Access to Inside Information Why do securities firms typically have some inside information that could affect future stock prices of other firms?

15. Sensitivity to Stock Market Conditions Most securities firms experience poor profit performance during periods in which the stock market performs poorly. Given what you know about securities firms, offer some possible reasons for these reduced profits.

16. Conversion to BHC Structure Explain how the credit crisis of 2008–2009 encouraged some securities firms to convert to a bank holding company (BHC) structure. Why might the expected return on equity be lower for securities firms that convert to this structure?

17. Financial Services Modernization Act How did the Financial Services Modernization Act affect securities firms?

18. Regulation FD What impact has the SEC's Regulation Fair Disclosure (FD) had on securities firms?

Critical Thinking Question

Regulation of Security Firms Should large securities firms be allowed to be independent and insulated from bank regulation, or should they be required to register as bank holding companies and subject to bank regulations? Write a short essay that supports your opinion.

Interpreting Financial News

Interpret the following comments made by Wall Street analysts and portfolio managers.

a. "The stock prices of most securities firms took a hit because of the recent increase in interest rates."

b. "Now that commercial banks are allowed more freedom to offer securities services, there may be a shakeout in the underwriting arena."

c. "Chaos in the securities markets can be good for some securities firms."

Managing in Financial Markets

Assessing the Operations of Securities Firms As a consultant, you are assessing the operations of a securities firm.

a. This securities firm relies heavily on full-service brokerage commissions. Do you think the firm's heavy reliance on these commissions is risky? Explain.

b. If this firm attempts to enter the underwriting business, would it be an easy transition?

c. In recent years, the stock market volume has increased substantially, and this securities firm has performed very well. In the future, however, many institutional and individual investors may invest in index funds or exchange-traded funds rather than in individual stocks. How would this affect the securities firm?

Flow of Funds Exercise

How Securities Firms Facilitate the Flow of Funds

Recall that Carson Company has periodically borrowed funds but contemplates a stock or bond offering so that it can expand by acquiring some other businesses. It has contacted Kelly Investment Company, a securities firm.

a. Explain how Kelly Investment Company can serve Carson, and how it will also serve other clients when it serves Carson. Also explain how Carson Company can serve Kelly Investment Company.

b. In a securities offering, Kelly Investment Company would like to do a good job for its clients, which include both the issuer and institutional investors. Explain Kelly's dilemma.

c. The issuing firm in an IPO hopes that there will be strong demand for its shares at the offer price, which will ensure that it receives a reasonable amount of proceeds from its offering. In some previous IPOs, the share price by the end of the first day was more than 80 percent higher than the offer price at the beginning of the day. This reflects a very strong demand relative to the price at the end of the day. In fact, it probably suggests that the IPO was fully subscribed at the offer price and that some institutional investors who purchased the stock at the offer price flipped their shares near the end of the first day to individual investors who were willing to pay the market price. Do you think that the issuing firm would be pleased that its stock price increased by more than 80 percent on the first day? Explain. Who really benefits from the increase in price on the first day?

d. Continuing the previous question, assume that the stock price drifts back down to near the original offer price over the next three weeks (even though the general stock market conditions were stable over this period) and then moves in tandem with the market over the next several years. Based on this information, do you think the offer price was appropriate? If so, how can you explain the unusually high one-day return on the stock? Who benefited from this stock price behavior, and who was adversely affected?

Internet/Excel Exercises

1. Go to www.goldmansachs.com. Using this website, describe the different types of financial services offered by Goldman Sachs. Summarize its main business. Is Goldman Sachs focused on brokerage, investment banking, or a combination of these services? Describe its performance over the last year. Explain why its performance was higher or lower than normal. Was the change in its performance due to the economy, recent interest rate movements, the stock market's performance, or changes in the amount of stock-trading or merger activity?

2. Retrieve information about Morgan Stanley (www.morganstanley.com) or another publicly traded securities firm of your choice. Go to the firm's website and retrieve its most recent annual report (look under "Investor Relations"). Review the security firm's recent performance. Has its income as a percentage of assets increased since the previous year? Explain what caused this change over the last year. How have the firm's operating expenses changed over the last year? Discuss how the firm's recent strategy and economic conditions may explain the changes in these components of its income statement.

3. Go to finance.yahoo.com, and enter the symbol MS (Morgan Stanley). Click on "5y" just above the stock price graph to review the stock price movements over the last five years. Then click on "Chart" and under "Comparison," select "S&P 500" to compare the trend of Morgan Stanley's stock price with the movements in the S&P stock index. Has Morgan Stanley performed better or worse than the index? Offer an explanation for its performance.

4. Go to finance.yahoo.com, enter the symbol MS (Morgan Stanley), and retrieve stock price data at the beginning of the last 20 quarters. Then go to fred.stlouisfed.org and retrieve interest rate data at the beginning of the last 20 quarters for the three-month Treasury bill. Record the data on an Excel spreadsheet. Derive the quarterly return of Morgan Stanley. Derive the quarterly change in the interest rate. Apply regression analysis in which the quarterly return of Morgan Stanley is the dependent variable and the quarterly change in the interest rate is the independent variable (see Appendix B for more information about using regression analysis). Is there a positive or negative relationship between the interest rate movement and the stock return of Morgan Stanley? Is the relationship significant? Offer an explanation for this relationship.

WSJ Exercise

Performance of Securities Firms

Using a recent issue of *The Wall Street Journal*, summarize an article that discusses the recent performance of a particular securities firm. Does the article suggest that the securities firm's performance was better or worse than the norm? What reason is given for the particular level of performance?

Online Articles with Real-World Examples

Find a recent practical article available online that describes a real-world example regarding a specific financial institution or financial market that reinforces one or more concepts covered in this chapter.

If your class has an online component, your professor may ask you to post your summary of the article there and provide a link to the article so that other students can access it. If your class is live, your professor may ask you to summarize your application of the article in class. Your professor may assign specific students to complete this assignment or may allow any students to do the assignment on a volunteer basis.

For recent online articles and real-world examples related to this chapter, consider using the following search terms (be sure to include the prevailing year as a search term to ensure that the online articles are recent):

1. [name of a specific securities firm] AND income
2. [name of a specific securities firm] AND operations
3. [name of a specific securities firm] AND risk
4. [name of a specific securities firm] AND earnings
5. securities firm AND underwriting
6. securities firm AND earnings
7. securities firm AND risk
8. securities firm AND regulation
9. securities firm AND operations
10. securities firm AND credit

25

Insurance Operations

CHAPTER OBJECTIVES

The specific objectives of this chapter are to:

- Explain how insurance premiums are determined.

- Describe how insurance companies are regulated.

- Describe the main operations of life insurance companies.

- Describe the main operations of other types of insurance companies.

- Explain the exposure of insurance companies to various forms of risk.

- Identify the factors that affect the value of insurance companies.

WEB

www.insure.com
Information about more than 200 insurance companies.

Insurance companies provide insurance for individuals, firms, and government agencies. They charge a fee (called a premium) for this financial service. They make a payment to the insured (or a named beneficiary) under conditions specified by the insurance policy contract. These conditions typically result in expenses or lost income to the insured party, so insurance is a means of financial protection.

Insurance companies invest the insurance premiums and fees received from other services until those funds are needed to pay insurance claims. In some cases, claims may occur several years after the premiums are received. Thus, the performance of insurance companies partly depends on the returns they receive from their invested funds. Their investment goals are to generate a high rate of return while maintaining risk at a tolerable level. They also need to maintain sufficient liquidity so that they can easily access funds to accommodate claims by policyholders. Those insurance companies whose claims are less predictable need to maintain more liquidity.

Common types of insurance offered by insurance companies include life insurance, property and casualty insurance, health insurance, and business insurance. Many insurance companies offer multiple types of insurance.

25-1 Setting Insurance Premiums

Insurance companies employ underwriters to calculate the risk of specific insurance policies. The companies decide which types of insurance policies to offer based on the premiums they can charge (cash inflows) versus the potential value of claims to be paid to policyholders (cash outflows).The premium charged by an insurance company for each insurance policy is based on the probability that it will have to provide a payment to the insured (or the insured's beneficiary) and the potential size of the payment. When insured parties are more likely to experience an event that will require the insurance company to provide a payment, their premiums will be relatively high. The premium charged is also influenced by the present value of the expected payment for the claim. In addition, the premium will contain a markup to cover overhead expenses and to provide a profit beyond expenses.

The premium may also be influenced by the degree of competition within the industry for the specific type of insurance offered. When many competitors offer the same type of insurance, the premium is likely to be lower.

Insurance companies tend to charge lower premiums when they provide services to all employees of a corporation through group plans. The lower premium represents a form of quantity discount in return for being selected to provide a particular type of insurance to the entire group of employees.

25-1a Adverse Selection Problem

When assessing the probability of a condition that will result in a payment to the insured (or the insured's beneficiary), insurance companies rely on statistics about the general population. However, they also need to consider the behavior of policyholders that can increase the likelihood of claims. The insurance industry faces an **adverse selection problem**, meaning that those who are most likely to need insurance are most likely to purchase it.

EXAMPLE

An insurance company representative arrives on a college campus and asks all students whether they want to purchase insurance in case any of the property (such as computer tablets) in their dorm rooms is stolen. Beth declines the offer because she always locks the door when she leaves her dorm room, and believes that there is no need to insure her property. Conversely, Randy decides to buy the insurance because he never locks his door and realizes that he may need the insurance.

Assume the insurance company sets the premium based on historical police reports showing that 3 percent of all students on campus have property stolen from their dorm rooms. Now consider that many careless students like Randy buy the insurance whereas many careful students like Beth do not. Because the students who purchase the insurance often forget to lock their dorm rooms, they are more likely to have property stolen than the norm. Therefore, more than 3 percent of these students will have property stolen. The insurance company set its premiums too low, because it based its premiums on a general sample, not on a sample of students who actually buy insurance. ●

As a result of the adverse selection problem, insurance companies need to assess the probability and potential size of claims made by the people who obtain insurance rather than the claims made by the population in general. In this way, they can set insurance premiums sufficiently high to reflect the likely claims by policyholders.

The adverse selection problem is reduced when insurance is required for all members of a group. For example, in most states, a driver must have a minimum level of insurance to legally operate a motor vehicle. Therefore, all drivers must purchase insurance, including safe drivers.

25-1b Moral Hazard Problem

Once individuals are covered by insurance, they may take more risks, as they recognize that they are protected by insurance. This type of behavior is known as the **moral hazard problem** in the insurance industry.

EXAMPLE

Refer back to the previous example in which the insurance company offers insurance to students in case property is stolen from their dorm rooms. Assume that Mina purchases this insurance even though she is usually very careful about locking her dorm room. Once she has insurance, she decides that she does not need to worry about locking her room because she is now insured if her property is stolen. At the time Mina purchased the insurance, she was a low risk to the insurance company because she was less likely to have property stolen than other students who were more careless than she was. But once she had insurance, she became a high risk to the insurance company because she changed her behavior as a result of having insurance. ●

WEB

www.naic.org

Links to information about insurance regulations.

Insurance companies must consider that some people will become more careless (which leads to more insurance claims) after they become insured, and attempt to set premiums to reflect the higher risk of claims.

25-4a **Property and Casualty Insurance**

Property and casualty (PC) insurance protects against fire, theft, liability, and other events that may result in economic or noneconomic damage. Property insurance protects businesses and individuals from the impact of financial risks associated with the ownership of property, such as buildings, automobiles, and other assets. Casualty insurance protects policyholders from potential liabilities for harm to others as a result of product failure or accidents. Property and casualty insurance companies charge policyholders a premium that should reflect the probability of a payout to the insured (or claimant) and the potential magnitude of the payout.

There are approximately 2,500 individual PC companies in the United States. The largest providers of PC insurance are State Farm, Berkshire Hathaway, Liberty Mutual, Allstate, Progressive, Travelers, and Nationwide. Although PC companies outnumber life insurance companies, the PC insurance business in aggregate is only approximately one-fourth as large as the life insurance business in aggregate (based on assets held). Nevertheless, the PC insurance business generates about the same amount of insurance premiums as the life insurance business. Many insurance companies have diversified their business and offer both life and PC insurance.

Life insurance and PC insurance have very different characteristics. First, PC policies often last one year or less, whereas life insurance policies cover a much longer term. Second, PC insurance encompasses a wide variety of activities, ranging from auto insurance to business liability insurance; by comparison, life insurance is more focused. Third, forecasting the amount of future compensation from claims to be paid is more difficult for PC insurance than for life insurance. Property and casualty compensation depends on a variety of factors, including inflation, hurricanes and tornadoes, terrorism, and the generosity of courts in lawsuits. Therefore, PC insurance companies need to maintain more liquid asset portfolios, so that they can liquidate investments if their policyholders experience an adverse event (such as a hurricane) that results in massive claims.

Cash Flow Underwriting A unique aspect of the PC insurance industry is its cyclical nature. As interest rates rise, companies tend to lower their rates so that they can write more policies and acquire more premium dollars to invest. In doing so, they are hoping that losses will hold off long enough to make the cheaper premiums profitable through increased investment income. As interest rates decline, the price of insurance rises to offset decreased investment income. This method of adapting prices to interest rates is called **cash flow underwriting**. It can backfire for companies that focus on what they can earn in the short run and ignore what they will pay out later. A company that does not accurately predict the timing of the cycle can experience inadequate reserves and a drain on cash.

Uses of Funds The primary uses of funds by PC insurance companies are investments in municipal securities and corporate bonds. Thus, the most obvious difference in the asset structure of PC companies relative to life insurance companies is the much higher concentration of their investments in government (municipal, Treasury, and government agency) securities and the lower concentration of their investments in stocks. Because PC companies may need to liquidate a large portion of their investments quickly to pay claims in response to an unexpected adverse event, they maintain liquid investments that can be easily sold in the secondary market. If PC companies invested heavily in stocks, they might be forced to liquidate stocks to pay claims at a time when their stock holdings had low valuations because of poor market conditions.

Property and Casualty Reinsurance PC companies commonly obtain reinsurance, which effectively allocates a portion of their return and risk to other insurance companies. This is similar to a commercial bank organizing a syndicate by inviting other banks to participate in a loan and share the risk and the return. A particular PC insurance company may agree to insure a corporation but spread the risk by inviting other insurance companies to participate in the coverage. Reinsurance allows a company to write larger policies because a portion of the risk involved will be assumed by other companies.

In recent times, the number of companies willing to offer reinsurance has declined significantly because of generous court awards and the difficulty of assessing the amount of potential claims. Reinsurance policies are often described in the insurance industry as "having long tails," which means that the probability distribution of possible returns on reinsurance is widely dispersed. Although many companies still offer reinsurance, their premiums have increased substantially in recent years. If the desire to offer reinsurance continues to decline, the primary insurers will be less able to "sell off" a portion of the risk they assume when writing policies. Consequently, they will be under pressure to more closely evaluate the risk of the policies they write.

25-4b **Healthcare Insurance**

Health insurance companies provide healthcare insurance to households, companies, and government agencies. This coverage can include hospital stays, visits to physicians, drugs, and surgical procedures. Health insurance companies serve as intermediaries between healthcare providers and the recipients of healthcare. Large companies in this field include Aetna, Cigna, and Humana.

Types of Healthcare Plans Insurance companies offer two types of healthcare plans: managed healthcare plans and indemnity plans. The primary difference between the two types of plans is that individuals who are insured by a managed care plan may choose only specified healthcare providers (hospitals and physicians) who participate in the plan. Individuals who are insured under an indemnity plan can usually choose any provider of healthcare services. The payment systems of the two types of plans are also distinctly different. The premiums for managed healthcare plans are generally lower, and payment is typically made directly to the provider. In contrast, indemnity plans may require that the insured pay the provider for services and then submit a claim to the insurance company for reimbursement.

Managed healthcare plans can be classified as **health maintenance organizations (HMOs)** or preferred provider organizations (PPOs). In most cases, HMOs require individuals to choose a primary care physician (PCP), who then acts as the "gatekeeper" for that individual's healthcare. Before patients insured under an HMO can see a specialist, they must first see a PCP to obtain a referral for the specialist. This helps to keep costs for the HMO down, because patients will not see high-cost specialists unless their PCP sees them first and determines whether a referral to a specialist is necessary. In contrast, PPOs usually allow insured individuals to see any physician without a referral. As a result, PPO insurance premiums are typically higher than HMO insurance premiums.

25-4c **Business Insurance**

Insurance companies provide a wide variety of insurance policies that protect businesses from many types of risk. Some forms of business insurance overlap with property and casualty insurance. Property insurance protects a firm against the risk associated with ownership of property, such as buildings and other assets. It can provide insurance against property damage by fire or theft.

Liability insurance can protect a firm against potential liability for harm to others as a result of product failure or a wide range of other conditions. This is a key type of insurance for businesses because of the increasing number of lawsuits filed by customers who claim that they suffered physical injury or emotional distress as a result of using products produced by businesses.

Liability insurance can also protect a business against potential liability for claims by its employees. For example, a business may be subject to a lawsuit by an employee who becomes hurt on the job or is fired. Key employee insurance provides a financial payout if specified employees of a business become disabled or die. Such insurance is intended to enable the business to replace the skills of the key employees so that the business can continue. Business interruption insurance protects against losses due to a temporary closing of the business. Credit line insurance covers debt payments owed to a creditor if a borrower dies. Fidelity bond insurance covers losses due to dishonest employees. Marine insurance covers losses due to damage during transport. Malpractice insurance protects business professionals from losses due to lawsuits by dissatisfied customers. Surety bond insurance covers losses due to a contract not being fulfilled. Umbrella liability insurance provides additional coverage beyond that provided by the other existing insurance policies.

25-4d Bond Insurance

Bond insurance protects investors that purchase bonds from the risk that the bond issuers will default on their bonds. Many municipal bonds are backed by insurance. Some municipalities are willing to pay for the insurance because it allows them to more easily sell their bonds at lower prices; thus, the insurance reduces their cost of borrowing. The risk of default may be minimized when an insurance company insures the bonds. Many insurance companies, including Ambac Financial Group and MBIA, provide bond insurance.

Of course, the insurance on bonds is only as good as the insurance company's ability to cover claims. Potentially both a bond issuer and the insurer backing the bond issuer might not satisfy their obligations, which could lead to major losses for institutional investors holding these bonds. A downgrade in the credit rating of a bond insurer signals that a greater likelihood that the insurance company will not be able to cover a claim in the event that the bond defaults. To compensate for the higher risk, bonds insured by this company will need to offer higher yields. Existing bonds insured by this insurer will experience a decline in price to reflect the higher risk of loss from holding these bonds.

25-4e Mortgage Insurance

Mortgage insurance protects the lender that provides mortgage loans in the event that homeowners cannot cover their payments and default on their mortgages. The insurance is usually intended to cover the lender's losses when the lender is forced to foreclose on the home and sells the property for less than the prevailing mortgage amount.

Mortgage lenders commonly require homeowners to obtain mortgage insurance unless they make a down payment of at least 20 percent of the home's cost. Sometimes, obtaining the insurance may allow a homeowner to qualify for a lower interest rate on the mortgage. Mortgage insurance is required for all mortgage loans guaranteed by the Federal Housing Administration. The insurance companies that sell mortgage insurance typically receive periodic insurance premiums for providing this insurance. In the event of a mortgage default, they cover the damages to the creditor.

Credit Default Swaps as a Form of Mortgage Insurance Some insurance companies provide insurance on mortgages by taking a position in credit default swaps, which are privately negotiated contracts that protect investors against the risk of default on particular debt securities. An institutional investor that previously purchased mortgage securities may become concerned that these securities could perform poorly. Therefore, it may be willing to engage in a credit default swap in which it will make monthly or quarterly payments to the counterparty.

Insurance companies commonly serve as the counterparty and have to make payments only if there is a default on the securities covered by the swap. In this event, the insurance companies have to pay the face value of the securities covered by the swap in exchange for those securities. When no defaults on the debt securities occur, the insurance companies benefit from their swap positions because they are not required to make payments. When defaults do take place, however, the insurance companies can incur large expenses to cover the payments.

Insurance companies reduce their exposure to various types of insurance through diversification. They have numerous policyholders, and an adverse event that causes an insurance claim from one policyholder is unlikely to happen to many other policyholders at the same time. However, credit defaults on mortgage-backed securities can occur across financial institutions at the same time if mortgage qualification standards are low and the economy is weak. Consequently, diversification among credit default swaps on mortgage-backed securities does not effectively reduce risk. Insurance companies that sold credit default swaps were highly exposed to mortgage conditions during the credit crisis of 2008–2009.

25-5 Exposure of Insurance Companies to Risk

The major types of risk faced by insurance companies are interest rate risk, credit risk, market risk, and liquidity risk.

25-5a Interest Rate Risk

Because insurance companies hold a large amount of fixed-rate, long-term debt securities (bonds and mortgages), the market value of their asset portfolios can be very sensitive to interest rate fluctuations. When interest rates rise, the values of their holdings of long-term bonds and mortgages decline. If they need to liquidate some of those long-term debt securities to cover claims at a time when interest rates are high, they may suffer losses on those investments.

25-5b Credit Risk

Since insurance companies purchase corporate bonds, mortgages, and state and local government securities, they are exposed to credit risk. To deal with this risk, some insurance companies invest only in securities assigned a high credit rating. They also diversify among securities issuers so that repayment problems experienced by any particular issuer will have only a minor impact on their overall portfolio.

Because long-term interest rates have been so low in recent years, some insurance companies have shifted more funds out of Treasury bonds and into corporate bonds (including junk bonds) that offer higher yields. However, by striving for higher returns, they become exposed to a much higher degree of credit risk.

25-5c Market Risk

Because insurance companies invest in stock, they are exposed to possible losses on their stock portfolios during weak stock market conditions. While they diversify among their stock investments in an effort to reduce their exposure, most stocks are very sensitive to general stock market conditions. Thus, a large decline in the overall stock market will typically result in a large decline in the stock portfolio of an insurance company.

25-5d Liquidity Risk

Another risk faced by insurance companies is liquidity risk. A high frequency of claims in a short span of time could force a company to liquidate assets at a time when the market value is low, thereby depressing its performance. Claims due to death are not likely to occur simultaneously, however, so life insurance companies can reduce their exposure to this risk by diversifying the age distribution of their customer base. If the customer base becomes unbalanced and is heavily concentrated in the older age group, life insurance companies should increase their proportion of liquid assets to prepare for a higher frequency of claims.

Property and casualty insurance companies are more exposed to liquidity risk because a single adverse event such as a massive fire or hurricane could trigger numerous claims by their policyholders. Therefore, they need to ensure sufficient liquidity within their asset portfolio in case such an event occurs. They may also attempt to diversify their insurance (impose limits on the amount of fire or hurricane insurance offered within a particular area) so that they are not overly exposed to a single adverse event.

25-5e Exposure to Risk during the Credit Crisis

As the credit crisis intensified in 2008, many insurance companies experienced losses. Many insurance companies that had invested some of their funds in mortgage-backed securities or in junk bonds experienced losses on their investments. Some insurance companies sold private mortgage insurance to offer protection on mortgages and had to cover insurance claims filed by creditors when homeowners defaulted on their mortgage payments. Other insurance companies incurred losses from their credit default swaps. Furthermore, many insurance companies experienced a decline in their stock portfolio value of more than 50 percent during the credit crisis.

25-5f Government Rescue of AIG

Before the credit crisis, American International Group (AIG) was the largest insurance company in the world, with annual revenue of more than $100 billion and operations in more than 130 countries. The company had sold credit default swaps that were intended to cover approximately $440 billion in debt securities against default. However, many of those debt securities represented subprime mortgages. In 2008, AIG experienced severe financial problems when many of those mortgage-backed securities defaulted.

If AIG had failed, all of the financial institutions that had purchased credit default swaps from AIG to protect against default on their mortgage-backed securities might have failed or suffered severe losses. Because the failure of AIG could have had a devastating effect on the insurance industry and the rest of the financial sector, the Federal Reserve bailed out AIG in September 2008 with support from the U.S. Treasury. The Fed may have viewed AIG as too big and too entangled with other financial institutions to fail. The bailout allowed AIG to borrow up to $85 billion from the Federal Reserve over a two-year period, and the government received an equity stake of about 80 percent of AIG. As part of the agreement, AIG was required to sell off some of its businesses to increase its liquidity.

The Fed's rescue of AIG occurred one day after it allowed Lehman Brothers to fail. Perhaps one reason for rescuing AIG and not rescuing Lehman Brothers was that AIG had various subsidiaries that were financially sound at the time. The assets in these subsidiaries served as collateral for the loans extended by the federal government to rescue AIG. Thus, the federal government perceived the risk of a loss to taxpayers due to the AIG rescue as low. Conversely, Lehman Brothers did not have adequate collateral available, so a large loan from the U.S. government could have been costly to U.S. taxpayers.

WEB

www.iii.org
Information about all aspects of the insurance industry from the Insurance Information Institute.

25-6 Valuation of an Insurance Company

Insurance companies (or insurance company units that are part of a financial conglomerate) are commonly valued by their managers to monitor progress over time or by other financial institutions that are considering an acquisition. The value of an insurance company can be modeled as the present value of its future cash flows. Thus, the value of an insurance company should change in response to changes in its expected cash flows (CF) in the future and to changes in the required rate of return (k) by investors:

$$\Delta V = f[\underset{+}{\underline{\Delta E(\text{CF})}}, \underset{-}{\underline{\Delta k}}]$$

25-6a Factors That Affect Cash Flows

The change in an insurance company's expected cash flows may be modeled as

$$\Delta E(\text{CF}) = f(\underset{-}{\underline{\Delta \text{PAYOUT}}}, \underset{+}{\underline{\Delta \text{ECON}}}, \underset{-}{\underline{\Delta R_f}}, \underset{?}{\underline{\Delta \text{INDUS}}}, \underset{+}{\underline{\Delta \text{MANAB}}})$$

where PAYOUT represents insurance payouts to beneficiaries, ECON represents economic growth, R_f represents the risk-free interest rate, INDUS represents industry conditions, and MANAB represents the abilities of the insurance company's management.

Change in Payouts The payouts on insurance claims are somewhat stable for most life insurance companies with a diversified set of customers. In contrast, the payouts on property and casualty claims can be volatile for PC companies.

Change in Economic Conditions Economic growth can enhance an insurance company's cash flows because it increases the level of income of firms and households and can increase the demand for the company's services. During periods of strong economic growth, debt securities maintained by insurance companies are less likely to default. In addition, equity securities maintained by insurance companies should perform well because the firms represented by these securities should perform well.

Change in the Risk-Free Interest Rate Some of an insurance company's assets (such as bonds) are adversely affected by rising interest rates. Thus, the valuation of an insurance company may be inversely related to interest rate movements.

Change in Industry Conditions Insurance companies are subject to industry conditions, including regulatory constraints, technology, and competition within the industry. For example, they now compete against various financial institutions when offering some services. As regulators have reduced barriers, competition within the insurance industry has become more intense.

Change in Management Abilities An insurance company has control over the composition of its managers and its organizational structure. Its managers can attempt to make internal decisions that will capitalize on the external forces (economic growth, interest rates, regulatory constraints) that the company cannot control. Thus, the management skills of an insurance company can influence its expected cash flows. In particular, skillful management is needed to determine the likelihood of events that could cause massive payouts to policyholders.

25-6b Factors That Affect the Required Rate of Return by Investors

The required rate of return by investors who invest in an insurance company can be modeled as

$$\Delta k = f(\underset{+}{\underbrace{\Delta R_f}}, \underset{+}{\underbrace{\Delta RP}})$$

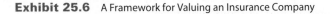

where R_f represents the risk-free interest rate and RP represents the risk premium.

The risk-free interest rate is usually expected to be positively related to inflation, economic growth, and the budget deficit level, but inversely related to money supply growth (assuming it does not cause inflation). The risk premium on an insurance company is inversely related to economic growth. It can also be affected by industry conditions (such as regulations) and management abilities.

Exhibit 25.6 provides a framework for valuing an insurance company based on the preceding discussion. In general, the value of an insurance company is favorably affected by strong economic growth, a reduction in interest rates, and strong management capabilities.

Exhibit 25.6   A Framework for Valuing an Insurance Company

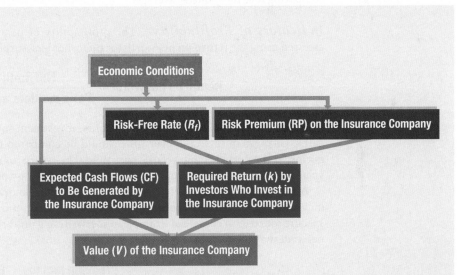

- A stronger economy leads to more services being provided by insurance companies and better cash flows. It may also enhance stock valuations, thereby increasing the valuations of stocks held by the insurance company.
- A lower risk-free rate results in more favorable valuations of the bonds held by the insurance company.
- The valuation of an insurance company is also influenced by industry conditions and the firm's management (not shown in the diagram). These factors affect the risk premium (and therefore the return required by investors) and the expected cash flows to be generated by the insurance company. In particular, property and casualty companies are exposed to court rulings that can result in them paying large damages awards, and health insurance companies are exposed to regulations regarding reimbursement for healthcare services.

25-6c **Indicators of Value and Performance**

Some of the more common indicators of an insurance company's value and performance are available in investment service publications. A time-series assessment of the dollar amount of life insurance and/or PC insurance premiums will indicate the growth in the company's insurance business. A time-series analysis of investment income can be used to assess the performance of the company's portfolio managers. However, the dollar amount of investment income is affected by several factors that are not under portfolio managers' control, such as the amount of funds received as premiums that can be invested in securities and market interest rates. In addition, a relatively low level of investment income may result from a high concentration in stocks that pay low or no dividends rather than from poor performance.

Indicators of Liquidity   Because insurance companies have unique characteristics, the financial ratios of other financial institutions are generally not applicable. An insurance company's liquidity can be measured using the following ratio:

$$\text{Liquidity ratio} = \frac{\text{Invested assets}}{\text{Loss reserves and unearned premium reserves}}$$

The higher the ratio, the more liquid the company is. This ratio can be evaluated by comparing it to the industry average.

Indicators of Profitability   The profitability of insurance companies is often assessed using the return on net worth (or policyholders' surplus) as a ratio, as follows:

$$\text{Return on net worth} = \frac{\text{Net profit}}{\text{Policyholders' surplus}}$$

Net profit consists of underwriting profits, investment income, and realized capital gains. Changes in this ratio over time should be compared to changes in the industry norms, as the norm is quite volatile over time. The return on net worth tends to be quite volatile for PC insurance companies because of the volatility of their claims.

Although a company's net profit reflects all income sources and, therefore, provides only a general measure of profitability, various financial ratios can be used to focus on a specific source of income. For example, underwriting gains or losses are measured by the net underwriting margin:

$$\text{Net underwriting margin} = \frac{\text{Premium income} - \text{Policy expenses}}{\text{Total assets}}$$

When policy expenses exceed premium income, the net underwriting margin is negative. As long as other sources of income can offset such a loss, however, net profit will still be positive.

Summary

- Insurance company premiums are influenced by the likelihood of a claim and the potential size of the claim. They also account for the potential adverse selection problem and the moral hazard problem.

- State agencies attempt to ensure that insurance companies are providing adequate services, and also approve the rates that insurers may charge. Insurance company agents must be licensed, and the specific wording of insurance policies must be approved by the state to ensure that the policies are not misleading. State regulators also evaluate insurance companies' asset portfolios to confirm that investments are reasonably safe and that adequate reserves are maintained to protect policyholders in case of a loss.

- Life insurance companies compensate the beneficiary of a policy upon the policyholder's death. They obtain most of their funds from annuity plans, investments, and premiums; stocks and corporate debt securities are their primary assets.

- Other types of insurance operations include property and casualty insurance, healthcare insurance, business insurance, bond insurance, and mortgage insurance.

- Insurance companies are exposed to interest rate risk because they tend to maintain large bond portfolios whose values will decline when interest rates rise. They are also exposed to credit risk and market risk as a result of their investments in corporate debt securities, mortgages, stocks, and real estate.

- The value of an insurance company is based on its expected cash flows and the rate of return required by investors. The payouts of claims (cash outflows) are somewhat predictable for life insurance firms, so they tend to have stable cash flows. In contrast, the payouts of claims for property and casualty insurance and other types of insurance services are subject to much uncertainty.

Point/Counterpoint

Should Insurance Companies Make Risky Investments?

Point No. Insurance companies can best serve their policyholders by maintaining adequate reserves in case claims are filed. If they make risky investments, they could experience liquidity problems and may not be able to serve their policyholders.

Counterpoint Yes. Insurance companies can increase their return by investing in riskier securities, which in turn may enhance their profits and valuation, and their stock price (if they are publicly traded). In this way, the investment policy maximizes the value of an insurance company for its owners.

Who Is Correct? Use the Internet to learn more about this issue and then formulate your own opinion.

Questions and Applications

1. **Life Insurance** How does whole life insurance serve as a form of savings for policyholders?

2. **Whole Life versus Term Insurance** How do whole life and term insurance differ from the perspective of insurance companies? From the perspective of the policyholders?

3. **Universal Life Insurance** Identify the characteristics of universal life insurance.

4. **Group Plan** Explain group plan life insurance.

5. **Assets of Life Insurance Companies** What are the main assets of life insurance companies? Identify the main categories. What is the main use of funds by life insurance companies?

6. **Financing the Real Estate Market** How do insurance companies finance the real estate market?

7. **Policy Loans** What is a policy loan? When are policy loans popular? Why?

8. **Government Rescue of AIG** Why did the U.S. government rescue AIG during the credit crisis in 2008?

9. **Managing Credit Risk and Liquidity Risk** How do insurance companies manage credit risk and liquidity risk?

10. **Liquidity Risk** Discuss the liquidity risk experienced by life insurance companies and by property and casualty (PC) insurance companies.

11. **PC Insurance** What purpose do property and casualty insurance companies serve? Explain how the characteristics of PC insurance and life insurance differ.

12. **Cash Flow Underwriting** Explain the concept of cash flow underwriting.

13. **Impact of Inflation on Assets** Explain how a life insurance company's asset portfolio may be affected by inflation.

14. **Reinsurance** What is reinsurance?

15. **NAIC** What is NAIC, and what is its purpose?

16. **Adverse Selection and Moral Hazard Problems in Insurance** Explain the adverse selection and moral hazard problems in insurance. Gorton Insurance Company wants to properly price its auto insurance, which protects against losses due to auto accidents. If Gorton wants to avoid the adverse selection and moral hazard problems, should it assess the behavior of insured people, uninsured people, or both groups? Explain.

Critical Thinking Question

Investment Policy Incentives of Insurance Companies Consider a life insurance company that needs to ensure that it can make a steady stream of payments over time to beneficiaries of its policyholders. Assume that the compensation for the insurance company's portfolio managers is tied to the return earned on the investments each year. Write a short essay that explains how the compensation plan

might lead to investment strategies that do not serve the needs of the policyholders.

Interpreting Financial News

Interpret the following comments made by Wall Street analysts and portfolio managers.

a. "Insurance company stocks may benefit from the recent decline in interest rates."

b. "Insurance company portfolio managers may serve as shareholder activists to implicitly control a corporation's actions."

c. "If a life insurance company wants a portfolio manager to generate sufficient cash to meet expected payments to beneficiaries, it cannot expect the manager to achieve relatively high returns for the portfolio."

Managing in Financial Markets

Assessing Insurance Company Operations As a consultant to an insurance company, you have been asked to assess the asset composition of the company.

a. The insurance company has recently sold a large amount of bonds and invested the proceeds in real estate. Its logic was that these actions would reduce the exposure of its assets to interest rate risk. Do you agree? Explain.

b. This insurance company currently has a small amount of stock. The company expects that it will need to liquidate some of its assets soon to make payments to beneficiaries. Should it shift its bond holdings (with short terms remaining until maturity) into stock in an effort to achieve a higher rate of return before it needs to liquidate this investment?

c. The insurance company maintains a higher proportion of junk bonds than most other insurance companies. In recent years, junk bonds have performed very well during a period of strong economic growth, as the yields paid by junk bonds have been well above those of high-quality corporate bonds. Very few defaults have occurred over this period. Consequently, the insurance company has proposed that it invest more heavily in junk bonds, as it believes that the concerns about junk bonds are unjustified. Do you agree? Explain.

Flow of Funds Exercise

How Insurance Companies Facilitate the Flow of Funds

Carson Company is considering a private placement of equity with Secura Insurance Company.

a. Explain the interaction between Carson Company and Secura. How will Secura serve Carson's needs, and how will Carson serve Secura's needs?

b. Why does Carson interact with Secura instead of trying to obtain the funds directly from individuals who pay premiums to Secura?

c. If Secura's investment performs well, who benefits? Is it worthwhile for Secura to closely monitor Carson's management? Explain.

Internet/Excel Exercises

1. Obtain a life insurance quotation online using the website www.eterm.com. Fill in information about you (or a family member or friend) and obtain a quotation for a $1 million life insurance policy. What are the monthly and annual premiums for the various term lengths? Next, leaving all other information unchanged, change your gender. Are the premiums the same or different? Do you think insurance premiums are higher or lower for insurance companies operating entirely through the Internet?

2. Select a publicly traded insurance company of your choice. Go to its website and retrieve its most recent annual report. Summarize the company's main business. Is it focused on life insurance, auto insurance, health insurance, or a combination of these? Describe its performance over the last year. Explain why its performance was higher or lower than normal. Was the change in its performance due to the economy, the impact of recent interest rate movements on its asset portfolio, the stock market's performance, or a change in the frequency and size of insurance claims?

3. Go to finance.yahoo.com, and enter the symbol MET (MetLife, Inc.). Click on "5y" just above the stock price graph to review the stock price movements over the last five years. Click on "Chart," then on "Comparison," and then on "S&P 500" to compare the trend of MetLife's stock price with the movements in the S&P stock index. Has MetLife performed better or worse than the index? Offer an explanation for its performance.

4. Go to finance.yahoo.com, and enter the symbol MET (MetLife, Inc.). Retrieve stock price data at the beginning of the last 20 quarters. Then go to fred.stlouisfed.org and retrieve interest rate data at the beginning of the last 20 quarters for the three-month Treasury bill. Record the data on an Excel spreadsheet. Derive the quarterly return of MetLife. Derive the quarterly change in the interest rate. Apply regression analysis in which the quarterly return of MetLife, Inc., is the dependent variable and the quarterly change in the interest rate is the independent variable (see Appendix B for more information about using regression analysis). Is there a positive or negative relationship between the interest rate movement and the stock return of MetLife? Is the relationship significant? Offer an explanation for this relationship.

WSJ Exercise

Insurance Company Performance

Using an issue of *The Wall Street Journal*, summarize an article that discusses the recent performance of a particular insurance company. Does the article suggest that the insurance company's performance was better or worse than the norm? What reason is given for the particular level of performance?

Online Articles with Real-World Examples

Find a recent practical article available online that describes a real-world example regarding a specific financial institution or financial market that reinforces one or more concepts covered in this chapter.

If your class has an online component, your professor may ask you to post your summary of the article there and provide a link to the article so that other students can access it. If your class is live, your professor may ask you to summarize your application of the article in class. Your professor may assign specific students to complete this assignment or may allow any students to do the assignment on a volunteer basis.

For recent online articles and real-world examples related to this chapter, consider using the following search terms (be sure to include the prevailing year as a search term to ensure that the online articles are recent):

1. [name of a specific insurance company] AND performance

2. [name of a specific insurance company] AND operations

3. [name of a specific insurance company] AND risk

4. [name of a specific insurance company] AND earnings

5. [name of a specific insurance company] AND management

6. insurance company AND operations

7. insurance company AND risk

8. insurance company AND regulation

26
Pension Fund Operations

Pension plans provide savings for employees that can be used for retirement. They serve as a key source of income for employees upon retirement. Pension plans invest the money set aside by employees for their retirement in the financial markets until those funds need to be distributed. For this reason, they serve as major institutional investors.

Pension plans can be categorized as private or public, depending on the profile of the employer. Private pension plans are created by private employers, including industrial, labor, service, nonprofit, charitable, and educational organizations. Public pension funds can be state, local, or federal. The best-known government pension fund is Social Security. In addition to that system, public pension funds serve employees who work in the public sector. States, counties, and cities commonly hire employees and offer pensions as an employee benefit. State employers channel their retirement contributions each pay period to a state pension fund that manages the fund for employees of the state. Public pension funds are governed by their respective state and local laws.

26-1 Types of Pension Plans

Pension funds are commonly categorized as defined-benefit or defined-contribution plans depending on how contributions are made and what level of benefits is provided.

26-1a Defined-Benefit Plans

A **defined-benefit plan** precisely specifies the benefits to be received by employees. The contributions are dictated by the benefits that will eventually be provided. A defined-benefit plan uses a formula to determine how much it will provide to employees upon retirement based on their salary level and their number of years of full-time service. However, the specific formula varies among employers. The retirement income will be provided by the pension fund as long as the retiree is living. For defined-contribution plans, the sponsoring firm's main responsibility is its contributions to the fund.

EXAMPLE
Quatz Co. has established a defined-benefit plan for employees with at least 20 years of full-time service. For these employees, the plan will pay annual retirement income equal to 50 percent of the employee's average annual salary during the five years in which their salary was highest. For employees with 30 years of full-time service, Quatz's defined-benefit plan pays a retirement income equal to 70 percent of the employee's average annual salary during the five years in which their salary was highest. ●

A defined-benefit plan requires the employer to set aside ("contribute") funds that can be invested until they are to be distributed to employees after retirement. Some defined-benefit plans might also require employees to contribute to the plan while they are employed. The employer is responsible for ensuring that the money set aside will grow over time (from investing strategies) so that it will be large enough to provide the defined benefits at retirement.

The amount of the monthly pension payments that will be provided to an employee upon retirement is commonly influenced by the employee's maximum salary level, which is not known until the time of retirement. The amount of the monthly pension payment is also influenced by the employee's retirement age and life expectancy, which also are not known while the employee is working. Consequently, the estimate of the amount of funds that should be set aside to cover an employee's retirement benefits is uncertain.

In recent years, many news reports have focused on public defined-benefit pension plans that might not be able to cover their obligations to participating employees, because those plans have not set aside sufficient funds or have made poor investment decisions with those funds. This topic is discussed in detail near the end of this chapter.

26-1b Defined-Contribution Plans

A **defined-contribution plan** provides benefits that are determined by the accumulated contributions made to the fund while the employee is employed and by the fund's investment performance. With a defined-contribution plan, the employer allocates money to the fund on behalf of the employees each pay period. Many plans also allow employees to make their own contributions to the fund, which are deducted from their paycheck each pay period. This feature allows employees to increase the savings that will be available to them upon their retirement.

Employees cannot access money in a defined-contribution plan until retirement unless they are willing to incur a penalty for early withdrawal. The employer typically offers several different investment options, such as stock mutual funds, bond funds, money market funds, and real estate funds. Employees can designate what proportions of their money should be allocated to particular types of investments. Thus, even if two employees have same amount of money set aside in their retirement accounts over time, the employee who makes better decisions about how to invest the money in the defined-contribution plan will have a larger account balance at the time of retirement.

26-1c Comparing Pension Plans

Employees' freedom to decide how to invest the money set aside for their retirement in a defined-contribution plan is a key characteristic that distinguishes these pension plans from defined-benefit plans; in the latter case, the managers of the pension fund determine how the money set aside for retirement is invested. Some employees may favor a defined-contribution plan if they prefer to make their own investment decisions with their retirement money. Conversely, other employees may favor a defined-benefit plan if they prefer to know the exact amount of benefits they will receive at retirement and do not want to be responsible for determining how to invest their retirement money. Employees with defined-benefit plans usually do not worry about how their pension fund money is invested until it is distributed to them, because the amount of retirement income that they will receive is defined by their plan.

If financial markets are weak for a few years, the investments made by many defined-benefit plans will likely perform poorly, but the obligations to the retirees covered by those plans are not affected by the weak market conditions. Because the defined-benefit plans are still obligated to cover the payouts to retirees, the employers will have to contribute additional cash to their defined-benefit plans to make up for the poor investment performance.

the credit crisis that began in 2008, many large companies experienced losses in their pension portfolios because of their investments in mortgage-backed securities and stocks. As a consequence, the gap between what they needed to pay their retired employees and the amount of funds available in their pension plans increased, and the companies' financial condition was not sufficiently strong to reduce this gap. When companies use more of their cash to boost underfunded pension plans, they have less cash to use for other purposes; in turn, their operating performance may suffer when they have to increase contributions to their pension plans. By 2015, financial markets had improved substantially, and many private plans were once again fully funded.

In the future, there will likely be some periods when investments yield poor performance, and many private pension plans will be underfunded again. The Pension Protection Act should prompt corporations to periodically determine whether their pension fund is underfunded, and if so, to set aside additional money to resolve the deficiency.

WEB

www.pensionfunds.com
News related to pension
funds.

26-4 Underfunded Public Defined-Benefit Pension Plans

Every government agency that offers a defined-benefit plan should automatically set aside funds each pay period for each employee who is participating in the plan to ensure that it will have sufficient funding for all participating employees upon their retirement. However, many public defined-benefit pension plans are not consistently allocating sufficient funds to cover future obligations.

ETHICS

26-4a Overestimated Rate of Return

Many government agencies assume that they will earn a high rate of return on their pension fund investments, which justifies setting aside a smaller amount of money to meet future obligations. But if the rate of return on their investments is lower than what they assumed, their pension plans can become underfunded.

EXAMPLE

The California state government has huge pension funds to accommodate the large number of state employees. The state commonly presumes that its pension funds will earn high annual returns on investments. This presumption allows the state government to allocate a smaller amount of money toward the pension funds so that it can provide more money for other government services. However, the California state pension funds are now underfunded by more than $300 billion, which suggests that the state may be unable to pay its obligations to state workers who retire in the future. ●

ETHICS

26-4b Political Motivation

Some pension funds are underfunded for political reasons. In particular, some governments may not set aside sufficient funding for their pension plans because they prefer to use the funds for other purposes. Such a strategy can lead to serious underfunding problems in the long run that will ultimately have to be corrected by either higher state taxes, reduced government employee pensions, or reduced spending on education or other services. Unfortunately, this problem has been largely ignored, because politicians are unlikely to be elected if they call for raising taxes and reducing government employee pensions to resolve the underfunded pensions problem.

26-4c Possible Solutions to Underfunded Pensions

Government officials might consider the following possible solutions to reduce their underfunded pensions. There is no easy or painless solution, however, and each strategy is subject to limitations.

Issue Bonds Some governments might attempt to correct their budget deficits caused by underfunded pensions by issuing debt. However, some governments with large pension underfunding that utilized this strategy have defaulted on their debt, including Harrisburg, Pennsylvania (2010); San Bernardino and Stockton, California (2012); Jefferson County, Alabama (2013); and Detroit, Michigan (2013). The defaults by Stockton and Detroit were directly influenced by the large degree of underfunded pensions.

The credit rating agencies recently downgraded the credit rating of bonds issued by the state of Illinois because of its substantially underfunded pension plan. This forced the state to pay a higher yield on the bonds it issued, which may impose an additional cost on Illinois taxpayers or lead to reductions in state government services to make up for the deficit. The credit rating agencies also downgraded the rating of specific bonds issued by the city of Chicago. Those bonds are now rated as junk, primarily because of the huge amount of underfunded pensions that make it difficult for Chicago to cover its cash outflow payments.

Use Aggressive Investment Management Strategy for the Pension Fund In some cases, a pension plan that is underfunded may attempt to correct its funding deficiency by implementing a more aggressive investment strategy to increase its return on investments. However, this strategy can backfire, because a risky investment strategy may result in losses that could cause the pension fund to be even more underfunded. Many pension funds have specific guidelines intended to limit the amount of risk they can assume.

Revise the Required Pension Contributions or Benefits Some government agencies have attempted to solve the problems caused by underfunded pensions by increasing the retirement age at which employees can start receiving their pensions, requiring employees to contribute a larger proportion of their salary to the pension fund, or reducing the retirement benefits to employees. However, these changes may apply only to new government employees, as the government employer may be contractually required to meet its obligations to the employees who were hired before the policies were revised. Therefore, these actions may not provide a quick cure for the underfunded pensions.

Increase Taxes or Reduce Other Government Services Some government agencies have considered raising taxes or cutting services to resolve the pension underfunding problem. The city of Chicago recently increased its sales tax to 10.25 percent in an attempt to replenish its underfunded pension fund. This solution is usually politically unpopular, as taxpayers do not embrace the idea that they should pay more taxes today to correct past mistakes by government officials that led to the underfunded pensions.

Hold Government Officials Accountable for Underfunded Pensions Government officials who used pension money for political favors or other reasons instead of allocating the money toward pension funds have rarely been held accountable for the problems they caused. They may even have become more popular while they were in office, because they had more money to spend on government services as a result of diverting funds from the government pension fund. That strategy may have provided immediate short-term benefits, with the adverse effects (underfunded pensions) going unnoticed for several years.

Laws could be improved to make government officials accountable if they allow pensions to be underfunded by a specific degree. However, determining the amount of underfunding is not an exact science, and public pension funds might be able to use creative accounting that would understate the degree of underfunding.

Shift from Defined-Benefit to Defined-Contribution Plans The pension underfunding problem is possible only with defined-benefit plans and not with defined-contribution plans, because the money to be allocated in defined-contribution plans is immediately set aside for employees in each pay period. Only a few states currently require their employees to subscribe to a defined-benefit plan; by comparison, many other states allow participants to subscribe to either a defined-benefit or a defined-contribution plan. A government's shift from a defined-benefit plan to a defined-contribution plan would not resolve any underfunding problems that already exist, but it could at least prevent additional underfunding in the future.

ETHICS

26-5 Corruption of Defined-Benefit Pension Funds

The management of each defined-benefit pension fund is guided by its trustees, who have a fiduciary responsibility to serve the retirees who receive pension benefits. The board of trustees determines whether the investment decisions for the pension fund are made internally or by one or more investment companies. The board also sets policies for the investment strategy that can be implemented by the portfolio managers who manage the pension portfolio. In doing so, it may impose constraints on the proportion of funds that can be invested in particular types of investments. The board of trustees must carefully consider the pension fund's future liabilities when establishing guidelines for investing. In general, the trustees need to ensure that the investments generate sufficient returns so that they can cover their future liabilities.

26-5a Bribes to Trustees

Trustees of defined-benefit plans are supposed to serve the interests of the employees rather than themselves. However, trustees may be tempted to make decisions that are mostly intended to benefit themselves at the expense of the pension fund participants that they represent. When trustees select a particular investment company to manage a public defined-benefit plan, they can generate millions of dollars of annual income for the investment company (from the fees that the company charges the pension fund for its portfolio management service). For this reason, bribes from investment companies to trustees have occurred.

In one case, officials who oversaw pension funds for government agencies in California accepted bribes in return for allowing particular investment companies to manage a portion of the pension money. In another case, the sole trustee of a New York pension fund accepted bribes of nearly $1 million to steer $250 million of pension fund money toward an investment in a particular private equity fund. Trustees of Detroit's pension plan were charged with taking bribes to steer more than $200 million in pension fund money toward specific investments.

Some trustees of public pension plans are politicians who are campaigning for other political positions. Investment companies may make "contributions" to a trustee's election campaign in the hope of being hired by the trustee as consultants to manage a portion of the pension funds. Pension funds might be able to prevent corruption if they could ensure that their trustees are not subject to potential conflicts of interest.

26-5b Payment of Excessive Benefits

Some trustees of public pension plans have engaged in actions that favor particular pension participants or are simply inappropriate. For several years, Detroit's pension fund made payments to some employees while they were still working and gave some retirees supplemental payments to which they were not entitled. These unwarranted payments, which amounted to billions of dollars, helped to cause the deficiency in Detroit's pension fund and contributed to the city's bankruptcy.

Chicago's pension funds have granted some city employees excessive pension benefits, even though its pension funds in aggregate may be underfunded by more than $40 billion. The state of Illinois's pension funds (separate from the pension funds of Chicago) made some unusually large pension payouts to certain state employees, which were attributed to political maneuvering. This is one reason why the state of Illinois's pension funds may be underfunded by more than $130 billion.

26-5c **Ineffective Oversight by Trustees**

Sometimes trustees of public pension funds are hired for political reasons and do not have the financial qualifications to adequately oversee the management of the pension funds. Consequently, some public pension funds have been mismanaged, and the taxpayers or the pension fund participants may ultimately have to incur the cost of political hiring decisions. For example, Detroit's pension fund made some very risky investments that were inconsistent with serving the retirement needs of its pension participants. Proper oversight could have prevented such risky investments by the pension fund.

The types of corruption described in this section occur only with defined-benefit pension plans, because the employer is responsible for investing the money in the pension fund. Such corruption is not possible with defined-contribution plans, because the pension participants (not the employer) are responsible for deciding how the money is to be invested. Therefore, some employers might consider switching their pension plans from defined-benefit to defined-contribution plans if they wish to avoid the risk of corruption.

26-6 **Pension Fund Management**

Some defined-benefit pension plans are managed by life insurance companies. Contributions to such plans, called insured plans, are often used to purchase annuity policies so that the life insurance companies can provide benefits to employees upon retirement. The insurance company becomes the legal owner of the assets and is allowed to maintain only a small portion of its assets as equities. Therefore insurance companies concentrate on investing the pension plan contributions as bonds and mortgages.

Other pension funds are managed by the trust departments of financial institutions, such as commercial banks. The trust department invests the contributions and pays benefits to employees upon retirement. Although the day-to-day investment decisions of the trust department are controlled by the managing institution, the corporation owning the pension fund usually specifies general guidelines that the institution should follow. These guidelines might include:

- The percentage of the portfolio that should be used for stocks or bonds
- A desired minimum rate of return on the overall portfolio
- The maximum amount to be invested in real estate
- The minimum acceptable quality ratings for bonds
- The maximum amount to be invested in any one industry
- The average maturity of bonds held in the portfolio
- The maximum amount to be invested in options
- The minimum size of companies in which to invest

Pension portfolios managed by trusts commonly concentrate their investments in stocks. Thus, they offer potentially higher returns than insured plans can achieve, but also have a higher degree of risk.

26-6a Asset Allocation of Pension Funds

Private pension portfolios are dominated by common stock. By contrast, public pension portfolios are somewhat evenly invested in corporate bonds, stock, and other credit instruments, although the specific allocation can vary substantially among pension funds.

Many pension funds also invest in private equity funds, which use the money to purchase majority or entire stakes in businesses. A private equity fund charges a fee such as 2 percent per year to invest in the fund. In addition, it may take a percentage of the profits from its specific investments. Some pension funds make risky investments in real estate, junk bonds, and international securities.

Return versus Risk   In determining their asset allocation, pension fund managers have to balance return against risk. If pension funds can achieve higher returns on their existing investments, they can more easily meet their obligations to the participants in the plan. However, the strategy of attempting to earn a higher return with risky investments can backfire and cause a large loss.

Many pension fund managers pursued risky investments prior to the credit crisis of 2008–2009, which resulted in major losses when the downturn occurred. Since then, some pension plans have imposed restrictions on the types of investments that their pension fund managers can pursue. Although such restrictions result in safer investments, these investments will likely generate relatively low returns.

The degree of risk assumed by pension fund managers may be influenced by their compensation incentives. Some pension fund managers are rewarded if the portfolio performs very well, but are not penalized if the portfolio performs poorly. Under these conditions, the portfolio managers have an incentive to take more risk than is appropriate.

Hedging Pension Fund Portfolio Risk   Pension fund portfolio managers who are concerned about their exposure to risk can implement strategies to hedge that risk. If they are concerned that the prices of their bonds might fall over the next month due to an increase in interest rates, for example, they could hedge by selling bond futures contracts.

If pension portfolio managers are worried about the exposure of their stocks to risk over the next month, they could sell stock index futures or buy put options on stocks to hedge this risk. Many portfolio managers periodically sell futures contracts on stock indexes to hedge against market downturns.

Passive Investment Strategy   Another way that pension funds might manage risk is to consider using a passive management strategy such as investing in indexed mutual funds, which would perform as well as market benchmarks that represent the general stock market, bond market, and real estate market. The allocation across investments could be based on guidance from the board of trustees (assuming that they have adequate expertise) on the proper long-term allocation across different types of investments.

A passive investment strategy has several benefits. First, the pension fund can ensure that its investment strategy is consistently aligned with the board's recommended long-term allocation across investments. Second, this strategy can ensure that the pension fund portfolio avoids excessively risky investments. Third, the transparency of the investment strategy is beneficial to participants in the plan who rely on the pension for their retirement benefits. Fourth, the fund can avoid the large fees that pension funds commonly pay to investment companies hired to manage their money. Fifth, it ensures that no money is diverted to alternative investments triggered by favors or bribes to anyone who oversees the pension fund.

Many pension fund managers might argue that passive investing is designed to achieve only the mean performance level for each type of market represented by an index, and they would like to achieve a much higher performance level than the mean. Yet all active investors cannot outperform the mean. Obviously, portfolio managers hired to actively manage pension portfolios would not favor a passive strategy, because they would not be needed if such a strategy was implemented.

Pension funds that are willing to accept market returns on bonds can purchase bond index portfolios that have been created by investment companies. The bond index portfolio may include investment-grade corporate bonds, Treasury bonds, and U.S. government agency bonds. It does not include the entire set of these bonds, but rather just enough of them to mirror the market's performance. Investing in a market portfolio is a passive approach that does not require any analysis of individual bonds.

Equity portfolio indexes that mirror the stock market are also available for passive portfolio managers. These index funds have become popular over time because they avoid the transaction costs associated with frequent purchases and sales of individual stocks.

26-6b Matched versus Projective Funding Strategies

Pension fund management can be classified according to the strategy used to manage the portfolio. With a matched funding strategy, investment decisions are made with the objective of generating cash flows that match planned outflow payments. An alternative strategy is projective funding, which offers managers more flexibility in constructing a pension portfolio that can benefit from expected market and interest rate movements. Some pension funds segment their portfolios, with a portion being used for matched funding and the rest for projective funding.

An informal method of matched funding is to invest in long-term bonds to fund long-term liabilities and in intermediate bonds to fund intermediate liabilities. The appeal of matching lies in its assurance that future liabilities are covered regardless of market movements. This method might be especially useful for defined-benefit plans. Matching limits the manager's discretion, however, because it allows only investments that match future payouts. For example, portfolio managers required to use matched funding would need to avoid callable bonds, because these bonds could potentially be retired before maturity. This requirement also precludes consideration of many high-yield bonds. In addition, each liability payout may require a separate investment to which it can be perfectly matched; this would require several small investments and increase the pension fund's transaction costs.

26-7 Performance of Pension Funds

Pension funds commonly maintain a portfolio of stocks as well as a portfolio of bonds. Because they focus on investing pension contributions until payments are provided, the performance of their investments is critical to pension funds' success.

26-7a Pension Fund's Stock Portfolio Performance

The change in the value of a pension fund's portfolio focusing on stocks can be modeled as

$$\Delta V = f(\Delta \mathbf{MKT}, \Delta \mathbf{MANAB})$$

where MKT represents general stock market conditions and MANAB represents the abilities of the pension fund's management.

Change in Market Conditions   The stock portfolio's performance is usually closely related to market conditions. Most pension funds' stock portfolios performed well during the 2003–2007 period when market conditions were strong, poorly during the credit crisis in the 2008–2009 period, and well when the market rebounded in the 2010–2018 period.

Change in Management Abilities   Stock portfolio performance can vary among pension funds in a particular time period because of differences in the fund's management abilities. The composition of the stocks in a pension fund's portfolio is determined by the fund's portfolio managers. In addition, a pension fund's operating efficiency affects the expenses that the fund incurs and, therefore, affects its performance. A fund that is managed efficiently so that its expenses are low may be able to achieve higher returns even if its portfolio performance is about the same as the performance of other pension funds' portfolios.

26-7b Pension Fund's Bond Portfolio Performance

The change in the value of a pension fund's bond portfolio (including mortgages or mortgage-backed securities) can be modeled as

$$\Delta V = f(\Delta R_f, \Delta \text{RP}, \Delta \text{MANAB})$$

where R_f represents the risk-free rate, RP represents the risk premium, and MANAB represents the abilities of the portfolio managers.

Impact of Change in the Risk-Free Rate   Prices of bonds tend to be inversely related to changes in the risk-free interest rate. During periods when the risk-free interest rate declines substantially, the required rate of return by bondholders decreases, and most bond portfolios managed by pension funds perform well.

In recent years, long-term interest rates have been very low. Consequently, the future return that can be earned by pension funds on low-risk long-term bonds is very low if the investor holds those bonds until maturity. However, there is significant interest rate risk because long-term rates could rise from their prevailing levels over time, which would cause the prices to decline.

Impact of Change in the Risk Premium   When economic conditions deteriorate, the risk premium required by bondholders usually increases, which results in a higher required rate of return (assuming no change in the risk-free rate) and lower prices on risky bonds. During periods when risk premiums increase, bond portfolios of pension funds that contain a high proportion of risky bonds tend to perform poorly.

Impact of Management Abilities   The performance levels of bond portfolios can vary as a result of differences in management abilities. If a pension fund's portfolio managers can effectively adjust the bond portfolio in response to accurate forecasts of changes in interest rates or shifts in bond risk premiums, that fund's bond portfolio should experience relatively high performance. In addition, a pension fund's operating efficiency affects the expenses it incurs. If a bond portfolio is managed efficiently so that its expenses are low, it may be able to achieve relatively high returns even if its investments perform the same as those of other pension funds.

As time passes, portfolio managers might change the composition of a pension portfolio, which can alter the portfolio's potential return as well as its risk. Because long-term interest rates have been so low recently, portfolio managers might be tempted to switch out of low-risk bonds into high-yield bonds. That is, they might attempt to offset the low long-term risk-free rate with a high-risk premium on the bonds. However, this strategy exposes the portfolio to higher credit risk, as the high-yield bonds are more likely to default on their payments.

Alternatively, portfolio managers seeking to achieve better returns than are available on low-risk bonds might invest more of their funds in stocks (assuming that there are no restrictions on the portfolio that would rule out such a strategy). This strategy also exposes the portfolio to higher risk, as the stocks may suffer significant declines in value when stock market conditions are weak.

26-7c Evaluation of Pension Fund Performance

A pension fund's performance can be evaluated by comparing it to a passive strategy benchmark representing the same mix of securities. For example, assume that an actively managed pension fund presently has a stock portfolio and a bond portfolio. The risk-adjusted returns on the fund's actively managed stock portfolio could be compared to a benchmark stock index (such as an exchange-traded fund representing the stock index). In addition, the risk-adjusted returns on the pension fund's actively managed bond portfolio could be compared to a benchmark bond index. This comparison can determine whether the portfolio managers of the pension fund are achieving better performance than if the pension fund used a passive management strategy.

Research on Pension Portfolio Performance   Some research has found that managed pension portfolios perform no better than market indexes. During the credit crisis, some pension portfolios actually performed much worse than benchmark market indexes because their managers invested heavily in risky mortgages and mortgage-backed securities. For example, the state of Washington lost $90 million on its investment in securities issued by Lehman Brothers (which filed for bankruptcy after experiencing severe losses in mortgage-related securities), and the state of New York lost hundreds of millions of dollars on its investment in similar securities.

Summary

- For defined-benefit pension plans, the benefits are dictated by a formula that is typically based on the employee's salary level and number of years of employment. For defined-contribution pension plans, the benefits are determined by the accumulated contributions and the returns on the pension fund investments.

- Pension funds participate in financial markets by investing in securities such as stocks and bonds. Many pension funds' investments require the brokerage services of securities firms. Some pension funds have taken active roles in governance over corporations.

- Private pension plans are subject to vesting rules and are monitored by the Pension Benefit Guaranty Corporation.

- Many defined-benefit pension plans are currently underfunded. One reason for the underfunding is employers' assumption of an overly optimistic rate of return. Other public pension funds are underfunded because the government agencies have granted generous retiree benefits without requiring sufficient

contributions to cover those future benefits when employees retire. Consequently, they have to correct the deficiency by raising taxes or cutting government services.

- Corruption, including bribery and political favors, has contributed to the underfunding problem for many defined-benefit public pension plans.

- Some pension funds use a matched funding strategy, in which investment decisions are made with the objective of generating cash flows that match planned outflow payments. Other pension funds use a projective funding strategy, which attempts to capitalize on expected market or interest rate movements.

- The valuation and performance of pension fund portfolios are highly influenced by market conditions. However, some pension portfolios are more exposed to risk than others. Notably, pension portfolios can suffer losses during weak market conditions. Pension fund managers have an influence on the pension portfolio performance, especially when they have the flexibility to adjust the relative proportion of stocks versus bonds in the portfolio.

Point/Counterpoint

Should Pension Fund Managers Be More Involved with Corporate Governance?

Point No. Pension fund managers should focus on assessing stock valuations and determining which stocks are undervalued versus overvalued. If pension funds own stocks of firms that perform poorly, the fund managers can penalize those firms by dumping those stocks and investing their money in other stocks. If pension funds focus too much on corporate governance, they will lose sight of their goal of serving the pension recipients.

Counterpoint Yes. To the extent that pension fund managers can use governance to improve the performance of the firms in which they invest, they can improve the funds' performance. In this way, they also improve the returns to the pension recipients.

Who Is Correct? Use the Internet to learn more about this issue and then formulate your own opinion.

Questions and Applications

1. **Private versus Public Pension Funds** Explain the general difference between the portfolio composition of private pension funds and public pension funds.

2. **Defined-Benefit versus Defined-Contribution Plans** Describe a defined-benefit pension plan. Describe a defined-contribution plan, and explain how it differs from a defined-benefit plan.

3. **Pension Fund Participation in Financial Markets** Explain how pension funds participate in financial markets.

4. **Governance by Pension Funds** Explain how a pension fund's governance of corporations can help to enhance the performance of the pension fund.

5. **Pension Plan's Vesting Schedule** Explain how a pension plan's vesting schedule works and what its purpose is.

6. **ERISA** Explain how ERISA affects employees who change employers.

7. **Tax Benefits of Pension Plans** Explain how pension plans provide tax benefits.

8. **Guidelines for a Trust** What type of general guidelines may be specified for a trust that is managing a pension fund?

9. **Management of Pension Portfolios** Explain the general difference in the composition of pension portfolios managed by trusts versus those managed by insurance companies. Why does this difference occur?

10. **PBGC** What is the main purpose of the Pension Benefit Guarantee Corporation (PBGC)?

11. **Exposure of Pension Funds to Interest Rate Risk** Why might pension funds be exposed to interest rate risk? How can pension funds reduce their exposure to interest rate risk?

12. **Pension Fund Investment Performance Evaluation** McCanna, Inc., has hired an investment company to manage its pension fund, which is invested in a stock portfolio and a bond portfolio. Explain how McCanna can evaluate the performance of the investment company in managing its pension fund money.

13. **Estimated Rate of Return and Underfunding** Explain how some government defined-benefit plans have become underfunded as a result of overestimating their rate of return on investment.

14. **Potential Impact of an Underfunded Public Pension Fund on Debt** Explain how an underfunded public pension fund can affect the debt rating of a city or state.

15. **Potential Corruption of Pension Fund Trustees** Explain the potential for corruption when a trustee has the power to determine who will manage a pension fund.

Critical Thinking Question

Aligning Incentives of Pension Funds Consider a state pension fund that needs to generate a series of fixed payments for its retirees. Assume that the compensation of the fund's portfolio managers is tied to the return earned on the investments each year. Write a short essay that explains how the compensation plan might lead to investment strategies that do not serve the needs of the retirees.

Interpreting Financial News

Interpret the following statements made by Wall Street analysts and portfolio managers.

a. "The city is now broke because of its pensions."
b. "Defined-contribution plans would prevent politicians from buying votes in a state."
c. "Public pension funds govern corporations but also need to govern themselves."

Managing in Financial Markets

Solutions to Pension Underfunding As a consultant to a state's underfunded pension fund, you have been asked to search for solutions to prevent underfunding in the future.

a. One explanation for the underfunding of the defined-benefit plan is that the economy was weak recently, so financial markets were weak, and this caused the underfunding. If so, the underfunding may not be a problem in the future. Do you think this explanation is sufficient, so there is no need to search for an alternative solution? Explain.
b. One possible solution is to convert the state's defined-benefit plan to a defined-contribution plan. Explain why this could be a viable solution to the problem.
c. Some state workers prefer a defined-benefit plan because they are afraid that they will make poor investments if they are forced to manage their own funds (as they would with a defined-contribution plan). Is that a sufficient reason to force the state to remain on a defined-benefit plan?

Flow of Funds Exercise

How Pension Funds Facilitate the Flow of Funds

Carson Company has a defined-benefit pension plan that provides generous benefits to its employees upon retirement.
a. Explain the role of the portfolio managers who manage the pension fund. What is their primary role?

b. Explain the trade-off between investing in bonds versus in stock for the purpose of providing future retirement benefits.
c. Explain how investment decisions on the pension fund would change if the defined-benefit plan was changed to a defined-contribution plan.

WSJ Exercise

Pension Fund Issues

Using an issue of *The Wall Street Journal*, summarize an article that discusses recent issues involving one or more pension funds.

Internet/Excel Exercises

Go to www.calpers.ca.gov/page/investments (the website of the California Public Employees Retirement System). How are the fund's assets allocated? What is the fund's current market value? Look at the fund's most recent investment report. What is the fund's rate of return? Has its rate of return increased or decreased in the last year? What is the fund's philosophy of corporate governance? What governance actions has it taken recently?

Online Articles with Real-World Examples

Find a recent practical article available online that describes a real-world example regarding a specific financial institution or financial market that reinforces one or more concepts covered in this chapter.

If your class has an online component, your professor may ask you to post your summary of the article there and provide a link to the article so that other students can access it. If your class is live, your professor may ask you to summarize your application of the article in class. Your professor may assign specific students to complete this assignment or may allow any students to do the assignment on a volunteer basis.

For recent online articles and real-world examples related to this chapter, consider using the following search terms (be sure to include the prevailing year as a search term to ensure that the online articles are recent):

1. [name of a specific pension fund] AND performance

2. [name of a specific pension fund] AND operations

3. [name of a specific pension fund] AND risk

4. pension fund AND management

5. pension fund AND operations

PART 7 INTEGRATIVE PROBLEM

Assessing the Influence of Economic Conditions across a Financial Conglomerate's Units

This problem requires an understanding of the operations and asset compositions of savings institutions (Chapter 21), finance companies (Chapter 22), mutual funds (Chapter 23), securities firms (Chapter 24), insurance companies (Chapter 25), and pension funds (Chapter 26).

A diversified financial conglomerate has six units (subsidiaries), with each unit focusing on its own specialization:

- Thrift operations
- Consumer finance operations
- Mutual fund operations
- Securities firm operations
- Insurance operations
- Consulting for pension funds (managing long-term bond portfolios for some pension funds)

As a financial analyst for the conglomerate's holding company, you have been asked to assess all of the units and to indicate how each unit will be affected as economic conditions change, as well as which units will be most affected.

In the past few months, all economic indicators have been signaling the possibility of a recession. Stock prices have already declined, as the demand for stocks has decreased significantly. It appears that the pessimistic outlook will last for at least a few months. The trading volume of stocks is expected to decline. Economic conditions are already somewhat stagnant and are expected to deteriorate further in future months. Thus, long-term interest rates will likely decline. During the next few months, firms will not consider mergers, new stock issues, or new bond issues.

Questions

1. Your assignment is to identify the units that will be less adversely affected by the recession. You believe that the units' different characteristics will cause some of them to be affected to a more significant extent than others are.

2. Currently, each unit employs economists who develop forecasts for interest rates and other economic conditions. When assessing potential economic effects on each unit, what are the disadvantages of this approach versus having just one economist at the holding company provide forecasts?

Final Review

Chapters 17 to 26 are focused on financial institutions. Here is a brief review of the chapters.

Chapter 17 explains how banks obtain most of their funds from deposits and allocate most of their funds toward loans or securities. Chapter 18 explains how banks are regulated according to the services they offer and the capital that they must maintain; it also explores how regulators monitor banks' risk over time. Chapter 19 explains how banks manage their sources and uses of funds (within regulatory constraints) in a manner geared toward achieving their return and risk preferences. Chapter 20 considers how a bank's performance is highly influenced by what it charges on loans versus what it pays on deposits (which affects its net interest margin), its income earned from services (noninterest income), and its level of noninterest expenses.

Chapter 21 explains that savings institutions are similar to banks in terms of the manner by which they obtain funds, but notes that they use most of their funds to invest in mortgages or mortgage-related securities. This results in a higher exposure to interest rate risk, although savings institutions can hedge that risk. Chapter 22 explains that finance companies differ from banks and savings institutions in that they typically obtain their funds by issuing commercial paper and target their use of funds toward consumers or small businesses. In general, the credit risk of their assets is higher than that of commercial banks or savings institutions. Chapter 23 identifies the types of mutual funds available and explains how performance and risk vary across funds. In general, a mutual fund's asset portfolio is much more risky than those of other financial institutions. Chapter 24 describes how securities firms channel funds through financial markets. The investment banking portion of a securities firm places new securities with investors, thereby helping corporations obtain financing. The brokerage portion of a securities firm channels funds between investors in the secondary market.

Chapter 25 explains how insurance companies obtain funds from the premiums they charge, and how they invest those funds in financial markets. Chapter 26 explains how pension funds rely on retirement contributions from employees or their respective employers, and how they invest those funds in financial markets.

This self-exam allows you to test your understanding of some of the key concepts covered in the chapters on financial institutions. It does not replace the end-of-chapter questions, nor does it cover all the concepts. Instead, it is simply intended to allow you to test yourself on a general overview of key concepts. Try to simulate taking an exam by answering the questions without using your book and your notes. The answers to this exam are provided at the end of the questions so that you can grade your exam. If you have any wrong answers, you should reread the related material and then redo the questions that you answered incorrectly.

This exam may not necessarily match the level of rigor in your course. Your instructor may offer you specific information about how this Final Self-Exam relates to the coverage and rigor of the final exam in your course.

Final Self-Exam

1. Flagstaff Bank currently has assets that are heavily concentrated in secured loans and Treasury securities, whereas Mesa Bank has assets that are concentrated in consumer loans and credit card loans. The managerial capabilities of the two banks are similar. Mesa Bank's performance was much better than that of Flagstaff Bank last year, but Flagstaff Bank's performance is much better than that of Mesa Bank this year. Explain why the relative performance of the two banks is likely to change over time.

2. The Sarbanes-Oxley Act of 2002 requires publicly traded firms to be more transparent in their reporting. This may reduce the asymmetric information problem between firms (including banks) and their investors. Do you think the Sarbanes-Oxley Act will eliminate the need for CAMELS ratings?

3. Kentucky Bank has a new board of directors who believe that the bank has opportunities for major growth and want to ensure that the CEO makes good investment decisions to expand the bank's business. To give the CEO a strong incentive to perform well, the board set the CEO's quarterly compensation in line with the return on equity. The CEO immediately decided to repurchase as many shares as possible while barely meeting the bank's capital requirements. Why would the CEO take this action? Will the compensation structure used by the bank remove agency problems?

4. Last year, Alabama Bank had a net interest margin of 3 percent, noninterest income was 1.5 percent of assets, noninterest expenses were 3 percent of assets, and loan loss reserves were 0.5 percent of assets. Alabama Bank wants to employ a strategy of using more of its resources to offer financial services. It expects that it can increase its noninterest income by 0.5 percent as a percentage of assets. What other components (or ratios) of the income statement may be affected by this strategy?

5. Maryland Savings Institution maintains most of its assets in fixed-rate mortgages with maturities of between 10 and 30 years. Most of its deposits have maturities of less than one year. Assume that the Fed implements a restrictive monetary policy.

   a. Explain how that monetary policy will affect interest rates.

   b. Assuming that interest rates change as expected, how will that affect the spread between interest revenue and interest expenses?

   c. Should Maryland hedge its asset portfolio based on its expectations? If so, how should it hedge? If it should hedge, explain any limitations of the hedge.

6. How do financial institutions vary in terms of their main uses of funds?

7. Explain the role that insurance companies and pension funds play in financial markets.

8. Explain why a stock market benefits more when financial institutions are investors than when individual investors invest all their money directly into the stock market themselves.

9. Discuss the following argument. Money market funds attract money from investors who do not know what else to do with their money. Thus, money market funds are merely a last resort when there are no better alternatives for investment. Since they invest only in short-term securities, they do not play a role in financing economic growth.

10. Closed-end funds tend to hold stocks that are less liquid than stocks held by open-end funds.

a. Do you think this characteristic is an advantage for closed-end funds that want to achieve high returns?

b. Why is it easier for closed-end funds to manage a portfolio of less liquid stocks than it would be for open-end funds?

11. Discuss the strategy of investing all of an investor's money in four mutual funds that focus on growth companies. The belief is that the investor is fully insulated from market conditions because each fund contains 40 different stocks.

12. For a given type of mutual fund classification, what is a key characteristic that causes some mutual funds to outperform others?

13. When a securities firm serves as an underwriter for an initial public offering (IPO), is the firm working for the issuer or the institutional investors that may purchase shares? Explain the dilemma.

14. Do stock analysts reduce market inefficiencies?

15. Why might the value of an insurance company be affected by interest rate movements?

16. Should financial institutions be regulated to reduce their risk? Offer at least one argument for regulation and one argument against regulation.

17. Consider the typical sources and uses of funds at commercial banks, savings institutions, and securities firms. Explain the risk of each type of institution based on its typical sources and uses of funds.

Answers to Final Self-Exam

1. Under favorable economic conditions, Mesa Bank should perform better because it earns higher returns on its loans as long as the borrowers repay their loans (higher risk). Under unfavorable economic conditions, Flagstaff Bank should perform better because Mesa will likely experience many loan defaults, but Flagstaff will not.

2. Even if investors have more information, they may not be able to detect banks that have financial problems. In addition, CAMELS ratings are intended to detect financial problems of banks early enough that there is time to correct the problems. This can prevent bank failures, leading to a more stable banking system.

3. The stock repurchase will reduce equity so that the profits in the near future will result in a higher return on equity. This will enhance the CEO's compensation but will not necessarily enhance the bank's value in the long run. In fact, the decreased equity will restrict the growth of the bank. Thus, this compensation structure will not remove agency problems.

4. Alabama Bank will incur more expenses when attempting to expand its financial services. This will increase the ratio of noninterest expenses to assets, and this increase could offset any increase in revenue.

5. **a.** Interest rates will rise.

    b. The spread will decrease because short-term deposit rates will increase, whereas long-term rates may not be affected as much or at all.

    c. Maryland should hedge. It could sell interest rate futures. However, if it does sell interest rate futures and interest rates decline, it will incur a loss on its interest rate futures position, which may offset most of its gain from operations.

6. Commercial banks serve corporate borrowers; savings institutions serve homeowners; finance companies serve consumers and small businesses; and mutual funds, insurance companies, and pension funds serve corporate borrowers (investing in stocks and bonds and money market securities issued by corporations).

7. Insurance companies and pension funds are suppliers of funds and add much liquidity to the financial markets. They may also make the stock market more efficient because if a stock's price deviates from its fundamental value, they may take a position to capitalize on the discrepancy, which should push the stock toward its fundamental value.

8. Institutional investors pool funds that come from many individuals and take much bigger stakes in a specific stock. Thus, the institutional investors have an incentive to make the correct investment choices (because of the large investment) and then to monitor the companies in which they invest. This practice results in more governance over companies than if stocks were owned only by small investors.

9. Money market funds provide liquidity to investors, which is necessary even when investors have alternative investments that pay higher returns. In addition, money market funds play a major role in financing the budget deficit because they invest heavily in Treasury securities. They also channel funds to corporations in the form of commercial paper. Since the Treasury and corporations frequently reissue short-term securities, they are sometimes using the short-term securities to finance long-term investment.

10. **a.** The investment in illiquid stocks may be an advantage because it allows the closed-end funds to pursue stocks that are not followed by most investors. These stocks are more likely to be mispriced than are other stocks.

    b. Closed-end funds do not have to accommodate redemptions, whereas open-end funds do. Thus, closed-end funds do not need to worry about selling some of their stock holdings just for the purpose of satisfying redemptions.

11. These mutual funds will all be adversely affected during a weak economy because firms that have high growth potential will probably experience weak performance when economic conditions are weak. There is not sufficient demand under these conditions.

12. Mutual funds with low expense ratios tend to perform better than those with higher expense ratios.

13. A securities firm attempts to satisfy the issuer of stock by ensuring that the price is sufficiently high, but it must also ensure that it can place all the shares. In addition, it wants to satisfy investors who invest in the IPO. If the investors incur losses because they paid too much for the shares, they may not want to purchase any more stock from that underwriter in the future.

14. Some stock analysts may be able to detect when a specific stock is underpriced or overpriced in the market, and they can communicate their opinion through their stock ratings, which may cause investors to capitalize on the information. This could push stock prices closer to their fundamental values and reduce market inefficiencies. During the stock market bubble that occurred in 2000, however, analysts were overly optimistic

about stocks and were not paying attention to fundamentals of the companies. Thus, they may have been a partial cause of the stock market bubble.

15. The value of an insurance company is partially influenced by the value of its asset portfolio, which contains bonds. The market value of those bonds is inversely related to interest rate movements.

16. Regulation may be able to reduce failures of financial institutions, which may stabilize the financial system. The flow of funds into financial institutions will be larger if the people who provide the funds can trust that the financial institutions will not fail. However, regulation can also restrict competition. In some cases, it results in subsidies to financial institutions that are performing poorly. Thus, regulation can prevent firms from operating efficiently.

17. Commercial banks are exposed to default risk due to their commercial and consumer loans. They are exposed to interest rate risk because the maturities of some of their assets (especially bonds and some term loans) may be longer than the maturities of their liabilities. Savings institutions are exposed to default risk due to their mortgage loans (although these loans are normally backed by the home) and consumer loans. They are exposed to interest rate risk because the maturities of their fixed-rate mortgages are longer than the maturities of their liabilities. Securities firms are exposed to market risk from taking equity positions and to default risk when providing bridge loans. Their operations are especially sensitive to financial market activity. When financial transactions such as mergers and stock trades decline, their business declines because they serve as intermediaries for many types of financial transactions.

Appendix A

Comprehensive Project

One of the best ways to gain a clear understanding of the key concepts explained in this text is to apply them directly to actual situations. This comprehensive project enables you to apply numerous concepts regarding financial markets and institutions discussed throughout the text to actual situations. The tasks in this project can be categorized as follows:

Part I. Applying Financial Markets Concepts

Part II. Applying Financial Institutions Concepts

Part III. Measuring Stock Performance

At the beginning of the school term, you should complete two tasks. First, compile the information on financial markets needed to fill in the blank spaces in steps (a) through (j) in Part I. This information will be needed when applying financial markets concepts in the questions that follow (Part I of the project). Second, obtain the information on financial institutions identified at the beginning of Part II. This information will be needed when applying financial institutions concepts in the questions that follow (Part II of the project).

Part I. Applying Financial Markets Concepts

The exercises on financial markets concepts require you to measure the change in the yields and values of securities over the school term and explain why those values changed. In doing so, you will apply the concepts in the chapters on financial markets to actual situations.

At the beginning of the school term and again near the end of the term, use an issue of *The Wall Street Journal* or a financial website such as Yahoo Finance (finance.yahoo.com) to obtain the information requested here. Your professor will identify the dates to use as the beginning and end of the term, and may possibly cite specific sources you should use to obtain the information you need. The dates will allow you sufficient time to assess the changes in the yields and values of securities so that you can answer the questions. Your professor will explain the specific format of the assignment, such as whether any parts are excluded or whether students should work in teams. Your professor will also indicate whether the answers will be handed in, presented to the class, or both. A commonly used format is to divide the project into parts and assign a team of students to present their answers to one specific part. Each student will be a member of one of the teams. All students may still be required to hand in answers to all parts of the project, even though their team's presentation focuses on only one part.

	BEGINNING OF TERM	END OF TERM

a. Stock market index information:

S&P 500 (stock) index level: _____ _____

Nasdaq Composite (stock) index level: _____ _____

b. Interest rate information:

Mortgage, fixed rate (30-year): _____ _____

Federal funds rate: _____ _____

Commercial paper rate (90 days): _____ _____

Certificate of deposit rate (3-month): _____ _____

Treasury bill rate (13 weeks): _____ _____

Treasury bill rate (26 weeks): _____ _____

c. Bond yield information:

Treasury long-term bond yield: _____ _____

Corporate bond yield: _____ _____

Junk bond yield: _____ _____

Tax-exempt (7–12 years) bond yield: _____ _____

d. Use stock exchange quotations to record the stock price and dividend of one stock from each stock exchange in which you would like to invest.

New York Stock Exchange: Stock price: _____ _____

Name of firm _____ Dividend: _____ _____

Nasdaq Market: Stock price: _____ _____

Name of firm _____ Dividend: _____ _____

e. Use futures prices quotations to record the recent ("settle") price of the following futures (select futures with the first settlement date beyond the end of the school term):

Treasury bond futures: _____ _____

S&P 500 index futures: _____ _____

British pound futures: _____ _____

f. Use an options quotations table to select a call option on a firm whose stock price you expect to increase (select the option with the first expiration month beyond the end of the school term):

Name of firm: _____

Expiration month: _____

Exercise price: _____

Stock price: _____ _____

Option premium: _____ _____

g. Use an options quotations table to select a put option on a firm whose stock price you expect to decrease (select the option with the first expiration month beyond the end of the school term):

Name of firm: _____

Expiration month: _____

Exercise price: _____

Stock price: _____ _____

Option premium: _____ _____

	BEGINNING OF TERM	END OF TERM

h. Use a currency exchange rate table in *The Wall Street Journal* or at a financial website to record exchange rates:

Exchange rate of the British pound (in $): _____ _____

Exchange rate of the Japanese yen (in $): _____ _____

Exchange rate of the Mexican peso (in $): _____ _____

i. Use currency options data (if available) to select a call option on a foreign currency that you expect will strengthen against the dollar (select the option with the first expiration month beyond the end of the school term):

Currency: _____

Expiration month: _____

Exercise price: _____

Currency's existing value: _____ _____

Option premium: _____ _____

j. Use currency options data (if available) to select a put option on a foreign currency that you expect will weaken against the dollar (select the option with the first expiration month beyond the end of the school term):

Currency: _____

Expiration month: _____

Exercise price: _____

Currency's existing value: _____ _____

Option premium: _____ _____

1. Explaining changes in interest rates (from Chapter 2)

a. Compare the 13-week Treasury bill rate (which is a proxy for short-term interest rates) at the end of the school term to the rate that existed at the beginning of the school term.

b. Recall that Chapter 2 offered reasons why interest rates change over time. Apply the concepts in that chapter to explain why interest rates have changed over the school term.

2. Comparing yields among securities (from Chapter 3)

a. What is the difference between the yield on high-quality corporate bonds and the yield on Treasury bonds at the end of the school term?

b. Apply the concepts discussed in Chapter 3 to explain why this premium exists.

c. What is the difference between the yield on long-term Treasury bonds and the yield on long-term municipal bonds at the end of the school term?

d. Apply the concepts discussed in Chapter 3 to explain why this difference changed over the school term.

3. Assessing the forecasting ability of the yield curve (from Chapter 3)

a. What was the difference between the 26-week T-bill yield and the 13-week T-bill yield at the beginning of the school term?

b. Does this imply that the yield curve had an upward or downward slope at the beginning of the school term?

c. Assuming that this slope can be primarily attributed to expectations theory, did the direction of the slope indicate that the market expected higher or lower interest rates over the school term?

d. Did interest rates move in the direction predicted by the short-term portion of the yield curve over the school term?

4. Explaining shifts in the yield curve over time (from Chapter 3)

a. Describe how the yield curve changed over the school term. Explain the changes in expectations about future interest rates that are implied by the shift in the yield curve over the school term.

5. The Fed's influence on interest rates (from Chapter 5)

a. How did the Fed change the federal funds rate over the school term?

b. Explain how other market interest rates changed over the school term. Did they move in tandem with the federal funds rate? Do you think the movements in interest rates over the school term were caused by the Fed's monetary policy? Explain.

6. Measuring and explaining premiums on money market securities (from Chapter 6)

a. What is the difference between the yield on 90-day commercial paper and the yield on 13-week T-bills at the end of the school term? Apply the concepts discussed in Chapter 6 to explain why this premium exists.

b. Compare the premium on the 90-day commercial paper yield (relative to the 13-week T-bill yield) that exists at the end of the school term to the premium that existed at the beginning of the term. Apply the concepts discussed in Chapter 6 to explain why the premium may have changed over the school term.

7. Explaining bond premiums and price movements (from Chapter 8)

a. What is the difference between the yield on junk (high-yield corporate) bonds at the end of the school term and their yield at the beginning of the school term? Apply the concepts discussed in Chapter 8 to explain why this premium exists and why it changed over the school term.

b. Compare the long-term Treasury bond yield at the end of the school term to the long-term Treasury bond yield that existed at the beginning of the school term. Given the direction of this change, did prices of long-term bonds rise or fall over the school term?

c. Compare the change in the yields of Treasury, municipal, and corporate bonds over the school term. Did the yields of all three types of securities move in the same direction and by about the same degree? Apply the concepts discussed in Chapter 8 to explain why yields of different types of bonds move together.

d. Compare the premium on high-yield corporate bonds (relative to Treasury bonds) at the beginning of the school term to the premium that existed at the end of the school term. Did the premium increase or decrease? Apply the concepts discussed in Chapter 8 to explain why this premium changed over the school term.

8. Explaining mortgage rates (from Chapter 9)

a. Compare the rate paid by a homeowner on a 30-year mortgage to the rate (yield) paid by the U.S. Treasury on long-term Treasury bonds at the end of the school term. Explain the difference.

b. Compare the 30-year mortgage rate at the end of the school term to the 30-year mortgage rate that existed at the beginning of the school term. What do you think is the primary reason for the change in 30-year mortgage rates over the school term?

9. Explaining stock price movements (from Chapter 11)

a. Determine the return on the stock market over your school term based on the percentage change in the S&P 500 index level over the term. Annualize this return by multiplying the return by $12/m$, where m is the number of months in your school term. Apply the concepts discussed in Chapter 11 to explain why the market return was high or low over your school term.

b. Repeat the previous question for smaller stocks by using the Nasdaq Composite instead of the S&P 500 index. What was the annualized return on the Nasdaq Composite over your school term?

c. Explain why the return on the Nasdaq Composite was high or low over your school term.

d. Determine the return over the school term on the stock in which you chose to invest. The return is $(P_t - P_{t-1} + D)/P_{t-1}$, where P_t is the stock price at the end of the school term, P_{t-1} is the stock price at the beginning of the school term, and D is the dividend paid over the school term. In most cases, one quarterly dividend is paid over a school term, which is one-fourth of the annual dividend amount per share shown in stock quotation tables.

e. What was your return over the school term on the stock you selected from the New York Stock Exchange? What was your return over the school term on the stock you selected from the Nasdaq market? Apply the concepts discussed in Chapter 11 to explain why you think these two stocks experienced different returns over the school term.

10. Measuring and explaining futures price movements (from Chapter 13)

a. Assume that you purchased an S&P 500 futures contract at the beginning of the school term, with the first settlement date being beyond the end of the school term. Also assume that you sold an S&P 500 futures contract with this same settlement date at the end of the school term. Given that this contract has a value of the futures price times $250, determine the difference between the dollar value of the contract you sold and the dollar amount of the contract you purchased.

b. Assume that you invested an initial margin of 20 percent of the amount that you would owe to purchase the S&P 500 index at the settlement date. Measure your return from taking a position in the S&P 500 index futures as follows. Take the difference determined in part (a) (which represents the dollar amount of the gain on the futures position) and divide it by the amount you originally invested (the amount you originally invested is 20 percent of the dollar value of the futures contract that you purchased).

c. The return that you just derived in part (b) is not annualized. To annualize your return, multiply it by $12/m$, where m is the number of months in your school term.

d. Apply the concepts discussed in Chapter 13 to explain why your return on your S&P 500 index futures position was low or high over the school term.

e. Assume that you purchased a Treasury bond futures contract at the beginning of the school term, with the first settlement date being beyond the end of the school term. Also assume that you sold this same type of futures contract at the end of the school term. Recall that Treasury bond futures contracts are priced relative to a $100,000 face value and the fractions are in thirty-seconds. What was the dollar value of the futures contract at the beginning of the school term when you purchased it?

f. What was the dollar value of the Treasury bond futures contract at the end of the school term when you sold it?

g. What was the difference between the dollar value of the Treasury bond futures contract when you sold it and the value when you purchased it?

h. Assume that you invested an initial margin of 20 percent of the amount that you would owe to purchase the Treasury bonds at the settlement date. Your investment is equal to 20 percent of the dollar value of the Treasury bond futures contract as of the time you purchased the futures. Determine the return on your futures position, which is the difference you derived in part (g) as a percentage of your investment.

i. The return that you just derived in part (h) is not annualized. To annualize your return, multiply your return by $12/m$, where m is the number of months in your school term.

j. Apply the concepts discussed in Chapter 13 to explain why the return on your Treasury bond futures position was low or high.

11. Measuring and explaining option price movements (from Chapter 14)

a. Assume that you purchased a call option (representing 100 shares) on the specific stock that you identified in Part I(f) of this project. What was your return from purchasing this option? [Your return can be measured as $(\text{Prem}_t - \text{Prem}_{t-1})/\text{Prem}_{t-1}$, where Prem_{t-1} represents the premium paid at the beginning of the school term and Prem_t represents the premium at which the same option can be sold at the end of the school term.] If the premium for this option is not quoted at the end of the school term, measure the return as if you had exercised the call option at the end of the school term (assuming that it is feasible to exercise the option at that time). That is, the return is based on purchasing the stock at the option's exercise price and then selling the stock at its market price at the end of the school term.

b. Annualize the return on your option by multiplying the return you derived in part (a) by $12/m$, where m represents the number of months in your school term.

c. Compare the return on your call option to the return that you would have earned if you had simply invested in the stock itself. Notice how the magnitude of the return on the call option is much larger than the magnitude of the return on the stock itself. That is, the gains are larger and the losses are larger when investing in call options on a stock instead of the stock itself.

d. Assume that you purchased a put option (representing 100 shares) on the specific stock that you identified in Part I(g) of this project. What was your return from purchasing this option? [Your return can be measured as $(\text{Prem}_t - \text{Prem}_{t-1})/\text{Prem}_{t-1}$, where Prem_{t-1} represents the premium paid at the beginning of the school term and Prem_t represents the premium at which the same option can be sold at the end of the school term.] If the premium for this option is not quoted at the end of the school term, measure the return as if you had exercised the put option at the end of the school term (assuming that it is feasible to exercise the option at that time). That is, the return is based on purchasing the stock at its market price and then selling the stock at the option's exercise price at the end of the school term.

12. Determining swap payments (from Chapter 15)

Assume that, at the beginning of the school term, you engaged in a fixed-for-floating rate swap in which you agreed to pay 6 percent in exchange for the prevailing 26-week T-bill rate that exists at the end of the school term. Assume that your swap agreement specifies the end of the school term as the only time at which a swap will occur and that the notional amount is $10 million. Determine the amount that you owe on the swap, the amount you are owed on the swap, and the difference. Did you gain or lose as a result of the swap?

13. Measuring and explaining exchange rate movements (from Chapter 16)

a. Determine the percentage change in the value of the British pound over the school term. Did the pound appreciate or depreciate against the dollar?

b. Determine the percentage change in the value of the Japanese yen over the school term. Did the yen appreciate or depreciate against the dollar?

c. Determine the percentage change in the value of the Mexican peso over the school term. Did the peso appreciate or depreciate against the dollar?

d. Determine the per unit gain or loss if you had purchased British pound futures at the beginning of the term and sold British pound futures at the end of the term.

e. Given that a single futures contract on British pounds represents 62,500 pounds, determine the dollar amount of your gain or loss.

Part II. Applying Financial Institutions Concepts

Obtain an annual report of (1) a commercial bank, (2) a savings institution, (3) a securities firm, and (4) an insurance company. The annual reports will allow you to relate the theory in specific related chapters to the particular financial institution of concern. The exercises in Part II of this comprehensive project require the use of these annual reports. The annual report for each financial institution can be obtained online at the firm's website or by calling its shareholder services department. Also, order a prospectus of a specific mutual fund in which you are interested. The prospectus can be obtained online at the website of the specific investment company that sponsors the mutual fund, or it may be obtained by calling the company.

1. Commercial bank operations (from Chapter 17)

For the commercial bank that you selected at the beginning of the term, use its annual report or any other related information to answer the following questions:

a. Identify the types of deposits that the commercial bank uses to obtain most of its funds.

b. Identify the main uses of funds by the bank.

c. Summarize any statements made by the commercial bank in its annual report about how recent or potential regulations will affect its performance.

d. Does it appear that the bank is attempting to increase its business in the securities industry by offering more securities services? If so, explain how.

e. Does it appear that the bank is attempting to increase its business in the insurance industry by offering insurance services? If so, explain how.

2. Commercial bank management (from Chapter 19)

For the commercial bank that you selected at the beginning of the term, use its annual report or any other related information to answer the following questions.

a. Assess the bank's balance sheet as well as any comments in its annual report about the gap between its rate-sensitive assets and its rate-sensitive liabilities. Does it appear that the bank has a positive gap or a negative gap?

b. Does the bank use any methods to reduce its gap and, therefore, to reduce its exposure to interest rate risk?

c. Summarize any statements made by the bank in its annual report about how it attempts to limit its exposure to credit risk on the loans it provides.

3. Commercial bank performance (from Chapter 20)

For the commercial bank that you selected at the beginning of the term, use its annual report or any other related information to answer the following questions.

a. Determine the bank's interest income as a percentage of its total assets.

b. Determine the bank's interest expenses as a percentage of its total assets.

c. Determine the bank's net interest margin.

d. Determine the bank's noninterest income as a percentage of its total assets.

e. Determine the bank's noninterest expenses (do not include the addition to loan loss reserves here) as a percentage of its total assets.

f. Determine the bank's addition to loan loss reserves as a percentage of its total assets.

g. Determine the bank's return on assets.

h. Determine the bank's return on equity.

i. Identify the bank's income statement items described previously that would be affected if interest rates rise in the next year, and explain how they would be affected.

j. Identify the bank's income statement items described previously that would be affected if U.S. economic conditions deteriorate, and explain how they would be affected.

4. Savings institutions (from Chapter 21)

For the savings institution (SI) that you selected at the beginning of the term, use its annual report or any other related information to answer the following questions.

a. Identify the types of deposits that the SI uses to obtain most of its funds.

b. Identify the main uses of funds by the SI.

c. Summarize any statements made by the SI in its annual report about how recent or potential regulations will affect its performance.

d. Assess the SI's balance sheet as well as any comments in its annual report about the gap between its rate-sensitive assets and its rate-sensitive liabilities. Does it appear that the SI has a positive gap or a negative gap?

e. Does the SI use any methods to reduce its gap and, therefore, to reduce its exposure to interest rate risk?

f. Summarize any statements made by the SI in its annual report about how it attempts to limit its exposure to credit risk on the loans it provides.

g. Determine the SI's interest income as a percentage of its total assets.

h. Determine the SI's interest expenses as a percentage of its total assets.

i. Determine the SI's noninterest income as a percentage of its total assets.

j. Determine the SI's noninterest expenses (do not include the addition to loan loss reserves here) as a percentage of its total assets.

k. Determine the SI's addition to loan loss reserves as a percentage of its total assets.

l. Determine the SI's return on assets.

m. Determine the SI's return on equity.

n. Identify the SI's income statement items described previously that would be affected if interest rates rise in the next year, and explain how they would be affected.

o. Identify the SI's income statement items described previously that would be affected if U.S. economic conditions deteriorate, and explain how they would be affected.

5. Mutual funds (from Chapter 23)

For the mutual fund that you selected at the beginning of the term, use its prospectus or any other related information to answer the following questions.

a. What is the investment objective of this mutual fund? Do you consider this mutual fund to have low risk, moderate risk, or high risk?

b. What was the return on the mutual fund last year? What was the average annual return over the last three years?

c. What is a key economic factor that influences the return on this mutual fund? (That is, are the fund's returns highly influenced by U.S. stock market conditions? By U.S. interest rates? By foreign stock market conditions? By foreign interest rates?)

d. Must any fees be paid when buying or selling this mutual fund?

e. What was the expense ratio for this mutual fund over the last year? Does this ratio seem high to you?

6. Securities firms (from Chapter 24)

For the securities firm that you selected at the beginning of the term, use its annual report or any other related information to answer the following questions.

a. What are the main types of business conducted by the securities firm?

b. Summarize any statements made by the securities firm in its annual report about how it may be affected by existing or potential regulations.

c. Describe the recent performance of the securities firm, and explain why the performance has been favorable or unfavorable.

7. Insurance companies (from Chapter 25)

For the insurance company that you selected at the beginning of the term, use its annual report or any other related information to answer the following questions.

a. How does the insurance company allocate its funds? (That is, what is its asset composition?)

b. Is the insurance company exposed to interest rate risk? Explain.

c. Does the insurance company use any techniques to hedge its exposure to interest rate risk?

d. Summarize any statements made by the insurance company in its annual report about how it may be affected by existing or potential regulations.

e. Describe the recent performance of the insurance company (using any key financial ratios that measure its income). Explain why its recent performance was strong or weak.

Part III. Measuring Stock Performance

This part of the project enables you to analyze the risk and return characteristics of one particular stock that you own or would like to purchase. You should input your data in Excel or an alternative electronic spreadsheet. Perform the following tasks.

a. Obtain stock price data at the end of each of the last 16 quarters, and fill in that information in Column A of your electronic spreadsheet. Historical stock price data are available at finance.yahoo.com and other financial websites. Your professor may offer some suggestions on where to obtain this information.

b. Obtain the data on dividend per share for this firm for each of the last 16 quarters, and input that information in Column B of your electronic spreadsheet. When you obtain dividend data, recognize that the dividend is often listed on an annual basis. In this case, divide the annual dividend by 4 to obtain the quarterly dividend.

c. Use "compute" statements to derive the quarterly return on your stock in Column C of your electronic spreadsheet. The return on the stock during any quarter is computed as follows. First, compute the stock price at the end of that quarter minus the stock price at the end of the previous quarter; then add the quarterly dividend; and then divide by the stock price at the end of the previous quarter.

d. Input the S&P 500 stock index level as of the end of each of the 16 quarters in Column D of your electronic spreadsheet.

e. Use "compute" statements to derive the quarterly stock market return in Column E, which is equal to the percentage change in the S&P 500 index level from the previous quarter.

f. Using the tools in an electronic package, run a regression analysis in which your quarterly stock return (Column C) represents the dependent variable and the stock market return (Column E) represents the independent variable. This analysis can be easily run by Excel.

g. Based on your regression results, what is the relationship between the market return and your stock's return? (The slope coefficient represents the estimate of your firm's beta, which is a measure of its systematic risk.)

h. Based on your regression results, does it appear that there is a significant relationship between the market return and your stock's return? (The t-statistic for the slope coefficient can be assessed to determine whether there is a significant relationship.)

i. Based on your regression results, what proportion of the variation in the stock's returns can be explained by movements (returns) in the stock market overall? (The R-squared statistic measures the proportion of variation in the dependent variable that is explained by the independent variable in a regression model like the one described previously.) Does it appear that the stock's return is driven mainly by stock market movements or by other factors that are not captured in the regression model?

j. What is the standard deviation of your stock's quarterly returns over the 16-quarter period? (You can easily compute the standard deviation of your column of stock return data by using a "compute" statement.) What is the standard deviation of the quarterly stock market returns (as measured by quarterly returns on the S&P 500 index) over the 16-quarter period? Is your stock more volatile than the stock market in general? If so, why do you think it is more volatile than the market?

k. Assume that the average risk-free rate per quarter over the 16-quarter period is 1 percent. Determine the Sharpe index for your stock (The Sharpe index is equal to your stock's average quarterly return, minus the average risk-free rate, divided by the standard deviation of your stock's returns.) Determine the Treynor index for your stock. (The Treynor index is equal to your stock's average quarterly return, minus the average risk-free rate, divided by the estimated beta of your stock.)

Appendix B

Using Excel to Conduct Analyses

Excel spreadsheets are useful for organizing numerical data and for executing computations. Excel not only allows you to compute general statistics such as average and standard deviations of cells, but also can be used to perform regression analysis. This appendix begins by describing the use of Excel to compute general statistics. Then, a background of regression analysis is provided, followed by a discussion of how Excel can be used to run regression analysis.

General Statistics

Some of the more popular computations are discussed here.

Creating a Compute Statement

If you want to determine the percentage change in a value from one period to the next, type the compute statement in the cell where you want to see the result. For example, assume that you identify the month and year in Column A and record the stock price of Amazon. com, Inc., at the beginning of that month in Column B. To assess the performance or risk characteristics of stocks, you should first convert the stock price data into "returns." This allows you to compare performance and risk among different stocks. Because Amazon does not pay a dividend, the return from investing in Amazon stock over a period is simply the percentage change in the price. Assume you want to compute the monthly percentage change in the stock price. In cell C2, you can create a compute statement to derive the percentage change in price from the beginning of the first month until the beginning of the second month. A compute statement begins with an equal sign (=). The proper compute statement to compute a percentage change for cell B2 is = (B2 − B1)/B1. Assume that in cell C3 you want to derive the percentage change in Amazon's stock price as of the month in cell B3 from the previous month B2. Type the compute statement = (B3 − B2)/B2 in cell C3.

Using the COPY Command

If you need to repeat a particular compute statement for several different cells, you can use the COPY command as follows:

1. Place the cursor in the cell with the compute statement that you want to copy to other cells.

2. Click "Edit" and then click "Copy" on your menu bar.
3. Highlight the cells where you want that compute statement copied.
4. Press the Enter key.

For example, assume that you have 30 monthly prices of Amazon stock in Column B and have already calculated the percentage change in the stock price in cell C2 as explained previously. [You did not have a percentage change in cell C1 because you needed two dates (cells B1 and B2) to derive your first percentage change.] You can place the cursor on cell C2, click "Edit" and then click "Copy" on your menu bar, highlight cells C3 to C30, and then press the Enter key.

Computing an Average

You can compute the average of a set of cells as follows. Assume that you want to determine the mean monthly return on Amazon stock shown in cells C2 to C30. Go to any blank cell (such as cell C31) and type the compute statement = AVERAGE(C2:C30).

Computing a Standard Deviation

You can compute the standard deviation of a set of cells as follows. Assume that you want to determine the standard deviation of the returns on Amazon stock. In cell C32 (or in any blank cell where you want to see the result), type the compute statement = STDEV(C2:C30).

Regression Analysis

Various software packages are available to run regression analysis. The Excel package is recommended because of its simplicity. The following example illustrates the ease with which regression analysis can be run.

Assume that a financial institution wishes to measure the relationship between the change in the interest rate in a given period (Δi_t) and the change in the inflation rate in the previous period (ΔINF_{t-1}); that is, the financial institution wishes to assess the lagged impact of inflation on interest rates. Assume that the data over the last 20 periods are as follows:

COLUMN A PERIOD	COLUMN B Δi_t	COLUMN C ΔINF_{t-1}
1	0.50%	0.90%
2	0.65	0.75
3	−0.70	−1.20
4	0.50	0.30
5	0.40	0.60
6	−0.30	−0.20
7	0.60	0.85
8	0.75	0.45
9	0.10	−0.05
10	1.10	1.35
11	0.90	1.10
12	−0.65	−0.80
13	−0.20	−0.35

COLUMN A PERIOD	COLUMN B Δi_t	COLUMN C ΔINF_{t-1}
14	0.40	0.55
15	0.30	0.40
16	0.60	0.75
17	−0.05	−0.10
18	1.30	1.50
19	−0.55	−0.70
20	0.15	0.25

Assume the firm applies the following regression model to the data:

$$\Delta i_t = b_0 + b_1(\Delta INF_{t-1}) + \mu$$

where

Δi_t = **change in the interest rate in period** t

ΔINF_{t-1} = **change in the inflation rate in period** $t - 1$ **(the previous period)**

b_0, b_1 = **regression coefficients to be estimated by regression analysis**

μ = **error term**

Regression Analysis Using Excel

In our example, Δi_t is the dependent variable and ΔINF_{t-1} is the independent variable. The first step is to input the two columns of data that were provided earlier (Columns B and C) into a file using Excel. First, click the Data Tab and see if you have the Data Analysis option. If not, you must install the free Analysis ToolPak add-in within Excel. (Select "File," then "Options," then "add-ins," then "Data Analysis.") The Data Analysis leads to a new menu in which you should click "Regression." For "Input Y Range," identify the range of the dependent variable (B1:B20 in our example). Then, for "Input X Range," identify the range of the independent variable (C1:CC20 in our example). Click "OK" and, within a few seconds, the regression analysis will be complete. For our example, the output is as follows:

SUMMARY OUTPUT	
Multiple R	0.96884081
R-square	0.93865251
Adjusted R-square	0.93524431
Standard error	0.1432744
Observations	20

ANOVA					
	df	SS	MS	F	SIGNIFICANCE F
Regression	1	5.653504056	5.653504	275.4105	2.34847E-12
Residual	18	0.369495944	0.020528		
Total	19	6.023			

	COEFFICIENTS	STANDARD ERROR	t-STAT	p-VALUE	LOWER 95%	UPPER 95%
Intercept	0.0494173	0.035164424	1.405321	0.176951	−0.024460473	0.123295
X Variable 1	0.75774079	0.045659421	16.5955	2.35E-12	0.661813835	0.853668

The estimate of the slope coefficient is approximately 0.76, which suggests that every 1 percent change in the inflation rate is associated with a 0.76 percent change (in the same direction) in the interest rate. The t-statistic is 16.6, which suggests that there is a significant relationship between Δi_t and ΔINF_{t-1}. The R-squared statistic suggests that approximately 94 percent of the variation in Δi_t is explained by ΔINF_{t-1}. The correlation between Δi_t and ΔINF_{t-1} can also be measured by the correlation coefficient, which is the square root of the R-squared statistic.

If you have more than one independent variable (multiple regression), you should place the independent variables next to each other in the file. Then, for the "X Range," identify this block of data. The output for the regression model will display the coefficient and standard error for each of the independent variables. The t-statistic can be estimated for each independent variable to test for significance. For multiple regression, the R-squared statistic represents the percentage of variation in the dependent variable that is explained by the model as a whole.

Using Regression Analysis to Forecast

The regression results can be used to predict future values of the dependent variable. In our example, the historical relationship between Δi_t and ΔINF_{t-1} can be expressed as:

$$\Delta i_t = b_0 + b_1(\Delta INF_{t-1})$$

Assume that last period's change in inflation (ΔINF_{t-1}) was 1 percent. Given the estimated coefficients derived from regression analysis, the forecast for this period's Δi_t is:

$$\Delta i_t = 0.0494 + 0.7577(1\%)$$
$$= 0.8071\%$$

Some obvious limitations should be recognized when using regression analysis for forecasting purposes. First, if the model does not include other variables that influence the dependent variable, the coefficients derived from the model may be improperly estimated, leading to inaccurate forecasts. Second, some relationships are contemporaneous rather than lagged, which means that last period's value for ΔINF could not be used. Instead, a forecast would have to be derived for ΔINF to use as input for forecasting Δi_t. If the forecast for ΔINF is poor, the forecast for Δi_t will likely be poor even if the regression model is properly specified.

Glossary

A

adjustable-rate mortgage (ARM)   Mortgage that requires payments that adjust periodically according to market interest rates.

adverse selection problem   In an insurance context, the problem for the insurance industry stemming from the fact that those who are most likely to purchase insurance are also those who are most likely to need it.

amortization schedule   Schedule developed from the maturity and interest rate on a mortgage to determine monthly payments broken down into principal and interest.

annuity plans   Plans provided by insurance companies that offer a predetermined amount of retirement income to individuals.

arbitrageurs   Firms or individuals that capitalize on discrepancies between prices of securities.

ask quote (ask price)   Price at which a seller is willing to sell.

asset stripping   A strategy of acquiring a firm, breaking it into divisions, segmenting the divisions, and then selling them separately.

asymmetric information   Information about a firm's financial condition that is not available to investors.

at the money   Refers to an option in which the prevailing price of the underlying security is equal to the exercise price.

B

back-end load   A withdrawal fee charged when money is withdrawn from a mutual fund.

balloon payment   A required lump-sum payment of the principal of a loan.

balloon-payment mortgage   Mortgage that requires payments for a three- to five-year period; at the end of the period, full payment of the principal is required.

banker's acceptance   Agreement in which a commercial bank accepts responsibility for a future payment; it is commonly used for international trade transactions.

bank holding company (BHC)   Company that owns a commercial bank.

basis risk   As applied to interest rate swaps, the risk that the index used for an interest rate swap will not move perfectly in tandem with the floating-rate instrument specified in a swap arrangement. As applied to financial futures, the risk that the futures prices will not move perfectly in tandem with the assets that are hedged.

behavioral finance   The application of psychology to make financial decisions.

Beige Book   A consolidated report of economic conditions in each of the Federal Reserve districts; used by the Federal Open Market Committee in formulating monetary policy.

best efforts   An arrangement in which an underwriter attempts to sell bonds at a specified price, but makes no guarantee to the issuer.

best-efforts agreement   Arrangement in which the securities firm does not guarantee a price on securities to be issued by a corporation but states only that it will give its best effort to sell the securities at a reasonable price.

691

bid quote (bid price)   Price a purchaser is willing to pay for a specific security.

Board of Governors   Composed of seven individual members appointed by the president of the United States; also called the Federal Reserve Board. The board helps regulate commercial banks and control monetary policy.

Bond Buyer Index   Index based on 40 actively traded general obligation and revenue bonds.

bond price elasticity   Sensitivity of bond prices to changes in the required rate of return.

Bretton Woods era   Period from 1944 to 1971, when exchange rates were fixed (maintained within 1 percent of a specified rate).

bridge loan   Funds provided as temporary financing until other sources of long-term funds can be obtained; commonly provided by securities firms to firms experiencing leveraged buyouts.

broker   One who executes securities transactions between two parties.

bullet loan   Loan structured so that interest payments and the loan principal are to be paid off in one lump sum at a specified future date.

C

call option   Contract that grants the owner the right to purchase a specified financial instrument for a specified price within a specified period of time.

call premium   Difference between a bond's call price and its par value.

call provision (call feature)   Provision that allows the initial issuer of bonds to buy back the bonds at a specified price.

callable swap (swaption)   Swap of fixed-rate payments for floating-rate payments whereby the party making the fixed payments has the right to terminate the swap prior to maturity.

CAMELS ratings   Characteristics used to rate bank risk: capital adequacy, asset quality, management, earnings, liquidity, and sensitivity.

capital   As related to banks, funds mainly composed of retained earnings and proceeds received from issuing stock.

capital appreciation funds   Mutual funds composed of stocks of firms that have potential for very high growth but may be unproven.

capital gain   The difference between the prices at which a stock is sold versus the price at which it was purchased.

capital market securities   Long-term securities, such as bonds, whose maturities are more than one year.

capital ratio   Ratio of capital to assets.

carve-out   Arrangement in which a corporation sells one of its units to new shareholders through an initial public offering.

cash flow underwriting   Method by which insurance companies adapt insurance premiums to interest rates.

chattel mortgage bond   Bond that is secured by personal property.

closed-end funds   Mutual funds that do not repurchase the shares they sell.

coincident economic indicators   Economic indicators that tend to reach their peaks and troughs at the same time as business cycles.

collateralized debt obligation (CDO)   A package of securities that are backed by collateral and are sold to investors.

collateralized mortgage obligations (CMOs)   Securities that are backed by mortgages; segmented into classes (or tranches) that dictate the timing of the payments.

commercial paper   Short-term debt instrument issued only by well-known creditworthy firms.

commission brokers (floor brokers)   Brokers who execute orders for their customers.

common stock   Securities representing partial ownership of a corporation.

convertible bond   A bond that can be converted into a specified number of shares of the firm's common stock.

corporate bonds   Long-term debt securities issued by corporations that promise the owner coupon payments (interest) on a semiannual basis.

covered interest arbitrage   Act of capitalizing on higher foreign interest rates while covering the position with a simultaneous forward sale.

credit default swap (CDS)   A privately negotiated contract that protects investors against the risk of default on particular debt securities.

credit risk   The risk of loss that will occur when a counterparty defaults on a contract.

crowding-out effect Phenomenon that occurs when insufficient loanable funds are available for potential borrowers, such as corporations and individuals, as a result of excessive borrowing by the Treasury. Because limited loanable funds are available to satisfy all borrowers, interest rates rise in response to the increased demand for funds, thereby crowding some potential borrowers out of the market.

currency call option Contract that grants the owner the right to purchase a specified currency for a specified price within a specified period of time.

currency futures contract Standardized contract that specifies an amount of a particular currency to be exchanged on a specified date and at a specified exchange rate.

currency put option Contract that grants the owner the right to sell a specified currency for a specified price within a specified period of time.

currency swap An agreement that allows the periodic swap of one currency for another at specified exchange rates; it essentially represents a series of forward contracts.

D

day traders Traders of financial futures contracts who close out their contracts on the same day that they initiate them.

dealers Securities firms that make a market in specific securities by adjusting their inventories.

debentures Bonds that are backed only by the general credit of the issuing firm.

debt-for-equity swap An exchange of debt for an equity interest in the debtor's assets.

debt securities Securities that represent credit provided to the initial issuer by the purchaser.

defensive operations The open market operations implemented to offset the impact of other conditions that affect the level of funds.

deficit units Individual, corporate, or government units that need to borrow funds.

defined-benefit plan Pension plan in which contributions are dictated by the benefits that will eventually be provided.

defined-contribution plan Pension plan in which benefits are determined by the accumulated contributions and on the fund's investment performance.

demand deposit account Deposit account that offers checking services.

demand-pull inflation Inflation caused by excess demand for goods.

Deposit Insurance Fund Reserve fund used by the FDIC to close failing banks. The fund is supported by deposit insurance premiums paid by commercial banks.

Depository Institutions Deregulation and Monetary Control Act (DIDMCA) Act that deregulated some aspects of the depository institutions industry, such as removing the ceiling interest rates on deposits and allowing NOW accounts nationwide.

derivative securities Financial contracts whose values are derived from the values of underlying assets.

designated market makers Agents who serve a broker function by matching up buy and sell orders on the New York Stock Exchange.

direct exchange rate The value of a currency in U.S. dollars.

direct lease loan Loan in which a bank purchases assets and then leases the assets to a firm.

dirty float System in which exchange rates are market determined without boundaries but are subject to government intervention.

discount brokerage firms Brokerage firms that focus on executing transactions.

duration gap Difference between the average duration of a bank's assets versus its liabilities.

dynamic operations Monetary policy implemented by the Federal Reserve to increase or decrease the level of funds.

E

economies of scale Reduction in average cost per unit as the level of output increases.

effective yield As related to international money markets, the yield on foreign money market securities adjusted for the exchange rate.

efficient market Market in which securities are rationally priced.

equity securities Securities such as common stock and preferred stock that represent ownership in a business.

equity swap   Swap arrangement involving the exchange of interest payments for payments linked to the degree of change in a stock index.

Euro-commercial paper (Euro-CP)   Securities issued in Europe without the backing of a bank syndicate.

Eurodollar certificate of deposit   Large U.S. dollar–denominated deposits in non-U.S. banks.

Eurodollar floating-rate CDs (FRCDs)   Eurodollar certificates of deposit with floating interest rates that adjust periodically to the London Interbank Offer Rate (LIBOR).

Eurodollar market   Market in Europe in which dollars are deposited and loaned for short time periods.

Eurodollars   Large dollar-denominated deposits accepted by banks outside the United States.

Euronotes   Notes issued in European markets in bearer form, with short-term maturities.

exchange-traded funds (ETFs)   Securities designed to mimic particular stock indexes and traded on a stock exchange just like stocks.

exercise price (strike price)   Price at which the instrument underlying an option contract can be purchased (in the case of a call option) or sold (in the case of a put option).

extendable swap   Swap of fixed payments for floating payments that contains an extendable feature allowing the party making fixed payments to extend the swap period if desired.

F

Federal Deposit Insurance Corporation (FDIC)   Federal agency that insures the deposits of commercial banks.

federal funds market   Market that facilitates the flow of funds from banks that have excess funds to banks that are in need of funds.

federal funds rate   Interest rate charged on loans between depository institutions.

Federal Home Loan Mortgage Association (Freddie Mac)   Federal agency that issues mortgage-backed securities and uses the proceeds to purchase mortgages.

Federal National Mortgage Association (Fannie Mae)   Federal agency that issues mortgage-backed securities and uses the funds to purchase mortgages.

Federal Open Market Committee (FOMC)   Composed of the seven members of the Board of Governors plus the presidents of five Federal Reserve district banks. The main role of the FOMC is to control monetary policy.

Federal Reserve district bank   A regional government bank that facilitates operations within the banking system by clearing checks, replacing old currency, providing loans to banks, and conducting research; there are 12 Federal Reserve district banks.

Federal Reserve System   A system that is involved (along with other agencies) in regulating commercial banks and responsible for conducting periodic evaluations of state-chartered banks and savings institutions with more than $50 billion in assets.

financial futures contract   Standardized agreement to deliver or receive a specified amount of a specified financial instrument at a specified price and date.

financial market   Market in which financial assets (or securities) such as stocks and bonds are traded.

Financial Services Modernization Act (Gramm-Leach-Bliley Act)   Legislation enacted in 1999 that allows affiliations between banks, securities firms, and insurance companies; repealed the Glass-Steagall Act.

firm commitment   An arrangement in which an underwriter guarantees the issuer that all bonds will be sold at a specified price.

first mortgage bond   Bond that has first claim on specified assets as collateral.

fixed-rate mortgage   Mortgage that locks in the interest rate paid by the borrower over the life of the loan.

floor brokers   Individuals who facilitate the trading of stocks on the New York Stock Exchange by executing transactions for their clients.

floor traders (locals)   Members of a futures exchange who trade futures contracts for their own account.

flotation costs   Costs of placing securities.

foreign exchange derivatives   Instruments created to lock in a foreign exchange transaction, such as forward contracts, futures contracts, currency swaps, and currency options contracts.

foreign exchange market   The financial market that facilitates the exchange of currencies.

forward contract   Contract typically negotiated with a commercial bank that allows a customer to purchase or sell a specified amount of a particular foreign currency at a specified exchange rate on a specified future date.

forward market   Market that facilitates the trading of forward contracts; commercial banks serve as intermediaries in the market by matching up participants who wish to buy a currency forward with other participants who wish to sell the currency forward.

forward rate   In the context of the term structure of interest rates, the market's forecast of the future interest rate. In the context of foreign exchange, the exchange rate at which a specified currency can be purchased or sold at a specified future point in time.

forward swap   An arrangement that involves an exchange of interest payments that does not begin until a specified future point in time.

freely floating system   System in which exchange rates are market determined without any government intervention.

full-service brokerage firms   Brokerage firms that provide complete information and advice about securities in addition to executing transactions.

fundamental analysis   Method of valuing stocks that relies on fundamental financial characteristics (such as earnings) about the firm and its corresponding industry.

fundamental forecasting   Forecasting based on fundamental relationships between economic variables and exchange rates.

G

gap   Rate-sensitive assets minus rate-sensitive liabilities.

Garn-St. Germain Act   Act passed in 1982 that allowed for the creation of money market deposit accounts (MMDAs), loosened lending guidelines for federally chartered savings institutions, and allowed failing depository institutions to be acquired by other depository institutions outside the state.

general obligation bonds   Bonds that provide payments that are supported by the municipal government's ability to tax.

Glass-Steagall Act   Act in 1933 that separated commercial banking and investment banking activities; largely repealed in 1999.

global crowding out   Given the international integration of money and capital markets, a government's budget deficit can affect interest rates in various countries.

graduated-payment mortgage (GPM)   Mortgage that allows borrowers to initially make small payments on the mortgage; the payments are increased on a graduated basis.

gross interest expenses   Interest paid on deposits and on other borrowed funds.

gross interest income   Interest income generated from all assets.

group life policy   Insurance policy provided to a group of policyholders with some common bond.

growing-equity mortgage   Mortgage in which the initial monthly payments are low and increase over time.

growth and income funds   Mutual funds that contain a combination of growth stocks, high-dividend stocks, and fixed-income bonds.

growth funds   Mutual funds containing stocks of firms that are expected to grow at a higher than average rate; they are appropriate for investors who are willing to accept a moderate degree of risk.

H

health maintenance organizations (HMOs)   Intermediaries between purchasers and providers of healthcare.

hedge funds   Mutual funds that sell shares to wealthy individuals and financial institutions and use the proceeds to invest in securities; they require a larger investment than open-end mutual funds, are subject to less regulation, and tend to be more risky.

hedgers   Participants in financial futures markets who take positions in contracts to reduce their exposure to risk.

high frequency trading (HFT)   Algorithmic trading in which robots have been programmed to make specific trades in response to the occurrence of specific characteristics of a financial security such as its price or volume movements.

high-yield funds   Mutual funds composed of bonds that offer high yields (junk bonds) and have a relatively high degree of credit risk.

highly leveraged transaction (HLT)   Credit provided that results in a debt-to-asset ratio of at least 75 percent.

I

impact lag   Lag time between when a policy is implemented by the government and when the policy has an effect on the economy.

imperfect markets   Markets where securities buyers and sellers do not have full access to information.

implementation lag   Lag time between when the government recognizes a problem and when it implements a policy to resolve the problem.

income before tax   As related to banks, an amount derived by summing net interest income, noninterest income, and securities gains and then subtracting from this sum the provision for loan losses and noninterest expenses.

income funds   Mutual funds composed of bonds that offer periodic coupon payments.

indenture   Legal document specifying the rights and obligations of both the issuing firm and the bondholders.

independent brokers   Agents who trade for their own account and are not employed by any particular brokerage firm.

index arbitrage   Act of capitalizing on discrepancies between prices of index futures and stocks.

index funds   Mutual funds that are designed to match the performance of an existing stock index.

indirect exchange rate   The value of a currency specified as the number of units of that currency equal to a U.S. dollar.

initial margin   A margin deposit established by a customer with a brokerage firm before a margin transaction can be executed.

installment loans   Loans to individuals to finance purchases of cars and household products.

Insurance Regulatory Information System (IRIS)   Organization that compiles financial statements, lists of insurers, and other relevant information pertaining to the insurance industry.

interest-inelastic   Insensitive to interest rates.

interest rate cap   Arrangement that offers a party interest payments in periods when the interest rate on a specific money market instrument exceeds a specified ceiling rate; the payments are based on the amount by which the interest rate exceeds the ceiling as applied to the notional principal specified in the agreement.

interest rate collar   The purchase of an interest rate cap and the simultaneous sale of an interest rate floor.

interest rate floor   Agreement in which one party offers an interest rate payment in periods when the interest rate on a specified money market instrument is below a specified floor rate.

interest rate futures   Financial futures contracts on debt securities such as Treasury bills, notes, or bonds.

interest rate parity   Theory that suggests the forward discount (or premium) depends on the interest rate differential between the two countries of concern.

interest rate risk   Risk that an asset will decline in value in response to interest rate movements.

interest rate swap   Arrangement whereby one party exchanges one set of interest payments for another.

in the money   Describes a call option whose premium is above the exercise price or a put option whose premium is below the exercise price.

investment-grade bonds   Bonds that are rated Baa or better by Moody's and BBB or better by Standard & Poor's.

investment-grade securities   Securities that are rated as "medium" quality or higher by rating agencies.

issue costs   Cost of issuing stock, including printing, legal registration, and accounting expenses.

J

junk bonds   Corporate bonds that are perceived to have a high degree of risk.

junk commercial paper   Low-rated commercial paper.

L

lagging economic indicators   Economic indicators that tend to rise or fall a few months after business-cycle expansions and contractions.

leading economic indicators   Economic indicators that tend to rise or fall a few months before business-cycle expansions and contractions.

letter of credit (L/C)   Guarantee by a bank on the financial obligations of a firm that owes payment (usually an importer).

limit order   Request by a customer to purchase or sell securities at a specified price or better.

liquidity   Ability to sell assets easily without loss of value.

load funds   Mutual funds that have a sales charge imposed by brokerage firms that sell the funds.

loan loss provision   A reserve account established by a bank in anticipation of loan losses in the future.

loan participation   Arrangement in which several banks pool funds to provide a loan to a corporation.

loanable funds theory   Theory that suggests the market interest rate is determined by the factors controlling the supply and demand for loanable funds.

locational arbitrage   Arbitrage intended to capitalize on a price (such as a foreign exchange rate quote) discrepancy between two locations.

long hedge   The purchase of financial futures contracts to hedge against a possible decrease in interest rates.

long-term capital gain   The gain on a stock position that was held for one year or longer.

long-term equity anticipations (LEAPs)   Stock options with relatively long-term expiration dates.

low-coupon bonds   Bonds that pay low coupon payments; most of the expected return to investors is attributed to the large discount in the bond's price.

M

M1   Definition of the money supply; composed of currency held by the public plus checking accounts.

M2   Definition of the money supply; composed of M1 plus savings accounts, small time deposits, MMDAs, and some other items.

M3   Definition of the money supply; composed of M2 plus large time deposits and other items.

maintenance margin   A margin requirement that reduces the risk that participants will later default on their obligations.

margin account   An account established with a broker that allows the investor to purchase stock on margin by putting up cash for part of the cost and borrowing the remainder from the broker.

margin call   Call from a broker to participants in futures contracts (or other investments) informing them that they must increase their equity.

margin requirements   The proportion of invested funds that must be paid in cash versus borrowed; set by the Federal Reserve.

market-based forecasting   Process of developing forecasts from market indicators.

market-makers   Individuals who facilitate the trading of stocks on the New York Stock Exchange and Nasdaq by standing ready to buy or sell specific stocks in response to customer orders.

market microstructure   Process by which securities are traded.

market order   Request by a customer to purchase or sell securities at the market price.

matched funding   Strategy in which investment decisions are made with the objective of matching planned outflow payments.

merger-conversion   Procedure used in acquisitions whereby a mutual savings and loan institution (S&L) converts to a stock-owned S&L before either acquiring or being acquired by another firm.

mixed forecasting   The use of a combination of forecasting techniques, resulting in a weighted average of the various forecasts developed.

money market deposit account (MMDA)   Deposit account that pays interest and allows limited checking, but does not specify a maturity.

money market mutual funds   Mutual funds that concentrate their investment in money market securities.

money markets   Financial markets that facilitate the flow of short-term funds.

money market securities   Short-term securities, such as Treasury bills or certificates of deposit, whose maturities are one year or less.

moral hazard problem   In a banking context, the deposit insurance pricing system that existed until the early 1990s, in which insurance premiums per $100 of deposits were similar across all commercial banks. This system created an indirect subsidy from safer banks to risky banks and encouraged banks to take excessive risks. In an insurance context, the problem for the insurance industry stemming from the fact that those who have insurance may take more risks because they are protected against losses.

mortgage-backed securities (MBS)   Securities issued by a financial institution that are backed by a pool of mortgages; also called pass-through securities.

multifund mutual fund   A mutual fund composed of different mutual funds.

Municipal Bond Index (MBI) futures   Futures contract allowing for the future purchase or sale of municipal bonds at a specified price.

municipal bonds   Debt securities issued by state and local governments; they can usually be classified as either general obligation bonds or revenue bonds.

mutual fund   An investment company that sells shares representing an interest in a portfolio of securities.

N

National Association of Insurance Commissioners (NAIC)   Agency that facilitates cooperation among the various state agencies when an insurance issue is a concern.

negotiable certificate of deposit (NCD)   Deposit account with a minimum deposit of $100,000 that requires a specified maturity; there is a secondary market for these deposits.

negotiable order of withdrawal (NOW) account   Deposit account that allows unlimited checking and pays interest.

net asset value (NAV)   Financial characteristic used to describe a mutual fund's value per share; estimated as the market value of the securities composing the mutual fund, plus any accrued interest or dividends, minus any expenses. This value is divided by the number of shares outstanding.

net exposure   In the context of futures markets, the difference between asset and liability positions.

no-load funds   Mutual funds that do not have a sales charge, meaning that they are not promoted by brokerage firms.

noise traders   Uninformed investors whose buy and sell positions push the stock price away from its fundamental value.

noninterest expenses   Expenses, such as salaries and office equipment, that are unrelated to interest payments on deposits or borrowed funds.

note issuance facility (NIF)   Commitment in which a bank agrees to purchase the commercial paper of a firm if the firm cannot place its paper in the market at an acceptable interest rate.

notional principal   Value to which interest rates from interest rate swaps are applied to determine the interest payments involved.

O

open-end funds   Mutual funds that are willing to repurchase the shares they sell from investors at any time.

Open Market Desk   Division of the New York Federal Reserve district bank that is responsible for conducting open market operations.

organized exchange   Visible marketplace for secondary market transactions.

origination   Decisions by a firm (with the help of a securities firm) on how much stock or bonds to issue, the type of stock (or bonds) to be issued, and the price at which the stock (or bonds) should be sold.

out of the money   Describes a call option whose premium is below the exercise price or a put option whose premium is above the exercise price.

P

participation certificates (PCs)   Certificates sold by the Federal Home Loan Mortgage Association; the proceeds are used to purchase conventional mortgages from financial institutions.

pass-through securities   Securities issued by a financial institution and backed by a group of mortgages. The mortgage interest and principal are sent to the financial institution, which then transfers the payments to the owners of the pass-through securities after deducting a service fee. Also called mortgage-backed securities.

Pension Benefit Guaranty Corporation (PBGC)   A federally chartered agency established as a result of ERISA to provide insurance on pension plans.

Pension Protection Act of 2006   Federal act that requires a company with an underfunded defined-benefit pension plan to increase its contributions to the pension plan so that it will eventually be fully funded.

plain vanilla swap   An arrangement that involves the periodic exchange of fixed-rate payments for floating-rate payments.

policy directive   Statement provided by the FOMC to the Trading Desk regarding the target money supply range.

portfolio insurance   The use of program trading combined with the trading of stock index futures to reduce the exposure of a securities portfolio to risk.

position traders   Traders of financial futures contracts who maintain their futures positions for relatively long periods (such as weeks or months) before closing them out.

prepayment risk   The possibility that the assets to be hedged may be prepaid earlier than their designated maturity; also applies to mortgages.

primary credit rate   The interest rate charged by the Federal Reserve System on short-term loans extended to banks.

primary market   Market where securities are initially issued.

prime rate   Interest rate charged on loans by banks to their most creditworthy customers.

private placement   Process in which a corporation sells new securities directly without using underwriting services.

projective funding   Strategy that offers pension fund managers some flexibility in constructing a pension portfolio that can benefit from expected market and interest rate movements.

prospectus   A pamphlet that discloses relevant financial data on the firm and provisions applicable to the security.

purchasing power parity (PPP)   Theory that suggests exchange rates adjust, on average, by a percentage that reflects the inflation differential between the two countries of concern.

put option   Contract that grants the owner the right to sell a specified financial instrument for a specified price within a specified period of time.

putable swap   Swap of fixed-rate payments for floating-rate payments whereby the party making floating-rate payments has the right to terminate the swap.

Q

quantitative easing   A central bank strategy to increase the money supply by purchasing government securities and other securities.

R

rate-capped swap   Swap arrangement, involving fixed-rate payments for floating-rate payments, in which the floating payments are capped.

real interest rate   Nominal interest rate adjusted for inflation.

recognition lag   The lag between the time a problem arises and the time it is recognized.

registered bonds   Bonds that require the issuer to maintain records of who owns the bonds and automatically send coupon payments to the owners.

registration statement   Statement of relevant financial information disclosed by a corporation issuing securities; it is intended to ensure that the issuing corporation provides accurate information.

repurchase agreement (repo)   Agreement in which a bank (or some other firm) sells some of its government security holdings with a commitment to purchase those securities back at a later date. This agreement essentially reflects a loan from the time the firm sold the securities until the securities are repurchased.

reserve requirement ratio   Proportion of deposits that must be retained by a bank as required reserves.

return on assets (ROA)   After-tax earnings divided by assets.

revenue bonds   Bonds that provide payments that are supported by the revenue generated by the project.

reverse repo   The purchase of securities by one party from another with an agreement to sell them in the future.

revolving credit loan   Financing arrangement that obligates the bank to loan some specified maximum amount of funds over a specified period of time.

S

Savings Association Insurance Fund (SAIF)   Insuring agency for savings and loan institutions from 1989 until 2006.

second mortgage   Mortgage used in conjunction with the primary or first mortgage.

secondary market   Market where securities are resold.

secondary stock offering   A new stock offering by a firm that already has stock outstanding.

securities   Certificates that represent a claim on the issuer.

Securities Act of 1933   Federal legislation intended to ensure complete disclosure of relevant information on publicly offered securities and to prevent fraudulent practices in selling these securities.

Securities Exchange Act of 1934   Federal legislation intended to ensure complete disclosure of relevant information on securities traded in secondary markets.

securities gains (losses)   Bank accounting term that reflects the gains or losses generated from the sale of securities.

Securities Investor Protection Corporation (SIPC) An organization that offers insurance on cash and securities deposited at brokerage firms.

securitization Pooling and repackaging of loans into securities, which are sold to investors.

semistrong-form efficiency Security prices reflect all public information, including announcements by firms, economic news or events, and political news or events.

shared-appreciation mortgage Mortgage that allows a home purchaser to pay a below-market interest rate; in return, the lender shares in the appreciation of the home's value.

Sharpe index Measure of risk-adjusted return; defined as the asset's excess mean return beyond the mean risk-free rate, divided by the standard deviation of returns of the asset of concern.

shelf registration Registration with the Securities and Exchange Commission in advance of a public placement of securities.

short sale The sale of securities that are borrowed with the intention of buying those securities to repay what was borrowed.

short-term capital gain The gain on a stock position that was held for less than one year.

sinking-fund provision Requirement that a firm retire a specific amount of its bond issue each year.

Smithsonian Agreement Agreement among major countries to devalue the dollar against some currencies and widen the boundaries around each exchange rate from 1 percent to 2.25 percent.

sovereign risk As applied to swaps, the risk that a country's political conditions could prevent one party in the swap from receiving payments due.

specialty funds Mutual funds that focus on a group of companies sharing a particular characteristic.

speculators Investors who take positions to benefit from future price movements.

spinoff Process in which the corporation creates a new independent firm from an existing division and distributes shares of stock representing that unit to its existing shareholders.

spot rate The prevailing exchange rate at which one currency can be exchanged for another currency.

standby letter of credit Agreement that backs a customer's financial obligation.

stock index futures Financial futures contracts on stock indexes.

stock index option An option that provides the right to trade a specified stock index at a specified price by a specified expiration date.

stop-buy order Order to purchase a particular security when the price reaches a specified level above the current market price; often used in short sales.

strong-form efficiency Security prices fully reflect all information, including private (insider) information.

subordinated debentures Debentures that have claims against the firm's assets that are junior to the claims of both mortgage bonds and regular debentures.

surplus units Individual, business, or government units that have excess funds that can be invested.

swap options (swaptions) Options on interest rate swaps.

systematic risk Risk that is attributable to market movements and cannot be diversified away.

systemic risk The spread of financial problems, among financial institutions and across financial markets, that could cause a collapse in the financial system.

T

technical analysis Method of forecasting future stock prices based on historical stock price patterns.

technical forecasting Forecasting that involves the use of historical exchange rate data to predict future values.

term insurance Temporary insurance over a specified term; the policy does not build a cash value.

term loan Business loan used to finance the purchase of fixed assets.

term structure of interest rates Relationship between the term remaining until maturity and the annualized yield of debt securities.

theory of rational expectations To the extent that businesses and households recognize that an increase in money supply growth will cause higher inflation, they will revise their inflationary expectations upward as a result.

time deposit Deposits that cannot be withdrawn until a specified maturity date.

time-series model   A model that examines moving averages and allows forecasters to develop rules.

Trading Desk   Located at the New York Federal Reserve district bank, it is used to carry out orders from the FOMC about open market operations.

triangular arbitrage   Buying or selling a currency that is subject to a mispriced cross exchange rate.

U

underwrite   Act of guaranteeing a specific price to the initial issuer of securities.

underwriting syndicate   Group of securities firms that are required to underwrite a portion of a corporation's newly issued securities.

universal life insurance   Insurance that combines the features of term and whole life insurance. It specifies a period of time over which the policy will exist, but also builds a cash value for policyholders over time.

usury laws   Laws that enforce a maximum interest rate that can be imposed on loans to households.

V

variable life insurance   Insurance in which benefits awarded by the life insurance company to a beneficiary vary with the assets backing the policy.

variable-rate bonds   Bonds whose coupon rates adjust to market interest rates over time.

W

weak-form efficiency   Theory that suggests that security prices reflect all market-related data, such as historical security price movements and volume of securities traded.

whole life insurance   Insurance that protects the insured policyholder until death or as long as premiums are promptly paid; the policy builds a cash value to which the policyholder is entitled even if the policy is canceled.

working capital loan   Business loan designed to support ongoing operations, typically for a short-term period.

writer   The seller of an option contract.

Y

yield to maturity   Discount rate at which the present value of future payments would equal the security's current price.

Z

zero-coupon bonds   Bonds that have no coupon payments.

zero-coupon-for-floating swap   Swap arrangement calling for one party to swap a lump-sum payment at maturity for periodic floating-rate payments.

Index